Natural Disasters

Natural Disasters

Volume I
Avalanches — Explosions

Editors

Marlene Bradford, Ph.D.
Texas A&M University

Robert S. Carmichael, Ph.D.
University of Iowa

Project Editor
Tracy Irons-Georges

SALEM PRESS, INC.
Pasadena, California   Hackensack, New Jersey

Editor in Chief: Dawn P. Dawson
Copy Editor: Lauren Mitchell
Research Supervisor: Jeffry Jensen
Acquisitions Editor: Mark Rehn
Production Editor: Joyce I. Buchea

Project Editor: Tracy Irons-Georges
Assistant Editor: Andrea E. Miller
Research Assistant: Jeff Stephens
Photograph Editor: Philip Bader
Layout: William Zimmerman

Copyright © 2001, by Salem Press, Inc.

Library of Congress Cataloging-in-Publication Data

Natural disasters / editors, Marlene Bradford, Robert S. Carmichael.
    p. cm.
Includes bibliographical references.
    ISBN 0-89356-071-5 (set : alk. paper) — ISBN 0-89356-072-3 (vol. 1 : alk. paper) — ISBN 0-89356-073-1 (vol. 2 : alk. paper) — ISBN 0-89356-082-0 (vol. 3 : alk. paper)
    1. Natural disasters. I. Bradford, Marlene. II. Carmichael, Robert S.
    GB5014 .N373 2000
    363.34—dc21

00-058763

First Printing

PRINTED IN THE UNITED STATES OF AMERICA

Publisher's Note

Every day, the news is filled with reports of the devastation that nature brings to human lives and property—houses lifted up and carried away by a powerful tornado, thousands buried under tons of debris after a strong earthquake, people desperately fleeing burning ash and lava spewed by a volcano long thought dormant. History records thousands of such disasters, and countless others have been forgotten to time. Unlike many disaster chronologies or earth science texts, *Natural Disasters* both explains the science behind such phenomena and chronicles hundreds of examples of these events.

This three-volume set is divided into twenty-three chapters by disaster type: Avalanches; Blizzards, Freezes, Ice Storms, and Hail; Droughts; Dust Storms and Sandstorms; Earthquakes; El Niño; Epidemics; Explosions; Famines; Fires; Floods; Fog; Heat Waves; Hurricanes, Typhoons, and Cyclones; Icebergs and Glaciers; Landslides, Mudslides, and Rockslides; Lightning Strikes; Meteorites and Comets; Smog; Tornadoes; Tsunamis; Volcanic Eruptions; and Wind Gusts. These disasters are explained in scientific terms. Every chapter then covers specific events, in chronological order, with narrative-style essays of facts, figures, and interesting stories. Events were chosen based on loss of life, widespread destruction, and notable circumstances. They range in time from 65,000,000 B.C.E. to the year 2000 and cover six continents. *Natural Disasters* is illustrated with photographs, maps, drawings, tables, and diagrams.

In creating this encyclopedia, the question of what constitutes a natural disaster had to be addressed. To what degree are the forces of nature to blame when a catastrophe strikes? To what extent can human error or interference be a factor before an event is considered "human-made"? Is a disaster measured by numbers of people killed and injured, or by the amount of disruption caused? When does a local tragedy become an event of broader significance? Why are some disasters more heartbreaking or spectacular, and thus more memorable, than others?

In selecting the types of disaster and the specific events covered, decisions were also made regarding scope and focus. For example, only wildfires—large-scale fires affecting cities or whole regions—are addressed individually in the "Fires" chapter; thus, tragic blazes in single buildings such as hotels or theaters are not featured, no matter how many lives were lost or how famous the circumstances. The chapters "Fog" and "Icebergs and Glaciers" discuss collisions and crashes involving ships, trains, and airplanes in which these natural conditions were a factor, although human error was often one link in the chain of events. In the "Explosions" chapter, the intentional use of bombs is not covered, but entries describe accidents involving dynamite and the inadvertent ignition of gas or coal dust. In addition, because many disasters could fall into several categories—earthquakes cause landslides and tsunamis, hurricanes create floods, droughts result in famines—numerous choices concerning chapter placement had to be made.

Each chapter begins with a general overview of the type of disaster. A few sentences define the natural phenomenon and its importance. Then the factors involved (animals, chemical reactions, geography, geological forces, gravitational forces, human activity, ice, microorganisms, plants, rain, snow, temperature, weather conditions, wind) and the regions affected (cities, coasts, deserts, forests, islands, lakes, mountains, oceans, plains, rivers, towns, valleys) are listed.

Several subsections of text follow. "Science" explains the science behind the phenomenon in general terms understandable to the layperson. "Geography" names and describes the continents, countries, regions, or types of locations where this disaster occurs. For example, some conditions (such as floods) occur worldwide, but some areas (such as river valleys) are more prone to these disasters than are other areas. "Prevention and Preparations" describes any measures that can be taken to prevent or predict the disaster, including the intentional triggering of events. The steps that can be taken in advance to avoid or minimize loss of life and property are discussed, including drills, warning systems, and evacuation orders. "Rescue and Relief Efforts" explains what is done in the aftermath of the disaster to find and treat casualties. The typical wounds received and any special challenges faced by rescue workers, such as aftershocks or similiar continuing threats to safety, are addressed. The efforts of relief organizations and programs are highlighted. "Impact" describes the typical short-term and long-term effects on humans, animals, property, and the environment of these disasters. A "Bibliography" lists general sources about the disaster type that are useful for further study, with annotations that discuss the content and value of these sources.

A section listing Notable Events follows, ranging from a few entries ("El Niño" and "Meteorites and Comets") to around a hundred ("Earthquakes" and "Hurricanes, Typhoons, and Cyclones"). Most of these sections begin with a "Historical Overview" that offers a broad sense of this type of disaster throughout history and around the world, beginning with the first recorded occurrences and offering highlights of notable events and trends up to the present day. In some cases, cultural views of the phenomenon over time and in various societies are discussed. Included with every "Historical Overview" is a boxed "Milestones" table listing major events, such as significant disasters, relevant scientific discoveries, and establishment dates for programs and classification systems.

Each event entry begins with a year and a general description of location or the popular designation for the disaster (such as Hurricane Hugo, the Black Death, or the Great Chicago Fire). The most accurate date when the event occurred is given; this may be a range of days or even months for a longer-term event such as a hurricane or a volcanic eruption. Then the most accurate place where the event occurred—one or more towns, cities, regions, states, or countries—is identified. This is the official place name, if any, according to government agencies; otherwise, it is the location most identified with the event. Magnitude on the Richter scale, either official or estimated, is given for earthquakes. The best speed estimate or official classification number is listed for hurricanes, if available. For tornadoes, the most reliable Fujita rating, according to the National Weather Service, is offered for disasters after 1950, when the modern classification system began. Temperature in Fahrenheit and/or Celsius is listed for heat waves, if available. Measurement on the Torino Impact Hazard Scale is provided for meteorites, and many eruptions are gauged by the Volcanic Explosivity Index. "Result" lists the best figures for total numbers of dead or injured, people left homeless, damage, structures or acres burned, and so forth. Then each entry provides readers with an account—before, during, and after—of the disaster, including both broad scientific and historical facts and narrative details. A section at the end of each entry entitled "For Further Information" lists books, chapters, magazines, or newspapers that offer specific coverage of that particular event.

At the back of each volume, a Time Line lists all events covered in the encyclopedia chronologically, and a Geographical List organizes all the events by region, country, or state. Volume 3 also features a Glossary that defines essential meteorological and geological terms, a General Bibliography offering sources for additional material, and a list of Organizations and Agencies that provide disaster relief. A comprehensive subject Index concludes the volume.

All articles in *Natural Disasters* were written by experts in the various fields of meteorological and geological studies, the vast majority of whom are academicians; their names and affiliations are listed in the front matter to volume 1. Special acknowledgment is extended to the Consultants, Marlene Bradford, Ph.D., and Robert S. Carmichael, Ph.D. We thank them all for their knowledge, their enthusiasm, and their dedication to this encyclopedia.

Contents

Contributor List

Amy Ackerberg-Hastings
Iowa State University

Richard Adler
University of Michigan-Dearborn

David Barratt
Independent Scholar

Alvin K. Benson
Brigham Young University

Milton Berman
University of Rochester

Margaret Boe Birns
New York University

Nicholas Birns
New School University

Mary Etta Boulden
Middle Tennessee State University

Marlene Bradford
Texas A&M University

John A. Britton
Francis Marion University

Mary Louise Buley-Meissner
University of Wisconsin-Milwaukee

Jeffrey L. Buller
Georgia Southern University

Edmund J. Campion
University of Tennessee

Robert S. Carmichael
University of Iowa

Robert E. Carver
University of Georgia

Nicholas Casner
Boise State University

Gilbert T. Cave
Lakeland Community College

Paul J. Chara, Jr.
Loras College

Monish R. Chatterjee
Binghamton University, SUNY

Jaime S. Colome
Cal Poly State University, San Luis Obispo

John A. Cramer
Oglethorpe University

Robert L. Cullers
Kansas State University

Loralee Davenport
Mississippi University for Women

Bruce J. DeHart
University of North Carolina at Pembroke

Judith Boyce DeMark
Northern Michigan University

M. Casey Diana
*University of Illinois at Urbana-
Champaign*

Gordon Neal Diem
*ADVANCE Education and Development
Institute*

Stephen B. Dobrow
Fairleigh Dickinson University

Margaret A. Dodson
Boise Independent Schools

Colleen M. Driscoll
Villanova University

John M. Dunn
Independent Scholar

Mary Bosch Farone
Middle Tennessee State University

Bonnie L. Ford
Sacramento City College

Soraya Ghayourmanesh
Nassau Community College

Sheldon Goldfarb
University of British Columbia

Nancy M. Gordon
Independent Scholar

Robert F. Gorman
Southwest Texas State University

Daniel G. Graetzer
University of Washington Medical Center

Hans G. Graetzer
South Dakota State University

Don M. Greene
Baylor University

Johnpeter Horst Grill
Mississippi State University

Irwin Halfond
McKendree College

C. Alton Hassell
Baylor University

Charles Haynes
University of Alabama

Diane Andrews Henningfeld
Adrian College

Mark C. Herman
Edison Community College

Jane F. Hill
Independent Scholar

Carl W. Hoagstrom
Ohio Northern University

William Hoffman
Independent Scholar

Robert M. Hordon
Rutgers University

Raymond Pierre Hylton
Virginia Union University

Karen N. Kähler
Independent Scholar

Grove Koger
Boise (Idaho) Public Library

Jacob P. Kovel
University of Kansas

Philip E. Lampe
University of the Incarnate Word

Jennifer S. Lawrence
Texas A&M University

Terrence A. Lee
Middle Tennessee State University

Victor Lindsey
East Central University

Donald W. Lovejoy
Palm Beach Atlantic College

David C. Lukowitz
Hamline University

Dana P. McDermott
Independent Scholar

Michelle C. K. McKowen
Independent Scholar

Louise Magoon
Independent Scholar

Carl Henry Marcoux
University of California, Riverside

Christine L. Martin
Spring Arbor College

Ralph W. Mathisen
University of South Carolina

Howard Meredith
University of Science and Arts of Oklahoma

Randall L. Milstein
Oregon State University

Lauren Mitchell
Independent Scholar

William A. Mitchell
Baylor University

William V. Moore
College of Charleston

Otto H. Muller
Alfred University

Anthony Newsome
Middle Tennessee State University

Robert J. Paradowski
Rochester Institute of Technology

D. G. Paz
University of North Texas

Nis Petersen
New Jersey City University

Darren J. Pierson
Texas A&M University

Erika E. Pilver
Westfield State College

Dorothy Potter
Lynchburg College

Victoria Price
Lamar University

Steven J. Ramold
University of Nebraska-Lincoln

Donald F. Reaser
The University of Texas at Arlington

Betty Richardson
Southern Illinois University, Edwardsville

Edward A. Riedinger
Ohio State University Libraries

James L. Robinson
University of Illinois at Urbana-Champaign

St. John Robinson
Montana State University at Billings

Charles W. Rogers
Southwestern Oklahoma State University

Neil E. Salisbury
University of Oklahoma

Elizabeth D. Schafer
Independent Scholar

Billy Scott
Fordham University

Rose Secrest
Independent Scholar

James B. Seymour, Jr.
Texas A&M University

R. Baird Shuman
University of Illinois at Urbana-Champaign

Gary W. Siebein
University of Florida

Donald C. Simmons, Jr.
Mississippi Humanities Council

Roger Smith
Independent Scholar

David M. Soule
Compass Point Research

Kenneth F. Steele, Jr.
University of Arkansas

Thomas R. Stephens
Texas A&M University

Joan C. Stevenson
Western Washington University

Dion C. Stewart
Adams State College

Toby R. Stewart
Adams State College

Leslie Stricker
Park College

Eric R. Swanson
University of Texas at San Antonio

Sue Tarjan
Independent Scholar

Leslie V. Tischauser
Prairie State College

Robert D. Ubriaco, Jr.
Illinois Wesleyan University

Rosa Alvarez Ulloa
Independent Scholar

Theodore Weaver
College of New Rochelle

Winifred Whelan
St. Bonaventure University

Wm. Michael Whitley
York College

Edwin G. Wiggins
Webb Institute

Thomas A. Wikle
Oklahoma State University

Mary Catherine Wilheit
Texas A&M University

Richard L. Wilson
University of Tennessee at Chattanooga

Lisa A. Wroble
Redford Township District Library

Jay R. Yett
Orange Coast College

Robinson M. Yost
Des Moines Area Community College

Natural Disasters

Avalanches

An avalanche is a large amount of snow, ice, rock, or earth that becomes dislodged and moves rapidly down a sloped surface or over a precipice. Avalanches are generally influenced by one or several natural forces but are increasingly being initiated by human activities. Landslide avalanches are defined as the massive downward and outward movement of some of the material that forms the slope of an incline. Unqualified use of the term "avalanche" in the English language, however, most often refers to a snow avalanche and generally refers to movements big and fast enough to endanger life or property. Avalanche accidents resulting in death, injury, or destruction have increased tremendously in direct proportion to the increased popularity of winter recreational activities in mountainous regions.

FACTORS INVOLVED: Chemical reactions, geography, geological forces, gravitational forces, human activity, ice, plants, rain, snow, temperature, weather conditions, wind

REGIONS AFFECTED: Cities, forests, mountains, towns, valleys

(AP/Wide World Photos)

Artificial avalanches may be triggered when humans, animals, or machinery—such as this snowmobile—contribute stress to the snow. (AP/Wide World Photos)

SCIENCE

The term "avalanche" relates to large masses of snow, ice, rock, soil, mud, and/or other materials that descend rapidly down an incline such as a hillside or mountain slope. Precipices, very steep or overhanging areas of earth or rock, are also areas prone to avalanche activity. Landslide avalanches are downward and outward movements of the material that forms the slope of a hillside or mountain. General lay usage of the term "avalanche" often relates to large masses of snow or ice, while the term "landslide" is usually restricted to the movement of rock and soil and includes a broad range of velocities. Slow movements cause gradual damage, such as rupture of buried utility lines, whereas high-velocity avalanches require immediate evacuation of an area to ensure safety.

A landslide avalanche begins when a portion of a hillside weakens progressively to the point where it is no longer able to support the weight of the hillside itself. This weakness may be caused when rainfall or floodwater elevates the overall water content of the slope, thus reducing the sheer strength of the slope materials. Landslides are most common in areas where erosion is constantly wearing away at the local terrain, but they can also be initiated by events such as earthquakes and loud noises. Some landslides only move sporadically—during certain seasons of the year—and may lie dormant for decades, centuries, or millennia; their extremely slow movements may go unnoticed for long periods of time. Slow-moving landslides are distinguished from creep—the slow change of a mountain's or hill's dimensions from prolonged exposure to stress or high temperatures—in that they have distinct boundaries and have at least some stable ground.

Natural avalanches can be triggered when additional stressors are provided in the form of the added weight of additional snow, either fresh snowfall or windblown snow, or when the cohesive strength of the snowpack naturally decreases, which serves to weaken the bonds between particles of snow. Artificial avalanches may be triggered when humans, animals, or machinery begin the downslide, due to their contribution of additional stress to the snow. Many avalanches in outdoor recreational areas are triggered by the weight of a single skier or the impact of small masses of snow or ice falling from above. Explosives can also trigger an artificial avalanche, either intentionally or unintentionally. When explosives are detonated to knock down potentially dangerous snow at a prescribed time and location, such as for maintenance of highways or ski areas, the public is temporarily evacuated from the area.

Ground that has remained relatively stable for as little as one hundred years or possibly as long as tens of thousand of years may begin to slide following alteration of the natural slope by human development, such as during grading for roads or building projects on hillsides. Landslide avalanches can also be started by deep cutting into the slope and removal of support necessary for materials higher up the slope, or by overloading the lower part of the slope with the excavated materials. Some have occurred where development has altered groundwater conditions.

GEOGRAPHY

Snow avalanches require a snow layer that has the potential for instability and a sloped surface that is steep enough to enable a slide to continue its downhill momentum once it has started. Slopes with inclines between 25 and 55 degrees represent the broadest range for avalanche danger, but a majority of avalanches originate on inclines between 30 and 45 degrees. Angles above 55 degrees are generally too steep to collect significant amounts of snow, as the snow tends to roll down the hillside very rapidly without accumulating. Slope angles of less than 25 degrees are generally safe, except for the remote possibility of very slow snow avalanches in extremely wet conditions.

When a layer of snow lies on a sloped surface, the constant force of gravity causes it to creep slowly down the slope. When a force imposed on a snow layer is large enough, a failure is triggered somewhere within the snow, thus stimulating the avalanche to begin to move rapidly downhill. There are two distinct types of failures that can occur within the snow prior to an avalanche. When a cohesionless snow layer rests on a slope steeper than its angle of repose, it can cause a loose-snow avalanche, which is often also called a point-release avalanche. This can actually be triggered by as little as one grain of snow slipping out of place and dislodging other grains below it, causing a chain reaction that continues to grow in size as the accumulated mass slips down the hill. The point-release avalanche generally appears as an inverted *V* shape on the snow and is typically limited to only the surface layer of snow cover. In this type of avalanche, the snow has little internal cohesion, no obvious fracture line, and no clear division where the sliding snow separates from the layers underneath.

In contrast, when snow fails as a cohesive unit, an obvious brittle fracture line appears and an entire layer or slab or snow is set in motion. Because creep formation causes the snow layer to be stretched out along the slope, the fracture releases stored elastic energy. The release of this energy may cause the fracture to spread across an entire slope or basin. Failure may occur deep within the snow layer, allowing a good portion or nearly all of the snow to be included in the avalanche. Slab avalanches are often larger and more destructive than point-release avalanches and can continue to slide on weaker layers underneath or actually upon the ground itself.

The specific shape of the slope may reflect the level of avalanche danger, with hazards being highest when snow accumulates on straight, open, and moderately steep slopes. One classic law of avalanches for mountaineers is that they face the least danger while moving on ridges, somewhat more danger while moving on the valley floor, and the most danger when moving directly upon the slope itself. Snow on a convex slope is more prone to avalanches, as it comes under tension because it tends to stretch more tightly over the curve of the hill. When coming down a convex slope, mountaineers may not know how steep the slope is until they pass the curve that temporarily obstructed their view and then discover that they are further down on the face than is safe. Bowls and cirques (steep-walled basins) have a shape that tends to accumulate snow deposited by the wind. Once an avalanche begins, it most often spreads to the entire face and dumps large quantities of snow into the area below. Couloirs (mountainside gorges) are enticing to climbers because they offer a direct route up a mountain, but they are susceptible to snow movement because they create natural chutes. Forested slopes offer some avalanche protection, but they do not guarantee safety. While slides are less likely to originate within a dense forest, they have been known to crush through even very high-density tree areas. Shattered trees provide clear evidence that a previous avalanche has occurred on the mountainside. A slope that has only bushes and small trees growing on it may indicate that the incline has experienced avalanches so often than the timber is not being given a chance to regrow.

While avalanches can occur anywhere in the world where snow falls on slopes, some countries and regions are prone to such events. In Europe, the Alps—a mountain range stretching through Italy, Austria, Germany, Switzerland, and France—has experienced many devastating avalanches. The Andes mountain range in South America has produced avalanches in Peru. In North America, areas of the Pacific Northwest—particularly Washington State, British Columbia, and Alaska—are most often affected.

PREVENTION AND PREPARATIONS

Snow avalanches are among the main hazards facing outdoor winter sports enthusiasts who drive through a mountain pass in an automobile or snowmobile, or hike, climb, snowshoe, hunt, or ski along a mountainside. The relative level of avalanche hazard and the conditions that occur to create the hazard at any given time are relatively easy for a trained professional to identify. The local news media generally report avalanche danger in heavily populated and well-traveled recreational areas. Unfortunately, there currently is no completely valid and reliable way to predict precisely where and when an avalanche will occur. Novice mountaineers can certainly benefit by being able to recognize the formation of different types of snow crystals and hazardous terrain and weather. They should keep in mind that avalanches can sweep even on perfectly level ground for more than 1 mile after the snow has reached the bottom of a slope.

Avalanche hazards can be assessed by examining the snow for new avalanches in the area. Cracks in hard snow may outline an unstable slab as snow that settles with the weight of a person moving on it. The sound of a loud thump may indicate that a hard slab is nearly ready to release. Snow stability can be tested by probing with a ski pole to feel for layers of varying solidity or by digging a pit to examine the layers for weakness. Some excellent advice for winter travelers is to always stop to rest or set up camp outside the potential reach of an avalanche.

Avalanche research has consistently shown that approximately 80 percent of avalanches occur during or just after a storm. Avalanche danger escalates when snowfall exceeds a level of 1 inch per hour or an accumulation of 12 inches or more in a single storm. Rapid changes in wind and temperature also significantly increase avalanche danger. Storms that begin with a low ambient temperature and dry snow on the ground and are followed immediately by a rapidly rising temperature are more likely to set off avalanche conditions. Snow that is dry tends to form poor chemical bonds and thus does not possess the strength to support the heavier, wet snow that rapidly accumulates on the surface. Rainstorms or spring weather with warm winds and cloudy nights creates the possibility of a wet-snow avalanche and causes a "percolating" effect of the water into the snow.

The manner in which the sun and wind hit a slope can often provide valuable clues regarding potential avalanche danger. In the Northern Hemisphere, slopes that face south receive the most sun. The increased solar heat makes the snow settle and stabilize more quickly than on north-facing slopes. Generally speaking, south-facing slopes are safer in winter, but there are certainly many exceptions to this rule as determined by local factors. South-facing slopes also tend to release their avalanches sooner after a storm. Thus, slides that begin on southern slopes may indicate that slopes facing other directions may soon follow suit. As warmer days arrive near the end of winter, south-facing slopes may actually become more prone to wet-snow avalanches, making the north-facing slopes safer. North-facing slopes receive very little or no sun in the winter, so consolidation of the snowpack takes much longer, if it occurs at all. Colder temperatures may create weak layers of snow, thus making northern slopes more likely to slide in midwinter. It is important to note that these guidelines should be reversed for mountainous areas south of the equator.

Windward slopes that face into the snow tend to be safer because they retain less snow—the wind blows it away. The snow that remains tends to become more compact through the blast of the wind. Lee slopes, which face the same direction the wind is blowing, collect snow rapidly during storms and on windy days as the snow blows over from the windward slopes. This results in cornice formation on the lee side of ridges, snow that is deeper and less consolidated, and the formation of wind slabs that can be prone to avalanches. Snow formation often indicates the prevailing wind direction, following the general rule that cornices face the same direction that the wind is blowing.

Attempts have been made to prevent avalanche damage by building artificial supporting structures or transplanting trees within anticipated avalanche zones. The direct impact of an avalanche has been effectively blocked by diversion structures such as dams, sheds, and tunnels in areas where avalanches repeatedly strike. Structural damage can be limited by the construction of various types of fencing and by building splitting wedges, V-shaped masonry walls that are designed to split an avalanche around a structure located behind it. Techniques have been developed to predict avalanche occurrence by analyzing the relationships between meteorological and snow-cover factors, which are often reported through the media. Zones of known or predicted avalanche danger are generally taken into account during commercial development of a mountainous area. The avalanche danger of unstable slope accumulations is often prevented through detonation, from explosives similar to grenades to the sending out of controlled acoustic waves.

RESCUE AND RELIEF EFFORTS

Search and rescue experts recommend that, when individuals know they are about to become caught in an avalanche, they should make as much noise as possible and discard all equipment, including packs and skis. They should try to avoid being swept away by grabbing onto anything stable, such as large rocks or trees. Those who become caught in a slide should attempt to stay on the snow surface by making swimming motions with the arms and legs or by rolling. It is also recommended to attempt to close the mouth in the event that the head begins to fall below the snow surface. If victims anticipate becoming completely buried and no longer moving with the snow, they should attempt to create a breathing space by putting their hands and elbows in front of their faces and inhaling deeply before the snow stops in order to expand the ribs. All available oxygen and energy should be conserved if victims anticipate that rescuers will soon begin making appropriate search and rescue efforts.

Avalanche search and rescue efforts should begin as soon as possible by companions of the victim, who should generally anticipate that there will not be time for professional help to arrive. Despite the shock of the moment, rescue procedures should begin immediately by noting and marking—with an object such as a ski pole—three critical positions on the snow. These positions include the point where the victim was first caught in moving snow, the point where the victim disappeared beneath the snow surface, and

the point where the moving surface of the avalanche eventually stopped. Accurately noting these three areas greatly reduces the area that needs to be searched, thus providing an increased chance of a successful search. Rescue beacons, small electronic devices which should be secured to all persons traveling together in a winter excursion party, have proven to be very effective tools in finding buried victims. The beacons can be switched to either transmit or receive signals at a radio frequency that is set to the transmit mode during the initial movement. Searchers who switch their beacons to receive mode immediately after an incident can often locate a buried victim in just a few short minutes. Procedures for avalanche rescue, such as setting up a probe line, have been established by search and rescue organizations and should be reviewed prior to a trip by all persons participating in winter activities within a potential avalanche zone.

IMPACT

The impact pressures resulting from high-speed avalanches and landslides can completely destroy or harm human and animal life and property. About

Rescue teams often use dogs to track the scent of humans buried under avalanches. (AP/Wide World Photos)

one-third of avalanche victims die from the impact; the remaining two-thirds die from suffocation and hypothermia. Movement of snow and other debris is most destructive when it is able to generate extremely high speeds. Small to medium avalanches can hit with impact pressures of 1 to 5 tons per square meter, which is generally enough force to damage or destroy wood-frame structures. Larger avalanches can generate forces that can exceed 100 tons per square meter, which is easily enough to uproot mature forested areas and destroy large concrete structures.

Measurements have shown that highly turbulent dry snow or dry powder creates avalanche speeds averaging 115 to 148 feet (35 to 45 meters) per second, with some velocities being clocked as high as 223 to 279 feet (68 to 85 meters) per second. These high speeds are possible only in dry-powder avalanches because these avalanches incorporate large amounts of air within the moving snow, thus serving to reduce internal frictional forces. Wet-snow avalanches comprise liquid or snow that is very dense, which creates less turbulent movement once the slide begins. With a reduction in turbulence, a more flowing type of motion is generated, and speeds are generally reduced to approximately 66 to 98 feet (20 to 30 meters) per second.

Persons who do not live in mountainous regions might mistakenly believe that damage caused by an avalanche is minimal when compared to the destruction caused by other environmental hazards such as tornadoes and floods. However, the frequency of accidents resulting in destruction, injury, or death has risen tremendously in direct proportion to the increased popularity of winter recreational activities in mountainous areas. An estimated 150 to 200 avalanche-related deaths occur per year, but it should be noted that these avalanche data are systematically and accurately recorded mainly in developed countries in North America, Europe, and northern Asia.

Daniel G. Graetzer

BIBLIOGRAPHY

Armstrong, B. R., and K. Williams. *The Avalanche Book.* Golden, Colo.: Fulcrum Press, 1986. An excellent text highlighting the damage assessment of all major avalanches in North America.

Cupp, D. "Avalanche: Winter's White Death." *National Geographic* 162 (September, 1982): 280-305. A documentation of the March, 1982, avalanche tragedy at California's Alpine Meadows ski resort that claimed seven lives, with heroic rescuers that saving the lives of four others. Also reports on how science attempts to deal with avalanches and to rescue quickly those caught in their paths.

Graydon, E. *Mountaineering: The Freedom of the Hill.* Seattle: Mountaineers Books, 1992. A presentation of both introductory and advanced information on the sport of mountaineering, with much practical information on avalanches and other hazards of snow travel and climbing.

La Chapelle, E. R. *The ABC of Avalanche Safety.* Seattle: Mountaineers Books, 1985. This very readable and applied-science text discusses different types of avalanches, how they form, and where they can be predicted to occur, in addition to giving general guidelines on safety when traveling in mountainous regions.

Logan, Nick, and Dale Atkins. *The Snowy Torrents: Avalanche Accidents in the United States, 1980-86.* Denver: Colorado Geological Survey, Department of Natural Resources, State of Colorado, 1996. This government document examines avalanche occurrences in the United States between 1980 and 1986.

Mears, Arthur I. *Avalanche Forecasting Methods, Highway 550.* Denver: Colorado Department of Transportation, 1996. In this booklet Mears discusses avalanche control and his studies in Colorado performed in cooperation with the Federal Highway Administration.

National Research Council Panel on Snow Avalanches. *Snow Avalanche Hazards and Mitigation in the United States.* Washington, D.C.: National Academy Press, 1990. Edited by committee chair D. B. Prior and panel chair B. Voight, this government report assesses avalanches and other related natural disasters in the United States and the efficiency of relief efforts by the government.

Parfit, M. "Living with Natural Hazards." *National Geographic* 194 (July, 1998): 2-39. An excellent writeup on natural hazard areas within the United States and some personal histories of persons whose lives have been affected by them.

USDA Forest Service. *Snow Avalanche: General Rules for Avoiding and Surviving Snow Avalanches.* Portland, Oreg.: USDA Forest Service, Pacific Northwest Region, 1982. Provides general guidelines for both recreational and serious outdoor enthusiasts for avoiding and surviving snow avalanches.

Notable Events

Historical Overview

Considered one of the greatest military commanders in the history of the world, Hannibal and his North African army were no match for the natural forces unleashed in 218 B.C.E. when an avalanche descended upon his invading army of thirty-eight thousand soldiers, eight thousand horsemen, and thirty-seven elephants. The rapidly moving snowmass, which wreaked havoc at Col de la Traversette pass in the Italian Alps and claimed nearly 40 percent of Hannibal's fighting force, dealt the general one of the most devastating losses of his entire military career. The historic and horrendous tragedy experienced by Hannibal was also one of the first documented avalanches in European history.

Like so many before and since, Hannibal either was unaware of the dangerous physical environment created by the heavy snows or chose to ignore the danger. Thousands of avalanches occur annually worldwide, but most cause little damage. Each year, however, avalanches consistently claim about 150 lives and cause millions in property losses.

The European Alps, where the lives of Hannibal's troops were claimed, have been the site of the most deadly avalanches in recorded history, although the greatest number occur in the much more sparsely populated Himalayas, Andes, and Alaska. During World War I an estimated 40,000 to 80,000 soldiers were killed and maimed in the Alps by avalanches caused by the sounds and explosions of combat.

Milestones

218 B.C.E.:	Hannibal loses 20,000 men, 2,000 horses, and several elephants in a huge avalanche near Col de la Traversette in the Italian Alps.
1478:	About 60 soldiers of the Duke of Milan are killed by an avalanche while crossing the mountains near Saint Gotthard Pass in the Italian Alps.
September, 1618:	An avalanche kills 1,500 inhabitants of Plurs, Switzerland.
1689:	A series of avalanches kills more than 300 residents in Saas, Switzerland, and surrounding communities.
January, 1718:	The town of Leukerbad, Switzerland, is destroyed by two avalanches that leave more than 55 dead and many residents seriously injured.
September, 1806:	Four villages are destroyed, and 800 residents are killed when an avalanche descends Rossberg Peak in the Swiss Alps.
July, 1892:	St. Gervais and La Fayet, Swiss resorts, are destroyed when a huge avalanche speeds down Mont Blanc, killing 140 residents and tourists.
March, 1910:	An avalanche sweeps through the train station in Wellington, Washington State, destroying 3 snowbound passenger trains and killing 96.
December, 1916:	Heavy snows result in avalanches that kill more than 10,000 Italian and Austrian soldiers located in the Tirol section of the Italian-Austrian Alps.
January, 1951:	A series of avalanches leaves 240 dead; the village of Vals, Switzerland, is completely destroyed.
January, 1954:	In one of the worst avalanches in Austrian history, 145 people are killed over a 10-mile area.
1962:	Melting snow rushes down the second-highest peak in South America at speeds in excess of 100 miles per hour, killing around 4,000 in Peru.
April, 1970:	A hospital in Sallanches, France, is destroyed by an avalanche that kills 70, most of them children.
1971:	An earthquake unleashes a huge avalanche of snow and ice, killing 600 and destroying Chungar, Peru, and surrounding villages.
1982:	13 students and teachers are killed by an avalanche in Salzburg, Austria.
June, 1994:	An earthquake in the Huila region of Colombia causes avalanches and mud-slides that leave 13,000 residents homeless, 2,000 trapped, and 1,000 dead.
November, 1995:	A series of avalanches kills 43 climbers in Nepal.
March, 1997:	A park geologist and a volunteer are killed by an avalanche while working on a project to monitor Yellowstone National Park geothermal features.
1998:	Three avalanches in southeastern British Columbia, Canada, leave 8 dead and several wounded.
February, 1999:	Avalanches in Galtür, Austria, kill 38 and trap 2,000.

Such massive loss of life, however, is not representative of avalanche disasters. In a more typical year the country of Switzerland, for example, has an average avalanche death rate of less than 25. An 1892 avalanche that destroyed the Swiss resort towns of St. Gervais and La Fayet, killing 140 residents and tourists, was considered a fairly deadly and unusual occurrence. As one of the most avalanche-prone nations, Switzerland committed considerable resources after the early 1900's to identify ways to avoid the loss of property and life. The leading avalanche research center in Europe is the Swiss Federal Snow and Avalanche Research Unit, which takes considerable pride in its successful Avalanche Warning System. Similar research programs are located in the United States, Japan, and other countries.

Despite the best efforts and intentions of warning systems, avalanches continue to claim the lives of unsuspecting victims each year. Even the most highly trained and skilled scientists are often vulnerable to the deadly force of avalanches. Many of the individuals killed by the 1980 Mount St. Helens volcanic explosion and the resulting 250-mile-per-hour avalanche, the largest in recorded history, were scientists on location to study the volcano. In March, 1997, a park geologist and a volunteer were killed by an avalanche while working on a project to monitor Yellowstone National Park geothermal features.

As a result of years of research and data collection, however, scientists have identified ways of diminishing the potential for destruction and loss of life resulting from avalanches. Federal, state, regional, and local governments may coordinate efforts to detect and identify potentially unstable snow-covered slopes by monitoring weather conditions; geographic data available through photogrammetry, the science and art of deducing the physical dimensions of objects from measurements on photographs; and satellite imagery.

Donald C. Simmons, Jr.

218 B.C.E.: Alps

DATE: 218 B.C.E.
PLACE: The Alps above Italy
RESULT: 20,000-36,000 people and thousands of horses dead

During the Second Punic War, scheming to attack the Romans from the north, Hannibal of Carthage marched his vast army across the Alps, where Alpine tribes repeatedly ambushed them. Guides from one tribe led Hannibal's 7-mile column through a narrow valley only to roll massive boulders from the clifflike slopes, crushing close to 20,000 men and animals.

After nine days of perilous travel, the despondent army reached the base of the final pass. Here, to make camp, they were forced to remove snow and ice from the frozen terrain. During the two days set aside for recuperation, it snowed. At dawn on the third day the army climbed to the summit, where Hannibal stood aside and gestured to the Italian plains below, saying that in "a battle or two" they would conquer Rome itself.

However, the seemingly easy descent proved detrimental to Hannibal's army. Soldiers and pack animals slipped on the paths above steep ice fields, then fell for thousands of feet, careened off cliffs, or impaled themselves on rocks below. Diminishing quickly, the troops marched on until they came to a place where a landslide had washed away a section of the path, leaving a rock face in its place. Hannibal and his engineers decided upon a detour, directing the men a few hundred feet above the cliff. The first soldiers climbed easily through the deep, fresh snow that had fallen on the hard packed ice beneath it, and they successfully arrived at the other side. The trampled snow eventually turned to slush and ice, upon which thousands slipped. Once a man lost his footing, he almost surely tumbled to his death.

Hannibal then resorted to the arduous task of rebuilding the path. The soldiers heated portions of the cliff to a glow by building massive fires upon them. They poured vinegar onto the hot rocks, causing them to crack and split. They pried the rocks apart using iron tools. A zigzagging path, wide enough for Hannibal's elephants, was chipped out of the mountain.

The exact number of casualties is disputed by scholars, but the historian Polybius writes that Hannibal himself claimed 36,000 men were lost while traversing the Alps, half of whom died coming down from the pass. Latin and Greek histories describe Hannibal's soldiers sliding to their deaths, but based on the accounts of new snow that fell on hard ice and the extraordinary number of deaths, some modern scholars believe Hannibal's men were caught in an avalanche.

Theodore Weaver

FOR FURTHER INFORMATION:

Livy. *The History of Rome, Book V.* Translated by B. O. Foster. Cambridge, Mass.: Harvard University Press, 1996.

Prevas, John. *Hannibal Crosses the Alps.* Staplehurst, England: Spellmount Press, 1998.

FOR FURTHER INFORMATION:

Cornell, James. *The Great International Disaster Book.* New York: Charles Scribner's Sons, 1982.

Davis, Lee. *Natural Disasters.* New York: Facts on File, 1992.

Probst, Eduard. *Leukerbad Loèche-les-Bains.* Bern, Switzerland: Buchverlag Verbandsdruckerie, 1974.

1718: Switzerland

DATE: January 17, 1718
PLACE: Leukerbad, Switzerland
RESULT: Estimated 55 dead

Leukerbad, a small community situated at an elevation of 4,629 feet in the Swiss Alps, has been famous for its curative thermal baths since before the Roman Empire. The town is surrounded on three sides by mountainous slopes that lead to towering walls of rock. In parts of the valley, structures with gothic detail dating back to the 1600's still stand, but in other locations there are only modern buildings, the old having been destroyed by avalanches.

In late December, 1717, snow fell continuously for ten days. During this period the temperature gradually rose so that heavy, wet snow accumulated atop crystalline, dry snow. On the morning of January 17, the weight of the heavy snow gave way to gravity, causing a small avalanche to tumble down from the mountains, killing and burying 3 people. Using long poles to probe the snow, as rescuers still do today, the villagers located and dug out the bodies.

The search crew returned to their homes in the evening, shortly before a second avalanche broke loose. This avalanche, which descended from the 10,000-foot Balmhorn peak, carried much more snow and bore directly into the town. Bathhouses, chapels, homes, and inns were crushed and buried. One man was buried in his cellar beneath the cementlike snow for eight days, then died shortly after being discovered. A group of people were in the Saint Laurentius Chapel when it was swept away by the avalanche. Approximately half of the population perished: 52 people according to one source, 61 according to another.

Theodore Weaver

1892: Switzerland

DATE: July 12, 1892
PLACE: St. Gervais, Switzerland
RESULT: 140 dead

The avalanche that took the lives of 140 people in the towns of St. Gervais and La Fayet, Switzerland, is unique for occurring during the summer. Snow can tumble down any slope steeper than 20 degrees, and although not entirely predictable, especially in magnitude, avalanches tend to fall down the same chutes time after time, giving people a general idea of how to avoid them. However, the St. Gervais avalanche was entirely unexpected, being triggered by summer heat and melting snow. At approximately 2 A.M. on July 12, 1892, a massive chunk of La Tête Rousse glacier broke free, and hundreds of tons of ice and debris slid down the 14,318-foot Mont Blanc. The avalanche bore through both villages, killing more than 90 percent of the population, most of whom were probably sleeping, and destroying the central structures. As avalanches of this size pick up speed, a layer of compressed air forms beneath the turbulent mass, allowing the snow to travel essentially without friction. Without making contact with snow, the wind that avalanches create can flatten a forest, displace large vehicles, and even tear a wooden house from its foundation.

Theodore Weaver

FOR FURTHER INFORMATION:

Bryant, Edward. *Natural Hazards.* New York: Cambridge University Press, 1991.

Chapman, David. *Natural Hazards.* New York: Oxford University Press, 1994.

Davis, Lee. *Natural Disasters.* New York: Facts on File, 1992.

1910: Washington State

DATE: March 1, 1910
PLACE: Wellington, Washington
RESULT: 96 dead, 22 injured, $1 million in damage

The Great Northern Railroad's westbound *Spokane Express* became trapped in heavy snowfalls while crossing the Stevens Pass in the Cascade Mountains, Washington State, on Thursday, February 24, 1910. Workmen were sent out to clear the railroad tracks, and by February 26 the train had managed to get through a tunnel at the summit, reaching the small village of Wellington some 2 miles beyond the western portal of the tunnel. However, it then became trapped again, along with a westbound mail train.

A sudden rise in temperature in the whole northwest region caused some minor avalanches; one of them killed some miners in northern Idaho on February 28. Elsewhere, flooding was reported. However, it was believed safe enough to let the trains stay where they were, rather than run them back into the tunnel. The decision taken by the train superintendent was to prove fatal.

At 4:20 A.M., Tuesday, March 1, a massive avalanche hurled the trains, with their sleeping passengers and workers, over the bottom ledge of the high line, to the bottom of the gorge 150 feet below. The wreckage, consisting of three locomotives, four electric engines, and carriages, lay buried beneath snow, loose stones, and uprooted trees. The station and a water tank were also destroyed. The hotel, store, and saloon were untouched.

Communication was difficult because the telegraph wires were down. The first full news of the disaster was brought by Thomas Wentzel, who had managed to reach Skykomish, 18 miles away. Rescue efforts were difficult because of the heavy, unstable snowfall and the danger of further avalanches. A rescue train dispatched from Everett could only get to within 10 miles of the disaster; from there, doctors and nurses had to don snowshoes. The railroad bunkhouse at Wellington became a temporary hospital for the 10 injured people.

It was not until late on March 2 that the superintendent could lead a medical party down to the wreck itself. First estimates suggested 40 dead among the passengers, with perhaps a further 30 workmen, but only

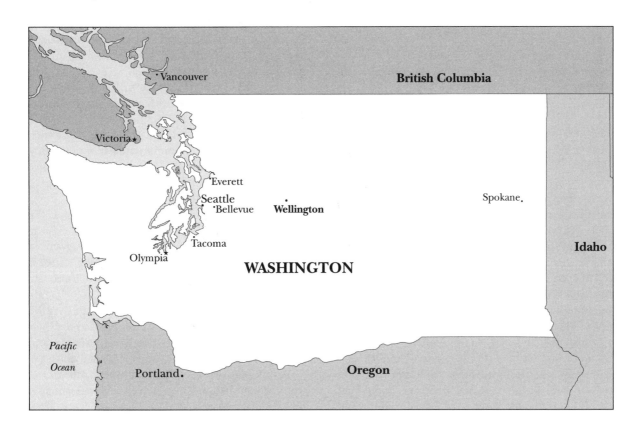

12 bodies could be removed at first. Several passengers had, in fact, left the train a few days before to walk to safety. A few others had been boarded in Wellington. Rescue efforts from the east were hampered by a slide at Drury, 6 miles east of Leavenworth, which destroyed a station and killed the watchman. Elsewhere, 6 laborers were killed by other avalanches.

By March 4, 40 people had been rescued, with 150 men trying to dig out the remainder. Some cars were still under 70 feet of debris. By now a cold rain had set in, bringing fear of further slides. Of the 700 sacks of mail from the mail train, 150 had been recovered; fortunately, the train had not been carrying passengers. The full count of 96 dead could not be confirmed for some time. As a result of the disaster, a much longer tunnel was constructed to cover the whole section of railroad vulnerable to avalanche activity.

David Barratt

FOR FURTHER INFORMATION:
Galagher, Dale, ed. *The Snowy Torrents: Avalanches in the U.S. 1910-1966.* Wasatch National Forest, Idaho: USDA Forest Service, 1967.
The New York Times, March 2-5, 1910.

1915: British Columbia

DATE: March 23, 1915
PLACE: Britannia Mine, near Vancouver, British Columbia, Canada
RESULT: 50 dead

Before the mid-1800's, the mountainous regions of North America were relatively unpopulated. Mines, then railroads, brought more people to the mountains, and as a consequence, the number of avalanche deaths increased significantly. In late March of 1915, hundreds of tons of snow broke loose above the Britannia Mine at Howe Sound and fell upon the bunkhouses, killing 50 miners and injuring many more. The snow ripped away an aerial tramway used to transport men and coal approximately 5,000 vertical feet from the mine to the beach. When the avalanche struck, most of the one thousand men employed by Britannia were at work in the mine. Had the slide occurred during a meal or at night, when the bunkhouses were full, the avalanche would have been much more deadly.

Theodore Weaver

FOR FURTHER INFORMATION:
Armstrong, Betsy. *The Avalanche Book.* Golden, Colo.: Fulcrum, 1986.
"Fifty Killed by Snowslide." *The New York Times,* March 23, 1915.

1916: Alps

DATE: December 13, 1916
PLACE: Italy
RESULT: Estimated 10,000 soldiers dead

In May, 1915, Italy declared war on the Austro-Hungarian Empire. At that time, Austria still held the province of Trentino in the southeastern extension of the Alps and the adjoining Dolomite Mountains. In May, 1916, Austria attacked Italy through the Trentino Alps and made some progress into northern Italy. Some 425,000 soldiers were in the Austro-Hungarian army and a similar number in the Italian. The latter army, reinforced, counterattacked and regained most of the lost territory.

From July, 1916, to February, 1917, fighting was mostly on a small scale, with the Alpine front line heavily defended, especially by artillery. Besides shelling each other, the two sides would undermine each other's positions and dynamite whole mountain summits in efforts to dislodge the other side. Soldiers were stationed at heights of up to 9,000 feet, up to seven months at a time.

More than any other front in World War I, the Austro-Italian front was influenced by weather conditions. The winter of 1916-1917 was extremely severe, with massive blizzards and gales sweeping through the area during most of December, 1916. It was not surprising, therefore, that dangerous snow conditions built up. In all efforts to gain advantage over the other side, however, each side continued to use their artillery and explosives. Disaster was inevitable, and on December 13, a series of avalanches slid down the Alpine slopes, sweeping away whole sections of the front line and supporting positions. It is estimated that 10,000 soldiers perished—heavier casualties than on any single day's fighting. However, the news of the disaster was entirely suppressed, and no account of it can be found in any contemporary record of the war, despite its being the worst avalanche disaster on record.

David Barratt

FOR FURTHER INFORMATION:
Reynolds, Francis J. *The Story of the Great War.* Vol. 6. New York: P. F. Collier & Son, 1916.

ing men made it back to the base via an aqueduct, a small tunnel, and a type of railway operated by a rope.

Theodore Weaver

FOR FURTHER INFORMATION:
Cortesi, Arnaldo. "21 Italian Soldiers Killed by Avalanches." *The New York Times,* January 29, 1931.
"Soldiers Caught by Avalanche." *The Times* (London), January 29, 1931.

1931: Italy

DATE: January 28, 1931
PLACE: Bardonecchia, Italy
RESULT: 21 dead

On January 26, 1931, three regiments of thirty men each set out to climb Mount Galambra to the northeast of Bardonecchia. When a heavy mist blew into the area and snow began to fall, two of the regiments turned back. Under the direction of a major and two captains, the third regiment of the Fenestrella Battalion marched on and successfully reached the summit. Hampered by heavy snow during the descent, the regiment stopped for the night in a hut halfway down the mountain.

Heavy snow continued to fall and drift, putting the men in clear avalanche danger. On the morning of the 27th, a captain led the men down the left side of the mountain, choosing this route because it was protected from above by a forest. A dry avalanche roared down the right side of the mountain at such a speed that it passed through the valley bottom and rushed up the other side, burying 8 soldiers and a captain. Of the 2 men dug out, 1 was injured, the other dead.

As the blizzard continued to rage and the path was blocked, the soldiers hiked back to the hut, where the injured man later died. Their food had run out, and they had no firewood. On January 28, intending to call for help at the base in Bardonecchia, a small squad set out ahead of the others. Of these men, only the sergeant major arrived at the base, and because of the threatening weather no rescuers could be sent.

In the vicinity of the first avalanche, 9 men in the following group were buried by what survivors described as a whirlwind-like snowslide. The 8 remain-

1951: Alps

DATE: January 20, 1951
PLACE: Switzerland, Austria, France, and Italy
RESULT: 240 dead, hundreds injured, thousands of acres of forest destroyed, buildings and cattle lost

The winter months of 1950-1951 in the Alpine areas of Switzerland, Austria, France, and Italy came to be known as "the winter of terror." In mid-January, 1951, there were some very unusual weather conditions in the whole region. Masses of warm air from the Atlantic met masses of cold air from the polar regions, resulting in very heavy precipitation. In some places, 10 to 15 feet of thick, wet snow fell in only three hours. In other places, 2 inches of snow per hour fell continuously for twenty-four hours. The weight of the new snow over a four-day period broke the crust of older layers of compacted snow, causing a massive series of avalanches all over the region on January 20.

In Switzerland, the eastern part of the country was the worst affected—at least 15,000 square miles from Andermatt and Wassen to the Austrian border. Scores of villages and valleys saw frantic local rescue operations, but such efforts were hampered by broken communications and continuing heavy snowfall. No trains could run, and most roads had to be closed because of avalanche warnings. One of the first avalanches occurred at Zernez, where an elderly roadworker died. Six rescuers digging for him were hit by a second avalanche and swept away. There were avalanches where none had occurred before.

The main Gotthard railroad line was cut in three or four places, and 60 people were reported trapped in a railroad tunnel between Chur and Arosa, with avalanches falling at both ends. It took a day for the men to fight their way out to a nearby village; Alpine tourists and skiers were trapped. In the ski resort of Andermatt, three avalanches crashed into the village. Barns and cattle were lost on a massive scale.

Worst hit in terms of casualties was Austria, with at least 120 deaths. Ten workers were killed at a sawmill in Carynthia when an avalanche crashed into it. Thousands of acres of forest were swept away, and whole villages were overwhelmed. Two locomotives were knocked from their tracks, and the whole railroad system in the Tirol was closed down.

A most remarkable story from Austria is that of Gerhard Freissegger. He was working on a hydroelectric scheme near Heiligenblut in the Austrian Alps and was trapped in a station hut when a massive avalanche struck. He was buried for ten days, heard a colleague die, and then had to wait for help a further two days after he had managed to scratch his way to the surface. At the time, it was the longest anyone had survived in an avalanche.

Italy and France also suffered damage. In Switzerland, the army was brought in to evacuate villages and mortar unstable slopes. In Austria, the Allied armies of occupation helped the local forces in their rescue efforts. The Swiss Avalanche Research Institute pronounced the death and damage sustained to be the worst in the history of the Alps.

David Barratt

FOR FURTHER INFORMATION:
The New York Times, January 21-23, 1951.

1952: Austria

DATE: February 11-13, 1952
PLACE: Melkoede, Austria
RESULT: 78 dead

A snowstorm that raged for ten days in Europe in 1952 wreaked havoc in many countries, with Austria bearing the brunt. In Germany, where the mail was delayed, 2,000 workers and 92 plows removed snow from Berlin streets. There were three accidental deaths in Stockholm, and Norwegian fire crews traveled by sled. Winds made church bells ring. In France, roofs collapsed under the weight of the snow.

On February 11, an avalanche engulfed a small ski resort in Melkoede, Austria, catching 50 in their sleep. The rush of snow killed 20 people and injured 10. Sixteen German skiers who had gone to Austria for the weekend, an innkeeper, his wife, and his son were among the dead. The twentieth man died in a hospital.

Experts in Davos, Switzerland, warned of imminent danger, and an entire village was evacuated in the Vaud Canton. A snowslide tore down barns and killed cattle in Isenthal on February 12. An avalanche in Leutasche, Austria, buried a family of 7. Four subsequent avalanches impeded the rescue effort, which was able to save only one twelve-year-old boy. On Brienzerrothorm Mountain in Austria, an avalanche flattened every building on its slope, including previously untouched chalets built in 1663.

Theodore Weaver

FOR FURTHER INFORMATION:
"Avalanche Toll 75; More Snow in Europe." *The New York Times*, February 14, 1952.
"19 Die as Avalanche Hits Austrian Resort." *The New York Times*, February 12, 1952.
"Tempêtes de neige sur l'Europe." *Le Monde*, February 14, 1952.

1952: Austria

DATE: December 23, 1952
PLACE: Lagen, Austria
RESULT: 23 dead

On December 23, 1952, a blast of air preceding an avalanche blew a bus of tourists off a bridge on the Flexenstrasse mountain road into the Aflenz River 18 feet below. The bus, which was equipped with Caterpillar tracks (two endless metal belts), was then partially covered with snow and rock. Sustaining only minor injuries, the bus driver ran back to Lagen to notify authorities, then insisted on aiding in the rescue effort until he collapsed and was taken to the hospital. Before the rescue crew arrived, the leader of a British ski group on board broke a window, and the survivors began to evacuate themselves. Of the 31 passengers, 23 died. The primary cause of death was lung injury resulting from the initial blast of air. The families of the deceased, 11 of whom were British, traveled to the Lagen church to identify the dead.

One father lost 3 children, and the leader of the British tour, a widower, lost his eleven-year-old son.

The Arlberg Pass had been intermittently closed throughout the day. The tour bus, which had been delayed by a minor breakdown earlier, was the last vehicle allowed to pass. The second-to-last car to pass carried Prince Henry of Bavaria.

Theodore Weaver

FOR FURTHER INFORMATION:
"British Victims of Avalanche." *The Times* (London), December 24, 1952.
"Crash Dead Identified." *The New York Times*, December 24, 1952.
"23 Killed by Avalanche." *The Times* (London), December 23, 1952.
"23 Skiers Killed in Alps Avalanche; Air Pressure Hurls Bus off Bridge." *The New York Times*, December 23, 1952.

1954: Alps

DATE: January 11-14, 1954
PLACE: Austria, Germany, Italy, and Switzerland
RESULT: 145 dead

A succession of avalanches in 1954 during a fierce winter blizzard buried families, farms, and entire villages throughout Austria, Germany, Italy, and Switzerland. Hundreds of Alpine villages, particularly in the Austrian province of Vorarlberg, were isolated when snow, wind, and avalanches dismantled communication. Telephone lines, roads, and rail systems were blocked. A passenger train approaching Lucerne, Switzerland, ran into the residue of an avalanche, derailing the locomotive and baggage car but causing no deaths. Less fortunate were the 3 dead and 7 missing when a snowslide buried the train station at Balaas. Six cars of the nearby express train, which was stopped between two other avalanches, were blasted off the tracks by a third avalanche.

Tons of snow descended upon the Austrian town of Blons, where 385 people lived in 117 houses. An avalanche roared into the village, killing 27 people and leaving 35 missing. A mountainous pile of snow dammed the Lutz River that runs through Blons, causing flooding in the village strewn with ice and debris. At daybreak, 300 rescuers in a nearby village set out for Blons on cross-country skis, and officials in Bregenz planned to dynamite a bridge to divert the river.

One man described how he was caught in the avalanche. Siegfried Jenny heard the avalanche when he left his house around 9 A.M. to help his father and brother with the pigs. He was instantly caught in the slide and swam with his arms for the second or two that he was engulfed. When he looked around, his brother, father, and the stable had disappeared. He remained at home for two days with a broken leg before receiving medical attention.

Near the Swiss border, more than 1,000 rescuers came to the Walser region, where avalanches crushed seven villages. They were able to dig out 207 people alive, many of whom were seriously injured. Farming families unable to flee the region took refuge in their cellars.

Among the 4 found dead in Germany's Bavarian Alps, a sixty-year-old woman was crushed when an avalanche collided with her farmhouse. Others in the Alpine region died when their roofs collapsed under the weight of snow. A church, a school, a stable, and an inn were flattened in the Swiss town of Riemenstalden. As winds, snow, and more avalanches hampered rescuers from six countries, many survivors struggled with inadequate supplies and shelter.

Theodore Weaver

FOR FURTHER INFORMATION:
"Aid Sped to Victims of Alps Avalanches." *The New York Times*, January 15, 1954.
"Alpine Avalanches Take Toll of 198 in 3 Countries." *The New York Times*, January 13, 1954.
"Alps Snow Victims Get Help by Plane." *The New York Times*, January 14, 1954.
"Avalanches Spread over West Europe." *The New York Times*, January 12, 1954.

1962: Peru

DATE: January 10, 1962
PLACE: Mount Huascarán, Andes mountain range, Peru
RESULT: Estimated 4,000 dead, $1.2 million in crop damage

Peru's Mount Huascarán during a rock and snow avalanche. (Courtesy National Oceanic and Atmospheric Administration)

Villagers living in the shadow of the 22,205-foot-high Mount Huascarán are accustomed to avalanches. Since 1702, avalanches and *aluviónes*, which are floods of liquid mud occurring with little or no warning, have wiped out villages or caused massive damage in the Río Santa Valley. *Aluviónes* usually transport boulders and huge blocks of ice, causing damage as they slide down the mountainside. Two devastating *aluviónes* in 1941 caused the geological survey to number the glaciers within the Andes mountain range in an effort to prevent further disasters. Glacier 511 was the culprit on January 10, 1962, when an overhanging edge of ice broke away at 6:13 P.M.

Shouts of *alud* or *apaqui*, meaning "avalanche," are familiar warnings. Those hearing the warnings take cover. Typical snow avalanches can take twenty minutes or more to descend the side of the mountain, allowing villagers to move to safe ground, according to reports of survivors of the January 10, 1962, avalanche. Two men standing in front of the church in Huarascucho talking with friends heard the roar of cascading ice from Mount Huascarán. One told the other it would take the avalanche twenty minutes to get there, but within five minutes the avalanche was a mere two blocks away.

Geologists, surveyors, and reporters worked to piece together the events of this 1962 glacial avalanche. The chunk of ice breaking away from glacier 511 was estimated to have begun as a block of ice about the size of two Empire State Buildings. Occurring after the equatorial rainy months, the nearly 5 million tons of ice literally rocketed down the mountainside cushioned by water and melting ice. It gathered snow, mud, trees, and boulders the size of houses, creating a massive, 40-foot-high tidal wave of debris. At 6:15 P.M. it smashed against a hill at the narrowest point of the gorge, bouncing in a new direction. Diverted from a direct course toward the city of Yungay, it instead buried Yanamachico. As it ripped through the village of Shacsha, a few villagers managed to escape by climbing to higher ground. The snow then crushed half the village of Huarascucho. By 6:18 P.M. the avalanche had wiped out the villages

Melting ice caused the edge of a huge glacier on the peak of Mount Huascarán in the Andes Mountains to break away in January, 1962. As it fell it caused a high-speed avalanche to descend on the Río Santa Valley in Peru. The avalanche destroyed nine towns, including totally burying seven small villages in up to 40 feet of ice and mud, and caused heavy destruction to three towns, wiping out vast sections as the tidal wave of snow moved through. The avalanche also caused *aluviónes*, or floods, which led to further damage. The two hardest-hit towns were Ranrahirca, Peru, from which only about 5 inhabitants survived, and Huarascucho, Peru, half of which was wiped out.

No one knows exactly how many people died during this disaster. Because the avalanche cascaded through the valley at dusk, as most villagers were sitting down to their evening meals, a majority of villagers were trapped in their homes. The avalanche also descended at tremendous speed. It traveled 9.3 miles in less than seven minutes, dropping a total of 8,600 feet in altitude from its starting point.

of Pongor and Uchucoto, before it hurtled upon the town of Ranrahirca, where the greatest number of fatalities occurred. It finally came to a stop at 6:20 P.M., after crashing into the Río Santa (Santa River), damming it with debris that caused flooding of up to 15 feet of water and wiped out two bridges farther down the river.

The avalanche struck in a zigzagging path, bouncing throughout its journey. Surveyors, as well as survivors of the disaster, noted five separate impact points marked in the path of the avalanche. It rolled across fertile bottomland, destroying about $1.2 million worth of crops. The amount of total property damage was not estimated by officials.

The avalanche was said to either kill or spare a person entirely. Fewer than two dozen people were hospitalized after the disaster. Although doctors arriving on the scene had little to do—because few survivors remained—they soon found themselves vaccinating the clean-up crews, survivors, and grieving families of victims against typhoid, typhus, and the dreaded mountain disease *verruga*, which is native to parts of the Andes and spread by the sandfly. So many victims remained buried in debris—and about 10,000 livestock were also decomposing—that water sources easily became corrupted. Bulldozers were used to clear away mud and debris in Huarascucho and Ranrahirca, and occasionally victims were discovered.

The casualties of many hamlets and villages, such as Pacucco, Shacsha, Yanamachico, Chuquibamba, Calla, and Uchucoto remained entombed beneath 60 or more feet of debris. Several bodies were carried down the river to the seaport of Chimbote, 100 miles away, where the Santa River meets the Pacific Ocean.

Despite the devastation, the mayor of Ranrahirca, Alfonso Caballero, was confident in his proclamation to build a new town nearby. The new town would also be called Ranrahirca, the Hill of Many Stones, with the main avenue named the Street of January Tenth. After surviving this catastrophe, no one believed such a devastating event would again take place. However, on May 31, 1970, an earthquake caused yet another glacial avalanche to descend upon the valley.

Lisa A. Wroble

FOR FURTHER INFORMATION:
"Avalanche Hits Peru, Nation of Disaster." *U.S. News & World Report*, January 22, 1962, 12.

Bryant, Edward. *Natural Hazards.* New York: Cambridge University Press, 1991.

Facklam, Howard. *Avalanche!* New York: Crestwood House, 1991.

McDowell, Bart. "Avalanche!" *National Geographic* 121, no. 6 (June, 1962): 856-879.

"Peru: Avalanche." *Newsweek*, January 22, 1962, 27.

Sutton, Ann, and Myron Sutton. *Nature on the Rampage: A Natural History of the Elements.* New York: J. B. Lippincott, 1962.

Uhrbrock, Don. "Valley Buried Alive." *Life* 52, no. 4 (January 26, 1962): 26-35.

1965: British Columbia

DATE: February 18, 1965
PLACE: Leduc Camp, near Stewart, British Columbia, Canada
RESULT: 26 dead, 17 seriously injured, mining camp mostly destroyed by snow and ice

The Leduc glacier in northwestern British Columbia, Canada, was the site of one of Canada's worst avalanche disasters. The glacier covered a large amount of low-grade copper ore, and the Granduc Mining Company created an ambitious mining project to get the ore out from under the massive sheet of ice. Two mining camps were built at either end of an 11-mile tunnel. On the morning of February 18, 1965, the camp at the Leduc glacier side of the tunnel was buried under a massive avalanche or glacial slide that trapped 40 people, the third avalanche in five weeks to hit the province.

Luckily for the survivors, the camp was able to radio a distress call while the slide was in progress, and the rescue operation was launched immediately. Rescue teams were brought in from both Canada and the United States, as the Granduc Mine was very close to the British Columbia-Alaska border. The remote nature of the mining site required rescue parties to travel either by air or by Caterpillar train. Many of the missing had been working in the tunnel when it was at least partially obstructed by the tons of snow and ice. While some were able to cut their own way to safety, others were rescued by the dozens of workers not hurt in the avalanche. Most of the missing had to rely on Canadian and American military and civilian rescuers for possible escape.

The rescue was a multinational land, air, and sea operation that included the Royal Canadian Air Force, the Royal Canadian Mounted Police, and the United States Coast Guard, in addition to civilians and other police agencies. The U.S. Coast Guard cutter *Cape Romain* was sent as a staging base to receive victims as they were airlifted out of the disaster area, as was the Alaskan ferry *Taku*. Unfortunately, the weather was rapidly changing and often made air travel in and out of the area extremely hazardous. The difficult weather conditions included alternating snow and rain with heavy wind gusts. Making the flights even more dangerous was the unique topography of the area. The glacier was surrounded by extinct volcanoes around 8,000 feet high, which only magnified weather effects. The overland rescue routes were blocked by snow and required bulldozing to keep them open, making air rescue the only real possibility.

Within two days, most of the survivors of the mining camp had been flown out of the area to Vancouver, the province's largest city, hundreds of miles to the south.

Rescue workers labored to try and free any possible survivors, but it became increasingly unlikely by the hour that any additional survivors would be found. Within four days the bodies of 14 of the missing 27 miners had been found. Despite the lessening chances of finding anyone still alive under the snow and ice, on February 21, 1965, the searchers uncovered Einar Myllyla, who had been buried alive under the avalanche. The carpenter had been able to survive because the snow that covered him also left a large air pocket, allowing him to breath for the slightly more than three days it took rescuers to find him. Myllyla, who at the time of the disaster had been only approximately 25 yards from where the radio operator had sent out the camp's distress call, though buried under 6 feet of snow, was found completely by accident after a bulldozer revealed his location. The rescue was made even more incredible by the fact that his location was directly under the makeshift helicopter landing area that had seen numerous aircraft land and take off for three days. Myllyla was subsequently airlifted out of the area and taken to a hospital in Ketchikan, Alaska, where he was treated for shock and various exposure-related maladies.

The rescue of Myllyla was the last discovery of any survivors from the Granduc mine. By February 26, 1965, worsening weather conditions required a halt of all active rescue operations. The authorities became fearful that conditions were becoming worse and that additional avalanches were a distinct possibility. This, coupled with the extreme length of time since the initial slide, ruled out any additional chances of finding any more survivors. Although only 19 fatalities had been confirmed by that date, 7 more bodies were later found, bringing the final death toll to 26.

The disaster at the Granduc mining camp led to a dramatic change in the planned copper mine. A new tunnel was designed that allowed excavation of the copper ore without exposing miners to the avalanche dangers at the Leduc glacier site. This resulted in the construction of a 10-mile-long tunnel under three glaciers and several mountains to access the mine. Despite the disaster at the Granduc mining camp, the newly designed mine was built and continued operations until 1984.

Darren J. Pierson

FOR FURTHER INFORMATION:

Fraser, Colin. "Death and Survival." In *Avalanches and Snow Safety.* New York: Charles Scribner's Sons, 1978.

The New York Times, February 19-25, 1965.

The Times (London), February 19-26, 1965.

1970: France

DATE: February 10, 1970
PLACE: Val d'Isère, France
RESULT: 42 dead, 60 injured

In what was called the worst avalanche in French history, more than 100,000 cubic yards of dry-powder snow slid down the Val d'Isère ski resort and smashed through the picture windows of a hotel operated by a nonprofit youth organization. The incident, which happened in the morning, killed 39 young skiers who were eating breakfast on the ground floor and injured more than 60 others. The massive snowslide was of relatively dry, cold snow. The hotel organization's technical counselor estimated that the avalanche had billowed up to 100 yards in height by the time it struck the hotel. A group of 3 ski-trail workers was hurtled into the air when caught in the avalanche, and a few parked cars were rolled across National Route 202.

One survivor described a deafening and horrible noise moments before the avalanche reached the hotel. Another, who suffered a deep cut on his arm, was caught on the stairs, washed down a hallway by snow, and thrown out a window. The snow buried one man up to his neck and was so solid that he could not budge; victims often had to be cut free with steel blades. Many were dug out alive despite severe storms and impassable roads, which hampered the rescue effort.

In the following days, people in high-risk areas were evacuated to public buildings that had been converted to shelters. Subsequent avalanches pushed 6 cars off roads but resulted in no injuries. An eight-month-old girl, who was injured when an avalanche careened into her hotel, later died in an ambulance when it came to an impasse on the road. French president Georges Pompidou declared the series of avalanches a national tragedy and sent the minister of the interior and the secretary of state to oversee the rescue effort. Two days after the first snowslide, the deserted youth hotel was struck by another avalanche.

Theodore Weaver

FOR FURTHER INFORMATION:
Farnsworth, Clyde H. "39 Die in France Under Snowslide." *The New York Times*, February 11, 1970.
Hess, John L. "Old Dangers Turning up in French Snow-slide Area." *The New York Times*, February 21, 1970.
"New Slides in French Alps Kill an Infant." *The New York Times*, February 13, 1970.

1971: Peru

DATE: March 19, 1971
PLACE: Chungar, Peru
RESULT: 600 dead

A minor earthquake in the Andes Mountains set off a landslide, which poured into a lake. Displaced water swelled over the shores and washed down a lower face, creating an avalanche of snow, mud, and rock similar to a wet avalanche, which is caused by running meltwater and characteristically accumulates mud and rock. The rush of snow and earth obliterated the village of Chungar, its road, and its bridge. Six hundred died in the village situated 55 miles north of Lima. The slide blocked the main route to Chungar, which takes eight hours to travel by foot from the nearest town. Search parties traversed a 13,000-foot mountain range and descended from the east into the rubble-strewn mining camp, which sits at 10,000 feet. The voyage took rescuers more than twenty-four hours to arrive from Lima, Cerro de Pasco, and Canta.

In the winter and spring, snow and mud avalanches are relatively common in Peru. Less than a year earlier, a landslide buried approximately 70,000 people in two towns beneath Mount Huascarán.

Theodore Weaver

FOR FURTHER INFORMATION:
"Avalanche Said to Kill 400 at Peruvian Mining Camp." *The New York Times*, March 20, 1971.
"Avalanche Strikes in Peru." *Christian Science Monitor*, March 20, 1971.

Peruvian survivors view destruction after a 1971 avalanche. (AP/Wide World Photos)

1982: Austria

DATE: January 31, 1982
PLACE: Salzburg, Austria
RESULT: 13 dead

After two days of unseasonably warm weather in the Salzburg region, an avalanche rumbled down from a steep, craggy ridge to engulf 19 cross-country skiers on the reclining expanse below. They were all students and teachers from Berchtesgaden, a private school located in Bavaria, Germany. The group had come on a school trip to the picturesque ski trails and pine forests in the Tenuen mountain range.

After the slide, which may have been triggered by boisterous shouting, one girl succeeded in digging herself out and located an inn, whose owner telephoned the police. Using gas lamps and portable searchlights, a rescue crew worked for seven hours into the night. Four youths and one adult were dug out alive. The rescue effort was called off under mounting fear of a second slide and as the chances of survival of the sole remaining victim dwindled. The next day, aided by trained avalanche dogs, the body of Oliver Jensen was found buried 16 feet down.

Hermann Tum, an experienced German ski instructor, had led the group on the Mount Elmau trail system. He had ignored an avalanche warning earlier in the day.

Theodore Weaver

FOR FURTHER INFORMATION:

"Avalanche in Austria Kills 11 in Ski Group." *The New York Times*, February 1, 1982.
"Avalanche Kills 12 Teenagers." *The Times* (London), February 1, 1982.
"Lost Boy Found 16 Feet Down." *The Times* (London), February 2, 1982.

1982: Alps

DATE: March 14, 1982
PLACE: French Alps
RESULT: 16 dead

Although avalanches are difficult to predict, snow engineers and geologists are quick to recognize the conditions that cause them. When a sunny, warm spell on March 14, 1982, followed two days of heavy snowfall, specialists at the Grenoble Center for the Study of Snow released warnings of high avalanche danger. Yet at the same time, tens of thousands of skiers flocked to the ski resorts to enjoy the fresh powder and good weather.

That afternoon, avalanches killed 16 skiers and mountaineers, almost all of whom had disregarded ski-area boundaries in pursuit of more adventurous terrain. Some had climbed to steep, south-facing chutes, where the new snow became increasingly heavy and unstable in the afternoon sun. Avalanches in high altitudes and away from regular runs in the Savoie Department took 8 lives. Two more deaths were confirmed in the Isère Department, where rescue crews probed the cementlike snow that resulted from even the smallest slides. One boy was washed away when an avalanche caught him above the top lift at the Arrondaz ski area. His friends managed to escape. In addition to the 16 who died, another 28 were rescued after being buried in the frozen, immobilizing substance. Two were left in critical condition.

Theodore Weaver

FOR FURTHER INFORMATION:

"Alps Toll Now 16." *The Times* (London), March 16, 1982.
"11 Killed, 20 Injured in Alps by Avalanches." *The New York Times*, March 15, 1982.
"11 Skiers Killed by Avalanches." *The Times* (London), March 15, 1982.
Francillon, Claude. "Douze personnes tuées par des avalanches." *Le Monde*, March 16, 1982.

1995: India

DATE: January 16-19, 1995
PLACE: Kashmir, India
RESULT: More than 200 dead, 5,000 motorists trapped

Unusually heavy snow fell in mid-January, 1995, in the northern Indian province of Kashmir. It is a mountainbound region, with different ranges of the

Himalayas forming natural borders with the outside world; communications are not easy at the best of times. The two main cities of Kashmir, Srinagar and Jammu, are connected by a narrow 110-mile highway that winds among the foothills of the Himalayas. It is an area with a heavy military presence, as the whole province is disputed territory between India and Pakistan.

The initial storm began on January 16; one of the first avalanches swept two buses off the highway. Most of the occupants were killed. At least three more buses were reported to have plunged off the road. Although 133 people were recovered fairly quickly by rescuers led by the police, many others were feared dead.

The main problem for the rescuers was the thousands of motorists stranded in the snowdrifts. About 400 people were able to take refuge in the 1.7-mile-long Jawahar road tunnel, and air force helicopters dropped food and blankets near the mouth of the tunnel for those stranded there. However, many of these people died of exposure awaiting rescue. It took two days and two nights for them to be rescued, with continuing drifts and avalanches outside the tunnel hampering efforts.

Up to 5,000 motorists were eventually rescued, but dozens more froze to death, trapped in their vehicles or trying to walk through drifts 10 feet deep. Helicopters shuttled up and down the 7,650-foot pass at the center of the 25 miles of blocked road, dropping supplies of food, blankets, snow-boots, shovels, and pickaxes. Many vehicles were not reached by such haphazard efforts, which were marked by considerable confusion. Police underestimated the severity of the disaster; the rescue operation only really got underway on Friday, January 20, mainly because of poor communication between the police and the armed forces. After it was discovered that the Indian army had up to 0.5 million soldiers in the province, it can be seen why much criticism was leveled at the authorities in this politically sensitive area. As a result, the Indian government ordered an inquiry to be set up, led by a high-ranking army officer who had served as adviser to the governor of Kashmir.

David Barratt

FOR FURTHER INFORMATION:
The New York Times, January 20-22, 1995.

1995: Iceland

DATE: October 27, 1995
PLACE: Flateyri, Iceland
RESULT: 20 dead

Storms were generic over Iceland on October 25, 1995: A car was blown off the road in Siglufjordur, metal roofing panels were wrenched off houses and a hotel, 90 people were evacuated from their homes in the West Fjords, winter conditions had arrived early, and the sun rose at 8:47 A.M. and set at 5:36 P.M. The next day approximately 200 electrical poles were snapped by winds; an avalanche descended on a herd of horses in Langidalur, killing 18 and sparing 3; and an avalanche crashed down on the harbor in Sugandafjor, splintering a storage building. Two men at the harbor in Isafjordur luckily escaped danger when rumbling snow rammed the waste-disposal plant where they worked.

At 4 A.M. on October 27, an "extremely large and quite unusual" avalanche, according to Mr. Egilsson of the Iceland Meteorological Office, propelled itself much farther than predicted and pulverized Flateyri (population 379). Snow buried 17 houses, only 1 of which had been built in an avalanche danger zone. While severe weather initially hampered the rescue effort, hundreds of villagers relied upon memory to locate buried houses. Twenty people either dug themselves out or were helped by neighbors. U.S. helicopters and the Icelandic Coast Guard then shuttled another 600 rescuers and trained dogs to Flateyri. Of the 4 more discovered alive, 1 was a twenty-seven-year-old woman who had been immobilized in the hardened snow for eight hours. An eleven-year-old girl survived for eleven hours. By the end of the day the death toll had risen to 19, leaving the body of a one-year-old girl missing for another two days.

Approximately nine months earlier, on January 17, 1995, an early-morning avalanche struck the Icelandic fishing village of Sudavik (population 230), killing 16. Of the 11 people dug out alive, many were children who had been asleep when buried and were wearing nothing but their underwear.

Theodore Weaver

FOR FURTHER INFORMATION:
"Flateyri, October 26, 1995." www.geophys.washing ton.edu/People/Students/throstho/flateyri.html.

Johnson, Helga. "Sixteen Feared Dead in Iceland Avalanche." *The Times* (London), January 17, 1995.

1996: India

DATE: March 16-18, 1996
PLACE: Kashmir, India
RESULT: 72 dead

On March 16, 1996, tons of snow overcame frictional resistance on the deeply cut slopes above the village of Kel, Azad "Free" Kashmir, India; the avalanche uprooted a pine forest on its way down. The snowslide killed 32 people in the military outpost, wiped away 2 houses, and washed over 5 others. Stormy weather and the remote location of the village slowed the rescue effort. Wet-snow avalanches, which consist of damp snow, are particularly common in the spring. Slab avalanches and dry-powder avalanches are more common during the coldest months of winter.

Two days after the avalanche in Kel, another avalanche came down on the village of Muzaffarabad, about one mile away. Since it descended at night, the 40 people who died were most likely asleep when buried by the snow.

Theodore Weaver

FOR FURTHER INFORMATION:
"40 Die in Second Kashmir Avalanche." *Los Angeles Times*, March 20, 1996.
"Kashmiris Start Talks with Delhi." *The Times* (London), March 16, 1996.
"32 Die in Kashmir Slide." *Los Angeles Times*, March 17, 1996.
"32 Lost in Kashmir Slide." *The New York Times*, March 16, 1996.

1999: France

DATE: February 9, 1999
PLACE: Chamonix, France
RESULT: 12 dead

A dry-powder avalanche rumbled down Mount Pléceret in the Chamonix Valley in February of 1999, ripping up forests and demolishing chalets in the villages of Le Tour and Montroc-le-Planet. The tons of dry snow transported cement blocks, gravel, cracked timber, and other debris through the valley bottom and up the other side of the mountain, where it came to a stop. Much of the destruction of the Chamonix avalanche resulted from the snow blasting through residential areas that, according to Chamonix mayor Michel Charlet, were zoned for construction.

Monitoring devices placed at 6,000 feet showed that the snow base increased to 18 feet during heavy snowfall three days before the slide. A dry-powder avalanche, such as the one at Chamonix, occurs when newly fallen or drifted powder slides down a slope on top of stable, hard snow. The avalanche de-

An avalanche descends upon Le Tour and Montroc-le-Planet in Chamonix Valley in the French Alps. (AP/Wide World Photos)

stroyed 17 chalets and buried 6 others. One home was wrenched from its foundation and skidded across the road; two other structures were displaced by 30 feet.

As an additional 16 inches of snow fell, 200 workers with sensory devices and rescue dogs probed the snow with poles, primarily looking for people buried in their homes. A twelve-year-old boy who lost both parents was trapped for five hours and was suffering from hypothermia when discovered. The mountain police brigade shoveled out a total of 20 survivors while working through the night.

Peter Borgaard, a hotel owner in Montroc, saw the avalanche engulf his building and trap customers and friends. Nathan Wallace, a native of California, survived the avalanche. "I've seen many avalanches," he said, "but not the type that come into your house and blow it away. It was more like a California earthquake." The avalanche collapsed the roof of his chalet. Of the 12 who died, the avalanche took 4 children and a twenty-eight-year-old British skier.

Theodore Weaver

For Further Information:

"Avalanche Kills 5 in the French Alps." *The New York Times*, February 10, 1999.

"Search Opens After Avalanche Kills at Least 10 in the French Alps." *The New York Times*, February 11, 1999.

1999: Washington State

Date: February 14, 1999
Place: Near Mount Baker, Washington
Result: 2 dead

On Valentine's Day, 1999, an avalanche swept down a chute just outside the boundary of the Mount Baker Ski Area, carrying away many and burying 2. A gust of wind propelled by the lumbering slide blasted 2 skiers off their feet but left them unharmed, and a few of the skiers thrown down the mountain in the wave of snow were able to dig themselves out.

Mickey Parker, who was celebrating his forty-fourth birthday with his son Justin, ducked under the boundary marker near Lift 8 and dropped into Rumble Gulch, a notoriously dangerous area. Parker stood on firm ground, just 150 feet behind his son,

A front-end loader clears snow from a 1999 avalanche in Washington State. (AP/Wide World Photos)

Avalanches in Evolène, Switzerland, bury buildings at a ski resort. (AP/Wide World Photos)

when the 500-yard slab broke loose and tumbled down on the nineteen-year-old. Eliot Behre watched the boy attempt to outrun the avalanche on his snowboard, then disappear. A rescue crew dug up Justin's body in just over an hour. An autopsy determined that he died of suffocation.

Another cornice that was poised to slide led County Sheriff Dale Brandland to call off the rescue effort and declare that they would not return to search for the body of Shawn Riches, a twenty-five-year-old accountant from Vancouver who was also lost under the hardened snow. Less than a month earlier, another snowboarder had disappeared in a Rumble Gulch avalanche and was presumed dead.

Theodore Weaver

FOR FURTHER INFORMATION:

Carter, Mike. "One Killed, One Lost Near Mt. Baker." *Seattle Times*, February 15, 1999.

Fitzpatrick, Tamara. "Search for Skier Called off; Avalanche Danger Too High." *Seattle Times*, February 16, 1999.

1999: Switzerland

DATE: February 21, 1999
PLACE: Evolène, Switzerland
RESULT: 10 dead

The heaviest snowstorms in the Alps in fifty years terminated with fatal snowslides in Austria, France, Italy, and Switzerland. The Evolène avalanches, which coincided with national school holidays, cascaded down the steep slopes above the Swiss town after massive drifts formed atop the crystalline crust of old snow. The avalanches engulfed a French couple and their teenage daughter, who were taking a walk, and left holes in the ground where chalets of affluent Europeans had stood. Searching for bodies, teams of rescue workers probed the snow, which was littered with splintered wood, entire trees, and tumbled cars. Deposits almost 20 feet deep blocked 10 roads, damaged the railroad system, and caused rivers to flood. Unrelenting weather hampered the effort to evacuate tourists with helicopters.

A few days later, an avalanche triggered by violent winds struck a chalet in Morgex, Italy, causing a steel beam to run through the chest of a fifty-two-year-old woman. Near Gargellen, Austria, a wave of rumbling snow blasted through the windows of a restaurant, killing a couple dining there. The death count for Austria rose to almost 40 when avalanches in Galtür smashed unprotected houses in the curvature of the valley. In Ischgl, where military helicopters brought meat, potatoes, tomatoes, cabbage, and milk to some 7,500 stranded tourists, Major Thomas Schonherr described the snow as being like cement full of pieces of wreckage.

Theodore Weaver

FOR FURTHER INFORMATION:

Stanley, Alexandra. "9 Die in Austria as Avalanches Sweep the Alps." *The New York Times*, February 24, 1999.

Whitney, Craig R. "As the Lucky Escape the Alps, a Snow Slide Claims Others." *The New York Times*, February 25, 1999.

1999: Austria

DATE: February 23-24, 1999
PLACE: Galtür and Valzur, Austria
RESULT: 38 dead, 10 houses destroyed, 2,000 trapped

The winter of 1998-1999 produced heavy snowfalls in the Alpine countries of Europe: Switzerland, Austria, southeastern France, and northern Italy. After several winters of little snowfall—and therefore poor skiing conditions—the snow was welcomed by skiers, hoteliers, tour operators, and local inhabitants involved in the tourist industry. Unfortunately, the snow produced a number of hazards and disasters, the worst of which befell the two neighboring Austrian villages of Galtür and Valzur.

These small but popular resorts, known as the Gem of the Tirol, lie almost at the end of the Paznaun Valley, which runs approximately 25 miles southwestward from Landeck, in the western Tirol. The valley nearly touches the neighboring Austrian province of the Vorarlberg and runs almost to the Swiss border. Conditions in the valley had been deteriorating for

six days before the first avalanche struck Galtür. The previous Wednesday, February 17, a storm had broken. The villages had been whipped by high winds and heavy snow, closing the main road down the valley. A small slide hit Galtür, "a wall of white and black," as an eyewitness described it, but it went largely unreported. The temperature rose sharply over the weekend of February 20-21, but snow continued to fall. Tourists were being told, however, that it was still safe at Galtür, even though notices of high avalanche risk had been issued at the main resort of Ischgl.

Meanwhile, conditions were deteriorating elsewhere in the Alps. On February 20, 100 tourists, including Queen Beatrix of the Netherlands and Princess Caroline of Monaco, had been flown to safety by helicopter from the Austrian ski resort of Lech. By Monday, February 22, the Chamonix Valley in the French Alps had been closed off because of the risk of avalanches, and the melting snow was causing flooding along the Rhine and elsewhere. In Valais, Switzerland, an avalanche was being reported every twenty minutes, and in the worst of them, 9 chalets and a car were swept away, leaving 8 people missing and 2 dead.

In western Austria (the Vorarlberg and Tirol), some 30,000 tourists were trapped in various ski resorts because of heavy snowfall, maximum avalanche warnings having been issued. In Galtür itself, Monday the 22d saw temperatures drop and the wind pick up again. On the same day, chamois (small goatlike antelope) were spotted coming down off the high mountains into the valley, an unusual event. The mood in the village was becoming uneasy.

The Avalanche. On Tuesday, February 23, a traditional ski race had been arranged around the village streets to alleviate the boredom of the skiers who had, by now, been unable to ski for a week. Many people, fortunately, left their chalets and hotels to gather in the main square to watch, despite blizzard conditions that afternoon. Suddenly a great wall of snow, some 45 feet high, rushed down on the village, demolishing a boardinghouse, ripping off the two top floors of two houses, and filling many other houses completely with snow, trapping those inside. Nobody had heard the avalanche coming; they were suddenly plunged into a darkness created by a thick white cloud, like very dense fog. The avalanche did not reach the main square, however, stopping just short of the church. People were immediately dazed and

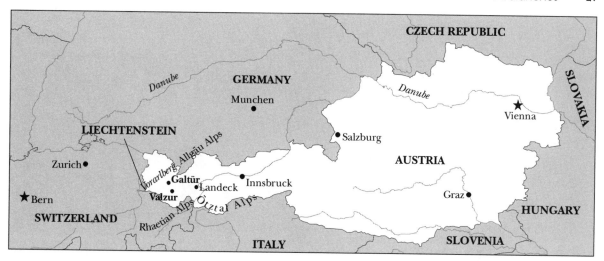

shocked, but locals began digging into the snow at once, as it takes only fifteen minutes to be suffocated if buried within the snow.

The avalanche had, in fact, forked into two parts, with the other branch going around the western part of the village, causing serious damage to chalets on the outskirts. The maximum speed was estimated at 180 miles per hour. The weather forecast continued to call for poor conditions, and new snow was expected. Because of this, relief efforts from the outside could not begin until early the next morning.

Digging Out. On Wednesday the 24th, the skies were clear for the first time in a week. At 7 A.M., two hundred Austrian soldiers and firemen arrived by helicopter to take over the rescue operations. Using dogs and scanning equipment, they managed to recover 18 corpses, including 3 children and a pregnant mother, but by the end of the day 15 people were still missing. A serious effort was also being made to helicopter out some 2,000 villagers and tourists to Landeck, but even with helicopters landing and taking off every two minutes many were left waiting when bad weather closed in again. Some people had only blankets and tea, according to a local doctor.

Worse was to follow. A second avalanche hit the neighboring village of Valzur on the 24th, destroying 4 houses and burying 6 people. The snowslide was 45 feet high and some 600 feet wide and was measured at traveling up to 180 miles per hour. Four bodies were immediately recovered, but 9 more remained missing.

Perhaps one of the most amazing rescues was at Valzur. A four-year-old boy, Alexander Walter, was found by rescue dogs after one hundred minutes; he was pronounced dead at first but was resuscitated in the helicopter and taken to the hospital at Zams, where he made a full recovery within six days. It was suggested that his young age had saved him, his body having closed down so as to need almost no oxygen.

The next day, Thursday, February 25, sunshine returned, but by then, the three-hundred-strong rescue team had begun to crumple with fatigue and the emotional strain of finding corpses. Counselors were helping them, parents who had lost children, and disoriented children. One German woman, for example, had survived, only to learn that her 2 children were dead. The Austrian helicopters had been joined by those from Italy and U.S. bases in Bavaria and were able to evacuate all those remaining who wished to leave.

Rescuers found 2 more bodies the next day at Galtür, bringing the total to 30, and 2 more in Valzur, bringing the final death toll there to 7. They were still looking for a girl believed to be in the ruins of the house where her parents' bodies had been discovered. The body of the fourteen-year-old German girl was finally found in the cellar on the 27th.

The victims were taken to St. Wilten monastery chapel, Innsbruck. Sunday, February 28, was declared a day of mourning by the Austrian prime minister, Viktor Klima. Thirty-eight bodies were buried that morning in a service attended by the prime minister and representatives from those countries affected—Germany, the Netherlands, and Denmark in particular. The disaster was the worst in Austria in

Avalanche victims in Galtür, Austria, are dug out by relief workers. (AP/Wide World Photos)

nearly fifty years, when in 1954 more than 50 people had been killed at Blons in the Vorarlberg.

Amazingly, some one thousand tourists chose to stay in Galtür to complete their holiday or wait for the roads to reopen, even though local authorities, backed by the Austrian government, had decided to evacuate the whole valley. At Ischgl, many returned to skiing on the slopes, though they too were unable to get out of the village.

Controversy. By now, serious criticisms were being leveled against the Austrian tourist industry for ignoring avalanche warnings from meteorologists and against tour companies for bringing out yet more skiers. The largest British tour operator, Thomsons, did finally cancel vacations to Galtür and four other destinations (St. Anton and Ischgl in Austria, Zermatt and Grindelwald in Switzerland), offering full refunds, but most operators merely shuffled their clients to different resorts. It was estimated that another fifteen thousand Britons alone were heading for the Alps at the weekend, while tourists who were stuck there had to hire private helicopters to get out. One German lawyer trapped at Ischgl threatened to sue the authorities for negligence.

Scientific Questions. The immediate scientific causes for the avalanche lie in the types of snowfall in the preceding months, although a very hot summer in 1998 had given rise to speculation that the winter would not be normal. In late January there were heavy snowfalls, but the snow was light and dry. This was followed by another snowfall in mid-February that was very wet and heavy, due to different temperatures. The snow base was therefore very unstable, the heavy snow not binding at all with the light snow, which in itself was not solid enough to act as a foundation. The second snowfall had been exceptionally heavy: 12.1 feet (3. 7 meters) of snow fell in February in the Galtür area, four times the average for the month.

This was not all, however. Gale-force winds at high altitudes, up to 95 miles per hour, had left some mountaintops bare, causing huge accumulations of snow on the sheltered slopes. The winds were then followed by rain, which made the snow even heavier and more unstable. These factors made the avalanche risk huge. Even so, Christian Weber, an Austrian avalanche expert, was quoted as saying, "With all our predictive mechanisms, we were not able to forecast Galtür. Avalanches are coming and crashing down in areas where they never happened before."

In the longer term, the joint effects of increased road traffic through the Alps—both heavy trucks and tourist cars—with the resultant increase in pollution, and of global warming are creating new climatic conditions, whose effects are not yet certain. The summers seem to be longer, delaying the snowfall. Such changing environmental factors raise serious questions over the future safety of skiing in the Alpine region.

Political Questions. As indicated, both the Austrian authorities and the tourist industry were blamed for the loss of lives. Although it is difficult to know whether the number of tourists in Galtür had any significant effect on the force of the avalanche, it is possible to question both the building regulations and the early warning systems. In Switzerland, new chalets are banned in all areas likely to suffer from avalanches; this is not so in Austria.

The other questions, about the number of tourists allowed in and the problem of dissuading them from coming, are more problematic. On the Tuesday of the Galtür avalanche, Hansjorg Kroll, chief of tourism of the Austrian chamber of commerce, is quoted as saying, "We must thank the Lord God for sending us this snow." With bookings up 30 percent over several poor seasons, there seemed every justification for such a statement. However, it is not merely the number of skiers that is significant, it is also the areas to which they are allowed to go. Although this does not seem to have been significant at Galtür, elsewhere avalanches were set off by skiers going off the trails. Where some warnings were posted for the areas, no one seemed to want to pay attention. Officials concluded that there was thus an urgent need to reassess the demands of the tourist industry, which is much needed for the local economy, against the needs for safety.

David Barratt

FOR FURTHER INFORMATION:
The Sunday Times (London), February 28, 1999.
The Times (London), February 23-March 1, 1999.

1999: Alaska

DATE: March 21, 1999
PLACE: Turnagain Pass, Alaska
RESULT: 10 dead

A warning sign alerts snowmobilers and skiers to the threat of avalanches near Palmer, Alaska, in 1999. (AP/Wide World Photos)

The Turnagain Pass Recreational Area lies 50 miles south of Anchorage, Alaska, in the Chugach Mountains of the Kenai Peninsula. It is a popular place for snowmobilers in the winter. One of their favorite activities is highmarking, or seeing how high up the slopes the drivers can take their snowmobiles. Although this is not illegal, it is discouraged by the local authorities, because the snowmobiles could tip over or even start an avalanche.

In mid-March, 1999, 8 feet of snow were dumped on top of older compressed snow, and avalanche warnings were given. One avalanche did occur at the Alyeska Resort in Girdwood, but no one was injured. When the warm spring sun came out on Sunday, March 21, hundreds of snowmobilers were tempted outside despite the warnings. Even when in the afternoon a small avalanche occurred in a side gully to one side of the snowmobile area, no one was deterred.

Twenty minutes later, at around 4 P.M., a 15- to 30-foot wave of snow 1 mile wide roared down the mountainside, sweeping away a number of snowmobiles and people. At first, it was thought only 6 people had been swept away, but the final count came to 10. About 140 searchers in nine teams searched for the missing people. Volunteers had 10-foot poles to prod the snow, which was 30 feet deep in places. Other rescuers used sniffer dogs, electronic sensors, and metal detectors. The search continued for several days.

The avalanche may have been the first indirectly attributable to snowmobiles. Both the National Weather Center and the U.S. Forest Service had issued warnings; had they been heeded, the avalanche, or at least the deaths, may have been prevented.

David Barratt

FOR FURTHER INFORMATION:
The Boston Globe, March 23-24, 1999.

Blizzards, Freezes, Ice Storms, and Hail

(AP/Wide World Photos)

Blizzards, freezes, ice storms, and hail are significant weather events that occur infrequently. When they do occur, they may seriously disrupt or curtail transportation, business, and domestic activities; destroy agricultural produce; cause tens of millions of dollars in damages; and result in significant loss of life to humans and animals. Blizzards, freezes, and ice storms are winter storms, while hail and hailstorms occur in the warmer weather of late spring, summer, and fall.

FACTORS INVOLVED: Geography, gravitational forces, ice, rain, snow, temperature, weather conditions, wind
REGIONS AFFECTED: Cities, coasts, deserts, forests, islands, lakes, mountains, plains, towns, valleys

SCIENCE

Blizzards, ice storms, and hail are significant weather events associated with dynamic interactions between masses of air. These interactions are influenced by altitude, latitude, temperature, moisture, geography, geology, cyclonic rotations, and the jet streams, as these air masses and the jet streams move from place to place.

Blizzards are severe winter storms that may occur when temperatures are 10 degrees Fahrenheit or lower, when winds blow at a minimum of 35 miles per hour, and when there is sufficient blowing or newly fallen snow to reduce visibility to less than 0.25 mile for at least three hours. Blizzards are produced by strong frontal cyclones that bring low temperatures and blowing snow. Blizzards in the Arctic, Antarctic, mountainous regions, or the continental tundra may have winds that blow in excess of 100 miles per hour, with subzero temperatures creating the legendary blizzards of the polar seas and polar areas.

Blizzard snow as well as the perpetual snow cover often found on high mountaintops, even in the tropics, results from the condensation and freezing of moisture contained within air masses that are forced up and over the mountains in a process called orographic lifting. Snow may also form when mid-Atlantic cyclones and upper-air troughs move over mountainous locations.

When freezing rain develops into a layer of ice, it cripples all modes of transportation and creates extremely hazardous conditions for humans and animals. (AP/Wide World Photos)

A ground blizzard is one in which previously fallen snow is blown around, often accumulating in large snow drifts that may exceed 10 feet in height. A whiteout is an especially dangerous type of blizzard in which visibility may be reduced to the point where the horizon, one's surroundings, and the sky become indistinguishable. During such blizzards, exposed humans and animals often suffer from disorientation and loss of the sense of direction.

There are several meteorological mechanisms that produce snow, potentially resulting in blizzards. There must be a constant inflow of moisture to feed growing ice crystals within appropriate clouds in the upper atmosphere. Convection may lift some of the moisture to higher, cooler regions of the atmosphere, where condensation may produce snow—or rain that will become snow—as it falls through cold atmospheric regions. Ice crystals falling from higher clouds may "seed" lower clouds, resulting in snowfall. Polar air masses from the north pick up significant quantities of moisture when they blow across relatively warmer bodies of water, such as the Great Lakes. This moisture may then dissipate into huge volumes of snow downwind, on land, creating blizzards. The Pacific Ocean is the source of moisture for most snowfalls and blizzards west of the Rocky Mountains; the Gulf of Mexico and the tropical north Atlantic Ocean are generally the sources of moisture for snowfalls and blizzards in the central and eastern portions of the United States and Canada.

When deep low-pressure systems (hurricanes) form over the eastern United States and approach the Atlantic Ocean, they can grow explosively as they are moving offshore, parallel to the coastline. Because winds around a hurricane generally blow in a counterclockwise direction, snow or rain, or both, will be accompanied by strong northeast winds, creating in winter a type of blizzard known as a northeaster. In summer the same systems can bring torrential rains, which may last for many days. Most major snowstorms and blizzards of the mid-Atlantic and New England states come from northeasters. If the system as it moves parallel to the coast should move slowly, or stall completely, the affected land areas may be battered for hours—or even days—by blizzard conditions and large amounts of snow or rain.

Ice storms are among the most destructive of all winter storms. They are caused by rain (liquid water) falling from an above-freezing layer of upper air to a layer of below-freezing air on or near the earth's surface. Rain may originate in cumulus clouds as molecules of supercooled water that coalesce with each other until they are heavy enough to fall as raindrops. If the raindrops are large enough and fall to earth rapidly enough to prevent their evaporation as vigra, and pass through regions of above-freezing temperatures in the atmosphere, they will fall to earth as rain. Vigra is precipitation that falls from clouds and evaporates before reaching the ground. The freezing rain coats everything with a layer of ice, called glaze. If the rain continues to fall, and continues to freeze, staggering amounts of ice may build up on roads, bridges, trees, utility poles, transmission towers, power lines, and buildings. The ice may vary in thickness from .04 inch to as much as 6 inches. Upon slight warming by the sun, ice on superstructures of bridges, buildings, power lines, and trees may loosen and fall in chunks or very large pieces known as ice slabs. This falling ice threatens the safety of anyone or anything below. Roads and bridges are generally closed when this danger exists. Ice storms cripple all modes of transportation, cause roadways and other thoroughfares to be closed, and create extremely hazardous conditions for humans and animals.

Hail is sometimes confused with sleet; they are not the same thing. Sleet is made of frozen raindrops that fall during winter storms. Hail is composed of balls of ice of varying shapes and sizes that fall from the interior of cumulonimbus clouds during thunderstorms. Thunderstorms are necessary for the production of hail. Atmospheric instability associated with thunderstorms creates the powerful updrafts and downdrafts necessary for the production of hail. Hail and hailstorms occur not during the winter but rather during the late spring, summer, and fall. During these seasons, heating of the earth's surface by the sun creates warm, rising air currents called thermals or updrafts, in a process called convection. The rising air masses contain moisture, salt particles from ocean spray, particles of kaolinite clay, volcanic dust, sulfur oxides, and other kinds of particles, which are collectively called aerosols.

As the rising air masses encounter the lower temperatures of the upper atmosphere, the moisture condenses, forming cumulonimbus clouds. Within these clouds are residual moisture present in a liquid, supercooled state; ice crystals; and aerosols. Supercooled water is water that remains in a liquid state at temperatures below which it would usually freeze. The name cumulonimbus means "heaped cloud which may produce precipitation." These clouds, also called thunderheads, are towering, often vertically extending themselves thousands of feet into the atmosphere. To the observer on earth they often appear puffy and lumpy and, because of upper-level wind shear, develop anvil-shaped tops. Their undersides often look dark and foreboding. Cumulonimbi are the clouds of greatest vertical extent, often measuring 10 miles or more from top to bottom.

Drops of atmospheric moisture brought by updrafts into the cold interiors of cumulonimbus clouds become supercooled and may begin to coalesce with and freeze around existing ice crystals or aerosols. Ice tends to freeze around particulate matter or other ice crystals, both of which serve as freezing nuclei, or nucleating agents. A nucleating agent is a substance that catalyzes the freezing of supercooled water into ice. Aerosols serve as nucleating agents. Updrafts within the clouds may lift the newly formed ice pellets to higher, cooler levels containing more supercooled water, which freezes them further, making them larger and heavier. When they are heavy enough for their movement to overcome the strength of the updraft, and the downward acceleration of gravity becomes the predominant force, they fall out of a cloud as hailstones. Downdrafts within a cloud may also push hailstones out and downward. Prior to exiting a cloud, hail may be bounced in trampoline fashion up and down within a cloud by competing updrafts and downdrafts. With each ascent, more supercooled water may freeze onto the ice pellets, making them still larger and heavier. Hailstones freeze in layers that look much like those of an onion. An examination of a cut hailstone shows these concentric layers. The number of layers provides a record of the number of times the hailstone was tossed up and down within the parent cloud. Hail may pass through several developmental stages and appear in pea-sized pieces called graupel, or soft hail. Hailstones may also be the size of baseballs or grapefruit.

The most frequent time for the production of hail is between 3 and 4 P.M., with almost all hailstorms occuring between 2 and 6 P.M., times that correspond to the period of maximum heating of the earth's surface by the sun. The development of the largest hailstones requires powerful updraft velocities and many trips up and down within a cloud. The largest documented hailstone fell in Coffeyville, Kansas, in September of 1970. It had a circumference of almost 18 inches and weighed almost 2 pounds. It would require an updraft velocity of almost 400 miles per hour to create a hailstone that size. In the United States, weather observers and reporters report hailstone sizes either in inches or in descriptive terms such as "quarter" (1 inch), "chicken egg" (2 inches), and "softball" (4.5 inches).

No one knows the maximum potential size of a hailstone. There are undocumented reports of basketball-sized hail having fallen in Manhattan, Illinois. Downdrafts from clouds may be powerful enough to slam the surface of the earth with wind gusts that exceed hurricane force, damaging property and causing airplane crashes. Powerful downdrafts are called microbursts, and they are second only to pilot error as the leading cause of airplane crashes. The amount of hail produced at any one time can be staggering. There are confirmed records of hail accumulations several feet deep, covering many square miles. It is not uncommon for snowplows to be used during the summer to clear haildrifts from roads. Melting hail is responsible for stream flooding and extensive property damage in many areas subject to hailstorms.

There are periodic reports of falling hail containing unusual items such as toads, frogs, snakes, worms, peaches and other fruits, fish, and even ducks. An explanation for such events suggests that powerful updrafts in appropriate places could be powerful enough to sweep up and convectively transfer these objects from the surface of the earth into cumulonimbus clouds, where they would be coated and recoated with ice prior to falling to earth.

GEOGRAPHY

Blizzards occur in regions where there is an abundance of moisture that can be transformed into snow and where temperatures are low enough to both encourage snow production and sustain falling or previously fallen snow. Additionally, blizzard-prone areas are affected by jet-stream-accompanied cyclonic events, such as cyclonic vorticity, troughs, and severe frontal cyclones, which may develop in conjunction with jet streams, causing higher-than-usual winds. These systems create storms at other times of the year; however, during winter months they result in heavy snowfall and other blizzard conditions. Blizzards occur most often in Canada, the northeastern U.S. plains states, the mid- and north Atlantic states, and downwind of the Great Lakes. Blizzards also occur in polar areas and at high altitudes at or near the summits of mountains, particularly in north, central, eastern, and western Europe.

Ice storms generally occur in a broad belt stretching from Nebraska, Oklahoma, and Kansas eastward into the mid-Atlantic and northeastern states. They can occur in any other places that experience winter weather. Ice storms are among the most devastating and deadly of all winter storms. A 1952 ice storm covered Louisiana, Arkansas, and Mississippi. It lasted from January 28 to February 4 and killed at least 22 people. During such storms an icy glaze of varying thickness coats all exposed surfaces and objects. During a November, 1940, storm in northeastern Texas, ice coatings of 6 inches and more were reported. Coatings 6 inches thick were also reported in a December, 1942, storm in New York State.

In February of 1994, an ice storm in the southeastern United States caused 9 fatalities and over $3 billion in economic damages. During that same storm, up to 4 inches of ice accumulated in some locations from Texas to North Carolina. Some utility customers were without power for a month; coping with lengthy power outages may create serious, life-threatening situations for the elderly, the very young, and the ill. An April, 1995, ice storm in Chicago resulted in the closing of Michigan Avenue, a main thoroughfare, because of great ice slabs falling from buildings and other high-rise structures.

Ice storms also cause trees to become overburdened with the weight of the ice, causing them to collapse onto power lines or other structures. When utility poles, transmission towers, and other such structures collapse because of accumulations of ice on trees, the fallen trees and utility poles and similar structures must be cut up or removed before any work on restoring power can begin. Lack of power seriously interferes with or shuts down such things as computers, elevators, escalators, heating systems, and hospital operations, among other things. Freezing rain and ice storms occur an average of twelve days per year around the Great Lakes and northeastern United States. Such storms also occur in Canada and Europe.

Large hailstones, such as those that fell on this car, can severely damage property and injure and kill humans. (AP/Wide World Photos)

Almost 5,000 hailstorms strike the United States each year, with perhaps 500 to 700 of them producing hailstones large enough to cause damage and injury. Hail forms in thunderstorms, but not all thunderstorms produce hail. The state of Florida has the greatest annual number of thunderstorms but has the lowest hail rate in the United States. Hail is most frequently found in "Hail Alley," a region that covers parts of eastern Colorado, Nebraska, and Wyoming. Hail is also common in the high plains, the Midwest, and the Ohio Valley. Cheyenne, Wyoming, is the so-called U.S. hail capital. The Pacific shorelines of the United States have the least hail. Hail in that region is produced by thunderstorms that blow on shore during winter storms. Northern India has the greatest frequency of large hail events. India also has the greatest number of human fatalities from hail. Hail belts around the world are generally found at mid-latitudes, downwind of large mountain ranges.

Hail occurs in Canada, central Europe, the Himalayan region, southern China, Argentina, South Africa, and parts of Australia. The highest documented frequency of hailfalls on earth has been in Keriche, Kenya, which averages more than 132 days of hail per year.

PREVENTION AND PREPARATIONS

Humans cannot prevent blizzards, ice storms, or hail. In 1948 the work of scientist Vincent Schaefer showed that adding finely divided dry ice crystals to cold clouds could induce precipitation. Further studies showed that, in addition to dry ice, crystals of either silver iodide or sodium chloride added to appropriate clouds would also spur precipitation. Each of these techniques was used in major efforts to suppress hail formation and/or modify the storm-producing potential of clouds. However, much of this work was terminated because of the lack of consistent positive results. Some states, from Texas to North Dakota, would continue modest efforts to control hail production, funded by the states themselves or jointly with federal agencies.

There are several steps that may be taken to lessen damage, injury, and loss of life from blizzards, ice storms, and hail. A very common response by many people to impending severe weather is to ignore it or assume that they will not be directly affected. This attitude should be replaced with one of greater respect and appreciation for these winter events, which can kill and cause hundreds of millions of dollars in damages. Information and forecasts about impending severe weather events for any area are readily available, well publicized, and continuously updated by radio and television weather services. These events often last for considerable periods of time, cause power outages, and make local or long-distance travel extremely difficult or impossible. For these reasons, prior to the onset of severe weather one should ensure that sufficient food, medical needs, auxillary lighting devices, water, snow shovels, and ice-melting aids are on hand. Automobiles should be fueled and should contain emergency items, even though travel or driving within or through the impacted areas should be avoided.

The occurrence of blizzards, ice storms, and hail is often unpredictable. Before the onset of such weather, one should be certain that insurance policies are in place to cover damages to personal property, agricultural produce, and livestock. Anyone caught outdoors during such events should seek immediate shelter. If one is trapped within an automobile, the chance of survival is increased by remaining with the vehicle, unless a safe place is visible outside. One should keep hazard lights on, make certain of adequate ventilation within the automobile, and make certain that snow or ice does not clog the exhaust pipe.

Mountain climbers and skiers often protect themselves from violent blizzards by digging holes in the snow, crawling in, and curling up in a fetal position to conserve body warmth. Snow is an excellent insulator. There can be a temperature difference of as much as 50 degrees 7 inches below the surface of the snow.

RESCUE AND RELIEF EFFORTS

Severe blizzards, ice storms, and hail may arise suddenly and be significantly more violent, extensive, or involved than previously forecast. Blizzards are one of the greatest potential killers of humans, livestock, and wildlife. They are often accompanied by freezing rain, hail, and sleet. During such events, humans, domestic animals, and livestock may be trapped away from adequate, safe environments and may require rescue and relief efforts from outside sources. Except for cases of the direst emergencies, rescue and relief efforts are generally mounted after the severe weather has subsided. Typical problems encountered during the storms are blocked, impassable roads and sidewalks; power outages; children, the elderly, and sick persons trapped in unheated dwellings; and travelers trapped in vehicles.

Most municipalities located within winter storm belts have dedicated public officials assigned to coordinate snow, ice, and hail removal and rescue efforts. Law enforcement agencies maintain law and order and prevent looting. Service organizations such as the National Red Cross and Salvation Army often have representatives available to assist in providing food, clothing, and shelter for those suffering from the effects of winter storms. When storm effects are very widespread, state governors may request that the president of the United States declare a state of emergency in the impacted area, making people and businesses in that area eligible for federal disaster relief funds. The National Guard is frequently called upon to aid travelers and others who face peril from blizzards and other severe winter storms. The Guard helps to maintain order and prevent looting. It also combats accumulations of snow, ice, and hail.

A 1979 blizzard that dropped more than 18 inches of snow in Cheyenne, Wyoming, and Denver, Colorado, moved eastward at a time when many people were traveling for Thanksgiving. The blizzard killed 125 people, and the National Guard rescued more than 2,000 travelers. Many were rescued by helicopter, while others were stranded in automobiles, hotels, motels, National Guard armories, and public buildings and auditoriums. An Ohio blizzard in January, 1978, stranded about 6,000 motorists. A state of emergency was declared, and the National Guard moved in to aid stranded motorists and exhausted utility repairpersons.

The most common injuries associated with severe winter storms are severe esposure to cold, hypothermia, frostbite, freezing to death, broken bones, and other injuries caused by slips, falls, and vehicle accidents. Each year thousands of Americans, especially the elderly, motorists, and hikers, die from exposure to cold. Although relatively uncommon, concussive injuries from falling hail are sometimes reported. In July, 1979, at Fort Collins, Colorado, an infant was killed in his mother's arms as she tried to shield him from falling hail. A 1953 hailstorm in Alberta, Canada, killed 65,000 ducks. Rescue and relief efforts must be directed not only toward humans but also toward livestock, other farm animals, and cats and dogs. Failure to do so may result in staggering losses.

IMPACT

Blizzards, ice storms, and hail cause hundreds of millions of dollars in damages; they also kill and injure hundreds of people each year. These storms can bring big-city traffic to a complete standstill, ground airplanes, make it difficult or impossible to get to or from work or school, and create power outages, food and fuel shortages, and additional hardships from heavy rains and flooding that often follow such storms. The impact on traffic is enormous. More than 85 percent of all ice storm deaths result from traffic accidents.

Billy Scott

BIBLIOGRAPHY

Battan, Louis J. *Weather in Your Life.* New York: W. H. Freeman, 1983. An introduction to meteorology and weather written for the layperson. Describes how the atmosphere influences humans and human behavior. Topics include weather forecasting; social implications of weather modification; effects of blizzards, ice storms, and hail on air transport; agriculture; and human health.

Byers, Horace Robert. *General Meteorology.* 4th ed. New York: McGraw-Hill, 1974. Presents a broad picture of atmospheric processes for serious students of meteorology and technology who already have a background in, or working knowledge of, mechanics, heat, and calculus. Chapters present topics in a sequential order, beginning with basic physical forces, leading on to complicated interactions of atmospheric components.

Christian, Spencer, and Tom Biracree. *Spencer Christian's Weather Book.* New York: Prentice-Hall General Reference, 1993. A weather primer written for laypersons. Briefly introduces readers to major weather-related topics, including storms, atmo-

spheric dynamics, weather reporting, and forecasting. Provides information for students and any others who might want to pursue a career in meteorology or weather reporting.

Eagleman, Joe R. *Severe and Unusual Weather.* New York: Van Nostrand, 1983. A detailed and thorough text that describes meterological phenomena that cause various kinds of storms. An excellent companion textbook to accompany courses in general meteorology or the earth sciences.

Erikson, Jon. *Violent Storms.* Blue Ridge Summit, Pa.: Tab, 1988. A story of weather through the ages, written in general terms. Discusses weather folklore, weather and the development of agriculture, inadvertent weather modification, rainmaking, and other aspects of voluntary weather modification. Provides a list and discussion of significant historical weather events.

Ludlum, David M. *National Audubon Society Field Guide to North American Weather.* New York: Alfred A. Knopf, 1997. A field guide for observing and forecasting weather. Contains more than three hundred color photographs of cloud types, storms, and weather-related optical phenomena. The book has thumb-tab references, visual keys, and images of historic weather occurrences.

_____. *The Weather Factor.* Boston: Houghton Mifflin, 1984. A collection of little-known facts about how weather and winter storms have influenced Americans from colonial times to modern times. Detailed accounts are provided about when and where storms occurred and descriptions of weather impact on events such as political campaigns, wars, sports events, and air transport.

Lyons, Walter A. *The Handy Weather Answer Book.* Detroit: Visible Ink Press, 1997. Contains photographs and many tables to illustrate and explain items and events described in the text. Uses a question-and-answer format to introduce general weather-related topics.

Riehl, Herbert. *Introduction to the Atmosphere.* New York: McGraw-Hill, 1978. A textbook of atmospheric sciences. Focuses on atmospheric processes as they relate to weather, weather disturbances and storms, natural climate controls, and weather forecasting.

Notable Events

Historical Overview

Throughout history, including modern times, blizzards and ice storms have been a serious threat to travelers. Travelers crossing the Alps have been trapped by sudden and unexpected snowstorms; this was the likely cause of death of a prehistoric man whose well-preserved remains were unearthed in the high Alps in the 1990's. The famous St. Bernard dogs, trained by the friars of the hospice founded around 982 C.E. by St. Bernard of Menthon, have rescued many travelers trapped in the mountain passes of Switzerland by sudden and unexpected snowstorms.

In the early fall of 1846, an unexpectedly early snowstorm in the Sierra Nevada trapped the Donner Party, a group of emigrants from the East seeking to reach California. The early storm was followed by many additional snowfalls, leading to the deaths of most of the members of the party. Some were believed to have resorted to cannibalism to relieve their hunger in the weeks immediately preceding their own deaths from starvation.

In the seventeenth century, Europe experienced what has been described as the most severe winters after the end of the Ice Age, particularly in the years 1643 to 1653. In the eighteenth century, severe weather played its part in initiating the French Revolution: A hailstorm damaged much of France's wheat crop in the summer of 1788, sparking strong inflation in the price of bread and rousing the anger of the working class.

Hailstorms occur mostly in the summertime as a result of unusual temperature inversions, and the threat they usually pose is the destruction of agricultural crops. The growth of major transportation capabilities has enabled the world to alleviate the risks of local starvation caused by such storms, but they can be devastating to local economies, particularly in parts of the world where the standard of living is low.

The nineteenth century experienced a period of lower average temperatures in winter that led to some startling developments. The lower temperatures and early frosts are believed to have played a part in the decline of agriculture in the Northeast. As evidence of the lower temperatures, the East River in New York City froze over in January of 1867. People used sleds for winter travel, and the frozen rivers and ponds provided ice that was cut, stored, and shipped south in the spring and summer in an era before mechanical refrigeration developed in the 1870's. The most striking event associated with this period of lower temperatures was the Great Blizzard of 1888, in which more than 400 people died as a result of being trapped outside or in unheated buildings. All travel came to a halt for several days.

Nevertheless, modern technology enticed several adventurers to believe they could overcome the enormous risks involved in exploring the world's coldest continent, Antarctica. Although a Norwegian explorer, Roald Amundsen, had managed to travel overland to the South Pole and return safely in 1911, the following year another explorer of the Antarctic, Robert Falcon Scott, together with four companions,

who managed to reach the South Pole a month after Amundsen, lost his life in a series of blizzards encountered on the return trip from the South Pole. People continuing a series of scientific expeditions and scientific observations carried out in Antarctica have due regard for the risks of winter weather.

In the middle of the twentieth century, colder weather hit the Northern Hemisphere, resulting in several blizzards of note. In February of 1962, a major storm centered in Germany led to the deaths of 343 people. Four years later, in January of 1966, the worst blizzard in seventy years struck the eastern United States. In 1972 heavy snow fell in Iran, a country whose climate normally does not experience such events except in the mountains to the north and east; 29 deaths resulted.

The development of predictive capabilities helped significantly to reduce the toll of such life-threatening storms. In 1960, the deployment of the first weather satellite made it possible to view the weather over large areas of the globe. These images enabled weather services all over the world to see major snowstorms and blizzards coming, and to alert travelers to the risks of travel. In 1967, the National Oceanographic and Atmospheric Administration (NOAA) began making public its maps of snow and ice cover all over the world. These maps revealed that in the early 1970's the snow and ice cover had begun to grow, and by 1973 it exceeded by 11 percent its extent in 1970.

Scientists began learning about the earth's climate and weather from the ice cores extracted from Greenland glaciers as early as 1966. These were analyzed by Danish scientists, as well as climatologists from other countries, and revealed that snowfall has been a variable event throughout history. It is concentrated, however, at high latitudes and high elevations. The lower temperatures that occurred in late medieval times, for example, wiped out the Norse settlers who had established a colony in Greenland around 1,000 C.E. Thanks to ice cores, scientists now have a clear chronological picture of snowfall over the entire period since the end of the last ice age, some twelve thousand years ago.

Between 1978 and 1980, the United States was hit by a series of blizzards. The Midwest was blanketed in late January of 1978, and in early February of that year the northeastern part of the country was targeted. There was another blizzard in the Midwest the following January, and in February of 1979 more than 18 inches of snow piled up in the District of Co-

Milestones

1643-1653:	Europe experiences its severest winters after the Ice Age.
July 13, 1788:	A severe hailstorm damages French wheat crop.
early October, 1846:	An early blizzard in the Sierra Nevada traps Donner Party.
January 23, 1867:	The East River in New York City freezes.
March 11-14, 1888:	The Great Blizzard of 1888 strikes eastern United States; 400 die.
February 17, 1962:	Major storms blanket Germany; 343 are killed.
January 29-31, 1966:	The worst blizzard in seventy years strikes the eastern United States.
February 4-11, 1972:	Heavy snow falls on Iran; 1,000 perish.
December 1-2, 1974:	Nineteen inches of snow falls on Detroit in the worst snowstorm in eighty-eight years.
January 28-29 and March 10-12, 1977:	Blizzards ravage the Midwest; Buffalo reports 160 inches of snow.
January 25-26, 1978:	A major snowstorm strikes midwestern United States, with 31 inches of snow and 18-foot drifts.
February 5-7, 1978:	The worst blizzard in the history of New England strikes the Northeast; eastern Massachusetts receives 50 inches of snow, and winds reach 110 miles per hour. All business stops for five days.
January 12-14, 1979:	Blizzards in the Midwest yield 20 inches of snow, with temperatures at -20 degrees Fahrenheit; 100 die.
February 18-19, 1979:	Snow blankets the District of Columbia.
March 1-2, 1980:	The mid-Atlantic region experiences a blizzard.
February 5-28, 1984:	A series of snowstorms strikes Colorado and Utah.
March 29, 1984:	A snowstorm covers much of East Coast.
January 7, 1996:	The East Coast is hit by another big snowstorm.
April 1, 1997:	The April Fool's storm strikes the Northeast.
January 5-12, 1998:	A major ice storm covers northeastern Canada.
February-March, 1999:	Heavy snowfall in the Alps triggers avalanches.

lumbia, bringing traffic to a halt. Washington, D.C., had not received that much snow since 1922. In March of 1980, the mid-Atlantic region was the victim of a blizzard. Twenty-eight inches of snow fell in tidewater Virginia, more than at any time in the preceding eighty-seven years. In April, 3 feet of snow fell in Colorado and Utah. The same storm became a blizzard in New England. Another year of heavy snowfall was 1984. In March, much of the East Coast was hit by heavy snows, leading to 8 deaths. The great popularity of skiing for recreation put many people at risk in these storms.

In January, 1985, a blizzard hit the Midwest, reaching as far south as San Antonio, Texas, which had a record snowfall of 13.5 inches. In November and again in December the Midwest experienced a series of blizzards, leading to 33 deaths. In 1986, it was Europe's turn. In the last week in January deep cold and snow caused many rivers and canals to freeze, and 33 people died. In January, 1992, an unusual snowstorm hit the Middle East, where it rarely snows except in the mountains. Jerusalem received as much as 18 inches of snow; 2 feet of snow fell in Amman, Jordan. In 1993 winds of 109 miles per hour (the Weather Service defines a blizzard as a snowstorm in which winds exceed 35 miles per hour) powered a blizzard along the entire East Coast, from Florida to Maine. The storm caused 213 deaths.

In 1996, a snowstorm covered much of the East Coast, and many highways were closed for as much as two days. Seventeen inches of snow fell on the District of Columbia, and the federal government shut down for two days. Parts of Pennsylvania received 31 inches of snow in this storm, and a few areas in New Jersey were blanketed by up to 37 inches of snow. The elevated trains in New York City had to shut down for a time.

On April 1 of the following year, what became known as the April Fool's snowstorm hit the Northeast. A sudden change in the path of this storm caught weather predictors by surprise. In May of 1997, 7 climbers on Mount Everest perished in a blizzard as they neared the peak of the mountain. Eight climbers had been killed the previous May in similar circumstances. The severe weather of 1996-1997 also proved fatal to at least 240 Hindu pilgrims attempting a pilgrimage to a cave in Kashmir; they were caught in a freak snowstorm on August 25, 1996.

What was termed a once-in-a-century ice storm devastated much of the Northeast as well as eastern Canada between January 5 and January 10, 1998. The storm dragged down power lines in much of the region, and crews had to be imported from southern states to help repair the damage, which took weeks. Many residents were without power for several weeks. The ice storm of 1998 was described as the most destructive storm in Canadian history. The Adirondacks in New York, as well as northern Vermont, New Hampshire, and Maine, were also hit. Damages in Canada exceeded half a billion dollars, and insurance claims totaling more than $1 billion were filed

in both countries. Seven people died in Maine as a result of this storm and 4 in New York State.

The threat posed by snow and ice was transferred to Europe in the early months of 1999. Heavy snows in the Alps in February and March, the heaviest in fifty years, triggered avalanches that trapped a number of skiers and other tourists. At least 31 people died in Austria and 18 in France. The lives lost in these events made it clear that people have yet to learn to heed the warnings that the weather services of the world are now able to provide: Travel remains a risky proposition under snowy and icy conditions.

Nancy M. Gordon

1360: France

HAIL
DATE: April 13, 1360
PLACE: Chartres, France
RESULT: Approximately 1,000 soldiers dead

The earliest stage of the Hundred Years' War (1337-1453) saw the armies of the English king Edward III try to conquer France. Despite initial successes in the 1340's, the job was still unfinished as of 1359, and the English king readied his armies for one decisive assault that would secure him the French crown. The invasion proceeded steadily through flat country until, on Monday, April 13, 1360, a freak storm devastated the armies near the cathedral town of Chartres. Lightning struck the heavily armored English infantry and cavalry, killing people outright. Huge hailstones frightened the horses of the cavalry, scattering them to the four winds. A chronicler of the time described the storm as "[A] foul day, full of myst and hayle, so that men dyed on horse back." At least two major leaders of the army were killed, so that, aside from the physical loss of troops, command was disrupted. The storm went down in English military lore as "Black Monday," perhaps the first time this phrase was used to describe any event. The more pious among the soldiers saw the storm as evidence of the hand of God punishing the overweening ambitions of their king, sentiments that served to damage the morale of Edward III's army and impede its momentum.

Given that few recorded large-scale hailstorms have caused fatalities in Europe, it was a devastating twist of fate that this onslaught occurred when a large mass of undomiciled people were in the open, without any cover or shelter. Given that this storm seriously retarded the efforts of Edward III and the English army to conquer France, it probably had the greatest direct historical impact of any hailstorm on record.

Nicholas Birns

FOR FURTHER INFORMATION:

Neillands, Robin. *The Hundred Years War.* London: Routledge, 1990.

Seward, Desmond. *The Hundred Years' War.* New York: Atheneum, 1978.

1784: South Carolina

HAIL
DATE: May 8, 1784
PLACE: Winnsborough, Fairfield County, South Carolina
RESULT: 4 or 5 dead

A deadly hailstorm in South Carolina hit the town of Winnsborough (spelled "Winnsboro" in many sources) in early spring of 1874. Ironically, the town was noted for having escaped serious damage during the recently concluded Revolutionary War, but the weather proved far more relentless than the troops of the British general Lord Cornwallis. The torrent of hail that assaulted the town and its surrounding "fair fields" was accompanied by thunder and lightning. The hailstones, measuring as much as 9 inches around, killed several persons (all of them apparently African Americans), and a great number of sheep, lambs, geese, and birds. The cotton farms of the area escaped serious damage because it was not harvest season, and the town's most prominent building, the then-vacant Mount Zion Institute, escape serious harm. Further details of the storm are sketchy, as this storm is known only through a contemporaneous Charleston, South Carolina, newspaper report. This storm was responsible for the only known deaths by hailstorms in the course of U.S. history until the Dallas hailstorm of 1995.

Analysis of the pattern of the storm is difficult because, at the time, weather systems were not under-

stood as dynamic. Instead of being considered as moving fronts, the weather of each community was seen, even by the best scientific minds in Charleston, as endemic and static. Thus the citizens of Winnsborough simply assumed that Winnsborough had a tendency to receive hail, not that any particularly unusual weather system had arisen to devastate the town.

Nicholas Birns

FOR FURTHER INFORMATION:

Sanders, Albert E., and William D. Anderson, Jr. *Natural History from Colonial Times to the Present.* Columbia: University of South Carolina Press, 1998.

South Carolina: The WPA Guide to the Palmetto State. Columbia: University of South Carolina Press, 1988.

1798: New England

BLIZZARD
DATE: November 17-21, 1798
PLACE: Parts of New England (Connecticut, New Hampshire, and Maine) and New York
RESULT: Hundreds dead

Known as "The Long Storm," this five-day blizzard covered New England and New York with several feet of snow. New York City and New Haven, Connecticut, received 12 inches, while 3 feet of flurries coated areas of New Hampshire and Maine. The Hudson and Connecticut Rivers were choked with ice and unnavigable, disrupting trade. *The Philadelphia Gazette* reported that President John Adams had traveled to New York, where a military parade was scheduled to be held in his honor but was canceled because of the blizzard. Additional newspaper reports noted that hundreds had died as a result of the intense storm.

Periodicals included accounts from travelers who had been in the areas affected by the blizzard. They told about the conditions that they had encountered and amounts of snowfall. The blizzard initiated an extended, harsh winter in New England. Officials were concerned about the spread of disease and care of the poor, infirm, widowed women, and orphaned children during the blizzard.

Elizabeth D. Schafer

FOR FURTHER INFORMATION:

Ludlum, David M. *The American Weather Book*. Boston: Houghton Mifflin, 1982.

_____. *Early American Winters*. Boston: American Meteorological Society, 1966.

_____. *Early American Winters II*. Boston: American Meteorological Society, 1968.

The Philadelphia Gazette, November 22-28, December 7, 1798.

1853: India

HAIL
DATE: May, 1853
PLACE: Northern and central India
RESULT: 84 people and 3,000 cattle dead

The Indian subcontinent is particularly vulnerable to hail because of its usual combination of humidity and high temperatures. Hailstorms are not frequent, but when they do occur they are phenomenal events. Many hailstorms of great intensity no doubt occurred in India in the past, and there exist anecdotal reports of some from various chronicles and records. It was not until the advent of British colonial rule in the eighteenth and nineteenth centuries, however, that verifiable records of the extent and damage of the hailstorms were kept.

The hailstorm that affected much of India in 1853 was notable for the range of its devastation, as the stones rained down indiscriminately on men, women, children, and livestock. The storm cut a wide swath through several provinces in central India, lashing 84 people to death and also killing 3,000 cattle. Another hailstorm of note occurred two years later, when, in 1855, particularly large hailstones fell on the town of Naini Tal, killing approximately 50.

Nicholas Birns

FOR FURTHER INFORMATION:

Blanford, Henry. *A Practical Guide to the Climates and Weather of India, Ceylon, and Burmah and the Storms of Indian Seas*. New York: Macmillan, 1889.

1886: U.S. Midwest

BLIZZARD
DATE: January 6-13, 1886

Cattle in a Blizzard on the Plains, *drawn by Charles Graham from a sketch by H. Worrall. This drawing appeared in* Harper's Weekly *on February 27, 1886.* (Library of Congress)

Place: U.S. Midwest, particularly Iowa
Result: 80 dead

The January, 1886, blizzard caught midwesterners by surprise. Employees of the United States Signal Service reported temperatures as low as 21 degrees Fahrenheit below zero. High winds blew snow into deep drifts, blocking railroads. Contemporaneous newspapers printed accounts across the United States about some of the blizzard's victims, whose ordeals were representative of many people's experiences. A Creston, Iowa, family froze to death in a sleigh.

William Cook, a Polk County, Iowa, farmer was returning home from the state capital at Des Moines. He was only 2 miles from home when he became confused about his direction in the driving snow. Cook steered his sleigh onto an ice-crusted pond. He struggled to rescue his team in the icy water, but his horses succumbed to hypothermia, still hitched to the sleigh. Cook began walking but could barely see because the blowing snow limited visibility and the landscape was entirely white. The exhausted Cook fell, freezing to death near his house and a haystack that might have saved his life if he had been able to see it.

By January 11, weather reports from Marshalltown, Iowa, indicated that the weather seemed to be improving. The sky cleared, and temperatures reached zero. Although the Illinois Central Railroad was still blocked, most other railroads cleared tracks enough for trains to move across Iowa. Records indicate that at least 80 people died during this blizzard that affected even the Deep South.

Elizabeth D. Schafer

FOR FURTHER INFORMATION:
"Dixie Turned to Iceland." *The New York Times*, January 14, 1886, p. 1.
"Results of the Cold Snap." *Burlington (Iowa) Weekly Hawk Eye*, January 14, 1886, p. 6.
"The Trail of the Storm." *The New York Times*, January 12, 1886, p. 1.

1888: The Great Blizzard of 1888

Date: March 11-14, 1888
Place: Northeastern United States
Result: 400 dead, $7 million in property damage

The Great White Embargo, the Great Blizzard of 1888, the White Hurricane—whatever name the folklore legends give it, the March 11-14, 1888, snowstorm was one of the biggest to hit the northeastern United States. A roaring blizzard, sustained for four days by hurricane-force winds, extended from Maryland to Maine. It claimed 400 lives and caused $7 million in property damage. Two hundred boats off the coast and in harbors were swamped and sunk, taking the lives of about 100 seamen. Countless numbers of wild birds, animals, and livestock froze to death. New York was hardest hit, with 200 deaths reported there alone. The stock exchanges on Wall Street closed for three days.

The day before the blizzard, March 10, 1888, was unusually mild. At 9:30 P.M. the thermometer registered in the mid-50's. It had been the warmest day of the year, during one of the mildest winters in seventeen years. However, the following afternoon—Sunday, March 11, 1888—a drizzling rain turned to a downpour, and the temperature steadily fell.

If the meteorological equipment of the time had been more sophisticated, and communication between Washington, D.C., and New York more efficient than telegraph messages, perhaps the U.S. Signal Service's weather observatory in New York could have been warned about a severe storm brewing off the coast of Delaware. There, two massive weather systems were headed for collision. Frigid Arctic air, coming from northwestern Canada, was traveling south along the eastern coast of North America at 30 miles per hour. Warm, moisture-packed air from the Gulf of Mexico headed north, into the Arctic air. The two huge systems clashed, resulting in a winter hurricane saturated with moisture and fueled by violent winds. As the system turned to travel northwest, it picked up speed.

The first winds of the storm reached small craft and fishing boats on Chesapeake Bay late Sunday afternoon. The mercury plummeted, and the downpour quickly changed to a blinding wall of snow. Anchor cables on boats snapped, causing them to run aground or smash into each other. Vessels in the open waters were overtaken by the churning waters and sank. The storm, dubbed "The White Hurricane," moved from Chesapeake Bay north to Boston.

By midnight in New York, the rain had been replaced by snow, and the winds were gusting to 85 miles per hour. To qualify as a blizzard, the wind must blow at 35 miles per hour or more. During a hurri-

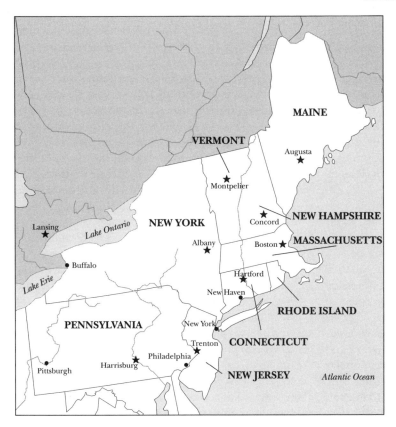

ing snow and falling temperatures, on elevated-train platforms for trains that did not arrive. An estimated 15,000 passengers were stranded in the trains, elevated above the streets, across the city. With no way to get down they were at the mercy of enterprising "entrepreneurs" who carried ladders to the train cars but charged a steep fee of one dollar per passenger for the short climb down to the street. One train, stalled on the tracks between stations, was hit by another from behind. The collision killed an engineer and injured 20 passengers. Winds picked up to nearly 100 miles per hour. Abandoned streetcars were pushed over in the these winds.

Fire stations were also immobilized. Many people, having no heat due to gas lines exposed above the ground, tried lighting fires in their homes to keep warm. When the fires raged out of control, fire trucks could not reach the victims, and the raging winds spread the fire. Property damage from fire alone was estimated at several million dollars. Those left homeless or trying to survive with walls or roofs missing from wind or fire damage often succumbed to the elements and died of exposure.

The financial district on Wall Street actually shut down for three days, something unheard of even today, because only 30 of 1,100 members of the stock exchange showed up Monday morning. People braving the elements on foot were later found frozen to death in snowdrifts along the sidewalks. One such victim was George D. Barremore, a merchant from the financial district. Finding the elevated trains closed down, he decided to walk to work. He apparently collapsed in a snowdrift and froze only 4 blocks from his home.

Those who did make it to work found the buildings deserted and the return trip home too hazardous to make. Many people camped out in hotel or business lobbies. By Monday evening New York City was at a standstill. Thousands were stranded in a city with hotels so overcrowded cots were set up in hallways and even bathrooms. Author Mark Twain was

cane, winds near the eye range from 74 miles per hour to as much as 150 miles per hour or more. The Great Blizzard of 1888 was virtually a hurricane with blizzard conditions. According to an eyewitness account from Arthur Bier, recorded in *Great Disasters* (Reader's Digest Association, 1989), "The air looked as though some people were throwing buckets full of flour from all the roof tops," sometime after midnight on March 12, 1888.

Disaster in New York City. New Yorkers awaking Monday, March 12, found 10 inches of snowfall with drifts as high as 20 feet. In many areas one side of the street was blown free of snow, while the other side had snow piled to the second-story windows of buildings. Used to heavy snowfalls and trying to go about their business as usual, many New Yorkers bundled up against the weather and headed off to work. As the temperature continued to drop, and the snow showed no sign of letting up, the city slowly ground to a halt. Horse-drawn street cars struggled to remain on snow-covered tracks. The elevated trains ran very slowly, eventually coming to a standstill on frozen tracks. Commuters waited in vain, among the swirl-

one such reluctant visitor. Having come in from Hartford, Connecticut, Twain is said to have sent word to his wife that he was "Crusoeing on a desert hotel." Some blizzard-tossed refugees found shelter on cots in the city's public buildings. One such location was the city's jails. At Grand Central Station an estimated 300 people slept on benches, since normal passenger traffic was immobilized. Business was brisk at pubs and places of entertainment, such as Madison Square Garden, where circus man P. T. Barnum performed to crowds of more than one hundred.

On Tuesday the East River was frozen. The ice bridge, connecting Manhattan and Queens, rarely formed because of the flowing waters of the river. Some adventurers bravely used the ice bridge as a shortcut between the two cities. When the tide changed, however, the ice bridge shattered, tossing some foolhardy travelers into the freezing waters of the river. Nearly 100 other adventurers were trapped on the ice floes and narrowly escaped with their lives.

On Tuesday afternoon the snow tapered off and the winds died down. By midday the thermometer began climbing from its 5-degree-Fahrenheit low. Wednesday, March 14, saw the snow yield to flurries. In the aftermath, a total of 20.9 inches had fallen, with drifts as high as 30 feet in Herald Square. This snowfall record would exist for at least the next sixty years.

Other Locations. New York saw light snowfall compared to other locations such as New Haven, Connecticut, which accumulated 45 inches. The driving winds there had also packed the snow into hardened drifts. Of the eastern cities, only Boston managed to avoid the worst of the storm. Alternating rain and sleet eventually led to an accumulated 12 inches of snow, but it did not bring the city to a standstill.

Traveling from Maryland to Maine, the Great Blizzard of 1888 affected one-quarter of the American population. High winds toppled telegraph poles from Washington, D.C., north to Philadelphia. Rail lines were blocked by the mangled cabling. In Philadelphia, freezing rain glazed the streets on March 12. When snow did fall, the ice-glazed streets were buried beneath 10 inches of drifts. Keene, New Hampshire, was blanketed in 3 feet of snow, and nearby Dublin received 42 inches. New York's state capital, Albany, received 47 inches, and Troy, New York, recorded 55 inches of snowfall—perhaps the largest amount of the Great Blizzard of 1888. City officials ordered paths plowed through the snow rather than having

the snow completely removed. In New York City, men and boys eagerly worked at the drifts—using axes and picks on those of hard-packed snow—and earning between $2 and $10 for shoveling people out. An estimated 700 wagons and 1,000 workers cleared away the snow, dumping it along the piers of the Brooklyn Bridge. The public bill for the cleanup came to $25,000.

Aftermath. By Friday, New York City was nearly back to normal. Bonfires lit to warm pedestrians, as well as the warming March sun, soon melted the mounds of snow piled alongside buildings and sidewalks. Cleaning up, restoring power, and counting the dead was a long task for the citizens. Melting snow revealed not only frozen bodies and dead animals but also heaps of debris discarded during the heavy snowfall. In areas outside New York hit by the blizzard, the melting snow revealed the bodies of thousands of dead birds, animals, and livestock.

The search for survivors was intense. In Brooklyn, at least 20 postal workers were pulled from the snow unconscious. New York's Republican Party leader, Roscoe Conkling, had collapsed in the snow from exhaustion. He became ill and died on April 18, making him the final victim of the White Hurricane.

Despite the devastation and loss of lives as a result of the Great Blizzard of 1888, it did have a positive impact on the largest cities shut down by the storm. To ensure that communications networks in the Northeast would never again be disrupted, the U.S. Congress decided that telegraph and telephone wires and public transit routes would be moved underground. Vulnerable gas lines and water mains, located above ground, were also redirected underground to safety. Within a quarter century, the subway systems for New York and Boston were proposed. New York's subway system was approved in 1894, with construction beginning in 1900.

Lisa A. Wroble

FOR FURTHER INFORMATION:

Allaby, Michael. *Dangerous Weather: Blizzards.* New York: Facts on File, 1997.

Davis, Lee. *Natural Disasters: From the Black Plague to the Eruption of Mt. Pinatubo.* New York: Facts on File, 1992.

Erickson, Jon. *Violent Storms.* Blue Ridge Summit, Penn.: TAB Books, 1988.

Ward, Kaari, ed. *Great Disasters.* Pleasantville, N.Y.: Reader's Digest Association, 1989.

Watson, Benjamin A. *Acts of God: "The Old Farmer's Almanac" Unpredictable Guide to Weather and Natural Disasters.* New York: Random House, 1993.

1888: India

HAIL
DATE: April 30, 1888
PLACE: Moradabad, Uttar Pradesh, India
RESULT: 246 people and 1,699 sheep and goats dead

The fertile central plains of the Indian subcontinent are used to an occasional hailstorm, experiencing roughly one per year. The period of greatest frequency for hailstorms is March and April. One April hailstorm not only stands out among the hailstorms of north central India but also has become legendary worldwide among meteorologists. The most deadly hailstorm on record occurred in the Uttar Pradesh city of Moradabad on April 30, 1888. Fierce winds assaulted the city, wreaking havoc and toppling structures. The hail descended swiftly and suddenly in huge torrents, clustering to the depth of 1 or even 2 feet. Even though it was midday, the sky was as dark as during a solar eclipse; several observers said they would have concluded that the storm was indeed an eclipse had not astronomical records indicated none was due.

The hailstorm killed 230 people at Moradabad and 16 others in the nearby town of Bareilly. The large death toll was a result of the hail striking when many of the city's men were farming and herding in the fields. There was no advance warning—there could be no possibility, technologically speaking, of a warning system in that time and place. The pounding effect of the hailstones was incredibly strong, and death was nearly always instantaneous. About 1,700 sheep and goats were also slain by the onslaught. The size of the hailstones was compared by observers to goose eggs and oranges. Everything breakable in the residences of Moradabad was shattered by the hailstorm, including windows and doors made of glass, verandas made of pucca, and roofs made of stucco. Because Moradabad was an agricultural trade center in Uttar Pradesh, the region's economy was disrupted for several months. Even though later storms were to be measured more accurately and studied

more thoroughly due to advances in meteorology, the Moradabad hailstorm attained near-legendary status and is the storm to which all subsequent hailstorms have been compared.

Nicholas Birns

FOR FURTHER INFORMATION:
Alter, James P. *In the Doab and Rohilkhand: North Indian Christianity, 1815-1915.* Delhi: I.S.P.C.K., 1985.
Cornell, James. *The Great International Disaster Book.* New York: Charles Scribner's Sons, 1982.

1891: U.S. Midwest

BLIZZARD
DATE: February 7-8, 1891
PLACE: Iowa, Nebraska, South Dakota, Wyoming, Minnesota, and Wisconsin
RESULT: 23 dead

Blowing snow began falling after 9 P.M. on February 7, 1891. For twenty hours, the blizzard raged across Iowa, Nebraska, South Dakota, Wyoming, Minnesota, and Wisconsin, heaping snow in drifts. Newspapers described conditions throughout the Midwest, remarking that residents of towns were not as severely affected as farmers in the country and livestock on the range. Weather reports from Cheyenne, Wyoming, stated that entire herds of cattle and sheep were frozen together.

The blizzard paralyzed railroads when snowdrifts formed on tracks. Outside Cheyenne, three Union Pacific trains carrying mail and passengers waited for snow removal; plows attached to train engines were used to clear snow from railroad cuts through mountains. In Omaha, Nebraska, the blizzard impeded streetcar traffic, and many people were stranded in their houses. Snowdrifts in southern Nebraska were 10 feet deep. At least 23 people died, including H. D. Huntington of Gordon, Nebraska, who became disoriented during the 200-yard walk between his house and store and was found 0.5 mile outside town.

Trains were able to move in Pierre, South Dakota, but northern winds ranging from 35 to 40 miles per hour interrupted travel in other parts of the state. Newspapers stated that the blizzard was most devastating in South Dakota, where temperatures reached

10 degrees Fahrenheit below zero at Aberdeen. The windstorm caused more problems than did the snow, blowing clouds of dust that lowered visibility. However, optimistic farmers hoped the blizzard's snow would help spring grass grow.

Elizabeth D. Schafer

FOR FURTHER INFORMATION:
"A Blizzard in the West." *The New York Times,* February 19, 1891, p. 1.
"Old Boreas' Blasts." *Burlington (Iowa) Daily Gazette,* February 9, 1981, p. 1.

1898: U.S. Northeast

BLIZZARD
DATE: November 26-27, 1898
PLACE: New York, Connecticut, and Massachusetts
RESULT: 455 estimated dead

Hit first by a storm approaching from the east over the ocean on Thanksgiving Day, then by a second gale from the west, New York City was inundated by snow in November of 1898. From 11 A.M. until midnight, snow fell. Northeast winds gusting over 40 miles per hour whipped snow into deep drifts. New York City's streetcars were delayed, canceling many trips, to the detriment of theater patrons wanting to return home. Ferries to Staten Island and Brooklyn also ran behind schedule or were stopped.

Trains were stopped in drifts as deep as 20 feet on Long Island and in Connecticut. Ships dropped anchors, waiting for the storm to end. Telegraph and telephone wires weighted down with snow snapped, severing communications. On Coney Island, stranded visitors talked in hotel lobbies about the 1888 blizzard and joined sleighing parties and snowball fights. Many New Yorkers dug tunnels through the snow from their apartments to the street. The city hired 2,000 workers using 700 carts to clear significant roads in retail sections of town.

Perhaps the worst casualties occurred in Massachusetts Bay, Boston Harbor, and along New England's southern coast. Approximately 100 ships were blown ashore by high winds. Another 40 vessels were destroyed by collisions with reefs or sandbars. Other ships sank. Crew members and passengers drowned

or died from hypothermia or injuries. At least 100 people died aboard the steamer *Portland,* which wrecked off Cape Cod. Almost every New England beach was covered with debris from ships or barges; bodies floated in the water or were found lashed to boats. Ice coated many ships, making identification difficult. Newspapers printed lists of damaged vessels and names of known casualties, but the total number of casualties was difficult to determine without complete passenger lists.

Elizabeth D. Schafer

FOR FURTHER INFORMATION:
"Delay on the Railroads" and "Streets Buried in Snow." *The New York Times,* November 28, 1898, p. 2.
"Effects of the Storm." *The New York Times,* November 27, 1898, p. 1.
"Havoc in New England." *The New York Times,* November 29, 1898, p. 1.

1922: U.S. East Coast

BLIZZARD
DATE: January 27-29, 1922
PLACE: Primarily Washington, D.C.
RESULT: 108 dead, 133 injured

More than 2 feet of snow blanketed Washington, D.C., during a blizzard that had formed in the Carolinas and Virginia. Snow fell steadily for several days, crippling the national capital's transportation. Street trolleys canceled service, and streets and sidewalks were not easily navigable because of the deep snow. Abandoned automobiles, several of them wrecked in collisions, crowded Pennsylvania Avenue. Considered one of the heaviest snowfalls in Washington, D.C., to that time, the snow accumulated but did not drift because minimal wind accompanied the blizzard.

Most government, business, and social activities were suspended during the blizzard. About 300 adventurous residents managed to reach the Knickerbocker Theater at the corner of 18th Street and Columbia Road in a residential neighborhood. While the audience enjoyed a comic motion picture that Saturday evening, the theater's roof suddenly collapsed underneath the weight of 3 feet of snow. Several tons of concrete and steel crushed the audience. Throughout the night, rescue workers removed bodies and looked for survivors. Approximately 100 people escaped from the theater, another 133 were injured, and 108 people died, including 5 members of 1 family. The theater's capacity was 2,000, but thankfully the storm resulted in many people staying home.

Investigators from the District of Columbia and the United States War Department studied the theater's structure to determine whether the design was flawed. Army engineers blamed poor materials for the catastrophe. President Warren G. Harding issued a statement of condolences for the victims, many of whom were prominent citizens, including a former Congressman. Evaluations of potentially hazardous buildings in the capital were initiated, and theater owners in other parts of the country assessed their buildings' strengths. The blizzard eventually dissipated over northeast Cape Cod.

Elizabeth D. Schafer

FOR FURTHER INFORMATION:

"Hundreds, Dead or Injured, Buried Under Ruins as Roof of Knickerbocker Theater Collapses; Rescuers Battle Storm That Paralyzes City." *Washington Post*, January 29, 1922, p. 1.

"Storm Cripples City." *Washington Post*, January 28, 1922, p. 1.

1939: Japan

BLIZZARD
DATE: December 12, 1939
PLACE: Off the coast of Japan
RESULT: 750 estimated dead

A blizzard blew the Russian steamer *Indigirka* ashore near the eastern banks of Hokkaido, Japan. One of that country's northern islands in La Perouse Strait, Hokkaido is located on the Russian route between fishing stations situated at Vladivostok and the Kamchatka peninsula. Thick snow hindered the crew of the steamer in stating the ship's accurate location when they issued an emergency signal. Several crew members drowned when small boats capsized en route to the coast. Others reached shore to seek help. Japanese rescuers on the ship *Karafuto Maru* sailed

to the wreckage strewn across a coast described as particularly precarious. They found 395 survivors and brought them to the town of Wakkanal, where the victims were treated for injuries and exposure. According to the survivors' statements, 39 crew members and more than 1,000 fishermen and their wives and children had been aboard the cramped steamer before the blizzard hit. Reports sent to Tokyo listed 87 confirmed casualties and suggested that more than 700 Russians remained missing, probably having drowned or frozen to death in the sea.

Elizabeth D. Schafer

FOR FURTHER INFORMATION:

"700 Believed Dead on Russian Vessel." *The New York Times*, December 14, 1939, p. 14.

"700 Lives Lost in Shipwreck." *The Times* (London), December 15, 1939, p. 8.

1940: U.S. Midwest

BLIZZARD
DATE: November 11-12, 1940
PLACE: Midwestern United States
RESULT: 157 dead

Characterized by light snowfall, high winds, and rapid temperature drops, this blizzard raced east from the Rocky Mountains across the Midwest. Above-zero thermometer readings quickly sank below zero on November 11, as winds attained speeds ranging from 20 to 80 miles per hour. Des Moines, Iowa, enjoyed a temperature of 54 degrees Fahrenheit at 6 A.M., which dropped to 22 degrees in three hours. Minot and Garrison, North Dakota, recorded the blizzard's lowest temperature of 19 degrees below zero.

Icy rain transformed into snow that drifted over roads and railroad tracks, stopping bus, car, and train traffic and closing schools. The blizzard affected an area stretching from Utah to Indiana and from Texas to Montana. Telephone lines were damaged by winds or heavy snow that cut communications. Airline flights scheduled at airports located between Chicago and Denver, Colorado, were canceled. Daily cattle trading stopped temporarily in Sioux City, Iowa, a significant midwestern livestock center. The weather also interrupted Armistice Day ceremonies.

In Canton, Illinois, high winds blew down a house, killing a Works Progress Administration worker. Buildings and trees were damaged in Chicago by the blizzard's gusts. An Iowa sports stadium was destroyed. Several thousand Thanksgiving turkeys froze to death in Iowa and Nebraska. Duck hunters stranded on islands in the Mississippi River during the blizzard suffered frostbite; the U.S. Coast Guard was called to rescue passengers from blizzard-blasted boats on Lake Michigan. The blizzard plagued search efforts for a U.S. Army airplane that crashed into Iowa's Spirit Lake. Three men died on that aircraft, adding to the blizzard casualties.

Elizabeth D. Schafer

FOR FURTHER INFORMATION:

"Blizzard Hits Iowa," "North Iowa Hunt Blocked by Blizzard," and "Storms Hit Many Areas." *Burlington (Iowa) Daily Hawk-Eye Gazette*, November 11, 1940, p. 1.

"Count Losses in Blizzard." *Burlington (Iowa) Daily Hawk-Eye Gazette*, November 12, 1940, p. 1.

"Storm Spares City as Nation Suffers." *The New York Times*, November 13, 1940, p. 25.

1941: China

FREEZE
DATE: January 31, 1941
PLACE: Shanghai, China
RESULT: More than 200 dead

Severe cold weather with temperatures well below zero killed more than 200 beggars in the city of Shanghai. Authorities said that more than 150 of the victims were children who lived in the streets of the city. The bitter temperatures hit the city's huge homeless population especially hard. The city had been under Japanese control since 1937 and was home to thousands of refugees from the Sino-Japanese War (1931-1945). Many of the children killed by the freezing temperatures had lost their parents in that bloody war and made their living by begging. The 13 million residents of China's second-largest city had suffered from war and extreme cold for much of the winter. Wartime shortages of food and coal added to their misery.

Leslie V. Tischauser

FOR FURTHER INFORMATION:
"Record Cold; Deaths, Shanghai." *The New York Times*, February 2, 1941, p. 5.

1941: U.S. Midwest

BLIZZARD
DATE: March 15-16, 1941
PLACE: North Dakota and Minnesota
RESULT: 151 dead

Even as war clouds loomed over the American horizon in 1941, nature showed that it too had its perils. On March 15, 1941, what was termed the most severe blizzard to ever hit these areas up to that point struck eastern North Dakota, northwestern Minnesota, and the surrounding regions. On that evening, a sudden and fierce windstorm struck without any advance warning. The wind speed rose to well over 50 miles per hour, and temperatures dropped suddenly, by a differential of up to 20 degrees Fahrenheit. This was the result of a cold front that penetrated the region in less than seven hours at a speed of 30 miles per hour. At the Grand Forks, North Dakota, airport, the temperature dropped 14 degrees in fifteen minutes; at other locations without on-site measurements, the spread was surely greater. The U.S. Weather Bureau determined that winds hit a high of 85 miles per hour at Grand Forks and 75 miles per hour at Duluth, Minnesota, about 200 miles to the east. The storm thus encompassed a large area.

The storm occurred on a Saturday night, when many people were out traveling and enjoying themselves. What started out as a weekend of joy and revelry turned into a terrifying and, in many cases, fatal ordeal. Thirty-two deaths were reported at Grand Forks in the first onslaught of the storm. Passengers left stalled automobiles that had been damaged by the storm and were caught on snowbound, impassable roads; some of the snowdrifts crested at a height of 7 feet. Many of the key transportation arteries of the area were blocked, a logjam compounded by the fact that many of these were key communication arteries as well, with phone lines running alongside them. U.S. Highway 2, which carried traffic from Duluth, Minnesota, into northern North Dakota, was completely stopped, as were U.S. Highways 75 and 81, key north-south roads linking the various areas scattered along the Red River Valley, one running on each side of the Minnesota-North Dakota border. Highway 59, running through Thief River Falls, Minnesota, was also immobilized, with several cars and their passengers immured in huge banks of snow; rescue efforts came too late. Other east-west roads slightly to the south were also rendered impassable, though only for a short amount of time. It took about twenty-four hours for Highways 2 and 59 to re-open.

Many passengers on these roads forayed out of their cars to try to find safety, only to freeze to death in the snowdrifts. One of the most poignant deaths was that of six-year-old Wilbert Treichel, whose parents tried to carry him to safety but could not prevent him from dying of expo-

sure in the bitter cold. Early Sunday morning, highway crews investigated the stalled cars, searching for survivors, but found most of the cars empty.

A particularly grisly death was that of two young girls, Florence and Kate Henry. Kate Henry was found pinioned at the front of a Northern Pacific Railway line; Florence Henry's body was found on the same railway line 2 miles away. This was one of the saddest of many cases in which young children were lost to the blizzard. There were heartening moments as well: Despite, or perhaps because of, their sparse populations and long distances, these areas of Minnesota and North Dakota had a strong sense of solidarity and community. This feeling emerged in response to the storm and helped comfort victims and, in some cases, save lives. It was in this regard that the Saturday night time period of the storm became a benefit. Four University of North Dakota students formed a human chain, rescuing people in danger of being hurtled away by winds and snowdrifts.

Often, seeking shelter from the storm was an accomplishment in itself. Two thousand people in Moorhead, Minnesota, remained in an arena all night after watching a basketball game. Theaters, hotels, and stores in towns and cities remained open all night, providing centers for people to seek shelter and information. People in these areas generally survived, though many suffered from frostbite.

The storm also affected people across the border and downstream in the Red River Valley, in the Canadian province of Manitoba. In Canada, these sorts of blizzard-producing storms are grouped under the category of "Alberta Low" or "Alberta Clipper." These storms usually begin just east of the Rocky Mountains as a result of a strong short-wave trough in a westerly to northwesterly flow. These winds move quite rapidly (over 50 miles per hour) in a southeasterly direction toward Manitoba or North Dakota. The storm was anticipated slightly more in Canada than in the United States because of the familiarity with Alberta Clippers. Also, the onset of the blizzard was slightly more gradual in Canada than below the border. At least 7 Manitobans were killed by Sunday evening.

News did not emerge immediately from all areas affected by the storm. It was thought that 30 fishermen embarking from Marquette, Michigan, had been lost on Lake Superior, their boat capsized by the storm. Fortunately, they turned up unharmed the next day, leaving at least one hopeful coda to the sad story of the storm's onslaught.

The many good deeds and valiant rescue efforts performed by ordinary citizens during the course of the storm meant that the story of the blizzard of 1941 was as much humanitarian as meteorological. This was especially true given the young age of many of the victims, with whom many Americans could empathize. As a result of the severity of the storm, combined with weather officials' complete inability to see it coming, the Weather Bureau realized that northern Minnesota and its environs needed more local autonomy in forecasting weather. The Minnesota office was detached from the former regional headquarters in Chicago and allowed to take responsibility for forecasting procedures throughout the state.

Nicholas Birns

FOR FURTHER INFORMATION:
Chicago Tribune, March 17, 1941.
Christian Science Monitor, March 17, 1941.
"45 Perish in North West." *The New York Times*, March 17, 1941, p. 1.
Grand Forks (N.D.) Herald, March, 1941.

1947: Western Europe

FREEZE
DATE: January 30-February 8, 1947
PLACE: Western Europe, especially England, France, and Germany
RESULT: At least 258 dead

A great winter storm hit most of Europe in late January, 1947. The snow and cold spread suffering over most of the continent emerging from the recent devastation of World War II (1939-1945). Blizzards hit London, Paris, and Berlin. Snow fell steadily in London for six straight days, closing schools, offices, and factories. Even "Big Ben," the clock over the Parliament buildings, was affected by the weather as it missed a note of its famous Westminster chimes when it struck 9 A.M.

Paris endured a major flu epidemic, which filled the city's hospitals. Even as far south as the French Riviera, where French citizens usually went to escape the ravages of winter, people witnessed snow and ice. Some areas of northern Italy reported receiving 28 inches of snow. Nine deaths from the cold were recorded as far south as Portugal.

British, American, French, and Soviet occupation authorities in Germany, which had been divided since 1945, reported that in the month of January, 37 people had frozen to death in Hamburg, more than 60 had died in Berlin, and 21 had succumbed to the cold in Schleswig-Holstein. Health authorities in the German capital said that 188 people were taken to hospitals with frozen hands or feet and 19,000 others had been treated for frostbite since the cold wave had begun. Floating ice on the Rhine River caused major problems for shipping, while the Elbe River, Germany's other main water route, was completely shut down because of ice. Occupation authorities in Wiesbaden had to call a halt to Nazi war crimes trials because of a severe shortage of coal.

The winter of 1947 was the coldest in modern European history. Thousands of factories shut down as electric power plants and gas plants were unable to produce enough energy to provide heat for them. Conditions in Germany were so bad that desperate people seeking heat for their homes looted trains carrying coal. Roads in northern Italy were blocked for days by snowdrifts. Over 100 deaths were reported in Germany due to the cold. All together, 258 people froze to death across Europe because of the subzero temperatures, which lasted for almost two weeks.

Leslie V. Tischauser

FOR FURTHER INFORMATION:
"Hamburg Health Officials Report Forty-eighth Death from Freezing." *The New York Times*, February 8, 1947.
"Storms and Cold Wave Continue." *The New York Times*, February 6, 1947, p. 7.

1948: U.S. South

FREEZE
DATE: January 24-31, 1948

PLACE: From the Great Plains to northern Florida
RESULT: 39 dead

The bitterly cold weather that hit the northern part of the United States in the last weeks of January, 1948, dipped well into the South, causing misery and distress in states unaccustomed to the cold. Much of the South was blanketed with heavy snow, and many cities, unaccustomed to dealing with the ravages of winter, shut down their schools and closed most roads.

Snow blanketed most of Arkansas, northern Louisiana, western Tennessee, northern Mississippi, and northern Alabama. Industrial users of natural gas were forced to close their factories in order to conserve the supply for homes.

President Harry S Truman, forced to deal with a weather crisis that stretched from the Great Plains to northern Florida, issued an executive order curtailing the use of fuel in government buildings and in government automobiles. He called upon Americans to use every possible means to conserve "fuel oil, gasoline, and gas" to make more fuel available for home heating.

Most southern states were hit hard. Residents from Tennessee to Florida, unaccustomed to subfreezing weather, faced 12 inches of snow and temperatures as low as minus 5 degrees Fahrenheit. Memphis, Tennessee, experienced 12 inches of snow, a record, and a temperature of 9 degrees Fahrenheit. Nashville had 7 inches of snow and also single-digit temperatures. One of the hardest hit places was Cotton Valley, Louisiana, where hundreds of families had been living in tents after being made homeless by a tornado on December 31, 1947. Snow drifted against tent walls and onto ceilings. Many tents collapsed when the snow melted from the heat of stoves, and tent-dwellers were drenched with a flood of cold water. Evacuation of the victims was impossible because of the already desperate and overcrowded conditions.

The cold wave eventually took the lives of 39 people in the southern states. Added to the 38 deaths attributed to subzero temperatures in the Midwest and eastern parts of the country, this made the last week of January and the first week in February among the deadliest in American history.

Leslie V. Tischauser

FOR FURTHER INFORMATION:
"Snow, Sleet, and Cold Sweeps Wide Area." *The New York Times,* January 25, 1948, p. 3.

1948: U.S. Midwest and East

FREEZE
DATE: January 29-February 5, 1948
PLACE: U.S. Midwest and East, particularly northern Minnesota and northwestern Wisconsin
RESULT: At least 39 dead

Extremely cold weather dominated the midwestern part of the United States during the last week of January, 1948, and gradually spread east. The freezing temperatures eventually set records in many communities. The coldest temperatures hit communities in northern Minnesota and northwestern Wisconsin. One small town in Wisconsin reported a temperature of 54 degrees below zero, a record low. Nine deaths were reported in Wisconsin because of the bitter weather.

Fuel shortages developed in many parts of the Midwest and the entire eastern half of the United States. The cold created an unusual demand for heating oil, quickly exhausting supplies. Many people used their kitchen stoves for extra heat, a dangerous practice that took at least 2 lives because of explosions. The drain on natural gas caused the shutdown of a major gas pipeline, and many factories and industrial plants had to shut down. As the cold wave spread across most of the eastern part of the country, President Harry S Truman issued an executive order directing all government buildings to cut back temperatures to 68 degrees Fahrenheit. He also placed a 40-mile-per-hour speed limit on government vehicles to conserve gasoline.

Even New York City was struck by the cold wave. The mayor set up a special committee to deal with the crisis. Fuel was limited, stores and factories were closed, and 2 homeless men froze to death. In the New England states 6 to 10 inches of snow added to the misery created by the cold wave. People from Massachusetts to Maine were subjected to one of the coldest winters in the region's history. In New Jersey, highways were closed because of the snow, wind, and cold. Conditions improved by early February in the Midwest and East, but by the end of the bitter weather 39 deaths were attributed to winter's wrath.

Leslie V. Tischauser

FOR FURTHER INFORMATION:
"Deaths Due to Cold Wave." *The New York Times,* February 11, 1948, p. 1.

1952: Sierra Nevada

BLIZZARD
DATE: January 14, 1952
PLACE: Sierra Nevada
RESULT: 26 dead, 226 stranded, $4.25 million in damage

Accompanying a storm system stretching from Canada to Mexico along the West Coast, the Sierra Nevada blizzard brought extreme weather, such as heavy rainfall, to nearby areas in California. The blizzard caused record cold temperatures in Los Angeles and San Francisco. Considered one of the worst winter storms ever to strike the High Sierra at the time, the January, 1952, blizzard stranded people at ski resorts and forced the evacuation of 2,000 people residing near the San Francisco Bay. Twenty-six people died because of the blizzard, which was blamed for an estimated $4.25 million in damage.

The rescue of the marooned streamliner *City of San Francisco* was perhaps the most publicized incident of the blizzard. A passenger train, the *City of San Francisco*, with 226 people including passengers and crew, was stuck on snowbound tracks in the High Sierras. Snowplows cleared tracks for rescue trains to travel east and west from different towns toward the streamliner. Equipped with food and medicine, the trains also brought dogs and sleds, military jeeps, and physicians to treat ill passengers. The engines pulled Pullman cars to transport the rescued people.

While the passengers of the *City of San Francisco* waited, skiers from a nearby resort brought food, blankets, and medicine. A helicopter dropped a radio transmitter. The stationary train was buffeted by 25- to 50-mile-per-hour winds. The crew burned wood from the baggage car to warm the passengers who suffered from exhaustion and exposure. Many people were overcome by carbon monoxide, and a doctor and military nurses on board resuscitated them. After three nights and four days, the last food and wood were used. Passengers bundled in coats and blankets until they were rescued later that day.

Elizabeth D. Schafer

FOR FURTHER INFORMATION:

"All 222 Stranded on Train Removed." *The New York Times*, January 17, 1952, p. 1.
"Sierra Snow Traps 226 on Train as New Storms Tie up Far West." *The New York Times*, January 15, 1952, p. 1.
"Trip Rugged, Iowan Says." *Burlington (Iowa) Daily Hawk-Eye Gazette*, November 16, 1952, p. 2.

1956: Europe

BLIZZARD
DATE: January-February, 1956
PLACE: Europe, from Siberia to the Mediterranean
RESULT: 907 dead, $2 billion in damage

In 1956 Europe endured two months of intensely frigid conditions that caused almost 1,000 weather-related deaths. Winter snowstorms blanketed the entire European continent as a series of blizzards hit from Siberia to the Mediterranean. The first recorded snow fell in North Africa, and the French Riviera received several inches of snow; snow also dusted Rome. Europe's major capital cities were paralyzed by the blizzards. The Seine River froze, and ice threatened low bridges over the Rhine River.

Northern European countries in Scandinavia generally experienced a more extreme winter, while the Mediterranean was devastated by the blizzard. The storms ruined crops and detrimentally affected economies. Spain suffered an estimated $100 million of agricultural losses. Citrus froze before it was picked. More than fifty thousand harvesting jobs were not needed, adding to unemployment woes in the southeast Mediterranean. Olive groves frosted in Spain and Greece. In other parts of the region, floodwater resulting from the blizzard caused millions of dollars of destruction. Turkey, in particular, was inundated by floodwater from the Thrace and Ceyhan Rivers.

Most deaths during the blizzard were caused by the unceasing cold. Europeans suffered from frostbite and exposure. In more macabre situations, people were attacked by wolves, boars, and other wild animals that abandoned their forest habitats covered with snow to scrounge for food near towns. A pack of blizzard-crazed wolves attacked schoolchildren in Kalambaka, Greece.

Airlifts brought food, clothing, and powdered milk to isolated villages. Pilots from the Netherlands flew naval helicopters to scatter seed for wild birds. In February, 1956, U.S. president Dwight Eisenhower promised 135,000 tons of America's agricultural surplus for Western Europe. Europe began to thaw by February 27, after 907 people died and $2 billion worth of damage was inflicted by the continuous blizzard.

Elizabeth D. Schafer

FOR FURTHER INFORMATION:

"Britain Swept by Blizzards." *The Times* (London), February 20, 1956, p. 8.

Hoffman, Michael. "European Economy Is Hard Hit by Cold Entering 24th Day." *The New York Times*, February 23, 1956, p. 1.

Lawrence, W. H. "President Offers Food to Europe Ravaged by Cold." *The New York Times*, February 20, 1956, p. 1.

1956: New England

ICE STORM

DATE: January 8-10, 1956

PLACE: New England, from New Jersey to Rhode Island

RESULT: 40 dead

Icy drizzle, driven by a gigantic Atlantic storm, glazed much of the northeastern part of the United States from January 8 to January 10, 1956. The storm, according to the United States Weather Bureau, was very unusual. One great disturbance was wheeling in a counterclockwise movement from a low-pressure center about 300 miles east of Cape Hatteras, North Carolina. At the same time, a stagnant high-pressure area over the northern Atlantic was preventing the normal eastward movement of air masses and driving bitterly cold Canadian air south into New England, New York, and Pennsylvania.

Storm warnings were posted from Atlantic City, New Jersey, to Block Island, Rhode Island. The Weather Bureau warned of a serious ice hazard for the region. Ice on windshields caused many accidents during the evening hours. Many cars did not have defrosters on their windshields, an improvement that did not grace most automobiles until the early 1960's. Motorists were forced to look out of their side windows, and, if they wore glasses, their lenses quickly frosted over. Many people complained

of the stinging ice pellets driven by the wind that cracked windows and caused their faces to bleed if they tried to walk outdoors.

Despite warnings from highway officials to stay home, many of the 40 deaths attributed to the extreme weather resulted from automobile and truck accidents on icy roads. Several people were killed on roads after stopping to clear ice from their windshields; they died when other vehicles skidded into them on the ice-coated roads. A National Guard airplane crashed during the ice storm, killing the 2 people on board.

New York City, Boston, Providence, and other coastal cities suffered icy conditions, and transportation slowed down throughout the three days of the storm. In eastern Massachusetts bus service in many cities was canceled, and hundreds of accidents were reported. Floods caused by heavy rains and melting snow from a January thaw forced hundreds of people in Nova Scotia to leave their homes. Thousands of other homes in Nova Scotia, Prince Edward Island, and southeastern New Brunswick were without heat, light, or telephone service after ice and sleet knocked down power and communication lines.

Leslie V. Tischauser

FOR FURTHER INFORMATION:

"Freezing Rain Glazes Street; Weather Bureau Calls It Worst Ice Storm in Three Years." *The New York Times*, January 9, 1956, p. 1.

1957: Iraq

HAIL

DATE: October 18, 1957

PLACE: Suleimaniyah, northern Iraq

RESULT: 27 dead

The *muhafazah* (government district) of Suleimaniyah is known for its extremes of weather. Its mountainous location makes it vulnerable to winter storms, while its position in semiarid terrain renders it prone to summer droughts. Thus, the largely Kurdish population of the town was not surprised by the hailstorms that erupted on October 18, 1957, after two months of virtually unchanging, stifling heat. What did startle Suleimaniyah's citizenry was the intensity and scale of the storm. Even though the temperature was above freezing, the ice-cold hail hurtled upon the town's inhabitants. The hail fell at the rate of nearly 100 miles per hour, killing 27 people and injuring hundreds. As with all underdeveloped countries, lack of advanced warning systems and communications infrastructure (including a virtually nonexistent Iraqi civil service) made it difficult either to prepare for the event or to respond to the needs of the victims in good time.

Nicholas Birns

FOR FURTHER INFORMATION:
Kubaysi, Amir. *Administrative Development in New Nations: Theory and Practice, with Reference to the Case of Iraq.* Baghdad: Al-Huriyah Print House, 1974.
Lytle, Elizabeth Edith. *The Geography of Iraq: A Bibliography.* Monticello, Ill.: Council of Planning Librarians, 1977.

1958: U.S. East Coast and Midwest

BLIZZARD
DATE: February 15-16, 1958
PLACE: Central, southern, and northeastern states
RESULT: About 500 dead

A shift in the west-east jet stream along the Canadian-U.S. border to a north-south direction brought record-breaking cold temperatures to the eastern two-thirds of the United States for fourteen days in 1958. Low temperatures associated with the blizzard included 33 degrees Fahrenheit below zero in Iowa, 37 degrees below zero in Wisconsin, 14 degrees in Atlanta, 27 degrees below zero in North Carolina, 4 degrees in New York City, and 4 degrees below zero in Boston.

The cold Arctic winds combined with moisture from the Gulf of Mexico on February 14 to bring heavy snow and a second week of freezing temperatures to the southern states. As the winds turned northward in the Carolinas, they triggered a classic northeastern coastal storm, bringing high winds, heavy snow, rough seas, and continued low temperatures to the mid-Atlantic states and the northeast on February 15 and 16.

Snowfall totals included 1 inch in Mississippi, 6 to 10 inches in the Carolinas, 13 inches in Washington, D.C., 23 inches on Long Island, 19 inches in Boston, 28 inches in western Massachusetts, and 42 inches in northeast Pennsylvania. Continued low temperatures, blowing snow, and occasional snow squalls around the Great Lakes and throughout the twenty-six-state region hampered snow-removal efforts during the week following the blizzard.

Heavy winds produced snow drifts up to 20 feet high, blocking roads and highways and causing thousands of motorists to abandon their cars along the roadways. Road, rail, and air transportation was brought to a halt, isolating towns and villages. Operation Haylift used helicopters to drop hay for stranded cattle in Pennsylvania, New York, and several midwestern states. Helicopters were also used to drop food to isolated towns and farmsteads and to rescue stranded motorists and rural residents.

The Pennsylvania Railroad was disabled for several days by snow drifts and short circuits in the trains' power systems. Ice on the Mississippi, Ohio, and Hudson Rivers stalled shipping. The demand for heating fuel reduced fuel oil inventories and natural gas line pressures, threatening the gas delivery system along the East Coast. Industrial plants were closed. The U.S. government did not consider the storm's effects to be beyond the power of states and counties and did not declare a disaster, but military equipment was released to assist with snow removal and the airdrops of food for humans and livestock.

The two-week cold wave finally ended February 22. The final death toll estimates ranged from 252 to 500, with deaths attributed to overexertion in snow removal, hypothermia from lack of heating fuel or burial beneath snowdrifts or snowslides, asphyxiation from blocked chimneys or faulty space heaters, automobile accidents, and drowning in 20-foot swells at sea caused by gale-force winds.

Gordon Neal Diem

FOR FURTHER INFORMATION:
The New York Times, February 15-21, 1958.

1967: U.S. Southwest

BLIZZARD
DATE: December 12-26, 1967

PLACE: Southwestern United States, especially New Mexico
RESULT: 51 dead

Between 4 and 5 feet of snow fell on southwestern states, especially remote areas of New Mexico, for more than one week in 1967. Native Americans were the primary population affected by this blizzard, with an estimated 60,000 people seeking shelter in log and mud dwellings called hogans. Near Grants, New Mexico, 200 Navajos waited in pickup trucks after they were caught in the storm while collecting piñon nuts. New Mexico governor David Cargo declared an emergency and ordered National Guard personnel to airlift food and supplies to the stranded people.

By December 18, the United States Air Force was utilizing helicopters for search and rescue missions as well as to drop relief parcels. Thirty-nine fatalities were confirmed, including 20 in Texas and several in California, New Mexico, Oklahoma, Missouri, and Oregon. On December 19, rescue crews delivered supplies to 24 Navajos before the storm intensified,

forcing the grounding of helicopters. Authorities counted 2 known Navajo deaths caused by the blizzard.

Additional snow fell on December 20, limiting airlift attempts. Crews managed to drop hundreds of tons of hay for sheep herds on the range in addition to some medicine and food for 5,000 people on a Hopi reservation. They also delivered supplies to a community of Utes and fodder for 6,200 livestock at Towaoc, Colorado. Rescuers evacuated Native Americans suffering from illness and injuries; airlifts continued even on Christmas Day.

Elizabeth D. Schafer

FOR FURTHER INFORMATION:

"Copter Takes Food to Snowbound Navajo Band." *The New York Times*, December 19, 1967, p. 26.

"Snow, Lashing Nation, Hits Southwest Hardest." *The New York Times*, December 16, 1967, p. 43.

"The Worst Is over in Navajos' Snow Crisis, Tribe's Counsel Reports." *The New York Times*, December 25, 1967, p. 27.

Navajo Indians wait outside their hogan for relief from a 1967 Arizona blizzard. (AP/Wide World Photos)

1972: Iran

BLIZZARD
DATE: February 4-11, 1972
PLACE: Northwestern and southern Iran
RESULT: 1,000 dead

An intense cold front accompanied by high winds caused heavy snowfall for one week in Iran. The snow drifted as deep as 10 to 26 feet in places. After suffering four years of drought, Iran was inundated with so much snow that authorities worried about flooding when a thaw occurred. The blizzard blanketed most of Iran, especially the northwestern and southern parts of the country. These remote regions were cut off from the capital at Tehran, which complicated rescue procedures and tallying of the missing, injured, and dead. Central Iran also suffered from the blizzard.

Villagers endured being trapped underneath heavy snowdrifts. Four thousand people at Ardekan, in southern Iran, waited for rescue beneath 26 feet of snow, as did villagers at nearby Kakkan and Kumar. All 18 villagers at Skeklab, near the Turkey border, died during the storm. Without effective quarantines, influenza spread among villagers, with 5 family members at Pirmeloh, southwest of Tehran, falling ill and infecting others in their village.

A week after the snow first fell, 6,000 villagers were still missing. Also, an American college student and 2 guides who had gone mountain climbing near Tehran were lost. Authorities said the mountain where they vanished had been coated with 39 inches of snow. A search team of 5 men looking for the hikers also disappeared. As sunshine penetrated storm clouds, enhanced visibility permitted rescuers to look for stranded trains and snowbound vehicles. Five passengers were found frozen in a car at Koheen Pass, 175 miles from Tehran, where they had waited for help for five days in temperatures around minus 13 degrees Fahrenheit. Iranian prime minister Abbas Hoveyda asked civil and military officials to assist rescue efforts, especially in northwestern Iran. Total deaths were estimated at 1,000.

Elizabeth D. Schafer

FOR FURTHER INFORMATION:
"Missing Put at 6,000 in Iranian Blizzard." *The New York Times*, February 11, 1972, p. 4.

"6,000 Lost in Iran as Snow Buries Village." *The Times* (London), February 11, 1972, p. 6.

1978: Scotland

BLIZZARD
DATE: January 29, 1978
PLACE: Scotland
RESULT: 8 motorists dead, 70 rescued from train

On January 28, 1978, Arctic weather produced enormous amounts of snow in northern Scotland. As snow fell rapidly that Saturday, people enjoying the weekend by skiing and mountain climbing were suddenly endangered by hazardous conditions in the Highlands and temperatures as low as 15.8 degrees Fahrenheit (minus 9 degrees Celsius). Some snowdrifts were estimated to be at least 50 feet deep before the storm ended. Scotland had not experienced such an intense blizzard for almost three decades. Even snowplows became stuck in drifts, and all of Scotland's primary roads and routes were blocked.

Unaware of how quickly snow was accumulating, many drivers remained in their cars, while others began walking to look for shelter. Military pilots flew helicopters searching for people to rescue. At least 200 people were safely removed from their automobiles. Some survived several days, eating snow. Rescue teams also located bodies of 8 people who died from exposure. Seventy people were assisted from a snowbound train derailed by a snowdrift north of Inverness. The train's driver had placed the passengers in the engine but was unable to move very far through the snow. The Scottish blizzard caused 85,000 people to lose electric services.

Elizabeth D. Schafer

FOR FURTHER INFORMATION:
Faux, Ronald, and Martin Huckerby. "Helicopters Lift 70 from Train Trapped in Blizzard." *The Times* (London), January 30, 1978, p. 1.

"Many Missing as Blizzards Continue in Scotland." *The New York Times*, January 31, 1978, p. 6.

"Motorist Tells of Four Days Buried in Snow." *The Times* (London), February 1, 1978, p. 1.

1993: U.S. East Coast

BLIZZARD
DATE: March 12-15, 1993
PLACE: Eastern United States, from Maine to Florida
TEMPERATURE: Record of 2 degrees Fahrenheit in Birmingham, Alabama
RESULT: 270 dead, 2.5 million homes without power

This mid-March blizzard paralyzed the United States east of the Mississippi River. During one weekend, a mixture of blowing snow and rain accumulated in twenty-six states, stretching from Maine to Florida. Record snowfall totals and low pressure readings were documented. Forming when three atmospheric disturbances converged into a low-pressure system in the Gulf of Mexico, the blizzard moved toward the Florida panhandle. The blizzard continued rapidly northeast across Georgia, the Carolinas, the mid-Atlantic states, and New England.

Beginning on March 12, the blizzard coated the southeastern United States with almost 1 foot of snow. Fifty-mile-per-hour winds formed drifts as deep as 6 feet, and the windchill caused bitterly cold temperatures. Historic accumulations included 20 inches in Chattanooga, Tennessee, and 13 inches in Birmingham, Alabama. A region unaccustomed to severe winters, the South was unprepared to deal with snow removal. Few cities had access to snowplows, and many residents had never dealt with snow. Most activities were canceled because of the blizzard. Interstate highways and airports were closed, stranding travelers. Approximately 2.5 million homes lost power.

Urban areas in the Northeast were not stricken as drastically as their counterparts in the South. Residents were familiar with blizzard conditions and able to cope better than southerners. The heavy snow caved in a roof atop a computer center in Clifton, New Jersey, interrupting service to automated teller machines across the country.

High winds following the blizzard's cold front produced surges along the western Florida coast. Waves eroded beaches and washed houses into the sea. Several people drowned. The blizzard was unique because its cold front produced thunderstorms and tornadoes, with approximately 60,000 lightning flashes. The entire Atlantic coast experienced hurricane-

level wind and waves, and gusts were measured as high as 93 miles per hour on Long Island. The blizzard subsided by March 15, leaving an estimated 270 people dead.

Elizabeth D. Schafer

FOR FURTHER INFORMATION:
Lott, Neal. *Water Equivalent vs. Rain Gauge Measurements from the March, 1993, Blizzard.* Asheville, N.C.: National Climatic Data Center, 1993.
McFadden, Robert D. "Storm Paralyzes East Coast; Snow Covers South; 33 Killed." *The New York Times,* March 14, 1993, p. A1.
Stevens, William K. "3 Disturbances Became a Big Storm." *The New York Times,* March 14, 1993, p. A38.

1995: Texas

HAIL
DATE: May 5, 1995
PLACE: Dallas and Tarrant Counties, Texas
RESULT: 17 dead, several millions of dollars in damage

The most damaging hailstorm ever to hit the United States occurred in Dallas and Tarrant Counties, Texas, on May 5, 1995. Texas is particularly susceptible to large-scale, rapidly moving weather systems that generate hail, often the size of tennis balls or baseballs. A particularly severe variety of thunderstorm called a supercell clustered in advance of a squall line and moved into Fort Worth just before coalescing with the squall line. The supercell updraft, which had been on the southwest flank of the storm, moved to the forward flank on the east side of the heavy precipitation core. After merging with the squall line, the storm evolved from a classic to an HP supercell configuration, one very likely to produce hailstorms. The storm lost speed as it moved from Tarrant into Dallas County and produced torrential rains, resulting in flash flooding and multiple deaths.

It was a Friday in spring and the weather was nice, so thousands of Texans were enjoying themselves at outdoor events, such as the annual "Mayfest" celebration. A sudden rain of stones of condensed ice was quite unwelcome. People suffered substantial inju-

Hailstones as big as softballs fell in Fort Worth, Texas, in May, 1995. (AP/Wide World Photos)

ries as a result of the hailstorm, including broken bones, lacerations, and deep bruises. The storm also occasioned more than $1.5 billion worth of property damage. Seventeen people were killed, breaking the record for deaths from a hailstorm in the United States held by the 1784 storm in Winnsborough, South Carolina, though strictly speaking all 17 deaths were due to flash flooding—not to the hail itself.

Though local governments responded rapidly to the crisis, their services were not the only resources available. The Dallas and Tarrant County RACES SKYWARN weather information networks provided lifesaving information to area governments and to the National Weather Service. Participants in the Dallas County RACES SKYWARN weather information network not only made reports but also shot video footage of the event. This video footage made it possible for weather officials to follow the storm from several vantage points, beginning on the west side of Dallas and ending on the east side of Dallas County, in the cities of Mesquite and Garland.

Life in the Dallas area was disrupted, and continental air travel was plunged into chaos. American

Airlines, one of the nation's major airlines, maintains a hub in Dallas, shuttling millions of passengers each day from plane to plane. The hailstorm caused major delays and many cancellations, not only disrupting traffic but costing American, one of the Dallas-Fort Worth area's major employers, millions of dollars in refunds and servicing. This was added to any general consideration of the economic effects of the storm of the Dallas-Fort Worth area.

Nicholas Birns

FOR FURTHER INFORMATION:
Dallas Morning News, May 6-May 10, 1995.
USA TODAY, May 8, 1995.

1996: The Blizzard of '96

DATE: January 6-12, 1996
PLACE: Eastern United States
RESULT: 154 dead, more than $1 billion in damage

The first indication that a major storm might strike the East Coast of the United States came on Wednesday, January 3, 1996, when European computer models predicted a strong storm for the following Saturday and Sunday. After U.S. computers confirmed European predictions, Friday evening forecasts warned that moderate to heavy snow might cover the Middle Atlantic states. Clockwise winds around a high pressure area in Canada pushed unusually frigid air southward, where it was overrun by a mass of mild, humid air from the Gulf of Mexico circulating around a low (an area of low barometric pressure) off the coast of the Carolinas. The two systems collided over the eastern United States: Warm, moisture-laden air rising over heavy cold air froze, falling as snow. When Albany, New York, reported a record low temperature of minus 19 degrees Fahrenheit at 5 A.M. Saturday, the Weather Service issued a winter storm watch, predicting 1 to 2 feet of snow for all major cities of the mid-Atlantic region; Sunday morning they upgraded the watch to a blizzard warning.

Snow began falling on Washington, D.C., at 9 P.M., Saturday, January 6. By 8 P.M. Sunday, Washington re-corded nearly 12 inches, a record for the date, and all traffic in the city halted. By then snow was falling in record amounts from Richmond, Virginia, to Boston, Massachusetts, with winds of 30 to 50 miles per hour piling up enormous drifts at airports and burying cars parked on the street. Washington's snowfall topped out at over 17 inches.

The worst blizzard in seventy years produced record snowfalls all along the East Coast. Lynchburg, Virginia, recorded 20 inches of snow in twenty-four hours. On Monday, January 8, Wilmington, Delaware, reported that 24 inches of snow had fallen the previous day, tying the one-day record. Newark, New Jersey, reported a record storm total of 27.8 inches; White House Station, New Jersey, set a new state record of 35 inches. Providence, Rhode Island, set a new January record of 32.1 inches. Philadelphia reported a record of 27.6 inches in twenty-four hours and 30.7 inches for a single storm, eclipsing the previous record of 21 inches. On Wednesday, Boston set a new snowfall record for January with 36.6 inches. New York City reported 20.2 inches at the official weather station in Central Park, while 27.5 inches fell on

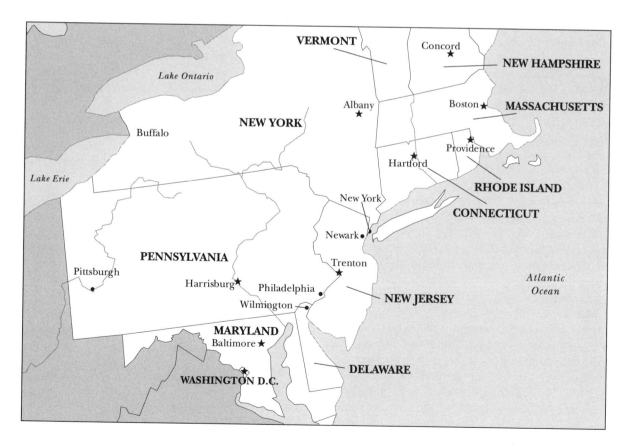

Staten Island and 24 inches at La Guardia Airport. On Tuesday, January 9, a rapidly racing storm from the west dumped another 4 to 6 inches of blowing and drifting snow on eastern cities, severely hampering attempts at street cleaning. On Friday, January 12, yet a third snowstorm hit cities from Washington, D.C., to Boston, dropping 3 to 6 additional inches of snow. As the blizzard and its two following storms paralyzed the Northeast, the Deep South experienced record low temperatures: Lake Charles, Louisiana, 21 degrees; Daytona Beach, Florida, 35 degrees; Key West, Florida, 45 degrees.

In city after city the storm forced school closings, halted mail delivery, shut down shopping malls, and prevented office workers from reaching their desks. In Washington, D.C., the federal government was closed for most of the week, although managing to partially reopen on Thursday. Friday's storm closed the government once again. Interstate highways became impassable because plows could not keep up with rapidly falling snow. Philadelphia allowed only emergency vehicles on its streets and was unable to reopen its schools until Tuesday, January 16, ten days after the blizzard began.

Air travel was hit especially hard, with most airports effectively shutting down on Saturday night. Twenty-foot drifts across runways and in front of hangars impeded snow removal efforts. By Tuesday most airports had reopened, but schedules were impossible to maintain. The airlines, alerted by blizzard warnings, had flown their planes out of East Coast airports before the storm; it took until the weekend for air traffic to approach normality.

Long-distance mail delivery was particularly hampered by the airlines' situation. Half of all first-class mail moves by air, where it shares space in cargo holds with passenger luggage. When passenger flights finally resumed, all seats on the first flights were filled, and cargo space was devoted to passenger luggage, which has priority over mail. Not until the weekend would the U.S. Postal Service finally clear the backlog of millions of pounds of packages and letters held up by the storm.

The accumulating weight of the snow damaged buildings across the East. A church roof collapsed in Harlem; a theater in Massachusetts was condemned as unsafe when its roof sagged; barn roofs collapsed in Pennsylvania; and supermarkets in Virginia, New York, and Massachusetts closed as their roofs gave way. Estimates of the blizzard's dollar cost varied widely, $1 billion being a conservative estimate. Insurance claims for property damage alone came to more than $600 million; extreme estimates of the storm's total cost ran as high as $3 billion. President Bill Clinton declared nine states and the District of Columbia disaster areas and promised federal help in paying for the expense of cleaning up after the storm's havoc.

Newspapers on Thursday the 10th reported 87 deaths due to the storm. Homeless people were found frozen in snowdrifts. Doctors at one New York hospital treated at least 12 people for carbon monoxide poisoning after they sat in their cars with the engines running and tailpipes stuck in the snow. Many deaths resulted from traffic accidents during whiteouts or loss of control on slick highways. The most spectacular crash occurred in Pittsburgh: Two commuter buses collided head on after one bus slid out of control on an icy bend, smashing into the left side of an oncoming bus, killing the driver and peeling away the side of his vehicle. At least 52 people were hospitalized, several with serious injuries. Final figures from the National Climatic Data Center totaled 154 storm-related deaths, 80 in Pennsylvania alone.

Milton Berman

FOR FURTHER INFORMATION:

National Climatic Data Center. *The Winter of '95-'96: A Season of Extremes.* Technical Report 96-02. Asheville, N.C.: Author, 1996.

The New York Times, January 4-14, 1996.

USA TODAY, http://www.usatoday.com/news/index/nsno000.htm.

Washington Post, January 4-14, 1996.

1996: Nepal

BLIZZARD

DATE: May 10-11, 1996

PLACE: Mount Everest, Nepal

WIND SPEED: 45 to 80 miles per hour

TEMPERATURE: With wind-chill factor, minus 94 to minus 148 degrees Fahrenheit

RESULT: 9 dead, 4 injured with severe frostbite

Extremes attract adventurers who seek to fly the fastest, descend the deepest, or climb the highest. For

most of the twentieth century, Mount Everest, the Earth's highest peak at 29,108 feet, has been the crowning goal for many mountaineers. Because of its location in the Himalayas between Tibet (where its name is Jomolungma) and Nepal (where its name is Sagarmatha), Mount Everest is often subject to extreme and unpredictable weather. The unexpected arrival of a savage blizzard on the high slopes of Everest during the spring of 1996, when the mountain was crowded with climbers, played an important role in the greatest tragedy in this mountain's long history of calamities.

By 1996, in the seventy-five years since the first attempt to climb Everest, more than 140 climbers had died. The largest single cause of death was avalanches, with falls into crevasses and from the mountain a weak second. Until the 1996 tragedy, there had been only 13 weather-related deaths. Furthermore, throughout most of the history of mountaineering on Everest, almost all deaths were of professional or highly skilled climbers. After 1985, however, climbing high mountains became a business, and populating the slopes of this dangerous mountain with amateurs of varying abilities was another factor that figured into the disastrous loss of life in 1996.

The leaders of the commercial companies that developed to meet the need of those who could pay $65,000 to reach the top of the world knew that their success depended on the vagaries of Everest's weather, and so clients were brought to the mountain in the spring to take advantage of the brief period of good weather between the decline of winter and the arrival of the summer monsoons. It was during this time period that, in 1953, Sir Edmund Hillary and his Sherpa guide, Tenzing Norgay, became the first people to reach the summit; their route, up the Khumbu Icefall and Glacier through the West Cwm and up the Southeast Ridge, became the standard way to the top. Because of the brief weather window, Everest's base

camp at 17,600 feet was crowded with more than four hundred people in the spring of 1996.

The Everest Expeditions. Some of these people had specific goals other than merely climbing Everest. For example, the film director David Breashears was shooting a $5.5 million giant-screen (IMAX) film about climbing the mountain. Others were part of commercial expeditions. For example, Rob Hall, who, like Hillary, was a skilled New Zealand climber, led the Adventure Consultants Guided Expedition. Among his clients was Jon Krakauer, an American journalist who had been assigned by *Outside* magazine to research an article on commercial climbing. Hall had already guided a record 39 climbers to the summit, but he was receiving competition from an American company, Mountain Madness Guided Expedition, led by Scott Fischer. Fischer was assisted by the guides Anatoli Boukreev, a Russian, and Neal Beidleman, an American. Among Fischer's clients was the millionaire socialite and journalist Sandy Hill Pittman, who was making daily reports of his trip on the World Wide Web.

As the clients acclimatized to the altitude, they also adapted to each other. Variations in economic backgrounds, states of health, and climbing ability did not make such adaptation easy. Nevertheless, Hall and Fischer guided their groups through the Khumbu Icefall, a river of glacial ice, to Camp 1, at 20,000 feet. Later, their clients trekked 4 miles and 1,700 vertical feet from Camp 1 to Camp 2, in the West Cwm, the earth's highest box canyon. While more than 100 climbers were going through the Icefall and up the West Cwm, a storm hit on April 21, with winds of over 60 miles per hour. Another storm arrived on April 23, with very strong winds pummeling the upper slopes, delaying the establishment of Camp 3 (at 24,000 feet) and Camp 4 (at 26,000 feet). When the weather stabilized, toward the end of April, oxygen cylinders and other materials necessary for the summit climbs were carried to the higher camps. By the first week in May, most clients had completed their acclimatization at the higher camps and were preparing for a summit bid. The IMAX climbers, who were higher on the mountain than the Hall and Fischer groups, decided against their attempt to reach the summit on May 9 because of a violent windstorm, which also hampered Sherpas setting up tents in the South Col (the plateau where Camp 4 was located).

The Ascent to the Summit. Despite the storm, Hall and Fischer brought their guides and clients to Camp

4 for a possible ascent on Friday, May 10. When the climbers awoke late Thursday night, the winds had died down, and they left the Col around midnight. Mount Everest above the South Col is called the Death Zone because the combination of the lack of oxygen, low temperatures, and high winds can quickly amplify small mistakes into tragedies. Each climber carried two oxygen cylinders (a third was available on the South Summit in a cache stocked by the Sherpas). Within two or three hours after leaving the South Col, Fischer's Mountain Madness climbers began to overtake Hall's group, and by 4 A.M. both groups were commingled. Though the groups were mixed, the philosophies of their leaders differed. For example, Hall taught his clients the Two O'Clock Turnaround Rule: If you are not on the summit by 2 P.M., go back down the mountain, no matter how close you are to the top.

Because there were so many climbers on the Southeast Ridge, the pace was slow and traffic jams

Climber Beck Weathers, who survived a harsh blizzard atop Mount Everest in 1996 but suffered severe frostbite and the eventual loss of his right hand. (AP/Wide World Photos)

occurred, such as at the Hillary Step, a steeply sloped tower of rock not far from the summit. Guides rigged ropes up this 40-foot cliff to help their clients conquer Everest's final obstacle. Boukreev, Fischer's chief guide, reached the summit several minutes after 1 P.M. Krakauer arrived about five minutes later. During the next few hours clients and guides from both Hall's and Fischer's groups reached the summit, along with others, and the weather, though very cold, did not appear threatening. Most climbers were worried about their dwindling supplies of oxygen, not about a storm. However, some guides noticed that clouds were filling the valleys below, obscuring all but the highest peaks. Unknown to the climbers, these innocent-looking puffs were actually the tops of thunderheads gradually moving up the mountain's sides.

Rob Hall reached the top at 2:30 P.M., thus breaking his own Two O'Clock Turnaround Rule. More ominously, Scott Fischer did not reach the summit until 3:40 P.M., and others arrived still later. In fact, Hall had left the summit to help his client Doug Hansen up the final section of the Southeast Ridge. Why Hall encouraged Hansen to continue his ascent so late in the day is one of the perplexing questions of the Everest tragedy. In 1995 Hall had turned Hansen back when he was close to the summit, and it is reasonable to speculate that it would have been particularly difficult for Hall to deny Hansen the summit a second time. After Hansen reached the top, Hall and his client began their descent and quickly ran into trouble. Beginning at 4:30, Hall repeatedly sent radio messages that he and Hansen were in trouble high on the summit ridge and urgently needed oxygen. Fischer, too, was in difficulty. On the summit he had told a Sherpa that he was not feeling well, and he experienced debilitating problems during his descent.

The Blizzard Strikes. The situation of the many climbers descending the Southeast Ridge was made even more difficult by the storm clouds which, by 5:15, had blanketed Everest's heights. Between 6:30 and 6:45 P.M., as dim daylight turned to darkness, Krakauer stumbled into Camp 4. By this time the storm was a full-blown blizzard, and visibility had dropped to 20 feet. Ice and snow particles carried by 80-mile-per-hour gusts froze exposed flesh. Despite these conditions, Hall had managed to get Hansen down to the top of the Hillary Step, but their progress then stopped. Fischer, too, was stranded on the ridge, and several of the clients of Hall and Fischer were lost in the snow and ice as they tried to descend to Camp 4 (one later compared their plight to trying to find a path in a gigantic milk bottle).

When the Mountain Madness clients did not return to Camp 4 by 6 P.M., Boukreev decided to discover their whereabouts, but the high winds and whiteout conditions made his search fruitless, and he was forced to return to camp. Meanwhile, Beidleman, Boukreev's fellow guide, had managed to get his group off the ridge and onto the broad expanse of the South Col, but they were on its eastern edge, far from the tents of Camp 4 about 330 yards to the west (a fifteen-minute walk in good weather). The storm was so intense that they could not see the lights of Camp 4, and only a few people in their group had headlamps with functioning batteries. Since their oxygen supplies had been depleted, they were all at the point of physical collapse. Some in Beidleman's group were Hall's clients (Yasuko Namba and Beck Weathers), while others were part of Fischer's group (Tim Madsen, Charlotte Fox, and Sandy Pittman). Failing to find Camp 4, the group decided to huddle and wait for the storm to subside.

Fearing they would all die, Beidleman later gathered a small group of the ambulatory climbers to make another attempt to find their camp. Wobbling into the wind, which occasionally knocked them down, they eventually stumbled into Camp 4 sometime before midnight. They told Boukreev that those left behind needed help. After his attempts to find volunteers for a rescue team were frustrated, Boukreev, on his own, made two long forays into the furious storm to bring the stranded climbers to safety. He eventually saw the faint glow of Madsen's headlamp and was thus able to save his life, along with those of Fox and Pittman (he assumed that Namba was dead, and he did not come across Weathers).

During the night, Rob Hall, still on the ridge, was in radio contact with base camp. Without Hansen, who was presumed dead, he had managed to descend to the South Summit. At 5 A.M. on Saturday,

May 11, base camp was able to arrange a telephone call from Hall to his wife in New Zealand. In this conversation and a later one at 6:20, she tried to get her husband to move down the mountain, but his legs were frozen, and he was too weak.

With daylight, there was a break in the storm, and a team was organized to locate the bodies of Beck Weathers and Yasuko Namba. The team found Namba partially buried in snow and, surprisingly, still breathing although judged to be near death. Namba did die, but Weathers was later able to rescue himself by walking directly into the wind and stumbling into Camp 4. He was bundled into two sleeping bags and given oxygen.

Another Storm. The gale that struck on Saturday evening was even more powerful than the one that had lashed the Col the night before. The storm collapsed Weathers's tent and blew his sleepings bags off him. With his badly frostbitten hands, he was unable to pull the bags back over his body. The storm was so intense that his anguished cries were unheard, and he had to suffer, unprotected, through yet another Everest blizzard. When the murderous winds abated and his condition became known to the other climbers, he was injected with dexamethasone, which helped him recover enough to stand and walk with assistance. He somehow managed to get to a lower camp, where a helicopter evacuated him to Kathmandu.

When the storm finally ended, the remaining members of Hall's and Fischer's groups descended the mountain, but the bodies of Rob Hall and Scott Fischer were left where they had died. By the time Krakauer reached base camp, 9 climbers from four expeditions were dead. Because all this drama on the high slopes of Everest had been closely followed by the world media, the tragedy generated great interest. Jon Krakauer's account of what happened appeared in the September, 1996, issue of *Outside* and in his book, *Into Thin Air,* which was published in April of 1997 and began its long run on the best-seller charts. In his book, Krakauer criticized some of Boukreev's decisions in the Death Zone. Boukreev defended his actions in his own book, *The Climb: Tragic Ambitions on Everest,* published in 1997. His views were given some sanction when, on December 6, 1997, the American Alpine Club honored him with their David A. Sowles Memorial Award for his courageous rescue of 3 climbers trapped in a storm on the South Col of Mount Everest. The controversy between Krakauer and Boukreev came to an end when Boukreev was killed in an avalanche on the slopes of Annapurna on Christmas Day of 1997.

Robert J. Paradowski

FOR FURTHER INFORMATION:
Boukreev, Anatoli, and G. Weston DeWalt. *The Climb: Tragic Ambitions on Everest.* New York: St. Martin's Press, 1997.
Coburn, Broughton. *Everest: Mountain Without Mercy.* Washington, D.C.: National Geographic Society, 1997.
Groom, Michael. *Sheer Will.* Milsons Point, New South Wales, Australia: Random House, 1997.
Jenkins, Steve. *The Top of the World: Clmbing Mount Everest.* Boston: Houghton Mifflin, 1999.
Krakauer, Jon. *Into Thin Air: A Personal Account of the Mount Everest Disaster.* New York: Villard, 1997.

1996: India

BLIZZARD
DATE: August, 1996
PLACE: Jammu and Kashmir, India
RESULT: Approximately 239 pilgrims dead

For a thousand years, Hindu pilgrims have annually trekked up the Himalayan mountains to visit a shrine to Shiva, one of Hinduism's major gods, located at Amarnath Cave at an elevation of 13,500 feet. Although August weather is usually temperate enough to enable people of all ages to participate in the march, Asian monsoons in 1996 produced massive amounts of moisture that initiated a tragedy along India's northern border with China.

More than 100,000 Hindus began the 27-mile ascent on August 23, unaware that a snowstorm would trap them en route. Pilgrims initially thought that the snow would subside and attempted to continue up the slope toward the temple. Incessant flurries prevented the Hindus from moving up the mountain to the shrine or down the slope to shelter. The Indian army deployed helicopters to attempt rescue of panicked pilgrims scattered along the mountain path, but the thick snowfall obscured pilots' visual abilities and interrupted their mission.

The stranded pilgrims, wearing minimal clothing because of religious tradition, endured the bitterly cold conditions of the high elevation worsened by deep snowdrifts. Pilgrims and their guides died from exposure to subfreezing temperatures, hunger, and dehydration. Many Hindus survived by reaching Amarnath Cave for shelter.

Authorities estimated at least 160 pilgrims had perished by August 26, stating that a more accurate count would be possible only when rescue crews gained access to the slope. On September 1, the official number of casualties was designated 239. Interior Minister Indrajit Gupta demanded that India's parliament investigate why the pilgrims were allowed to embark on the pilgrimage without being aware of a potential blizzard.

Elizabeth D. Schafer

FOR FURTHER INFORMATION:
Burns, John F. "Saved from Himalayan Blizzard, Hindus Recall 'Pilgrimage to Hell.'" *The New York Times,* August 27, 1996, p. 1.
"Freak Storm Kills 65 Pilgrims, Traps Thousands in Kashmir." *The New York Times,* August 24, 1996, p. 2.

1996: Europe

FREEZE
DATE: December, 1996-January, 1997
PLACE: Across Europe, including Bulgaria, Poland, Romania, Germany, Italy, Russia, and Turkey
RESULT: More than 200 dead

Extremely cold temperatures and heavy snow covered most of Europe in late December, 1996, and early January, 1997. The bitter winter was the coldest to affect Europe after the mid-1980's. Death tolls from the freezing weather set records in many countries; Bulgaria and Poland reported 13 fatalities, and Romania had 22. Most of the victims were homeless or elderly. In Poland, where temperatures fell to 35 degrees Fahrenheit below zero, most of the deaths were reported to be alcohol-related. (Intoxicated people have less resistance to the cold because alcohol speeds the loss of body heat.) Officials in all three countries reported that shelters set up for the homeless were filled to capacity.

In parts of Germany, the thermometer fell less severely, to minus 4 degrees Fahrenheit, but at least one homeless man was found dead. River traffic was closed because the frozen water and ice in the North and Baltic Seas was 2 to 4 inches thick. The Danube and Rhine Rivers were completely frozen, as were several canals connecting river traffic. In central Italy, heavy snow blocked roads and isolated mountain villages for several days. Temperatures in the mountains fell to 22 degrees below zero. Snow fell as far south as Rome, where it had not been seen in over a decade.

In Russia and Turkey dozens of people were killed in remote villages. When the cold spell began to ease after more than two weeks, more than 200 people had died across Europe. It was the most deadly winter since the 1940's.

Leslie V. Tischauser

FOR FURTHER INFORMATION:
"Death Toll Rises Above 220 in Eleventh Day of Europe's Freeze." *The New York Times*, January 4, 1997, p. A2.

1998: Canada

ICE STORM
DATE: January 5-12, 1998
PLACE: Northeastern Canada
RESULT: 15 dead, billions of dollars in damage

The ice storm that hit northeastern Canada from January 5-12, 1998, was among the most costly and devastating in Canadian history. The Canadian government reported that more than 3 million utility customers lost power and that damages to roads, forests, buildings, bridges, and power lines exceeded $3 billion. Montreal and most of Quebec received more freezing rain in a three-day period than over any other such period since records were kept. In just one day more than 2.13 inches of freezing rain fell on the region, enough for more than 3 feet of snow if the temperature had been a few degrees colder.

The ice storm was a disaster for Canadian farmers and maple-sugar makers. Quebec's ten thousand maple-syrup producers reported a loss of about $10 million. Farmers reported more than $1 billion in lost livestock and crops. Losses to apple growers were

estimated to be 20 percent of their trees. In many orchards trees were completely stripped of their branches and resembled telephone poles. Dairy farmers were also hard hit when processing plants were shut down and they were forced to throw away huge quantities of raw milk. Power companies suffered huge losses because of toppled utility poles and transmission towers. Thousands of Canadian soldiers provided crucial help for rural residents in the provinces of Quebec, Ontario, New Brunswick, Newfoundland, and Nova Scotia.

Weather experts said the storm resulted from an inversion of the southern (warm) and northern (very cold) jet streams. Usually, colder air rests above warm air. In January, 1998, however, the warm air sat above the Arctic air moving into the region. Moisture high up in the atmosphere started as rain, or snow from even higher elevations turned into rain as it fell through the inverted southern jet stream. It would not have time to freeze as it fell through the thin layer of colder air that settled close to the ground. The moisture would fall onto buildings, wires, trees, and roads, where it froze.

Fifteen deaths were attributed to the ice storm. Most of the deaths resulted from highway accidents and hypothermia.

Leslie V. Tischauser

FOR FURTHER INFORMATION:
Swanson, Stevenson. "'The Situation'—An Icy Grip Holding Tight Quebec; Northeastern U.S. Without Power After 10 Days." *Chicago Tribune*, January 16, 1998, p. 3.

1998: U.S. Northeast

ICE STORM
DATE: January 9, 1998
PLACE: New England and New York
RESULT: 5 dead, thousands forced from their homes

An ice storm that plagued Canada for most of the first week of January, 1998, hit New England and New York on January 9. In Maine, more than 200,000 customers lost their electric power, and many residents were without heat. The storm was actually a series of

Ice envelops branches and power lines in Watertown, New York, in 1998. (AP/Wide World Photos)

storms that hit one after another, leaving no time for freezing rain and sleet to melt between the weather activity. In a two-day period, meteorologists measured more than 3 inches of precipitation from the system. That amount was unusually high for any ice storm. Rapidly falling temperatures accompanied the storm and made the situation even worse for area residents.

The severity of the storm was blamed on a collision between cold Arctic air and warm southern air that met over New England. Because hot air rises, the warm air moved over the cold air, forcing the Arctic air to remain in place. The result was the creation of an immense amount of moisture, which fell as freezing rain.

In Canada about 3 million homes were without power, and more than 100,000 people sought refuge in shelters. The government declared a state of emergency, and 11,000 army troops were sent to communities in Nova Scotia and New Brunswick to help with the cleanup.

In New York the Red Cross opened forty-four shelters, which housed more than 3,600 people to whose homes power was cut off. Other residents of the state sought refuge in churches, fire stations, and warming centers. In Niagara Falls, melting snow flooded a trailer park, knocking over more than 200 mobile homes. President Bill Clinton declared the area a federal disaster zone, enabling residents to apply for low-cost government loans to help rebuild.

In New Hampshire and Vermont, Red Cross shelters provided relief to thousands of residents. In New York, 3 deaths were blamed on the weather. One worker was killed trimming tree branches, another person died of carbon monoxide poisoning from a faulty heater, and a third person died from hypothermia. Maine officials counted 2 deaths, both as a result of carbon monoxide poisoning. Thus, the total number of deaths in the United States linked to the storm stood at 5.

Leslie V. Tischauser

FOR FURTHER INFORMATION:
"Ice-Creamed." *Boston Globe,* January 14, 1998, p. A14.

1999: The Blizzard of '99

DATE: January 1-4, 1999
PLACE: U.S. Midwest and East Coast
RESULT: More than 100 dead, airline and rail traffic disrupted, hundreds of cars damaged in chain-reaction accidents, several hundred thousand homes without power

A fast-moving winter storm developing over the Texas Panhandle on New Year's Eve tracked across Texas on Friday, January 1, curved northeast toward the Great Lakes, and battered the Midwest with high winds from New Year's Day to January 3. The blizzard dropped 15 or more inches of snow over Illinois, Indiana, Ohio, Wisconsin, and Michigan. Winds off Lake Michigan, gusting to over 60 miles per hour, piled up snowdrifts faster than Chicago's street plows could move them. The blizzard reduced visibility at O'Hare Airport to zero at times and left 22 inches of snow on the ground. The National Weather Service ranked the storm as the second-worst blizzard of the twentieth century in Chicago, just an inch short of the 23 inches dropped in January, 1967. After the snow ended on Sunday, a cold wave brought record low temperatures of minus 20 degrees Fahrenheit or less throughout the region, hampering recovery efforts. Congerville, Illinois, recorded the all-time state minimum temperature of minus 36 degrees on January 5. Not until Saturday, January 16, did Chicago's temperature rise above freezing. President Bill Clinton declared Illinois and Indiana disaster areas and promised the region federal aid in cleaning up after the storm.

On one of the busiest travel days of the year, every form of transportation was either blocked or badly delayed by the storm. Chicago is the rail hub of the United States, and problems there held up priority freight shipments destined for the East and West Coasts for one to four days. At Chicago, Detroit,

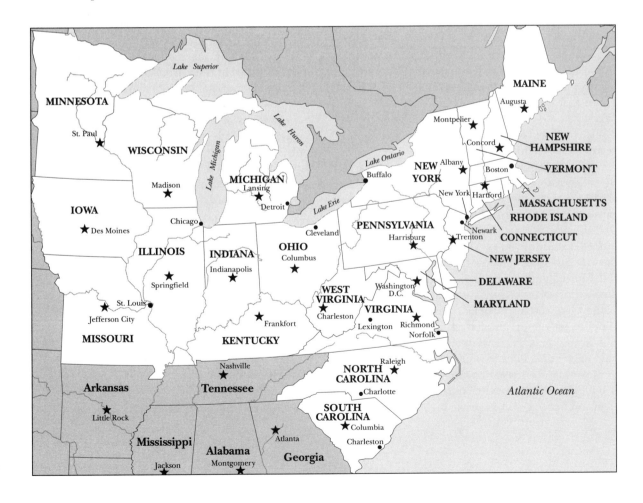

Indianapolis, and Milwaukee, airlines canceled thousands of flights and stranded hundreds of thousands of angry passengers eager to return home after the New Year's holiday. More than 200,000 travelers were stranded at O'Hare Airport for up to four days before finding flights. Cancellations and flight delays spread across the country in a domino effect. Trans World Airlines (TWA) canceled four hundred flights out of its St. Louis headquarters. Many midwesterners in Pasadena, California, for the New Year's Rose Bowl game found their vacations in the sun extended for an extra two to four days, a situation about which few complained. Airline spokesmen estimated that it might take until Tuesday, the 5th, before travel throughout the United States could return to normal.

More than 2,500 major auto and truck accidents occurred on slick highways and interstates. Driving snow and icy roads were blamed for a 60-car pileup in Wisconsin on Saturday, January 2, that left one driver dead and many injured. A 130-mile stretch along Interstate 65 in Indiana was closed for two days, stranding hundreds of travelers. Snowplows buried thousands of cars in snowdrifts: A striking photograph from Chicago showed an 8-foot-high snowbank with a line of protruding side-view mirrors, the only indication that cars were underneath. It took a week to free all buried vehicles. Mail was delayed, and schools remained closed for several days as the region slowly recovered from the storm.

Many deaths resulted from storm-caused accidents. Early reports indicated that 3 persons died in separate train accidents on the Chicago suburban rail system, 39 died in automobile accidents, 2 froze to death, and at least another 36 suffered fatal heart attacks, mainly due to overexertion while shoveling snow. Death totals well over 100 were expected when full information became available. The blizzard created a shortage of blood in hospitals throughout the nation. The Midwest is a major source of fresh blood supplies, but donors found it difficult to reach collection sites. What blood was collected could not be shipped to areas in need until the storm subsided.

By Sunday the storm had spread to the East Coast. From the Carolinas to New England, snow turned to sleet and freezing rain, covering highways with ice. A 15-vehicle pileup on Interstate 81 near Lexington, Virginia, killed 4, injured 23, and shut down the highway for hours, creating a 14-mile traffic backup. Slick roads triggered a chain-reaction crash in New Jersey that involved 50 cars. Heavy rain and ice caused over 200 accidents on the New York Thruway and downed power lines from the Carolinas to Connecticut, leaving hundreds of thousands of homes in the dark. The ice closed Newark International Airport for a day and caused cancellations and delays at the New York area's Kennedy and La Guardia Airports. At Buffalo, New York, the storm produced lake-effect snow from Lake Erie beginning on January 2 and continuing for fourteen days, eventually accumulating 59.5 inches, the highest two-week total in the city's history and the third highest total ever recorded for January.

The National Weather Service provided accurate forecasts of the course and severity of the storm, though not everyone took advantage of its warnings. Midwestern shoppers, however, prudently cleaned out supermarket shelves on Friday, New Year's Eve. Remembering the difficulties experienced in clearing snow from side streets during the last severe blizzard, in 1978, officials in Chicago put 850 snow removal vehicles into service; 240 were normally used when heavy snow was predicted. In contrast, Detroit, having a long-standing policy of clearing highways, large avenues, and streets in front of schools but leaving residential streets to thaw on their own, utilized only 59 plows. In 1999, however, the temperature failed to reach above freezing for ten days, seldom climbing above 20 degrees in the daytime and falling as low as 10 below zero at night. Throughout the city, neighborhood streets remained impassable, and residents vented their anger at Detroit's public officials.

Milton Berman

FOR FURTHER INFORMATION:

National Climatic Data Center. *Climate-Watch, January 1999*. Asheville, N.C.: Author, 1999.

_____. *January 1999 Blizzard: Impacts of the New Years 1999 Blizzard in the Midwest*. Asheville, N.C.: Author, 1999.

The New York Times, January 4-16, 1999.

Washington Post, January 4-16, 1999.

Droughts

A drought is an extended period of below-normal precipitation. It is a dry period that is sufficiently long and severe that crops fail and normal water demand cannot be met.

(AP/Wide World Photos)

FACTORS INVOLVED: Animals, geography, human activity, plants, temperature, weather conditions, wind
REGIONS AFFECTED: Cities, coasts, deserts, forests, islands, lakes, mountains, plains, rivers, towns, valleys

SCIENCE

Drought can be defined as a shortage of precipitation that results in below-normal levels of stream flow, groundwater, lakes, and soil moisture. It differs from other geophysical events such as volcanic eruptions, floods, and earthquakes because droughts are actually nonevents—that is, they result from the absence of events (precipitation) that should normally occur.

71

Drought also differs from other geophysical events because it has no recognizable beginning (as opposed to an earthquake) and takes time to develop. Drought may be recognized only when plants start to wilt, wells and streams run dry, and reservoir shorelines recede.

Most droughts occur when slow-moving subsiding air masses dominate a region. Commonly, air circulates in continental interiors, where there is little moisture available for evaporation, thereby providing little potential for precipitation. In order for precipitation to occur, the water vapor in the air must be lifted so that it has a chance to cool, condense into dust particles, and eventually, if conditions are favorable, precipitate. Clearly, there is little opportunity for these conditions to occur when the air is dry and descending.

Another climatological characteristic associated with droughts is that, following their establishment within a particular area, they tend to persist and even increase in areal extent. Air circulation is influenced by the drying-out of soil moisture and its unavailability for precipitation further downwind. Concurrently, the state of the atmosphere that produces the unusual circulation associated with droughts can induce surface temperature variations that in turn foster further development of the unusual circulation pattern. As a result, the process feeds on itself, making the drought last longer and intensify until major atmospheric circulation patterns change.

Drought-identification research has changed over the years from a time when the size of the precipitation deficit was the only factor considered, to the present, when sophisticated techniques are applied to the quantitative assessment of the deviation of the total environmental moisture status. These techniques facilitate better understanding of the severity, duration, and areal extent of droughts.

Early in the twentieth century, drought was identified by the U.S. Weather Bureau (now the National Weather Service) as any period of three weeks or more when the precipitation was 30 percent or more below normal. (Note that normal is defined as the average for a thirty-year period, such as 1951-1980 or 1961-1990.) The initial selection of three weeks for defining a drought was based entirely on precipitation. Subsequent research has shown that the moisture status of a region is affected by other factors besides precipitation.

Further developments in drought identification during the mid-twentieth century involved examination of the moisture demands that are related to evapotranspiration, the return of moisture to the atmosphere by the combined effects of evaporation and plant transpiration. Some drought-identification studies have examined the adequacy of soil moisture in the root zone for plant growth. The objective of this research is to determine drought probability based on the number of days when the moisture storage in the soil is zero. The U.S. Forest Service used evapotranspiration in developing a drought index for use by fire-control managers. The index was used to provide an indicator of flammability that could lead to forest fires. It had limited applicability to nonforestry users as it was not effective for showing drought as a measure of total environmental moisture stress.

W. C. Palmer developed a drought-identification index in 1965 that became widely adopted. The Palmer Drought Index (PDI) defines drought as the period of time, generally measured in months or years, when the actual moisture supply at a specified location is always below the climatically anticipated or appropriate supply of moisture. Evapotranspiration, soil moisture loss, surface runoff, and precipitation are the required environmental parameters. The PDI values range from +4.0, for an extremely wet moisture status, to –4.0, for extreme drought. Normal conditions have values close to zero. Although the PDI has been used for decades and recognized as an acceptable procedure for including evapotranspiration and soil moisture in drought identification, it has been criticized. For example, the method determines a dimensionless parameter ranging from +4.0 to –4.0 that cannot be compared to variables such as precipitation, which are measured in units (inches) that are immediately recognizable. In addition, the index is not very sensitive to short drought periods, which can negatively affect crops.

In order to overcome these problems with the PDI, other researchers have used water-budget analysis to identify changes in environmental moisture status. The procedure is similar to the Palmer method, as it includes precipitation, evapotranspiration, and soil moisture. However, the values for moisture status deviation are dimensional and expressed in the same units as precipitation—inches. Drought classification using this method yields values ranging from approximately +1.0 inch, for an above-normal moisture status, to –4.0 inches, for extreme drought. As in the PDI, the index is close to zero for normal conditions.

GEOGRAPHY

Many regions of the world have regularly occurring periods of dryness. Three different forms of dryness have a temporal dimension; they are known as perennial, seasonal, and intermittent. Perennially dry areas include the major deserts of the world, such as the Sahara, Arabian, Kalahari, and Australian Deserts. Precipitation in these large deserts is not only very low (less than 10 inches per year) but also very erratic. Seasonal dryness is associated with those parts of the world where most of the precipitation for the year occurs during a few months, leaving the rest of the year rainless. Intermittent dryness pertains to those areas of the world where the total precipitation is reduced in humid regions or where the rainy season in wet-dry climates either does not occur or is shortened.

The major problem for humans is a lack of precipitation where it is normally expected. For example, the absence of precipitation for a week where daily precipitation is the norm is considered a drought. In contrast, it would take two or more years without any rain in parts of Libya in North Africa for a drought to occur. In those parts of the world that have one rainy season, a 50 percent decrease in precipitation would be considered a drought. In other regions that normally have two rainy seasons, the failure of one could lead to drought conditions. Thus, the very word "drought" itself is a relative term, since it has different meanings in different climatic regions. The deficiency of precipitation in one location is therefore not a good indicator of drought, as each place has its own criteria for identifying drought.

PREVENTION AND PREPARATIONS

Droughts cannot be prevented, but their effects may be ameliorated. There are two main options for managing droughts: increasing the supply of water and decreasing the demand.

There are several supply enhancement measures that can be instituted. For example, reservoir release requirements can be relaxed. This occurred on the Delaware River during the severe drought of the early 1960's, when the required flow of 3,000 cubic feet per second at Trenton could not be met without jeopardizing the water-supply needs of New York City. Accordingly, the reservoir releases in the upper Delaware were temporarily relaxed. Many states require low flow or conservation flows to be maintained in the channel below a reservoir for waste assimilation and aquatic health. If a drought is severe enough, the conservation flows can be temporarily reduced or even eliminated. Other measures include the temporary diversion of water from one source, such as a recreational lake, to a water-supply reservoir. Interconnections with other water-supply purveyors may be encouraged or mandated. New sources of water could also be obtained from buried valleys that contain stratified glacial deposits with large amounts of groundwater.

Demand reduction measures include appeals for voluntary conservation. If these do not work, then mandatory water-use restrictions can be imposed. Bans on outside uses of water, such as lawn watering and car washing, are common.

Lack of precipitation in 1998 prevented crops from growing to maturity, putting many farmers' livelihoods at risk. (AP/Wide World Photos)

RESCUE AND RELIEF EFFORTS

Drought in the developed world affects crops and livestock but generally does not pose a threat to life, as it does in the developing world. Industrialized societies have existing transportation networks that enable supplies and foodstuffs to be shipped to affected regions. If there are crop and livestock losses, governments can provide disaster relief in the form of low- or no-interest loans to affected farmers, as happened in the eastern United States in the summer of 1999.

The situation in the developing world is much more grim. Governments often lack the money and resources to distribute supplies to rural populations. Food supplies coming from overseas donors may not reach the intended victims because of inadequate transportation infrastructures. Some relief efforts that could be successful include drilling of deeper wells so as to tap undeveloped water sources. This takes much time, but the extra water may inadvertently encourage more people to stay in an area that may not be sustainable.

IMPACT

Droughts have had enormous impacts on human societies since ancient times. Crop and livestock losses have caused famine and death. Drought has caused ancient civilizations to collapse and forced many people to migrate. Water is so critical to all forms of life that a pronounced shortage can decimate whole populations.

The effects of drought are profound, even during modern times. For example, the dry conditions in the Great Plains in the 1930's in conjunction with intensive farming resulted in the Dust Bowl, which at one time covered more than 77,000 square miles, an area the size of Nebraska. An estimated 10 billion tons of topsoil was blown away, some of it landing on eastern cities. The Sahel region south of the Sahara in Africa had a severe drought from 1968 to 1974, which decimated local populations. Famine and disease killed several hundred thousand people (100,000 in 1973 alone) and 5 million cattle that were the sole means of support for the nomadic populations.

Robert M. Hordon

BIBLIOGRAPHY

Benson, Charlotte, and Edward Clay. *The Impact of Drought on Sub-Saharan African Economies: A Preliminary Examination.* Washington, D.C.: World Bank, 1998. A look at the effects of often-occurring droughts on African life.

Bryson, Reid A., and Thomas J. Murray. *Climates of Hunger.* Madison: University of Wisconsin, 1977. A descriptive discussion of the profound effect of climate on human societies, going back to ancient times.

Dixon, Lloyd S., Nancy Y. Moore, and Ellen M. Pint. *Drought Management Policies and Economic Effects in Urban Areas of California, 1987-92.* Santa Monica, Calif.: Rand, 1996. This report examines the impacts of the 1987-1992 drought in California on urban and agricultural water users.

Frederiksen, Harald D. *Drought Planning and Water Resources: Implications in Water Resources Management.* Washington, D.C.: World Bank, 1992. This short report of thirty-eight pages contains two papers on drought planning and water-use efficiency and effectiveness.

Garcia, Rolando V., and Pierre Spitz. *Drought and Man: The Roots of Catastrophe.* Vol. 3. New York: Pergamon Press, 1986. Food insecurity and social disjunctions that are caused by drought are discussed, using case studies of northeastern Brazil, Tanzania, and the Sahelian countries.

Mather, John R. *Drought Indices for Water Managers.* Vol. 38. Newark: University of Delaware, Center of Climatic Research, Publications in Climatology, 1985. A technical monograph on the variety of drought indices that have been developed by researchers.

Russell, Clifford S., David G. Arey, and Robert W. Kates. *Drought and Water Supply.* Baltimore: The Johns Hopkins University Press, 1970. A scholarly study of the losses experienced by municipal water supply system customers in Massachusetts during the 1962-66 drought.

Tannehill, Ivan R. *Drought: Its Causes and Effects.* Princeton, N.J.: Princeton University Press, 1947. A classic technical but non-mathematical book on the climatology of droughts.

Wilhite, Donald A., and William E. Easterling, with Deborah A. Wood, eds. *Planning for Drought: Toward a Reduction of Societal Vulnerability.* Boulder, Colo.: Westview Press, 1987. A collection of 37 short chapters on the large number of issues pertaining to drought, including social impacts, governmental response, and human adaptation and adjustment.

Notable Events

Historical Overview

Drought is the absence of precipitation. It is a problem particularly where precipitation is marginal, usually because of topographic factors. For example, precipitation is less than 20 inches a year over much of the Great Plains of the United States; the area farther west, until the Rocky Mountains are reached, normally has less than 10 inches per year. In this case, precipitation is low because the Rocky Mountains exist between the Great Plains and the Pacific Ocean: Oceans are the source of moisture that becomes precipitation—either rain or snow. The mountains force most rain clouds to drop their moisture before the clouds have passed over the mountains. This is why rainfall is high in the Pacific Northwest and low in the region to the east of the Rocky Mountains.

Precipitation is often marginal in areas where rainfall is seasonal. This condition prevails in much of Africa and in Asia, where precipitation occurs in the form of seasonal monsoons. For central Asia, precipitation that should come in the form of monsoons is interrupted by the Himalaya Mountains, which lie between central Asia and the Indian Ocean, the source of moisture in that region.

Precipitation is also affected by long-term climatic trends. In general, when the climate is warmer, it tends also to be drier; when the climate is colder, it tends to be wetter. Some climatologists believe that the recurring droughts in northern and eastern Africa reflect a warming trend in the climate. Mean temperatures in the 1990's were higher than any recorded after the end of the Ice Age. These climatological trends are believed to be responsible for a prolonged drought in the American Southwest that undermined the Anasazi Indian culture of that region beginning in the thirteenth century. It is also possible that a comparable drought in central Asia led to the wave of Mongol invasions of Europe in the thirteenth century and the Turkish invasions of the fourteenth century.

While droughts occur with fairly regular frequency in areas of marginal precipitation, they represent an important historical event when they last more than one year. This was the case of the droughts believed to be responsible for the elimination of the early English colonies in Virginia in the sixteenth century. Droughts played a somewhat similar role in the late nineteenth century in the Great Plains of the United States, where farming settlement had been heavily promoted by the government through low-cost sales of public land. The process of moving the roving Native American tribes to reservations had been predicated on the assumption that they would be replaced by permanent white settlers. However, after droughts hit the newly established farms between 1887 and 1896, many of the settlers abandoned their residences.

The twentieth century saw repeated recurring droughts in the sub-Saharan portion of Africa. One that occurred between 1910 and 1915 led many of the pastoral tribes inhabiting the area to move onto marginal land at higher elevation, land less able to support the tribes as their numbers grew. This same area was subjected to recurring droughts in the second half of the twentieth century, which spread to eastern Africa. Because this area has many subsistence farmers, who are unable to survive a lost harvest, the drought problem led to much unrest, with large numbers of people migrating in search of food. The conditions in the Sudan and in Somalia and Ethiopia resulted in repeated calls for emergency food supplies.

In South America, drought is not uncommon along the Pacific coastline, particularly in Chile and

---

Milestones

1270-1350:	A prolonged drought in the U.S. Southwest destroys Anasazi Indian culture.
1585-1587:	A severe drought destroys the Roanoke colonies of English settlers in Virginia.
1887-1896:	Droughts drive out many early settlers on the Great Plains.
1899:	The failure of monsoons in India results in many deaths.
1910-1915:	First in a series of recurring droughts affects the Sahel region in Africa.
1933-1936:	Extensive droughts in the southern Great Plains destroy many farms, creating the Dust Bowl, in the worst drought in more than three hundred years in the United States.
1960-1990:	Repeated droughts occur in the Sahel, east Africa, and southern Africa.
1977-1978:	The western United States undergoes a drought.
1982-1983:	Droughts affect Brazil and northern India.
1986-1988:	Many farmers in the U.S. Midwest are driven out of business by a drought.
1998:	A drought destroys crops in the southern Midwest and causes ecological damage on the East Coast.
1999:	A major drought strikes the U.S. Southeast, the Atlantic coast, and New England.

Peru. Because the winds tend to blow from east to west, little moisture is moved over the Pacific coastline of South America, and the Andes Mountains prevent moisture that arises from the Atlantic Ocean from reaching the lands to the west of the mountains. Droughts also affect parts of Brazil that are well inland from the Atlantic. Droughts in this area have been increasing since the seventeenth century; at least 8 occurred in the twentieth century.

Many parts of Australia also suffer from recurrent droughts. The continent is located outside the main global circulation patterns that bring clouds and rain to inland areas, with the result that only the fringes of the continent are used for intensive cultivation. Most of Australia is suited only to grazing herds that can utilize the sparse vegetation and then move on.

Probably the most famous drought in American history was that which hit the southern part of the Great Plains region in the early 1930's. Lands that even under the best of conditions receive only marginal precipitation had been "broken to the plough" in the first two decades of the twentieth century. When precipitation failed to materialize in the early 1930's, many subsistence farmers were driven from the land in what came to be known as the Dust Bowl, as winds blew the unprotected soil off the land.

Another drought affected the Great Plains, even the northern Great Plains, in the late 1980's. Many farmers who had borrowed money to extend their farms were unable to pay back the loans and lost their farms when their crops failed. Another drought hit the southern Great Plains in 1998, destroying a large portion of the cotton crop in Texas. In 1999 the drought conditions moved to the southeastern United States, devastating crops in that region. Coupled with high temperatures, this drought captured public attention.

Nancy M. Gordon

1968: North Africa

Date: 1968-1974

Place: Sahel region of sub-Saharan Africa, especially Mali, Mauritania, Niger, and Burkina Faso

RESULT: 22 million affected in four countries, 200,000-500,000 estimated dead, millions of cattle and livestock lost

One of the major characteristics of drought is that it only slowly develops into a humanitarian catastrophe. This was true of the five-year drought in the Sahel region of sub-Saharan Africa from 1968 to 1974. This region of Africa, lying in a very fragile semi-arid zone just south of the Sahara, from the West African countries of Mauritania, Mali, Burkina Faso (then known as Upper Volta), and Niger to the central and East African countries of Chad and Sudan, is highly susceptible to drought. Many people in the region practice nomadic herding, which is the main livelihood, on substantial tracts of land that can support little else in the way of economic activity. The drought and famine of 1968-1974 centered primarily in the west, with Mauritania, Mali, Burkina Faso, and Niger being the most acutely affected. Still, during the height of the dry seasons, neighboring countries to the south, such as Senegal, Guinea, the Ivory Coast, and Ghana, were affected by migrants seeking relief.

The first few years of a drought place stress on nomadic herding populations, but well-established coping mechanisms permit them to adjust. Herds are moved to areas that will support meager pasture and water supplies. As drought persists, herders sell off livestock in order to purchase other foods. As drought enters a third or fourth year livestock begin to die as water and pasture resources diminish or disappear. People, too, begin to die. Weakened by malnutrition, they are more susceptible to disease. Measles, cholera, and meningitis interact with malnutrition to hasten death. In the Sahel during the drought, measles was a prevalent killer.

Many United Nations agencies, governmental agencies, and private organizations were present throughout the period of the drought. The deterioration of the food supply and of the nomadic economy did not go unnoticed. However, not until the fall of 1972, after several years of persistent and deepening drought, did food agencies start sounding the alarm that the situation bordered on crisis. In October, 1972, an internal report of the U.S. Agency for International Development (AID) portrayed the situation in the Sahel in very stark terms, characterizing much of the development aid previously invested in the area as having been wasteful or counterproductive and woefully lacking in the collection of perti-

nent data. It called the situation one of extensive deterioration, especially for the rural and nomadic populations. Wells dried up as water tables dropped for lack of recharge. Coping mechanisms had been exhausted. Harvests had failed extensively. Each year, hope for rain and a break in the drought had been met by little or no rain. The situation was ripe for crisis in the fall of 1972, and relief-agency contingency planning in the fall months was a belated response to a disaster that was well underway. Failure to anticipate the need for animal feed and veterinary medicines, as well as larger amounts of food, medicine, and other relief aid for the human population of the Sahel, during the winter of 1972-1973 led to a huge loss of livestock in 1973, and this, coupled with delayed humanitarian aid, placed the nomadic population at severe risk. Local governments were also lackadaisical in their response to the crisis among the rural population.

In March of 1973, the governments of the Sahel countries formally declared the region a disaster area. Subsequently, the U.S. government declared the Sahel a disaster area, paving the way for the involvement of AID's Office of Foreign Disaster Assistance. By midyear, humanitarian assistance and food aid began making its way to Sahelian countries in large amounts. More than twenty countries supplied assistance totaling in excess of $150 million. The United States provided about one-third of the total. There is little doubt that these efforts, which were in high gear during the summer of 1973, averted an even more staggering loss of life. As it was, famine-related deaths in 1973 alone substantially exceeded 100,000, while losses of livestock ranged from 30 to 50 percent, a devastating blow to that segment of the population engaged in pastoralism.

Food aid continued to reach the Sahel into 1974, as the countries attempted to cope with the lingering effects of the sustained drought and the famine. Recovery was slow but observable in subsequent years, illustrating that droughts often take time not only to develop and engender famine, but also to ease. The record of assistance was not encouraging. Not only was food aid late in coming, it was often poorly distributed. Corruption among host governments hampered relief efforts, and often the nomadic populations most in need of assistance were last to benefit from it.

The rather mixed performance of the international aid-giving community to the western Sahel drought and famine caused aid agencies to consider the need for better data collection, early warning mechanisms, and logistical systems for food delivery. As history has shown, even better emergency detection and response systems are only as good as the will to use them.

The Sahel has always been prone to drought and thus to famine. The 1968-1974 drought was devastating but demonstrated that international response could help to avert widespread mortality. When the Sahel region was visited again by a more extensive drought a decade later, international officials were in a better position to respond, even though the threat to life was even more daunting and extensive.

Robert F. Gorman

FOR FURTHER INFORMATION:

Brown, Barbara. "The United Nations and Disaster Relief in the Sahel." *Disasters* 1, no. 2 (1977): 145-150.

Sheets, Hal, and Roger Morris. *Disaster in the Desert: Failures of International Relief in the West African Drought.* Washington, D.C.: Carnegie Endowment for International Peace, 1974.

1981: Africa

DATE: 1981-1986

PLACE: 22 African countries, including Angola, Botswana, Burkina Faso, Chad, Ethiopia, Kenya, Mali, Mauritania, Mozambique, Namibia, Niger, Somalia, South Africa, Sudan, Zambia, and Zimbabwe

RESULT: 120 million people in 22 countries affected, several million forced to migrate, significant loss of life and of livestock

Africa is the fastest growing and poorest continent in the world. Much of the northern half of the continent is prone to drought, as are large areas of south-

An emergency rations line to feed Ethiopians suffering from food shortages caused by drought. (AP/Wide World Photos)

ern Africa. Only in Africa's midsection, where rain forests still exist, is drought unlikely. The only part of Africa that has experienced a well-documented, long-term trend toward decreasing rainfall is the western portion of the Sahel region, which experienced a moderate to severe drought for more than thirty years. Apart from the Sahara Desert, the Kalahari Desert, and the western Sahel, drought in other parts of Africa is cyclical and local in nature. However, during the early 1980's, almost all of the countries bordering on the Sahara, including all of the countries of the Sahel (Mauritania, Mali, Burkina Faso, Niger, Chad, Sudan), as well as Ethiopia, Kenya, and Somalia in the horn of Africa, experienced extended periods of drought ranging from a year to two or more years at a time. Southern Africa was hit hard too, with Mozambique, Zimbabwe, Zambia, Angola, Botswana, Namibia, and South Africa all experiencing drought. Seriously complicating the situation in several countries, including Ethiopia, Sudan, Mozambique, and Angola, were civil wars that further disrupted economic and agricultural activity.

During the first few years of drought, nomadic and sedentary populations in Africa engage in a variety of coping strategies to avoid starvation. Nomads seek out water holes and pasture in areas less affected by drought, and as drought is prolonged they sell off herds to purchase necessary food and migrate even farther in search of pasture and water. After a year or two of drought, depending on the quantity of harvests, farmers begin to consume seed meant for the following year's planting; an additional year of drought puts them at the brink of starvation. Members of the family often migrate to the cities to earn money so that family members can purchase food on the wider market, and livestock and valuables are sold. Eventually, starvation sets in, as it did in Ethiopia in 1983, and hordes of people begin migrating toward the cities, where their misery becomes more visible.

In Ethiopia and the western Sahel regions, extended droughts in the previous decade had put vulnerable portions of the population at risk even before the drought of the early 1980's. Renewed drought in both areas, coupled with war in Ethiopia, provoked a serious crisis. In Ethiopia, tens of thousands died, hundreds of thousands fled into the Sudan, and hundreds of thousands more became internally displaced inside war-torn Ethiopia, where the government ignored reports of famine as long as it affected rebel-held territories. When famine spread into government-controlled areas, international attention was sought, and gradually relief supplies began to reach the beleaguered populations in both government-controlled and rebel-held areas.

Although the famine in Ethiopia captured most of the world's attention, provoking the famous Band Aid recording of "Do They Know It's Christmas?" and the Live Aid concert that raised millions for drought and famine relief in Africa, the effects of drought extended far beyond Ethiopia. An estimated 120 million Africans in 22 countries were in need of assistance. Harvest failure owing to drought and civil war in 1984 put 4 to 5 million Mozambicans at great risk. In the Sahel region about a third of the livestock either was sold or died. In Mali alone, livestock losses reached the 50 percent level, placing 1.5 million Malian nomads at risk. Drought and harvests in the Sudan were regional in scope, but by 1985 more than 8 million Sudanese were at risk of famine, about equal to the numbers of Ethiopians threatened by starvation in the same year.

The United Nations, governments, and private humanitarian groups eventually mobilized massive amounts of humanitarian aid to stave off starvation, and gradually most of the affected countries recovered, some more quickly than others. The United Nations Office for Emergency Operations in Africa (UNOEOA) was created in 1984 in order to coordinate international responses to the widespread African drought emergency and to assist the governments of the affected countries. The office continued long after the drought eased, as a mechanism for early warning and information dissemination as well as for promotion of economic development in the region. Without the latter, most experts believe that many countries in Africa will remain highly vulnerable to famine in the future.

Robert F. Gorman

FOR FURTHER INFORMATION:

Berry, Leonard, and Thomas E. Downing. "Drought and Famine in Africa, 1981-86: A Comparison of Impacts and Responses in Six Countries." In *The Challenge of Famine: Recent Experience, Lessons Learned,* edited by John Osgood Field. West Hartford, Conn.: Kumarian Press, 1993.

Deng, Francis M., and Larry Minear. *The Challenges of Famine Relief: Emergency Operations in the Sudan.* Washington, D.C.: Brookings Institution, 1992.

Varnis, Stephen L. *Reluctant Aid or Aiding the Reluctant? U.S. Food Aid Policy and Ethiopian Famine Relief.* New Brunswick, N.J.: Transaction, 1990.

1986: California

DATE: Winter, 1986, to spring, 1992
PLACE: Primarily Southern California
RESULT: Increased water prices, loss of water for agricultural production, water rationing

In contrast to droughts that occur in poor countries, where loss of livelihood and loss of life from drought and resulting famines can be extensive, the case of Southern California during the late 1980's and early 1990's illustrates how wealthy countries and economies are able to forestall and prevent disastrous loss of life. People in Southern California experienced considerable inconvenience during the drought years, and, especially in the agricultural sector, losses of revenue were felt. Nonetheless, famine never became a reality because the resources, transportation systems, logistical capacities, and wealth of California were available to help the state cope with five years of little rainfall. In a Third World country, five years of drought typically provokes a devastating famine, but not in California.

Instead, the drought in California provoked a statewide political battle over the use of increasingly dwindling water resources. Indeed, the battle extended even beyond California, as political leaders there looked to neighboring states and regions for possible relief. A request for Oregon to sell surplus water to California was rebuffed, and in 1991, after four years of drought, a scheme to pump water to California from Alaska via a plastic undersea pipeline was even considered. However, that scheme was obviated by timely precipitation in the winter of 1992.

California produces more agricultural products than any other state in the United States. Much of this food is grown in the interior valleys of Southern California, which are exceptionally fertile but do not receive enough annual rain to ensure predictable harvests without irrigation. California is blessed with geological features, such as mountain ranges, that collect a good deal of Pacific moisture in the form of snow. By means of canals, water from Northern California rivers and mountain ranges is brought to the more arid but arable valleys of Southern California. However, when the winter snows and spring rains fail to materialize for several consecutive years, water reserves for agriculture and for use in the numerous and very large urban centers of California become increasingly scarce. As drought hit Northern California, that area balked at the idea of sending water resources to the south.

Concern over the effects of drought on California's water supply began after light mountain snowfall in the winter of 1986-1987. In this, the first year of the drought, editorials appeared in California newspapers concerning the ongoing dispute between the north and the south over water rights. Concern was expressed by journalists and legislators that California's population and economic growth were outstripping the state's water supplies. Environmentalists expressed concern over the draining of reservoirs and of natural lakes, such as Mono Lake. Drought in the Pacific Northwest caused further nervousness.

By 1988, after another year of drought, calls for conservation of water became more frequent. California's Water Resources Department declared the state critically dry but not yet drought-stricken. Still, proposals to line water canals to preserve more water were aired, and in Los Angeles the city council adopted a mandatory water-saving device ordinance to cut down on the waste of water. In 1989, as the drought continued, disputes arose between environmentalists; the sports, fishing, and recreation industries; and farmers over the allocation of water resources. Threats to cut by 50 percent the delivery of water to Central Valley farmers failed to materialize but indicated the growing concern over dwindling water resources as reservoirs in Northern California began to drop dangerously low.

By 1990, California was looking to the Colorado River system and the Columbia River in Oregon for more water. Water-conservation measures were widespread in Southern California, and discussion about mandatory rationing schemes was prevalent. When the drought entered its fifth year in 1991, Governor Pete Wilson urged Californians not to panic. Water deliveries to Southern California were reduced. In Los Angeles, nervous residents began watering their lawns with gray water, in violation of city codes. In March, the seemingly fantastic Alaska water pipeline plan was broached. Then, finally, heavy winter snow and rain partially replenished reservoirs and eased the drought conditions.

California continues to grow, and its demand for water continues to rise. The next time a lengthy drought occurs, the pressures of water resources will be even more acute.

Robert F. Gorman

FOR FURTHER INFORMATION:

DeBare, Ilana. "Dry Winter in State Stirs Concern About Water Supply in 1988." *Los Angeles Times,* February 19, 1987, p. I28.

Dye, Lee. "Drought Idea: Pipe in Water from Alaska." *Los Angeles Times,* March 25, 1991, p. A1.

Simon, Richard. "Oregon Pulls Plug on Hahn's Pleas for Water." *Los Angeles Times,* May 11, 1990, p. B3.

1998: U.S. East Coast and Midwest

DATE: July, 1998-November, 1999
PLACE: The Northeast, Middle Atlantic states, and Midwest
RESULT: Billions of dollars in damage to crops

Dead hay fields and undergrown cornstalks typical of many farms in the U.S. Midwest and East in 1998. (AP/Wide World Photos)

In summer, 1998, a drought was detected in the eastern and midwestern United States and continued through 1999 because insufficient rain and snow maintained dry conditions. Experts declared it the worst American drought since the 1930's Dust Bowl. The National Oceanographic and Atmospheric Administration (NOAA) called it the most severe drought ever documented in the Middle Atlantic states. Some scientists stated that the weather phenomenon La Niña was responsible for the 1990's drought: Abnormally cold water in the central Pacific Ocean shifted the jet stream's path and altered weather patterns in North America. Other climatologists suggested that global warming caused the drought.

Counties in states along the eastern seaboard and as far west as New Mexico were declared federal disaster areas. The drought economically impacted both agricultural producers and consumers because low yields resulted in higher prices at the market and minimal profits for farmers. The U.S. Department of Agriculture issued relief funds approved by Congress to assist farmers and arranged for shipments of hay to feed starving livestock where grazing ranges were scorched. Drought-related losses included the reduction of jobs on farms and in manufacturing of agricultural equipment. Industries that relied on water for manufacturing had to limit production during the drought.

In July, 1999, the National Drought Policy Commission was established to develop drought laws and programs. Water resource managers were concerned about reservoirs being emptied and groundwater sources that fed public aquifers and private wells being tainted. Authorities enacted water-use restrictions to prohibit people from carelessly watering dying lawns and filling swimming pools. The levels of rivers, streams, and lakes were lowered, damaging aquatic habitats and preventing recreational activities. The salinity of East Coast inlets increased, causing ecological damage. The drought affected tourism in New England states because fall foliage was ruined. Bird migration patterns were altered, and confused wildlife wandered into urban areas, looking for water and posing potential health hazards. The drought created conditions favorable for forest fires to engulf millions of acres.

Researchers cited archaeological evidence, such as tree rings, that revealed that the region affected by the 1990's drought had suffered droughts lasting several decades during the previous seven hundred years. NOAA scientists studied climatic cycles and determined that intense droughts like the 1930's Dust Bowl occurred twice each century, with minor two-year droughts happening once every twenty years. This historical information supplemented by experiments during the 1990's drought—corn planted with organic mulch maintained soil moisture and flourished despite lack of rain—offered solutions for future droughts. The hurricanes that soaked the East Coast in autumn of 1999 replenished some groundwater sources, and, ironically, flooding became the primary concern in previously drought-stricken areas.

Elizabeth D. Schafer

FOR FURTHER INFORMATION:

Borenstein, Seth. "Summer Drought May Have Marked Beginning of Another Dust Bowl Period." *Washington Post,* December 15, 1998.

Monastersky, Richard. "Acclimating to a Warmer World." *The Weekly Newsmagazine of Science* 156 (August 28, 1999): 136.

Suplee, Curt. "El Niño/La Niña: Nature's Vicious Cycle." *National Geographic* 195 (March, 1999): 73-95.

Dust Storms and Sandstorms

(AP/Wide World Photos)

Dust storms and sandstorms are composed of airborne and windblown clouds of soil particles, mineral flakes, and vegetative residue that impact climate, air temperature, air quality, rainfall, desertification, agricultural productivity, human health, and human habitation of the land.

FACTORS INVOLVED: Geological forces, human activity, plants, rain, weather conditions, wind
REGIONS AFFECTED: Deserts, plains, valleys

SCIENCE

Dust storms result from wind erosion, desertification, and physical deterioration of the soil caused by persistent or temporary lack of rainfall and wind gusts.

Dust storms develop when wind velocity at 1 foot above soil level increases beyond 13 miles per hour, causing saltation and surface creep. In saltation, small particles are lifted off the surface, travel 10 to 15 times the height to which they are lifted, then spin downward with sufficient force to dislodge other soil particles and break down earth clods. In surface creep, larger particles creep along the surface in a rolling motion. The larger the affected area, the greater the cumulative effect of saltation and surface creep, leading to an avalanche of soil particles across the land, even during moderate wind gusts. The resulting soil displacement erodes the structure and texture of the remaining soils, reduces the moisture content of the soil, exposes bedrock, and limits the type of vegetation sustainable on the remaining soil.

Dust storms remove smaller and lighter soil particles, leaving behind the larger and denser particles and granular minerals associated with deserts, and erode rock surfaces, creating dust and granular particles. As soils become drier and more dense, and as ground cover is reduced, the number and intensity of subsequent dust storms increases. Arid or semiarid soil eventually becomes desert. Atmospheric dust increases soil and air temperature by trapping heat in the lower atmosphere. Dust may also reduce soil and air temperature by reflecting the sun's heating radiation back into space. Changes in air temperature, coupled with dust in the atmosphere and drier land surfaces, reduce local rainfall, encouraging desertification.

Dust storms result from the dislodging of small, light soil particles, mineral flecks, and decomposing vegetation matter. Dust storms rise miles into the atmosphere and have both local and global impacts. Sandstorms result from dislodging larger, heavier particles of soil and rock. They tend to occur in conjunction with desert cyclones. Sandstorms remain close to ground level and have primarily local impacts. Dust and sandstorms may occur simultaneously.

There are many types of dust storms. Haze reduces visibility to three-fourths of a mile or less and results from persistent wind gusts across arid soils or across temporarily dry or disturbed semi-arid soils. Dust devils lift silt and clay particles several hundred yards into the air. Tornadoes generate local vortices that lift silt, clay, mineral flecks, and vegetation residue more than a mile high and transport it hundreds of square miles. Cyclones form at the leading edge of thunderstorm cells, extending across a front of several hundred miles, generating winds up to 150 miles per hour, and lifting particles and debris several miles into the upper atmosphere and jet stream for distribution around the globe.

GEOGRAPHY

Dust storms and sandstorms of global significance originate in the arid deserts and semiarid lands covering 36 percent of the earth's land surface. Major deserts are located in northern Africa, northeast Sudan, southwest Africa, the Arabian Peninsula, southwest Asia, the Middle East, northern and western China, central Australia, southwest North America, and parts of southern and western South America, the Caucasus of Russia, central Spain, and the southern coast of the Mediterranean Sea. In addition, dust storms arise when normally semiarid lands periodically become arid, undergo abnormally strong windy periods, or have their vegetation removed by humans or nature. These areas include sub-Saharan Africa, the U.S. Midwest, the northern coast of the Mediterranean, the steppe of central Asia, and all lands immediately adjacent to deserts.

Globally significant storms cover areas of several hundred to several thousand square miles and transport dust from one continent to another. Locally significant dust storms originate in overly cultivated agricultural fields, residential or commercial developments denuded of ground cover, major road construction sites, and any lands experiencing a temporary drought. Local storms are often confined to only a few square miles in area.

Locales with the highest frequency of dust storms are Mexico City and Kazakhstan in central Asia, with about 60 storms per year; western and northern China, with 30 storms each year; West Africa, with 20 storms; and Egypt, with 10 storms. Storms of the longest known duration occurred in the southwestern United States, with a storm of twenty-eight days in Amarillo, Texas, in April, 1935, and a storm of twenty-two days in the Texas Panhandle in March of 1936.

PREVENTION AND PREPARATIONS

The number and intensity of dust storms and sandstorms are reduced through soil-conservation practices, such as covering the soil with vegetation, reducing soil exposure on tilled land, creating wind barriers, installing buffer strips around exposed soils, and limiting the number and intensity of soil disturbing activities on vulnerable arid and semiarid soils. Vegetative cover slows the wind at ground level, protects soil particles from detachment, and traps blowing or floating soil particles, chemicals, and nutrients. Because the greatest wind-erosion damage often occurs during seasons when no crops are growing or when natural vegetation is dormant, dead residues and standing stubble of the previous crop often remain in place until the next planting season. Planting grass or legume cover crops until the next planting season, or as part of a crop rotation cycle or no-till planting system, also reduces dust.

No-till and mulch-till planting systems reduce soil exposure to wind erosion. No-till systems leave the soil cover undisturbed before inserting crop seeds into the ground through a narrow slot in the soil. Mulch-till planting keeps a high percentage of the dead residues of previous crops on the surface when the new crop is planted. Row crops are planted at right angles to the prevailing winds to absorb wind energy and trap moving soil particles. Crops are planted in small fields to prevent avalanching caused by an increase in the amount of soil in particles transported by wind as the distance across bare soil increases.

Because wind breaks to slow wind speeds at the surface of the soil, good wind barriers include tree plantings, cross-wind strips of perennial shrubs, and high grasses. The protected area is ten times the height of the barrier. Alley cropping is used in areas of sustained high wind; crops are planted between rows of larger, mature trees.

Strip farming reduces field width, thereby reducing wind erosion. Large fields are subdivided into narrow cultivated strips. Planting crops along the contour lines around hills is called contour strip cropping. Planting crops in strips across the top of predominant slopes is called field stripping. Crops are arranged so that a strip of hay or sod, such as grass, clover, alfalfa, or a close-growing small grain, such as wheat or oats, is alternated with a strip of cultivated row crop, such as tobacco, cotton, or corn. In areas of high wind, the greater the average wind velocity, the narrower the strips. Blown dust from the row-crop strip is trapped as it passes through the subsequent strip of hay or grain, thereby reducing dust. Contour strip cropping or field stripping can reduce soil erosion by 65 to 75 percent.

Dust blows around children pumping water in the Colorado Dust Bowl in 1935. (AP/Wide World Photos)

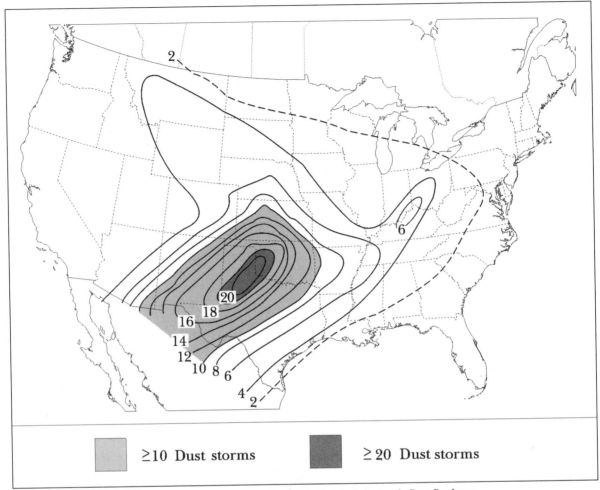

The number of dust storms occuring in March, 1936, during the Dust Bowl years.

Limiting land-disturbing activities by humans on highly vulnerable arid and semiarid soils reduces the number and intensity of both dust storms and sandstorms. Deserts are especially vulnerable to impacts of animal herds and motor-vehicle traffic. Many fragile desert plants, shrubs, and trees are easily destroyed by animal or human activity, especially foraging and vehicle traffic. The surface of the desert consists of a thin layer of small and microscopic plants, microorganisms, and insects, whose combined activities produce a thin crust that limits the impact of wind on the surface of the desert. When this crust is broken by surface traffic, the underlying sands and minerals are vulnerable to wind erosion. Natural repair to the broken crust and natural revegetation processes may take decades or centuries.

RESCUE AND RELIEF EFFORTS

Little can be done to protect humans, buildings, or crops from the impact of dry-wind tornadoes or cyclones producing major dust storms or sandstorms, but soil-conservation measures reduce the number and intensity of these storms. The effects of these storms on humans is partly ameliorated by remaining indoors, by wearing heavy clothing or remaining inside vehicles when outdoors, and by covering the nose and mouth to prevent the ingestion of dust, spores, and pollens.

IMPACT

Sandstorms and dust storms have moved sufficient soil particles over the centuries to reshape continents; alter the distribution of plant and animal life; alternately heat and cool the earth; and silt rivers, lakes, and oceans. The volume of annual wind-blown dust is approximately equal to the volume of soil transported each year through water erosion. Approximately half a billion tons of dust is borne aloft each year, with more than half that dust deposited in the world's oceans.

The desertification processes associated with sandstorms and dust storms impacted the historic rise and fall of many civilizations, including the early Pueblo Indians of the American Southwest, the Harappan civilization of southwest Asia, the city-states of Arabia, and the caravan empires of sub-Saharan Africa. Dust storms on agricultural lands cause soil nutrient loss, reduce the moisture-retaining capacity of the soil, and concentrate salts and fertilizer acids in the soil, thereby reducing agricultural production. Efforts to replace lost topsoil with fertilizers have proven futile. Crop yields are reduced by up to 80 percent.

Sandstorms kill people and animals and damage, destroy, or bury roads, buildings, machinery, and agricultural fields. Many people and animals are killed each year by the force of the storms or by ingestion of wind-borne particles. In 1895, more than 20 percent of the cattle in eastern Colorado died of suffocation in a particularly intense dust storm.

Dust storms are a major source of air pollution and a major distribution vehicle for mold spores, pollens, and other harmful airborne particles. One pathogen causing "valley fever" or "desert rheumatism" kills approximately 120 people each year in the United States alone. Sandstorms and intense dust storms contribute to traffic accidents and disrupt mass-transportation systems. In many southwestern American states, dust storms are responsible for up to 20 percent of all traffic accident fatalities.

Gordon Neal Diem

BIBLIOGRAPHY

Morales, Chister, ed. *Saharan Dust: Mobilization, Transport, Deposition.* Chichester, England: John Wiley & Sons, 1979. The editor presents numerous scientific papers and recommendations from a workshop held in Sweden sponsored by the Scientific Committee on Problems in the Environment.

Pewe, Troy L., ed. *Desert Dust: Origin, Characteristics, and Effect on Man.* Boulder, Colo.: Geological Society of America, 1981. This collection of scientific papers provides detail on the causes and effects of sand- and dust storms.

Sundar, Christopher A., et al. *Radiative Effects of Aerosols Generated from Biomass Burning, Dust Storms, and Forest Fires.* Washington, D.C.: National Aeronautics and Space Administration, 1996. The book discusses global heating and cooling from dust storms.

Tannehill, Ivan Ray. *Drought: Its Causes and Effects.* Princeton, N.J.: Princeton University Press, 1947. Discusses the effects of drought on dust storms.

U.S. Department of Agriculture. *Soil Erosion by Wind* (Agriculture Information Bulletin Number 555), *Crop Residue Management to Reduce Erosion and Improve Soil Quality* (Conservation Research Report 39), and *Universal Soil Loss Equation with Factor Values.* These undated public-information booklets and a variety of *Conservation Practice Job Sheets* describe appropriate soil-conservation measures to limit dust storms.

Worster, Donald. *Dust Bowl: The Southern Plains in the 1930's.* New York: Oxford University Press, 1941. Describes the dust storms of the southwestern United States.

Notable Events

1932: Dust Bowl

DATE: 1932-1938
PLACE: Great Plains and the southwestern United States
RESULT: 500,000 homeless

Six years of severe drought combined with overuse and improper exposure of the soil in the semi-arid and arid prairie regions of southeastern United States led to Dust Bowl conditions, wind erosion of the soil, and the displacement of 500,000 farmers and townsfolk in the region. Dust Bowl conditions include extensive and prolonged lack of rainfall extending over several years; depletion of soil moisture to the point where plant life cannot be sustained; increased heat in summer and increased cold in winter due to the effect of airborne dust particles on atmospheric heating and cooling; the transformation of soil into particles of dust, sand, and minerals; and an increase in the frequency and intensity of wind due to the combined effects of rapidly fluctuating daily air temperature, low humidity, and a decline in the vegetative barriers and ground covers.

Homesteaders Arrive. Before settlement in the late nineteenth and early twentieth centuries, natural, deep-rooted prairie grasses held the soil in place. The grasses that established themselves on the prairie soil were able to survive severe and prolonged drought, hot summers, and cold winters. During most of the eighteenth and nineteenth centuries, the region of the Great Plains was known to most citizens as "The Great American Desert." In the post-Civil War period, railroads were given government land grants to encourage the western expansion of rail services. Promotional literature produced by the railroads and the national government encouraged set-tlement in the Great Plains, either along railroad lines or in homestead areas established in the western territories by the government. The older idea of the Great Plains as a desert was replaced by a new myth of an agricultural empire in the "Garden of the World" and a new marketing dictum that "rain follows the plow." This mistaken idea that settlement could change the climate encouraged farmers to continue plowing and planting their lands as the years of drought progressed, and discouraged the use of new agricultural techniques for semiarid soils even after these techniques were developed.

A period of western migration encouraged eastern, midwestern, and European immigrant farmers to relocate to the area. Government land-grant and homesteading programs, land marketing schemes by railroad companies, national policies encouraging increased agricultural production, and the invention of mechanized farming tools and tractors encouraged and supported this migration to the previously untilled land. The native grasses were plowed under, using the agricultural techniques of the day, exposing the newly turned soil to potential erosion. Most settlement and soil exposure occurred during periods of normal or increased rainfall, and the growing crops replaced the prairie grasses as protectors of the soil. Many farmers enjoyed bumper yields in the years preceding the drought.

The settlement of the American Great Plains was similar to the patterns experienced in semiarid areas of Australia, South Africa, and the Russian steppes. The settlers were primarily individuals with agricultural experience limited to the humid agricultural conditions of Western Europe or the eastern half of North America. The settlers began with an inaccurate perception of the possibilities and limitations of agricultural production in these arid and semiarid areas and lacked an adaptive technology to cope with extended drought. A severe drought in the Great Plains in the 1890's did not deter optimism concerning the agricultural potential of the region.

Years of Drought. The drought beginning in 1932 led to agricultural failure and to the repeated exposure of the land to wind erosion. Once tilled lands began to suffer wind erosion, the blowing dust together with the drought conditions caused the natural grasses on untilled land to wither and die, exposing more soil to erosion. Left unprotected, topsoil was lifted into the air, creating "black blizzards" of dust. The previously rich topsoil was blown away. On many farms, topsoil was eroded down to the clay base or to the bedrock. In many cases, even the clay began to fragment and become airborne in the wind. The loss of land fertility plus repeated crop failures led to the bankruptcy of thousands of farmers and the townspeople who provided services to the farmers. Many of these people became displaced migrants, with many traveling further west to California or returning to the East in search of jobs and new land.

The harvest of 1931 produced a bumper crop of wheat, depressing the market price in the midst of the Great Depression, a national and worldwide decline in economic activity which began in the 1920's and which had already depressed prices for agricultural products. Farmers responded by increasing the acreage under cultivation hoping to restore lost income by increasing output, thus further reducing prices and exposing more land to potential erosion. The 1932 agricultural year began with a late freeze followed by violent rainstorms, a plague of insects, and a summer drought affecting 50 million acres in Kansas, Oklahoma, Texas, New Mexico, Colorado, and parts of Nebraska, South Dakota, and North Dakota. Drought conditions continued without relief until 1937 and gradually extended east, west, and north, involving most of North America in some form of drought. Lakes Michigan and Huron dropped to their lowest levels on record.

Black Blizzards. The first great dust storm, or black blizzard, occurred in November, 1933. Vast quantities of dust particles were carried thousands of feet into the atmosphere by winter winds, blocking out the sun for several days at a time. Gritty dust and dirt blew into houses and other buildings under windowsills or through door jambs, covering and contaminating floors, food, bed clothes, furniture, and drinking water and damaging machinery and

Nebraska farmers migrating to the West after Dust Bowl conditions forced them to abandon their farms. (AP/Wide World Photos)

tools. Dust storms continued to occur regularly during the next few years. In parts of Texas and Oklahoma as many as 100 separate dust storms were recorded in a single year. In March of 1936, there were twenty-two days of dust storms over the Texas Panhandle. In April, 1935, twenty-eight days of dust storms occurred in Amarillo, Texas.

Storms in April, 1934, and February, 1935, were so severe that they darkened the skies over the entire eastern half of the United States, with dust from the Dust Bowl falling on Washington, D.C., New York City, and ships at sea. The finest dust particles were carried as far as Europe. An estimated 350 million tons of topsoil was blown away from what had been one of the world's richest agricultural areas.

Within the most severely affected areas of the Dust Bowl, crops sprouted only to wither and die. Drifts of dirt and sand smothered the remaining prairie grasslands, killed trees and shrubs, and blocked roads and railroad lines. Blowing dust scrubbed the paint off buildings and automobiles, caused human respiratory sickness, and created massive dry-weather electrical storms generating substantial wind gusts but no rainfall. Hundreds of people died of respiratory ailments. Cattle and wildlife starved or died of thirst. Birds found it impossible to nest successfully.

Government Action. In 1936-1937, Congress debated and eventually enacted a Soil Conservation Act, intended to relieve the economic impact of the Dust Bowl conditions and prevent future wind or water erosion of the soil. Dr. Hugh Hammond Bennett, working with the Roosevelt administration as the chief proponent of the bill, encouraged a congressional vote on the bill just as dust from a Dust Bowl black blizzard shrouded Washington, D.C., in a brown haze. The act allocated $500 million to subsidize farmers who converted from growing grain crops, such as corn and wheat, to soil-building crops, such as hay and legumes. These measures both helped stabilize the soil and helped reduce grain production, resulting in agricultural prices rising to pre-Depression levels. The Soil Conservation Act called for the establishment of agricultural and conservation education programs, the planting of trees around farms and along roads as windbreaks, and establishment of Soil Conservation Districts in each state. Later renamed Soil and Water Conservation Districts, these units of local government, encouraged by the national government and established in each state by acts of the state legislature, are an important force in encouraging farmers to add "best management practices" to their farming techniques, constructing vegetative barriers to reduce wind and water erosion of the soil, and protecting the soil and water resources of America.

Actions by the national government came too late for many farmers forced off the land due to mortgage foreclosures or the near-total loss of topsoil from their lands. Many migrated west to California or returned east to the industrial cities with only a few clothes and possessions and no money. Those with no skills other than farming worked as migrant farm laborers wherever they could find a harvest to work. These migrants put strains on the already overburdened government-welfare programs in these states and increased labor competition pressures. The migrants experienced anger and discrimination in the areas to which they migrated. Several states and many local governments enacted laws intended to prevent the migration and settlement of Dust Bowl migrants into their areas.

In 1937, the drought ended, and those who could return to agricultural production did, using new farming methods designed to protect the soil from both wind and water erosion. The 1937 crop yield nationwide was the largest on record. The good weather continued throughout the critical years of World War II, and the improved agricultural methods continued to protect the soil.

Gordon Neal Diem

FOR FURTHER INFORMATION:

Saarinen, Thomas F. *Perception of the Drought Hazard on the Great Plains.* Chicago: University of Chicago Press, 1966.

Smith, Henry Nash. *Virgin Land: The American West as Symbol and Myth.* New York: Vintage Books, 1950.

Stamp, L. D., ed. *A History of Land Use in Arid Regions.* Paris: UNESCO, 1961.

United States Great Plains Committee. *The Future of the Great Plains.* Washington, D.C.: U.S. Government Printing Office, 1936.

1991: California

DUST STORM
DATE: November 29, 1991
PLACE: Coalinga, California
RESULT: 17 dead in 104-vehicle pileup

Dust from agricultural fields barren from years of drought was driven by 40-mile-per-hour winds shrouding heavily traveled Interstate 5 in a locally significant dust storm that caused traffic accidents resulting in 17 dead, 150 injured, and 55 hospitalized. The storm occurred along a 4-mile section of the highway in midafternoon on a Saturday, reducing visibility to zero. The sudden blackout caused motorists to brake frantically, resulting in rear-end collisions.

More than 100 cars, many carrying travelers returning from the Thanksgiving holiday, and a number of trucks were involved in a series of chain-reaction collisions. Eleven tractor-trailer trucks crashed into each other in a 1.5-mile section of highway. Victims reported a mile-long column of wrecked vehicles that resembled a war zone. Thousands of motorists were trapped on the highway until after the reopening of the highway around 7 P.M. that day. Crews experienced continued high winds, sand, and dust, making it difficult to clear the roadway of the accident. Thousands more motorists were rerouted by the closing of the Interstate for more than 150 miles—from Bakersfield to Los Banos—because of fear of more local dust storms.

Critics claimed the disaster could have been averted had the California Highway Patrol issued warnings concerning road conditions. Motorists reported dust squalls with near-zero visibility on Friday evening and again Saturday morning, just two hours prior to the accidents. The Highway Transportation Safety Council claimed that more than 7,000 motorists were killed between 1985 and 1995 in limited-visibility accidents like the one on Interstate 5 and urged an improved system for warning motorists of the danger.

Many farmers in central California's San Joaquin Valley did not plant crops in 1991 after experiencing several years of drought in the valley. The barren land was exposed to the effects of locally heavy wind gusts, cyclone winds, and dust devils. The result was a significant twenty-four-hour "black blizzard" similar to those produced during the Dust Bowl days in the 1930's American Great Plains. Two months following this dust storm, the San Joaquin Valley reported a record outbreak of valley fever, a flu-like respiratory infection spread through dust storms. More than 1,000 victims suffered from the fever in January of 1992. Spring rains in 1991 caused a fungus growth, which produced spores with the onset of summer drought. These spores became airborne during the wind-storm and lodged in the lungs of their victims, where they bloomed to produce the potentially deadly disease coccidioidomycosis, known popularly as "valley fever" or "desert rheumatism." Valley fever is also common in portions of Arizona.

Interstate 5 experienced similar dust storms during two days in December, 1978, when 7 people were killed and 47 injured in three chain-reaction collisions as dust storms shrouded the highway. The interior valley region of California suffered a regionwide great dust storm on December 20, 1977, when drought, overgrazing, crop failures, diminished native vegetation, and the general lack of windbreaks on agricultural lands exposed the entire San Joaquin Valley and much of California to the effects of wind gusts of more than 150 miles per hour. More than 25 million tons of soil was lifted from the San Joaquin grazing lands alone within a twenty-four-hour period.

Gordon Neal Diem

FOR FURTHER INFORMATION:

"14 Killed, 114 Hurt in I-5 Pileups." *Los Angeles Times*, November 30, 1991, p. 1.

"I-5 Is Reopened After Pileup That Killed 17: Traffic Workers Battle Winds and Sand Clouds to Clear Highway of 104 Vehicles That Crashed in Dust Storm." *Los Angeles Times*, December 1, 1991, p. A1.

Schmidt, R. T., and D. H. Howard. "Desert Fungus: An Endemic Disease and What to Do About It." *Quarterly of the Los Angeles County Museum of Natural History* 7 (1968/1969): 12-15.

"Valley Fever Outbreak Hits Record Level." *Los Angeles Times*, January 30, 1992, p. A3.

Wilshire, H. W., J. K. Nakata, and Bernard Hallet. "Field Observations of the December 1977 Windstorm, San Joaquin Valley, California." In *Desert Dust: Origin, Characteristics, and Effect on Man: Special Paper 186*, edited by Troy Pewe. Boulder, Colo.: Geological Society of America, 1981.

1995: Arizona

DUST STORM
DATE: April 9, 1995
PLACE: Arizona, along Interstate 10
RESULT: 10 dead in 24-car pile-up

Downtown Phoenix, Arizona, in the midst of a dust storm. (AP/Wide World Photos)

A locally powerful dust storm with winds of 50 miles per hour suddenly reduced visibility to zero on a Sunday afternoon along a half-mile stretch of Interstate 10, leading to a series of chain-reaction automobile accidents that left 10 dead and 20 injured. The accident was the worst associated with a dust storm in Arizona history. Fallen trees and branches and disrupted electric service hampered emergency rescue efforts. Thousands of motorists were affected as the Interstate was closed because of the accidents and the drifts of sand covering the roadway.

The windstorm lasted only a few minutes and caused panicked motorists to brake suddenly, causing one 24-car pile-up and a second fatal accident involving 4 automobiles, 2 tractor-trailer trucks, and a pickup truck hauling a motor home. In the fatal accident, a Chevrolet Blazer continued full-speed into the wall of dust, colliding with slowed traffic on the road ahead. Highway Patrol officers described the portion of highway as a long straight stretch with nothing to look at, which lulls drivers into a false sense of security.

Meteorologists claimed the same hemispheric weather conditions generating this locally significant dust storm along the Arizona-New Mexico border also produced locally significant windstorms in California on the same day, resulting in downed tree limbs, sporadic electrical outages, and large waves at sea. One surfer drowned when a large wave knocked him off his surfboard. The winds fanned any accidental fires and were responsible for the death of an elderly woman unable to escape the flames that engulfed her California home.

Interstate 10 is especially dangerous on hot summer afternoons, when high-speed traffic is often suddenly blinded by blowing dust clouds that create zero visibility. Nearly 900 dust-storm-related accidents were recorded in Arizona between 1968 and 1975, with 36 fatalities and 720 injuries, many occurring along Interstate 10 between Phoenix and Tucson. The increased traffic volume; increased land disturbance; agricultural, construction, and off-the-road vehicle traffic; and grazing activities along the arid and semi-arid stretches of Interstate 10 increased both the number and intensity of these storms. Dust from the April 9, 1995, storm was lifted from recently plowed and dry fields adjacent to the highway.

The Arizona Department of Transportation devised various warning road signs and radio warnings to inform motorists of blowing dust hazards in an effort to reduce the number of accidents. Motorists often fail to heed these warnings or to follow instructions to pull off the roadway during periods of temporary low visibility. Efforts to reduce blowing dust include land-use and land-disturbance restrictions along highways, treatment of the soil in order to stabilize the surface, and reestablishment of native vegetation on barren soils.

Previous accidents related to dust storms in Arizona include a June 28, 1970, 14-vehicle chain-reaction crash on Interstate 10, with 8 people killed, and a July 14, 1964, 13-vehicle crash north of Tucson, which also killed 8 people.

Gordon Neal Diem

FOR FURTHER INFORMATION:

Idso, S. B. "Summer Winds Drive Dust Storms Across the Desert." *Smithsonian* 9, no. 5 (1974): 68-73.

Krammer, Jerry, and Jim Walsh. "Desert Dust Storms Nothing to Sneeze at, Weekend Crash Highlights Deadliness." *Arizona Republic*, April 11, 1995, p. B1.

"Winds Kill at Least 8 in Arizona Dust Storm, Cut off Power Locally." *Los Angeles Times*, April 10, 1995, p. 10.

1996: Sudan

SANDSTORM
DATE: May 3, 1996
PLACE: Khartoum, Sudan
RESULT: 53 dead in plane crash

A sudden evening sandstorm covered the runway of Khartoum's airport with dirt and sand, causing a Sudanese domestic airliner to be diverted to a landing strip under construction at Haj Yusef, a suburb 10 miles north of Khartoum. Reduced visibility due to the extension of the sandstorm to the alternative landing site caused the plane to land short of the runway and crash into an unoccupied house near the landing strip, killing 48 passengers and 5 crew members. Many of the passengers were students from Bahr al-Ghazal University in southern Sudan.

The deadly sandstorm arose suddenly on Friday evening and quickly swept across much of the Sudan. Desert dust storms, or *haboobs*, form on the leading edge of decaying thunderstorm clouds and advance at speeds of up to 200 miles per hour. The storms may measure up to 300 miles in width and rise off the surface of the soil from 656 to 8,202 feet (200 to 2,500 meters).

Gordon Neal Diem

FOR FURTHER INFORMATION:

Idso, S. B. "Dust Storms." *Scientific American* 235, no. 4 (1976): 108-114.

———. "Summer Winds Drive Dust Storms Across the Desert." *Smithsonian* 90, no. 5 (1974): 68-73.

"Sandstorm Cited in Crash of Sudan Plane: 53 Dead." *The New York Times*, May 5, 1996, p. 12.

1997: Egypt

SANDSTORM
DATE: May 2, 1997
PLACE: Across Egypt
RESULT: 12 dead, 50 injured

The most violent sandstorm to sweep across North Africa in thirty years reduced visibility to near zero across much of Egypt and killed 12 people, most under the crush of fallen trees, walls, and other objects. Winds of more than 60 miles per hour uprooted trees; diverted air traffic from Luxor, Aswan, and Cairo; and caused widespread damage to buildings and crops. Utility outages were caused, and the storm started 56 fires and caused 23 traffic accidents. The storm occurred during the Muslim sabbath, threatening travelers on the roadways and picnickers afloat in excursion boats on the Nile River.

The sandstorm blew in from the Libyan desert in the mid-afternoon, moving northeast. As the storm moved, the sky turned from clear blue to gray, then to glowing red, then to an eerie white because of the mass of sand suspended in the air. The city of Cairo was plunged into midday darkness.

Spring sandstorms are common in Egypt. Sandstorms are known as *Khamaseen*, the Arabic word for "fifty," because sandstorms can occur for fifty days at a time in Egypt during April and May. Egypt usually experiences ten major sandstorms per year. Winds of as little as 6 miles per hour begin lifting particles of dust, clay, and sand from the soil. As wind speed increases, more and larger particles are lifted into the air, until the atmosphere becomes saturated with dust and sand, reducing visibility to zero, disorienting travelers, and threatening to suffocate anyone attempting to breathe the air. In combination with high winds, the airborne sand abrades painted surfaces and the sides of buildings and cars.

On the same day, 36 people died in the Niger Desert of the southern Sahara after a truck became lost in another major desert sandstorm.

Gordon Neal Diem

FOR FURTHER INFORMATION:

"Earthweek: Diary of the Planet for the Week Ending May 9, 1997." *Toronto Star*, May 21, 1997, p. B6.

Nasrawi, Salah. "Powerful Sandstorm Rages Through Egypt, Killing at Least 8." *Associated Press*, May 2, 1997.

Earthquakes

(Courtesy National Oceanic and Atmospheric Administration)

Earthquakes often cause violent shaking that can persist for several minutes. This shaking can destroy buildings, bridges, and most other structures. It also can trigger landslides, tsunamis, volcanic eruptions, and other natural disasters.

FACTORS INVOLVED: Geological forces, gravitational forces
REGIONS AFFECTED: Cities, coasts, deserts, forests, islands, mountains, plains, towns, valleys

SCIENCE

Earthquakes are produced by sudden slips of large blocks of rock along fractures within the earth. This abrupt displacement generates waves that can travel vast distances and cause immense destruction when they reach the surface of the earth.

To get an idea of how this occurs, imagine a man trying to slide a very heavy crate across the floor. At first, it will not budge at all. He pushes harder and harder, until, quite suddenly, the crate slips across the floor a few inches before coming to rest again. This motion is called strike-slip motion and is thought to be the way in which most earthquakes occur. Next, imagine what would have happened if, instead of pushing directly on the crate, the man had instead pushed on a big spring, compressing it further as he pushed harder. When the crate suddenly slid across the floor, the spring would have expanded again, continuing to push the crate, even though the man was standing still. The energy stored in the spring is called elastic strain energy. Major earthquakes usually result from the accumulation of a great deal of elastic strain energy as plates move past each other with relative velocities of a few centimeters per year. After a number of decades, the accumulated elastic strain energy is sufficient to cause a sudden slip. With the crate example, the slip surface is between the bottom of the crate and the floor. Within the earth, it is a fracture in the rock called a fault.

Many faults are vertical fractures, which come to the surface of the earth and are readily apparent from the offsets they produce in rivers, mountain ranges, and anthropogenic structures. The San Andreas fault in California is a well-known example. More often, earthquakes occur on faults that are not vertical but have a substantial slope to them. The quakes may occur along a segment of such a fault, which is buried deep beneath the surface of the

earth. Often these faults can be followed up to the surface, using geological and geophysical methods, where their surface exposures can be mapped. Sometimes the faults do not extend to the surface; these are called hidden faults.

A portion of the energy released by slippage is transmitted away from the site in the form of elastic waves (waves that travel through a material because of its ability to recover from an instantaneous elastic deformation). Within the interior of the earth, there are two types of waves: P waves and S waves. A P wave is a sound wave, consisting of alternating regions of compressed and rarefied media. All materials—solids, liquids, and gases—transmit P waves. An S wave distorts the material through which it is trying to travel. If that material is capable of recovering from a distortion, the S wave will travel through it. Solids are defined as materials with this capability. As P waves and S waves reach the surface of the earth they can generate surface waves there. These surface waves, which are also elastic waves, are considerably more complex, travel more slowly, and are usu-

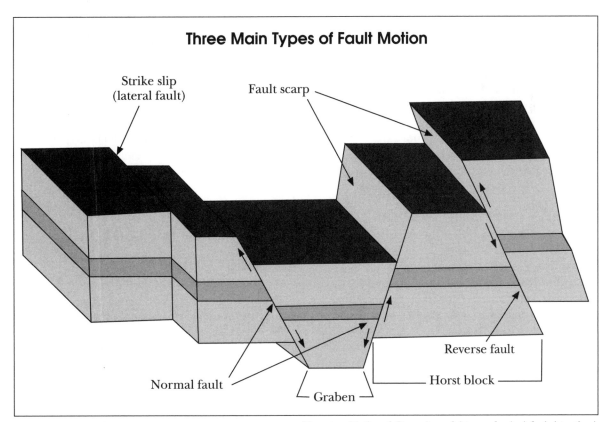

Three Main Types of Fault Motion

Strike slip
(lateral fault)

Fault scarp

Normal fault

Graben

Horst block

Reverse fault

(Courtesy National Oceanic and Atmospheric Administration)

ally much more damaging than P waves or S waves.

As elastic waves travel through different materials, they are filtered and transformed. Sometimes, particularly when traveling through mud or unconsolidated materials, the energy can be concentrated in waves with a period of a second or two. Many buildings resonate at such low frequencies, and the effect of a long series of these waves passing under such a building is like pushing someone on a swing: Each additional push is very small, but because the timing of the push is in harmony with the swinging, each push adds to the amount the swing moves. Because of this, regions far from an earthquake, if they are underlaid by mud, may experience much greater devastation than areas closer to the earthquake that are underlaid by bedrock.

Any major earthquake produces a series of elastic waves that can be detected just about anywhere on earth. From these waves scientists can determine the location and size of the earthquake. The location on the surface of the earth above the point where the earthquake is thought to have happened is called the epicenter. Seismic data measure the size of an earthquake using some form of the Richter scale. Useful from a scientific perspective, such seismically determined sizes do not tell the whole story. If the epicenter is in an uninhabited area, even a large earthquake may cause no fatalities and produce little damage. In contrast, if the epicenter of a small earthquake is in a densely populated region characterized by thick accumulations of mud, death and destruction may be great. Another measure of earthquake size, the Modified Mercalli scale, calculates the intensity of shaking at the surface. Observations of damage and perceptions of witnesses are used to estimate this intensity.

In traveling from their source to the seismograph that records them, seismic waves propagate through regions of the earth about which little is known. Differences in composition, temperature, and other factors within a particular region of the earth may result in either early or late arrivals for waves moving through that region. Because the same region will be traversed by waves from many earthquakes, careful studies, compiling large sets of data acquired over de-

Comparison of Magnitude and Intensity

Richter Magnitude	Mercalli Intensity	
2 and less	I-II	Usually not felt by people
3	III	Felt indoors by some people
4	IV-V	Felt by most people
5	VI-VII	Felt by all; building damage
6	VII-VIII	People scared; moderate damage
7	IX-X	Major damage
8 and up	XI-XII	Damage nearly total

cades of work, have been able to decipher much about the interior of the earth. Through the 1960's these different regions were represented as depth ranges. This produced a model for the earth in which properties varied as a series of spherical shells. As more sophisticated digital instruments came into use, lateral variations could be addressed. The computations required are similar to those in medicine in a computed tomography (CT or CAT) scan and form the basis for the field of seismic tomography.

GEOGRAPHY

Earthquakes are not randomly distributed on earth: Most occur along tectonic plate boundaries. The surface of the earth is made up of a dozen or so tectonic plates, which are about 62 miles thick and persist with little deformation within them for hundreds of millions of years. Tectonic plates comprise the crust (either oceanic or continental crust) and a portion of the earth's mantle beneath it. The boundaries between them are named according to the relative motions between the two plates at that boundary. Plates diverge from each other along ridges (generally beneath the oceans, but occasionally running through a continent, such as the East African Rift Valley). Plates move past each other along transform faults, such as the San Andreas fault in California. They also converge, with one plate moving beneath the other, along subduction zones.

The forces driving these motions are among the most powerful on earth and have been moving the plates around for at least the last five hundred million years. Discovering and understanding this tectonic system was one of the principal achievements of the earth sciences during the latter half of the twentieth century.

Many geographic features are the result of interactions between the plates. Most subduction zones occur near coastlines, have a trench lying offshore, and have a string of volcanic mountains a little way in from the shore. This geography dominates the western coast of Central and South America. Often a chain of islands develops if the subduction zone involves two plates carrying oceanic crust. The Aleutian Islands off the coast of Alaska are a good example of this phenomenon. Most of the Pacific Ocean is surrounded by subduction zones, which are responsible for the earthquakes and volcanoes of the "Ring of Fire," a dramatic name given to this region before plate tectonics was understood. (One early theory held that the moon had been ejected from the Pacific Ocean, and the Ring of Fire was the wound that remained in the earth.)

A plate carrying a continent subducting beneath another continental plate may create gigantic mountain ranges and immense uplifted regions such as the Himalayas. They were formed as the subcontinent of India drove into the southern edge of the Eurasian plate. In the process, wedges of crust were forced out to the side, forming some of the eastern portions of China and Indochina. The compression, occurring in a north-south direction, ejected these wedges to the east, much as a watermelon seed squeezed between the thumb and forefinger may be squirted across a table. Hence this process is called "watermelon-seed tectonics." Other places where it is thought to occur are Turkey and the Mojave Desert in California.

Although most earthquakes occur along plate boundaries, a few, including some very large ones, take place in plate interiors. The cause of these intraplate earthquakes is not well understood. It is generally believed, however, that future earthquakes will occur where earthquakes have occurred in the past, and

these locations are considered to have substantial seismic risk. The very southeastern corner of Missouri, near the city of New Madrid, is one such area, having had a series of violent earthquakes in 1811 and 1812. Charleston, South Carolina, is another, as it was nearly destroyed by an earthquake in 1886.

PREVENTION AND PREPARATIONS

Earthquakes are caused by the intermittent motion of tectonic plates past each other. Any attempt to stop the motion entirely is doomed to failure, as it only ensures greater motion at some later time. The only other way to prevent earthquakes is to increase their frequency, thereby avoiding a huge, damaging earthquake by inducing a large number of smaller, less harmful ones. Various scenarios have been proposed in which two sections of a fault are temporarily "locked" and the region between them is encouraged to slip, releasing the accumulated strain energy a little bit at a time. Because the risks involved in such an undertaking are great, and because the confidence in either locking or unlocking a section of the fault is small, such scenarios are rarely taken very seriously.

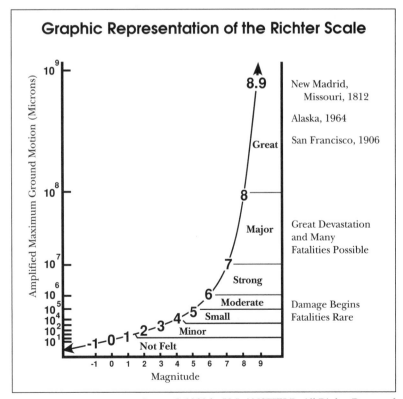

A model of the first seismograph, an instrument to detect earth tremors, made in China in 132 C.E. (photo by R. Carmichael)

As prevention seems unlikely, preparation is of particular importance. Efforts here involve understanding the science involved, identifying places at particular risk for earthquakes (forecasting), and identifying and then observing precursory phenomena (which may lead to predicting impending earthquakes).

There are two premises on which forecasting is based: If there once was a damaging earthquake at some location, there is likely to be another one there at some time, and if that place recently had a big earthquake, there is unlikely to be another one there soon. Understanding faults, plate tectonics, and the earthquake process permits incorporation of these two premises into a concept of seismic gaps: Faults are identified along which damaging earthquakes have occurred in historic times. That portion of each fault which slipped during each historic earthquake is then mapped out. Segments that have had large strain-releasing earthquakes in the past, but not for the last thirty years or so, can then be picked out as the locations most likely to have damaging earth-

quakes in the near future. These seismic gaps represent places where there is a gap in the release of seismic energy and that are thus "due" for an earthquake. Although obviously useful, such forecasts are not specific enough for extensive preparations.

An earthquake prediction states a time, place, and magnitude for an expected earthquake. Scientists use a variety of precursors to give them clues about when and where future earthquakes will occur. Laboratory experiments during which rock samples are made to fracture and slip under controlled conditions have revealed some interesting phenomena. Just prior to failure, the volume of the sample being compressed actually increases. Sensitive microphones glued to the rock can detect a number of tiny noises inside the samples; tiny cracks within the sample grow longer and open wider. As they grow longer they fracture the rock just ahead of their tips, making the noises. As the cracks open wider they make the volume of the sample increase. When they grow sufficiently to interconnect, the rock fails. This behavior is called dilatancy and explains a number of precursory phenomena.

Ground deformation occurred prior to the Nigata, Japan, earthquake of 1964. Although dilatancy had not yet been discovered, the survey data revealed this deformation previously existed. Similarly, anomalous radon fluctuations were observed prior to earthquakes in the Garm District of Russia during the early 1960's. Dilatancy can explain these, too, as the opening cracks draw water in from surrounding regions at an enhanced rate, increasing the levels of radon in the springwater.

Dilatancy also affects seismic waves. The P wave velocity is affected by the amount of water in the growing cracks, whereas the S wave velocity is not. A drop in the ratio of the velocities of these two waves can indicate growing cracks. The length of time that this ratio remains depressed can indicate the size of the impending earthquake. The eventual rise in this velocity can indicate when the earthquake will occur. In 1971 this approach led to the first successful prediction of an earthquake, in the Adirondack Mountains of New York State.

Unfortunately, not all earthquakes are preceded by indications of dilatancy. If it does occur, however, it may provide a prediction of a major earthquake as much as a year or two in advance of the event. With that much warning, a great deal could be done to reduce the number of people killed and injured by the earthquake. Most important, water levels in reservoirs behind dams could be lowered. Large meetings and conventions could be rescheduled. Emergency service personnel and volunteers could be trained, and people could be evacuated or schooled in earthquake survival.

RESCUE AND RELIEF EFFORTS

Earthquakes damage and destroy buildings, infrastructure, and lines of communication. Because the crucial connections between the affected area and the outside world, often called lifelines, may be severed, rescue and relief operations are likely to depend on local resources. Setting up reserves of water, fuel, and generators is an obvious prudent step, which most communities in earthquake-prone areas take. Less apparent is the need to identify human resources, on a neighborhood scale, who can help in such a disaster. As an example, a person who was trained as an army cook might be invaluable in a neighborhood field kitchen.

As in any mass casualty incident, triage will be essential—and unpleasant. In triage, treatment is allocated to victims based on how severely they are hurt and how likely they are to survive if given treatment. Because resources are limited, some living, badly hurt victims will not be treated, effectively being left to die. The triage officer making these decisions must be medically trained yet cannot actively treat patients. Such unpleasant work requires considerable training and discipline.

Once treatment has begun, additional complications may be anticipated. Normal protocols often call for radio communications between Emergency Medical Service (EMS) personnel and medical doctors or hospital staff. After an earthquake this is likely to be impossible: Too many radios trying to transmit crowd the airwaves. Hospitals are likely to fill quickly. Ambulances may be used as first-aid stations, at least during the early stages of the rescue effort.

Fatalities are likely to be from head or chest injuries or from respiratory distress brought on by burial. Those with compromised cardiovascular systems, caused by disease, age, or injuries, will be at greatest risk. Cultural and temporal variables can be important. A major earthquake during rush hour in Los Angeles might result in deaths and injuries from collisions on, and collapses of, the freeways. This could result in retired people being relatively spared. An earthquake at night in an economically depressed area in South America might kill most victims by collapsing their heavy adobe homes on them. In this case, infants young enough to sleep next to their mothers might survive better than the rest of their families.

The extrication of victims from collapsed and damaged buildings after an earthquake presents some special problems. Big earthquakes are usually followed by a series of smaller earthquakes called aftershocks for days after the initial event. A large initial earthquake will have sizable aftershocks, some of which are capable of producing extensive damage to undamaged buildings. A major earthquake, however, damages many buildings structurally, without causing their collapse. Weakened and then subjected to aftershocks, they represent death traps for rescue personnel. Great care must be taken to put as few of these people at risk as possible. Trained, organized groups—professional or volunteer—will most likely be more disciplined than the general population.

Plaintive cries for help, adrenaline coursing through the bloodstream, and the overwhelming sense of powerlessness engendered by a massive disaster can combine to put more people at risk. Debris may be pulled off a pile covering a whimpering child, who is scared but unhurt, and unwittingly added to another pile, burying a seriously hurt and unconscious individual.

As lifelines are restored, additional assets can be brought in to assist with extrication and medical services. To be effective, these need to be deployed where they are most needed, and priorities need to be established. Prior planning can anticipate many of the needs that will develop, but an overall command system must be in place to ensure that the right tools end up in the right places. Immediately after an earthquake neighborhoods and localities need to be able to function as independent entities, but eventually the rescue operation needs to evolve into a well-coordinated regional effort.

IMPACT

The impact of a devastating earthquake is profound, widespread, and long-lasting. Rescue efforts bring media attention, which in turn encourage assistance for the victims in the form of funds, clothes, and other materials. Sometimes the media portrays a disaster as an unfolding human interest story; much of the critically important work is less likely to make the news. Governments also often provide relief, but, more important, they restore the lifelines necessary for everyone's survival and the infrastructure required to return life to "normal." It is sobering to consider how much time may be needed to accomplish this. Electricity and phone service, taken for granted by most people, need wires and poles if they are to be delivered. After an earthquake in which landslides occur, many of those lines and poles are destroyed, as are many of the roads needed to bring in new lines and poles from outside the affected region. The roads that are in service are needed first to transport victims, rescue personnel, and equipment. Water and sewer distribution systems are other obvious high-priority systems to restore. Less apparent is the need for effective transportation if a modern metropolitan area is to remain viable. Elaborate networks of expressways, subways, rapid transit, trains, and buses are especially vulnerable to disruption by earthquakes and require enormous amounts of money and time to rebuild.

The financial resources necessary for recovery will not be available within the affected region, and they may not be immediately available within the country.

As governments borrow money to accomplish the tasks immediately required, credit may tighten elsewhere, having serious consequences for the economy as a whole. For example, the San Francisco earthquake of 1906 is thought by many to have been an important contributing factor to the Panic of 1907.

The productivity and economic viability of the affected area are likely to remain depressed for a long time. Small companies, unable to afford a period of inactivity, may fail. Larger companies may transfer personnel and contracts to other localities. Industrial facilities may be so expensive to rebuild that other alternatives, such as relocating offshore, might become attractive. More significant, and much more difficult to predict, will be the long-term effect an earthquake has on the reputation of the area in which it occurs. Businesses dislike uncertainty. The extent and duration of earthquake-caused disruptions will be considered when companies evaluate the region in future decisions concerning location.

Earthquakes will also have an impact on how residents evaluate their own situation. Fear and the presence of danger will motivate some people to move away. For others, the quality of life will never entirely recover: Although people may remain in the area, concerns and worries about seismic risks will add stress to their lives. Such impacts may be very long-lasting.

A technologically advanced society is very fragile. Many systems are interdependent, and an entire economy depends on their working together. A serious earthquake interferes with this, killing and injuring some and inconveniencing and frightening nearly everyone. Perhaps the greatest impact of the next big earthquake will be the realization of this fact, suddenly thrust upon the population by events entirely beyond its control.

Otto H. Muller

BIBLIOGRAPHY

Bolt, Bruce A. *Earthquakes.* New York: W. H. Freeman, 1993. In a manner suitable for a beginning student, this popular book presents the knowledge and wisdom of a man who studied earthquakes for decades. While technical details are generally not developed at length, the author's familiarity with all types of seismological information is apparent.

Brumbaugh, David S. *Earthquakes, Science, and Society.* Upper Saddle River, N.J.: Prentice Hall, 1999. This book covers earthquakes and their impact on society with a thorough, yet easily understood, approach. It explains the physics underlying earthquakes and seismology with unusual clarity. Seismic tomography, seismic refraction, and internal reflections are treated well.

Coch, Nicholas K. "Earthquake Hazards." In *Geohazards*. Englewood Cliffs, N.J.: Prentice Hall, 1995. A good treatment of the subject at an introductory level. Generally restricted to earthquakes within the United States, but it also includes good discussions of tsunamis.

Heppenheimer, T. A. *The Coming Quake: Science and Trembling on the California Earthquake Frontier*. New York: Random House, 1988. This very readable book describes the study of earthquakes from a human perspective. The author narrates a history of scientific developments, giving details of the people involved and their emotional involvement in their work.

Keller, Edward A., and Nicholas Pinter. *Active Tectonics: Earthquakes, Uplift, and Landscape*. Upper Saddle River, N.J.: Prentice Hall, 1996. Looking at earthquakes from the perspective of how they alter the landscape, this book provides some uncommon insights. Although it requires little in the way of background knowledge from its readers, it manages to develop considerable understanding of fairly complex technical material. Little attention is paid to the impact of earthquake disasters on society.

Kimball, Virginia. *Earthquake Ready*. Culver City, Calif.: Peace Press, 1981. This book details much of what can be done to prepare for and survive an earthquake.

Lundgren, Lawrence W. "Earthquake Hazards." In *Environmental Geology*. 2d ed. Upper Saddle River, N.J.: Prentice Hall, 1999. Includes case studies of five earthquakes that occurred between 1975 and 1995.

Notable Events

Historical Overview

Most cultures have oral histories describing earthquakes, and some have myths or legends attributing their cause to such sources as gods, catfish, or frogs. The Chinese history of earthquakes goes back at least to a device that could detect earthquakes, made by the Chinese scholar Chang Heng in about 132 C.E. However, the written record of a scientific approach to earthquakes, which is generally available to Western students, begins in the eighteenth century. A major earthquake occurred in Lisbon, Portugal, in 1755, which caused many scholars to begin thinking about earthquakes.

Scientific academies sponsored expeditions to Italy after several major earthquakes there. Investigators plotted damage to try to pinpoint where the events had occurred. In general they found concentric patterns, with the greatest damage in the center, but sometimes there were isolated pockets of intense damage far from the rest. This early work has been developed over the centuries, leading to the construction of maps showing what is now called the intensity of shaking, and using a scale, usually the Modified Mercalli scale, to try to quantify the event. Less successfully, the early investigators tried to plot the directions in which fallen pillars were aligned, in order to determine the directions in which the earth moved. Current knowledge suggests that the surface motions and building responses are far too complex for such an approach to have much value.

In 1872 a huge earthquake in Owens Valley, California, near the Nevada border, raised the Sierra Nevada as much as 23 feet (7 meters) along a fault. American geologist Grove Karl Gilbert, on observing the field evidence, concluded that the earthquake was the sudden release of accumulated elastic energy that had built up across the fault for a considerable period of time. When the frictional resistance along the fault was exceeded, an abrupt movement would occur, resulting in an earthquake. This was the first time the association of earthquakes with faults was recognized.

Additional information was sought on the frequency, timing, and duration of earthquakes, so scientists developed instruments. During the latter half of the eighteenth century many different designs were used in the construction of many seismographs. Attention was directed at local events until 1889, when a recording made at Potsdam, Germany, showed a distinct earthquake, but no earthquakes had been felt in the vicinity. It turned out that an earthquake had occurred in Japan on that date, and that the seismic waves had traveled thousands of miles before being recorded in Germany. Waves that have traveled such distances are called teleseisms.

Because a great deal of theoretical work on the theory of elasticity had already been done, the understanding of how and why these waves traveled such great distances developed rapidly. Recognizing the value of the information these waves might provide to the study of the interior of the earth, scientists expended considerable efforts to refine, redesign, build, and deploy seismographs in laboratories throughout the world, particularly in the United States and Japan.

By 1906, British geologist Richard Dixon Oldham had established the existence of the earth's core, correctly interpreting the absence of certain waves at certain points on earth as being the result of a fluid interior. Also in 1906, a great earthquake and subsequent fire had devastated San Francisco; movement on the San Andreas fault was obvious. In some places the offset reached almost 20 feet (6 meters). American geologist Harry Fielding Reid examined the field evidence and used several survey results to deter-

Milestones

January 23, 1556:	830,000 people die in Shaanxi, China, the greatest death toll from an earthquake to date.
November 1, 1755:	During church services on All Saints' Day, worshipers in Lisbon, Portugal, die in stone cathedrals or in tsunamis; as many as 50,000 perish.
December 16, 1811; January 23 and February 7, 1812:	In the sparsely settled region of New Madrid, Missouri, the largest historic earthquakes in North America to date rearrange the Mississippi River and form Reelfoot Lake.
January 9, 1857:	The San Andreas fault at Fort Tejon, California, in the northwest corner of Los Angeles County, ruptures dramatically. Trees snap off near the ground, landslides occur, and buildings collapse into rubble.
April 17, 1889:	The first teleseism is recorded in Potsdam, Germany, of an earthquake on that date in Japan.
April 18, 1906:	The San Andreas fault slips 20 feet near San Francisco. Much of the city is severely damaged by the earthquake, and a fire starts when cinders escape a damaged chimney, leveling the city.
1910:	American geologist H. F. Reid publishes a report on the 1906 San Francisco earthquake, outlining his theory of elastic rebound.
September 1, 1923:	143,000 people die as a result of the Great Kwanto Earthquake, centered in Sagami Bay, Japan.
early 1930's:	Charles Richter, working with Beno Gutenburg at the Seismological Laboratory of the California Institute of Technology, develops the Richter scale.
1958:	H. Jeffreys and K. E. Bullen publish seismic travel time curves establishing the detailed, spherically symmetrical model of the earth.
May 22, 1960:	A large earthquake, measuring 8.5 on the Richter scale, strikes off the coast of Chile, making the earth reverberate for several weeks. For the first time, scientists are able to determine many of the resonant modes of oscillation of the earth.
March 27, 1964:	The Good Friday earthquake near Anchorage, Alaska, with a Richter scale magnitude of 8.6, causes extensive damage near the southern coast of Alaska and generates tsunamis that damage vessels and marinas along the western coast of the United States.
February 9, 1971:	In the first serious earthquake to strike a densely populated area in the United States since 1906, a moderate (Richter scale magnitude 6.6) earthquake causes $1 billion in damage in Sylmar, California.
February 4, 1976:	A slip over a 124-mile stretch of the Motagua fault in Guatemala kills 23,000.

May 18, 1980:	An earthquake occurs beneath Mount St. Helens, Washington, which causes a large landslide high on that mountain. This landslide exposes a pressurized magma chamber, which explodes with a north-directed lateral blast.
September 19, 1985:	A major (Richter scale magnitude 8.1) earthquake off the coast near Michoacán, Mexico, kills 10,000 people, injures 30,000, and causes billions of dollars worth of damage.
October 17, 1989:	An earthquake in the Santa Cruz Mountains, in the vicinity of Loma Prieta, California, kills 67 and produces more than $5 billion worth of damage in the San Francisco-Oakland area.
January 17, 1994:	A moderate earthquake, with a magnitude of 6.7, strikes the northern edge of the Los Angeles basin near Northridge, California. There are 57 deaths, and damage is estimated at $20 billion.
January 17, 1995:	The most costly natural disaster to date occurs when an earthquake strikes Kobe, Japan. The death toll exceeds 5,500, injuries require 37,000 people to seek medical attention, and damage is estimated at $50 billion.
August 17, 1999:	More than 17,000 die when a magnitude 7.4 quake strikes northwest Turkey.

mine how the relative motion decreased with distance from the fault. His results quantified Gilbert's conclusions, let him estimate when the last important strain-relieving earthquake had taken place, and even let him guess when the next earthquake might occur along this segment of the fault. This has become known as the theory of elastic rebound.

By the early 1930's entire laboratories had been constructed to study earthquakes and their elastic waves. To permit workers to compare data, American scientist Charles Francis Richter, working with American seismologist Beno Gutenburg, suggested that they should all use a particular kind of seismograph, a logarithmic scale, and the same equations for how seismic wave amplitudes decreased with distance from their source. This was the basis for the Richter scale, which has evolved considerably but is still in use.

After World War II, the Cold War developed, with the Soviet Union and the United States building and testing nuclear warheads. To detect underground nuclear tests anywhere in the world, the United States deployed a network of sensitive seismographs that vastly increased both the quality and quantity of seismological data available to scientists all over the world. The same earthquake would now be recorded at dozens of locations, and details of the earth's interior were gradually revealed.

By 1958 the general model of the earth had been defined. By averaging the results from many earthquakes, recorded by many seismographs, scientists Sir Harold Jeffreys and Keith Edward Bullen compiled a graph of travel time curves. From these the seismic velocities within the earth could be determined as a function of depth. With additional constraints provided by other knowledge of the density distribution, reasonable estimates for the pressure, temperature, and composition of the earth were derived.

At the same time, geologists were shifting their attention to the ocean floor. By the 1960's a picture was emerging of a planet with an outer surface made up of a dozen or so plates that moved past each other, and sometimes over the tops of each other, at rates on the order of centimeters per year. This plate tectonic model provides the source of the deformation ultimately responsible for earthquakes. Movement of the plates past each other occurs in a spasmodic fashion, with elastic energy gradually building up until the strength of the material and the friction-resisting motion on a fault are overcome; then, a sudden displacement occurs, producing earthquakes.

When a gong or a cymbal is struck, vibrations occur at many different frequencies. The same thing can happen to the earth if it is struck by a large enough earthquake. This happened in 1960, when an earthquake off the coast of Chile made the earth resonate for several weeks. Scientists detected these very low frequencies, which have periods of about an hour, using instruments called strain meters. These data further refined our understanding of the earth.

With advances in electronics, communications, and computers, a new generation of digital seismographs was developed and deployed. New mathematical developments such as the Fourier transform permitted scientists to interpret the data these seismographs obtained. It became possible to examine how seismic velocities varied from place to place at the same depth. These studies, called seismic tomography, revealed that the internal structure of the earth was more complex than just a series of spherical shells with different seismic properties.

Otto H. Muller

---

464 B.C.E.: Sparta

DATE: 464 B.C.E.
PLACE: Sparta, Greece
RESULT: About 20,000 dead, extensive destruction to the city

Greece sits astride the Eurasian Plate, and, even in antiquity, earthquakes in this region have not been uncommon. The writings of both the Greek philosopher Aristotle and the historian Strabo include references to earthquakes in the region, ascribing them to underground motions of hot winds.

Little exists in the way of first-person accounts that describe the Spartan earthquake of 464 B.C.E. However, indirect references by historian Thucydides and other contemporary writers imply the quake was particularly devastating, with implications both to Sparta itself and to subsequent history.

At the time of the earthquake, the population of Laconia, the province in which Sparta was located, is estimated to have been between 38,000 and 50,000 persons, depending upon the source. Sparta itself was believed to have accommodated approximately 9,000 to 10,000 persons.

Destruction of property in the city-state of Sparta was extensive. Reference is made to the loss of the gymnasium; it is therefore likely that most major buildings were either damaged or destroyed. The loss in population within Sparta in the years following the earthquake may be inferred. Factors in addition to the earthquake contributed to such losses, but by the time of the Battle of Leuctra (371 B.C.E.), Sparta was able to put only 700 men under the age of fifty-five onto the battlefield.

The earthquake also resulted in historical implications. The city of Thásos, on the island by the same name, had been under siege by the Athenians since the previous year. Thásos had asked Sparta to provide aid and rescue. Following the earthquake, however, the Helots, Spartan serfs, began a revolt and fled to Mount Ithome in Messenia. Because of the uprising, along with the large number of deaths within both the army and the population as a whole, the Spartans could not join the fight against Athens.

Richard Adler

FOR FURTHER INFORMATION:
Huxley, G. *Early Sparta*. New York: Barnes and Noble, 1970.
Schlatter, Richard, ed. *Hobbes's Thucydides*. New Brunswick, N.J.: Rutgers University Press, 1975.
Thucydides. *The History of the Peloponnesian War.* Translated by Richard Crawley. New York: E. P. Dutton, 1968.

---

373 B.C.E.: Greece

DATE: 373 B.C.E.
PLACE: Helike and Bura, Greece
RESULT: Thousands dead, Helike and Bura destroyed

The region of southern Greece bordering on the Gulf of Corinth is well known for its frequent seismic activity. Ancient Greek writers, including Thucydides (c. 459 B.C.E-c. 402 B.C.E), described the destruction resulting from several severe earthquakes in ancient times. In 373 B.C.E., an earthquake destroyed the city of Bura. A tsunami triggered by the earthquake swept inland and submerged the city of Helike (also known as Helas and Eliki), the most important city in what is now the prefecture of Achaea, located on the southwestern shore of the Gulf of Corinth. Some of the most descriptive accounts of the devastation are found in the writings of the Greek geographer Strabo (64 or 63 B.C.E.-after 23 C.E.), and in the accounts by Greek geographer Pausanias (143-176 C.E.) written following a visit to the region.

The tsunami completely submerged Helike, and even centuries later the walls of the city could still be seen in the sea, with the waters higher than treetops. The Temple of Elikonian Poseidon was likewise destroyed. Apparently, the earthquake struck at night, since accounts described the inhabitants as being in their homes, while the darkness prevented any chance at escape. At least 10 Spartan ships, anchored along the shore, were swept away by the waters. About 2,000 men were sent by the Achaeans to aid in a rescue, but the devastation was so extensive that the bodies had simply been washed away.

It would appear the inhabitants of the cities may have had at least some prior warning. Author Claudius Aelianus (170-235 C.E.), in a third century description of the events, wrote that rodents and other creatures had fled the city several days earlier. Whether this is a realistic account or merely a later embellishment is unclear. Any prior warning that may have occurred was never acknowledged by the inhabitants.

Richard Adler

FOR FURTHER INFORMATION:

Aelianus, Claudius. *On the Characteristics of Animals.* Translated by A. F. Scholfield. Vol. 2. Cambridge, Mass.: Harvard University Press, 1992.

Gere, James, and Haresh Shah. *Terra Non Firma.* New York: W. H. Freeman, 1984.

Jones, H. L., trans. *The Geography of Strabo.* Cambridge, Mass.: Harvard University Press, 1960.

Pausanias. *Pausanias: Description of Greece (Attica and Corinth).* Translated by W. H. Jones. Vol. 1. Cambridge, Mass.: Harvard University Press, 1992.

217 B.C.E.: North Africa

DATE: June, 217 B.C.E.
PLACE: North Africa
RESULT: 50,000-75,000 dead

A massive earthquake struck the northern rim of Africa in June, 217 B.C.E. More than 100 cities along this part of the continent were reportedly destroyed, with heavy loss of life. The earthquake was felt across the Mediterranean Sea, where cities in Italy felt the tremors, though no damage was reported. At the time of the earthquake, Hannibal and his troops from Carthage were destroying the Roman legions in a battle at Trasimeno Lake in Italy.

Richard Adler

FOR FURTHER INFORMATION:

Nash, Jay. *Darkest Hours.* Chicago: Nelson-Hall, 1976.

365: Egypt

DATE: July 21, 365
PLACE: Alexandria, Egypt
MAGNITUDE: Approximately 8.0
RESULT: More than 50,000 dead, extensive destruction to buildings, including lighthouse

In 1996 archaeologists discovered ancient ruins of Alexandria beneath the Mediterranean. The city was destroyed by an earthquake and tidal wave in 365 C.E. (AP/Wide World Photos)

A large earthquake centered in the Hellenic Arc off the coast of Greece resulted in an enormous sea wave, which inundated the coastal areas of lower Egypt. Writers described the tsunami as it flowed over Alexandria as destroying all surrounding villages except those situated on high ground. Salt water covered previously fertile land.

In Alexandria itself, 50,000 houses were flooded or destroyed, and 5,000 people died. Ships were caught up in the waves and carried over the sea walls. The town of Tinnis, west of Alexandria, was destroyed. The anniversary of the flood, referred to as the "birthday of an earthquake," became the subject of a yearly celebration in Alexandria.

Later geological evidence suggests that what appeared to be a single quake probably represented at least two successive earthquakes. Evidence also suggests the period between the years 350 and 550 may have represented one of the most geologically active in the Mediterranean region.

Richard Adler

FOR FURTHER INFORMATION:

Ambraseys, N., et al. *The Seismicity of Egypt, Arabia, and the Red Sea.* Cambridge, England: Cambridge University Press, 1994.

Russell, K. "The Earthquake Chronology of Palestine and Northwest Arabia from the Second Century Through the Mid-Eighth Century A.D." *Bulletin American Schools of Oriental Research* 260 (1985): 37-59.

526: Syria

DATE: May 29, 526
PLACE: Antioch, Syria (now Antakya, Turkey)
MAGNITUDE: 9.0 (estimated)
RESULT: About 250,000 dead

Antioch was founded around 300 B.C.E. by the Syrian emperor Seleucus I. Rome captured Antioch in 25 B.C.E., making it into a colony called Caesarea Antiochia. Antioch quickly became a political center for Rome, and Saul of Tarsus (Saint Paul) selected it as the center of his mission in the Roman province of Galatia around 50 C.E. Antioch subsequently became an important, wealthy city of the eastern Roman (Byzantine) Empire, surrounded by olive plantations and home to a silk industry. Located on the Orontes River about 20 miles (32 kilometers) from the northeastern shore of the Mediterranean Sea, Antioch also prospered in trade.

Prominent in Christian worship during the sixth century was the feast of the Ascension, a celebration of Jesus Christ's final rise into heaven that conventionally took place forty days after Easter. A holiday on the same scale as Easter or Christmas, Ascension came on May 30 in the year 526. Antioch, home to thousands of people, swelled with thousands of visitors who had come to worship in its many magnificent churches and to eat, drink, and celebrate in its many inns the night before Ascension.

On the evening of May 29, at a time when most of the people in Antioch were inside buildings, the earthquake struck. Many buildings collapsed or caved in instantly, killing thousands of people. To escape the crushing walls, many fled to marketplaces and other open spaces within the city. One such person was Patriarch Euphrasius, religious leader of Antioch, who reportedly fled to the open space of the Circus (a circular, outdoor arena), only to be killed by a falling obelisk. Bishop Asclepius of Edessa and other prominent members of the Christian Church were also killed.

Some buildings withstood the initial shock but were destroyed by great fires caused by the earthquake. Rain following the earthquake further weakened structures, causing them to collapse days later. John Malalas, an eyewitness to the earthquake, reported that Antioch's Great Church, built under the command of Constantine the Great, survived for five days after the earthquake, then caught fire and burned to the ground. According to eyewitness accounts, eventually the entire city was destroyed, except for a few buildings on the nearby slope of Mount Silpius. On Ascension Day, according to authors reporting from eyewitness accounts, the survivors gathered at the Church of the Kerateion for a service of Intercession, indicating that the region south of the inner city might have survived the initial damage. In all, an estimated 250,000 people were killed by the earthquake, fires, and aftershocks. Miraculous escapes from the crushing debris were reported. Pregnant women, who had been buried underneath the debris for twenty-one days, were excavated still alive and healthy. Some of these women had even given birth while buried but were still rescued in good condition.

Another reported miracle occurred three days after the earthquake, on a Sunday. Above the northern part of the city, a vision of the Holy Cross appeared in the sky and hovered for more than an hour. The survivors of the earthquake who witnessed this vision reportedly fell to their knees, wept, and prayed. Mount Silpius, which stood underneath the manifestation, was thenceforth called Mount Staurin in its honor. ("Staurin" was colloquial Greek for "cross.")

After the earthquake, many survivors gathered whatever possessions they could and fled the city. Many of these refugees were killed by people in the country. A number of robbers were reported entering the city to strip corpses of jewelry and other valuable goods and to gather up the gold and silver coins that the earthquake had scattered about. Accounts of this period tell of the robbers meeting divine justice after molesting corpses. One story tells of a Roman official called Thomas the Hebrew who, after the earthquake, stationed himself and his servants 3 miles away from Antioch at the Gate of Saint Julian. Thomas, with his band of obedient robbers, successfully gathered together a large amount of money and luxurious goods over a period of four days. Apparently healthy with no signs of ailment, Thomas then suddenly collapsed and died as a divine punishment for his bad deeds, and all that he had amassed was distributed among needy survivors.

News of the Antioch earthquake quickly reached Emperor Justin I (ruled 518-527) in Constantinople, the eastern capital of the Roman Empire. The emperor had served in Antioch during his military career and had fond memories of the city. He ordered the imperial court to wear mourning, and he suspended all public entertainments in Constantinople. On Pentecost, which is celebrated fifty days after Easter, Justin walked to the church of Saint Sophia in Constantinople in mourning. Rebuilding Antioch became his first priority. First, the emperor sent several government officials with large amounts of gold to seek out survivors and give them monetary relief. These officials were also ordered to assess the damage to Antioch and estimate how much money would be needed for restoration.

Once this was determined, the restoration began, although it was a slow process hindered by a second earthquake in November of 528. Residents of Antioch and nearby areas continued to emigrate from the region. Despite setbacks, Antioch was gifted by Emperor Justinian I (ruled 527-565) with several churches, a

hospice, baths, and cisterns in celebration of his rise to emperor. After the second earthquake, he deemed the city free of taxation. Antioch had made little progress, however, when the Persians sacked the city in 540. In 542, remaining Antioch residents were hit by a devastating plague, thus destroying any hope of regaining the once-powerful city's grandeur.

Rose Secrest

FOR FURTHER INFORMATION:

Downey, Glanville. *A History of Antioch in Syria.* Princeton, N.J.: Princeton University Press, 1961.
"Killer Quake at Antioch: A Stroke of Nature's Fury Destroys a Brilliant Metropolis." In *Great Disasters: Dramatic True Stories of Nature's Awesome Powers.* Pleasantville, N.Y.: Readers Digest Association, 1989.

1290: China

DATE: September 27, 1290
PLACE: Chihli, China
MAGNITUDE: Approximately 6.0-7.0
RESULT: 100,000 dead

Chihli, now known as Hebei Province, lies within the North China Plain in the region of inner Mongolia. Even in the thirteenth century, the region was among the heaviest populated in China. On September 27, 1290, one of the most destructive earthquakes recorded occurred in the region. Little is chronicled concerning the earthquake, but estimates are that over 100,000 persons were killed.

Richard Adler

FOR FURTHER INFORMATION:

Gongxu, Gu, ed. *Catalog of Chinese Earthquakes (1831 B.C.-1969 A.D.).* Beijing: Science Press, 1989.

1556: China

DATE: January 23-24, 1556
PLACE: Shaanxi Province, China
MAGNITUDE: 8.0-8.3
RESULT: More than 830,000 dead, enormous property damage

The 1556 earthquake that struck the Wei River Valley of Shaanxi Province in 1556 is considered the most destructive on record. Approximately 830,000 soldiers and civilians were identified among the dead. A large number of people identified as missing likely were killed as well. The initial quake, occurring late in the evening, affected a tract of land about 300 miles in length. Witnesses described the sound as that of mountains rumbling. Land along the outskirts of the shift were uplifted to form mounds or became depressed into gullies. About 50 percent of the city walls, temples, houses, and offices were destroyed in the cities along the fault.

Hardest hit were the cities of Huaxian, Weinan, and Huayin. In Huaxian, the topography of the land was completely altered by the quake. Every wall of the city was demolished, along with most of the houses and public buildings. The death toll was in the tens of thousands, representing over 60 percent of the city's population. In Weinan, land fissures as deep as 60 feet were created. At least 50 percent of the population perished. All the peaks of nearby Mount Wuzhi collapsed. A similar level of destruction and death was observed in Huayin. Similar but less extensive damage was observed throughout the province. Hundreds of temples were destroyed in the region. Landslides triggered by the quake contributed to the extensive destruction.

Richard Adler

FOR FURTHER INFORMATION:

Gongxu, Gu, ed. *Catalog of Chinese Earthquakes (1831 B.C.-1969 A.D.)*. Beijing, China: Science Press, 1989.

The Ming Dynasty, 1368-1644, Part I. Vol. 7 in *The Cambridge History of China*, edited by Frederick Mote and Denis Twitchett. Cambridge, England: Cambridge University Press, 1988.

1692: Jamaica

DATE: June 7, 1692
PLACE: Port Royal, Jamaica
MAGNITUDE: X on the Modified Mercalli scale (estimated)
RESULT: About 3,000 dead, more than 1,000 homes and other structures destroyed

In the late seventeenth century, the Jamaican city of Port Royal was a major trade center for the New World. Situated on a cay, or small low island, off the Palisadoes sands on Jamaica's southern coast, this Caribbean seaport owed its prosperity largely to smuggling and plundering. By the 1690's, Port Royal boasted at least 6,500 inhabitants and more than 2,000 densely packed buildings, some of which were constructed on pilings driven into the harbor.

Formerly a popular haunt for pirates, the city retained a reputation for hedonism and godlessness. Typical contemporaneous accounts called it "the most wicked and sinful city in the world" and "one of the lewdest [places] in the Christian World, a sink of all filthiness, and a mere Sodom." Those citizens who warned that Port Royal's widespread drunkenness, gambling, and debauchery were inviting divine retribution believed their fears realized when, in the spring of 1692, a devastating earthquake destroyed most of the city.

Earthquakes were nothing new to Port Royal. Jamaica lies along the boundary between the Caribbean and North American tectonic plates and is seismically active. Since 1655, when England captured Jamaica from Spain and founded the port, settlers had reported earth tremors almost every year. However, most of these quakes caused little or no damage. One of the more severe quakes, which occurred in 1688, was large enough to destroy 3 houses and damage many other structures. The major earthquake that would follow it four years later was to prove far more destructive.

On Tuesday, June 7, 1692, between 11 A.M. and noon, a series of three strong earthquakes struck Port Royal within a period of a few minutes. After the third and most severe quake, a large tsunami pounded the seaport, snapping the anchor cables of ships moored in Kingston Harbor, smashing those ships nearest the wharves, and pouring into the city. In this case, not the crest but the trough of the tsunami struck land first, pulling out the harbor waters, then sending them back to finish off the town. The tsunami submerged half the town in up to 40 feet of water, pulling down what remained of the structures, causing hundreds more fatalities, and capsizing the vessels at anchor in the harbor.

One of Jamaica's two warships, the HMS *Swan*, had recently had its ballast removed during maintenance; the tsunami tossed this relatively light ship from the harbor into the middle of town and depos-

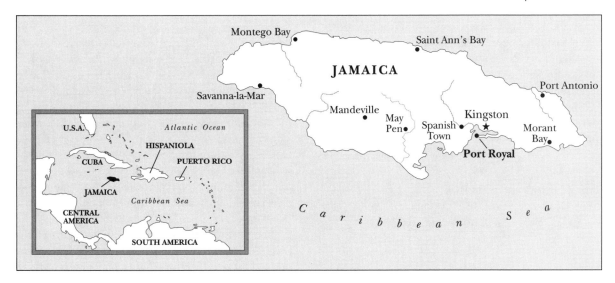

ited it upright on top of some buildings. Such a ride through the city would have revealed streets littered with corpses, of those killed by both the quake and the tsunami, and those washed out of tombs by the waves. While the ship's masts and rigging were lost and its cannons dislodged, the *Swan* remained intact enough to serve as a refuge for more than 200 people, who survived the devastation by clinging to the boat.

Multiple eyewitness accounts of the disaster describe the earth swallowing up whatever or whoever stood upon it, leading modern researchers to conclude that liquefaction played a major role in the devastation of Port Royal. In liquefaction, a process observed in loose, fine-grained, water-saturated sands subjected to shaking, the soil behaves like a dense fluid rather than a wet solid mass. This phenomenon is believed to be what caused "the sand in the streets [to] rise like the waves of the sea," as one witness reported, and many of Port Royal's buildings to topple, partially sink, or disappear entirely. Much of the city's population was also engulfed by the flowing sands.

The disaster killed roughly 2,000 people in Port Royal and left almost 60 percent of the city submerged below Kingston Harbor. Of those buildings left standing, most were uninhabitable. Two of the city's three forts, which had been heavily manned in anticipation of French attack, sank beneath the harbor. Several ships that had been moored in the harbor disappeared. Fill material that English settlers had dumped in the shallow marshy area between Port Royal and the Palisadoes to connect the cay to the sandspit was washed away. In Kingston Harbor,

the bodies of the drowned floated with corpses the tsunami tore from the cemetery at the Palisadoes.

The devastation in Jamaica was not confined to Port Royal. In the settlement of Spanish Town, located 6 miles inland from Kingston Harbor, almost no buildings were left standing. On the island's north coast, roughly 1,000 acres of woodland slid into St. Ann's Bay, killing 53 Frenchmen. Plantations and sugar mills throughout Jamaica were damaged or destroyed. The island suffered about 1,000 fatalities in addition to those killed at Port Royal.

The evening of the disaster, with aftershocks still rattling Port Royal, pillaging and stealing began among the ruins of the city. Looters had free run of the seaport for almost two weeks. During this time, law-abiding citizens took refuge aboard ships in Kingston Harbor. With few doctors and limited medical supplies, many of the injured soon died. Still more survivors succumbed to illness spread by unhealthy conditions aboard the crowded rescue ships. Injury and sickness claimed about 2,000 more lives in the weeks immediately following the disaster.

Survivors hesitated to return to Port Royal and rebuild. What was left of the city appeared to be sinking gradually into Kingston Harbor, and there was concern that the entire island would slip beneath the water. Aftershocks large enough to feel persisted for at least two months after the June 7 disaster, contributing to the people's doubts concerning Port Royal's safety. Members of the Council of Jamaica (who were in Port Royal for a meeting on the day the quake struck) and Port Royal's remaining residents decided to establish a new town across the harbor, a settlement that later became Kingston.

While Port Royal was too important strategically for the English to abandon entirely, it never regained its importance as a commercial center. It became primarily a base for the British navy, and for the remainder of Jamaica's history as a British colony its civilian population remained small.

Karen N. Kähler and David M. Soule

FOR FURTHER INFORMATION:

Marx, Robert F. *Pirate Port: The Story of the Sunken City of Port Royal.* Cleveland: World, 1967.

1703: Japan

DATE: December 30, 1703
PLACE: Edo (now Tokyo), Japan
MAGNITUDE: 8.0 (estimated)
RESULT: About 37,000 dead

The city of Edo, sometimes known as Yedo or Jeddo, stood where the eastern part of the central city of Tokyo exists today. The city was named Edo (meaning "estuary") because it stood at the point where the Sumida River enters Tokyo Bay. The area has been inhabited since prehistoric times. A castle was built in the area in 1457, at a strategic position where the Sumida River separated the provinces of Musashi to the west and Shimofusa to the east.

Edo was not an important city until the beginning of the seventeenth century. In 1600, Tokugawa Ieyasu defeated other military commanders at the Battle of Sekigahara. Tokugawa established himself as shogun (hereditary military dictator) of Japan, with his headquarters at Edo. The Tokugawa shogunate, also known as the Edo *bakufu* (tent government), lasted until 1867. It was the most powerful central government that had ever been established in Japan. The shogunate held power over the emperor, the symbolic ruler of Japan; the daimyos, military governors of the provinces; religious establishments; and all relations with foreigners. It brought peace to Japan for the first time in several hundred years.

The strength of the shogunate made Edo by far the most important city in Japan, much more so than Kyoto, the ancient capital of Japan and residence of the emperor. By the early eighteenth century, Edo had more than 1 million residents and was the largest city in the world. The stability of the government brought a time of economic prosperity and a flowering of artistic creativity known as the Genroku period (1688-1704). At this time, Japan was isolated from all foreign influence by the shogunate, which banned all foreigners from Japan, with the exception of a few Dutch traders confined to a small island near the city of Nagasaki. Thus, the Genroku period saw the development of uniquely Japanese art, such as haiku in poetry, kabuki in theater, and wood-block prints in the visual arts.

The earthquake of 1703 devastated Edo at the height of its political importance, economic development, and artistic flourishing. The disaster struck only a few years after large fires had heavily damaged both Kyoto (1692) and Edo (1698). On December 30, 1703, the earthquake destroyed a large part of the city. About 37,000 people died as a direct result of the earthquake. Modern seismologists estimate that the epicenter of the earthquake was located at 35.4 degrees north and 139.4 degrees east, a point located a few miles west of Edo. This area, known as the Kanto, is the largest lowland in Japan, a generally mountainous country.

The earthquake was also directly responsible for loss of life and destruction of property in large areas outside Edo. The force of the earthquake created tsunamis (tidal waves), which struck the southern coast of Honshū, the island on which Edo was located. As it is today, Honshū was by far the largest and most heavily populated island in the chain of islands that make up Japan. The area struck by the tsunamis included the Kii Peninsula at the eastern end of the Inland Sea and the Bonin Islands, as well as a large portion of the Tokaido (meaning "eastern sea road"), which linked the cities of Kyoto and Edo. The Tokaido ran more than 300 miles, mostly close to the Pacific shore of Honshū. Although the Tokaido suffered extensive damage from the tsunamis, it continued to be used as the main thoroughfare between the two most important cities in Japan. The highways and railroads that link Tokyo and Kyoto today still use the same route as the Tokaido.

Although it was not a direct result of the earthquake, another disaster struck Edo within a few days. A fire, beginning in the Mito mansion in the Yotsuya District of the city, spread throughout Edo. The destruction was particularly rapid because a hurricane, which struck Edo at the same time, caused the fire to move quickly to all parts of the city. The earthquake, tsunamis, fire, and hurricane did enormous damage to Edo and other areas of Japan. The total number of lives lost to this series of disasters may have been as many as 150,000. The devastation of Edo may have contributed to the end of the Genroku period of prosperity and creativity.

Japan suffered several disasters within a few years after the Edo earthquake of 1703. In late 1707, Mount Fuji, a volcano located about 60 miles southwest of Edo, erupted. The eruption lasted several days and covered a large area with ashes. Although there was little loss of life, the ashes ruined much of the farmland in the area. The shogunate paid a large amount of money to remove the ashes in order to make the land productive again. As of the end of the twentieth century, Mount Fuji, the highest mountain in Japan, had not erupted since 1707. This disaster was soon followed by another fire in Kyoto, which destroyed a large part of the city. In April of 1708, heavy storms caused flooding in the agricultural region known as the Kinai, ruining the crops.

Despite the large number of disasters which struck Japan in the late seventeenth century and early eighteenth century, the strength of the shogunate was undiminished until the emperor regained political power in 1867. By 1868, when the imperial capital of Japan was moved from Kyoto to Edo, which was renamed Tokyo (meaning "eastern capital"), the city had more than 1.2 million inhabitants. Despite an even more destructive earthquake in 1923, followed by massive bombing by the United States toward the end of World War II, by the 1980's Tokyo had a population of more than 8 million.

Rose Secrest

FOR FURTHER INFORMATION:

Heck, H. H. "Japanese Earthquakes." *Bulletin of the Seismological Society of America* 34, no. 3 (July, 1944): 117-136.
Sansom, George. "The Shogunate, 1680-1716" and "Genroku." In *A History of Japan: 1615-1867*. Stanford, Calif.: Stanford University Press, 1963.

1755: Lisbon Earthquake

DATE: November 1, 1755
PLACE: Lisbon, Portugal
MAGNITUDE: In the 8.0 range on the Richter scale (estimated), X for the central city and IX for the outskirts on the Modified Mercalli scale (estimated)
RESULT: 5,000-50,000 or more dead

During the eighteenth century Portugal enjoyed one of its greatest periods of wealth and prosperity. Gold had been discovered in its colony of Brazil, which held the largest deposits then known of this precious metal. Moreover, extensive diamond fields were also found there. The greater part of this wealth flowed to the mother country and concentrated principally in the capital, Lisbon.

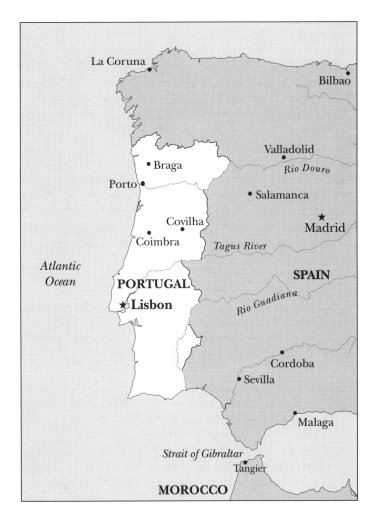

The population of Portugal was almost 3 million, with about 10 percent residing in Lisbon. This city, on the north bank of the Tagus River, was situated where the river, flowing from the northeast, bent gradually to the west and entered the Atlantic. The city was shaped like an amphitheater. It was flat in its central area, where the ports, together with the major commercial and royal government buildings, were located. In the low hills rising and arching around the center were houses, shops, churches, monasteries, and convents. A magnet of world trade, the city housed a cosmopolitan population. In addition, an exceptionally large proportion of its populace were members of the Catholic clergy and religious orders.

Destruction: Quake, Fire, Flood. The serenity and assurance of this city were irrevocably shaken on November 1, 1755, the holy day of All Saints. An earthquake of unprecedented strength and consequences struck the city, leaving it by dusk a broken ruin of its former self. For about ten minutes during midmorning the earth shook, rolled, and collapsed underneath the city three times. The shaking was so severe that the damage extended throughout southern Portugal and Spain and across the Strait of Gibraltar into Morocco.

Near the port area, the quake leveled numerous major buildings and destroyed the royal palace. The king was not, however, in residence. Many of the city's over 100 religious buildings were damaged or leveled. Because it was a holy day and Lisbon was known for its religious fervor, most churches were filled with morning worshipers. They were crushed under the crashing walls and roofs. Aftershocks at almost hourly intervals caused further damage. Indeed, aftershocks of less frequent intervals but great violence would continue well into the next year.

Fires began to appear in the city, progressively becoming a general conflagration fed by a northeast wind. Lasting for almost a week, these fires charred part of the outskirts and the entire central part of the city. Their damage was the costliest because they destroyed the contents of opulent churches and palaces, consuming paintings, manuscripts, books, and tapestries.

In a final assault, three seismic waves from the sea struck the central harbor and coastal area just before midday. Some of these tsunamis towered at over 20 feet. What the quake had not shaken nor fires destroyed, water in crashing cascades now leveled. Thus, within a few morning hours, quake, fire, and flood had destroyed one of the major ports of Europe.

Deaths from this destruction were, in the hysteria immediately following the events, estimated in the tens of thousands, as high as 50,000 or more. A systematic, contemporary attempt through parish surveys to account for the dead was unsuccessful due to its uneven application. Modern estimates now go as low as 5,000 or 15,000 for the fatalities of this disaster.

However, not only death but also fear, hunger, and disease followed the destruction. To flee the conflagration and repeated tremors, thousands tried to escape the city for the countryside, struggling over blocked roads and passages. Prisoners escaped from jails and assaulted the living and the dead. Food could not be brought into the city. The thousands who had been injured but not killed languished without care, hospitals destroyed and caregivers having fled or been killed. Infectious diseases began to spread.

Rebuilding. The king's principal minister, Sebastião de Carvalho, later known as the Marquis of Pombal, energetically took control of recovery and rebuilding. Public health needed immediate attention. Bodies that had not burned in the fires were collected on boats that were sunk in the Tagus. The army was called in to put out fires and clear streets and passages of debris. Anyone caught stealing was immediately executed. Prices for food and building materials were fixed. Field tents for shelter and feeding were erected.

The reconstructors of the city gave priority to replanning its layout. The new plan eliminated the old twisting, narrow streets. The flat central part of the city was redesigned to have straight streets that crossed at right angles in a grid pattern. These streets were 60 to 40 feet wide. Near the harbor area a spacious plaza was built, called Commerce Square.

To expedite construction, buildings were prefabricated. The sizes of doors, windows, and walls were standardized. To protect these buildings against future earthquakes, their inner frames were made of wood that could sway but not break under pressure. The style of building for these structures was a kind of simple or plain baroque and came to be known as "pombaline." These buildings were made according to the most advanced standards of hygiene so that there was adequate circulation of air and measures for sanitation. Because of the great wealth that Portugal commanded from its colonies, principally Brazil, Lisbon and other Portuguese cities recovered relatively quickly.

Consequences. One tragically ironic consequence of the Lisbon earthquake was that as the result of the extensive rebuilding, the city's port and central area came to be among the best planned and constructed in eighteenth century Europe. Another consequence was in terms of economic nationalism. Great Britain dominated Portuguese imports of manufactured goods. Indeed, much of the wealth that Portugal received from Brazil passed to English hands due to these purchases of British goods. To pay for the rebuilding, a tax was placed on the import of certain British products. This measure sought not only to raise revenue for reconstruction but also to make British goods more expensive and thereby encourage the production of native Portuguese products at a relatively lower price.

The consequences of the earthquake were not only in terms of engineering and economics but also in theology and philosophy. In fact, it was in these areas that the quake had its most resonant social significance. No sooner had the quake struck than the clergy of Lisbon began preaching that the disaster represented the wrath of God striking against the city's sinful inhabitants. So strong was the fervor of these preachers that they aroused parts of the populace into paroxysms of hysterical fear. This hysteria made dealing with the crisis in an organized, rational manner difficult. The civil authorities begged the clergy not to preach such fear, but their admonitions were only somewhat successful.

Western Europe as a whole was in the midst of a period known as the Enlightenment, or Age of Reason. Pombal, with his rational, utilitarian views of government, was representative of this movement. Against the religious hysteria, reasonable men argued that the Lisbon earthquake needed to be studied not as a supernatural event but as a natural one. They demonstrated that thunder and lightning were known to be natural events, so an earthquake should also be considered as such. The Lisbon earthquake thus prompted a great debate between the emerging rational forces of the modern age and the declining religious emotions of the medieval.

A further philosophical debate also occurred among those who were followers of the Enlightenment. Many of them believed that in a reasoned, organized world everything happened for the best. Thus, they explained that while the earthquake in Lisbon was a horrible disaster, it nonetheless resulted in a rebuilt and modernized city.

Others argued that one could not be so sanguine and optimistic about the world. Among the leading voices of this point of view was the French philosopher and poet Voltaire. In a long poem written immediately after the earthquake and in a later, famous novel, *Candide* (1759; English translation, 1759), he argued that the Lisbon tragedy proved the existence of irrational, totally unbeneficial evil in the world.

The young hero, Candide, voyages the world, traveling throughout Europe, America, and Asia, encountering perils and dangers at every corner. He is in Lisbon during the earthquake. Numerous times he or his friends are tortured or almost killed. People around them lead miserable lives. He pursues a girl for a love that is ultimately futile. Accompanying Candide is a teacher, the philosopher Pangloss, who believes that everything that happens in the world happens for the best. Pangloss adheres to this belief to the end of the novel, despite all the horrors he witnesses. Ultimately, therefore, the reader of *Candide* learns that the superficiality and rigidity of the thought of Pangloss and people like him betray the inherent error of their position.

Voltaire maintained that it was naïve and self-serving to say that evil was always balanced by good. There were people everywhere who suffered for no reason and who would never be personally benefited for their suffering. He argued that those who believed that everything that happened was for the best were those who wanted to keep things as they were, who wanted acceptance of the status quo. Such an attitude ignored those who suffered under the conditions of the present and failed to respond effectively to alleviate their suffering. If ignored over a long period, such suffering could prove unbearable and violent. In relation to these arguments it should be noted that less than half a century after the Lisbon earthquake, the suffering and outrage of these masses burst forth against the Old Regime in the French Revolution.

The Lisbon earthquake resounded in Europe not only as a physical event but also as a cultural one. Its force shook not only the earth but also men's minds, in terms of old and new ideas.

Edward A. Riedinger

FOR FURTHER INFORMATION:

Brooks, Charles B. *Disaster at Lisbon: The Great Earthquake of 1755.* Long Beach, Calif.: Shangton Longley Press, 1994. This work is a reassessment of the

Lisbon earthquake based on the findings of modern science.

Davison, Charles. *Great Earthquakes, with 122 Illustrations.* London: Thomas Murby, 1936. The first two dozen pages of this work illustrate scenes of the Lisbon earthquake.

Dynes, Russell Rowe. *The Lisbon Earthquake in 1755: Contested Meanings of the First Modern Disaster.* Newark: Disaster Research Center, University of Delaware, 1997. This short book analyses attitudes toward the Lisbon earthquake in terms of the ways in which, as a modern disaster, relief was organized for it.

Kendrick, T. D. *The Lisbon Earthquake.* London: Methuen, 1956. This history of the Lisbon earthquake has become a modern classic, concisely describing the physical nature and results of the phenomenon along with its immediate religious and cultural consequences.

Laidlar, John, comp. *Lisbon.* Vol. 199 in *World Bibliographical Series.* Oxford: ABC-Clio Press, 1997. This annotated bibliography gives brief summaries of books and articles on Lisbon, most in English, for various subjects, such as history, geography, economy, and the arts. There are extensive entries for the earthquake of 1755, in addition to earthquakes that occurred at other times in the city's history.

Maxwell, Kenneth. *Pombal: Paradox of the Enlightenment.* Cambridge, England: Cambridge University Press, 1995. This study, by a leading scholar of Portuguese history, places Pombal and his policies regarding the Lisbon earthquake within the larger context of the famous minister's philosophy and objectives for government and society.

Mullin, John K. "The Reconstruction of Lisbon Following the Earthquake of 1755: A Study in Despotic Planning." *Planning Perspectives* 7 (1992): 157-179. This article examines the four alternative plans that were considered for the rebuilding of Lisbon and includes illustrations of plans.

1783: Italy

DATE: February 5-March 28, 1783

PLACE: Calabria and Sicily, Italy

MAGNITUDE: 7.5-8.0 on the Richter scale (estimated); XII on the Modified Mercalli scale (estimated)

RESULT: About 34,000 dead in the two strongest quakes, about 1,500 drowned in tsunamis, 181 towns destroyed

At 1 P.M. on February 5, 1783, the southern Italian province of Calabria was shaken by a severe earthquake. Within two minutes, 109 settlements were destroyed, and 32,000 inhabitants were buried. At midnight the cities of Reggio di Calabria and Messina (the former on the Italian mainland, the latter nearly opposite it on the island of Sicily) were destroyed in a second tremor. That same night 1,500 inhabitants of the mainland town of Scilla who had fled to the nearby beach or who had taken shelter on their boats were drowned. The sea, which had withdrawn from the narrow Strait of Messina due to the shocks and the ensuing landslides along its shores, had swept back into its channel with 20-foot waves.

As terrible as they were, these events were merely the first in a continuing series of quakes to plague the region. After several lesser shocks, another major earthquake shook the region on March 28, killing 2,000 more inhabitants. A doctor living near the center of the activity recorded a total of 949 quakes of various strengths, and by year's end an estimated 80,000 people had died—either directly or indirectly—from drowning, fire, exposure, or disease. The following year there were 151 major and minor earthquakes. The series did not cease until the end of 1786, by which time one authority had counted 1,700 shocks. All in all, 181 towns were eventually destroyed.

Calabria occupies the "toe" of the Italian peninsula, and it is separated from the island of Sicily by the narrow Strait of Messina. The major shocks were detected as far north as Naples, about one-third of the way up the Italian peninsula, and throughout most of Sicily. Quakes occurring on March 20 and 26, 1784, were felt in the Greek islands of Zante and Cephalonia, eastward across the Adriatic Sea.

The area most affected by this series of quakes was about 500 square miles in extent, with its epicenter located near the towns of Oppido and Monteleone in southern Calabria. Within this area, destruction was often total. Some communities were obliterated—swallowed so completely that no trace of them remained. In other communities the damage seemed arbitrary. Observers recorded with wonder that in some towns the grandest buildings were saved and the poorest destroyed, while in others the opposite was the case. The quay at Messina sank more than a foot.

land 400 feet across loosened by the initial earthquake slid an amazing 4 miles down a ravine. One observer recorded in prosaic but frightening terms an incredible phenomenon: "Two mountains on the opposite sides of a valley walked from their original position until they met in the middle of the plain, and there joining together, they intercepted the course of a river." Yet another lake—dubbed Lago del Tolfilo—was formed when water from an underground spring filled a newly opened chasm; subsequent efforts to drain it were unsuccessful. Some authorities recorded the formation of 50 lakes, while others counted more than 200, large and small. In other cases fields were reduced to mud by the shaking of the ground and by the freeing of underground springs, which in turn overflowed lower ground. In the worst case, a river of mud over 200 feet wide and 15 feet deep inundated what remained of Scilla.

Amid such overwhelming destruction, accounts often stressed the seemingly miraculous survival of individuals. In 1783, for instance, an infant was dug out alive after being buried for three days. That same year two mules and a chicken were rescued after twenty-two days, two pigs after thirty-two days.

The destruction in Calabria was appalling. And yet, as famed geologist Charles Lyell noted in the second volume of his landmark work *Principles of Geology* (1832), this series of earthquakes was neither more powerful nor more destructive than those that had shaken other regions. It was, however, the first to be recorded and studied by scientists with any care. Various officials of the Kingdom of Naples made reports to the court, and the Royal Academy of Naples sent a deputation of scientists and artists to record the damage at first hand. British scientist Sir William Hamilton also visited the region. The result was a significant

In level areas, fractures in the ground resembled "cracks on a broken pane of glass." A new ravine nearly a mile long and over 100 feet wide was recorded, and others, wider or deeper, were also noted. One observer was shown a chasm into which 100 goats had vanished. Villagers themselves were swallowed and then disgorged—alive or dead—by subsequent eruptions of boiling water freed by the quake. The land was so shaken that inhabitants commonly experienced a phenomenon like seasickness.

Mountains and cliffs collapsed, with one particular mountain, Zefirio, split in two. A number of narrow but fertile river valleys in Calabria were destroyed, leading to the starvation of their inhabitants. Several rivers reversed their courses or were dammed with debris to form new lakes. In one case a mass of farm-

step forward in humankind's knowledge of the geological forces that have shaped the planet.

Grove Koger

FOR FURTHER INFORMATION:

Davis, Lee. *Natural Disasters: From the Black Plague to the Eruption of Mt. Pinatubo.* New York: Facts on File, 1992.

Dolomieu, D. de. "A Dissertation on the Earthquakes in Calabria Ultra in the Year 1783." In *A General Collection of the Best and Most Interesting Voyages and Travels in All Parts of the World,* edited by John Pinkerton. Vol. 5. London: Longman, Hurst, Rees, and Orme, 1809.

Lacaita, James Philip. "On Earthquakes in Southern Italy." *The American Journal of Science and Arts,* 2d ser. 28 (November, 1859): 210-215.

Lyell, Charles. "Earthquake in Calabria, 1783." In *Principles of Geology.* Vol. 2. London: J. Murray, 1832.

Ritchie, David. *The Encyclopedia of Earthquakes and Volcanoes.* New York: Facts on File, 1994.

1797: Ecuador

DATE: February 4, 1797
PLACE: Quito, Ecuador
RESULT: 40,000 dead

A number of earthquakes struck northern South America in February, 1797. Quito, Ecuador, was among the most heavily damaged cities in the region. Most of the population of 40,000 persons was killed, and the movement of the earth significantly altered the structure of the region. The earthquake activated the volcanoes of Cotopaxi and Chimborazo, raining lava on the town of Ambato. Other heavily damaged towns included Cotocollao, Nono, and San Antonio.

Richard Adler

FOR FURTHER INFORMATION:
Nash, Jay. *Darkest Hours.* Chicago: Nelson-Hall, 1976.

1811: New Madrid Earthquakes

DATE: December 16, 1811-March 15, 1812

PLACE: Missouri; also Arkansas, Illinois, Kentucky, Indiana, and Tennessee
MAGNITUDE: Estimated 8.6 (December 16, 1811), 8.4 (January 23, 1812), 8.8 (February 7, 1812), with other quakes estimated up to 7.0
RESULT: 1,000 estimated dead, 5 settlements and 2 islands destroyed

In 1811, the New Madrid region encompassed the states of Kentucky and Tennessee, as well as the territories of Missouri, Mississippi, Indiana, and Illinois. Within this sparsely populated region, the town of New Madrid, Missouri, with a population of about 1,000, dominated boat traffic on the Mississippi River from the mouth of the Ohio to Natchez, Mississippi. Founded in 1789 by Colonel George Morgan, New Madrid was the third-largest city between St. Louis and New Orleans. It was situated at a point where high banks seemingly would protect it against even the highest flood and at a point where the current brought river traffic close to the western bank on which the town stood. Farmers, hunters, and fur trappers came to the town for supplies; riverboats stopped to buy and sell provisions.

New Madrid County stretched from the Mississippi River to within 30 miles of what would become the Missouri state western border. It included land 60 miles deep into what became Arkansas. Settlers in the entire county numbered only 3,200, but census figures did not include unknown numbers of slaves and Native Americans. These figures also would not have included isolated hunters and fur trappers.

The Earthquakes. In 1811, scientific knowledge could not have provided information about the New Madrid seismic zone, which includes northeastern Arkansas, southeastern Missouri, southern Illinois, western Tennessee, and western Kentucky. The towns of Cape Girardeau, Missouri; Carbondale, Illinois; Paducah, Kentucky; Memphis, Tennessee; and Little Rock, Arkansas, mark the boundaries of the zone; only Cape Girardeau existed in 1811. The unique events of 1811 and 1812 brought this zone, later, to national attention. The number of earthquakes and tremors, the length of time they continued, and the geographic area affected made the New Madrid earthquakes unique in U.S. history. The sparse population and the absence of multistory buildings were credited for the low death rate, of about 1,000, during the quakes. In addition, many settlement residents had moved from log homes into tents after the initial quake. The death rate, however, may have been far higher than contemporary or later estimates. Deaths among Native Americans, slaves, and travelers on the Mississippi are not known.

The first tremors were felt about 2 A.M. on December 16, 1811. According to an anonymous New Madrid resident writing to a friend, the earth moved, houses shook, and chimneys fell, to the accompaniment of loud roaring noises and the screams and shouts of frightened people. At 7:15 A.M., a more serious shock occurred.

The shocks would continue. The Richter scale for measuring earthquake intensity had not been invented, but, in Louisville, Kentucky, engineer and surveyor Jared Brooks devised an instrument to measure severity, using pendulums and springs to detect horizontal and vertical motion. Working in Louisville, hundreds of miles from the probable epicenters, he recorded 1,874 separate shocks between December 16, 1811, and March 15, 1812. In New Madrid, according to eyewitness reports, quakes were an almost daily occurrence until 1814. The most violent shocks were felt on December 16, 1811; January 23, 1812; and February 7, 1812. Epicenters for the first two quakes were probably in northeastern Arkansas, about 60 miles south of New Madrid; the last was most likely in southern Missouri.

Eyewitnesses reported experiencing nausea and dizziness, sometimes severe, from the constant motion, saying that they could not maintain their balance during the worst of the quakes. Fissures, some as long as 600 to 700 feet, appeared in the earth. Various accounts told of eerie lights, dense smog, sulfurous smells, and darkness at the time of the quakes. Many pointed to unusual animal behavior before the quakes. Naturalist John Jacob Audubon, riding in Kentucky, was one of several people who found that horses refused to move for moments before the quakes. Bears, wolves, panthers, and foxes appeared in some of the settlements. After the quakes, panicked animals presented problems.

General Geographic Effects. Settlements along the Mississippi River were obliterated by quakes and subsequent flooding or landslides. Other settlements were abandoned. Little Prairie, Missouri, was destroyed on December 16, 1811. As water rose, almost the entire population of the town fled, wading through waist-deep water, carrying children and belongings. They were surrounded by wild animals and snakes also struggling for their lives. Among humans and animals alike, the sick and injured had to be abandoned. The Little Prairie refugees finally reached New Madrid on Christmas Eve, only to find that town in ruins. New Prairie eventually was entirely flooded by the Mississippi River. Big Prairie, Arkansas, near the later town of Helena, was destroyed the same day, also by flood. Point Pleasant, Missouri, was destroyed by bank slides into the Mississippi on January 23, 1812, and in January and February, Fort Jefferson, Kentucky, was lost to landslides. New Madrid itself suffered serious damage from December through February and was finally obliterated by floods in April and May, 1812.

Decades later, New Madrid was reestablished north of the original site. Other settlements, such as Spanish Mill, Missouri, were abandoned when their economic base was destroyed. As the configurations of river channels changed, Spanish Mill was left without enough water to run its mill and without direct access to river traffic.

The land was also changed by the formation of many new lakes, some of them large, during the course of the quakes. These included Big Lake, on the Arkansas-Missouri border, 10 miles long and 4 miles wide, and Reelfoot Lake in Tennessee, 65 square miles when first formed. Native Americans reported that their villages were destroyed and that many persons drowned in the formation of the lakes. Elsewhere, large tracts of ground sank. Near Piney River, Tennessee, 18 or 20 acres sank until treetops were level with surrounding ground; the same thing happened to a smaller tract on the Illinois side of the River near Paducah, Kentucky.

Ultimately, the earthquakes were felt over an area of about 1 million square miles, including two-thirds of what were then the United States and its territories. Residents of St. Louis, approximately 200 miles from the epicenter, felt the first shocks around 2:15 A.M. on December 16, 1811. Windows and doors rattled, some chimneys were destroyed, and some stone buildings fell. At Natchez, Mississippi, 300 miles south, four shocks were felt on December 16. Tremors were felt from Washington, D.C., to Boston, Massachusetts; and from Charleston, South Carolina, and Savannah, Georgia, north to upper Canada and south to Mexico and Cuba. To the east, considerable damage was reported in Louisville, Kentucky. In Cincinnati, Ohio, the first quake tore down chimneys; the quake of February 7, 1812, destroyed brick walls. Almost 800 miles away, in Washington, D.C., residents woke on December 16, 1811, to the slamming of doors and the rattling of furniture and dishes. Dolley Madison, wife of U.S. president James Madison, was awakened by the shock, which also caused scaffolding around the U.S. Capitol to collapse. The quakes triggered landslides in North Carolina, where, at the statehouse in Raleigh, legislators adjourned, alarmed by the building's motion. In Charleston, South Carolina, clocks stopped, furniture moved, and church bells rang. During the severe quake of February 7, bells rang in Boston, more than 1,000 miles from New Madrid.

The River and River Traffic. While damage to the Mississippi River and to river traffic was probably more severe than to the land itself, the extent is unknown. The number of boats, workers, and passengers and the amount of cargo on the river is impossible to gauge. Traffic probably was heavy, however, since the Mississippi was the only efficient means of transportation between the midwestern United States and the Gulf of Mexico.

Contemporary accounts point to dramatic effects of the earthquakes. One anonymous traveler saw violent movement of boats at the moment of the first quake. As the traveler watched, massive trees snapped in two. Another, hearing the crash of trees and the screaming of waterfowl, watched as riverbanks began their fall into the water. Eyewitnesses reported that the water changed from clear to rusty brown and became thick with debris tossed up from the bottom. Dead trees shot up from the riverbed into the air. Fissures, opening at the river's bottom, created whirlpools; water spouted. The quakes also created great waves, which overwhelmed many boats. The largest of the quakes caused the river to heave and boil.

The Mississippi was too dangerous to navigate after dark. River maps were unreliable; stumps and sandbars could shift. Thus, boats moored for the night. Those moored to river islands remained relatively safe, but many boats moored to the western shore were crushed by falling banks.

The most terrifying experience occurred on February 7, 1812, when the most violent of the quakes caused a huge series of waves in the river, in a phenomenon called a fluvial tsunami. This began about 3:15 A.M., when boats were still moored. Flooding New Madrid, the tsunami caused the Mississippi to run backward for a period that seemed, to observers, to last several hours. Lakes were created as the river poured into newly formed depressions, and thousands of acres of forest were dumped into the turbulent water.

The quake created temporary waterfalls, one about half a mile north of New Madrid and the other 8 miles downstream. A boatman, Captain Mathias Speed, had experienced the tsunami. Forced to cut his boat loose from the sinking bar to which it was moored, he found himself moving backward up the river. Safe on shore, he watched the disastrous effects of the waterfalls. River pilots had no way to anticipate the new hazards. Speed and his men counted 30 boats going over the falls. Twenty-eight capsized in the three days before the falls vanished as the river bottom settled. Those on shore could do nothing except listen to the screams for help. There were few survivors.

The first of the quakes, however, helped prove the value of steamboats. The *New Orleans*, commanded by Nicholas Roosevelt, was making its initial Mississippi River voyage in December of 1811. Provided with 116 feet of length, a 20-foot beam, and a 34-cylinder engine, as well as intelligent navigation, the boat arrived safely at New Orleans, despite the pilot's despair because all the normal navigation markers of the river had vanished. Since no one along the river had previously seen steam-driven craft, some blamed the subsequent disasters on the steamboat.

By the end of the quakes, the configuration of the river was altered. Many small islands vanished without a trace. Of the larger islands, some several miles in length, two were lost. Island #94, known as Stack or Crows Nest Island, inhabited by river pirates, disappeared on December 16, while island #32, off the Tennessee shore, disappeared on the night of December 21 while the *New Orleans* was moored there. Elsewhere, dry land became swamp, and wetlands were uplifted and dried. Smaller rivers that had flowed into the Mississippi were diverted, the shape of New Madrid Bend was changed, and three inlets to the Mississippi were destroyed.

Betty Richardson

FOR FURTHER INFORMATION:
Bagnell, Norma Hayes. *On Shaky Ground: The New Madrid Earthquakes of 1811-1812.* Columbia: University of Missouri Press, 1996.

Fuller, Myron L. *The New Madrid Earthquake: A Scientific Factual Field Account.* Washington, D.C.: Government Printing Office, 1912.

Logsdon, David, ed. *I Was There! In the New Madrid Earthquakes of 1811-1812 (Eyewitness Accounts by Survivors of the Worst Earthquake in American History).* Nashville: Kettle Mills Press, 1990.

Penick, James, Jr. *The New Madrid Earthquakes of 1811-1812.* Rev. ed. Columbia: University of Missouri Press, 1981.

Stewart, David, and Ray Knox. *The Earthquake America Forgot: 2,000 Temblors in Five Months.* Marble Hill, Mo.: Guttenberg-Richter, 1995.

1812: Venezuela

DATE: March 26, 1812
PLACE: Caracas, Venezuela
RESULT: 15,000 dead

The Caracas earthquake of 1812 destroyed over 90 percent of the city. Destruction was heaviest in the northern part of the city, near the mountains of La Silla. Approximately 10,000 persons were killed in the city, with another 5,000 reported deaths in the surrounding towns of La Guaya, Antimano, Baruta, and San Felipe. Troops cremated the dead in an attempt to prevent the spread of disease. Nevertheless, another 5,000 died from illnesses over the next month.

One reason the death toll was so high was because the earthquake occurred on Holy Thursday. The churches of Trinity and Alta Gracia in the north side of the city collapsed, burying all the worshipers in the debris. The San Carlos barracks was swallowed by fissures, killing every soldier in the regiment. Priests considered the earthquake a sign of God's displeasure with the ongoing revolt against Spanish rule, which resulted in revolutionary troops deserting towns they had occupied, betraying their leader, Miranda.

Richard Adler

FOR FURTHER INFORMATION:
Nash, Jay. *Darkest Hours.* Chicago: Nelson-Hall, 1976.
Ritchie, David. *Encyclopedia of Earthquakes and Volcanoes.* New York: Facts on File, 1994.

1822: Chile

DATE: November 19, 1822
PLACE: Valparaiso, Chile
MAGNITUDE: 8.5 (estimated)
RESULT: 10,000 dead, extensive damage to several cities

At approximately 10:15 P.M. on November 19, 1822, a large earthquake struck the region around Valparaiso, covering a region along the coast of some 270,000 square miles. The towns of Quillota, Casa Blanca, and Melipilla were described as heaps of rubble. Most houses in Valparaiso, Almendal, and Merced were rendered uninhabitable. While a quake of such high intensity was unexpected, frequent minor shocks had preceded the event during the previous year. Other quakes had previously occurred in the region dating back at least three hundred years.

Much of what is known about the 1822 earthquake is due to the records kept by Maria Graham, living in Quintero, 30 miles north of Valparaiso. Graham described a series of at least three vibrations that lasted a total of five minutes, causing the houses to reel like "ships on the ocean." Extensive areas of shoreline were uplifted, rendering dry land where none had previously been seen for a length of 100 miles. Similar observations were noted by British scientists Charles Darwin and Sir Charles Lyell when they visited the area some years later. Aftershocks of lower intensity continued for several days. Two moderate earthquakes occurred during the next ten years.

Richard Adler

FOR FURTHER INFORMATION:
Darwin, Charles. *Voyage of the Beagle.* Amherst, N.Y.: Prometheus Books, 1999.
Davison, Charles. *Great Earthquakes.* London: Thomas Murby, 1936.

1835: Chile

DATE: February 20, 1835
PLACE: Concepción, Chile
MAGNITUDE: At least 8.1
RESULT: 70 villages destroyed

Chile, situated on the west coast of South America, is astride one of the globe's tectonic zones of colliding crustal plates. Advancing from the west is the East Pacific (Nazca) oceanic plate, moving inexorably at 2 inches (5 centimeters) per year. The South American continent's plate is moving westward in opposition, at 1.2 inches (3 centimeters) per year. The resulting titanic collision creates a long narrow trench just offshore as the oceanic plate bends and dives down

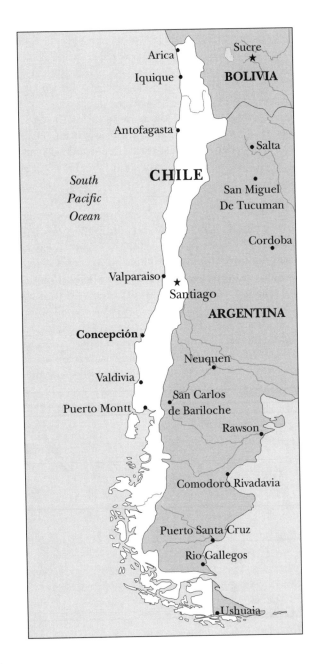

(subducts) at about a 45-degree angle under the South American plate. The collisional stresses cause major earthquakes, some shallow and others originating down to depths of 400 miles (650 kilometers). Partial melting of the lower crust results in a string of periodically active volcanoes running down the coast—part of the "Ring of Fire" rimming the Pacific. The resulting mountain building from the deformation, uplift, and volcanism created the Andes Mountains.

A great earthquake occurred in mid-Chile on February 20, 1835. By coincidence, the English survey ship HMS *Beagle* was visiting coastal Chile at the time, on the ship's 1831-1836 scientific voyage around the world. The naturalist on board was Charles Darwin, who at the start of the trip was twenty-two years old and had just graduated from Cambridge University. Darwin was a meticulous and astute observer of natural phenomena, both biological and geological, and a careful chronicler of his experiences. He is probably best known for his biological observations and insight, laying the foundation for modern evolutionary theory with his concept of the development and adaptation of life-forms through the slow process of natural selection. However, while on the same trip he noted a variety of geological formations and fossils in rock and was impressed by the effect that natural forces had on shaping the earth's surface. The latter included the gradual uplift of the Andes Mountains by earthquakes and resulting deformation.

On February 20, 1835, Darwin wrote that he "happened to be on shore, and was lying down in the wood to rest myself" at Valdivia, 186 miles (300 kilometers) south along the coast from Concepción. He felt the shock, which he estimated to last two minutes in total, from a very severe earthquake. Darwin wrote, "The Earth, the very emblem of solidity, has moved beneath our feet like a thin crust over a fluid." The rocking and undulations of the ground caused great alarm among the people, violent shaking of the wooden buildings locally, and a recession and advance of the sea at the coast, which we would now attribute to a tsunami generated by the earthquake's deformation near the coast.

On March 4 the *Beagle* and Darwin entered the harbor at Concepción. Reports and evidence detailed that 70 villages had been destroyed, ground fissures had opened up, and a "great wave" (and two following ones) rushed up 23 feet at the head of the Bay of Concepción above high-tide level to strew wreckage and debris along the coast. A cannon and carriage weighing about 4 tons was moved 15 feet, a schooner ship was left 600 feet inland, trees were uprooted, and heavy rocks were thrown up on shore.

Captain FitzRoy of the *Beagle* found mussel shells on an offshore island, still adhering to rocks that had risen 10 feet above sea level; the rocks and mussels had formerly been below the waterline, where the inhabitants had previously dived for them. Noting that the land around the Bay of Concepción had been raised by 2 to 3 feet, Darwin wrote that

> the most remarkable effect of this earthquake was the permanent elevation of the land—it would be far more correct to speak of it as the cause (of the earthquake). . . . The elevation of this province is particularly interesting, from its having been the theatre of several other violent earthquakes, and from the vast numbers of seashells scattered . . . up to a height of certainly 600, and I believe 1,000 feet.

His inference of uplift, which we would now understand in terms of plate tectonic collisions, earthquake faulting, and crustal deformation to build mountain chains, was reinforced when he later found ancient beaches, limestone rock (formed on seafloors), and marine fossils (of seashells, among others) at elevations of thousands of feet in the nearby Andes.

The earthquake occurred at 11:30 in the morning of February 20. The epicenter is now estimated to have been at 36.830 degrees south latitude, longitude 73.03 degrees west, just south of Concepción. The major shock, estimated to be of magnitude 8.1-8.5, was followed by many smaller aftershocks—three hundred in the first twelve days.

Several volcanoes within a few hundred miles erupted at the same time as the earthquake and ground deformation occurred. Darwin made an intuitive observation—which would not be generally understood until the plate tectonics model was fully developed 130 years later—that the causes of earthquakes and volcanic eruptions are identical.

Concepción, now a metropolitan area with population of half a million people, is on the narrow coastal plain of Chile. The Andes rise 124 miles (200 kilometers) to the east, to elevations of over 2.5 miles (4,000 meters). The Peru-Chile trench parallels the coast, 155 miles (250 kilometers) offshore. The collision of tectonic plates caused other great earthquakes to strike this location in the twentieth century. In January of 1939 a magnitude 8.3 earthquake occurred at Chillan, about 62 miles (100 kilometers) east of Concepción; about 50,000 people were killed. In May, 1960, an earthquake occurred 186 miles (300 kilometers) south of Concepción. It had the world's biggest recorded magnitude in historic time, calculated (by different magnitude scales) as 8.5 to 9.5. At least 5,700 died. As long as the earth's internal heat continues to drive plate tectonics and the movement of seafloors and continents, Chile will be visited by some of the world's greatest earthquakes.

Robert S. Carmichael

FOR FURTHER INFORMATION:

Darwin, Charles. *The Voyage of the Beagle.* Harvard Classics 29. New York: P. Collier and Son, 1909.

Moorehead, Alan. *Darwin and the Beagle.* New York: Harper and Row, 1969.

U.S. Geological Survey/National Earthquake Information Center, wwwneic.cr.usgs.gov.

1857: Fort Tejon Earthquake

DATE: January 9, 1857
PLACE: Fort Tejon, California
MAGNITUDE: 7.9-8.0
RESULT: 1 dead, many buildings damaged

Fort Tejon, located in the Grapevine Canyon on the route between the central valley of the state and Southern California, was originally established as an army post in 1854 as a means to oversee and control the local Native American tribes. The rapid influx of white settlers during the 1849 gold rush had resulted in conflicts with the American Indian tribes in the region; the fort was eventually abandoned in 1864.

The Fort Tejon earthquake of 1857 was among the ten strongest recorded quakes to occur in the contiguous United States. Fortunately, it occurred during a time in which California was sparsely populated, and most of the damage was confined to the post. The fort was situated about 4 miles from the San Andreas fault, near the site at which it intersects with the Oarlock fault. At about 8:20 A.M. on January 9, 1857, the fault ruptured along a line from present-day Parkfield in the Cholame Valley to Wrightwood, a distance of over 200 miles. The surface rupture scar is still clearly visible, more than 150 years later. Displacement due to the rupture was nearly 30 feet. The heaviest damage to populated areas occurred in the fort, with 5 buildings being heavily damaged and most of the other buildings showing mild to moderate damage. A woman at nearby Reed's Ranch was killed in the collapse of an adobe house. Another man dropped dead in Los Angeles, about 60 miles south of the fort, from what may have been a heart attack. The mission in Ventura was heavily damaged, as the church tower collapsed.

The earthquake, combined with numerous aftershocks, diverted the flow of rivers in areas around San Diego and Santa Barbara. The movement of the Kern River was reversed, while the water in Tulare Lake north of the fort overflowed its banks by a level of 4 feet. Artesian wells in the Santa Clara Valley ceased to flow.

There is some evidence that the earthquake of 1857 may have broken the fault line for about 1 mile both northwest and southeast from the epicenter, actually located closer to Parkfield. This portion of Southern California has been relatively quiet since the 1857 quake. However, earthquake researchers in 1996 found evidence that the Elkhorn Thrust, in an area near the San Andreas fault, may have slipped during the 1857 quake, resulting in the possibility that another shift in the San Andreas fault might potentially result in a "double earthquake" in the Los Angeles area.

Richard Adler

FOR FURTHER INFORMATION:

Anderson, Don. "The San Andreas Fault." *Scientific American* 225, no. 5 (November, 1971): 52-68.

Sieh, Kerry. "Slip Along the San Andreas Fault Associated with the Great 1857 Earthquake." *Bulletin of the Seismological Society of America* 68, no. 4 (1978): 1421-1448.

Townley, Sidney. "Earthquakes in California, 1769-1928." *Bulletin of the Seismological Society of America* 29, no. 1 (1939): 21-252.

1859: Ecuador

DATE: March 22, 1859
PLACE: Quito, Ecuador
RESULT: 5,000 dead

Approximately sixty years after the devastating earthquake of 1797, Quito, Ecuador, was subjected to another powerful earthquake in March, 1859. At 8:30 A.M., a six-minute tremor destroyed numerous government buildings and churches. Among the structures destroyed were the Government Palace and the Archepiscopal Palace, as well as many of the large cathedrals. Churches that fell included the Chapel of El Sagrario, the Temple of the Augustines, the Temple of Santa Clara, and the Church of Recoleta de Dominicos.

Richard Adler

FOR FURTHER INFORMATION:

Nash, Jay Robert. *Darkest Hours*. Chicago: Nelson-Hall, 1976.

1863: Philippines

DATE: July 3, 1863
PLACE: Manila, Philippines
RESULT: 1,000 dead

The earthquake that struck Manila in July, 1863, was the most devastating in Philippine history to that time. Two severe shocks took place at 7:30 P.M., at a time when most of the city's inhabitants were either shopping in the market area or worshiping during Vespers services.

Nearly all government buildings, churches, and hospitals were destroyed. The giant dome of the Binondo Cathedral collapsed, burying hundreds. The Church of St. Domingo collapsed, as well as the convents of St. Clara, St. Rosa, and St. Catalina, killing nearly all nuns and friars. Fissures that opened in parts of the city caused additional casualties among residents trying to flee.

The banks of the Pampanga River caved inward, and the waters washed away buildings and warehouses, destroying millions of dollars of tobacco, the major economic product of Manila. The governor of the Philippines and his son had been riding in the hills when the earthquake struck, and they barely felt the tremors. Reportedly, their major concern when they returned was that their food was cold.

Richard Adler

FOR FURTHER INFORMATION:
Nash, Jay Robert. *Darkest Hours.* Chicago: Nelson-Hall, 1976.

1868: California

DATE: October 21, 1868
PLACE: Northern and Central California
MAGNITUDE: 7.0
RESULT: 40 dead, extensive property damage

At 7:53 A.M. on October 21, 1868, an earthquake ruptured the southern segment of the Hayward fault along a line from Berkeley to Fremont, California. It was followed by a second shock approximately ninety minutes later. The quake was felt over much of Northern California and Nevada. Because much of the destruction occurred in San Francisco, the incident became known as the "great San Francisco earthquake," until it was superseded by the terrible quake of 1906.

Witnesses quoted in the local newspaper described the damage and ensuing chaos associated with the quake. People ran panic-stricken into the streets, often wearing only minimal amounts of clothing. Heavy damage in the city was confined primarily to the downtown area and the Chinese Quarter, bounded by Kearny, Stockton, Washington, and Pacific Streets. City Hall became a "dilapidated ruin." The Jewish Synagogue on Broadway was heavily damaged, as were the City, County, and Marine Hospitals. Four persons were killed by falling cornices and chimneys, while a fifth was killed in the collapse of the wall of an unfinished building.

Witnesses in the Santa Cruz Mountains near Pescadero described the swaying of redwood trees, with the loss of large branches. Large sections of rock were dislocated. Damage was also extensive in the city of San Jose.

Following the earthquake, engineers recommended that buildings no longer include cornices and that buildings not be placed on "made ground," land created by filling in San Francisco Bay. However, the recommendations were soon forgotten, and many of the same engineering mistakes contributed to the extensive destruction in the 1906 earthquake.

Richard Adler

FOR FURTHER INFORMATION:
Aldrich, M., et al. "The Report of the 1868 Haywards Earthquake." *Bulletin of the Seismological Society of America* 76 (1996): 71-76.
Hansen, Gladys. *San Francisco Almanac.* San Francisco: Chronicle Books, 1995.
Wollenberg, C. "Life on the Seismic Frontier: The Great San Francisco Earthquake of 1868." *California History* 7, no. 4 (Winter, 1992/1993): 494-509.

1872: Owens Valley Earthquake

DATE: March 26, 1872
PLACE: Owens Valley, Inyo County, California
MAGNITUDE: 7.8
RESULT: Approximately 30 dead

At approximately 2:30 A.M. on March 26, 1872, an earthquake was felt and reported by the weather observer in San Francisco. Movement in the city was light, and most people in the early hours of the morning were not even aware of the quake. However, the epicenter of the earthquake occurred along the Owens Valley fault on a line running a few miles east of the Sierra Nevada escarpment. It was here that the greatest level of damage and loss of life was found.

The quake, the largest in California since the 1868 San Francisco earthquake, was felt from Oregon to as far south as Mexico; fault scarps formed along a length of over 100 miles. Greatest damage occurred in the town of Lone Pine, where the largest horizontal displacement (over 7 feet) was reported. In the first shock, 52 of the 59 adobe and stone houses were destroyed, and 27 people were killed in the town. Additional fatalities were reported in other parts of Owens Valley, as major buildings in every town in Inyo County suffered damage. Property losses were reported as greater than $250,000. The earthquake caused clocks to stop and awakened people in San Diego (south), Red Bluff (north), and Elko, Nevada (east), an area encompassing more than 15,000 square miles.

Among the most vivid of the descriptions was that by naturalist John Muir, who was working as a caretaker near Sentinel Rock in Yosemite Valley. He described the sensation as that of walking on the deck of a ship during a storm. Muir witnessed and described the destruction of Eagle Rock a short distance away, as the quake triggered a rockslide that poured into the valley. Muir reported that aftershocks and trembling continued over a period of nearly two months. Other reports confirmed that more than one thousand aftershocks occurred during this interval.

Richard Adler

FOR FURTHER INFORMATION:

Muir, John. *Our National Parks.* Boston: Houghton, Mifflin, 1901.

Townley, Sidney. "Earthquakes in California." *Bulletin of the Seismological Society of America* 29, no. 1 (1939): 21-252.

1881: Turkey

DATE: April 3, 1881
PLACE: Chios Island, Turkey
RESULT: 5,000-7,000 dead

The island of Chios, located in the Aegean Sea 53 miles west of Smyrna on Asia Minor, was the scene of a massive earthquake in April, 1881. Approximately 7,000 persons in the population of 80,000 were killed during three large tremors, and another 15,000 were injured. Forty-four towns were heavily damaged or destroyed. In the district of Kampos, located on the southern portion of the island, 10 villages were destroyed. The town of Kalimasia, the largest on the island, suffered 670 dead among the population of 1,000.

In the seaport of Castro, 95 percent of the 3,000 buildings collapsed during the earthquake. The Convent of Neamonti, built on the slope of a cliff, collapsed into the sea, carrying dozens of nuns with the debris. Only a single nun survived. Chios Island, which according to local legends was the birthplace of the writer Homer, had previously been the scene of tragedy. In 1822, it had been invaded by the Greek army. Later, Turkish retaliation had resulted in the massacre of half the population.

Richard Adler

FOR FURTHER INFORMATION:

Nash, Jay Robert. *Darkest Hours.* Chicago: Nelson-Hall, 1976.

1885: India

DATE: June 2-July 8, 1885
PLACE: Kashmir, India
RESULT: 3,100 dead

During the months of June and July, 1885, a series of earthquakes struck the Kashmir region of India. The first quake occurred on June 2 in the city of Serinagur. Earthquakes continued during the following weeks. Eventually, dozens of towns and cities were heavily damaged, with the deaths of approximately 3,100 persons. At least 5,000 others were injured. Whole herds of cattle were described as being swallowed up within the fissures that formed in the region.

Richard Adler

FOR FURTHER INFORMATION:

Nash, Jay Robert. *Darkest Hours.* Chicago: Nelson-Hall, 1976.

1886: Charleston Earthquake

DATE: August 31, 1886
PLACE: Charleston and surrounding towns in South Carolina
MAGNITUDE: 7.6 (estimated)
RESULT: More than 100 dead, 122 commercial buildings destroyed, more than 14,000 chimneys collapsed, about $5.5 million in damage (in 1886 dollars)

The largest historic earthquake in the southeastern United States, the second largest in the eastern United States, and one of the largest earthquakes to ever occur in eastern North America took place in Charleston, South Carolina, in 1886. On August 27 and 28, a series of foreshocks rattled the small town of Summerville, approximately 16 miles northwest of Charleston. On August 31, the quake initially was barely perceptible in Charleston, but then, a rumbling sound became a roar, and all movable objects began to shake and rattle. The tremor became a rough, rapid quiver, reaching Charleston at 9:51 P.M. The major shock lasted only thirty-five to forty seconds but resulted in extensive damage at Charleston.

This old photograph shows damage to a building at Charleston College after the 1886 earthquake. (Courtesy National Oceanic and Atmospheric Administration)

Hardly a structure was left undamaged in the city, and only a few buildings escaped serious damage. Most of the brick buildings built after 1838 were constructed with inferior mortar that failed to hold the bricks together during the earthquake. Damaging secondary effects included fires, ruptured water lines, damaged wells, and flooding from a cracked dam in Langley, South Carolina. Because the event took place prior to seismological instrumentation, estimates of its location and size must come from observations of the damage and effects caused by the earthquake.

Most of what we know of the 1886 Charleston earthquake and the resulting damage is contained in a comprehensive report published by C. E. Dutton (1889) of the United States Geological Survey (USGS). Two epicentral locations are recorded for this earthquake. One epicenter was at Woodstock, a railroad stop on the Southern Railway, about 21 miles northwest of Charleston, and the other was at Ravenel, a small town 23 miles southwest of Charleston. The main shock was felt over an area of 5 million square miles, including distant points such as New York City, Boston, Milwaukee, Chicago, Bermuda, and Cuba. Structural damage was reported several hundred miles from Charleston in central Alabama, central Ohio, eastern Kentucky, southern Virginia, and western West Virginia. The main quake was followed two minutes later by an aftershock, as well as many other shocks over the following three years. Associated aftershocks were even reported well into the 1920's. In fact, of 435 or more earthquakes reported in South Carolina between 1754 and 1975, more than 300 are listed as aftershocks of the 1886 Charleston earthquake.

More than 500 square miles of extensive cratering and fissuring occurred in the epicentral regions. The formation of sand craterlets and the ejection of sand were also widespread, but no surface faulting was observed. Many acres of ground were overflowed with sand, and craterlets as much as 21 feet across were formed. In a few locations, water from the craterlets spouted to heights of over 15 feet. Fissures over 3 feet wide extended parallel to canal and stream banks. A series of wide cracks opened parallel to the Ashley River, and several large trees were uprooted when portions of the riverbank slid into the river.

About 3 miles northwest of Charleston, railroad tracks were bent laterally and vertically, with some stretches twisted into s-shaped curves. Extensive damage occurred to over 50 miles of track, and one locomotive was thrown off of the tracks by the quake. At Summerville, many houses settled into an inclined position, some displaced by more than 1 foot. Many long chimneys were crushed at their bases, allowing the whole chimney to sink down through the floors of the affected structures. Based upon the nature of the chimney damage and the absence of any overturned piered structures, the predominant motion is interpreted to have been vertical.

In all the large cities within a radius of 250 miles of Charleston, there was universal fright and concern among the people. In the Charleston area, the people were in a state of panic, but they soon gathered their wits and resources to recover from the devastating event. Buildings that could be salvaged were repaired or rebuilt, using long iron rods for reinforcement. Some businesses in Charleston reopened only two days after the quake. The Charleston earthquake of 1886 remains one of North America's great geological mysteries. The exact cause of this earthquake has still not been determined. No fault is known to be exposed at the surface within 60 miles of where the earthquake occurred. The historic record suggests that the Charleston-Summerville area had a continuum of low-level seismic activity prior to 1886 and that it continued in the same area throughout the twentieth century. Many studies funded by the USGS, the Nuclear Regulatory Commission, the National Science Foundation, and the Federal Emergency Management Agency have provided pieces of the puzzle about the 1886 earthquake mechanism. Through the examination of a variety of geophysical data during the 1990's, it appeared that movement within a concealed fault system buried beneath the coastal plain of the Carolinas and Virginia may be the source of the 1886 quake. However, determination of the fault's existence is complicated by layers of coastal sediment that lie above the projected fault. The sediment acts as a buffer, preventing seismic activity from drastically altering the landscape.

It is very important that the specific source of the 1886 earthquake and its tectonic setting be determined. This information will permit evaluation of expectable future earthquakes in the Charleston region. In addition, it will help to determine whether the Charleston region differs in any significant tectonic fashion from other parts of the eastern United States.

Alvin K. Benson

FOR FURTHER INFORMATION:
Bolt, B. A. *Earthquakes.* New York: W. H. Freeman, 1988.
Dutton, Clarence E. "The Charleston Earthquake of August 31, 1886." In *United States Geological Survey, Ninth Annual Report 1887-88.* Washington, D.C.: U.S. Geological Survey, 1889.
Keller, E. A. *Environmental Geology.* 6th ed. New York: Macmillan, 1992.
Press, F., and R. Siever. *Understanding Earth.* New York: W. H. Freeman, 1997.
Sieh, K., and S. LeVay. *The Earth in Turmoil.* New York: W. H. Freeman, 1998.

1887: Riviera

DATE: February 23, 1887
PLACE: Italy and France
MAGNITUDE: 6.0 on the Richter scale (estimated); X on the Modified Mercalli scale (estimated)
RESULT: About 2,000 killed, some villages completely destroyed, hundreds of buildings damaged or toppled

The Mediterranean coasts of Italy and France were shaken by a short but severe series of earthquakes shortly after 6 A.M. on February 23, 1887. The quakes were felt strongly in the coastal cities of Genoa and San Remo, both in Italy; Monte Carlo, Monaco; and Nice, France. In some locations two shocks were felt, in others three, in still others five. The quakes were noted as far away as Switzerland and central Italy. In the days following, weaker shocks were recorded along the Riviera as well as on the French island of Corsica and the Italian island of Sicily.

More than 1,500 people lost their lives on the Italian Riviera, where *The New York Times* described the damage as "immense and widespread." Worst hit was the Riviera de Ponente, the coastal region stretching southwestward from Genoa, in which every commu-

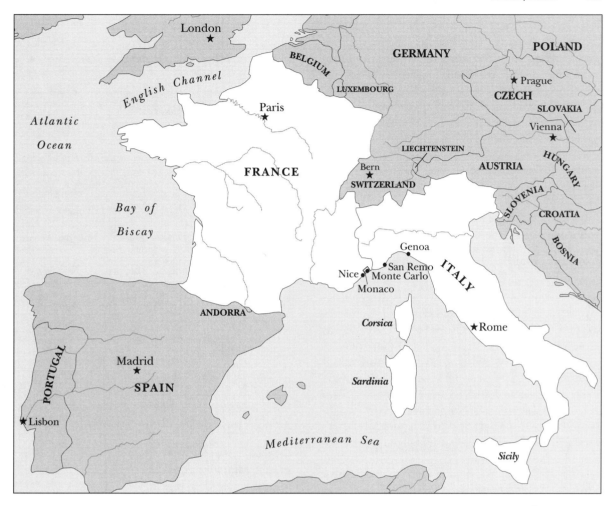

nity suffered damage and hundreds of buildings were toppled. The church in Bajardo, in which many of the town's residents had taken shelter after the first shock, was destroyed by a subsequent shock, crushing 300. Most of these were then buried in a mass grave in the town cemetery. Nearly equal numbers were killed in Bussana, where only the church steeple remained standing, and in Diano Marina. In the latter town most casualties resulted when the inhabitants, having fled the first shock, returned to their homes and were caught by the second. Survivors subsequently set up camp on the beach. The imminent collapse of the penitentiary in Oneglia resulted in the transport of its 500 prisoners to Genoa by train.

In Genoa itself the Ducal Palace and many other public buildings were damaged. Most Genoans slept outside after the initial shock, and some 20,000 of them tried to flee the city by rail. In the Italian city of San Remo, west of Genoa, over 300 residents were reported killed.

The situation was somewhat different across the border, where the shocks were milder and events sometimes took on the character of a comic opera. In the late nineteenth century the French Riviera became a prestigious destination. A contemporary magazine called it "perhaps the most attractive spot on the earth's surface" and noted the presence on its shores of throngs of tourists and wealthy invalids drawn by its beauty and mild climate. Because many of those caught in the tumult were English and American, the Riviera earthquakes received more than their share of attention in English-language newspapers. Ironically, few, if any, of the region's foreign visitors suffered any harm.

In the ports of the French Riviera the sea fell 3 feet at the first shock but afterward rose 6 feet. The damage to the cities themselves was no more than moderate, except to new, cheaply built tenements, many of which collapsed. In Nice, as in many southern European cities, an important and colorful festival was just concluding. It was the morning of Ash Wednesday, the day after Mardi Gras. Some celebrations were winding down, while others were still in progress. The streets were filled with costumed revelers when the walls began cracking and tiles began falling from the roofs. The streets were further swollen as panic-stricken sleepers rushed from their rooms. As the city's open public spaces filled, 2,000 frightened English, American, and Russian tourists set up camp in the countryside above the city. Subsequently some 15,000 visitors left Nice, most by train for the French capital of Paris, and some clad only in their nightclothes and furs. (Parisian hotel-keepers were reported to be delighted by the influx of wealthy visitors during what would normally be the city's slow season.) By the end of the week, another 8,000 frightened tourists had crowded into the port of Marseilles to the west.

Nearby Mentone was harder hit, with most official buildings weakened or toppled. Because the town's bakeries were also destroyed, bread was rushed from Nice. Alarmingly enough, large crevices were also reported to have opened in the town's cemetery. Yet after the initial disaster, the town actually enjoyed an influx of curiosity seekers.

The Prince of Wales—the heir to the British throne—had recently visited Nice but was staying in Cannes, a few miles down the coast to the southwest, when the quakes struck. He was urged by the British government to return home as soon as possible "to allay anxiety." The prince did subsequently leave Cannes, but only for the French capital.

Monte Carlo, which is built upon a rock and which therefore suffered only slight damage, saw its population swollen by thousands of "refugees" from nearby French communities. In recognition of the gravity of the situation, gambling (from which the principality of Monaco derived most of its income) was suspended. Moreover, a band was instructed to set up to play "for the purpose of restoring confidence to the frightened people."

Contemporary reports indicated that an almanac, the *Italian Soothsayer*, had predicted earthquakes between February 15 and 23. Interestingly enough, several natural signs portending earthquakes were also noted at the time. Horses, for instance, became restless and recalcitrant before the quakes struck. An Ameri-

can tourist sleeping in the open air in Nice after the first shock reported that each subsequent shock was preceded by "hot, heavy gusts of wind from the sea."

Grove Koger

FOR FURTHER INFORMATION:
"Another Shock at Nice." *The New York Times*, February 26, 1887, p. 1.

Davis, Lee. *Natural Disasters: From the Black Plague to the Eruption of Mt. Pinatubo*. New York: Facts on File, 1992.

"Home from the Riviera." *The New York Times*, February 27, 1887, p. 1.

Nash, Jay Robert. *Darkest Hours*. Chicago: Nelson-Hall, 1976.

"The Riviera Earthquake." *The New York Times*, February 25, 1887, p. 1.

"Southern Europe Shaken." *The New York Times*, February 24, 1887, p. 1.

"What Paris Talks About." *The New York Times*, February 24, 1887, p. 1.

1891: Japan

DATE: October 28, 1891
PLACE: Mino-Owari, Japan
MAGNITUDE: Approximately 7.9
RESULT: 7,300 dead, extensive damage in provinces of Mino and Owari

The Mino-Owari plain, near the central plain on the main island of Japan, was the major rice-producing region in the country. At 6:37 A.M. on October 28, 1891, a severe earthquake struck the region and surrounding provinces over a region of 94,000 square miles. From Nagoya to Gifu in the center of the region, described as a continuous 20-mile street, not a building was left undamaged. Nearly 200,000 houses in the provinces were entirely destroyed, and another 80,000 were badly damaged. Loss of life was relatively small, considering the extent and size of the quake. This probably reflected the low-density concentration of the population in the provinces.

Aftershocks continued for several years, totaling approximately two thousand. Most of these were comparatively weak.

Richard Adler

FOR FURTHER INFORMATION:

Davison, Charles. *Great Earthquakes.* London: Thomas Murby, 1936.

Milne, John. *The Great Earthquake in Japan, 1891.* Yokohama, Japan: Lane, Crawford, 1891.

1897: India

DATE: June 12, 1897
PLACE: Assam, India
MAGNITUDE: 8.8
RESULT: 1,542 dead, extensive destruction in Assam and surrounding cities

The Himalayas form much of the northern border of India. Formation of the mountains was the result of collision between two tectonic plates, resulting in continual geological instability in the area. The region around Assam has been subjected to frequent earthquakes, among which are the strongest on record.

At approximately 5 P.M. on the afternoon of June 12, 1897, a powerful earthquake shook the region around Assam and Shillong in northern India. Much of the scientific information recorded about the earthquake came from the work of Richard Dixon Oldham, a British geologist who investigated the quake. Under the auspices of the Indian government, Oldham published a work that became the classic in study and descriptions of Indian earthquakes. It was determined that the magnitude of the earthquake reached 8.8, approximately 50 times that of the San Francisco earthquake of 1906.

The earthquake devastated an area of 160,000 square miles, a region the size of California. The quake was felt over an additional 250,000 square miles. Lasting about two to three minutes, the temblor was described as producing undulations of the ground from 8 to 10 feet, at a height as great as 3 feet. Telephone poles, originally anchored in a straight line, were displaced 15 feet. Hundreds of aftershocks were felt for weeks.

Oldham described river channels that had been 15 feet in depth completely filled with sand and dirt. Railway rails were bent or thrown. Initially, 6,000 persons were reported killed, though this estimate was later lowered to slightly more than 1,500. Property damage in Assam and outlying towns and cities was devastating. In Assam and Shillong, all stone build-ings collapsed. A landslide triggered by the quake in Cherrapunji caused 600 deaths. A tsunami in Goalpara also caused heavy loss of life.

Richard Adler

FOR FURTHER INFORMATION:

Luttman-Johnson, H. "The Earthquake in Assam." *Journal of the Society of the Arts* 46 (1988): 473-493.

Oldham, Richard. *Report on the Great Earthquake of 1897.* 1899. Reprint. Calcutta: Geological Survey of India, 1981.

1899: Alaska

DATE: September 10, 1899
PLACE: Yakutat, Alaska
MAGNITUDE: 8.2
RESULT: Tsunamis along the Alaskan coast

Several earthquakes occurred during the week of September 4, 1899, along the coast of Alaska. The most severe of these occurred on September 10 in the Yakutat Bay region. This quake has been recorded as the sixth most severe in North America. Its effects were felt over an area of 300,000 square miles, with an uplift of 48 feet (14.5 meters) recorded on the west coast of Disenchantment Bay. A tsunami was generated in Yakutat Bay which reached over 34 feet (10.5 meters) in height, while other tsunamis developed along other portions of the Alaskan coast.

Fortunately, the area of the earthquake affected primarily unsettled portions of the Alaskan coast. Settlers, prospectors, and residents of Yakutat village reported more than 50 shocks, 2 of which were severe. Shocks were also felt in the Chugach Mountains near Prince William Sound, and in Juneau and Skagway, southeast of the bay.

The United States Geological Survey Team did not investigate the earthquake until some six years later. At that time, they determined that portions of Muir Glacier had shattered, and that avalanches had been generated in at least 9 other glaciers. Uplifted beaches were observed, but the only deaths had occurred among shellfish and barnacles.

Richard Adler

FOR FURTHER INFORMATION:

Coffman, Jerry, ed. *Earthquake History of the United*

States. Boulder, Colo.: United States Department of Commerce, 1982.

Stover, Carl, and Jerry Coffman. *Seismology of the United States, 1568-1989.* United States Geological Survey no. 1527. Washington, D.C.: United States Government Printing Office, 1993.

1902: Russia

DATE: February 13, 1902
PLACE: Caucasia, Russia
MAGNITUDE: 5.3
RESULT: 2,000 dead and injured, more than 9,000 buildings destroyed or damaged

An earthquake in the Caucasian region of southeastern Europe, between the Black Sea and the Caspian Sea, rocked the then-Russian town of Shamahka and its surrounding area, leaving some 25,000 people without shelter or food. Continuing tremors over the following several days made the work of excavating bodies of victims all the more difficult. Among the dead were many women who at the time of the main shock were gathered in the various bathhouses in the area.

To make things even worse, a volcano eruption at Marasy, east of Shamahka, occurred. As a result, the course of the River Geonchalkn was altered. This mountainous area of picturesque country covered with luxuriant vegetation, 2,230 feet above the level of the Black Sea, was turned almost instantaneously into a burial ground of dead and living. Hundreds of people were disentombed alive during the days following the quake. More than 126 villages were destroyed or damaged. Of more than 9,000 buildings that were destroyed or damaged, there were 11 churches and 41 mosques; 3 schoolhouses were seriously damaged. Most of the victims were Mussulmans, one of two major ethnic groups inhabiting the area.

Victoria Price

FOR FURTHER INFORMATION:
"25,000 Homeless at Shamahka." *The New York Times,* February 16, 1902, p. 4.
"2,000 Dead at Shemakha." *The New York Times,* February 18, 1902, p. 1.

1902: Guatemala

DATE: April 18-19, 1902
PLACE: Western Guatemala, Department of Quezaltenango, with the epicenter on the southern slope of the volcano Santa María
MAGNITUDE: 7.5 (initial shocks), 8.2 (third shock)
RESULT: More than 2,000 dead, more than 50,000 homeless, more than $50 million in damage

Guatemala is located at the juncture of five tectonic plates; seismic activity is thus quite regular and frequently intense. Twice in the country's colonial past (in the sixteenth and eighteenth centuries) earthquakes destroyed the capital. Most quakes occur in central and western Guatemala and are sometimes associated with volcanic eruptions along the western *cordillera* (mountain ranges) of the country. Earthquakes in the area of Quezaltenango have been recorded since 1625, but at the time, none had been as destructive as that of April 18, 1902.

On the evening of April 18, 1902, torrential rains fell throughout highland Guatemala, amid a major lightning and thunderstorm, flooding many cities and towns and putting out of commission the recently installed electric power plant at Quezaltenango. Just before 8:30 P.M. local time there was a loud explosion and an intense flash of light as the first shock arrived. Many inhabitants of the city immediately sought shelter from the falling houses by fleeing to the streets. The streets were then pitch black and were only a few yards wide, providing little shelter from collapsing buildings. The streets were also hilly and winding and were soon flowing with water and mud. This combination of conditions made the potential refuge of the outdoors a death trap, as many were buried under the falling debris and mud.

Subsequent shocks of equal or greater magnitude continued the destruction of most of the city's buildings until about 8 A.M. on April 19, when the tremors ceased temporarily, only to return on the 20th. In many areas, bridges and roads buckled and deep fissures opened. Cracks appeared in older buildings in Guatemala City, and many people prayed in the streets; some went mad, and others committed suicide. Fires broke out in many areas following the first quakes, adding to the destruction and panic.

The quake was felt from southern Mexico to Nicaragua and Belize. Damage was greatest from Chiapas, Mexico, to Amatitlan, southeast of Guatemala City.

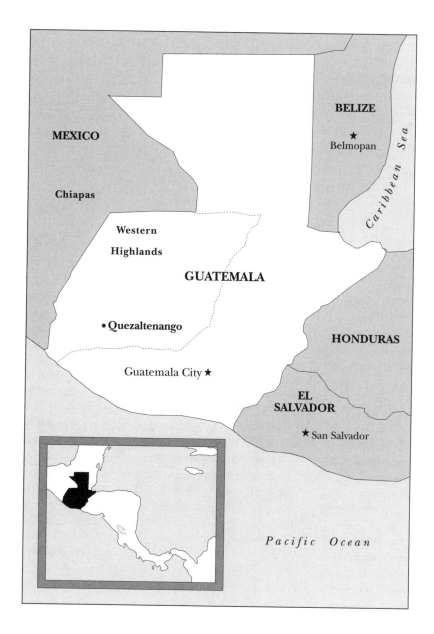

ous recession, making refinancing of loans and further foreign investment difficult to achieve.

This earthquake, along with another on January 18, near Ocós, marked the beginning of a series of seismic activities on the fringes of the Caribbean tectonic plate and in Central America and helped establish 1902 as a year of record seismic activity worldwide. For Guatemala this meant a continuous stream of quakes in the same area. Within a few weeks of the first earthquake a number of previously inactive volcanoes became active, including Colima, west of Guadalajara in Mexico; Soconusco, in Chiapas, Mexico; Tacaná, on the Mexico-Guatemala border, which erupted disastrously in June; and Ilopango, near the Guatemala-El Salvador border.

Extremely destructive activity began soon after in the eastern Caribbean—a series of eruptions of La Soufrière on the island of St. Vincent on May 7 and the first of several eruptions of Mount Pelée on Martinique on May 8. Severe earthquakes were recorded in the Virgin Islands, Jamaica, and on the northern coast of South America. The destruction was climaxed by the violent eruption of Santa María in Guatemala on October 24, 1902.

The compact nature of the debris in the Department of Quezaltenango made both rescue and early estimates of casualties difficult. Damage was done to much of the coffee crop at a time when coffee prices were already depressed, as well as to the railway and to the new power plant. Telegraph lines were knocked out, making reporting the disaster difficult. Relief efforts were made by the Guatemalan government, but pleas for aid and information came chiefly from foreign consuls and visitors. This earthquake and the series of quakes and eruptions that followed occurred when the Guatemalan economy was in serious recession, making refinancing of loans and further foreign investment difficult to achieve.

This eruption again destroyed much of Quezaltenango and the entire coffee crop, covering the towns, cities, and plantations with more than 3 feet of ash.

St. John Robinson

FOR FURTHER INFORMATION:

Claxton, Robert H. "Earthquakes." In *Encyclopedia of Latin American History & Culture*, edited by Barbara Tanenbaum. New York: Charles Scribner's Sons, 1996.

Grosvenor, Gilbert H. "Volcanoes." *National Geographic*, June, 1902, 204-208.

Nash, Jay Robert. *Darkest Hours.* New York: Pocket Books, 1977.
The New York Times, May 9, 11, 16, 24; June 8; August 17; September 28, 1902.

1902: Turkestan

DATE: December 16, 1902
PLACE: Andijan, Turkestan
MAGNITUDE: 6.4
RESULT: 10,000 dead, about 15,000 houses destroyed

On a cold December day, with temperatures close to freezing, an earthquake struck an area of Turkestan, west of the Mongolian Desert and east of the Caspian Sea. The town of Andijan, with a population of 30,600, was totally destroyed. According to one report some ten days after the initial quake, more than 15,000 houses, belonging to both native Turkomans and Russians, were lost. Shocks were also felt in New Marghelan and in surrounding villages. Shocks and swaying of the earth continued for over a week. The railway system leading into and out of Andijan was also destroyed for a considerable distance. Because of the disruption of all means of communication, it was difficult to obtain information quickly.

Among those killed by the earthquake were city officials, soldiers, and many children. The surviving population was threatened with starvation while they waited for rescue teams to bring in food and clothing. Railway cars were used as temporary dwelling places. Andijan is a major cotton-producing center; about 40 million pounds of cotton are harvested annually. Thus, the surviving inhabitants made no plans to leave this very productive region. However, of the 20 cotton gins in the town, 19 were destroyed.

Andijan has existed for more than four hundred years, and, since there have been other earthquakes over the years, the general population chose to take such disasters in stride, to rebuild, and to go on with their lives there.

Victoria Price

FOR FURTHER INFORMATION:
"The Andijan Earthquakes." *The New York Times*, December 27, 1902, p. 9.
"Earthquake Destroys Town." *The New York Times*, December 18, 1902, p. 9.

"Earthquakes at Andijan." *The New York Times*, December 26, 1902, p. 5.

1903: Armenia

DATE: April 29, 1903
PLACE: Armenia, especially Melazguird and surrounding villages
RESULT: 785 dead

Historically, Armenia has long been subject to earthquake activity. At about 2 A.M. on April 29, a strong earthquake lasting about one minute was felt in Armenia. The areas of greatest shock were those between Lake Van and the Russian frontier and as far north as Baibourt. It was reported that Melazguird, a town in which about 80 percent of the population are of the Mussulman ethnic group, was virtually destroyed. Considerable damage occurred in surrounding villages, including Patnotx, Hadjili, Mollah Ibrahim, Zoussicko, and Molla Mustapha. At least 17 other villages were partially destroyed.

The seismic disturbance appeared to have been in the neighborhood of Mount Sipan. Among the casualties were a number of British military personnel. The telegraph operator was seriously injured, and his wife and sister were killed. The telegraph instruments were finally retrieved with great difficulty from the debris. In addition to the toll of human fatalities, many cattle and sheep also perished.

Victoria Price

FOR FURTHER INFORMATION:
Nature, May 28, 1903, 85.

1905: India

DATE: April 4, 1905
PLACE: Kangra, India
MAGNITUDE: 8.7
RESULT: More than 20,000 dead

At approximately 6:50 on the morning of April 4, 1905, a violent earthquake shook the district of Kangra in northern India. In less than three minutes, all of the valley of Kangra was destroyed and over

20,000 persons were killed. Severe aftershocks continued for another twenty minutes. While most of the towns and cities in the district suffered damage, the heaviest destruction occurred in the cities of Kangra and Dharmsala.

Kangra lay in a valley in the southeast corner of the province of Punjab, approximately 130 miles from Lahore. The area was described as one of immense scenic beauty, green and lush. An army regiment was also situated in the region, which was home to a large number of Hindu temples, including the Temple of Maharani, commonly referred to as the "Bhoon." The city had grown around a fortress, Fort Kangra, which had been established by a Hindu prince some nine hundred years earlier. No records existed that described any earlier destruction. Therefore, the 1905 earthquake was probably the most severe natural disaster to strike the region.

The earthquake struck while most people were asleep. All 1,600 homes in Kangra were destroyed, as well as all the Hindu temples, including the Bhoon. At the moment of the earthquake, a large number of visitors were in the Bhoon, and the collapse of the shrine trapped many of the people in the rubble. Fort Kangra was also destroyed, but because of the early hour, only 7 men were killed. It was estimated that the total number killed in or around Kangra was about 20,000.

Dharmsala, a city located about 5 miles from Kangra, was also nearly destroyed. Out of a population of 3,000, approximately 2,700 were killed. Included in the destruction were civil and military stations located in the town, including an encampment of Gorkha soldiers. Over 100 soldiers were killed, along with many of their European officers. Ironically, the only building in the encampment that withstood the earthquake was that of the treasury, which was much sturdier than the other buildings.

Kotwali, about 2 miles from Dharmsala, likewise suffered significant destruction. The town was situated along the side of a hill, with the police station and jailhouse, both constructed of stone, located above most of the town. During the earthquake, both buildings collapsed and spilled down the hill, killing some 300 persons.

Comparable levels of destruction were reported from numerous towns in the valley. In Palumpar, the site of picturesque gardens as well as temples, 3,000 died. In Mandi, 750 people were reported killed.

Even weeks later, bodies were still being recovered from the ruins.

Richard Adler

FOR FURTHER INFORMATION:
Baduwi, Munshi Abdul. *Earthquakes of India . . .*, 1905. Translated by Muneeb Cheema. Cooperative Institute for Research in Environmental Sciences (CIRES), University of Colorado, 1998.

1905: Italy

DATE: September 8 and 14, 1905
PLACE: Calabria, Italy
MAGNITUDE: 7.9
RESULT: 5,000 dead, several hundred injured, at least 18 villages destroyed

At 2:55 A.M., a shock lasting eighteen seconds was felt at Catanzaro, the capital of the region of Calabria, located in the toe of the boot-shaped peninsula of Italy. Soon afterward, shocks were also felt in the towns of Keggio, Monte Leone, Martinaro, Sterfaconi, Piscapio, Triparni, Sammaro, Cassaniti, Maida, Olivadi, and Messina in Sicily; tremors were felt to some extent as far north as Naples and even Florence. The earthquake was recorded as being located at the coordinates of 39.4 north and 16.4 east. Parents aroused from their sleep rushed screaming and half-clothed into the streets, carrying babies and dragging their children out of their houses. Many of them were calling on the Virgin Mary and the saints for help. The confusion was increased by cries from the jails, where prisoners were in a state of panic from fright; however, they were kept in bounds.

By daylight, since there was no repetition of the tremors, those whose villages had not been destroyed returned to their homes; however, about 18 villages were ruined. Some of the villages had fatalities, while others had varying numbers of injured people. All the structures collapsed in several villages; in others, buildings were left standing, but with foundations so weakened that they were considered unsafe for entry. Six days later, on September 14, three fresh shocks caused considerable damage at Cosenza, one of the three provinces of the region of Calabria. In Catanzaro, the buildings that housed the courts of law threatened to collapse, and lawyers refused to enter them. Doctors, troops, and engineers were rushed to the area to tend the wounded, evaluate the damage, and begin the job of rescue and salvage.

Victoria Price

FOR FURTHER INFORMATION:

"Earthquake Kills 370, Wrecking 18 Villages." *The New York Times*, September 9, 1905, p. 1.

1906: Colombia, Ecuador

DATE: January 31, 1906
PLACE: The border of Colombia and Ecuador
MAGNITUDE: 8.9
RESULT: Structural damage, several hundred dead

Two earthquakes struck Guayaquil, Ecuador, during the morning of January 31, 1906, when plate boundaries slipped. The first tremor hit at 9 A.M., and another earthquake rocked the area an hour later. A brief news account printed the next day described the tremors as being long-lasting and intense, causing severe damage and panicking the local population. Five days after the earthquakes struck, newspapers reported that cable communications had been disrupted between islands in the West Indies and countries in northern South America.

Ten days later, newspapers published reports of earthquakes that shook Ecuador and Colombia on January 31. Articles said that residents of Esmeraldas Province in northwestern Ecuador had traveled to Guayaquil after earthquakes had destroyed structures throughout Esmeraldas, including the Government House. The earthquakes also affected houses in Manabi Province. Adjacent to Colombia, Pinguagi was flooded when tremors caused sea surges, and many people drowned. At least 90 bodies were washed onto the beach at Tumaco, Colombia, and nearby Guncada was also covered by ocean waves, which drowned 200 people. Simultaneously with the earthquake, the volcano Cumbal in Colombia had erupted.

Elizabeth D. Schafer

FOR FURTHER INFORMATION:

"Earthquakes in Guayaquil." *The New York Times*, February 1, 1906, p. 1.

"Havoc by Earthquakes." *The New York Times*, February 15, 1906, p. 1.

"West Indies Still Cut Off." *The New York Times*, February 5, 1906, p. 1.

1906: Taiwan

DATE: March 17, 1906
PLACE: Kagi, Taiwan
MAGNITUDE: 7.1
RESULT: 1,228 dead, estimated $45 million in damage

During the early morning hours of Saturday, March 17, 1906, the island of Taiwan was shaken by an earthquake; the shaking lasted until late that night. The tremors were also felt in Japan, to the north. It was reported that the prosperous towns of Datiyo, Raishiko, and Shinko were completely destroyed, but Kagi sustained greater loss of life. An estimated 7,000 buildings were shaken down. As soon as makeshift sheds could be constructed or open-air sites chosen, the government resumed its business transactions. At Datiyo, many of the dead were found in the open fields to which the people had fled before succumbing to their injuries. According to Fusakichi Omori, for many years the most distinguished of Japanese seismologists, this earthquake was caused by a slip on a compound fault, the Chinsekiryo fault in the western branch and the Baishiku fault in the eastern branch.

Victoria Price

FOR FURTHER INFORMATION:

"Formosa Again Stricken." *The New York Times*, April 15, 1906, p. 4.

Macelwane, James B. *When the Earth Quakes*. Milwaukee, Wis.: Bruce, 1947.

Richter, Charles F. *Elementary Seismology*. San Francisco: W. H. Freeman, 1958.

1906: San Francisco Earthquake

DATE: April 18, 1906
PLACE: The northern coast of California, from King City to Humboldt Bay

The San Francisco earthquake of 1906 caused Union Street to buckle and become offset. (Courtesy National Oceanic and Atmospheric Administration)

MAGNITUDE: About 8.3
RESULT: Approximately 700 dead, 400 injured, 200,000 homeless, 28,188 buildings burned in San Francisco, and about $500 million in damage

In 1906, fifty-seven years after the 1849 gold rush, San Francisco was an active up-to-date city of 400,000. Although its central business district still included a handful of Spanish and Mexican adobe structures and comparatively few wooden buildings, the city comprised masonry and brick structures and newer multistory, steel-framed office blocks. Churches and public buildings of diverse construction were scattered throughout the city, while most residences, primarily wooden, were either closely spaced or shared common walls. In addition, most of the central business district, the waterfront, and the warehouse district was built on filled-in marshes, mudflats, and shallow water. Some newer commercial development and most of the residential district were perched on steep bedrock hills.

Before the 1906 earthquake, effective public utilities and fire and police departments served the bustling city. Numerous ferries crisscrossed the bay, steamers connected the city with Sacramento, and many railroad lines radiated from the busy city in all directions. The private Spring Valley Water Company pumped water through wrought iron or cast iron pipelines from the Crystal Springs, San Andreas, and Pilarcitos lakes, all impounded along the San Andreas fault, to University Mound, College Hill, and Lake Honda reservoirs inside the city. In turn, these reservoirs discharged water into the city's water mains. Additional water from Alameda Creek and Lake Merrit entered the city via a pipeline beneath the South Bay. Several hundred firefighters manned 41 fire engines, 9 trucks, and 7 "chemical" engines as well as monitor and ladder trucks. Seven hundred police officers were assisted by sheriff's deputies, state militia, and the army's garrison at the Presidio.

Reasons for the Earthquake. Most San Franciscans in 1906 did not expect a major earthquake.

Prior to the 1906 earthquake, frequent small earth tremors caused trivial damage and occasional consternation. Spanish records from the second decade of the nineteenth century describe memorable earthquakes at the Presidio. In 1857, a severe earthquake centered on the San Andreas fault at Fort Tejon in Northern California significantly damaged the city. Another quake in 1865 damaged City Hall and downtown buildings. In 1868, a severe earthquake across the bay at Haywards caused damage in downtown San Francisco and resulted in 5 deaths. Milder earthquakes occurred in 1890 and 1898. As a result, advanced construction codes had been adopted in San Francisco, and many buildings were designed to be fireproof. Thus, San Franciscans on the eve of the 1906 major earthquake judged the city well prepared to resist damage, but geologists and insurers were deeply concerned.

Earthquakes result from sudden, instantaneous lurches in a fault's movement, thought to be caused by temporary "freezing" of the fault that is followed by rupture. If the fault does not "freeze," movement is continuous and there are no major earthquakes. The San Andreas fault, responsible for the 1906 earthquake, is a right lateral transform fault separating the Pacific Ocean Plate from the North American Plate between Cape Mendocino and Baja California. This fault began shifting in latest Cretaceous period, and by the present epoch cumulative movement has totaled about 370 miles. Thus, California as far north as Point Reyes and Santa Cruz was part of northern Baja California about seventy million years ago.

Today, movement on the San Andreas fault ranges up to 1.5 inches per year, requiring continual small repairs to structures spanning the fault trace. During the San Francisco Earthquake, apparently more than 240 miles of the San Andreas fault broke loose and shifted. Fissures with displacements mark the San Andreas fault from Point Arena, 100 miles northwest of San Francisco, to San Juan Bautista, 85 miles southeast. Severe damage at Priest Valley, 60 miles farther southeast, suggests an additional 60 miles of fault movement that failed to crack the surface. In addition, submarine observations in the later twentieth century traced fault-line topography to the San Andreas fault's juncture with the Mendocino Fracture Zone, a westward-trending fracture system passing far into the Pacific Plate.

Wherever displacement could be observed on the fissure, land southwest of the fault trace moved northward relative to the northeastern block. Just north of Tomales Bay this horizontal displacement was about 16 feet. Here the southwest block was lifted about 1 foot relative to the northeastern block. These displacements decrease to the north and south. Earthquakes along the San Andreas fault in historic time include 1812, Wrightwood (estimated magnitude, 7.0); 1838, San Francisco peninsula (7.0, estimated); 1857, Fort Tejon (8.0, estimated); 1906, San Francisco (8.3, estimated); and 1989, Loma Prieta (7.1, recorded).

The Earthquake. The San Francisco Earthquake struck central California with a magnitude of about 8.3, on Wednesday, April 18, 1906, at 5:12 A.M. Fortunately, most people were still safely at home. In and around San Francisco, severe shaking lasted for about one minute. Before the main shocks, however, many observers noted two substantial preliminary shocks lasting several seconds. More than 1,000 aftershocks of intensity as great as V on the Modified Mercalli scale were recorded between April 18 and June 10 by a seismograph in Berkeley, California. Oscillatory ground movement during the main shock was principally horizontal and was estimated, in the city, at more than 2 inches on bedrock or firm ground. This was greatly amplified, however, on unconsolidated soil or sediment. Damage was substantial in a belt 20 to 40 miles wide paralleling the San Andreas fault from Eureka to Priest Valley. Thus, Santa Rosa, Salinas, San Mateo, Oakland, Berkeley, Vallejo, Petaluma, San Rafael, San Mateo, Palo Alto, and San Jose, in addition to San Francisco, suffered damage. Destruction was greatest adjacent to the fault trace, decreasing with distance from the trace. Indeed, the shock was felt as far away as Coos Bay, Oregon (390 miles); Los Angeles, California (350 miles); and Winnemucca, Nevada (340 miles). In addition, minor damage occurred 90 miles away on the east side of the San Joaquin Valley. As far away as Steamboat Springs, Nevada, wells and springs were affected by rising or falling water, interruption, stoppage and initiation of spring flow, and incursion of mineralized water.

Damage to buildings differed greatly according to construction type and quality. Least damaged were buildings with solid foundations set on bedrock. Solidly built and well-braced one- or two-story wooden buildings suffered relatively little. The steel frames of structures as high as nineteen stories generally did not collapse, but masonry walls and cornices often shook loose. Most, however, were gutted by fire that caused poorly insulated beams to soften and crumple. Heavy, well-constructed brick or stone buildings were also relatively resistant to damage, but poorly constructed masonry, or masonry with lime mortar, collapsed or disintegrated. Brick and stone clamped or braced by steel endured, as did massive concrete and brick fortifications. Finally, the single reinforced concrete building in the city of San Francisco, the Bekin Storage warehouse, survived with minor damage, as did the reinforced concrete portion of the Stanford University Museum.

Federal buildings, such as the mint and post offices, along with well-built churches, suffered least among masonry structures. However, shoddily constructed local governmental buildings, victims of low-bid and perhaps corrupt construction practices, such as the San Francisco and Santa Rosa city halls, the Agnews Insane Asylum, and the San Jose hall of records, were demolished. Private buildings differed greatly in their resistance. Many spires and towers collapsed.

The amount of damage was also greatly affected by the distance from the fault trace, topography, and the substratum, or soil foundation. For example, buildings straddling the fault trace were sheared. Although strong wood or steel-frame buildings generally did not break apart, they were twisted or rotated. Incredibly, a few stayed put, allowing the earth to shift beneath them, while larger structures either bent or were sliced apart but still stood. Concrete and earth-fill dams resisted damage. The earthen dams of the San Andreas and Pilarcitos reservoirs, built across the fault trace, survived the shearing. The massive concrete dam of the Crystal Springs Reservoir, immediately adjacent to the fault trace, also was undamaged. Buildings on weak or insecure foundations slid down slopes, while adjacent buildings with firm foundations attached to bedrock were relatively unharmed. Structures in the path of landslides and mudflows were severely damaged or destroyed.

Buildings not set on firm foundations reaching bedrock either collapsed or were severely damaged. For example,

the Ferry Building, which rested on piles that reached bedrock, did not collapse; buildings on bedrock hills downtown and in the Western Addition were not very damaged. Approximately 20 percent of San Francisco, including the waterfront, the South of Market District, and most of the central business district, was built on filled-in mudflats and marshes. There, shaking was amplified by the soft, semiliquid substratum and generated actual wave movement; outright liquefaction also removed support for the buildings.

The earthquake reshaped the landscape in many ways. Fissures opened along the fault trace were, perhaps, most striking. Characteristically, these open

A house on Howard Street in San Francisco that was tipped by the 8.3-magnitude earthquake. (Courtesy National Oceanic and Atmospheric Administration)

rifts were generally about 5 feet wide and 10 feet deep. They sometimes occurred in zones as big as 50 feet wide. They were discontinuous, in many places consisting of a series of overlapping individual ladder breaks and somewhat inclined to the trace of the fault. In some places fissures did not open, and the fault trace was identifiable only by offset structures. Mudflows and landslides also occurred wherever blocks of surficial material shifted during the shock. These were concentrated along stream channels, where unstable land slumped into stream channels or on steep hillsides. In a landslide a coherent block of ground moves downhill in a more or less coherent mass, while in a mudflow, the dislodged material behaves as a liquid and flows.

In addition, liquefaction of water-soaked, unconsolidated subsoil was widespread. Parts of the mudflats in Tomales Bay simply flowed off into deep water. Here and at Bolinas, waves of compression, generated by shock along the fault trace, sent concentric giant ripples outward on the surface of the liquefied, unconsolidated material. After the shock passed, stability was restored in the liquified material and the ripples froze in place. Such frozen waves disrupted buildings, streets, and car tracks on the filled land in San Francisco. Compression at depth also spewed liquified sediment up to form mud volcanoes or craters on the surface.

The Fire. Although the event is referred to as the San Francisco Earthquake, the principal devastation was inflicted by the resultant fire. American cities of the time, including San Francisco, were largely built of wood. Consequently, nineteenth century American history records many great fires, such as the 1871 Great Chicago Fire. Actually, downtown San Francisco had been gutted by fire six times prior to 1906. As a consequence, most commercial builders favored brick, stone, and steel, but wood remained predominant in house-building. Immediately after the major earthquake shock, at least 10 large fires started among the closely spaced wooden buildings south of Market Street and in Chinatown, north of Market Street. Shattered chimneys, broken gas lines, and scattered fires readily ignited houses.

About 57 fires were reported before noon, despite the destruction of the city's modern alarm system. Also, Fire Chief Dennis Sullivan's fatal injury complicated the department's response. The capacity of the fire department to respond was far exceeded, and when an engine reached a fire, the firefighters found little or no water in the hydrants. The earthquake had broken the large mains bringing water into the city as well as the network of mains serving the hydrants from the subsidiary reservoirs. Thus, San Francisco's large, well-equipped fire department remained essentially unable to throw water on fires beyond reach of hose lines from the Bay Shore or one of the relatively undamaged reservoirs.

Mayor Eugene Schmitz and Fire Chief John Doughty implemented fatally injured Chief Sullivan's emergency plan to pump water up Market Street through linked hoses, to establish a fire line along the city's broadest street. The already-blazing South of Market District was thus abandoned. Unfortunately, with Chinatown already ablaze and flames already jumping the street in a few places, the Market Street fire line soon failed. At the same time, a determined effort was made to check the westward advance of flames out of the South of Market District and into the Mission District. Frederick Funston, commanding the garrison at the Presidio in the temporary absence of his superior officer, General Adolphus Greeley, immediately ordered his troops into the city to fight fire and maintain order. Since he acted without official orders and without consulting his superior officers or civil authorities, his unconstitutional act was privately deplored by the War Department. The disciplined work of most of his men, however, as well as that of naval reinforcements, prevented looting and the breakdown of order. Thus, Funston, who eventually met with Mayor Schmitz and established cooperation with the police and fire departments, became a public hero and escaped discipline.

Strong measures were imperative to check the fire's spread. At 2 P.M., Mayor Schmitz obtained an opinion from a judge to clear the way for dynamiting buildings. Then, around 3 P.M., nine hours after the earthquake, he posted a proclamation announcing that gas and electricity had been cut off and warned people of the fire danger from damaged chimneys, gas pipes, and fixtures. Furthermore, he authorized summary execution of looters or persons defying the police or military. To enforce all of this, Schmitz also swore in 1,000 armed volunteer patrolmen. Although the proclamation of summary execution was illegal, Funston's men continued shooting looters and people ignoring orders. In this they were joined by police, the militia, and Schmitz's volunteers. Although the shootings effectively prevented civil disorder, there were many accusations of unwarranted, summary execution by rifle or bayonet. Most of this agitation was directed against relatively undisciplined militia and vigilantes, but controversy over the Army's role persisted.

In addition, Schmitz organized a committee of 50 prominent citizens to advise and assist him in fighting the fire. This committee first met at the Hall of Justice but relocated to Portsmouth Square when the building burned. By 8 P.M. on the first day, the fire front was a 3-mile-long crescent, and light from the flames was visible for at least 50 miles. Also by this time, Funston had met with the mayor and his committee at the Fairmount Hotel to outline plans to control the fire with a barrier of dynamited buildings. Thereafter, his troops set up a cordon along Van Ness Avenue, preventing entrance into the area to the east as troops forced all civilians out of the same area. Troops were also set to guard property west of Van Ness, and the dynamiting began on the east side of the avenue. Funston had made himself the de facto military governor of the city.

The fire continued spreading for a second day. On Thursday, April 19, the mansions on Nob Hill, the Fairmount Hotel, and the Barbary Coast below Telegraph Hill burned before 6 A.M. By 11 A.M., the U.S. Navy Pacific Squadron arrived, including the hospital ship the *Preble* and a water tender that immediately went to work bringing water to the city's fire engines. Sailors landed for demolition work, and Marines were deployed to protect waterfront property. In contrast to the Army, the militia, and the volunteers, they drew no criticism for misbehavior or wanton shooting. The Army, with the active participation of Funston's wife, Eda, set up a refugee camp on the grounds of the Presidio and in Letterman Hospital. Additional rations were ordered from Army stocks in Los Angeles and Seattle.

Ultimately, 20,000 people were estimated to be camping out in the Presidio. Other refugees, including the staff and patients from many of the city's hospitals, camped out in even larger numbers in Golden Gate Park. The inhabitants of St. Mary's hospital, however, escaped *en masse* on the steamer *Medoc*, which then stood offshore, eventually docking in Alameda. President Theodore Roosevelt requested that the Red Cross, insofar as possible, supervise relief operations at San Francisco. This first such effort established the Red Cross as the principal responder to mass disaster relief in America. By Thursday after-

noon, thousands of people had gathered along the waterfront, where the fire department, aided by a Navy fire-fighting detachment and using more than 20 engines to pump water from the bay, had succeeded in saving almost all of the dock area. Every six minutes the Southern Pacific Railroad sent ferries loaded with refugees across the Bay without charge. In addition, a large number of Bay Boatmen also evacuated many, in some cases at exorbitant fees. Ultimately, the railroad transported 300,000 people across the Bay by ferry or onward by train to any point in North America. In time the wind changed, and by 4 P.M. the fire front was no longer wind-driven. Also, the water mains from Lake Honda had been repaired so that some water became available to the fire department. A small group of troops managed to organize a successful defense of part of the Russian Hill neighborhood. At 5 P.M., the Army, with the aid of a naval demolition squad, began blasting houses on the east side of Van Ness Avenue. This was soon supplemented by artillery fire.

The third day of the fire began with flames jumping the Van Ness Avenue fire line at midnight, but the fire department successfully checked this advance, and the firebreak was essentially maintained. At 5 A.M., Mayor Schmitz confronted Funston and ordered the cessation of dynamiting. One last blast, however, spread burning debris into an unburned area north of Green Street, and the fire, driven by the wind, expanded north and east. In the absence of troops to drive them away, Russian Hill residents successfully saved their neighborhood using water gathered in bathtubs, wet sheets, and even wine on the flames. At 5 P.M., Funston defied the mayor and ordered artillery bombardment along the Van Ness Avenue fire line. At 5:30 P.M. firefighters reported that the fire along Van Ness Avenue was out, and at 6 A.M. the following Friday morning, the Mission District was declared safe. At 7:15 A.M., the last flames were extinguished along the waterfront—seventy-two hours after the fire started.

Ultimately the fire was extinguished by a combination of factors. Fire lines established along Van Ness, Dolores, Howard, and Twentieth Street finally held when the wind either died down or shifted to oppose the fire's advance. Restoration of water service from the Honda Reservoir enabled firefighters to hold at Van Ness Avenue, and water pumped from the bay enabled firefightershters to save the waterfront. Ultimately, 4.7 square miles burned. Only a few isolated spots within the outer bounds of destruction survived: the south half of Russian Hill, a few downtown blocks, and part of Telegraph Hill. The strongly built mint, which contained a well in the basement, was successfully defended. The post office, thanks to thick walls and a determined crew of postal employees, managed to stave off the fire. The Palace Hotel also survived for six hours, until its cisterns were emptied and the roof sprays were cut off. Several additional buildings with solid walls and fire-resistant shutters or wired glass also stood unburned in the midst of the burned-out area.

After the Fire. Because of the total confusion, actual enumeration of casualties was impossible, and many corpses were totally consumed by fire. Casualty estimates range from 450 to 1,000, with 700 the generally agreed estimate. While General Adolphus Greeley's official report listed 458 dead in San Francisco, only 315 dead were cited by city authorities. Four hundred injured were treated by medical authorities that kept records, and approximately 200,000 were left homeless. Subsequent to the fire, an outbreak of bubonic plague, caused by rats driven throughout the city, caused at least 160 recorded deaths.

Insurance companies were overwhelmed. The Fireman's Fund, for example, incurred liabilities of $11.5 million against total assets of $7 million. Companies reorganized under bankruptcy and paid claims, 55.6 percent cash and 50 percent in company stock. Only 6 major companies were able to pay claims without delay and in full. Fifty-nine companies spent months or even years fighting legal battles to avoid meeting their commitments.

Rebuilding San Francisco began immediately and, in the rush, plans that would have made the city more fire- and earthquake-resistant were essentially ignored. By December, 1906, plans were under way for the 1915 Panama Pacific International Exposition. By that year the city was rebuilt. Building codes were revised following publication of the California Earthquake Commission report. The codes curbed use of brickwork, outlawed heavy ornamental cornices, required improved bracing of steelwork, specified integration of walls and frames of buildings, and required installation of automatic sprinkler systems. In addition, a supplementary fire main system of saltwater, additional reservoirs within the city, refurbished cisterns, and acquisition of fireboats were recommended.

Earthquakes and other great disasters give rise to fanciful stories that persist in popular memory. The motion picture *San Francisco* (1936) dramatically shows a crevice suddenly opening in a crowded city street. Panicked people fall into it, to be engulfed when it promptly slams shut. This event never occurred. Also, a picture of dead cows in an open fissure at the south end of Tomales Bay has been published repeatedly as evidence of animals dying by falling into a fissure. In actuality, a rancher used the crevice to dispose of a dead cow, but the more dramatic story persists.

Folklore also has it that the San Francisco fire was stopped through heroic efforts by the Army to dynamite firebreaks, when in reality the dynamited wreckage of a building burns just as easily as the building, and even more readily if the building has stone or brick walls. Sober analysts of the California Earthquake Commission and of the Fire Underwriters heavily discount blowing up buildings as a way of stopping fires. A rumor that the U.S. mint was assaulted during the fire by an armed gang intending to rob it was repeated as historical fact in a San Francisco paper as late as 1956. Another incident wherein the carcass of a bull shot while charging and taken to Letterman Hospital to help feed refugees led to a rumor that dead horses from all over the city were being fed to unsuspecting victims.

Perhaps the most important result of the 1906 earthquake was that it made Californians actively conscious of the inevitability of periodic major earthquakes and the need for preparation. Thus, after every major quake, the California Uniform Building Code has been strengthened where found lacking. Also, continuing research on earthquake prediction provides growing understanding of what to expect and how to react. In spite of this, San Francisco again suffered severe damage in the 1989 Loma Prieta earthquake, escaping a major fire only because, fortuitously, winds were calm.

M. Casey Diana

FOR FURTHER INFORMATION:
Bolt, Bruce A. *Earthquakes.* San Francisco: W. H. Freeman, 1988.
Gere, J. M., and J. C. Shah. *Terra Non Firma.* San Francisco: W. H. Freeman, 1984.
Gilbert, G. K., Richard L. Humphrey, John Stephen Sewell, and Frank Soulé. *The San Francisco Earthquake and Fire of April 18, 1906, and Their Effects on*

Structures and Structural Materials. Washington, D.C.: Government Printing Office, 1907.

Iacopi, Robert. *Earthquake Country.* Menlo Park, Calif.: Lane Books, 1964.

Jordan, David Starr, ed. *The California Earthquake of 1906.* San Francisco: A. M. Robertson, 1907.

Lawson, A. C., et al. Report of the State Earthquake Commission. *The California Earthquake of April 18, 1906.* Washington, D.C.: Carnegie Institute of Washington, 1908.

Norris, Robert M., and Robert W. Webb. "San Andreas Fault." In *Geology of California.* 2d ed. New York: John Wiley & Sons, 1990.

Robinson, Andrew. "Earthquakes." In *Earth Shock.* London: Thames and Hudson, 1993.

Saul, Eric, and Don Denevi. *The Great San Francisco Earthquake and Fire, 1906.* Milbrae, Calif.: Celestial Arts, 1981.

Thomas, Gordon, and Max Morgan Witts. *The San Francisco Earthquake.* New York: Stein & Day, 1971.

1906: Chile

DATE: August 16, 1906
PLACE: Valparaiso, Chile
MAGNITUDE: 8.6
RESULT: 20,000 dead, more than $200 million in damage

At about 8 P.M. on Thursday, August 16, 1906, a strong earthquake struck Valparaiso, Chile, leaving no more than 10 buildings undamaged in the business area of the city. The most severe shock lasted three and a half minutes. Thousands of inhabitants who were left homeless were huddled like sheep on some undamaged vessels in the harbor, where they sought refuge. As houses fell into the streets, electricity was knocked out, making communication within and out of the city impossible for some time. It was also impossible to keep a complete staff of cable operators on duty. They left the building intermittently when new tremors were felt, many of them leaving to see about the safety and survival of their families. At one point, only one person remained on duty.

Adding to the terror and destruction were fires that broke out throughout the area; heavy rain showers helped to extinguish them quickly. Damage and destruction were even greater in the outlying countryside. Fissures in the earth measuring more than 100 feet wide and 50 feet deep were reported. Bridges were down, and tunnels were wrecked. Troops in Valparaiso were called out to control looting. The outlying villages of Quillota, Liai, Illapel, Vallenar, San Felipe, Vina del Mar, Quilpue, and Limache were in ruins. All telegraph and telephone lines were severed, and even the observatory seismograph was rendered useless by the violence of the quake.

Victoria Price

FOR FURTHER INFORMATION:
"Big Region Wrecked by Chilean Earthquake." *The New York Times,* August 4, 1906, p. 4.
"Earthquakes Shake Valparaiso All Day." *The New York Times,* August 18, 1906, p. 1.

1907: Jamaica

DATE: January 14, 1907
PLACE: Kingston, Jamaica
MAGNITUDE: 6.5
RESULT: 1,400 dead, more than $10 million in damage

Without warning, an earthquake rocked the Kingston area of Jamaica at 3:33 P.M. on a clear afternoon on Monday, January 14, 1907. The quake occurred near the date of the new moon, which some claimed was the time when earthquakes were most likely to occur in Jamaica. Seismographs in the area were put out of commission at the beginning of the shock. A large number of buildings and homes were destroyed either by the quake or by the ensuing fires; the fires were confined largely to the docks and the warehouse area of the city. The event was accompanied by loud noise and a notable darkness after the shock, and the air was saturated with dust from falling mortar. It was reported that all houses within a 10-mile radius of Kingston were damaged, if not destroyed. The shocks continued throughout the day and night. Frightened people fled their homes and camped out.

Jamaica has a history of devastating hurricanes, earthquakes, and fires, but after each disaster, the people have risen from the ruins and improved the city's appearance with reconstruction. However, as time passed, the threat of famine and disease caused authorities to urge all survivors to leave the city. The stench of burning flesh pervaded the area. Looting became a problem as well. By the time rescue squads had time to survey the situation, it was estimated that well over 1,000 persons had lost their lives and at least 90,000 were homeless. In addition to the native population, there were large numbers of foreign tourists and convention attendees in the area who were affected.

Victoria Price

FOR FURTHER INFORMATION:

Davison, Charles. "The Kingston Earthquake." *Nature,* January 24, 1907, 296.

Fuller, Myron. "Notes on the Jamaica Earthquake." *Journal of Geology* 15 (1907): 696-721.

"Quake and Fire Wreck Kingston." *The New York Times,* January 16, 1907, p. 1.

1908: Italy

DATE: December 28, 1908
PLACE: Strait of Messina
MAGNITUDE: 7.5
RESULT: 120,000 dead, numerous communities destroyed or severely damaged

In 1900 the Italian island of Sicily in the Mediterranean had a population of 3.8 million people. The island is separated from the province of Calabria on the Italian mainland by the 20-mile-long Strait of Messina. The strait is only 2 miles wide in the north, near the city of Messina, but expands to 10 miles in the south, near Reggio di Calabria. Even though

much of the population of both Sicily and Calabria was employed in agriculture, one-fourth of it was concentrated in towns with populations of over 25,000, which proved disastrous during the earthquake in 1908. The Sicilian port city of Messina, which is located on the northern coast of the strait, claimed a population of 158,812 in 1905. It became Italy's fourth largest port, from which much of the citrus export was shipped to northern Europe. Ten miles southeast of Messina across the strait in Calabria is Reggio, another important Italian port city, with a population of 45,000 in 1908.

Sicily and the southern Italian region of Calabria are on the edge of the line that marks the collision between the European and the African continental plates. The mountain range that runs down the length of Italy and curves in southern Italy becomes the Calabrian Arc. The Messina Strait is on the southern point of the Calabrian Arc. The severe curvature of the Calabrian Arc causes lateral stretching of the earth's crust under the strait. Most of the earthquakes in Sicily and Calabria result from movement along the Messina fault, a fracture in the earth's crust that is 43 miles (70 kilometers) long and almost 19 miles (30 kilometers) wide. Between 1793 and 1908, twenty different earthquakes racked Messina and Reggio, although many were minor disturbances.

Quake. Earthquakes that reached at least 7 on the Richter scale have occurred repeatedly in Sicily and Calabria. An earthquake in 1783 resulted in 29,515 casualties, and another one in Calabria on September 8, 1905, produced property damage in excess of $10 million (1905 value). The most devastating earthquake to strike this region after 1783, however, occurred on December 28, 1908. The epicenter of this 7.5 Richter scale earthquake was in the Messina Strait. The focus of the earthquake was 5 miles (8 kilometers) below the strait. Several weeks before December 28, shock waves were recorded in the region.

The day before the catastrophe was a mild day in Messina. That evening Giuseppe Verdi's opera *Aïda* was being performed at the local theater. People came from Reggio di Calabria, across the strait, to attend the performance, and the hotels in town were completely full. At 5:21 A.M., while it was still dark and most people were sound asleep, the ground moved for thirty-five seconds and destroyed or damaged an area from Terresa to Faro on the Sicilian coast and from Lazzaro to Scilla on the Calabrian coast. The shock, which some survivors compared to the noise of a fast train going through a tunnel, was most intense at the northern entrance to the strait, but it was felt in an area 100 miles in radius.

The earthquake's 30-mile path of destruction directly affected 40 communities north and south of Messina on both sides of the strait. The devastation was greatest in large towns, such as Messina and Reggio. Aftershocks were felt as late as early January, 1909. The initial shock was followed by a tsunami, or tidal wave, which reached heights of 8 feet in Messina and 15 feet in Reggio. The waves extended 219 yards (200 meters) inland and reached the island of Malta 115 minutes after the earthquake. In Messina the force of the water pushed a 2,000-ton Russian steamer from a dry dock into the bay. On the shore, embankments collapsed 6 feet under water, and

cracks appeared on the ground 109 yards (100 meters) long and half a yard (0.6 meter) deep. In Reggio the wharf was wrecked, and freight railroad cars near a major ferry station overturned.

Few deaths resulted from either the tsunami or fires. Most of the 120,000 people who perished died because poorly constructed houses collapsed in the densely populated towns of Messina and Reggio. One-third of the population living in the 30-mile impact area perished. In Messina the dead included soldiers of the local garrison, who died when their military barracks collapsed, and the U.S. Consul and his wife. The last survivors, a boy and two siblings, were rescued from the ruins eighteen days after the earthquake. Until order was restored by the Italian military, a number of criminals, who were freed when the prison in Messina collapsed, added to the carnage by pillaging. Witnesses claimed that former prisoners cut off fingers and ears of earthquake victims in order to collect wedding rings and other jewelry.

Gauged by the Modified Mercalli scale, the epicentral intensity of the destruction measured XI, which was only one level below the highest measurement possible on this scale. Both housing and infrastructure came down in clouds of dust and stones. The quake immediately destroyed the region's municipal electric, gas, and water facilities. Ports and banks were damaged or destroyed, and the telegraph cable was cut. The principal street in Messina, Corso Cavour, was demolished. In addition, 87 of Messina's 91 churches were destroyed, including the famous Norman cathedral. More than 1 million tons of debris had to be removed from Messina alone.

In addition to the destruction of the towns' infrastructure, in Messina and Reggio a majority of housing was completely destroyed. The most important reason for the extent of the destruction was the fact that most buildings were poorly built. In this poverty-stricken land, housing had to be constructed by local labor using available local material. Most walls were erected by using rounded stones held together with weak mortar. Walls had weak girders and unsupported cross beams to support the weight of heavy roofs. These shortcomings of local construction had a long tradition. They were well known to French geologist Déodat de Gratet de Dolomieu, who described the poorly constructed housing in Messina in the aftermath of the earthquake of 1793. After that natural disaster, the Bourbon government of the kingdom of Sicily recommended construction of two-story timber-frame houses with the space between the timbers filled with stone embedded in mortar. This type of construction, called *baraccata*, was not enforced. Only the very rich could afford houses that were constructed adequately. A few of these *baraccata* buildings actually survived the earthquake of 1908 in Messina and in Castiglione. A doctor's house in Messina outlived the quake because its foundations were nearly 5 feet thick and the masonry was made of expensive lime and puzzolan mortar.

Response. Predictably, immediate reaction to the misery caused by the earthquake varied. The historian Gaetano Salvemini, a professor at the University of Messina who lost his whole family, lamented that he should have killed himself too. In one small Sicilian community that was not destroyed by the shock, people gathered in the church after the tremor. From there they followed their priest, who was carrying a statue of a saint to the center of the village in order to seek divine protection for the community.

Journalists who visited destroyed communities reported that the population was apathetic, not religious, and gave the appearance of stupefaction and "mental paralysis." Outside Italy, the Russian poet Aleksandr Blok, reflecting on the achievements of modern civilization, asked whether fate was attempting to show how elemental forces could humiliate humankind, which in its hubris thought it could control and rule nature through technology.

Messina received foreign assistance two days before Reggio, where communications were interrupted longer. At first, help came from a variety of foreign ships, although one Italian warship in the region appeared soon after the catastrophe. The north German steamer *Theropia* left Naples on the afternoon of December 28 and reached the strait by daybreak the next day to offer assistance. By December 30, Russian and British warships were actively involved in rescue work. The wounded were sent to Naples by ship and to Palermo and Catania by train.

Survivors of the 1908 earthquake in the Strait of Messina. (AP/Wide World Photos)

Because of the initial lack of communication, the Italian government in Rome reacted slowly. Early reports suggested the loss of a few thousand people. Only after receiving a report from the prefect of Messina twenty-four hours after the disaster did the government appreciate the seriousness of the situation. King Victor Emmanuel III arrived in Messina by December 30. The pope offered financial assistance, but, because of health reasons, he could not make the journey to the stricken area. Systematic relief work did not come until a week later, when the Italian premier sent soldiers and imposed martial law. On January 9, 1909, the army secured Messina and helped in the rescue work. Looters were shot on sight. Military control lasted until February 14.

The world community reacted to the catastrophe with both an outpouring of sympathy and massive financial aid. By February 27, 1909, forty-three foreign countries, including even Peru, had provided assistance to this Italian region. The United States Congress voted for an assistance package of $800,000, and the Red Cross donated $1 million to the relief work by April, 1909. Additional funds were raised by a variety of papers and journals, ranging from the *Christian Herald* to *The New York Times*. The New York paper devoted front-page coverage to the earthquake from December 29, 1908, to January 6, 1909. In addition, it published appeals for help from various American organizations, particularly the Italian American community.

In Italy a Committee to Aid was organized to assist the victims and to guide reconstruction. This committee included a number of politicians who wanted the aid to benefit primarily landowners and professionals rather than the masses. Peasants were urged to return to work on local citrus-fruit farms rather than rely on welfare in other parts of Italy. The duke of Aosta suggested that because of their poverty, the poor had lost little in the earthquake. The most extreme solution to the problem of recovery was suggested by the journalist Giuseppe Piazza, who thought that the Italian navy should bombard the ruins of Messina to the ground so that the city could be abandoned. Nonetheless, the population recovered and reached 177,000 by 1921. Also, by 1912, commerce in Messina reached 1909 levels and its port was again Italy's fourth-largest. Still, the earthquake left reminders. In 1958, 10,000 inhabitants of Messina still lived in "temporary" housing that had been built in 1909.

One long-term consequence of the earthquake was that it stimulated scientific studies on earthquake engineering. In early 1909 a committee was appointed, composed of 9 engineers and 5 professors of engineering. Its task, as defined by the Ministry of Public Works, was to recommend earthquake-resistant buildings, which could be afforded by rural communities that had to rely on local raw material. The committee published its findings in Rome in 1909. Like many earlier studies after previous earthquakes, it summarized the weakness of housing construction in Messina and Reggio, ranging from poor mortar quality to unrestrained support beams. The committee recommended two-story wood-frame houses with walls filled with masonry. Based on these and subsequent findings, the Italian government between 1923 and 1930 passed more stringent construction laws, which in 1930 were more rigorous than those issued in earthquake-ridden Japan at that time. The task of meeting the challenge of earthquakes in this region is not finished. In 1970, the Italian government initiated studies on how to build a 2-mile (3-kilometer) single-span bridge across the Strait of Messina.

Johnpeter Horst Grill

FOR FURTHER INFORMATION:

Bosworth, R. J. B. "The Messina Earthquake of 28 December 1908." *European Studies Review* 11 (1981): 189-206.

Freeman, John R. *Earthquake Damage and Earthquake Insurance.* New York: McGraw-Hill, 1932.

Hobbs, William H. "The Latest Calabrian Disaster." *The Popular Science Monthly* 74 (February, 1909): 134-140.

Hood, Alexander Nelson. "Some Personal Experiences of the Great Earthquake." *The Living Age* 43 (May 8, 1909): 355-365.

Mulargia, F., and E. Boschi. "The 1908 Messina Earthquake and Related Seismicity." In *Earthquakes: Observation, Theory, and Interpretation*, edited by E. Boschi and H. Kanamori. Amsterdam: North-Holland, 1983.

The New York Times. December 28, 1908-January 6, 1909.

Perret, Frank A. "The Messina Earthquake." *The Century: Illustrated Monthly Magazine* 55 (April, 1909): 921-928.

Wright, Charles W. "The World's Most Cruel Earthquake." *The National Geographic Magazine* 10 (April, 1909): 373-396.

1915: Italy

DATE: January 13, 1915
PLACE: Avezzano, Italy
MAGNITUDE: 7.5
RESULT: 30,000 dead, 20,000 estimated injured

The strongest earthquake felt in Italy in over one hundred years occurred in the area of Avezzano, in the Abruzzi region about 63 miles east of Rome, on January 13, 1915. The seismograph record at Georgetown, in Washington, D.C., began at 2:23 A.M. and lasted for fifteen minutes, ending at 2:38. The maximum activity was at 2:30 (8:30 A.M. Roman time). Undulations of the quake could be felt from below Naples, some 300 miles to the south, to Ferrera in the north, also about 300 miles, and almost completely across the width of the country. The neighboring town of Sora was devastated; some of the other villages that sustained heavy death tolls were Pescina, Paterno, Samelino, Celano, Cenchio, Marai, Castelliri, and Cocoa. In Rome, which was long believed to be immune to earthquakes, at least 50 palaces and churches were damaged. So severe was the quake that it registered in England, Scotland, and the Isle of Wight.

Many towns were completely destroyed; in one town alone, more than 8,000 died. In Avezzano itself, only 800 survivors could be found on the day after the earthquake, and the only city official to survive was the chief of police. Though wounded, he joined in the rescue efforts. King Victor Emmanuel III came to the area to direct rescue efforts. All around, rescuers were led to half-buried victims by their cries. One survivor described the area as "a huge cemetery."

Although the weather was cold and clear on the day of the quake, by the third day, strong, cold wind and rain made the already tragic scene desperate. Food was collected, but blocked roads made it very difficult to get it to the victims. Such insurmountable conditions inevitably brought some complaints of slowness in rescue, but there was praise for the 50,000 soldiers who went almost without food in order to give it to the survivors, and many of whom worked day and night without sleep.

Victoria Price

FOR FURTHER INFORMATION:
"Hunger and Cold Swell Death List of Earthquake." *The New York Times*, January 17, 1915, p. 12.

"Toll of Slain by Earthquake Now over 25,000." *The New York Times*, January 16, 1915, p. 1.

1920: China

DATE: December 16, 1920
PLACE: Gansu Province, China
MAGNITUDE: 8.6
RESULT: More than 200,000 dead, 4 major cities devastated, extensive destruction to hundreds of towns and villages

On December 16, 1920, a devastating earthquake struck Gansu Province, located in north-central China. The fracture zone ran from Haiyuan in the southeastern portion of the province, to Jintai, a distance of approximately 120 miles. The destruction encompassed a region of some 28,000 square miles. Damage was intensified by shock waves that caused several landslides throughout the region.

Gansu Province is characterized by a large number of plateaus and mountains, particularly along its southern border, and was home to millions of Chinese. Agriculture represented the major means of livelihood for the local peasants, reflecting the rich soil found in parts of the province. In particular, the Yellow River Valley was a rich agricultural area.

The extensive devastation was the result in part of the agricultural methods practiced by the people. Much of the soil is in the form of loess, a rich loamy deposit that has a yellow-brown color as a result of the high level of iron. The names of the Yellow River and Yellow Sea reflect the washing of such deposits into the water. The ability of loess to form stable vertical terraces contributed in part to such agricultural practices as were observed in the province, as well as the actual living conditions of the people. Villages were often developed in the province by cutting into the loess cliffs and building houses. Much of the devastation was a direct result of the collapse of these terraces.

During the earthquake, large sections of land either collapsed into valleys or were thrown upward into small hills. Four cities in the province were completely destroyed. In Haiyuan over 70,000 persons were killed. Survivors described the displacement of rivers, and black water flowed from rifts in the land.

In Guyuan more than 30,000 persons were killed as the city walls and watch towers collapsed. The city walls of other cities were likewise destroyed, with 9,000 persons in Jingning and 10,000 persons in Tongwei dying. In the region of Huining, the combination of avalanches and direct destruction of homes by the earthquake killed nearly 14,000 persons; rescuers reported no sign of life for dozens of miles. In the city of Longde, 20,000 persons died, and an estimated 50,000 domestic animals were killed. All the temples in the area were also destroyed. In addition to the complete destruction of 4 major cities, the earthquake resulted in extensive destruction and death in dozens of smaller cities and villages.

Portions of northern China are particularly prone to earthquakes, and some of the most devastating disasters in human history have occurred there. Ironically, the 1920 earthquake in Gansu Province was the first in nearly three hundred years.

Richard Adler

FOR FURTHER INFORMATION:

Gongxu, Gu, ed. *Catalog of Chinese Earthquakes (1831 B.C.-1969 A.D.)*. Beijing, China: Science Press, 1989.

Willis, B., et al. *Research in China*. Vol. 1. Washington, D.C.: Carnegie Institution, 1907.

1923: The Great Kwanto Earthquake

ALSO KNOWN AS: Great Kanto Earthquake, Great Tokyo Fire
DATE: September 1, 1923
PLACE: Kwanto area (including Tokyo and Yokohama), Japan, with the epicenter in Sagami Bay
MAGNITUDE: 8.3
RESULT: 143,000 dead

Over the past several centuries a major earthquake has struck the Kwanto District in Japan approximately every seventy years. Early in the twentieth century, seismologist Akitune Imamura, after lengthy studies, discovered that Tokyo was sitting on a seismic gap that would be corrected only when an earthquake of substantial size occurred. He predicted that that there would soon be a very strong earthquake in the Kwanto District of Japan, an area that includes Tokyo and the seaport of Yokohama, 17 miles to the south. Imamura further predicted that the quake and consuming fires that would follow would result in over 100,000 casualties. This prediction was well publicized but was dismissed as irresponsible. It was, however, shortly fulfilled.

At one minute before noon on Saturday, September 1, 1923, the quake struck. Its epicenter was in Sagami Bay, 50 miles southeast of Tokyo near the island of Oshima. The initial shaking lasted for about five minutes and was followed shortly thereafter by a tsunami, or a tidal wave, that washed people and houses out to sea. In some of the smaller inlets the tsunami reached heights of up to 40 feet, resulting in many drownings. The tsunami had one advantage, however, in that it extinguished many fires that otherwise would have been uncontrollable.

Immense holes appeared in the streets, and buildings were tilted at strange angles. Tokyo's largest building, the twelve-story Asakusa Tower, split in two and collapsed. The earthquake knocked out the seismograph at the central weather bureau in Tokyo. The seismograph at Tokyo Imperial University was still functioning, however; it recorded a series of 1,700 earthquakes and aftershocks that struck the Tokyo area over the following three days.

Fires followed the initial quake and in general did more damage than the quake itself. They were caused primarily by overturned charcoal braziers or hibachis that were being used to cook the noonday meal. Since the city was built largely of wood, the fires burned out of control. Gas mains ruptured by the quake and leaking oil from above-ground storage tanks added to the conflagration. A condition called a fire tornado was soon created, with a wind of such velocity that it would lift a person off the ground. These crisscrossed the city and either burned people alive or suffocated them with dense fumes of carbon monoxide. More than 30,000 people were reportedly killed at a single location, a park on the east bank of the Sumida River, when such a fire storm descended on refugees that had gathered there. Fire fighting was greatly hampered because much of the equipment was destroyed or could not be moved because of the rubble that blocked the roads. Water was not available to fight the fire because the water mains were ruptured by the quake. Safe havens were hard to find; bridges and narrow streets became deathtraps as fleeing people could neither go forward nor turn back. Hundreds of people who had attempted to cross one of the large bridges that spanned the Sumida River found themselves trapped and incinerated when walls of fire swept the bridge from both banks.

A party of 200 children on an excursion train trip were buried alive by a falling embankment. Hundreds of people tried to escape in small boats, only to be drowned by waves caused by aftershocks or to be burned to death in burning oil slicks. The liner *Empress of Australia* was able to save several thousand people by loading them aboard and heading out to sea to ride out the disaster.

The quake devastated a region of 45,000 square miles. In Yokohama, Japan's chief port, eyewitness accounts tell of the earthquake announcing itself as an underground roar, followed almost immediately by a frantic shaking. Communications were completely

destroyed. The city authorities finally succeeded in getting messengers through to the capital begging for help, to little avail since that capital suffered the same plight. A great cultural loss was sustained with the destruction of the Imperial University Library, which contained one of the world's oldest and greatest collection of rare books, original documents, and priceless art objects.

The typical Japanese house of wood and paper construction was well suited by reason of its flexibility to withstand shaking, but the heavy tile roofs often collapsed, trapping the occupants. For the most part, steel-framed and reinforced concrete buildings remained standing with only moderate damage, but altogether 60 percent of the buildings in Tokyo and 80 percent in Yokohama were flattened by the quake or destroyed by the fires that followed.

The earthquake tested the design of the newly opened 250-room Imperial Hotel, a project of the famous American architect Frank Lloyd Wright. The hotel, financed by the royal family, was meant to be a showpiece. When the earthquake struck, many of Tokyo's notables were attending a party to mark its opening. Although he was not a seismic engineer, Wright incorporated into his design features that he thought would safeguard his structure from earthquake damage. He ruled out a deep foundation in the alluvial mud upon which the structure was built; he intended that the structure should float like a ship. He was mistaken in this theory, as experience gained in the quake demonstrated that soft earth amplifies the seismic shocks. The solidly constructed buildings in Tokyo with deep foundations withstood the quake better than the central section of the hotel, which sank 2 feet into the ground.

The hotel did survive, however, and Wright's other safe-

This view of the Kwanto area of Japan shows almost complete destruction following the 1923 earthquake. (Library of Congress)

guards proved to be quite effective. They included reinforced and tapered walls and separation joints that isolated parts of the structure. The use of a light copper roof prevented collapse, which had entombed so many Japanese in their homes with heavy tile roofs. Rather than embedding utility pipes and conduit in concrete, as was the practice, Wright had them laid in a trench or hung in the open so that they would flex and rattle but not break in any seismic occurrence. Fortuitously, the hotel was designed with a large reflecting pool in front. This served as a fire-fighting reservoir that protected the hotel from the fires that raged following the quake when water was unavailable from the municipal system. The hotel stood until 1968, when the land upon which it rested became too valuable to accommodate it.

Aftermath. Aftershocks continued to shake the region following the quake. A soaking rain followed on the third day, which helped extinguish the fires that were still raging. Food shortages were rampant, and riots broke out, but there was no looting and little profiteering. Members of the Korean community were attacked as rumors accused them of setting fires

and poisoning the wells. Several hundred were killed by vigilantes before the authorities could reestablish order.

A week after the quake 25,000 people were still living in the open. The prince regent, who later became Emperor Hirohito, tried by his presence to calm the terrorized citizens. He led relief operations and ordered the gates of the Imperial Palace opened to refugees. Many of the refugees returned to their homes looking for loved ones. Messages seeking missing family members were posted on public buildings, and collection centers for stray children were set up around the city. One of the biggest problems was disposing of dead bodies, many of which lay undiscovered in the rubble. Usually when located they would be piled up and cremated. The Sumida River was full of bloated and discolored corpses.

Within forty-eight hours of the earthquake, ships of the U.S. Pacific fleet arrived in Japanese ports, laden with water, food, and medicine. The American Red Cross set a goal of $5 million for relief supplies. Japan's low foreign debt and good credit rating made funds for rebuilding readily available. The most immediate effect on the economy was unemployment. An estimated 9,000 factories were destroyed. Massive reconstruction operations somewhat alleviated the unemployment problem, but the drain on the Japanese economy was ruinous. Foreign exchange dwindled, leading to a tight monetary policy that stifled growth.

A master plan for reconstruction was formulated under the leadership of the new home minister, Shimpei Goto. Narrow streets were to be replaced with broad avenues that would provide better access in and out of the area in a future quake and also act as firebreaks. Flammable wooden structures were to be banned in favor of fireproof structures limited in height. Before these plans could be implemented, however, those rendered homeless by the quake went to work rebuilding their houses in the old manner, resulting in the flammable and congested neighborhoods reappearing. Despite the threat of future earthquake damage, high-rise buildings, refineries, and chemical plants have been built on soft reclaimed land beside Tokyo Bay. Even a nuclear power station has been constructed at Shizuoka, about 100 miles from the center of Tokyo.

Plans and Forecasts. Seismologists were of one mind that there would be a major earthquake in Tokyo or adjoining areas in the early twenty-first century. They cited as the most likely area the heavily industrialized Tokai region down the coast from Tokyo, which had not experienced a great quake since December 24, 1854. Studies indicate that tectonic forces have accumulated, and strains of these forces have deformed the adjacent land, indicating that the breaking points are inevitable. Following a historical pattern, this may be triggered by a sizable quake near Odawara, which is located a few miles south of Yokohama. The Japanese government designated this area for intensive civil defense measures. When a quake strikes, Tokyo will receive considerable damage but the industrial heartland in the Shizuoka prefecture will be devastated both by the quake and the tsunami that will follow.

Another place of concern is directly under Tokyo itself, where a *choka-gata* ("directly below") quake is likely to strike. A quake of this type struck in 1988, but because it was 55 miles under the surface, there was little damage.

Japan is the world leader in planning for earthquake survival. Disaster teams are trained and at the ready; stores of food, water, and blankets are on hand. Clearly marked evacuation routes have been laid out and reinforced against quake damage. An extensive public education campaign has instructed the population as to what to do in the event of a quake. Earthquake drills in schools and places of employment are a usual practice. Lines of apartment complexes are strung out to act as firebreaks in the event of a major conflagration among the crowded wooden houses behind them. The Tokyo fire department has detailed emergency plans to deal with a quake. Because a major quake will rupture water mains, it is likely that water will not be available from hydrants to fight the inevitable fires, so earthquake-resistant fire cisterns and underground water storage areas have been constructed. Measures have been taken to deliver water from the sea and streams for fire-fighting use.

On a national level, if unusual seismic activity is detected, six members of the Earthquake Assessment Committee are contacted immediately. They then analyze data and decide whether or not to advise the prime minister to warn the nation that a major earthquake is imminent.

Gilbert T. Cave

FOR FURTHER INFORMATION:
Hadfield, Peter. *Sixty Seconds That Will Change the World: The Coming Tokyo Earthquake.* Boston: Charles E. Tuttle, 1991.

1927: China

DATE: May 23, 1927
PLACE: Xining, China
MAGNITUDE: 8.3
RESULT: Perhaps 200,000 dead

Internationally reported as a mysterious earthquake, this tremor was detected by seismographs on three continents. Because China was undergoing a period of political strife, leaders were more focused on those issues than disseminating news of natural disasters. The seismograph at Kew Observatory in England recorded vibrations for four hours, and the seismograph at West Bromwich, also in Great Britain, was broken by the earthquake's force. The seismograph at Georgetown University in Washington, D.C., began recording the earthquake at 5:47 P.M. and continued measuring its magnitude until 8:15 that night, when the needle jumped off the machine.

Scientists decided that the earthquake had happened in eastern China, comparing its intensity to a March, 1927, earthquake in Japan. Authorities at the Coast and Geodetic Survey pinpointed China's isolated Gansu Province as the most likely site, saying the earthquake would have begun on May 23 because of China's proximity to the International Date Line. Experts described a December, 1920, earthquake in Gansu to suggest what might have transpired in 1927. Globally, newspapers briefly mentioned the enigmatic earthquake because they were concentrating on U.S. aviator Charles Lindbergh's pioneering flight to Paris. Chinese news releases told only about military concerns.

Elizabeth D. Schafer

For Further Information:
"England Recorded Quake: Kew Official Locates Severe Shock in Eastern China." *The New York Times*, May 24, 1927, p. 13.
"Experts Believe Lost Quake Hit Kansu, China; Recall 1920 Upheaval That Killed 100,000." *The New York Times*, May 28, 1927, p. 5.
"Great Earthquake Recorded 7,500 Miles from Washington." *The New York Times*, May 23, 1927, p. 1.

1931: New Zealand

Date: February 3, 1931
Place: Napier and Hastings, New Zealand
Magnitude: 7.9
Result: 212 dead, 950 injured, 10,000 homeless

An earthquake that, at the time, was the most disastrous in New Zealand's history occurred in the early morning hours on Tuesday, February 3, 1931. A low rumbling gave only brief warning of a two-minute-long rocking, followed by the roar of falling masonry. The quake rocked the district of Hawke's Bay, with the center of intensity being Napier and Hastings, an area of about 30,000 people; these cities were almost completely destroyed. Downed communication lines and railway bridges made it difficult to determine the extent of death and damage.

What the quake did not ruin, fire destroyed, and thousands of people were left homeless. Added to the distress, the quake was followed by heavy landslides. Part of a buff dominating the harbor collapsed into the sea. Hundreds who escaped serious injury poured out into the streets; others were trapped in the ruins and were injured or killed. In Hastings, rescue work proceeded quickly, but Napier had to contend with fires that were even more destructive than the quake itself. The water supply failed, and the fire destroyed everything in its path until it was stopped by vacant land. Care of the injured was hampered by the fact that the hospital and the nurses' home were destroyed.

Few houses escaped some kind of damage, but even if their houses were habitable, many were afraid to enter for fear of new shocks, so improvised shelters were hastily put up on the beaches. Numerous buildings were destroyed or severely damaged. Napier Cathedral was burned and unroofed; Te Aute Native College and the Napier Municipal Theatre were damaged beyond repair, as were some of the schools. Prime Minister George William Forbes stated that the government would change national building regulations to minimize the likelihood of similar earthquake destruction in the future.

Victoria Price

For Further Information:
Andrews, Allen. *Earthquake.* London: Angus & Robertson, 1963.
Eiby, G. A. *About Earthquakes.* New York: Harper & Brothers, 1957.
Richter, Charles F. *Elementary Seismology.* San Francisco: W. H. Freeman, 1958.

1933: Long Beach Earthquake

Date: March 10, 1933
Place: Long Beach, California
Magnitude: 6.2
Result: 117 dead, 2,100 private homes damaged beyond habitation, $60 million in damage

After schoolchildren had returned home from their schools, at 5:54 P.M. on Friday, March 10, 1933, a violent tremor shook the Long Beach area of South-

A school that partially collapsed during the Long Beach earthquake. (Courtesy National Oceanic and Atmospheric Administration)

ern California, causing the collapse of several local schools and severely damaging other buildings. Even though the fatality count was about 117, the potential for a far greater death toll was high, since only a few hours earlier, the schools had been full of children.

The center of the quake was offshore, several miles southeast of Newport Beach. Some drivers reported that their cars suddenly became unmanageable, and lampposts began falling into the streets. Gas tanks exploded, and transformers were hit and disabled. Ironically, on that day the physicist Albert Einstein was visiting the University of California at Long Beach to discuss earthquake motions with some university scientists. They were so engrossed in their discussion that they were unaware of the quake around them until they saw students and faculty fleeing the university buildings.

Among the many kinds of buildings, those most prone to earthquake damage are brick buildings that have not been reinforced with steel and poured-concrete framing. Unfortunately, Long Beach had many buildings of this type, which accounted for the large number of buildings destroyed. In May of 1933, the California legislature passed the Field Act, which gave the State Division of Architecture the authority to review and approve public-school building plans and specifications, and which provided for state supervision of actual construction of school buildings. In 1959, Long Beach enacted a code requiring steel reinforcement and poured-concrete framing for new buildings.

Victoria Price

FOR FURTHER INFORMATION:

Iacopi, Robert. *Earthquake Country.* Menlo Park, Calif.: Lane Books, 1964.

Meyer, Larry L. *California Quake.* Nashville: Sherbourne Press, 1977.

Ritchie, David. *Superquakes! Why Earthquakes Occur and When the Big One Will Hit Southern California.* New York: Crown Press, 1988.

Yanev, Peter. *Peace of Mind in Earthquake Country.* San Francisco: Chronicle Books, 1974.

1934: India

Date: January 15, 1934
Place: Bihar, India, and Nepal
Magnitude: 8.4
Result: 10,000 dead, 10,000 homeless

An earthquake reported to have hit the largest area recorded prior to 1934 shook India at 2:40 P.M. on January 15, 1934. The areas most affected were northern Bihar, Orissa, and the country of Nepal. The area of destruction was elliptical in shape, with a minor axis extending 90 miles along the valley of the Ganges from Lahore to Calcutta and a major axis spanning 300 miles. Scarcely a house was left standing in Muzzafarpur, a city of about forty thousand people. Airmen flying over the area reported seeing giant cracks in the earth through which water was pouring into the fields to a depth of between 5 and 6 feet. Several people were killed when the railway station collapsed at Jamalpur.

While the loss of life was great, experts believed that the toll would have been substantially greater if the quake had not occurred in the early afternoon, when many people were outside working in the fields. There was considerable damage to crops. At least 12 towns had to be virtually rebuilt. The greatest burden was to the farmers, whose livelihood depended on tilling the land, because much of the land was so violently disrupted as to be uncultivable. According to one reporter, Hindu astrologers had predicted the earthquake, based on the convergence of seven planets into Capricorn.

Victoria Price

FOR FURTHER INFORMATION:

"The Earthquake in India." *Current History,* May, 1934, 223.

Heck, Nicholas Hunter. *Earthquakes.* New York: Hafner, 1865.

1939: Chile

Date: January 24, 1939
Place: Chillan, south central Chile
Magnitude: 8.3
Result: 50,000 killed, 60,000 injured, $30 to $40 million in property damage

On January 24, 1939, about 50,000 people were killed when an earthquake devastated several cities in the south central areas of Chile. The town of Chillan was the most heavily affected area, representing 10,000 of the casualties. At that time, Chillan had approximately 40,000 inhabitants, and the surrounding regions about three times that amount, meaning that the population, though not large, was sufficiently concentrated for an earthquake to cause serious harm in terms of the human population and damage to the natural resources and transportation/communication networks.

Chileans were used to earthquakes; many had occurred there, most particularly the famous 1906 earthquake that killed tens of thousands in Chillan. Chile was internationally known for the frequency of its earthquakes—one serious earthquake every three years, by El Salto Observatory's measurements.

Chileans classified earthquakes into two types: the temblor or tremor, and the *terramoto* or earth render. A temblor occurs in this area every six months or so; when this pattern is not maintained it is often a danger signal, a hint of an impending *terramoto*. In Chile, earthquakes tend to be cumulative in their course. First an oncoming tumult sounds, then a slight ripple, then silence. Another big quake usually follows, during which food on plates or hangings on walls slip. This pattern would continue until a huge wave would arrive, sweeping everything in its way into rubble.

Although the *terramoto* of 1939 began less gradually than in this scenario, in general this order of events was followed. Within minutes, the cities of Chillan and Concepción were totally obliterated to a pile of rubble. Confusion prevailed as auditoriums and other public buildings collapsed, killing everyone inside. Amateur short-wave radio operators frantically tried to establish contact with the outside world, especially the seaport at Talcahuano.

The earthquake's progress annihilated not only the physical contours of the region but also its social infrastructure. Communications were cut not only in Chillan (at that time in Nuble Province, now in B'o-B'o Province) but also in the major cities of neighboring Concepción and Linares Provinces (Concepción and Talca). The disruption of telephone and railroad service necessitated the Chilean navy and military taking control of the area.

The newly inaugurated Chilean president, Pedro Aguirre Cerda, declared martial law in the affected provinces and promised massive and immediate aid; he was joined by the International Red Cross and Pan American-Grace Airways (which was permitted by the U.S. Civil Aeronautics Board to amend its schedule so as to participate). Aguirre Cerda's program stressed government spending on social projects, and the Chillan earthquake relief was an early opportunity to put this policy into action. Aguirre Cerda passed up the opportunity to make political speeches and capitalize on the visibility given him by the tragedy, preferring to inspect the damage in person. On January 26, El Salto Observatory issued a report measuring the approximate magnitude and extent of the earthquake; the recently devised Richter scale was one of the indexes consulted. Julio Bustos, the observatory's director, said a sudden change in barometric pressure was the major factor in the unusually accelerated progress of the earthquake.

Fortunately, the weather in Chillan and Concepción was relatively mild, even in the winter; a scant hundred or miles or so to the south, this would not have been the case. Thus, the location of the earthquake was an advantage, as severe weather would have decisively impeded relief efforts. Another variable, building construction, was not as favorable, as, despite previous quakes in the area, few edifices possessed the structural stability needed to withstand the seismic energy.

Every circumstance seemed to work against those caught in the midst of the earthquake. There was a food and water shortage, and a rainstorm that swept over the area about a week after the earthquake threatened not only discomfort but also disease. An antityphoid effort by government and private aid services (including burying the dead in open pits to avoid epidemics) helped deflect any wide-scale public health crisis.

United States newspapers expressed fears for the safety of several U.S. delegates to a Pan-American Highway Conference in Chile, but these turned out to be unwarranted. Two Americans were killed in the quake, and 4 were injured. To the Chileans themselves the deaths of a few foreigners were overshadowed not only by the devastating collective loss of life but also by the money and effort needed to clean up the situation. The range and scope of earthquake relief was hotly debated in the Chilean legislature, but a comprehensive program was passed on March 10. In the immediate aftermath of the earthquake, and with minor tremors still occurring in the area, many

opined that the very sites of Chillan and Concepción would have to be moved (as indeed they had been once before). In the end the decision was made to rebuild more or less on the former sites, but with considerably enhanced safety requirements for buildings and a considerably more prepared citizenry.

President Aguirre Cerda awarded the medal "de Merito" to the Red Cross, Pan American-Grace Airways, and many other individuals and agencies that had participated in the relief effort. A large cross was built in memory of the people who died in the quake. This memorial commemorates not only the lives lost in the earthquake but also the valiant response of the people of Chillan to the devastation of their community.

Nicholas Birns

FOR FURTHER INFORMATION:

Bizzarro, Salvatore. *Historical Dictionary of Chile.* 2d ed. Metuchen, N.J.: Scarecrow Press, 1987.

Galdames, Luis. *A History of Chile.* Translated and edited by Isaac Joslin Cox. Chapel Hill: University of North Carolina Press, 1964.

Griffin, Charles. "Quake Ruins 20 Towns; Concepción City Wiped Out; Loss of Life in Thousands." *The New York Times,* January 26, 1939, p. 1.

Lambert, Charles James. *Sweet Waters: A Chilean Farm.* London: Chatto & Windus, 1952.

Loveman, Brian. *Chile: The Legacy of Hispanic Capitalism.* 2d ed. New York: Oxford University Press, 1988.

1939: Turkey

DATE: December 27, 1939

PLACE: Erzincan, Turkey

MAGNITUDE: 7.9-8.0 on the Richter scale (estimated); XI on the Modified Mercalli scale (estimated)

RESULT: 32,000-40,000 lives lost, about 140,000 buildings destroyed, city of Erzincan destroyed

Turks refer to the city of Erzincan as the "city of earthquake disaster." In 1047, 1457, 1583, 1666, and 1784 this major city in eastern Turkey, along with many of its surrounding villages, was destroyed by earthquakes. The December 27, 1939, earthquake struck the provincial capital at about 2 A.M. local time on a freezing, snowy winter night. Most of the residents were in their homes asleep. Many still had coal fires burning in their homes. Within minutes, the entire city, sitting at an elevation of 3,937 feet (1,200 meters), was reportedly totally destroyed by the shaking and accompanying fires. In a total affected area of about 60,000 square miles (including Sivas and Samsun Provinces), up to 40,000 people died and about 50,000 were injured as rock, adobe, and masonry homes and buildings collapsed. Thousands became homeless and huddled under makeshift tents in the bitter cold. Communications lifelines, such as power lines, roads, bridges, and railways, were severely hampered by earthquake devastation coupled with heavy snow amounts.

The concentrated damage was in a basin (about 12 miles east to west, 9 miles north to south) that rests on about 300 feet of fine to coarse granular alluvium. The epicenter of the main shock was 39.8 degrees north and 39.4 degrees east, on the North Anatolian fault. This fault system is seismically similar to the San Andreas fault in California. Strong aftershocks continued for several days.

Erzincan is a strategically located city on the main road and rail route from the Caucasus region in the east to Ankara and Istanbul in the west. The Turkish Third Army Headquarters is located there. Located near the Euphrates River about 435 miles (700 kilometers) east of Ankara, Erzincan was the scene of two wars with the Russians and was occupied by the Russians in World War I. Many Armenians migrated from the area prior to the 1939 earthquake. Just over fifty years later, on March 13, 1992, Erzincan was again devastated by powerful earthquake disaster.

William A. Mitchell

FOR FURTHER INFORMATION:
Ambraseys, N. N. "Some Characteristic Features of the North Anatolian Fault Zone." *Tectonophysics* 9 (1970): 143-165.

"Earthquake in Turkey." *Life Magazine* 8 (January 29, 1940): 20-21.

"Erzincan, Turkey Earthquake Reconnaissance Report." *Earthquake Spectra: The Professional Journal of the Earthquake Engineering Research Institute* 9 (July, 1993): 7-8.

"Turkey: 16 Miles Under." *Time* 35 (January 8, 1940): 24.

1948: Japan

DATE: June 28, 1948
PLACE: Fukui, Japan
MAGNITUDE: 7.3
RESULT: 5,000 dead, 21,750 injured, over 39,000 homes destroyed

On June 28, 1948, as postwar reconstruction was getting under way in the city of Fukui, 250 miles west of Tokyo on the western side of the island of Honshū, the city was demolished by a massive earthquake that started at 5:13 in the afternoon. The quake, which left around 5,000 dead and which destroyed more than 39,000 homes, was the first natural disaster to strike postwar Japan.

The Daiwa department store in Fukui, Japan, is left in ruins after a 7.3-magnitude earthquake. (AP/Wide World Photos)

Fukui is subject to earthquakes, as is all of Japan, because the country lies in a region where three of the earth's tectonic plates come together, causing earthquakes when they meet. Within seconds after the first tremor, all communication lines were down. Highways were blocked by huge piles of rubble that rose and fell as the convulsions continued. Even many of the modern steel and concrete buildings that had survived bomb attacks during World War II toppled.

People were seen carrying dead family members on their backs, with children clinging to their parents. Beneath the rubble there were cracks in the earth 1.5 feet wide. Streetcar tracks buckled into various grotesque shapes. The water supply was cut off, leaving water from a moat around a local castle as the lone source.

The time of the earthquake affected the amount of damage by fire. As suppertime approached, almost every house had charcoal-filled stoves burning for meal preparation; when the quake hit, houses became like kindling wood as overturned stoves touched off fires. After a reporter who happened to be on assignment for another purpose saw the devastation, especially that from fire, he initiated a campaign to promote the storage of earthquake kits containing an ax, crowbar, and wire cutters; families were urged to keep these kits in a familiar place outside their home.

Victoria Price

For Further Information:
Mydans, Carl. "Worse than B-20's." *Time*, July 12, 1948, 24.

"Silk to Cinders." *Newsweek*, July 12, 1948, 37.

Walker, Bryce, et al. *Planet Earth: Earthquake.* Alexandria, Va.: Time-Life Books, 1982.

1949: Ecuador

Date: August 5, 1949
Place: Ecuador, especially the towns of Guano, Pelileo, Patate, and Pillaro
Magnitude: 6.8
Result: 6,000 dead, 20,000 injured

On Friday, August 5, 1949, a severe earthquake struck an area of Ecuador extending 1,500 square miles along the slopes of the Andes Mountains approximately 100 miles south of Quito, the capital. The most devastated area was the rich farming and industrial area in the central portion of the country.

Hardest hit were the towns of Guano, Pelileo, Patate, and Pillaro, all of which practically disappeared in the devastation. In Pelileo, a town of 3,500 residents, only 300 survived, while not a single house was left standing. A landslide blocked a drainage canal in the town, resulting in flooding that drowned many of the residents. In Patate, over 1,000 people were killed. In the town of Ambato, approximately 450 people were killed and 90 percent of the buildings were destroyed or made unusable, including 5 textile mills.

The population of the area prior to the quake was approximately 300,000; about one-third of this population was rendered homeless. Property damage exceeded $20 million. Compounding the tragedy was the crash of a Shell Oil Company plane that was carrying rescue workers to the scene, resulting in 34 deaths.

Richard Adler

For Further Information:
"1,400 Dead in Ecuador Earthquake; New Shocks Cause Panic in Ambato." *The New York Times,* August 7, 1949, p. 1.

Time 54, no. 7 (August 15, 1949): 27.

1950: India

Date: August 15, 1950
Place: Assam, India
Magnitude: 8.7
Result: 30,000 dead, over $2.5 million in damage

The people of Assam awakened on August 15, 1950, anticipating the celebration of their third year of independence from Great Britain; little did they realize that the day would become unforgettable for a very different reason. When the earthquake struck at 7:40 P.M. in northeastern India, in the Himalayan villages in the states of Assam and West Bengal, the Darjeeling tea country, seismographs were so severely jarred that scientists in Japan, the United States, and Venezuela were unable to determine where the quake had originated. The only earthquake to date that had been more violent took place in 1897, ironically also in Assam.

Trying to piece together the details was made all the more difficult because telephone and telegraph lines were down. The only thing that kept the death toll down was the fact that the area was sparsely populated—little comfort to over 2,000 who lost their homes and suffered severe property damage. The earth opened and swallowed up many towns completely, while other villages were flooded from torrential rains and huge fissures in the ground. Shipping on the lower Brahmaputra River was interrupted by a tide of tens of thousands of uprooted trees and the bodies of dead and dying fish, elephants, tigers, and other wild animals. Landslides dammed up the river up in the mountain areas. The Indian air force sent bombers in to free the dams, but before they could do so, the water burst free and floodwater inundated vast stretches of land. Thousands of people, as well as cattle, were marooned in the flooded areas.

Brahman priests conducted ceremonies of propitiation to the god of destruction and to the goddess of the earth. Peasants were reported to have sat, numb with sleeplessness and terror, watching glasses half-filled with water for signs of more tremors, which continued for four more days.

Victoria Price

FOR FURTHER INFORMATION:
"Record Quake in Assam." *Science News Letter,* August 26, 1950, 132.
Richter, Charles F. *Elementary Seismology.* San Francisco: W. H. Freeman, 1958.

1952: Kern County Earthquake

DATE: July 21, 1952
PLACE: Kern County, California
MAGNITUDE: 7.5
RESULT: 14 dead, millions of dollars in damages

The second strongest earthquake of the twentieth century in California when it occurred, this tremor affected 100,000 square miles. Beginning at 4:52 A.M. Pacific Daylight Time, the earthquake's epicenter

was 75 miles north of Los Angeles in Tehachapi, a mountain town with 2,000 residents. Some seismologists thought that the Garlock fault slipped to initiate the earthquake, while other scientists believed a smaller fault caused the tremors. Witnesses said that the earthquake rocked Tehachapi, causing buildings to collapse along the town's main street. Most of the casualties were found in the rubble of these structures.

Damage totaling an estimated $2.5 million included shattered windows, broken chimneys, and chipped plaster. Landslides coated Highway 99, a crucial trucking route. A railroad tunnel caved in soon after a passenger train with 150 people aboard roared through it, and three other tunnels were damaged. Inmates at the Tehachapi Prison for Women were housed in tents while inspectors examined the prison's structure. The earthen dam that protected the aqueduct that was Los Angeles's primary water source was cracked. The earthquake also triggered a fire, igniting at an oil refinery near Bakersfield.

Elizabeth D. Schafer

FOR FURTHER INFORMATION:
"California Feels Steady Tremors." *The New York Times,* July 23, 1952, p. 8.
"11 Killed by Quake; Three-State Area on Coast Shaken." *The New York Times,* July 22, 1952, pp. 1, 9.

1954: Algeria

DATE: September 9, 1954
PLACE: Algeria, especially the town of Orleansville
MAGNITUDE: 6.8
RESULT: 1,600 dead, more than 5,000 injured

The rich land with its beautiful gardens in the Cheliff River Valley of Algeria hides the bedrock underneath. Because Algeria is located in an area that averages some 45 shocks each year, many people pay little attention to the tremors, but at 1:07 on the morning of September 9, such a strong convulsion occurred that, in only twelve seconds, the principal town of Orleansville and much of its valley was a mass of rubble, wreckage, and floodwater.

Orleansville, a trade center of 32,500, was built on the site of an ancient Roman city. When the earthquake struck, 35 construction workers were asleep on the unfinished third floor of the latest building to be constructed in the city; the building and the workers alike were hurled to the ground into a mass of destruction, as if they were a deck of cards thrown into the air. Near the construction site, the Cathedral of St. Peter and St. Paul toppled over, and its steeple bell bounced into piles of rubble, while a statue of the Virgin Mary stood beside a cross almost unhurt after falling 6 feet.

Army barracks, a sports stadium, the police headquarters, a hospital, a prison, and the post office all fell down like children's building logs being knocked over. The desk register of hotel guests in a palatial hotel became a death toll list when the hotel swayed and plunged downward. A shepherd outside the city reported that he saw the earth opening up all around him and his sheep disappearing into the enormous crevices in the earth. With a broken rib, he crawled home to find his entire family crushed in the ruins of their cottage.

The area worst hit extended from Orleansville 24 miles to the port city of Tenes on the Mediterranean; from there it extended about 50 miles east to Miliana. At least 10,000 French and Algerians were left homeless. Vauban, a town of 2,000 people 15 miles east of Orleansville, was demolished. Following the initial quake, there were aftershocks on September 9, 10, and 16.

Victoria Price

FOR FURTHER INFORMATION:
"Algeria: Twelve Seconds." *Time* 64 (September 20, 1954): 36.
"Algerian Catastrophe." *Life* 37 (September 20, 1954): 41.

1957: Iran

DATE: July 2, 1957
PLACE: Northern Iran
MAGNITUDE: 7.4
RESULT: More than 2,000 dead, at least 5,000 injured, estimated $12.5 million in damage

On July 2, 1957, for 250 miles on either side of the stately peak of the 18,600-foot-high Mount Dema-

vend in the Elburz range north of Tehran, the earth shuddered and heaved in a devastating earthquake that destroyed more than 120 towns and villages over an area of more than 50,000 square miles. The arc of destruction reached from Mianch, near the Soviet border in Azerbaijan in the northwest, to Veramin, south of Tehran, and to Gurgan, near the Soviet frontier in the northeast.

The region is both a winter and a summer resort area. Communications were disrupted, a network of irrigation canals became blocked, and sliding earth made roads impassable. In two villages alone, rescue workers on horseback and on foot found more than 400 bodies. When word reached Shah Mohammad Reza Pahlavi, he ordered all-out relief efforts to be made and returned home with Queen Soraya from a vacation in Switzerland. In addition to homelessness, hunger, thirst, and disease, the situation was made even worse by the presence of packs of maddened, hungry wolves.

Victoria Price

FOR FURTHER INFORMATION:
"Shah Back to Aid Victims of Quake." *The New York Times,* July 13, 1957, p. 4.

1960: Morocco

DATE: February 29, 1960
PLACE: Agadir, Morocco
MAGNITUDE: 5.9
RESULT: 12,500 dead, city reduced to ruins, area abandoned

On Monday, February 29, 1960, a devastating series of earthquakes occurred under Agadir, Morocco, a resort and port city on the Atlantic coast. Two earthquakes occurred approximately one hour apart, the first lasting approximately twelve seconds and the second a slightly shorter period of time.

Agadir had been a sprawling city with a population of 45,000 people. It lay on a bay, with gentle rolling hills rising farther inland. The Atlas Mountains lay to the south. The warm winter temperatures made the city an ideal resort for visiting tourists. Many of the inhabitants worked in small factories, metalworks, or fish canneries. The presence of small industry was a

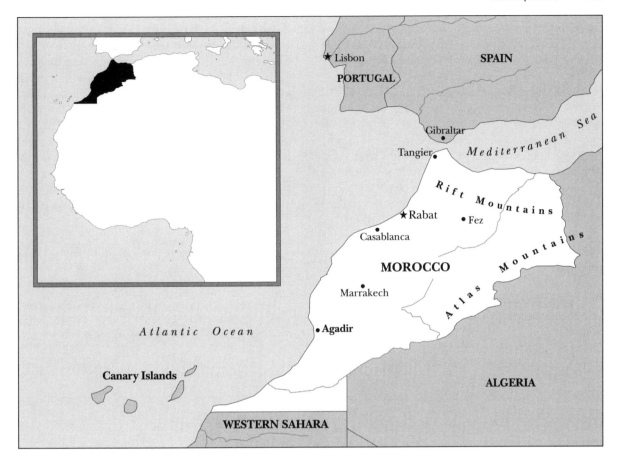

major cause for the growth of the population from 6,000 people only three decades earlier. As a port city, Agadir was a major shipping point for products mined in the Atlas Mountains and the sardines collected from the ocean.

Prior to the earthquake, Agadir's most important historical reference was as the site at which a world war had nearly been triggered. In 1911, competition over spheres of influence had resulted in the dispatch to Agadir of the warship *Panther* by William II of Germany. In response, France was prepared to send troops into Agadir. Only a compromise through British pressure averted war.

"Mild" earthquakes were not unknown in the area; in fact, two small but noticeable tremors had occurred one week earlier. However, severe earthquakes had never been known to occur in that region of northern Africa. The only earthquake remotely comparable to that in Agadir had occurred in 1954 in Orleansville, Algeria, situated at the opposite end of the Atlas Mountains.

At 11:49 P.M. on February 29, a major earthquake lasting approximately twelve seconds shifted the earth under Agadir by more than 4 feet. In that span of time, over 70 percent of the city was destroyed. A second earthquake occurred about one hour later, resulting in additional devastation. Compounding the severity of the disaster was a tsunami generated in the Atlantic Ocean, which swept 300 yards into the city. It was believed the tsunami was triggered by a "turbidity current," an undersea landslide, which had been triggered by the quake. The city was left in total darkness and without any telephone or electrical service.

At daybreak, the level of the disaster became apparent. In the Casbah, every building had collapsed, killing over two-thirds of the 2,500 inhabitants. The mosque in the Casbah was destroyed, leaving only the minaret standing. The old Moroccan quarter known as Tal Borj was similarly destroyed. The Jewish population of Agadir was devastated, with 1,500 of the city's 2,200 Jewish inhabitants killed. At least 50 tourists were killed when the Es Saada Hotel, lying on the edge of the European quarter of the city and described as the most luxurious building in Agadir, collapsed. Of the 3 Americans killed in the earthquake, 2 were victims of the hotel's collapse.

Accounts of the earthquake describe a night of terror followed by an equally terrifying day. Screams and shouting could be heard under the debris of collapsed buildings. Huge fires were triggered in portions of the city, burning alive many who were trapped in the wreckage. One description reported by the pilot of a relief plane that flew over the city said it looked like a "giant foot" had squashed the city flat.

The absence of any history of major earthquakes in the region had resulted in little reinforcement added to the modern buildings that had risen since the 1930's. Exceptions were found in the modern tourist hotels that had been built in the city. Except for the Es Saada Hotel, most of the tourist hotels withstood the earthquake without major structural damage.

At daybreak, the survivors of the city headed inland to other villages. Hundreds of people lined the roads out of the city, the survivors walking "as if in a daze." A French naval base that lay approximately 4 miles south of the city, and which was untouched by the earthquake, served as a camp for the fleeing inhabitants. The United States began an airlift of the injured to the air bases at Benguérir and Nouaseur, northeast of Agadir.

The Moroccan government and its ruler, King Mohammed V, divided the city into ten sections, with a government official in charge of digging out the debris for each section. French sailors from the nearby base brought fire-fighting equipment, replacing the equipment destroyed in the quake. The United States sent transport planes and bulldozers from bases in Europe. A cruiser, the *Newport News*, was dispatched with emergency food and medical supplies. A recovery team was also sent from the American base at Kenitra. By noon the next day, American flights of injured to the French base had to be stopped. The base had only a single landing strip, and thirty-five planes were already crowded onto the field there. By the second day, 150 American relief flights had evacuated over 2,000 injured people to several additional bases.

As the days passed, the danger of disease began to increase. Many of the dead were buried in mass graves. American Army engineers dug a large trench 100 feet in length, while Moroccan troops rolled or bulldozed the bodies into the grave. Antiseptic masks were distributed to the relief workers, and the Moroccan army began a campaign of spraying dichloro-diphenyl-trichloroethane (DDT) in the hardest hit areas. A complicating factor was the insistence by Muslim Imams (religious leaders) that the bodies be close to the ground surface, increasing the danger of disease. As a result, the bodies were sprinkled with lime prior to being covered with dirt. The precise number of dead was unclear, with estimates ranging from 8,000 to nearly 13,000.

Richard Adler

FOR FURTHER INFORMATION:

"Agadir Working to Bar Epidemic." *The New York Times*, March 4, 1960, p. 4.

Howe, Marvine. "1,000 Feared Dead as Quakes Wreck Moroccan Resort." *The New York Times*, March 2, 1960, p. 1.

Time 75, no. 11 (March 14, 1960): 26-27.

1960: Chile

DATE: May 21-30, 1960
PLACE: Valdivia and Puerto Montt, Chile
MAGNITUDE: 8.5
RESULT: More than 5,000 dead, more than 25,000 injured, more than 2 million homeless, about $550 million in damage

Located in southern Chile between the high, rugged Andes Mountains and the great ocean depths of the Peru-Chile trench, the cities of Valdivia and Puerto Montt were rocked by a major foreshock on May 21, 1960. On May 22, another foreshock shook the towns. Only seconds later, as walls were still crumbling down from the foreshock, the largest earthquake ever instrumentally recorded was initiated. For four minutes, the quake intensified. Then, for an instant, the shaking seemed to slacken, but it again increased with tremendous force. Finally, after seven minutes of shaking, the tremor stopped. At its peak, at about 3:11 P.M., the principal quake measured an astounding 8.5 on the Richter scale, which yields a moment magnitude value of 9.5. By contrast, the moment magnitude calculations for the 1906 San Francisco earthquake produced a magnitude of 7.9. After the main quake on May 22, significant aftershocks were still being recorded by May 30, and surface waves generated by the quake were being recorded thirty days after the main event. The earth was literally ringing like a bell for over a month.

The Chilean earthquake of 1960 was caused by a jerking downward movement of the Nazca oceanic plate beneath the continental South American Plate. Over a period of many days, this movement involved an area of approximately 620 miles in length by 180 miles in width between the two plates, an area almost the size of the state of California. It is estimated that the Nazca Plate slid 50 feet beneath South America during that time. The epicenter for the earthquake was located approximately 100 miles off the coast of Chile. The focal depth was estimated to be 20 miles below sea level.

About thirty minutes prior to the main quake, a large foreshock had sent most of the alarmed people out into the streets. As the people were still milling about, discussing the terror of the foreshock and calming their jitters, the main shock arrived and collapsed most of their homes. Because most of the buildings and homes were vacated, many lives were saved.

The earthquake was devastating to the southwestern coast of Chile. The people were not ready for such a large earthquake, and most buildings had not been built to withstand such great forces. Coastal towns, particularly Valdivia and Puerto Montt, suffered enormous damage because of their proximity to the center of the quake. Huge landslides and massive flows of earthen debris and rock tumbled down the mountain slopes. Some large landslides changed the course of major rivers or dammed them, creating new lakes. Land along the coast, especially in the port city of Puerto Montt, settled as a result of the ground movement during the quake, flooding this land with ocean water.

Being familiar with earthquake events, many Chileans headed for high ground in anticipation of a tsunami. About fifteen minutes after the main earthquake, the ocean rapidly rose, reaching 15 feet above sea level. Then the water quickly retreated with an incredible hissing and gurgling noise, dragging collapsed homes, buildings, and boats into the ocean. At about 4:20 P.M., the second tsunami arrived along the Chilean coast with a speed of 125 miles per hour and waves reaching 26 feet high. Passengers who had taken to small boats to escape the shaking of the earthquake were crushed, and any coastal buildings still standing were wrecked. The third tsunami wave rose over 35 feet high but traveled at only about 60 miles per hour. These tsunamis took more than 1,000 Chilean lives.

Not only did the 1960 quake devastate over 600 miles of Chilean coastline from Concepción on the Chilean coast to the south end of Isla Chiloé, but it also sent an oceanwide tsunami racing across the Pacific at speeds of up to 500 miles per hour. Due to the Chilean earthquake, the ocean floor had shifted, producing enormous ripples in every direction. From the time that the first foreshocks of the Chilean quake were registered at the Honolulu Observatory in Hawaii, scientists at the Warning Center remained in a state of tense alert. The first large foreshock on May 21 had generated a tsunami that produced a small, but noticeable, wave in Hilo Bay. On May 22, news reports from Chile told of the destructive tsunamis and damage along the coast of South America, and scientists in Hawaii predicted the generation of a large, destructive tsunami that would reach Hawaii.

The Chilean tsunami was predicted to arrive in Hawaii at 9:57 A.M. on May 23, and it arrived at 9:58, approximately fifteen hours after it had originated off the coast of southern Chile. Sixty-one people drowned, including sightseers who wanted a good view of the incoming tsunami. After the tsunami had passed by Hawaii, the estimated damage to the islands was over $70 million. From Hawaii, the tsunami raced on to the Philippines, where it killed 32, and then to Japan, where over 200 more people were killed. Waves 5 feet high reached the shores of Crescent City, California, and over $500,000 in damages occurred along the West Coast of the United States. The amount of energy associated with this tsunami was so great that it was recorded on Pacific Ocean tide gauges for about one week, as the energy pulses continued to bounce back and forth across the Pacific Ocean basin.

Alvin K. Benson

FOR FURTHER INFORMATION:
Abbott, P. L. *Natural Disasters.* Dubuque, Iowa: William C. Brown, 1996.
Dudley, W. C., and M. Lee. *Tsunami!* Honolulu: University of Hawaii Press, 1988.
Hamblin, W. K., and E. H. Christiansen. *Earth's Dynamic Systems.* 8th ed. Upper Saddle River, N.J.: Prentice Hall, 1998.

Lomnitz, C. *Fundamentals of Earthquake Prediction.* New York: John Wiley & Sons, 1994.

Press, F., and R. Siever. *Understanding Earth.* New York: W. H. Freeman, 1997.

Sieh, K., and S. LeVay. *The Earth in Turmoil.* New York: W. H. Freeman, 1998.

1962: Iran

DATE: September 2, 1962
PLACE: Eastern Iran
MAGNITUDE: 7.1
RESULT: 10,000 dead, many injured

The night before a severe earthquake in a triangle of hill country in the east of Iran, in the capital city of Tehran some 100 miles away there was a full minute in which the ground rocked. Before the next day was over, 3,500 of the 4,200 inhabitants in this area of the west were buried in the ruins of one township. The rest moved about in shock, mourning lost ones. Similar destruction reduced another 150 villages to rubble.

The ground opened up and swallowed its victims, burying them alive. Landslides blocked approaches to the hardest hit area, so that the few survivors with their improvised tools of poles and rafters could not reach the trapped. Many stood helplessly listening to the tortured cries of those enclosed within the rubble. By the time a donkey caravan reached them, help was useless for many of the victims. The night had been cold, but when the sun arose, the temperature soared to 100 degrees Fahrenheit. The Iranian army joined American units already there, bringing water trucks, since the entire local water supply was cut off. Many survivors left without family attempted suicide. A 100-bed evacuation hospital unit was ferried to Qazvin and set up on a sun-baked parade ground; staff worked seventeen hours nonstop to treat survivors and fight potential disease. Other nations joined the United States in donating medicines and supplies.

Victoria Price

FOR FURTHER INFORMATION:
Andrews, Allen. *Earthquake.* London: Angus & Robertson, 1963.

1963: Yugoslavia

DATE: July 26, 1963
PLACE: Skopje, Yugoslavia
MAGNITUDE: 6.0
RESULT: 1,100 dead, 3,000-4,000 estimated injured

Skopje, located in the northwestern part of the southernmost republic of Macedonia in Yugoslovia, was hit by an earthquake that registered on seismograph stations all over the world. Seismologists stated that it was remarkable that an earthquake of a relatively small magnitude could have caused such severe damage and could have been concentrated in so small a region. The region of greatest damage was entirely within the city of Skopje. About 10 percent of the buildings collapsed, and another 65 percent were damaged beyond economical repair, although there was no foundation damage. The area of greatest damage was in Old City, where there was much adobe construction with heavy tile roofs, but some of the

A weeping man carries his dying baby through crowds of people left homeless by the 1963 Skopje, Yugoslavia, quake. (AP/Wide World Photos)

most spectacular damage was in the Freedom Square vicinity of New City.

An unusual feature of this earthquake was the lack of fire damage. This was due partly to the fact that the quake occurred at 5:17 on a summer morning when no artificial heat was in use; also, the operating personnel at the power plant cut power immediately after the quake struck. A seismic building code was put into effect in Yugoslavia in 1948, but in Skopje, the lateral force provisions of the code had not been followed in many instances.

Victoria Price

FOR FURTHER INFORMATION:

American Iron and Steel Institute. *Earthquakes.* New York: Author, 1975.

1964: The Great Alaska Earthquake

ALSO KNOWN AS: Good Friday Earthquake, Black Friday
DATE: March 27, 1964
PLACE: Alaska
MAGNITUDE: 8.3-8.6, possibly as high as 9.2
RESULT: 131 dead, $500 million in damage

The 1964 Great Alaska Earthquake was one of the highest in magnitude ever recorded, between 8.3 and 8.6 on the Richter scale. This magnitude has since been revised to 9.2, making it the strongest earthquake ever recorded in North America. It released as much as eighty times the energy of the 1906 earthquake of San Francisco. The quake took place 125 miles below the earth's surface but near the shore, so that most of the damage was caused by waves heaving up onto the land and sweeping away whatever was in their path.

Reasons for the Earthquake. Normally the Pacific Plate moves in a northwesterly direction at a rate of about 5 to 7 centimeters per year. The continents, the ocean basins, and everything else on the surface of the earth move along on these plates that float on the underlying convecting material. However, where the plates come together, as is the case in southern Alaska, the movement causes the earth's crust to be compressed and warped, with some areas being depressed and others uplifted.

As far as scientists can understand, in 1964 the Pa-

cific Plate subducted, or slid under, the North American Plate at the head of Prince William Sound, 56 miles (90 kilometers) west of Valdez and 75 miles (120 kilometers) east of Anchorage. It caused the earth under the water in the harbor to split open and crack. A tsunami, or harbor wave, resulted. Water rushed in at great force to fill the open areas and was pushed up by the section of the seafloor that was uplifted. In the Alaska earthquake, 100,000 square miles of earth uplifted or dropped. Areas north and northwest of the epicenter subsided as much as 7.5 feet. Areas south and southeast rose, over wide areas, as much as 6 feet. Locally, the uplift was much greater: 38 feet on Montague Island and more than 50 feet on the seafloor southwest of the island. The Homer Spit and all the coastline of the Kenai Peninsula sank 8 feet. Cook Inlet and Kachemak Bay protected Seward, but the Seward area dropped 3.5 feet. Tsunamis devastated every town and village along the outer coast and the Aleutian Islands. Also, horizontal movements of tens of feet took place in which the landmass moved southeastward relative to the ocean floor, moving more earth farther than any other earthquake ever recorded, both horizontally and vertically. The area of crustal deformation stretched from Cordova to Kodiak Island. Beginning in Prince William Sound, it moved toward Kodiak at 10,000 feet or about 2 miles per second. The shock was felt over a range of 50,000 miles.

The strong ground motion caused many snowslides, rockfalls, and landslides both on land and on the ocean floor. It smashed port and harbor facilities, covered plants and salmon beds with silt, disturbed and killed salmon fry, leveled forests, and caused ocean saltwater to invade many coastal freshwater lakes. In areas where the land sank, spawning beds, trees, and other vegetation were destroyed. In areas where the seafloor rose, marine animals and plants that need water for survival were forced above ground.

It is thought that the duration of the quake was three to four minutes; however, no seismic instruments capable of recording strong ground motion were in Alaska at the time. The quake served as a test of manufactured structures under extreme conditions and as a guide to improvements in location and design.

An earthquake sends out waves known as aftershocks. There were 52 large aftershocks in Alaska, which continued for a year after the quake. The first 11 of these occurred on the day of the quake, and 9

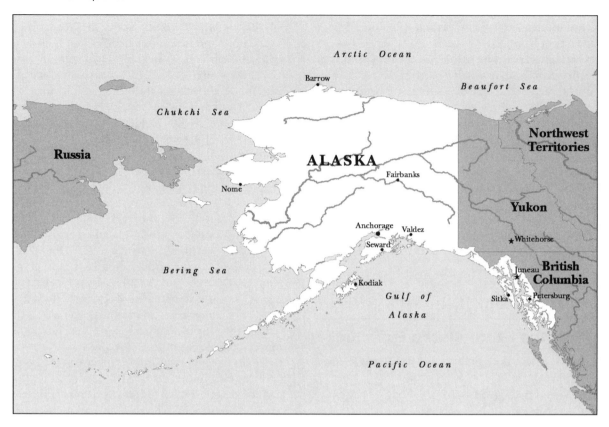

more happened in the next three weeks. The aftershock zone spanned a width of 155 miles (250 kilometers), from 9 miles (15 kilometers) north of Valdez, for 497 miles (800 kilometers) to the southwest end of Kodiak Island, to about 34 miles (55 kilometers) south of the Trinity Islands.

Geography. South central Alaska and the Aleutian Islands compose one of the most active seismic regions in the world. One thousand earthquakes are detected every year in Alaska, thirty-seven of which measure 7.25 or more on the Richter scale. Anchorage itself rests on a shelf of clay, sometimes called "Bootlegger Clay," named for Bootlegger Cove, once a rendezvous for rumrunners. This clay assumes the consistency of jelly when soaked with water. In 1959 the U.S. Geological Survey cited a number of places along the bluffs of Anchorage where the clay had absorbed water. However, people did not attend to the report, and the geologists were referred to as "catastrophists" because they predicted a catastrophe where seemingly there was none. When the quake hit, many homes and businesses, especially on the west side of city, sank out of sight.

Thanks to the Good Friday holiday, there were very few fishing boats on the water at the time of the quake. However, one boat, the *Selief,* had been sailing toward the harbor with $3,000 worth of Alaskan king crab in its hold. The captain of the ship heard warnings on the radio, but, unable to avoid the tsunami, he found himself uplifted by the waters and deposited about six blocks inland from the shore. Another boat, a freighter, was docked in the harbor and unloading its cargo in Valdez. When the quake hit, 31 men, women, and children, who were standing by and watching, were swept away and killed by the wave. The boat rose about 30 feet and then dropped, rose again, and dropped. The third time it was able to get free from its mooring and move out to sea. Two men died of falling cargo, and another died of a heart attack.

Effects of the Earthquake. The Alaska earthquake has been called the best-documented and most thoroughly investigated earthquake in history. Within a month, President Lyndon B. Johnson appointed a Federal Reconstruction and Development Commission for Alaska, a commission that thoroughly researched every aspect of the disaster. The committee divided itself into panels, each representing the major disciplines involved in the data gathering: engineering, geography (human ecology), geology, hydrology, oceanography, biology, and seismology. Each of these panels gathered scientific and technical information.

Other prevention measures for the future included the establishment of the Alaska Tsunami Warning Center (ATWC) in 1967, located in Palmer. Strong-motion seismographs and accelerographs were installed in Anchorage shortly after the quake. Risk maps for Anchorage, Homer, Seward, and Valdez, based on extensive geological studies, were prepared by the Scientific and Engineering Task Force of the Reconstruction Commission and were used as a basis for federal aid to reconstruction and as guides to future builders.

The earthquake provided seismologists with a rich field of study, but it also turned the nation's attention again, and sharply, to the problems of improving the elements of a national natural-disaster policy: zoning and construction codes, prediction and warning systems, rescue and relief organizations, disaster data collection and analysis, and disaster insurance and reconstruction aids.

There were 131 lives lost in the earthquake, a very small number for so great a catastrophe. There are several reasons for this. First, the earthquake happened on a holiday, when the schools were empty and most offices were deserted. Second, it was an off-season for fishing, so there were very few boats in the harbors. Third, there were no fires in residential or business areas, and fourth, there was a low tide at the time, which left some room for water to flow. Most people who died were swept away by tsunamis, 16 of whom were in Oregon and California. The extensive military establishment provided resources that reduced the loss of life, eased some of the immediate suffering, and restored needed services promptly.

The office of Emergency Planning, under the provisions of the Federal Disaster Act, provided additional aid. This included transitional grants to maintain essential public services, an increase in the federal share of highway reconstruction costs, a decrease in the local share of urban renewal projects, debt adjustments on existing federal loans, federal purchase of state bonds, and grants for a state mortgage-forgiveness program. In all, the earthquake generated $330 million of government and private funds for rescue, relief, and reconstruction.

Because Anchorage is the most populated and most developed area in Alaska, most of the financial losses occurred there. A J. C. Penney building was destroyed, and a Four Seasons apartment building,

The Great Alaska Earthquake caused this bridge over the Cooper River to fall. (Courtesy National Oceanic and Atmospheric Administration)

A boat beached by the tsunami that followed the Great Alaska Earthquake. (Courtesy National Oceanic and Atmospheric Administration)

which was under construction and was not yet occupied, totally collapsed. Many other buildings were damaged beyond repair. The Denali Theater on Fourth Avenue in Anchorage was showing a late afternoon matinee when the entire building sank 15 feet. All five hundred children were able to crawl out, once the building stopped shaking. Almost all the schools in Anchorage were demolished.

Railroads twisted, and a diesel locomotive was thrown 100 yards from the track. Oil storage tanks at Valdez, Seward, and Wittier ruptured and burned. Many bridges, ports, and harbor facilities were destroyed. An incredible 75 percent of Alaska's commerce was ruined—$750 million worth. A landslide at Turnagain Heights destroyed about 130 acres of residential property, including 75 houses. Another landslide at Government Hill caused severe destruction.

A wide area outside the state of Alaska also felt the effects of the quake. Buildings in Seattle, 1,000 miles away, swayed. The tsunami hit Vancouver Island, California, Hawaii, and even Japan. Water levels jumped abruptly as far away as South Africa; shock-induced waves were generated in the Gulf of Mexico. An at-

mospheric pressure wave was recorded in La Jolla, California. The day became referred to as Black Friday, because of the death and destruction.

Winifred Whelan

FOR FURTHER INFORMATION:

Hatfield, Fred. *North of the Sun: A Memoir of the Alaskan Wilderness.* New York: Birch Lane Press, 1990. Contains interesting narratives about people's experiences in the quake.

Herb, Angela M. *Alaska A to Z: The Most Comprehensive Book of Facts and Figures Ever Compiled About Alaska.* Bellevue, Wash.: Vernon, 1993. This book contains alphabetical listings of a variety of facts and figures on Alaska. The listings are concise and brief, about one paragraph each in length. There is a special section on the Good Friday earthquake, as well as one on earthquakes in general.

Hulley, Clarence C. *Alaska: Past and Present.* Portland, Oreg.: Binsfords & Mort, 1970. Relates some personal stories of people who experienced the quake. Gives an account of the damage, rescue efforts, and reconstruction.

Lane, Frank. *The Violent Earth.* Topsfield, Mass.: Salem House, 1986. The author describes the history of measuring earthquakes, beginning in 120 C.E. by Chinese astronomers. He then describes the 1964 quake. The book also explains other natural disasters, such as floods and volcanic eruptions.

Murck, Barbara W., Brian Skinner, and Stephen C. Porter. *Dangerous Earth: An Introduction to Geologic Hazards.* New York: John Wiley & Sons, 1997. This book illustrates various natural disasters, such as volcanoes, floods, tornadoes, and hurricanes, and it clearly explains the terminology connected to these phenomena.

National Research Council Committee on the Alaska Earthquake. *The Great Alaska Earthquake of 1964.* Vols. 1 and 2. Washington, D.C.: National Academy of Sciences, 1969-1970. These volumes are a scientific report on the earthquake and contain multiple reports and diagrams, the result of the committee's research. The description given in the preface summarizes the findings.

Smith, Richard Austin. *The Frontier States: Alaska, Hawaii.* New York: Time-Life Books, 1968. This book contains pictures of the devastation caused by the quake, as well as some factual information.

Ward, Kaari, ed. *Great Disasters: Dramatic True Stories of Nature's Awesome Powers.* Pleasantville, N.Y.: Reader's Digest Association, 1989. A special section on the Good Friday earthquake shows graphic scenes as well as a sidebar on how earthquakes are measured.

one survivor had driven about halfway across the valley in the village of El Cobre, his truck suddenly began to leap up and down and to veer from side to side on the dirt road. As he struggled to keep the truck on the road, he saw a dam that rose high above the village begin to collapse. He hurried on to safety, and when he looked back, the village of El Cobre was an oozing river of mud; the 60 houses in the village were nowhere in sight. His family—a wife and five children—was in his house somewhere under the mud on the opposite side of the valley. After various attempts to build a makeshift bridge across the valley failed, he had to wait until rescue workers with bulldozers could plow a path to it the next morning. He found his twelve-year-old son unharmed, but hours later, when he finally reached the ruins of his collapsed house, he found the dead bodies of the others. There being nothing he could do, the man left to help with rescue efforts elsewhere, and after digging among the ruins, he heard a sound: It was a white rabbit—the only living thing around.

The earthquake lasted for a full minute across an area of 130,000 square miles. The most seriously hit was the copper mining village of El Cobre, located just under the dam that broke. The village became a tent village as salvage efforts continued. Since approximately 15 percent of all world earthquakes occur in Chile, the people have learned that rebuilding is a part of living in that earthquake-prone country.

Victoria Price

FOR FURTHER INFORMATION:
"Chile: The Shakes Again." *Time,* April 9, 1965, 34.

1965: Chile

DATE: March 28, 1965
PLACE: Central Chile
MAGNITUDE: 7.5
RESULT: 470 dead, estimated $100 million in damage

At 11:53 A.M. on a bright, warm Sunday, an earthquake jolted central Chile about 80 miles north of the capital city of Santiago. A 230-foot-high dam broke, drowning about 400 people. Many fires broke out in central Chile as a result of the quake, and seismology stations around the world were jolted. When

1966: Turkey

DATE: August 19, 1966
PLACE: Eastern Turkey
MAGNITUDE: 6.9
RESULT: 2,500 dead, 1,747 injured, $40 million in estimated damage

Anatolia, in a windswept area of eastern Turkey, is a harsh land that is prone to earthquake activity; one villager reported that he rebuilt his house eighteen times between 1946 and 1998. At 2:25 in the afternoon on August 19, 1966, a devastating quake hit the area. Farmers, who had returned to their wheatfields after taking a lunch break, reported hearing a gathering roar that sounded to them like rolling stones. Then the earth began to convulse. First, it shook back and forth, and then it heaved up and down. One U.S. Peace Corpsman, who was building a silo, observed houses splitting and people screaming and praying.

Huge fissures opened in the roads, whirling dust in the air made the atmosphere look unnatural, and mud-clay huts collapsed into heaps of rubble. Many of the area buildings were built of adobe with heavy earthen roofs, and were easily destroyed, but many of the newer post and slab buildings of reinforced concrete also collapsed. Landslides did additional damage, as did the many aftershocks, which continued up to two weeks after the initial earthquake. Following what was said to have been the worst earthquake in twenty-three years, villages in the three provinces near the then-Soviet frontier and Turkey's Mount Ararat lay in ruins. Even by the end of the first week, damage was estimated at $40 million, and there was concern about how much rebuilding could be done before the onset of a snowy winter.

Victoria Price

FOR FURTHER INFORMATION:

"More than 500 Killed by Earthquake in Turkey." *The New York Times*, August 20, 1966, p. 2.

1968: Iran

DATE: August 31, 1968
PLACE: Northwestern Iran, especially the town of Kakhk
MAGNITUDE: 7.8
RESULT: 12,200 dead, 1,820 seriously injured, more than 100,000 homeless, damage estimated at $25 million

Iran is located in the Alpide belt, one of the earth's more active seismic zones. This huge fault in the earth's surface runs from the Azore Islands, some 800 miles off the coast of Portugal; through Gilbraltar on the south coast of Spain; the Himalayas on the border between India and Tibet and in Kashmir, Nepal, and Bhutan; and in to Burma and Crete. Along this path there average some 3,000 earth-

quakes per year, half the total number of quakes recorded on the earth. On August 31, 1968, at 2:17 on a sunny Saturday afternoon, an earthquake occurred which killed 6,000 of the 7,000 inhabitants of the medium-sized town of Kakhk, destroyed 14 other villages, and severely damaged another 16.

One survivor in Kakhk reported that there was a sudden roar, and the earth began to rise and fall. When he looked back from some distance, the village was gone. Houses made of sun-baked mud brick, which in a dry environment could withstand the erosion of time, came tumbling down at the first convulsion. The death toll among women and children was especially high. Groups of soldiers were organized to dig for bodies and to scrape shallow graves; there were too many dead and too few able-bodied living to make coffins. A mosque was 1 of only 3 buildings left standing. When it appeared evident that no more of the dead could be recovered, the authorities ordered that bulldozers plow over the vast area of ruins and that crop-dusting planes dust the area with disinfectants.

Victoria Price

FOR FURTHER INFORMATION:

"Many Are Feared Killed as Earthquake Hits Iran." *The New York Times*, September 1, 1968, p. 1.

"Worst Quake Since 1939." *U.S. News and World Report*, September 16, 1968, 13.

1970: Peru

DATE: May 31, 1970
PLACE: Northern Peru
MAGNITUDE: 7.7
RESULT: Approximately 70,000 dead, 140,000 injured, 500,000 homeless, 160,000 buildings destroyed or damaged

The scene of this disaster is known for its rugged beauty. Towering, snow-capped mountains with steep, rocky slopes overlook the valley of the Santa River, which flows to the north through the Department of Ancash and then turns west until it empties into the Pacific Ocean. This narrow valley—about 5 miles at its widest point—runs for 125 miles parallel to Peru's Pacific shore and is dotted by a series of towns and

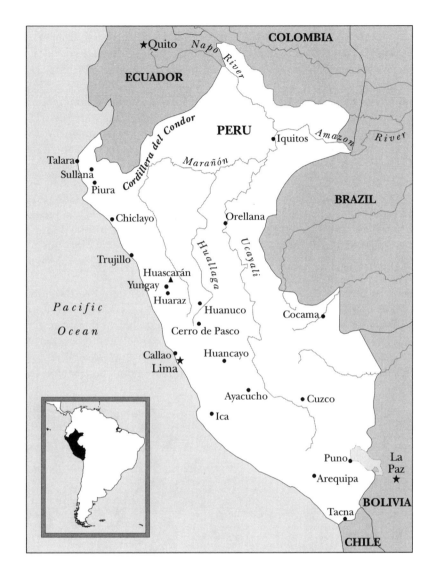

The Santa River Valley, also known as the Callejón de Huaylas, has a long record of human settlement. Archaeologists have found remains of the Chavin culture that date back as far as 800 B.C.E. The Inca Empire reached into the area in the 1460's, only to be superseded by the Spanish conquistadors in the 1530's. The Spanish controlled most of the agriculture in the valley during the colonial period (1530's-1820's), but the population became heavily mestizo—a mixture of Native Americans and Europeans.

The independence of Peru from Spain brought few changes in the society and the economy, with much of the best land in the valley in the hands of a few landowners well into the twentieth century. Yungay, an important political center, was also a leading market for the peasant farmers who bought and sold foodstuffs and textiles. By the 1960's, however, a new dynamism took hold in Yungay. A paved highway provided easy access to people and goods outside the region. Yungay had a dependable source of electricity, and plans were in place for the construction of a large hotel for visiting mountain climbers and tourists.

small cities. For example, Yungay, an old town with roots in the colonial era, was by the 1960's a forward-looking community with an interest in tourism.

One of the region's greatest assets is its physical environment. Looming 14,000 feet above the valley floor are the twin peaks of Mount Huascarán, which measure 22,190 and 21,860 feet above sea level. The peaks are prominent in a section of the Andes Mountains that also includes glaciers and, at lower altitudes, cold lakes drained by streams that feed the Santa River. The monumental Huascarán attracts mountain climbers from around the world because of the extraordinarily steep slopes that rise at angles of 45 to 90 degrees. At the base of these mountains are large boulders, evidence of the area's geological instability.

In spite of its location in the Andes, a mountain chain well known for earthquakes, the Callejón de Huaylas had experienced relatively few cataclysmic events before 1970. The three most serious events, however, did furnish forebodings of geological conditions that harbored the potential for a major disaster. The large avalanche of 1725 that destroyed the colonial city of Ancash was caused by the breaking of a high mountain glacier that sent tons of ice hurtling downward, picking up rocks and debris as it crashed into the unsuspecting city in the valley below. Another city, Huaraz, was inundated by the bitterly cold waters of a mountain lake that spilled into the valley in 1941. In 1962 another large avalanche overran the community of Ranrahirca. These events all involved loss of life, injuries, and property damage, but, in comparison with the earthquake of 1970, they also served as warnings of a disaster of much greater magnitude.

Earthquake and Avalanche. The Sunday afternoon of May 31, 1970, was a time of relaxation for the people of the valley, with extended family visits, casual strolls through town plazas, and leisurely meals at local restaurants. This pleasant scene ended abruptly at 3:23 P.M. with the first rumblings in the ground. The Callejón de Huaylas and, indeed, all of Peru rests on or near the place in the earth's crust where two major tectonic plates come together. The Nazca Plate, gradually moving beneath the Pacific Ocean, tends to push under the South American Plate, causing the latter to rise. On May 31, the Nazca Plate's movement become sudden and intense, pushing the edge of the South American Plate upward. This extraordinary tectonic shift broke off a large section of Huascarán overlooking the Callejón de Huaylas—probably 0.5 mile wide and 0.75 mile long. The huge mass crashed down upon a glacier, adding

large chunks of ice to the avalanche that, because of the steep slope, accelerated as it moved downward, reaching a speed of approximately 200 miles per hour. The rock and ice collided and shattered into smaller segments that, in spite of the fragmentation, weighed tons when they reached the valley floor.

Yungay was in the path of the avalanche. Within four minutes a great mass of rock, ice, soil, and water covered the 10 miles from Huascarán to the town. Eyewitnesses described the mass as being as high as a ten-story building as it roared across the valley floor to bury Yungay and nearby villages beneath a sea of mud and rock that, after settling for several days, was over 15 feet deep. Approximately 3,500 of Yungay's population perished beneath the huge avalanche. Only an estimated 200 survived.

A portion of the avalanche veered to the north along the Santa River, crushing virtually everything in its path. Included in the debris of this mass were bodies and houses from Yungay. Another section, or lobe, of the avalanche crossed the river bed and rolled about 200 feet up the mountain slope on the

Victims of the 1970 Peru earthquake view the wreckage in Huaraz. (AP/Wide World Photos)

western side of the valley. As these lobes of the avalanche moved to the north and west, they carried boulders the size of automobiles and deposited them considerable distances from Huascarán, some reportedly as far north as the Cañón de Pato, approximately 25 miles from Yungay.

The earthquake that caused the avalanche also produced devastating results in areas not reached by the mass of rock, ice, and debris. For example, the city of Huaraz, about 35 miles south of Yungay, experienced the collapse of many of its structures, including portions of the cathedral on the main plaza and the homes of both rich and poor. All through the valley, walls made of adobe crumbled and roofs caved in. In Huaraz and other communities, some cemeteries were so severely shaken that monuments collapsed and tombs broke open. Recently built highways and bridges that linked towns and cities in the Santa River Valley were destroyed. The violent shaking of the earth also destroyed the region's electric-power grid, as well as water and sewer lines. Within a few minutes most of the human-made structures in the Callejón de Huaylas were in ruins or covered by thick layers of rock and mud. Surveys after the earthquake indicate that more than 160,000 buildings were destroyed or damaged—approximately 80 percent of the structures in the area. Although the impact of the earthquake was most intense in the Callejón de Huaylas, buildings collapsed throughout the Department of Ancash, including those in cities and villages along the Pacific coast.

Aftermath. Seismographic records made clear to the outside world that a powerful earthquake had struck the Callejón de Huaylas, but the survivors in the devastated valley had to struggle without external aid for four days. Airplanes and helicopters dispatched by the Peruvian government encountered billowing clouds of dust that extended as high as 18,000 feet, blocking visual observation of most of the valley. The destruction of telephone lines and highways prevented communication and the movement of people. Meanwhile, the survivors attempted to care for themselves. The only hospital in the valley was in the city of Huaraz, and it quickly became the gathering place for the injured. The hospital structure was damaged but remained standing as five doctors attended to a steady stream of hundreds of patients over the four-day period between the earthquake and the arrival of outside aid.

Finally, on June 5, the atmosphere cleared enough for pilots to find relatively clear drop zones and landing strips. The Peruvian air force dropped 70 tons of food and other supplies by parachute and transported over 400 injured residents to outside medical facilities by helicopter. Later on the same day, a landing field near Huaraz was sufficiently repaired to accommodate small transport planes. By June 9, Peruvian engineers had repaired highways into the valley, opening the way for emergency vehicles. On the same day, Peruvian president Juan Velasco Alvarado established the Committee for the Reconstruction and Rehabilitation of the Affected Zone (CRYRZA), a government agency that was responsible for supervision of efforts to supply material aid and the implementation of long-term plans for the rebuilding of communities. Soon military and other emergency aircraft from Argentina, Brazil, the United States, Canada, France, and the Soviet Union arrived not only with much-needed supplies but also with experienced crews who soon joined with the Peruvian air force to provide a continuous flow of relief and evacuation missions. Medical personnel, engineers, government officials, and volunteers worked with the survivors on the necessary tasks: the burial of the dead, the erection of shelters for the living, and the distribution of food and medicine throughout the valley.

Recovery. The reconstruction of communities began within weeks after the earthquake, but the complicated processes of reestablishing the physical infrastructure, such as roads, public buildings, private homes, and commercial establishments, as well as the institutions of local government and private businesses, required many months and, in some cases, years. For example, Yungay had virtually disappeared, buried beneath the avalanche, but, within a year, approximately 1,800 people had moved into its vicinity to build a new community with the same name. By the middle of 1971, Yungay had a functioning local government, primary and secondary schools, and a revived commercial sector. Huaraz also rebuilt quickly, highlighted by the construction of a modern airport with the capacity to handle small jet aircraft. By 1980, all the valley's cities were linked to a modern electric power grid and the new highway system that ran down the Santa River Valley to the Pacific coast.

This recovery, although impressive in many ways, was not free of acrimony and accusations. The distribution of aid was more prompt in some areas than in others, causing angry complaints from those who felt neglected. Some of the materials to be used in home construction were not suitable for the mountain environment. Finally, frustrated locals accused government officials of incompetence and corruption as some reconstruction projects dragged on for months and, in a few cases, years.

Much uncertainty remained about the future safety of of the inhabitants of the valley. The geological conditions that had caused the disaster remained: an unstable land prone to earthquakes surrounded by steep-sided mountains with high-altitude glaciers and lakes. A key to the safety of the region was the Santa Corporation, a government agency charged with the responsibility of monitoring the buildup of ice and snow on the mountain summits and changes in the conditions of glaciers and lakes. The Santa Corporation was primarily responsible for avoiding another disaster soon after the events of May 31, 1970. The earthquake had thrust a large boulder into the stream that customarily drained Lake Orkococha, located on the flank on Mount Huascarán. As a result, the level of that lake was much higher than normal and threatened to spill over its banks, causing a flood on the valley floor. Working furiously, an international team of mountain climbers cut a new drainage channel for the lake by June 7, thereby averting a second disaster for the people of the valley. The Santa Corporation's duties were taken over by a new government agency called Ingeomin in 1977.

John A. Britton

FOR FURTHER INFORMATION:

Bode, Barbara. *No Bells to Toll: Destruction and Creation in the Andes.* New York: Scribner, 1989.

"Death by Glacier." *Scientific American* 223, no. 2 (August, 1970): 46.

Levy, Matthys, and Mario Salvador. *Why the Earth Quakes: The Story of Earthquakes and Volcanoes.* New York: W. W. Norton, 1995.

The New York Times, June, 1970.

Oliver-Smith, Anthony. *The Martyred City: Death and Rebirth in the Andes.* Albuquerque: University of New Mexico Press, 1986.

1971: Sylmar Earthquake

DATE: February 9, 1971
PLACE: Sylmar, California
MAGNITUDE: 6.6
RESULT: 65 dead, $1 billion in damage

A freeway that was compressed and uplifted by the Sylmar earthquake. (Courtesy National Oceanic and Atmospheric Administration)

Shaking the San Fernando Valley at 6 A.M. on February 9, 1971, this earthquake lasted one minute. A seismograph at the California Institute of Technology was shaken inoperable. Some seismologists decided that the earthquake was caused by the Soledad Canyon fault; others blamed an alignment of the sun, moon, and earth, which resulted in the earth being pulled different ways by solar and lunar forces. The earthquake's epicenter was north of Los Angeles at Newhall.

Patients in the tuberculosis and emphysema wards at the San Fernando Veterans Hospital were trapped when the stucco structure collapsed. Other casualties occurred at the Olive View Sanitarium. Freeways crossing the area were damaged, but few motorists were traveling, which prevented the casualty rate from being higher. Also, building codes implemented after a deadly 1933 earthquake in the vicinity improved structural resilience.

Perhaps the most dangerous damage caused by the earthquake happened at the Van Norman Lake Reservoir and Dam, where concrete supports were shaken off and the structure cracked. Governor Ronald Reagan ordered the evacuation of nearby residents, and 7 billion gallons were pumped out of the reservoir into the Los Angeles River to prevent potential flooding. Los Angeles's oldest building, the Avila Adobe, suffered damage. Electrical disruptions affected tracking stations monitoring the Apollo 14 mission.

Elizabeth D. Schafer

FOR FURTHER INFORMATION:

Roberts, Steven V. "Threat of Flooding Eases in California; 57 Now Dead in Quake." *The New York Times*, February 12, 1971, p. 16.

Wright, Robert A. "Heavy Quake in Los Angeles Area Kills at Least 35; Hundreds Hurt; Houses, Hospitals, Freeways Hit." *The New York Times*, February 10, 1971, pp. 1, 30.

1972: Iran

DATE: April 10, 1972
PLACE: Southern Iran
MAGNITUDE: 7.0
RESULT: 5,044 estimated dead, 1,336 injured

An earthquake victim carries his belongings through the streets of Ghir, a village in southern Iran. (AP/Wide World Photos)

Southern Iran experienced a strong earthquake at 5:38 A.M. on April 10, 1972. The communities of Ghir and Karzin, with a combined population of 18,000, were flattened, and approximately 45 villages were damaged. Because the quake hit an agricultural region, casualties were composed mostly of women and children—men having already gone outside to work in the fields. Unsteady houses made of adobe, sticks, and stones crashed down on sleeping occupants. The Geophysics Institute at Shiraz University reported four additional earthquakes and more than one thousand minor tremors that occurred after the main earthquake, destroying structures that had withstood the first tremors.

Exact casualties were unknown for some time because of ineffective radio communications. Shah Mohammad Reza Pahlavi approved relief and rescue missions, designating his brother, Prince Mahmoud, to travel to the damaged towns to oversee workers. Provincial governor-general Manouchehr Pirouz flew in an observation airplane over the damaged villages. The volcano Kazerun began erupting simultaneously with the first earthquake, and flooded rivers washed away bridges, impeding efforts to deliver supplies. A total of 1,650 bodies were found, and 1,800 people were missing. One boy was rescued forty-eight hours after the earthquake.

Elizabeth D. Schafer

FOR FURTHER INFORMATION:

"Iran Quake Area: Rubble and Tears." *The New York Times*, April 13, 1972, p. 9.

"Iran with 4,000 Killed, Rescuing Quake Victims." *The New York Times*, April 12, 1972, p. 2.

"Quake Hits Iran; Toll Estimated at 2,000 to 4,000." *The New York Times*, April 11, 1972, p. 1.

1972: Nicaragua

DATE: December 23, 1972
PLACE: Managua, Nicaragua
MAGNITUDE: 6.2
RESULT: 10,000 dead, 150,000 injured, 250,000 homeless, $1 billion estimated in damage

Shortly after midnight on December 23, 1972, a series of tremors lasting two and one-half hours struck the city of Managua, the lakeshore capital of the Central American nation of Nicaragua. The quake left about 75 percent of the city a barren ruin, brought down the communications network and the electricity grid, and disrupted the gas, water, and sewer system. Without water the Managuans were crippled in their attempts to extinguish the fires raging throughout the city.

Twenty-four hours after the quake a large portion of the city was still aflame, and many fires would continue to smolder for days. The destruction rendered homeless some 250,000 people, more than half of the city's population. Most of these survivors fled the city immediately after the quake struck, carrying what few belongings they could collect, in favor of neighboring towns and the relief stations hastily established outside the city. First estimates numbered 10,000 to 12,000 fatalities and 150,000 injured. The exact number of fatalities was never ascertained because of the number of corpses missing under the rubble of flattened buildings.

Fearing that the untold number of decaying and unburied corpses littering the city would cause an epidemic, President Anastasio Somoza ordered the city to be evacuated, the remainder of the city to be leveled and covered with lime, and any remaining bodies to be cremated where they lay. Despite the evacuation order, many survivors stayed in the city to look for their belongings or loot the numerous destroyed homes, markets, and warehouses. Because of this Somoza issued orders to the emergency stations within the city to discontinue the provision of food in the hope that these remaining survivors would evacuate, and he issued orders to the police to shoot looters on sight.

The earthquake that caused this mayhem registered only 6.2 on the Richter scale, normally not considered by seismologists to be a major quake. The severity of the quake and its aftermath resulted less from the quake's magnitude and more from its actual location and the type of construction commonly used in Managua. Nicaragua, situated astride the Central American isthmus with coasts on both the Atlantic and Pacific, is located along the "Ring of Fire," the ring of submarine trenches, volcanoes, and earthquake fault lines that encircle the basin of the Pacific Ocean. Managua, only 25 miles from the Pacific Coast, is located atop a volcanic region; from the city it is possible to see an active volcano. It is also an area of significant seismic activity; four parallel fault lines run directly under Managua.

Earthquakes had demolished the city in 1885 and 1931. Seismologists from the National Earthquake

Information Center in Boulder, Colorado, placed the focus of the 1972 earthquake directly under the city. Experts noted that all four of the fault lines located under Managua were in motion during this quake, causing violent shaking in both horizontal and vertical directions. Such shaking, not normal for an earthquake of such moderate magnitude, was attributed to the quake's extremely shallow focus, less than 9 miles directly below the city. The subsequent confinement of the enormous physical energy of the earthquake into such a small area, on top of which lay compacted volcanic debris instead of rock, assured that the city and the majority of its structures, poorly built of brittle materials, would be shaken to their foundations and brought down.

In ruins, the city came to a standstill. The quake destroyed, or rendered unusable, at least 4 major hospitals, with a total capacity of 1,650 beds. The medical system lost a total of $55 million worth of supplies, equipment, and space, making the provision of medical relief to the vast number of injured nearly impossible without the provision of assistance from abroad.

An international aid effort consisting of governmental and volunteer organizations was mounted. Neighboring Costa Rica was first on the scene with medical aid, followed by numerous other countries, among them the United States and Cuba. The American military flew in with mobile hospitals and set them up on the outskirts of the city to attend to the injured. Still, disruption of communications and the crippling of the transportation system and the electricity supply made distribution of relief and medical aid extremely difficult. The effort was not without its own tragedies. Among those answering the call to aid was thirty-eight-year-old Roberto Clemente, a native of Puerto Rico and an All-Star baseball player for the Pittsburgh Pirates. Minutes after his plane took off from San Juan airport on the last day of 1972, hoping to deliver $150,000 in relief supplies, it crashed. He and his four companions were killed. In addition, criticisms were leveled at the government in general and President Somoza in particular for official mismanagement of the emergency and the relief effort, and even misappropriation of the relief funds given to Nicaragua.

Although the actual physical destruction caused by the quake was confined to the city of Managua, the political, commercial, and industrial importance of the capital city ensured that the earthquake would in fact affect the entire country for a long time. At least 50 percent of Nicaragua's commercial sector and 70 percent of its industrial production were centered in Managua. Estimates of the monetary value of total losses due to the earthquake were placed as high as $1 billion. This was a staggering figure for a nation whose gross national product the previous year amounted to $760 million and whose national budget for the year 1972 had been set at $120 million. With the city in ruins and its productive base crippled, tax losses for the year 1973 were estimated to be $38.6 million. It was probably the poor, however, who suffered the most. Approximately 95 percent of the small businesses in Managua, those that employed the vast majority of Managuans as bakers, tailors, or cobblers, lay in ruins. The quake affected most severely the people unable to have afforded property insurance for their now-destroyed homes. Theirs was a long road to recovery.

Rosa Alvarez Ulloa

FOR FURTHER INFORMATION:

Encyclopedia Brittanica Book of the Year 1973. Chicago: William Belton, 1973.

Mallin, Jay. *The Great Managua Earthquake.* www.story-house.com/op/events/great1.html.

The New York Times, Sunday, December 24, 1972, p. 1.

1973: Mexico

DATE: August 29, 1973
PLACE: Southern Mexico
MAGNITUDE: 6.5
RESULT: 575 dead, 4,000 injured, 400,000 homeless

At 3:51 A.M. on August 29, 1973, southern Mexico was rocked by an earthquake along the Zacomboxo fault. The states of Puebla, Veracruz, and Oaxaca received the most damage. Eighty people died when a five-story apartment building collapsed in Orizaba, near the epicenter. At the time, the earthquake was considered one of the worst in recent Mexican history. Cracks 100 yards wide opened up in the ground, and buildings, including colonial-era churches, disappeared into these gaping holes. Crevices were opened on the extinct volcano Pico de Orizaba.

Although disrupted communications prevented exact casualty figures, the Mexican government confirmed 575 deaths soon after the earthquake and said that at least 1,000 people had been hurt. Mexican president Luis Echeverría Alvarez requested donations of supplies and blood to help victims, many of whom had been without shelter since a hurricane devastated the region a month before the earthquake. Heavy rainfall plagued rescue attempts, and many deaths were attributed to flooded conditions. At least 400,000 people became homeless because of the earthquake, with 4,000 wounded and 575 dead.

Elizabeth D. Schafer

FOR FURTHER INFORMATION:

"More than 500 Die in Mexican Quake and Toll Is Rising." *The New York Times*, August 29, 1973, p. 1.

"Rain Adds to the Plight of Mexican Quake Victims." *The New York Times*, August 30, 1973, p. 12.

Severo, Richard. "Mexico Counts Quake's Toll: 527 Dead and 4,000 Injured." *The New York Times*, August 31, 1973, p. 3.

1974: Pakistan

DATE: December 28, 1974
PLACE: Northern Pakistan
MAGNITUDE: 6.3
RESULT: More than 4,000 dead

This earthquake shook an isolated part of northern Pakistan along a 70-mile stretch of the Indus River that ran parallel to the Karakoram Highway atop a mountain chain. Beginning at dusk, the earthquake caused mosque roofs to cave in while many Pakistanis were saying their evening prayers. Men finishing outdoor chores saw their houses collapse on their families. The tremor's epicenter was at the village of Pattan, population 4,000, where an estimated 500 people died, 2,000 were hurt, and 400 buildings were crushed because they were constructed from mud bricks. Boulders from the mountains fell downhill, flattening houses that withstood the earthquake.

Survivors were evacuated by helicopter to a military hospital at Rawalpindi. The area between Pattan and Somar Nullah suffered the earthquake's greatest impact. A bazaar with 100 stores was destroyed at nearby Beesham, and 6 other towns experienced casualties. Earthquake damage sealed off communities in higher altitudes, and runners were sent to contact those places. Helicopters dropped medicine, clothes, and food.

During daylight, survivors searched rubble for people and property. At night, they slept outside in the frigid zero-temperature weather. A total of 15,000 people were injured during the earthquake, and an estimated 4,000 died, as compared to a 1935 Pakistani earthquake that killed 30,000.

Elizabeth D. Schafer

FOR FURTHER INFORMATION:

"Pakistan Estimates Quake Killed 4,700 in 9 Towns." *The New York Times*, December 31, 1974, p. 1.

"Quake Destroys Pakistan Village." *The New York Times*, December 30, 1974, p. 5.

1975: China

DATE: February 4, 1975
PLACE: Haicheng, China
MAGNITUDE: 7.3
RESULT: 1,300 estimated dead

This earthquake shook a crucial industrial compound in Manchuria, which was the epicenter of the tremor. Seismographs around the world detected the earthquake. Western newspapers received a message about the earthquake from Hsinhua, China's official press agency. The news release acknowledged that an earthquake had occurred. No casualties or damage costs were listed, although the report did suggest that relief work was being pursued in Yingkou and Haicheng sections of Liaoning Province and that Chairman Mao Zedong had sent a delegation to examine damage and provide emergency medical assistance. Journalists filled in details about such activities by using information from reporters in nearby countries.

The area that was most devastated was a center of iron and steel production. Experts estimated that the region processed a minimum of 6 million tons of steel annually. Tremors were felt as far away as Peking, China, and Vladivostok, Russia. Seismologists believed that the railroad between the manufacturing site at Mukden and the port at Dairen was probably damaged because the epicenter was determined to be 20 miles east of the railway. Although specific casualties were not reported, journalists knew that millions of people lived within a 50-mile radius of the epicenter. The earthquake probably destroyed crucial hydroelectric, petrochemical, and aluminum plants, mills, and factories that produced machinery necessary for domestic uses such as transportation.

Elizabeth D. Schafer

FOR FURTHER INFORMATION:

Lelyveld, Joseph. "Chinese Quake Struck Industrial Area." *The New York Times*, February 7, 1975, p. 1.

1975: Turkey

DATE: September 6, 1975
PLACE: Lice, Turkey
MAGNITUDE: 6.8
RESULT: 2,500 dead

Occurring along the Anatolian fault, this earthquake struck southeastern Turkey in the Diyarbakir Province. Between 1939 and 1975, 35,000 people had died in 14 quakes situated on this fault. The tremor started at noon on September 6, 1975, and aftershocks continued all day. The earthquake leveled buildings and triggered fires. The city of Lice, where 8,000 people (primarily ethnic Kurds) lived, was the epicenter. Approximately 75 percent of the buildings in Lice were ruined. Palu in Elazig Province also suffered severe structural damage.

Most survivors being devout Muslims, they prayed outside on the first day of the holy month of Ramadan, beginning a month-long fast, and relief workers experienced difficulty in convincing people to eat emergency rations. Engineers restored communications, and military troops airlifted water tanks and sanitary toilets for victims to use. Soldiers, armed with

A school damaged by the 1975 earthquake in Lice, Turkey. (Courtesy National Oceanic and Atmospheric Administration)

submachine guns, prevented looting by guarding entrances to Lice. Medical personnel provided typhus injections to mitigate disease outbreaks. Disaster relief became a political issue as government rivals, heckled by protesters, toured Lice and nearby communities and criticized each other's reconstruction plans. Total casualty figures were estimated at 2,500. More than 3,500 injured people were transported to urban hospitals. Many of the 10,000 homeless traveled to the city of Diyarbakir to live with relatives.

Elizabeth D. Schafer

FOR FURTHER INFORMATION:

"Big Earthquake in Turkey Leaves at Least 1,000 Dead." *The New York Times*, September 7, 1975, p. 1.

"Death Toll in Turkish Quake Now at 1,700." *The New York Times*, September 8, 1975, p. 3.

Pace, Eric. "Grim Mood Dominates Turkish Rescue." *The New York Times*, September 9, 1975, p. 2.

"Turks Called Lax on Quake Relief." *The New York Times*, September 10, 1975, p. 5.

1976: Guatemala

DATE: February 4, 1976
PLACE: Guatemala City, Guatemala
MAGNITUDE: 7.5
RESULT: About 23,000 dead, more than 70,000 injured, more than 1 million homeless, about $2 billion in damage

On February 4, 1976, at 3:04 A.M., a great earthquake struck the Central American republic of Guatemala. Many people scattered out into the darkness of a bitter cold morning. Daylight revealed a scene of utter chaos. More than one-third of the buildings in the capital city, Guatemala City, were destroyed. There was no water, no electricity, and initially, no organization to address the growing problems. Relatives and neighbors dug frantically through piles of rubble, hoping to locate survivors.

Aftershocks continued to shake the area, bringing down loosened mortar and igniting fires. At least twenty aftershocks were reported on February 4, and aftershocks as large as 4.7 on the Richter scale were still being recorded on February 10. Because Guatemala City is located on an elevated plain almost 1 mile above sea level, the foundation soils remained generally intact, and liquefaction was not a problem because the water table is deep below the ground level. However, since many of the more modern residences were built along the steep slopes of the city, many foundations failed as a result of the landscaping.

The seismological station at Boulder, Colorado, recorded the earthquake's magnitude at 7.5 on the Richter scale and placed its epicenter about 120 miles northeast of Guatemala City. The quake was felt over an area of about 60,000 square miles and was accompanied by the most extensive surface faulting in the Western Hemisphere since the 1906 San Francisco earthquake. Teams of rescue workers tried desperately to reach towns and villages that had been devastated to the north and east of the capital city. Thousands of survivors were stranded without food, drinking water, or medicine, and thousands of injured people awaited the arrival of help of any kind.

On the morning of February 5, long lines of people formed outside many shattered shops with the hope of purchasing food, but few opened that day. One of the hardest hit areas was the slum district of Guatemala City, where most of the shanty buildings had collapsed during the main earthquake event. The unfortunate inhabitants were now living in improvised shelters made out of sheets, tablecloths, and scavenged pieces of corrugated iron and tin. The capital city was placed under a state of emergency, and troops patrolled the streets to provide aid and to control looting and violence.

During the afternoon of February 5, a team of United States Army disaster relief experts flew to Guatemala City from the Panama Canal Zone, and American relief organizations began to airlift tons of food to the area. Vaccine supplies sent from Great Britain and the United States helped to avert any epidemics. Great Britain sent thousands of dollars, tents, blankets, and medical supplies to help the victims of the earthquake. America sent 20 Air Force helicopters into the highland areas to help the American Indian people living there. At least 80 percent of their fragile dwellings had been destroyed, and they had little food or water.

Relief workers worked hard to reach some of the devastated villages, while others cut makeshift landing strips out of the scrub and brush to enable doctors and other relief specialists to fly into the Indian settlements to airlift the wounded to medical facili-

Relief was slow in arriving after the 1976 Guatemala City quake because of downed bridges, such as this one at Aguas Calientes. (AP/Wide World Photos)

ties. By February 10, all the hospital beds in Guatemala City were filled, and the injured were then placed in the buildings of a trade fair in the capital city, or taken to an American field hospital set up at Chimaltenango, 40 miles northwest of the capital city. The magnitude of the disaster ruled out proper burial of the dead. Instead, communal graves were dug for the remains of thousands of victims, some in properly constructed coffins and some, as supplies ran out, in makeshift enclosures.

The 1976 Guatemala earthquake was particularly devastating because of the weak adobe construction in Guatemala and the timing of the earthquake. Families were sleeping when the quake hit, and most of the adobe-mud brick walls collapsed, sending wood beams and tile roofs crashing down onto the sleeping occupants. The most common injuries were broken backs and smashed pelvises. Homes collapsed over an area of approximately 3,500 square miles, leaving more than 1 million people homeless. However, within a few weeks of the earthquake, many inhabitants in the villages around Guatemala City were breaking up the fallen adobe bricks, releveling their lots, and building new adobe houses before the May rains arrived.

The source of the 1976 Guatemala earthquake was a rupture along the Motagua fault, which is the boundary between the Caribbean and North American Plates. The focus of the earthquake was located toward the eastern end of the ruptured fault at a depth of about 6.2 miles under the earth's surface. Lateral movement along the fault averaged over 3 feet, with a maximum movement nearly 16 miles north of Guatemala City. Ground rupture parallel to the fault could be seen for a distance of more than 155 miles. The breakage ran roughly east to west, from a point about 16 miles north of the capital city eastward as far as the Gulf of Honduras. The ruptured zone varied in width from 3 to 10 feet, with a maximum width in some places of over 29 feet. The fault rupture offset roads, fences, and railroad tracks.

A few days after the main earthquake, fresh ground rupture was also found about 3 miles west of Guatemala City along the Mixco fault, which trends northward. Instead of the prominent lateral displacement that had been found along the Motagua fault, vertical displacement was the primary feature along the Mixco fault as viewed at several road crossings, curbs, and house foundations. It is very probable that the extensional motion of the rocks on the south end of the Motagua fault caused the crust to drop down along the Mixco fault, generating aftershocks. Maximum vertical displacements ranged from 2 to 3.5 feet on the east side of the Mixco fault.

Alvin K. Benson

FOR FURTHER INFORMATION:

Bolt, B. A. *Earthquakes*. New York: W. H. Freeman, 1988.

Canning, John, ed. *Great Disasters*. Norwalk, Conn.: Longmeadow Press, 1976.

Sieh, K., and S. LeVay. *The Earth in Turmoil*. New York: W. H. Freeman, 1998.

1976: Italy

DATE: May 6, 1976
PLACE: Gemona, Italy
MAGNITUDE: 6.5
RESULT: 939 dead, 80,000 homeless

Striking during the night, this earthquake transformed the lives of its survivors. Before the tremor hit, residents of communities in northwestern Italy retained almost clannish ties with their families and neighbors. After the earthquake, many victims moved to other areas of Italy and were separated from their friends, homeland, and traditional lifestyles. The earthquake was triggered by the northward movement of the plates underneath the Adriatic Sea and the Alps. The resulting tremors were felt around the Mediterranean, in Yugoslavia, and as far away as Belgium. Monuments and art were damaged in Venice, where buildings swayed during the earthquake and electricity was disrupted.

The epicenter was near Gemona, Maiano, and Udine, Italy, in the Friuli region. The main tremor and two strong aftershocks leveled most of the houses and a medieval castle in Gemona. Surrounding villages suffered similar damage, and roads and communications were destroyed by landslides, preventing rescuers from reaching victims quickly. Officials determined that 939 people died and 80,000 people became homeless because of the earthquake. Survi-

vors lived in tents and railway cars while they waited for government aid, which was delayed. Winter weather worsened conditions, and approximately two-thirds of the survivors moved to Adriatic coast communities or immigrated to Italian neighborhoods in the United States. The government finally provided public housing for all the survivors twelve years after the earthquake.

Elizabeth D. Schafer

FOR FURTHER INFORMATION:

"New Tremor Shakes Northeastern Italy." *The New York Times*, May 10, 1976, p. 2.

Shuster, Alvin. "Hundreds Killed, Many Are Missing in Italian Quake." *The New York Times*, May 8, 1976, pp. 1, 8.

1976: China

DATE: July 28, 1976
PLACE: Tangshan, northeastern China
MAGNITUDE: 8.0
RESULT: About 250,000 dead (the highest death toll for a natural disaster in the twentieth century), 160,000 seriously injured, almost entire city of 1.1 million people destroyed

China has a long recorded history of earthquakes. Geologically, it is a region of complex tectonic relationships. The Indian Plate is pushing northward in the southwest, forming the Himalayas and elevated Tibetan Plateau, and oceanic plates are approaching and colliding in the southeast and east.

Historically, China is a vast region that has had a large population for millennia, as well as a relatively advanced culture, with recorded history extending back well over two thousand years. When the Communist Party took power in 1949 and the People's Republic of China began, a search was initiated by 130 historians to document the history of seismic activity. They found that there had been more than ten thousand earthquakes recorded in China in the previous three thousand years—over five hundred of them of disaster proportions.

Setting. Tangshan is a large, thriving industrial city at 39.4 degrees north latitude and 118.1 degrees east longitude in Hebei Province of northeast China, 100 miles (160 kilometers) southeast of the capital of

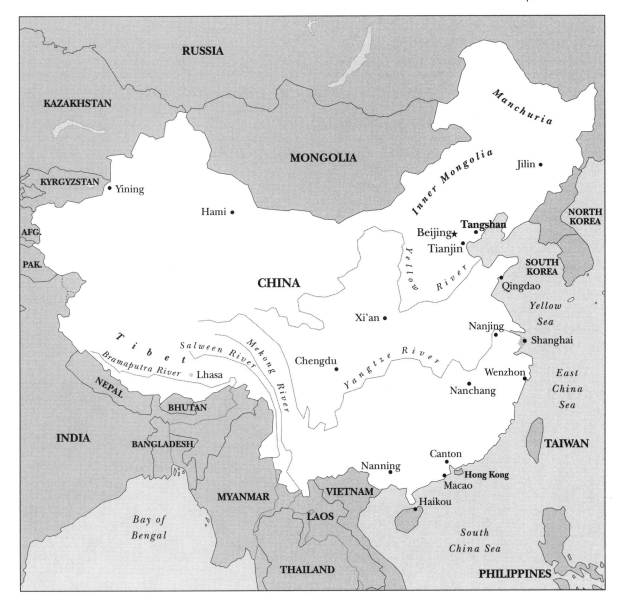

Beijing. It is about 25 miles (40 kilometers) from the Gulf of Chihli, on the Yellow Sea. Its name derives from the T'ang dynasty (618-907 C.E.) and the word for mountains, "shan." In the early 1970's it had a population of 1.1 million, much industrial production, and China's largest coal mine, at nearby Kailuan. There was little expectation that Tangshan was to become the site, in terms of death and destruction, of the worst natural disaster of the twentieth century, with the second highest death toll in the recorded history of earthquakes—exceeded only by a great earthquake in January, 1556, in Shaanxi (or

Shensi), central China, in which 830,000 died when buildings and caves collapsed at night.

The important Beijing-Tianjin-Tangshan region of northeast China was being intensely studied for potential seismic risk. By the early 1970's the Chinese government had begun a major effort to investigate earthquake prediction, using the State Bureau of Seismology, other agencies, and an extensive network of field stations to monitor various geophysical and geological properties of the local earth, which were thought to be possible precursors that might herald an impending earthquake. This effort resulted in a spectacular success in 1975, when seismologists detected an increasing frequency of minor earthquakes in the region of Haicheng, northeast of Tangshan, along with some regional ground deformation. They thought this could indicate an upcoming, larger earthquake.

On February 4, 1975, their warning resulted in the evacuation of well over 1 million people from their homes, factories, and other workplaces—into the cold, without civil resistance. A few hours later, at 7:36 P.M., the Haicheng area was hit by a magnitude 7.3 earthquake, which destroyed 90 percent of the buildings of Haicheng as well as nearby towns and villages. There were only 1,328 deaths, however, compared to the doubtless tens of thousands who would have died without the advance warning and evacuation. A later report noted that the seismologists who had predicted the quake were "worshipped as saviours."

Unfortunately, nature would not easily yield its secrets and intentions. Despite much work in earthquake prediction in seismically active areas in the United States, Japan, Russia, and China, Haicheng remained the only major earthquake that had been predicted correctly—or with a short-term notice—by the year 2000. After the Haicheng event, various seismic stations in China issued their own predictions for local earthquakes, but none occurred.

The Tangshan area had likewise been monitored since 1974 for changes in such conditions as microseismicity (number and location of very small earthquakes), ground elevation, local sea level, gravity and magnetic fields, radon gas in groundwater, and even drought conditions. There was sufficient concern that on July 15, 1976, there was a meeting of technical experts in Tangshan. However, it was felt that there was no indication of potential seismic activity exceeding magnitude 5, which was the threshold at which it would be reported to the civil authorities. Some thought an earthquake might be possible in the next few years, but there were no minor precursory foreshocks warning that a quake was imminent. There were also meetings in Beijing of the State Bureau of

The aftermath of the 1976 Tangshan earthquake. (Courtesy National Oceanic and Atmospheric Administration)

Seismology on July 24 and 26, regarding the possibility of a future earthquake in the Beijing-Tianjin-Tangshan area. While there was no technical reason for immediate concern, it was also true that an alert leading to evacuation would be very disruptive to life, production, and other economic activity in the large cities in the region.

Since the area is of intraplate nature, which is far away from the seismically and tectonically active margins of the crustal plates, earthquakes there are expected to be infrequent and of only moderate size. Human knowledge of crustal fracturing, stress, and potential for faulting (slippage, which causes earthquakes) is imperfect. There had been major earthquakes in the general region of Tangshan in September, 1679, and in September, 1290 (with 100,000 deaths).

The Quake. Without warning, at 3:42 A.M. on July 28, 1976, a massive earthquake struck the Tangshan area. There was a loud rumbling and roaring sound, followed by violent jerking back and forth. The earthquake (including subsequent aftershocks) leveled 20 square miles (50 square kilometers) of the densely populated industrial center of the city, flattened or severely damaged 97 percent of the buildings and three-quarters of Tangshan's 916 multistory structures (only 4 remained essentially intact), and left a ruin of crumbled buildings, fallen smokestacks, and rubble. Falling buildings, cement floor slabs, and beams immediately crushed thousands of people. Most of the disaster's victims survived the initial shock only to suffocate or succumb to injuries after hours and days trapped in the dusty wreckage.

There was no electrical power, no water, no telecommunication systems, no functioning hospital, no transport routes, and no immediate search and rescue help. With 300 miles of railroad track ruined, 231 highway bridges damaged, and rivers without crossings, relief could not arrive quickly. It was over a day before the first of an eventual 100,000 army troops and 50,000 others could arrive. For ten days the workers did not have the necessary heavy equipment and cranes to clear the rubble and retrieve many people.

The city was initially shrouded in total darkness (it being nighttime) and a dense gray fog of soil, coal dust, and smoke. According to the local Chinese authorities, 242,769 people died and 164,851 were seriously injured. Other reports and international databases listed the official death toll as 250,000 to 255,000, and early estimates by visitors placed it even higher.

The earthquake had a magnitude of 7.8 as determined by Chinese seismologists, and 8.0 in the international database maintained by the U.S. Geological Survey/National Earthquake Information Center. Its focus, where rupture began, was at a relatively shallow depth of 14 miles (23 kilometers), and its epicenter was calculated at 39.5 degrees north and 117.9 east—virtually right under Tangshan. Later that same day, at 6:45 P.M. on July 28, there was a major aftershock, with magnitude 7.4 at the same focal region. It finished off most of the buildings that had survived the first shock. Within forty-eight hours of the initial earthquake, there were more than nine hundred aftershocks having magnitude of at least 3.0, including sixteen with magnitude at least 5.0.

Aftereffects. A second disaster was averted at the large Douhe River reservoir 9 miles (15 kilometers) northeast of Tangshan. The embankment dam was cracked and weakened, and if it collapsed it would have flooded the city. Furthermore, after the earthquake a heavy rain started, and the water level was rising. The floodgate could not be opened quickly to let out the reservoir water gradually and unstress the dam, because its electrical power was disabled. Fortunately, troops working manually for eight hours managed to get the floodgate open.

At the large coal mine complex, about 10,000 people were in the underground workings when the earthquake struck. The surface buildings were destroyed, but the large-amplitude surface wave vibrations—usually the most damaging of the seismic waves—became less intense with depth, and the deep workings were somewhat less affected. However, there was no electricity, no hoist cages for workers, and no water pumps to keep the workings from flooding with groundwater. Remarkably, only 17 mine workers died; the others managed to dig through the rubble and climb to safety or be rescued. Five men were brought up alive after fifteen days, having no food and only filthy water to drink.

Relief and Reconstruction. The search and recovery of bodies was a slow and difficult task, with the stench of decaying bodies of people and animals, lack of clean water and sanitation, and increasing danger of an epidemic. Relief aid (clothing, tents, heavy equipment, and medical supplies) was offered by the United Nations, the United States, Great Britain, Japan, and others, but the Chinese government declined it. In retrospect, this denied timely and useful assistance. However, at the time, China was in its Cultural Revolution—a decade-long era which would last until September, 1976, when Chairman Mao Zedong died—and the Chinese wanted to display their self-reliance and not engender a dependent mentality and considered any outsiders and their assistance to be "interference by others."

It was also not an easy time for the State Bureau of Seismology and those engaged in earthquake monitoring and prediction. When the earthquake occurred, the recording seismographs in Beijing were driven off the scale by the large vibrations, and others around the country could not pinpoint the epicenter other than being somewhere around Beijing. So, with much of the telecommunication systems in the area disabled, scientists set out in vehicles in all directions to try to find the epicenter and greatest damage. After being credited with the success of predicting the Haicheng earthquake the previous year, the seismologists became ridiculed, and the failure to predict the devastating Tangshan event became blame for negligence. Anger and abuse were directed at those identified locally as earthquake experts, as if the inability to reliably predict one of nature's great uncertainties was somehow willful and deserving of punishment.

Within two years, a massive reconstruction effort had restored the city's industrial production to what it had been. By 1986, ten years after the earthquake, restoration was mostly complete, although some citizens were still in temporary shelters, and the population of Tangshan had increased to 1.4 million. Because it was now recognized that the city was on a major crustal fault, reconstruction was carried out to make structures more earthquake-resistant. Waterpipes were made with flexible joints so they could withstand vibration, embankments were reinforced around nearby reservoirs, and hazardous industries were moved outside of town. One factory that had been destroyed in the great earthquake has been left as a memorial to the thousands lost.

Robert S. Carmichael

FOR FURTHER INFORMATION:
De Blij, H. J. *Nature on the Rampage.* Washington, D.C.: Smithsonian Institution, 1994.
Qian, Gang. *The Great China Earthquake.* Beijing: Foreign Language Press, 1989.
U.S. Geological Survey/National Earthquake Information Center. www.neic.cr.usgs.gov.

1976: Philippines

DATE: August 17, 1976
PLACE: Mindanao, Philippines
MAGNITUDE: 7.8
RESULT: As many as 8,000 dead

Shaking Mindanao, the biggest island in the southern Philippines, this earthquake began at dawn. The earthquake's epicenter was located in the Moro Gulf. Caused by shifting plates beneath the Philippine Islands, the earthquake was perceived as an apocalyptic event by superstitious residents of the islands, who did not comprehend the geological causes of the tremors.

The earthquake shattered fishermen's shacks and created a tsunami at least 18 feet high, which washed away coastal villages. Other settlements slipped into large fissures that tremors caused to open in the ground. Waves flooded populated regions and pulled people into the ocean, drowning them. Roads buckled, and fires ignited the buildings that withstood aftershocks. Casualties totaled 5,000 dead, 3,000 missing, and 150,000 homeless, with Mindanao suffering the most losses. Places encountering high fatalities included Malabang, Pagadian City, Margosatubig, and Zamboanga City.

Eyewitnesses described panicked people and soldiers who yelled, shot guns, and pounded drums and gongs to scare aware evil spirits they believed caused the earthquake. The 21st Infantry Battalion sheltered survivors in its camp at Sangali, providing food and cholera inoculations. Relief workers were frustrated that people planned to rebuild on the island's beaches despite the risks of another earthquake.

Elizabeth D. Schafer

FOR FURTHER INFORMATION:
"Quake Dead Exceed 3,100 in Mindanao." *The New York Times,* August 18, 1976, p. 1.
Villadolid, Alice. "14 Victims of Quake Are Buried." *The New York Times,* August 20, 1976, p. 5.

1976: Turkey

DATE: November 24, 1976
PLACE: Turkey
MAGNITUDE: 7.9
RESULT: 5,000 dead

At the time, this earthquake was the strongest to shake Turkey since 1939. Muradiye on Mount Ararat was the earthquake's epicenter. Inhabited primarily by Kurdish peasants who were agriculturists, an ethnic minority in Turkey, this region was remote in many ways. The Kurds were embroiled in constant conflict with Turkish officials regarding governmental policies. As a result, survivors were hesitant to trust relief workers, not only because they were not Kurds but also because they represented the Turkish government.

Many peasants resisted relief workers' efforts to place them in temporary camps. Farmers wanted to remain with their herds, fields, and buildings that had survived the earthquakes. They hoped to mend damage. Their families also insisted on returning home. Aftershocks and blizzards aggravated already miserable conditions. Officials estimated that 5,000 people died because of this earthquake and thousands were left homeless.

Elizabeth D. Schafer

FOR FURTHER INFORMATION:
Pace, Eric. "Turkish Quake Toll Passes 3,000 Mark; Snow Slows Relief." *The New York Times*, November 26, 1976, p. 1.
"Turkish Quake Toll Expected to Rise." *The New York Times*, November 27, 1976, p. 1.

though some survivors were rescued eight days after the earthquake. Officials spread chlorine over the rubble to prevent disease from spreading.

Seventy miles away, Zimnicea, a town located on the bank of the Danube River, was destroyed. Dumitru Sandu, the town's mayor, described how he saw the earth move in waves as he rushed outside. He estimated that 80 percent of Zimnicea had been leveled and stated that utilities had been disrupted. He and residents wrapped themselves in blankets and sat beside fires in the streets because they were afraid another earthquake would strike. Many oil factories at Ploiesti, north of the capital, were ruined, with 2,000 structures leveled. This loss hindered Romania's efforts to secure economic autonomy from the Soviet Union. Total casualties were estimated to be about 1,500 dead, including 80 to 90 people in adjacent Bulgaria. Thousands of people were injured and left homeless as a result of the earthquake.

Elizabeth D. Schafer

FOR FURTHER INFORMATION:
Browne, Malcolm W. "Rumanians Fear That Earthquake Has Seriously Impaired Industry." *The New York Times*, March 7, 1977, p. 1.
Hofmann, Paul. "Rumanian Leader Doubts U.S. Data on Quake Danger." *The New York Times*, March 11, 1977, p. 3.

1977: Romania

DATE: March 4, 1977
PLACE: Vrancea, Romania
MAGNITUDE: 7.5
RESULT: 1,541 dead

Considered the strongest earthquake to rock Romania when it happened, this tremor was felt throughout Central Europe and as far away as Moscow and Rome. Vrancea was the earthquake's epicenter; the capital city, Bucharest, and surrounding rural areas suffered intensive damage. Eyewitnesses compared the scene to World War II bombing damage. Buildings collapsed or were split in two, and the streets were filled with brick, plaster, and concrete rubble in addition to furnishings from residences. Many people died while trapped beneath piles of debris, al-

1978: Iran

DATE: September 16, 1978
PLACE: Tabas, Iran
MAGNITUDE: 7.7
RESULT: 25,000 dead

Northeastern Iran was shaken on a Saturday night by what was described as the strongest earthquake to hit that region at the time. One decade prior, a 6.5 earthquake killed 12,000 people in this agricultural region near the Afghanistan border. The earthquake's epicenter was at the densely settled city of Tabas, an oasis and market center located on the route that thirteenth century trader Marco Polo had traveled to China.

The earthquake leveled Tabas and as many as 40 nearby settlements, killing a total of 25,000 people.

Official estimates stated that 15,000 of Tabas's 17,000 residents died in the earthquake. Most deaths occurred because of the unsteady dwellings constructed from dried mud, which collapsed upon occupants. Other victims fell into fissures the earthquake created in fields. Exact casualties could not be determined because so many people were buried by earthquake debris.

Two schools and a bank in Tabas withstood the earthquake because they had steel frames. The earthquake was felt in two-thirds of Iran, and buildings were jolted 400 miles away in Tehran. The Iranian army deployed soldiers, medical personnel, and relief workers to assist victims, and a tent city was erected on the city's airstrip.

Elizabeth D. Schafer

FOR FURTHER INFORMATION:
"Death on the Silk Road." *The New York Times*, November 7, 1978, p. 50.

Tomkins, Richard. Untitled report. The New York Times News Service and the Associated Press. Microfilmed with regular issues of *The New York Times* because of a newspaper strike. September 20, 1978, p. 34.

1980: Algeria

DATE: October 10, 1980
PLACE: Al-Asnam, Algeria
MAGNITUDE: 7.5 and 6.5
RESULT: 6,000 dead

Occurring on the Muslim Sabbath day, two tremors shook Al-Asnam (now known as Ech-Cheliff) at half past noon. A 1954 earthquake had demolished the city, known then as Orleansville, which was reconstructed on the same site. The first tremor measured 7.5 in intensity and shook for two minutes, of which the initial thirty seconds were the most destructive. The second tremor registered 6.5 on the Richter scale. Casualties were high because most of the city's 125,000 residents were in their homes, participating in religious activities.

The earthquakes devastated 80 percent of the city, ruining the city's primary mosque, a high school, and a hospital, in addition to government and business buildings. Tremors opened fissures along hillsides and in fields adjacent to the Mediterranean Sea. The Algerian government was unprepared to initiate rescue efforts and exaggerated casualty statistics to as high as 25,000 deaths.

Relief caravans jammed the highway between the capital at Algiers and Al-Asnam, and military guards erected checkpoints to permit entry only to traffic necessary to assist rescue. Searchers looked for survivors, using generators to illuminate floodlights. Six people lived on lemonade for two weeks before they were freed from the rubble that trapped them. The earthquake killed approximately 6,000 people, injured 60,000, and rendered 250,000 homeless.

Elizabeth D. Schafer

FOR FURTHER INFORMATION:
"At Least 17,000 Dead in Algeria's Quake, Relief Agency Says." *The New York Times*, October 12, 1980, p. 1.

Markham, James M. "Algerians Search for Signs of Life in Quake Rubble." *The New York Times*, October 13, 1980, p. 1.

1980: Italy

DATE: November 23, 1980
PLACE: Campagnia, Italy
MAGNITUDE: 7.2
RESULT: 3,000 dead

Beginning to shake southern Italy at 7:34 P.M., when two plates collided, this earthquake's epicenter was at Eboli, a community south of Naples. Especially devastating because it happened on a Sunday night, the earthquake killed many of its victims who were attending Mass ceremonies, including children preparing for their First Communion at the thousand-year-old church in Balvano. The village of Conza Della Compagna was leveled, and 80 percent of its residents were killed. People rushed into streets, leaving stoves turned on, which ignited fires that could not be easily extinguished because water lines had ruptured. Prisoners rioted when the earthquake damaged their cell walls.

Although Italian physicians had planned a labor strike, they tended to the wounded. Rescuers were

A survivor of the 1980 earthquake emerges from the remains of his house in Laviano, Italy, with few possessions intact. (AP/Wide World Photos)

hampered by fog and damaged roads and railways. Isolated Apennine Mountains settlements such as Pescopagano suffered extreme damage and lacked necessary equipment such as bulldozers and cranes to move debris. Almost 10,000 workers searched for people, many of whom died waiting for help. Military helicopters dropped supplies and airlifted the injured to hospitals. Aftershocks shook the area for weeks afterward; at least 200 towns were damaged, 3,000 people died, 7,000 were injured, 1,500 were missing, and 300,000 became homeless. The government erected tents for survivors who endured frigid winter weather while greedy local officials embezzled relief funds.

Elizabeth D. Schafer

FOR FURTHER INFORMATION:

"400 Dead in Quakes in Southern Italy; Damage in 29 Cities." *The New York Times*, November 24, 1980, p. 1.

Tanner, Henry. "Death Toll in Italian Quake Rises to 3,000." *The New York Times*, November 27, 1980, p. 6.

1982: North Yemen

DATE: December 13, 1982
PLACE: Dhamar region, North Yemen
MAGNITUDE: 6.0
RESULT: 1,507 dead, 1,538 injured, 400,000 homeless

Yemen was shaken for forty seconds by an afternoon earthquake, the epicenter being at Marib, located in the Dhamar region. A seismograph in the east African country of Djibouti measured the earthquake at 6.0 intensity and detected three aftershocks within five hours. Approximately 11 villages were flattened, and 27 communities suffered some degree of damage. Exact casualties were unavailable because residents did not keep population records, but officials confirmed that 1,507 people had died and 1,538 were admitted to hospitals. At least 250 children were in a school when it collapsed. Officials believed that hundreds of victims might have been buried beneath the debris of their homes and other buildings. As many as 400,000 residents were homeless after the tremor.

Dhamar, 60 miles south of Yemen's capital city of San'a, was the hideout for Communist guerrillas who provoked conflicts with government forces. President Ali Abdullah Saleh admitted that Yemen lacked legal control after the earthquake, and looting was rampant. The military, police, and citizens were requested to maintain order. Indigenous tribesmen, Boy Scouts, and refugee Palestinian guerrillas joined rescue teams, and 49 survivors were found alive four days after the earthquake.

Elizabeth D. Schafer

FOR FURTHER INFORMATION:

"Earthquake Toll in Yemen Area Is Put at 1,082." *The New York Times*, October 15, 1982, p. A1.
"Yemen Quake Said to Kill 335." *The New York Times*, December 14, 1982, p. A8.
"Yemen Quake Toll Is Now 1,340." *The New York Times*, December 16, 1982, p. A8.

1985: Mexico City Earthquake

DATE: September 19, 1985
PLACE: Mexico City, Mexico
MAGNITUDE: 8.1
RESULT: 10,000 estimated dead, 30,000 injured, 2,850 buildings destroyed, 100,000 units damaged

Topography. Mexico City, the nation's capital, is located in the Valley of Mexico, situated between two towering mountain ranges, the Sierra Madre Occidental and the Sierra Madre Oriental, in the south central part of the country. The city itself is situated on a plateau surrounded by a series of mountains that include a string of volcanoes. The valley proper has an altitude ranging from 6,800 to 7,900 feet above sea level. Its floor, on which the modern city has been built gradually over the past five hundred years, is not geologically stable. Beneath the massive concentration of high-rise buildings, extensive freeways, and the marginal dwellings of the poor lies a weak foundation of watery shale rather than a firm base of bedrock, for the city was extended over areas that in precolonial times were lakes.

Contributing to the lack of stability has been the continuous pumping of water from the city's subterranean underpinnings, resulting in a constant shifting and weakening of its buildings' foundations. Structural engineers have developed techniques utilizing permanent hydraulic jacks to keep new high-rises level, but much of the older construction must be subjected to constant adjustment and realignment of its foundations in order to keep buildings from sustaining serious damage. The same is true for transportation and communication facilities—the freeways and the power and water lines.

Hundreds of earthquakes have been recorded in the past five centuries, since the Spaniards first entered Mexico. However, many of the low-lying edifices, built during the colonial era, have managed to survive the recurrent quakes better than the multistory buildings constructed in later times. In the case of relatively new construction, only the high-rises built in accordance with the latest scientific knowledge on quake resistance have weathered the tremors to which the city is constantly exposed.

The People. Archaeologists state that primitive tribes lived in the Valley of Mexico as early as fifteen thousand years ago. The area's appeal can be traced to the availability of fresh water, attracting humans and animals alike. The surrounding mountains also acted as a natural trap for game, making their capture less difficult to the prehistoric hunter. As the number of humans increased, the availability of this wild game dwindled. The shortage led ultimately to the evolution of an agricultural society, one that grew its sustenance from planned crops rather than depending entirely on the vagaries of the hunt.

The area's rich soil, combined with regular rainfall, led to the development of a substantial society, capable of building impressive stone structures for use as palaces, temples, and granaries. Civilizations such as the Teotihuacán and Toltec empires flourished for centuries, followed by that of the Aztecs, who held sway throughout central Mexico until the arrival of the Spanish conquistadores. The precolonial city constructed by the indigenous peoples dazzled the Spaniards on their arrival in the Valley of Mexico. The Aztecs had organized the city's functions in a manner superior to that which the Europeans had experienced at home. The treatment of sewage, for example, far exceeded in sophistication that found in European cities at the time.

In the process of their conquest of the Aztecs, the Spaniards laid waste to much of what was precolonial Mexico City, but they retained the location as the capital of what they called New Spain. A European-styled city rose from the ashes of the Aztec empire. Despite frequent fires and earthquakes—more than 340 quakes had been registered in the capital since the beginning of the colonial era—many examples of the initial Spanish colonial architecture can still be found throughout the city.

The Spaniards intermingled with the indigenous population from the beginning of their occupation. The conquistadores married into the noble families of the native peoples or made the Indian women their concubines. Today Mexico City's population is an amalgamation of European and Amerindian strains, giving the society a heterogeneous character.

More than 20 million people lived in greater Mexico City as early as 1986. This area includes the city itself and also the surrounding federal district. More than a quarter of the country's total population is crammed into the Valley of Mexico and its environs. Because the capital contains Mexico's economic and political seats of power, a constant influx of citizens seeking political advantage and employment opportunities pours into Mexico City in a continuous stream, many condemned to eke out a precarious existence.

During the second half of the twentieth century Mexico's society became more urban than rural. Living in the cities became the goal of the country's rural poor. As a result, virtually any open space within greater Mexico City became home to economic refugees. These poverty-stricken families from the countryside seized small plots of land wherever they could, built shacks from any material they could find, and fought the local authorities to retain custody of them. The new arrivals sought work of any type in order to sustain themselves; thus, factories throughout the crowded city and its surrounding area often employ workers under illegal and unsafe conditions. These poorly paid workers are crowded into poorly constructed commercial buildings that constantly threaten their health and well-being. Congestive traffic conditions and the accompanying pollution have made the capital a poor-quality residential area for many, if not most, of its inhabitants. Moreover, only roughly one-third of its citizens can afford to rent or own homes in its formal real-estate market.

The Quake. At 7:18 on the morning of September 19, 1985, Mexico City experienced a devastating earthquake. Technical experts described the event as a clash between two opposing seismic forces, the Cocos and the North American tectonic plates. The epicenter was determined to be deep in the Pacific Ocean, approximately 250 miles west of the Mexican coastline. Mexico City sits on what has been termed the "Ring of Fire" surrounding the Pacific Ocean and extending to Australia, Japan, Alaska, the western United States, Central America, and the western coasts of the countries of South America.

While some general damage occurred throughout Mexico's smaller southern cities and its rural areas, the capital itself experienced the greatest destruction. The quake measured 8.1 on the Richter scale. The tremor itself lasted over three minutes, shaking the city to its core. The damage was concentrated in the north, central, and eastern parts of the city.

The very nature of the ground beneath the city, with its lack of a solid rock base, resulted in extensive damage throughout its many districts, but especially in its very center. Dozens of the older hotels that lacked earthquake protection in the city's center collapsed, killing and injuring thousands of visitors. The

The Mexico City earthquake reduced many buildings to rubble. (Courtesy National Oceanic and Atmospheric Administration)

Regis, the Diplomático, the Versailles, the Romano (all of its occupants were killed), and the De Carlo were among those most seriously affected. While the upscale Del Prado survived the quake itself, it was rendered uninhabitable.

The Regis, formerly a luxury hotel but over time one that had deteriorated to second-class status, was 90 percent occupied when the quake struck. A few guests managed to jump to safety from the second floor. The stairway between the first and second floor as well as the front of the building had collapsed in the initial tremor. A few minutes later the rest of the edifice blew up as a result of accumulated gas within its ruins.

Both the Navy ministry nearby, as well as a secondary school, the National College of Professional Education, suffered major damage. Navy personnel dug with their hands to try to free their fellow sailors. Several hundred students at the school were entombed in the ruins of their classrooms. They had been in class for only twenty minutes.

The poorly constructed, overcrowded factories in the city suffered major damage as well. Four hundred production centers were destroyed, over 800 garment workers were killed, and thousands were left without work once the tremors had ceased. The factories proved to be particularly vulnerable to quakes for two reasons: the poor construction of the buildings in which they were housed, and the fact that the floors of the buildings themselves were stressed by the heavy loads of machinery and rolls of material that they bore.

Several major high-rises in the Tlatelolco complex failed to survive the first tremors. In 1968 Tlatelolco had been the scene of the massacre of an estimated 300 students by the army at the instigation of the government. This 103-building housing development, containing the living quarters of many government workers, suffered major damage, leaving the hundreds that survived the initial quake without shelter. Forty-three of the 103 buildings were rendered immediately uninhabitable.

The development's thirteen-story Nuevo León Building ended up in ruins, with more than half of its 3,000 residents trapped in the wreckage. The remaining rubble alone stood four stories high. Prior to the quake, many of its occupants had complained to authorities about the poor condition of the building. Some of the accusers claimed that the builders had paid bribes to government inspectors to overlook the quality of the materials used in its construction. Survivors from the surrounding buildings dug with their hands in an effort to free the Nuevo León's victims.

Famous tenor Placido Domingo had relatives trapped on the sixth floor in one of Tlatelolco's highrises. He led a brigade of volunteers that banded together to pull people from the rubble and provide food and water for survivors and volunteers.

When aid workers using public and private vehicles took the victims of the Tlatelolco disaster to the National Medical Center they were turned back. All of its major buildings had been devastated. Seventy of the center's physicians, nurses, and other employees had been killed. Several hundred patients had been crushed at the site as well. Some experts maintained that the medical buildings themselves were of substandard construction and that building regulations had been ignored during their erection. Five major hospitals within the city were destroyed, and an additional 22 were heavily damaged. The loss of hospital beds alone numbered 4,200, about 30 percent of the city's existing capacity. Following the quake, a number of complaints arose about the marginal construction of many of the recently built government structures. The material used proved to be inferior to what had been specified in the contracts between the government and the builders.

The headquarters of the television station Televisa suffered immense damage. More than 77 of its employees perished in the building's collapse. Nevertheless, the station managed to get back on the air after five hours of broadcast suspension. The station could not send filming units into the streets since many were blocked by debris, but the station did manage to report on the quake utilizing helicopters flying over the city.

A second—less severe, but still powerful—earthquake occurred less than thirty-six hours after the initial temblor. Technicians rated this subsequent quake 5.6 on the Richter scale. The tremor resulted in the postponement of rescue efforts. Further loss of life occurred among injured and trapped victims from the first disaster. The Pino Suárez high-rise building at Tlatelolco, damaged in the earlier quake, collapsed in the second, killing many rescue workers.

The statistics at the end of the first day showed the following: The quake had contaminated the city's water supply, and it had severed both electrical and telephone service. The telephone center on Victory Street was destroyed, effectively closing down telephone communications from and to Mexico City. Initially, news concerning the quake could be transmitted only by some of the city's 1,800 licensed ham-radio operators. More than 250,000 citizens found themselves temporarily without shelter. Adequate food supplies still existed, but getting them to the needed areas presented serious logistical problems. However, groups of citizen volunteers set up kitchens and tents in the streets next to excavation sites and began preparing food and drink for both victims and volunteers.

Five days after the initial quake, officials at Mexico's national university began to assemble a list of the missing, because the computers there were more sophisticated than those available to the government. Nevertheless, the delay in initiating a program seeking to identify the missing, dead, and injured led to a great deal of confusion for friends and relatives trying to locate those whose whereabouts were unknown. No program had been prepared for the government's computer facilities to be utilized in such an emergency.

The Government. After 1929 Mexico's federal, state, and regional governments were controlled by a single political entity, the Partido Revolucionario Institucional (PRI). The party has been accused of maintaining continuous control of the government by engineering elections, not only at the federal level but also in state and regional political contests. At the time of the 1985 earthquake, it was left to the country's president to personally appoint Mexico City's mayor, who was also named to the presidential cabinet. The responsibility for governing the city and providing for the welfare of its citizens lay with the office of the president.

Despite its claim to have a disaster plan for Mexico City to be implemented in the event of an emergency, when the earthquake struck, the Mexican government officials, initially at least, seemed to be helpless in the face of the tragedy. The extensive nature of the damage rendered previous planning inoperable. The city had an insufficient number of firefighters to meet the emergency. It also lacked the heavy construction equipment needed to begin removal of the thousands of tons of masonry rubble. The police and the army did little more than cordon off the damaged areas; they did not respond to the plight of the injured or aid in the removal of the dead. Some police were accused by onlookers of looting the damaged structures or taking bribes to allow businessmen

to recover their records without addressing the need for first aid for injured employees. The police expelled a reporter on the scene who had observed the pilferage and who planned to expose the corruption.

More scandals involving the police surfaced with the unscheduled release of some prisoners held in local jails damaged by the quakes. They testified to the use of torture by their captors during interrogations. Corpses of prisoners killed by the quake also bore evidence of systematic brutalization after the rescuers exhumed the bodies from a building occupied by the office of the attorney general.

When the manual laborers assigned by the government to aid in rescue efforts arrived on the scene, their equipment proved to be totally inadequate to meet the formidable task of removing the huge piles of debris resulting from the demolished buildings. Only when private contractors moved their own bulldozers and tractors to the sites could any meaningful shifting of the debris be accomplished.

Immediately following the quake, Mexican president Miguel de la Madrid announced publicly that Mexico had adequate resources to meet the emergency and that foreign aid would not be needed. In one instance, a team of French rescue workers with trained dogs was prevented by Mexican officials from beginning search operations at a devastated building. The president reversed his decision two days later; the delay cost the lives of many of the trapped and injured who could have been rescued by the many teams of foreign workers who then entered the country. President de la Madrid, essentially a bureaucrat, lacked the necessary leadership characteristics needed in the president of a stricken country facing this type of catastrophe.

Ultimately, 60 foreign countries aided in the rescue effort. Thirteen specialty brigades from outside the country, with tools and bloodhounds, worked tirelessly at the sites of devastation to find both the injured and the dead. The Israelis sent a team of 25 along with 17 tons of equipment. Because of the constant threat of quakes in their own country they had developed special equipment for locating and recovering those who had been trapped. In total, some 250 foreign governments, international relief agencies, and nongovernmental organizations of various types offered their services to Mexico. To complement these high-profile efforts, a group of young students from El Salvador drove several hundred miles from their Central American country in a battered passenger car, seeking to help in whatever capacity they could. Airplanes from the United States, the Soviet Union, France, Argentina, the Dominican Republic, Algeria, Switzerland, Colombia, Canada, Peru, Italy, Cuba, Spain, and Panama brought in tons of relief supplies for distribution to the injured and homeless.

Rescue. The citizens of Mexico City themselves became the major participants in the rescue effort. Forming brigades of volunteers similar to the one led by Placido Domingo, working with a modicum of tools acquired from local hardware stores, and sometimes with only their bare hands, the teams sought to save the lives of their trapped and injured fellow citizens. They formed human chains and passed debris and broken concrete from hand to hand. In most cases the brigades consisted of friends or coworkers. Some slightly built rescuers, nicknamed moles, crawled through tiny openings in the ruins, risking their own lives, in an effort to aid the living and to recover the bodies of the dead. One of these heroes, Marcos Efrén Zariñana, slightly over 5 feet in height, became known as "the Flea." Observers credited him with personally saving a number of lives. The diminutive rescuer edged his way through tunnels too small for other workers to enter in order to pull out victims.

Citizens formed their own committees to distribute food, clothing, and blankets directly to the survivors. They did not trust government officials to even carry out these tasks. They continued to upbraid the police and the soldiers for failing to take a positive role in the rescue efforts. The army defended itself vociferously, maintaining that it had been given orders only to secure the afflicted areas and to prevent looting.

Consequences. There were many economic and political consequences of the 1985 Mexico City earthquake. The government immediately began a rapid updating of building codes. It established for the first time a centralized national civil defense system. Nongovernmental organizations such as the Mexican Red Cross and the Catholic Church began to coordinate with one another their plans for addressing major emergencies such as the Mexico City earthquake.

The quake dealt Mexico a serious economic blow. The final estimate of the country's financial loss amounted to the equivalent of at least 4 billion U.S. dollars, possibly as much as $10 billion. The city lost hundreds of thousands of dollars in its normally lucrative tourist revenue. Moreover, hundreds of mil-

lions of dollars in wages literally disappeared when local businesses ceased to function. Reconstruction and rehabilitation costs were equivalent to 6 percent of the whole country's annual gross national product. The World Bank alone provided over half a billion dollars in reconstruction loans. The paid insurance losses exceeded any previous earthquake catastrophe except for those occurring in San Francisco in 1906 and Tokyo in 1923. The heavy concentration of industry in the capital further demonstrated that the nation's economic structure was ill served by allowing the bulk of its industry to locate in such narrow confines.

Some events developed after the catastrophe that the government had not foreseen. The PRI, although still the foremost political organization throughout Mexico, lost the support of many citizens of Mexico City. The general public saw the party as closely aligned with the government itself. Initially at least, the two together were seen as to have failed to contribute effectively to the rescue effort.

Eventually a citywide organization of ordinary citizens was formed to protest the manner in which the country's political leadership responded to the quake. Named the United Victim Network, its leaders pressured the office of the president to meet the needs of the homeless. The government, in an effort to regain support, and faced with a series of street demonstrations by this disaffected group of citizens, sometimes numbering in the thousands, took over some 600 acres of downtown real estate and, with the financial help of the World Bank, constructed dwellings for some 70,000 local citizens who were without housing. It added some small parks and playgrounds as well. Despite this highly publicized program, the government failed to win back the allegiance of most of the city's population.

The PRI's presidential candidate, Carlos Salinas de Gortari, barely won the national election held in 1988, three years following the quake. The opposition accused the government of fraud in tallying the votes. No questions of closeness arose in the case of the Mexico City vote, however—75 percent of the capital's voters backed his two opponents, Cuauhtémoc Cárdenas of the leftist Partido Democratico Revolucionario (PDR) and Manuel Clouthier of the Partido Acción Nacional (PAN).

In the years immediately following the quake, Mexico City's citizens continued to demonstrate their opposition to the existing political system. They had come to resent the country's president unilaterally selecting their mayor, a resentment kindled by the ineffectual handling of quake relief by the mayor's office. Finally, under pressure from an aroused and increasingly vociferous citizenry, the federal government capitulated and acquiesced to legislation enfranchising the city's residents.

Over a decade later, a further example of the rejection of the government's direct control of the reins of city government occurred when, in 1997, its citizens elected Cárdenas of the PRD its first popularly elected mayor over Alfredo del Mazo, the candidate chosen by the government and the PRI. The 1985 earthquake had changed forever the way that Mexico City was to be governed.

Carl Henry Marcoux

FOR FURTHER INFORMATION:

Centeno, Miguel Angel. *Democracy Within Reason: Technical Revolution in Mexico.* University Park: Pennsylvania State University Press, 1994.

D'az Cervantes, Emilio. *The Placido Domingo Brigade: A Manual Against Disaster.* Mexico City: Ediciones Castillo, 1995.

Foweraker, Joe, and Ann L. Craig. *Popular Movements and Political Change in Mexico.* Boulder, Colo.: Lynne Rienner, 1990.

Gil, Carlos B., ed. *Hope and Frustration: Interviews with Leaders of Mexico's Political Opposition.* Wilmington, Del.: Scholarly Resources, 1992.

Kandell, Jonathan. *La Capital: The Biography of Mexico City.* New York: Random House, 1988.

Morris, Stephen D. *Political Reformism in Mexico: An Overview of Contemporary Mexican Politics.* Boulder, Colo.: Lynne Rienner, 1995.

Poniatowska, Elena. *Nothing, Nobody: The Voices of the Mexico City Earthquake.* Philadelphia: Temple University Press, 1995.

Quarantelli, E. L. *Organizational Response to the Mexico City Earthquake of 1985: Characteristics and Implications.* Newark: University of Delaware Disaster Research Center, 1992.

1987: Ecuador

DATE: March 5-6, 1987
PLACE: Ecuador
MAGNITUDE: 7.3

RESULT: 5 dead, 12 missing, disruption of oil exports

In the wake of the 1987 earthquake in Ecuador, three provinces were declared emergency areas. News coverage of earthquakes occurring in the mountains by the Colombian border focused on how oil exports were affected. The trans-Andean petroleum pipeline that transported oil 350 miles from fields located in the jungle to the Pacific port at Balao was ruptured along a 25-mile section. Officials projected that all shipments of crude oil from Ecuador would cease for four months until the pipeline could be repaired and oil reserves replenished.

The Ecuadorian government had stockpiled enough oil for 35 days. Officials decided to import oil for the remaining three months while waiting for the pipeline to be restored fully. Repairs cost a minimum of $100 million. Ecuador, which pumped an average of 260,000 barrels daily in 1987, was economically damaged by the earthquake because oil composed two-thirds of that country's exports and 60 percent of the government's revenues. After the earthquake, President León Febres Cordero canceled payment toward the nation's foreign debt in order to use the money for reconstruction costs.

Elizabeth D. Schafer

FOR FURTHER INFORMATION:

"Ecuador Declares Emergency Following Earthquake." *Washington Post,* March 7, 1987, p. A30.

"4-Month Disruption of Ecuador Oil." *The New York Times,* March 9, 1987, p. D3.

1987: Whittier Earthquake

DATE: October 1, 1987
PLACE: Whittier, California
MAGNITUDE: 6.1
RESULT: 6 dead, 100 injured

At 7:42 A.M., October 1, 1987, an earthquake shook Los Angeles for thirty seconds. Considered the most powerful earthquake to hit the area since 1971, the tremors knocked down walls, shattered glass, and rocked automobiles on freeways as commuters drove to work and school. The epicenter was near Whittier, former U.S. president Richard M. Nixon's home-

A parking garage that partially collapsed after the Whittier earthquake. (Courtesy National Oceanic and Atmospheric Administration)

town. California Institute of Technology scientists identified the Whittier fault, which parallels the San Andreas fault, as the earthquake's cause.

Six people died during the earthquake. Debris accounted for 100 people being hurt. Local hospitals evacuated patients and interrupted ongoing surgical procedures until the earthquake concluded. The earthquake started fires, and smoke hung over the stricken areas. Aftershocks continued throughout the day. Looters took advantage of the disaster, and store employees emptied window displays to prevent thefts.

Freeways were closed until overpasses could be scrutinized for potential risks to motorists. Rides at Disneyland's theme park were inspected for damage before patrons were permitted entry to the theme park. People working in underground stores and on construction cranes high above the city during the earthquake had terrifying perspectives of the tremor's effects. Recent South American immigrants slept in tents in parks because of their familiarity with earthquakes in their native countries. The earthquake increased awareness of the need to prepare for a possibly more catastrophic quake that seismologists have predicted will occur at some point along California's faults.

Elizabeth D. Schafer

FOR FURTHER INFORMATION:

Cummings, Judith. "6 Die as Severe Earthquake Hits Los Angeles Area." *The New York Times,* October 2, 1987, p. A1.

"Quake Aftershocks Continue; Damage Rises to $75 Million." *The New York Times,* October 4, 1987, p. 26.

Stevenson, Richard W. "California Begins Cleanup After Quake." *The New York Times,* October 3, 1987, p. 7.

1988: Armenia

DATE: December 7, 1988
PLACE: Armenian Soviet Socialist Republic
MAGNITUDE: 6.9 and 5.8

RESULT: More than 60,000 dead, 15,000 injured, 500,000 homeless, at least 450,000 buildings destroyed, including 7,600 historical monuments, estimated $30 billion in damage

On December 7, 1988, devastation struck Soviet Armenia. Between 11:41 and 11:45 A.M. two tremors measuring 6.9 and 5.8 on the Richter scale destroyed or severely damaged the cities of Spitak, Leninakan (now Gyumri), Kirovakan (now Vanadzor), and Stepanakert and more than 100 villages. Erivan (now Yerevan), the capital, suffered damage, and the shock waves spread out some 150 miles into neighboring Georgia, Azerbaijan, Turkey, and Iran. The quakes were shallow, the most destructive kind. The point on the fault between two massive subterranean tectonic plates where enough pressure was exerted to create the focus of the earthquake was approximately 13 miles below the surface. The corresponding mark of the focus on the surface of the earth, the epicenter, was about 20 miles northwest of Kirovakan, 26 miles northeast of Leninakan, and 3.25 miles from Spitak, a city of 30,000 that was virtually erased from the face of the earth. Approximately 99 percent of its population vanished, buried under the rubble. About 80 percent of Leninakan, Armenia's second largest city, with a population of 290,000, was destroyed; 80 percent of Stepanakert, a city of 16,000, was destroyed.

The quakes occurred at the worst possible time, just before noon on a working weekday. In addition, the damaged or destroyed areas had more than 150,000 unregistered refugees from neighboring Nagorno-Karabakh, a small, predominantly Armenian province in Azerbaijan that was forcibly attempting to oust the Armenians. The quakes caused a rupture 8 miles long and 2 feet wide; the force of the subterranean shock could be compared to the explosion of 100 nuclear bombs.

Devastating as the quakes were, in intensity they were relatively mild. In comparison, the 1985 Mexico City earthquake registered 8.1 on the Richter scale, the 1964 Alaskan earthquake was 9.2, and the 1939 Chile quake was 8.3. On the Richter scale, a magnitude 7.0 quake is ten times more powerful than a magnitude 6.0 quake and one hundred times more powerful than a magnitude 5.0 quake. Although all of these earthquakes were of greater intensity than that of Armenia, none were as costly in terms of human life. What set the Armenian earthquakes apart is the large number of buildings the quakes either damaged or destroyed. Damaged or collapsed buildings are more deadly than earthquakes themselves.

Reasons for the Scope of the Destruction. The first reason was the nature of the quakes. Usually, major earthquakes are preceded by a series of foreshocks, mild tremors that give authorities time to prepare and potential victims time to seek safety. The Armenian quakes came without warning, although some people had noted beforehand peculiar animal and bird behavior. The two tremors were of about equal intensity. This meant that whereas the first tremor badly damaged buildings, the second, or aftershock, four minutes later, caused them to collapse, often on their occupants.

Soviet seismologists defended their lack of preparedness, maintaining there had been no major earthquake in the area since 1046, when the ancient Armenian capital of Arni was destroyed by a quake. However, the area had experienced a series of quakes over the years. In 1667, a quake had taken 80,000 lives. The fault at the heart of the 1988 earthquake appears on a geological map dated 1971. The Caucasus Mountain range, in which Armenia is located, is a seismic area crisscrossed by fault lines and filled with extinct volcanoes. Soviet scientists were known to have acknowledged that a major quake in the area was long overdue.

A second reason was poor urban planning. In earthquake-prone areas provisions should be made for "areas of survival," or free space to which people can escape from the danger of collapsing buildings. There was no such provision in the Armenian cities. Buildings were placed close together so that the areas between them, including the streets, were filled with debris from the earthquakes. This not only failed to afford escape but also did not provide the firm, cleared ground the Caterpillar carriages of the moveable cranes needed to lift the heavy debris.

Inappropriate building design and faulty construction also contributed greatly. Substandard construction was probably the major reason for the scope of the Armenian catastrophe. Most of the newer buildings, both offices and apartment houses, eight or nine stories high, were prefabricated. Slabs of concrete rested on cement-block walls. When the quakes occurred, the unconnected elements toppled. The quality of the concrete was also inferior, unable to withstand strain and prone to crumbling. When the supports were destroyed, the slabs col-

When the outside world did become aware of the disaster, the extent of the support, especially from the 6 million Armenians scattered throughout the world, was unparalleled. The total value of aid, estimated at $500 million, was the largest international response ever to a national disaster. The day after the quakes a French team of doctors, anesthesiologists, and medical technicians—together with supplies—was ready to leave for Erivan. However, they had to wait two days before permission was given to land—two days in which thousands died. President Gorbachev was in New York at the time but canceled his trip to fly back to the Soviet Union. He visited Armenia on December 10, ostensibly to take charge of the rescue operation, which had suffered from lack of leadership. The position of landlocked Armenia surrounded

lapsed together like gigantic millstones, trapping many of the occupants of the buildings between them. After the quakes, lifting these huge slabs was beyond human efforts; the much-needed cranes and other heavy equipment arrived too late to save many victims. In rural areas, many of the houses were made of mud brick, with stone roofs that collapsed on the occupants. In rebuilding the decision was made to limit the height of buildings to three or five stories and to pour concrete on the site.

Another reason was ineffective assistance. The sheer scope of the tragedy, involving nearly 19 percent of the country's population, was beyond the capability of the Armenian authorities; help was needed from the outside. With thousands of badly injured trapped beneath the wreckage, every hour of delay meant additional loss of life. It was only because of *glasnost*, or the open-discussion policy of Soviet president Mikhail Gorbachev, that the outside world became aware of the disaster. (The 1948 earthquake in the Soviet republic of Turkmen that killed 110,000 was concealed for forty years.) Also, Soviet acceptance of outside help was unprecedented.

by alienated states made a desperate situation even worse because the necessary heavy equipment had to come by land. The only working rail line was from Erivan to Baku, the capital of Armenia-hostile Azerbaijan. Supplies came by air in such quantities that the Erivan and Leninakan airports became bottlenecks.

Meanwhile, aid workers desperately tried to free the victims whose cries and groans became ever fainter. In the end only 5,000 of as many as 80,000 were pulled from the wreckage. Most tragic was the death of more than 15,000 children, particularly in a country with a negative growth rate. By December 14, the Red Army wanted to clear all people from the damaged areas and to level the sites with bulldozers and sow them with lime and other disinfectants to halt the possible spread of disease from the decomposing bodies beneath the ruins. Desperate intervention by survivors still searching for possible living victims delayed the decision a few more days. As late as December 15, a living person was pulled from the wreckage. By December 17, foreign relief workers were ordered to leave;

by December 23, efforts to locate more survivors ceased.

The injured who did survive faced another ordeal: inferior medical treatment. Relief doctors estimated Soviet medicine lagged a half-century behind that of the West. Not only were basic medications either in short supply or lacking but there was also a lack of sophisticated equipment, such as dialysis machines. One of the more urgent problems was to deal with "crush syndrome." When subjected to great external pressure, the kidneys shut down and toxemia or poisoning begins. Only the use of dialysis machines that serve to cleanse the blood can keep the victim alive. At Erivan's central hospital, 80 percent of the 600 survivors suffered from crush syndrome. Several dialysis machines were brought in by air, but not enough to save all who needed their use.

There were also psychological problems to solve. In a society such as Armenia's, where the extended family and clan take precedence over the individual, the loss of such support is emotionally devastating. There was scarcely a person in the entire republic that had not lost a relative; entire families disappeared. Hundreds wandered aimlessly with blank eyes through the ruins, clearly in need of counseling or psychiatric services, which were not readily available.

The poor health of the victims was a factor in the death rate. Relief workers, especially those trained in nutrition, noted that low resistance caused by poor dietary habits raised the mortality rate among the earthquake victims. Further undermining their health was frequent evidence of alcohol and tobacco abuse.

Lack of authority was also to blame. Despite its officially being called a "union" of quasi-independent republics, the Soviet Union was a dictatorship, with authority tightly controlled by Moscow. Despite Gorbachev's pledge to "take charge" in Armenia, centralized authority to direct the complicated relief operation, especially in the distribution of supplies, was sporadic and ineffective. Relief workers often did not know where to go or what to do, and there was much duplication of effort and plundering and disappearance of supplies. A number of the bureaucrats who normally would have been available for administrative duties lay dead beneath the rubble. Units of the Red Army that had been sent to the disaster area did not participate in the relief efforts; they merely enforced curfews and blocked access to the ruined sites.

Assessing the Damage. Given the secretive nature of the Soviet system it was impossible to arrive at accurate figures for the cost of the earthquakes. The Soviets estimated that 55,000 people had been killed. Relief workers estimated far more—possibly as many as three times that number. Especially devastating to Armenia was the loss of trained professionals and of children—a loss impossible to evaluate in monetary terms.

More than 500,000 were left homeless; Soviet authorities indicated a wish to resettle about 70,000 in other parts of the Soviet Union. Gorbachev pledged $8.5 billion for restoration purposes, the same amount of money that was allocated to repair the nuclear disaster at Chernobyl two years before. Authorities estimated that at least triple that amount would be needed to restore the cities, using earthquake-resistant and more expensive building techniques. In addition to the buildings, extensive damage was done to the infrastructure—to light, sewer, water, and gas lines and to the transportation system.

Help from Moscow never arrived. The Soviet Union was dissolved December 4, 1991. Armenia had declared its independence on September 21, 1991, to face the formidable task of rebuilding a shattered land.

Nis Petersen

FOR FURTHER INFORMATION:
Brand, D. "When the Earth Shook." *Time*, December 19, 1988, 34-36.
Coleman, Fred. "A Land of the Dead." *Newsweek*, December 19, 1966, 19-23.
Kerr, Richard A. "How the Armenian Quake Became a Killer." *Science* 243 (January 13, 1989): 170-171.
Novosti Press Agency. *The Armenian Earthquake Disaster.* Translated by Elliott B. Urdang. Madison, Conn.: Sphinx Press, 1989.
Verluise, Pierre. *Armenia in Crisis: The 1988 Earthquake.* Translated by Levon Chorbajian. Detroit: Wayne State University Press, 1995.

1989: Loma Prieta Earthquake

DATE: October 17, 1989
PLACE: Northern California, in an area extending from Watsonville and Santa Cruz in the south to San Francisco and Oakland in the north

MAGNITUDE: 7.0 or 7.1 on the Richter scale (U.S. Geological Survey recorded this earthquake at 7.1, but other geologists recorded it at 7.0)

RESULT: 67 dead, more than 3,000 injured, more than $5 billion in damage

History. The worst earthquake in American history did not take place in the West, where there are many fault lines, but rather in Missouri. Although the February 7, 1812, New Madrid earthquake (one of a series in the region) took place long before the development of the Richter scale in 1935, contemporary reports by witnesses led seismologists to conclude that the New Madrid earthquake was in the range of 8.8 to 11 on the Richter scale. The 1812 earthquake caused the earth to shake over an area of 5 million square miles. Two later destructive American earthquakes were the San Francisco earthquake of April 18, 1906, and the Good Friday earthquake of March 27, 1964, in Alaska. Although these two earthquakes resulted in extensive property damage and many deaths, they extended over smaller areas than the New Madrid quake. The Alaska earthquake was recorded at 9.2 on the Richter scale and caused shaking of the earth

over approximately 500 square miles, whereas the San Francisco earthquake caused shaking of the earth over an area of 300 square miles and was estimated between 8.2 and 8.3 on the Richter scale.

The populations of San Francisco and Los Angeles are now much larger than they were in the first decade of the twentieth century. Were an earthquake of the magnitude of the New Madrid earthquake of 1812 or of the Good Friday earthquake of 1964 to occur near Los Angeles or San Francisco, it is probable that the number of deaths would be in the hundreds of thousands. It is not impossible that similar earthquakes might occur in California, which has the largest population of any American state.

After the terrible destruction and loss of life caused by the San Francisco earthquake, governmental officials and architects began to ask themselves what could be done to make buildings and bridges more resistant to seismic shocks caused by earthquakes, but few changes in building practices and codes were implemented until after the 1971 Sylmar earthquake near Los Angeles.

In 1972, the California legislature created a Seismic Safety Commission and instructed its members

The San Francisco-Oakland Bay Bridge, which was scheduled to be reinforced one week after the Loma Prieta earthquake. A portion of the upper level failed during the quake. (Courtesy National Oceanic and Atmospheric Administration)

to make recommendations to make California buildings and bridges more earthquake-resistant. This commission concluded that the major destruction caused by earthquakes is not generated by the shaking itself but by the aftereffects, when improperly constructed buildings, dams, and bridges collapse. The collapse of these structures and fires caused by the bursting of underground gas lines contribute significantly to property damage and the loss of life right after earthquakes. The commission demonstrated that buildings built with reinforced bricks were more quake-resistant than those built with regular bricks.

The commission also demonstrated that wood-frame houses, even when constructed in conformity with existing building codes, were much more prone to quake damage than were houses built with reinforced brick. This had been known for a long period of time, but it was not financially feasible to ask people to tear down their wood-frame houses and to replace them with houses built with reinforced bricks. Also, the installation of additional steel rods tends to make dams and bridges more stable. The California Seismic Safety Commission pointed out that bridges and dams built before 1972 were not sufficiently reinforced, and it recommended that the government of California begin retrofitting, or reinforcing, these structures.

In addition, this commission pointed out that construction should be discouraged in areas that were highly susceptible to damage from earthquakes. This recommendation was impractical because far too much construction had already occurred in areas such as the Marina District in San Francisco, which was created by filling in the land with sand, mud, and rocks. The foundation on which such construction was built was very susceptible to earthquakes—the ground tends to liquefy during severe seismic shocks. In addition, houses and businesses were built in very hilly areas, such as the Oakland Hills, during the first seven decades of the twentieth century. By 1972 it would have been impossible to move people and businesses from such areas. The government of California decided to create new building codes designed to make houses and public structures more quake-resistant and to undertake the retrofitting of existing dams, bridges, roads, and public buildings.

The reinforcement of existing structures was, however, a very expensive undertaking, and large tax decreases implemented in California in the 1970's and 1980's left the state government with insufficient means to complete this work in a timely manner. Ironically, the Bay Bridge, which connects San Francisco and Oakland, was scheduled to be reinforced just one week after the Loma Prieta earthquake. A portion of the upper level of this bridge collapsed during the Loma Prieta earthquake.

The Quake. Northern Californians expected October 17, 1989, to be a joyous day for the region of San Francisco and Oakland. The Oakland Athletics and the San Francisco Giants, the two major-league baseball teams from Northern California, had qualified for the World Series, and a game was scheduled to begin around 5:30 P.M. local time in San Francisco's Candlestick Park. The game was being broadcast live on American television. As camera operators were filming pregame activities, the transmission of images to television screens around the world was interrupted. Television viewers were not sure what was happening until reporters outside Candlestick Park began to inform the world that an earthquake had occurred.

The quake occurred on a sunny day during rush hour. The roads and bridges from Watsonville to San Francisco were filled with cars and people, and others were in their homes waiting for the World Series game to begin. The epicenter of the earthquake was located on the San Andreas fault in the Santa Cruz Mountains, to the east of the cities of Santa Cruz and Watsonville. The nearest landmark to the epicenter was Loma Prieta Mountain, which is why seismologists refer to this quake as the Loma Prieta earthquake.

Television reporters were already in San Francisco to cover the World Series game, so news traveled quickly. Initial reports stressed the damage done to the cities of San Francisco and Oakland, but extensive damage also occurred on the campus of Stanford University, in the nearby city of Palo Alto, in Santa Cruz, and especially in the largely Hispanic town of Watsonville, which was the closest city to the epicenter itself. Although authorities from the state and federal governments and volunteers from the Red Cross thought they they were sufficiently prepared for a natural disaster, each earthquake results in unexpected problems. The situation in Watsonville illustrates this point.

Effects in Watsonville. Since the San Francisco earthquake of 1906, the demographics of California have changed greatly. California is a much more ethnically and linguistically diverse state than it was dur-

The two-level Cypress freeway was rebuilt on a new site after its collapse in the Loma Prieta earthquake. (AP/Wide World Photos)

ing the first decade of the twentieth century. Like many cities throughout California, Watsonville has a large Latino population, and it is surrounded by wealthier cities such as those in the Silicon Valley and in the suburbs of Santa Cruz, where the population is largely Anglo-American. Watsonville was 60 percent Latino in 1989, and most houses were of older wood-frame construction, built long before the implementation in the 1970's of stricter building codes. Since it was located close to the epicenter of this accident, structural damage in Watsonville was very significant.

The major industries near Watsonville are farming and food production. These labor-intense industries pay poorly, but they attract large numbers of emigrants from Mexico and Central America, who often receive even lower salaries in their native countries. Between 1984 and 1989, the population of Watsonville had increased by 38 percent, but non-Latinos still dominated the municipal government of Watsonville, since many of the recently arrived Latinos were not yet American citizens. This earthquake destroyed almost 10 percent of all apartments and

houses in Watsonville, but the property damage affected the Latino neighborhoods more than the Anglo neighborhoods, largely because the structures in the Latino communities had been completed decades before and were of wood-frame construction and therefore not very resistant to seismic shocks.

When soldiers in the California National Guard and representatives from the Federal Emergency Management Agency (FEMA), the Red Cross, and the state of California arrived in Watsonville, an immediate problem became evident to almost everyone. Those who wanted to help the survivors did not speak Spanish and could not communicate with the Latino majority in Watsonville. Since so much housing in Watsonville had been destroyed, the Red Cross had no choice but to create makeshift disaster centers and housing enclosures located far from the Latino neighborhoods in Watsonville. The threat of aftershocks in the communities of Watsonville was simply too great for people to be allowed to stay near their severely damaged homes and apartment houses, but many Spanish-speaking residents did not understand why they were being forced to leave their neighborhoods for distant regions of Watsonville; they believed that this represented yet another example of Anglo racism against Latinos. Recent antagonism between Anglo and Latino communities in Watsonville only exacerbated relationships between these two groups in the days immediately following the Loma Prieta earthquake.

The various emergency organizations dealt with the problem by bringing in bilingual workers who could communicate with the Latino majority in Watsonville. The presence of bilingual workers who understood Latino culture helped to diffuse a volatile situation. The events in Watsonville helped the Red Cross, the California National Guard, and FEMA to understand that preparation for natural disasters required them to take into account not only problems related to health and housing but also the changing linguistic and cultural fabric of states such as California. Something positive, however, did result from the traumatic events in Watsonville. Anglos and Latinos learned to cooperate with each other in order to create a more unified city and to reduce political and cultural divisiveness.

In Watsonville, as in other cities affected by this earthquake, people discovered that their regular homeowner's insurance policies did not cover earthquakes. Earthquake insurance is extremely expensive, and it often includes very high deductibles and limits on the maximum liability for insurance companies. Individuals whose homes were destroyed by this earthquake had no choice but to turn to the federal government for loans to help them rebuild their residences. Such loans had to be repaid, and this created major financial crises for affected Californians. Companies and universities also suffered financially as a result of the Loma Prieta earthquake.

Stanford University. The case of Stanford University clearly indicates the gravity of the problems faced by universities and businesses. Stanford University was founded in 1885, and its campus is located near the San Andreas fault. Many of its older buildings were constructed with unreinforced bricks and are thus less quake-resistant than buildings constructed with reinforced bricks. For many years Stanford University paid for earthquake insurance, but by 1985 the annual premiums became so prohibitively expensive and the coverage so limited that the trustees of Stanford University concluded that it would be inadvisable to continue coverage against earthquakes.

In his book *Magnitude 8*, Philip L. Fradkin explains that Stanford University was offered in 1985 earthquake coverage for an annual premium of $3 million, with a deductible of $100 million and coverage for a mere $125 million worth of damage above the deductible. Although Stanford University suffered damages that amounted to $160 million as a result of the Loma Prieta earthquake, the decision not to renew earthquake insurance coverage in 1985 was perfectly understandable. Universities, private businesses, and homeowners often cannot afford such extremely expensive policies that offer such limited coverage. A typical homeowner's policy comes with a deductible of $250 to $500 and frequently includes full-replacement coverage. With earthquake insurance, the deductible is usually at least $6,000, and full-replacement coverage is not offered.

Daly City, San Francisco, and Oakland. Located almost 60 miles north of the Loma Prieta epicenter is Daly City, a bedroom community south of San Francisco. In Daly City, many people chose to live on the palisades, which offer exquisite views of the Pacific Ocean. Many houses were built on the cliffs in Daly City and appreciated greatly in value during the 1970's and 1980's. People were oblivious to the dangers involved in building houses on cliffs near the San Andreas fault. Many houses built on the palisades in Daly City were forced from their foundations during the Loma Prieta earthquake and were structurally destroyed. These houses had been built on an old garbage dump that had been covered with sand. The ground on which these beautiful and expensive houses had been built in Daly City was of insufficient strength to resist seismic shocks, and the ground liquefied during the Loma Prieta earthquake.

Just north of Daly City are San Francisco and Oakland. They both suffered extensive damage during the Loma Prieta earthquake, although not because the two cities had failed to enforce new building codes or to prepare for earthquakes. Office buildings and public structures constructed with reinforced bricks and additional steel rods in both cities did not suffer structural damage during the Loma Prieta earthquake; large buildings did not collapse as they had during the 1906 San Francisco earthquake. The San Andreas fault runs through these two cities, and the danger of earthquakes is extremely high. Athough property damage in both Oakland and San Francisco was very extensive, especially in the Oakland Hills, the three places that suffered the greatest damage were the Marina District of San Francisco, the Nimitz Expressway in Oakland, and the Bay Bridge. Houses on the cliffs in Daly City should never have been built there because the ground was not strong enough to resist earthquakes, contributing significantly to the property damage. Those who filled in the land in Daly City did not realize that they were creating a very dangerous situation for future residents. A similar error was made in San Francisco during the late nineteenth century and especially right after the 1906 earthquake.

Municipal officials and developers concluded that filling in the lagoon in San Francisco would be financially advantageous because it would permit extensive growth in both housing and economic development. The area filled in was called the Marina District, which includes such famous places as Fisherman's Wharf, Market Street, Embarcadero Street, and Candlestick Park. At first, the lagoon area was filled in with sand and rocks, but starting in 1912 municipal officials used a mixture of 30 percent mud and 70 percent sand to fill in the area. In 1915, a world's fair was held in San Francisco's new Marina District; afterward, the wooden buildings were taken down and buried in the mixture of mud and sand. The wood deteriorated and made the land even less earthquake-resistant.

Unlike the residents of Watsonville, those who lived in San Francisco's Marina District were mostly wealthy and Caucasian. Many of the structures in the Marina District were also built well before the stringent building codes of the 1970's. The combination of a poor ground foundation and inadequately reinforced buildings created conditions favorable for disaster. On October 17, 1989, wood-frames houses in the Marina District collapsed in large numbers, and gas mains and pipes burst because the ground of mud and sand was too weak to protect them. When the natural gas was released into the air, it provoked a series of dangerous fires. Although the gas supply was quickly cut off to the Marina District by the utility companies, the damage had already been done. Many houses collapsed as a result of the earthquake, but many more houses and commercial structures were destroyed by the numerous fires.

Although San Francisco had a professionally trained fire department and established procedures for dealing with emergencies, their ability to deal with so many fires at the same time was severely limited. Television cameras transmitted to viewers around the world images of the fires, which lasted throughout most of the night of October 17-18. Geologists determined that the way in which the Marina District ground was filled significantly increased the liquefaction of the land and made the effect of the sesimic shocks much worse in the Marina District. Sections of San Francisco that had not been developed on filled land were much more quake-resistant than the Marina District. Even after the Loma Prieta earthquake, construction continued in the Marina District, because the land there is so valuable. Builders were required to reinforce buildings and to respect stringent building codes, but there is no guarantee that the Marina District will not suffer extensive damage when the next earthquake takes place near San Francisco. Had people known in the late nineteenth century and the early twentieth century what geologists know today, the Marina District would never have been developed, and Stanford, near the San Andreas fault, and houses in hilly regions in Oakland and Daly City would not have been constructed.

Freeway Collapses. Two other major catastrophes in the San Francisco region were the collapse of the Nimitz Expressway and a section on the upper level of the Bay Bridge. The Nimitz Expressway in Oakland was built between 1954 and 1957. It did meet construction codes in effect at that time, and its engineers thought that it was safe, but it was not sufficiently reinforced to cope with an earthquake of the magnitude of 7.0 or 7.1. A total of 41 people died, either on the two levels of the freeway or below the freeway. Many people driving on the lower level were crushed to death when the upper level collapsed on their cars. The death toll would most certainly have been much higher had the earthquake occurred even a few minutes later. The earthquake took place at 5:04 P.M., and by that time most commuters had not yet reached the Nimitz Expressway for their trip home from work. Had this freeway collapsed even fifteen minutes later, hundreds would probably have been killed.

The two major bridges into San Francisco, the Golden Gate Bridge and the Bay Bridge, were constructed in the 1930's. Although the Golden Gate is the more famous of the two bridges, the Bay Bridge is used more heavily because it connects Oakland and San Francisco. In 1989, the Bay Bridge was double-deck, and people thought that it was safe. During the Loma Prieta earthquake, however, bolts that connected the east and west ends of supports came apart, causing a portion of the upper level to collapse. Amazingly, only one driver was killed, when his car fell from the upper level to the lower level. Luck and effective defensive driving by people on the upper and lower levels of the Bay Bridge prevented a large loss of life.

It took a full month to restore this bridge to regular service. The damage to bridges between Watsonville and San Francisco could have been much worse: Only 18 of the more than 4,000 bridges had to be closed for repairs after the Loma Prieta earthquake.

Results. The impact of the Loma Prieta earthquake on Northern California was quite significant. Economists have estimated that between $5.6 and $5.8 billion had to be spent to repair houses, roads, public and commercial buildings, and bridges damaged or destroyed by the Loma Prieta earthquake. At least 67 people were killed as the direct result of this earthquake, but it is difficult to determine how many fatal heart attacks were caused by the trauma of this earthquake. Between 3,000 and 4,000 people were seriously injured, putting a strain on medical personnel between Watsonville and San Francisco. It is impossible to describe the psychological damage experienced by people who survived this temblor. When the Loma Prieta earthquake occurred, California was already suffering from a national economic downturn, which affected the Golden State more severely than other American states. The temporary or permanent closing of businesses in an economically important region of Northern California exacerbated an already bad economic situation.

Edmund J. Campion

FOR FURTHER INFORMATION:
Bolt, Bruce A. *Earthquakes Newly Revisited and Expanded.* Rev. ed. New York: W. H. Freeman, 1993. This revised edition of a book originally published in 1978 explains clearly how and why earthquakes take place. Describes the effect of the Loma Prieta earthquake on Northern California. It is clearly written, and nonspecialists will have no difficulty understanding this book.
Chameau, J. L., G. W. Clough, et al. "Liquefaction Response of San Francisco Bayshore Fills." *Bulletin of the Seismological Society of America* 81, no. 5 (October, 1991): 1998-2018. Explains clearly why areas like San Francisco's Marina District are more susceptible to seismic shocks than areas developed on more solid foundations.
Fradkin, Philip L. *Magnitude 8.* New York: Henry Holt, 1998. This book, written by a geologist for the general public, describes the social devastation created by the Loma Prieta earthquake of 1989 and other major American earthquakes, including the 1964 Good Friday earthquake in Alaska and the 1994 Northridge earthquake in Los Angeles.
Hanks, Thomas C., and Gerald Brady. "The Loma Prieta Earthquake, Ground Motion, and Damage in Oakland, Treasure Island, and San Francisco." *Bulletin of the Seismological Society of America* 81, no. 5 (October, 1991): 2019-2047. A clearly written study that describes accurately why the Nimitz Expressway and the Bay Bridge collapsed on October 17, 1989. This special issue of this scholarly journal deals exclusively with the Loma Prieta earthquake.
Maclean's, October 30, 1989, 52-57. These illustrated articles from a popular Canadian weekly magazine describe very well the devastation caused by the Loma Prieta quake.
Newsweek, October 30, 1989, 22-48. Numerous articles in this issue of the weekly magazine not only describe the loss of life and property damage caused by the Loma Prieta earthquake but also examine the psychological effect of quakes on survivors.
Time, October 30, 1989, 30-51. Numerous articles from this weekly magazine describe the destruction caused by this temblor and explain how the Red Cross and governmental agencies prepare for natural disasters such as earthquakes.

1990: Iran

DATE: June 21, 1990
PLACE: Northwestern Iran
MAGNITUDE: 7.7
RESULT: More than 50,000 dead, more than 135,000 injured

At approximately 12:30 A.M. on Thursday, June 21, 1990, a major earthquake struck a densely populated region of northern Iran that bordered on the shores of the Caspian Sea. The initial quake, measuring 7.7 on the Richter scale, was followed twelve hours later by an aftershock measuring 6.5. Approximately one hundred aftershocks of less intensity continued throughout the following day.

Most of the damage occurred in the provinces of Zanjān and Gīlān, fertile agricultural regions northwest of the Iranian capital of Tehran that spread over some 20,000 square miles. The region was noted for lush plains, hilly farmland, and vineyards, and it was the source of wheat and fruit for much of the country. The beaches along the sea were favorite resort areas. Dozens of towns and villages were destroyed by the earthquake, with over 400,000 people out of the population of 2.7 million rendered homeless. The quake occurred while most people were sleeping or watching on television the World Cup soccer match being played in Italy. Consequently, most victims were buried in their homes beneath tons of concrete that collapsed over their heads.

While the June 21 earthquake was reported by seismologists to be the strongest recorded quake in the area's history, earthquakes in northern Iran were relatively common and had been recorded since 700 C.E. Iran lies on the earthquake belt that extends from Turkey through the Caucasus Mountains into the Himalayas, the region along which the Arabian Plate is sliding across the Eurasian Plate. Twelve other earthquakes with magnitudes exceeding 7.0 were reported in northern Iran between 1960 and 1989, with nearly 40,000 victims in the two quakes of 1968 and 1978. The 1988 earthquake in Armenia, which killed 60,000 people, had its epicenter only several hundred miles north of that which caused 1990 Iranian tremor and was the result of the same fault line that has plagued Iran.

The epicenter for the 1990 disaster was in the Caspian Sea just north of Rasht, capital of Gīlān province. It was believed to lie along the fault line under the Elburz Mountains on the edge of that sea. The earthquake also burst a dam just south of Rasht, resulting in a flood that covered a portion of the region and destroyed additional agricultural areas.

The province of Zanjān was hit the hardest. Fifty-four towns and villages were reported destroyed, with dozens of others having suffered severe damage. In the towns of Ab-Dar and Bouin, every building was destroyed and every resident was either killed or injured; over 1,000 died in Ab-Dar alone. Nearly 2,000 were reported killed in Tarom-e Oleya. The town of Abbar was completely destroyed. The devastation in Gīlān province was nearly as extensive. In the towns of Loushan, Rudbar, and Manjil, south of Rasht and

with a combined population of approximately 100,000 people, 80 percent of the buildings were damaged. Pilots described a continuous scene of devastation between Rasht and Loushan, a distance of 80 miles. In Rudbar, every house was destroyed.

Eyewitness accounts provided the most vivid descriptions of the severity of the devastation. Pilots flying helicopters over the region described mile after mile of collapsed buildings, rubble, and survivors clawing through the wreckage in attempts to locate people buried beneath the debris. The quake caused hillsides to slide over the roads, isolating villages and preventing relief convoys from reaching them. For a time, bad weather hindered even the airlifting of personnel or relief supplies.

At the time of the earthquake, Iran was subject to diplomatic isolation by most of the Western world. From 1980 to 1988, Iran had been at war with Iraq. Occupation by Iranian students of the United States embassy in 1979 and the holding of American hostages for over a year were still fresh in the minds of Americans. Despite the animosity, offers of assistance were rendered by many countries in the world. In addition to members of the former Communist bloc, such as Poland and the Soviet Union, assistance was offered by Israel, France, Great Britain, Turkey, and Greece. President George Bush, on behalf of the United States, offered assistance through the Red Cross in Geneva.

The Iranian government refused the offers of assistance from Israel and South Africa, but the extent of the devastation forced the government to accept assistance from most of the other countries. While blood donations were refused, Iran did accept donations of blood plasma. The European Community headquartered in Brussels pledged over $1.2 million in aid to the earthquake victims. Japan offered over $1.5 million in supplies and medical equipment. The value of relief supplies from the United States, rendered through the International Red Cross, eventually totaled approximately $300,000.

It was initially hoped that the extent of aid from Western countries, including that from the United States, might convince the Iranian government officials to liberalize their policy toward such countries. However, while Iran was willing to accept aid from the West, the government continued the actions that had led to the ostracism in the first place. Indeed, even those foreign workers who had been allowed into Iran to aid in the relief process were told to leave the country within one week.

In addition to the cost in human lives and the billions of dollars in damage to the infrastructure of the province, the earthquake had destroyed the major agricultural region of the country. Irrigation systems were destroyed, agricultural workers were killed, and the crops they had planted were lost. The economy, which had only recently been recovering from the long war with Iraq, was now reeling under the additional blows of the agricultural and human disaster.

Richard Adler

FOR FURTHER INFORMATION:
Chua-Eoan, Howard. "The Hour of Doom." *Time* 136 (July 2, 1990): 28-29.
McFadden, Robert. "Thousands of Iranians Die as Major Earthquake Destroys Many Villages in the North." *The New York Times*, June 22, 1990, p. 1.
The New York Times, June 23, 1990, p. 1.

Limited amounts of heavy machinery, infrared devices, sensitive microphones, and acetylene torches to cut through steel reinforcing concrete hampered rescue workers. American military personnel, doctors, nurses, and engineers assisted rescue crews. President Corazon Aquino toured the affected provinces as strong aftershocks rocked the area. Total casualties amounted to 429 dead, 1,225 injured, and 1,000 missing.

Elizabeth D. Schafer

FOR FURTHER INFORMATION:
"Earthquake in the Philippines Kills at Least 258, Including 48 Children in One School." *The New York Times*, July 17, 1990, p. A3.
Erlanger, Steven. "Hopes Dying in the Rubble in Philippines." *The New York Times*, July 19, 1990, p. A3.
"Manila Assesses Damage and High Cost of Quake." *The New York Times*, July 20, 1992, p. A3.

1990: Philippines

DATE: July 16, 1990
PLACE: Luzon, Philippines
MAGNITUDE: 7.7
RESULT: 429 dead

Shaking the main island of the Philippines, Luzon, this earthquake's epicenter was located in Nueva Ecija Province, north of the capital city, Manila. Most casualties occurred because people were crushed by flattened buildings or injured by stampeding crowds escaping from high-rise office buildings. The Christian College of the Philippines, a six-story school, was leveled, trapping 250 schoolchildren, teachers, and administrators underneath beams, concrete slabs, and rubble. Rescuers used ropes and motor oil to pull some of the people to safety, but 48 children died from dehydration and injuries.

Other victims were tourists and residents at resort hotels in the mountain town of Baguio, where 117 people died. A nearby chemical factory caught on fire. Thirty workers perished at the gold and copper mine at Tuba in Benguet Province. The earthquake cratered roads and runways, collapsed bridges, and triggered landslides, hindering travel by land and air. Radio stations conveyed messages when telephone service was disrupted.

1992: Turkey

DATE: March 13 and 15, 1992
PLACE: Erzincan, Turkey, with a major aftershock in Pulumur, 43 miles (70 kilometers) southeast
MAGNITUDE: 6.8 on the Richter scale, maximum intensity of VIII to weak IX on the Modified Mercalli scale; 6.1 aftershock
RESULT: Officially 541 dead (more than 2,000 rumored dead), thousands injured, more than 200 multistory buildings destroyed, 50,000 to 60,000 homeless, 172 towns and villages damaged, $1.2 billion in damage

This earthquake disaster occurred in the provincial capital of Erzincan, which has often been devastated by earthquakes in its past (in 1047, 1457, 1583, 1666, 1784, and 1939). The great Erzincan earthquake disaster of 1939 is known, and frequently talked about, by many Turks. The city was rebuilt after that event, and on March 13, 1992, the population within the city limits was 91,000. Another 209,000 people lived in the surrounding 4,595 square miles (11,900 square kilometers) of the Erzincan Province. Erzincan lies about 621 miles (1,000 kilometers) east of Istanbul and 435 miles (700 kilometers) east of Ankara and is on a major rail and road route connecting eastern and western Anatolia.

At 7:19 P.M., on a freezing Friday evening during Ramadan, the holy month of fasting, many residents of Erzincan were sitting in their homes, in one of several restaurants in the city, or in the business center, waiting for the special evening meal. Some were in mosques for Friday prayers. It was already dark, with a cloud of smoke, from coal and wood stoves, hovering over the city. People in the surrounding villages were also anticipating the evening meal. Then the earthquake struck. Within seconds thousands of people were out in the streets in the darkness, most with no flashlights, a few with their car lights turned on, lifting heavy debris without equipment and with their bare hands, desperately searching for their relatives and friends. Survivors were screaming, praying, and crying, in near shock from the physical and emotional trauma.

For at least seventeen seconds the shaking was strong enough to bring down power lines, interrupt the water lines, and destroy thousands of buildings. Dozens of men were praying in the Demirkent mosque when the minaret collapsed and pierced the roof, killing 27. The four-story Uratu Hotel, the four-story Vakif Business Center, the Erzincan Municipality Complex, the Nursing Student Dorm, the State Hospital, the Military Hospital, the Social Security Hospital, several banks, many of the buildings along Fevzipasa Street and other main streets, in addition to scores of six-story apartment buildings, were totally demolished or experienced major damage.

Most of the 91,000 residents of Erzincan and thousands of villagers in the 137 communities were now homeless, and others were unwilling to go back inside their shelters. Aftershocks were a serious concern. The survivors built temporary shelters from plastic sheets or scrap material collected from the area. Search and rescue was fairly well organized within forty-eight hours. National organizations, along with numerous international organizations, provided support. The Turkish army has a large headquarters in Erzincan, and it provided search and rescue relief within the military area, quickly expanding to the city. The military and police force provided security.

The city quickly received aid and assistance from neighboring Erzurum Province to the east. Erzurum had experienced a severe earthquake disaster in November, 1983, and Erzincan residents provided comfort and support at that time. The national government and other provinces responded with emergency aid and assistance, and the government began a reconstruction program of thousands of prefabricated homes for the survivors.

William A. Mitchell

FOR FURTHER INFORMATION:
"Earthquake Hits Eastern Turkey, Leveling Villages and Killing 500." *The New York Times*, October 31, 1983.

Earthquake Research Institute. *The Erzincan Earthquake of 18 November 1983*. Ankara: Ministry of Reconstruction and Resettlement, 1983.

Gulkan, Polat. "Special In-country Report." *Earthquake Spectra: The Professional Journal of the Earthquake Engineering Institute* 9 (July, 1993): 149.

Mileti, Dennis S. *Disasters by Design: A Reassessment of Natural Hazards in the United States*. Washington, D.C.: John Henry Press, 1999.

Mitchell, William A. *Organizational Response for the Rural Victims: The Erzurum-Kars Earthquake, October 10, 1983*. Colorado Springs, Colo.: USAF Academy Department of Geography, 1985.

Tobin, Graham A., and Burrell E. Montz. *Natural Hazards: Explanation and Integration*. New York: Guilford Press, 1997.

1992: Landers and Big Bear Earthquakes

DATE: June 28, 1992
PLACE: Southern California, in the desert area of Landers and the mountain community near Big Bear Lake
MAGNITUDE: 7.3 (Landers), 6.2 (Big Bear)
RESULT: 3 dead, 397 injured, more than 4,630 structures damaged or destroyed, $92 million in damage

The Landers earthquake was the largest to hit California since the Kern County earthquake of 1952 (magnitude 7.5) and the biggest U.S. earthquake since the magnitude 9.2 that shook Alaska in 1964. The Landers quake rattled a contiguous land area of approximately 64,377 miles (103,600 kilometers) and was felt by people not only in California but also in southern Nevada, western Arizona, and southern Utah. As far away as Boise, Idaho, tall buildings

A cement floor in a house 20 yards from the fault scarp developed a long crack after the Landers and Big Bear earthquakes. (Courtesy National Oceanic and Atmospheric Administration)

quake would occur on the San Andreas fault within three days. Fortunately, the forecasted San Andreas quake never came. Aftershocks of the Joshua Tree quake did not die off as quickly as most California aftershock sequences. During May and June of that year, seismic activity shifted northward. By mid-June, there were small earthquakes occurring in the immediate vicinity of what would be the Landers hypocenter. Hours before the Landers quake, several small quakes occurred within half a mile of the hypocenter of the upcoming main shock.

The Landers earthquake struck on a Sunday morning at 4:57. Its epicenter was located between the towns of Landers and Yucca Valley, in a lightly populated area of California's Mojave Desert roughly 106 miles (170 kilometers) east of Los Angeles. Fault slip moved northward from the hypocenter, with the rupture front traveling at an average speed of 1.2 miles (2 kilometers) per second. The total duration of rupture was twenty-four seconds. The Landers quake was characterized by complex faulting unusual for California: right-lateral surface rupture occurring on a series of staggered, unconnected strike-slip faults. (These faults—the Johnson Valley, Landers, Homestead Valley, Emerson, and Camp Rock faults—are all part of the fault system that composes the principal element of the Pacific-North American Plate boundary in Baja and California.) Other nearby faults also experienced triggered slip, minor rupture, and rupture during large aftershocks. The total length of ground rupture associated with the Landers earthquake was over 44 miles (70 kilometers), the longest surface rupture in the United States since the 1906 San Francisco earthquake. Average slip was 10 to 13 feet (3 to 4 meters), with maximum slip reaching 20 miles (6 meters).

In the first hour of the aftershock series, there were so many tremors that the ground never stopped shaking. A little more than three hours after the Landers quake came its most severe aftershock. At 8:05 A.M., while television news coverage of the Landers quake was being broadcast from the Califor-

swayed, and water sloshed from swimming pools near Denver, Colorado. Yet the Landers quake caused comparatively few casualties and relatively little damage for its size, largely due to its occurrence far from densely populated areas.

The two months before the Landers quake comprised a period of intense seismic activity in the area south of what would be the Landers epicenter. The largest of these preshocks was the magnitude 6.1 Joshua Tree earthquake of April 28, 1992. This quake was close enough to the San Andreas fault for the U.S. Geological Survey to declare a Level B San Andreas Hazard—that is, a 5 percent to 25 percent probability that a magnitude 7.5 or greater earth-

nia Institute of Technology, a magnitude 6.2 quake struck near the mountain resort community of Big Bear Lake. The epicenter of the Big Bear quake was about 5 miles (8 kilometers) southeast of Big Bear Lake and 25 miles (40 kilometers) east of the city of San Bernardino—over 25 miles (40 kilometers) west of the Landers rupture. Although the Big Bear earthquake did not rupture the ground surface, data from its aftershocks allowed seismologists to determine that movement along a left-lateral strike-slip fault trending northeast generated the quake. The Big Bear quake was felt over a large area of Southern California, southern Nevada, and western Arizona.

The greatest structural damage from the Landers earthquake occurred in the desert communities of Landers, Yucca Valley, and Joshua Tree. Chimneys fell, masonry walls toppled, concrete pads cracked, and houses shifted off their foundations. Mobile homes were jolted off their underpinnings, causing major interior damage. Extensive damage to water mains and tanks interrupted water service, which would not be fully restored for several weeks. Power loss disrupted service for up to a day for about 600,000 customers in Southern California, including some as far away as Los Angeles and Santa Barbara. In the epicentral area, radio stations without backup power were unable to broadcast until electrical service was restored. Roads were damaged and offset by surface rupture.

In Big Bear Lake there were several fires as well as structural damage. Landslides and rockfalls blocked mountain roads and impeded cleanup efforts. The Landers and Big Bear earthquakes destroyed 77 homes and 27 businesses and damaged 4,393 homes and 146 businesses. One fatality occurred during the Landers quake when a chimney fell on a three-year-old child. Another two deaths resulted from heart attacks. There were 397 injuries reported, 25 of them serious. Had earthquakes of this magnitude occurred in a more densely populated area, casualties and damage would have been considerably greater. Propagation of fault rupture northward, toward a very sparsely populated area, also kept the Landers quake from having a more severe impact on people and property.

In the minutes and hours after the Landers quake, there was an increase in seismic activity throughout the western United States. Occurring up to 777 miles (1,250 kilometers) away from the Landers epicenter, this surge of seismicity was noted particularly in areas

of late Quaternary volcanism and geothermal activity. This onset of seismic activity in locations well beyond the boundaries of the Landers aftershock zone coincided with the passage of large-amplitude seismic waves from the Landers main shock. Researchers have yet to reach a consensus as to how large earthquakes like the Landers quake can trigger seismicity at great distances.

Karen N. Kähler

FOR FURTHER INFORMATION:

Earthquakes and Volcanoes 23, no. 5 (1992). Special issue on the Landers-Big Bear earthquakes on June 28, 1992.

Kerr, Richard A. "Landers Quake's Long Reach Is Shaking Up Seismologists." *Science* 259 (January 1, 1993): 29.

Yeats, Robert S., Kerry Sieh, and Clarence R. Allen. *The Geology of Earthquakes.* New York: Oxford University Press, 1997.

1992: Indonesia

DATE: December 12, 1992
PLACE: Flores Island, Indonesia
MAGNITUDE: 7.5
RESULT: 2,500 dead

This earthquake struck a remote region of eastern Indonesia 1,100 miles from the capital at Jakarta. On a Saturday afternoon, tremors shook Flores Island. The earthquake's epicenter was in the Savu Sea, approximately 20 miles from Maumere, a town populated by 40,000 people at that time. Tremors were felt 800 miles away in Irian Jaya Province.

The earthquake was especially devastating because it triggered tsunamis as high as 80 feet, which washed away people and buildings. Entire coastal villages were leveled by waves that moved ashore as far as 1,000 feet inland. Officials confirmed 1,232 deaths, of which 1,120 were in Maumere. Many victims were impoverished farmers who processed coconuts for oil. Survivors said they climbed coconut trees to escape from drowning.

Provincial Governor Hendrik Fernandez toured the island, sadly realizing that a quarter-century of economic development had been wiped out, including schools, government structures, and mosques. A

A woman creates a makeshift shelter after her home was destroyed by the 1992 Indonesia quake. (AP/Wide World Photos)

tropical rainstorm impeded rescue efforts, and survivors feared damaged buildings and the canvas and plastic tents they were living in would collapse from the weight of rainwater. The Indonesian army claimed its personnel had located and buried 2,484 earthquake victims found in debris and on beaches and were still searching other areas.

Elizabeth D. Schafer

FOR FURTHER INFORMATION:

"Earthquake in Indonesia Kills at Least 147." *The New York Times*, December 13, 1992, p. 27.

"Indonesia Starts Mass Burials of Quake Victims; Toll Put at 2,500." *The New York Times*, December 16, 1992, p. A7.

"More than 1,200 Known Dead in Quake in Eastern Indonesia." *The New York Times*, December 14, 1992, p. A3.

1993: India

DATE: September 29, 1993
PLACE: Maharashtra, India
MAGNITUDE: 6.4
RESULT: 9,748-30,000 dead, 150,000 homeless

At 3:56 A.M. on September 29, 1993, a series of five tremors struck western India in Maharashtra state when the Indian subcontinent and the Asian landmass collided. Because they occurred only 4 miles beneath the earth's surface, destruction was intensified. An estimated 1,000 casualties were reported at the epicenter in Khilari, population 15,000, where at least three-fourths of the homes were leveled, trapping people underneath rubble. Approximately 22 people died in nearby Osmanabad. The earthquake was felt hundreds of miles away in Madras and

Bangalore. The vibrations were so intense that seismographic results were smeared. Considered the worst Indian earthquake in fifty years, the tremors hit an agricultural region where farmers grew sugar cane, grapes, and sunflowers.

The government newspaper reported that more than 8,500 people had died and stated that casualty figures would increase because thousands were believed to be buried by debris and in isolated villages that rescuers had not yet reached. Later, state television said 10,000 people had died, while police officials stated there were 12,000 casualties. Most deaths occurred while people were sleeping in flimsy houses made of mud bricks with thatch or corrugated metal roofs. At least 40 villages were affected.

Despite torrential rain, mass cremations of corpses were conducted to prevent disease spreading among survivors, who included those who had been outside celebrating the birthday of Ganesh, the Hindu elephant god of wisdom, when the earthquake began.

Elizabeth D. Schafer

FOR FURTHER INFORMATION:

Gargan, Edward A. "In India Quake Zone, a Land of Funeral Pyres." *The New York Times,* October 2, 1993, p. 1.

"High Toll in India Quake" and "Quake Hits India; 1,000 Feared Dead." *The New York Times,* September 30, 1993, pp. A1, A8.

1994: Northridge Earthquake

DATE: January 17, 1994

PLACE: Southern California, in an area extending from the San Fernando Valley to Los Angeles and Santa Monica

MAGNITUDE: 6.7

RESULT: 57 dead, more than 9,000 injured, approximately $20 billion in damage

Several different faults extend from Alaska to Mexico, and earthquakes with magnitudes exceeding 5.0 on the Richter scale occur rather frequently in areas of North America located near the Pacific Ocean. However, the epicenters of most of these serious earthquakes have not been located near heavily populated regions. The worst American earthquake was centered in New Madrid, southeastern Missouri, on February 7, 1812. Although the Richter scale was not developed until 1935, contemporary reports have enabled seismologists to conclude that this earthquake had a magnitude between 8.4 and 8.8 and caused the earth to shake over 5 million square miles. That area of the United States was not then heavily populated, however, and only about 1,000 people died. On March 27, 1964, the Good Friday earthquake took place in Alaska; it was recorded at 9.2 on the Richter scale. It caused tsunamis, giant waves which drowned 120 people in relatively sparsely populated areas of Alaska such as Valdez, Seward, Kodiak Island, and the Kenai Peninsula. Only 131 people died as a result of this earthquake. An earthquake of magnitude 9.2, 10.0, or 11.0 in a heavily populated area of California, for example, would most certainly result in hundreds of thousands of deaths.

Lessons from Other California Quakes. Before the Northridge earthquake of January 17, 1994, many earthquakes had occurred in California, but the three which affected the lives of large numbers of people were the San Francisco earthquake of April 18, 1906; the Sylmar earthquake of February 9, 1971; and the Loma Prieta earthquake of October 17, 1989. When the 1906 San Francisco earthquake took place, the population of San Francisco was around 400,000. This earthquake measured 8.2 or 8.3 on the Richter scale and shook the earth over an area of approximately 300 square miles. It caused numerous fires when gas mains burst, and approximately 700 people died.

Not many lessons were learned from the 1906 San Francisco earthquake. Developers and government officials did not then realize that it was extremely dangerous to build on hilly areas and land reclaimed from the sea by filling the water with a combination of sand, mud, and rocks. In both the greater San Francisco and the greater Los Angeles regions, houses, bridges, dams, and public buildings were constructed near faults and in areas where the ground was highly susceptible to seismic shocks.

During the 1971 Sylmar earthquake, centered just to the north of Los Angeles, 65 people died, 47 of them in the collapse of the San Fernando Veterans Administration Hospital. This hospital, completed in 1925, was not designed to resist seismic shocks. People did not realize that public buildings should be constructed with reinforced bricks or that installing

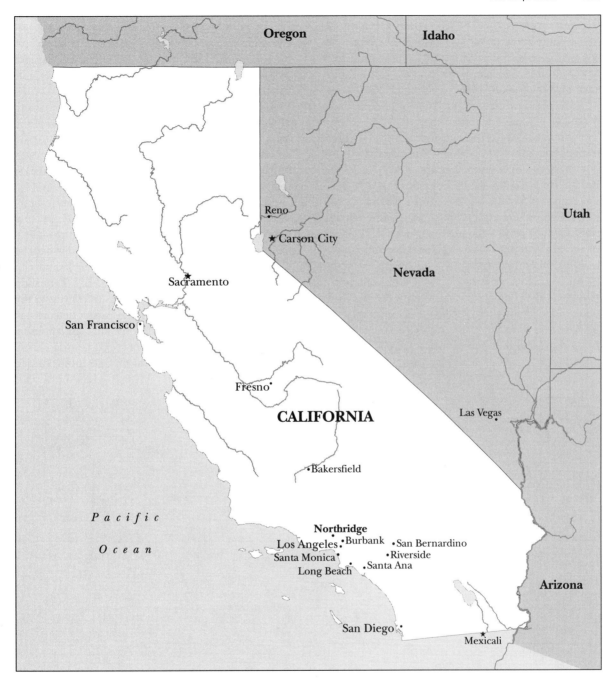

additional steel rods and wrapping more of them around existing rods made buildings more resistant to seismic shocks.

The deaths of so many people in the San Fernando Veterans Administration Hospital persuaded the California legislature to act quickly. In 1972, it created a Seismic Safety Commission and in-

structed the members to make recommendations to the governor and state legislators so that houses, public buildings, and other structures could be made more earthquake-resistant. The commission recommended that strict building codes be implemented in California to improve the safety of buildings and public structures throughout California. New building codes approved in the 1970's required builders to install more steel rods than had been previously required in new construction and to use reinforced bricks. In addition, the Seismic Safety Commission strongly recommended that existing bridges, dams, and overhead highways be "retrofitted," or reinforced with additional steel rods.

The changes implemented after the Sylmar earthquake dramatically decreased the number of deaths and the amount of property damage caused by the Loma Prieta earthquake of October 17, 1989, which was recorded at 7.1 on the Richter scale. The result was 67 deaths, more than 3,000 injuries, and damage well in excess of $5 billion dollars. However, only 18 of the more than 4,000 bridges and overhead highways in the region between San Francisco to the north and Santa Cruz and Watsonville to the south had to be closed for repairs as a result of this earthquake. Had not so many bridges and highways been retrofitted during the 1970's and 1980's, the loss of life and the amount of property damage would have been much higher.

The number of deaths and the property loss caused by an earthquake depend on a variety of factors. The epicenter and the time of an earthquake play major roles in determining the number of fatalities and the amount of damage. The epicenter of the Loma Prieta earthquake was located 70 miles south of San Francisco and Oakland, in the middle of the Santa Cruz Mountains and several miles from the cities of Watsonville and Santa Cruz. This distance significantly decreased the effect of this earthquake on very heavily populated cities such as San Francisco and Oakland and their surrounding communities.

The Northridge Earthquake. In 1994, the residents of Southern California were not as fortunate as their neighbors in Northern California in terms of location. The Northridge earthquake on January 17 originated in the heavily populated San Fernando Valley of Los Angeles, just 20 miles northwest of the downtown area. (The epicenter was later determined to be not in Northridge but in Reseda, an adjoining community.) The focal point of the Northridge earthquake was 12 miles below the surface, and it caused

A house is shifted from its foundation by the powerful Northridge earthquake. (FEMA)

the ground to shake over a wide area. Serious damage occurred as far west as Sherman Oaks and Fillmore; north to Santa Clarita; as far east as Glendale, Pasadena, and Los Angeles; and south to Santa Monica. It is fortunate, however, that this earthquake struck the greater Los Angeles area at 4:31 A.M. Had it struck during rush hour, the loss of life on Southern California highways would have been exceedingly high. Moreover, Southern Californians were fortunate indeed that the magnitude was not higher than 6.7. An earthquake of the magnitude of the 1964 Good Friday earthquake or the 1906 San Francisco earthquake would have killed far more people and resulted in property damage well in excess of the $20 billion caused by the Northridge earthquake.

When this earthquake took place, people were sleeping in their apartments, trailers, and houses. Sixteen were killed when the three-story Northridge Meadows apartment complex collapsed. The victims all lived on the first floor, which was flattened by the weight of the two floors above. Some of the victims died in their sleep, while others had been jolted awake moments before the collapse but had no means of escape. Many were crushed instantly, and some slowly suffocated in the rubble before help could reach them. Emergency personnel were able to rescue all those who lived on the second and third floors, but few were pulled out alive from the first floor.

This apartment complex was made of stucco, which is not very resistant to seismic shocks. To make matters worse, the carports on the first floor were supported by a series of single steel supports, which buckled and collapsed. Many stucco apartment complexes, like the Northridge Meadows apartment complex, were built in the 1950's and 1960's to accommodate the large influx of people who had moved to the greater Los Angeles region. Such apartment complexes were much cheaper to build than buildings constructed with reinforced bricks. It should be remembered, however, that people did not know at the time that such apartment houses would perform so poorly during earthquakes. Building codes in effect during the twenty years before the 1994 Northridge earthquake would have prohibited the construction of stucco apartment complexes with carports supported by single steel columns. Other similar apartment complexes collapsed in such widely separated cities or communities as Fillmore, Van Nuys, Los Angeles, and Sherman Oaks. In

affected areas, apartment houses built with reinforced bricks and reinforced with more steel rods than had been required before the 1970's performed rather well during this earthquake and did not collapse.

Trailer parks also suffered greatly either as a direct result of the seismic shocks or because of the fires that occurred when underground gas mains burst and ignited when the gas encountered a fire source. Over one hundred trailers were destroyed by fire, but quick and effective action by firefighters and other emergency officers resulted in the loss of just one life in trailers, an extraordinary figure because the fires began while almost all the residents were asleep. Fires of intensity equal to those seen in San Francisco's Marina District right after the 1989 Loma Prieta earthquake broke out in many different regions of the San Fernando Valley and the rest of Los Angeles.

Damage in the San Fernando Valley. Since Northridge was very near the epicenter of this earthquake, it is not surprising that this community suffered such extensive damage on that Monday morning of January 17, 1994. Part of the precast concrete parking garage for the Northridge Fashion Center collapsed. Both this parking garage and the adjoining mall suffered major structural damage. No loss of life occurred, however, because there were no customers in the mall or garage at such an early hour of the morning. Only one employee was at the site—a man driving a steam cleaning truck in the parking garage was trapped for several hours before being rescued. Had the earthquake taken place a few hours later, when the mall would be open for business on the Martin Luther King, Jr., holiday, thousands might have been killed or seriously injured.

Seismic shocks also caused a similarly built precast concrete parking garage on the campus of California State University, Northridge (CSUN), to collapse, destroying the cars inside. Many other buildings there suffered major structural damage. However, there was no loss of life on the campus. It is fortunate that this earthquake took place on Martin Luther King, Jr., Day because all state and federal offices were closed, as were all schools and universities. More students would have been on campus had this disaster not occurred on the third day of a long weekend.

Both of these two parking garages and the Northridge mall had been constructed after the implementation of strict building codes in the 1970's, but these structures could not resist the seismic shocks since they were located so close to the epicenter of this 6.7 earthquake.

In other areas of the San Fernando Valley, office buildings, private homes, and public buildings constructed after 1972 performed generally quite well during the earthquake because they were in conformity to codes which required that buildings be relatively resistant to seismic shocks.

Liquefaction. A common result of earthquakes is liquefaction of the ground. This phenomenon occurs when the ground upon which houses and structures have been built is primarily soft material such as sand or clay, not bedrock. When encountering seismic shocks, the ground itself weakens and behaves like water.

This effect had been noticed in 1989 in San Francisco's Marina District, which had been reclaimed from the sea by filling the area with massive amounts of mud, sand, and rocks. This combination appeared to make the ground stable, but liquefaction caused the collapse of many buildings and structures which had conformed to strict building codes. The buildings themselves were sound, but the ground on which they had been constructed was too weak to support structures during a major earthquake.

Geologists who studied the Northridge earthquake concluded that liquefaction caused major landslides in the Santa Susana Mountains, which literally changed the shape of the terrain, and in residential areas such as Pacific Palisades where houses built on cliffs overlooking the Pacific Ocean came loose from their foundations and slid down hills. The ground on which these expensive homes had been built was simply not solid enough to resist seismic shocks. In hindsight, it becomes clear that houses should not be built on cliffs located near faults.

The problem of liquefaction was by no means limited to mountain ranges and houses built on palisades. Much of what now appears to be stable ground in Southern California was, in fact, created by draining wetlands. Those who drained the wetlands thought that they were helping people by making more land available for housing and business, but ironically they had created a disaster waiting to happen. The Santa Monica Freeway was built over land reclaimed from marshes. The ground on which this heavily traveled expressway was built was not as earthquake-resistant as the architects and contractors had thought. A portion of the Santa Monica Freeway collapsed not because of structural deficiencies but rather because some of the ground on which it was built liquefied during the Northridge earthquake and the ground itself was no longer strong enough to support the weight of the freeway.

Other overhead highways collapsed because even well-constructed and reinforced highways could not resist such strong shocks emanating from such a close epicenter. Amazingly, only one motorist died as a result of the collapse of a highway. In the darkness of the early morning and with the power out, police officer Clarence Dean could not see that a portion of Highway 14 on which he was driving had collapsed. He drove his motorcycle over the edge and was killed instantly. During the Loma Prieta earthquake, 41 people were killed when a portion of the Nimitz Expressway collapsed in Oakland; that earthquake took place at 5:05 P.M., when many people were driving on the highways and bridges of the San Francisco Bay area. There was very little traffic on the highways in and around Los Angeles when the Northridge earthquake struck at 4:31 A.M. on a national holiday. At another time of day, hundreds if not thousands of deaths could have occurred on the usually heavily traveled highways around Los Angeles.

Fire and Flood. Another serious problem faced by residents and emergency personnel following the Northridge earthquake was the extremely large numbers of fires which occurred throughout the affected areas. Fires were fought over an area extending 25 miles in all directions from the epicenter. The Los Angeles Fire Department had to extinguish 476 earthquake-related fires on January 17, 1994, in Los Angeles County alone, and the earthquake caused dangerous fires in surrounding counties as well.

The community of Granada Hills experienced simultaneous flooding and massive fires, when water mains and gas mains burst. A gas main explosion on Balboa Boulevard in Granada Hills was the worst fire caused by the Northridge earthquake. People living in that area had to flee their homes and apartments in their pajamas. firefighters brought water trucks with them because the water main had burst and they could not obtain water from fire hydrants. Another earthquake-related fire began when 40,000 gallons of gasoline spilled onto the street in Pacoima and caught fire. Emergency personnel managed to extinguish this inferno, and although there was extensive property damage in Pacoima, no one was killed.

There was also environmental damage when a pipeline burst and spilled 150,000 gallons of crude

The Interstate 5 and SR14 freeways collapsed during the Northridge earthquake. (Courtesy National Oceanic and Atmospheric Administration)

1994 in order to make the hospitals of Southern California more resistant to seismic shocks. It was expected that the hospitals might experience minor structural damage during severe earthquakes but that they would not collapse. These newly built or reinforced hospitals were designed to continue operating after a major earthquake. Although patients had to be evacuated from the Veterans Administration Hospital in Sepulveda and from St. John's Hospital in Santa Monica, no one was killed in either hospital, and most hospitals in the greater Los Angeles continued normal operations despite the Northridge earthquake. Two other hospitals, Olive View Medical Center and Holy Cross Medical Center, both in Sylmar, had to cease operations temporarily because of flooding and the loss of electrical power, but neither hospital had very extensive structural damage. The systematic reinforcement of existing hospitals and the construction of new, quake-resistant ones enabled medical personnel to meet the needs of the thousands of people injured as a result of the Northridge earthquake.

Effects. The effect of the Northridge earthquake on the greater Los Angeles region was profound. By early 1994, California, especially Southern California, was slowly beginning to recover from an economic downturn that had begun in the late 1980's.

The Northridge earthquake caused at least $13 billion in damage, but most estimates place the actual damage as close to $20 billion. In comparison, the Loma Prieta earthquake, which took place four years before the Northridge earthquake, caused property damage of between $5 billion and $6 billion. Massive assistance from the federal government helped the state of California restore the infrastructure in and around Los Angeles, and interest-free loans from the federal government made it possible for individuals to rebuild their homes and for business owners to rebuild their establishments. As was the case for the Loma Prieta earthquake, most property owners in the Los Angeles region did not carry earthquake insurance because such insurance is almost prohibitively expensive and comes with very high deduct-

oil into the Santa Clara River. Toxic specialists were able to control this potentially dangerous situation, and the river itself did not catch fire. A chemical fire started in a science building of the campus of CSUN, and another potentially dangerous situation occurred when a train derailment resulted in the release of 8,000 gallons of sulfuric acid. In both cases, prompt response by representatives from various local, state, and federal environmental agencies permitted control of the situation and the prevention of an environmental disaster.

It is very fortunate that the federal government, the state of California, and hospital administrators learned a valuable lesson from the 1971 Sylmar earthquake. People realized that it was necessary to reinforce existing hospitals and to build new hospitals so that they would not collapse during earthquakes. Considerable money was spent between 1971 and

ibles and very limited coverage. Regular homeowner's insurance does not cover damage caused by earthquakes. Loans from the federal government remain the only real option for most people.

Emergency officials from local, state, and federal governments; members of the California National Guard; and volunteers from the Red Cross, the Salvation Army, and other nonprofit organizations met the immediate needs of the survivors. Makeshift housing was created for people whose homes and apartments had been destroyed. Food and bottled drinking water were distributed to those who had lost almost everything but their lives during this terrible earthquake. The federal government gave housing vouchers to survivors so that they could rent homes or apartments until they could return to their former places of residence. The Federal Emergency Management Agency (FEMA) coordinated relief operations. In the days after the Loma Prieta earthquake, emergency personnel realized that they had not hired enough Spanish-speaking people to assist Latino victims of that earthquake. Emergency organizations learned from this experience, and there were enough bilingual personnel from both government agencies and volunteer organizations to assist Spanish-speaking survivors of the Northridge earthquake.

It took several months to repair the many highways which had suffered serious damage. Traffic on the remaining highways and bridges in Southern California was even worse than usual because travelers could no longer use such frequently traveled highways as the Golden Gate Freeway and the Santa Monica Freeway. Using financial incentives, the federal government and the state of California had these damaged highways rebuilt in record time and made sure that they met strict building codes. By 1995, Southern California had basically recovered economically from the property damage caused by the Northridge earthquake, but it is difficult to assess the psychological damage experienced by survivors who had lost their homes and their personal possessions. Although property damage caused by the earthquake was very high, Southern Californians were thankful that no more than 57 people had died during this disaster. With a different set of circumstances, it could have been much worse.

Edmund J. Campion

FOR FURTHER INFORMATION:
Bolt, Bruce A. *Earthquakes*. Rev. ed. New York: W. H. Freeman, 1993. This revised edition of a book first published in 1978 explains clearly how earthquakes take place. Given its date of publication, this textbook does not deal with the Northridge earthquake, but it does explain well the devastating effect of major earthquakes on many different regions of the world.

Bulletin of the Seismological Society of America, 86, 1, Part B. Although written for seismologists and geologists, the articles in this issue describe well the initial seismic shocks, aftershocks, liquefaction, and structural failure during the Northridge earthquake.

Earthquakes and Volcanoes 25, nos. 1-2 (1994). These two issues of a scholarly journal deal exclusively with the Northridge earthquake. Several articles describe very clearly the landslides, liquefaction, and structural damage caused by the Northridge earthquake. Includes color photographs of many badly damaged structures.

Fradkin, Philip L. *Magnitude 8*. New York: Henry Holt, 1998. This book, written by a geologist for the general public, describes very well how the Northridge earthquake seriously disrupted daily life throughout the greater Los Angeles region.

Hall, John F., ed. *Northridge Earthquake January 17, 1994. Preliminary Reconnaissance Report*. Oakland, Calif.: Earthquake Engineering Research Institute, 1994. This very useful report published just three months after the Northridge earthquake contains ten chapters, each of which examines a different aspect of this earthquake. The report describes clearly the damage done to hospitals, highways, and buildings both by the seismic shocks themselves and by the accompanying fires.

Newsweek, January 31, 1994, 16-37. Numerous illustrated articles in this issue examine the physical destruction and social disruption caused by the Northridge earthquake.

Sieh, Kerry, and Simon Le Vay. *The Earth in Turmoil: Earthquakes, Volcanoes, and Their Impact on Humankind*. New York: W. H. Freeman, 1998. As its subtitle indicates, this book explores the profound social disruption caused by earthquakes and tornadoes.

Time, January 31, 1994, 26-46. Numerous illustrated articles describe the destruction caused by the Northridge earthquake. They also describe how governmental agencies prepare for major earthquakes.

1994: Bolivia

DATE: June 9, 1994
PLACE: Northern Bolivia
MAGNITUDE: 7.5
RESULT: 253 dead, 300 missing

This earthquake, which had its epicenter in northern Bolivia, was unusual for several reasons. Rocking South America on a Wednesday night, the tremor occurred exceptionally deep within the earth. Because it happened so far beneath the earth's surface, the earthquake, despite its strength, did not produce significant damage to people or property. Also, the earthquake's depth resulted in its shock waves traveling thousands of miles so that the tremors were felt as far north as Canada.

Beginning at 8:36 P.M. in Bolivia, the tremor was located 200 miles northeast of La Paz in an area with low population, which minimized destruction of buildings and deaths of humans and livestock. The earthquake occurred approximately 400 miles below ground level in rock that seismologists described as being elastic. Because the rock was flexible, it absorbed some of the earthquake's force and also enabled the shockwaves to move laterally through adjoining earth layers to distant sites in North America. In La Paz, people were evacuated from buildings that moved when the tremor began. Rescuers confirmed that 253 people died due to the earthquake, and 300 people were reported missing and had possibly perished. Coincidentally, on the Monday before the Bolivian earthquake, a tremor had struck Colombia and triggered an avalanche.

Elizabeth D. Schafer

FOR FURTHER INFORMATION:
"Deep Quake in Bolivia." *The New York Times,* June 10, 1994, p. A5.
Farah, Douglas. "In Colombia's Remote Valleys, Quake's Trauma Emerges." *Washington Post,* June 10, 1994, p. A1.

1995: Kobe Earthquake

ALSO KNOWN AS: Hyogoken Nanbu earthquake
DATE: January 17, 1995

PLACE: Kobe, Japan
MAGNITUDE: 7.2
RESULT: 5,502 dead, 37,000 injured, more than 100,000 buildings ruined, more than $50 billion in damage (the most financially costly natural disaster ever)

The city of Kobe (pronounced KOH-beh) lies on the southern coast of Japan's main island of Honshū. Situated on the Inland Sea between the islands of Honshū and Shikoku, it is Japan's second largest seaport and an important center for shipbuilding, steelmaking, and other commerce and industry. Its population of 1.4 million is densely concentrated along the narrow coastal plain that fronts inland mountains.

Without warning, just before dawn on the wintry morning of January 17, 1995, the Kobe area was struck by an earthquake that would be the most devastating seismic event in earthquake-prone Japan since the Tokyo quake of 1923, and the most expensive natural disaster in history to date. The epicenter was 20 miles (32 kilometers) southwest of downtown Kobe, at 34.6 degrees north latitude and longitude 135 degrees east. This was about 19 miles (30 kilometers) south of the coastline, near the tip of Awaji Island. Slippage occurred on the Nojima fault, including surface rupture along at least 6 miles (9 kilometers) with displacement (slip) up to 5 feet (1.5 meters), and perhaps 6.5 feet (2 meters) depth. The total length of the ruptured fault at depth was 19 to 31 miles (30 to 50 kilometers). The movement was lateral (strike-slip), with the fault oriented to the northeast toward the northern portion of the city of Kobe. The focus (zone of initial slip) was at a depth of 13 miles (21 kilometers) below the tip of Awaji Island.

This event has been called the Hyogoken Nanbu earthquake, for the local Hyogo prefecture (province) but is more commonly known as the Kobe earthquake for that nearby city. While it was not a truly great earthquake in magnitude and energy release, it had devastating consequences to people and urban structures because of its proximity to Kobe and the densely populated corridor along the coast, because of the orientation of the rupture directly toward the city, and because of the shallowness of the rupture.

The magnitude of the main shock was 7.2 on the Richter scale, and 6.9 on the moment-magnitude scale. It occurred at 5:46 A.M. local time on January

Mitsubishi Bank was destroyed by the Kobe earthquake in 1995. (AP/Wide World Photos)

17, which was 8:46 P.M. January 16, Universal time (Greenwich Mean Time). Aftershocks continued for many months after the initial major shock. In the seven days after, there were nineteen aftershocks having magnitudes 4 to 5. People reported that the approaching seismic waves created a rumble, then a roar, followed by strong vibrations both vertically and horizontally. The wrenching vibrations lasted about twenty seconds.

Aftereffects. The casualties and destruction were staggering. At least 5,502 people were killed, mostly from immediate crushing or entrapment in the rubble. This figure included 28 who were killed in a landslide at Nishinomiya, a town just east of Kobe. Early reports revealed 27,000 injured, but this was later raised to 36,896. As many as 310,000 people had to be evacuated to temporary shelters, including school gymnasiums and city offices, and over 70,000 were

still in them two months later. Initially, many residents had to camp out in the freezing January weather, having lost their homes or being afraid of more damage and collapse from the continuing aftershocks. According to the international edition of *Newsweek* for January 30, 1995,

> Everything but misery was in short supply. Many people spent the nights in the open air because no one could provide them with shelter. One moment they were well-dressed, propertied, and secure; the next they were refugees shuffling through rubble-strewn streets fretted by flame, lugging possessions on their backs, surrounded by the corpses of loved ones and neighbors.

Approximately 200,000 buildings were destroyed or damaged. More than 50,000 were reduced to rubble or complete collapse, thousands of others were so damaged that they had to be torn down, and others were consumed in the subsequent fires. While some modern structures, especially those built to an earthquake-resistant code (with reinforcing and bracing) instituted in 1981, were relatively unscathed, many suffered damage. Some collapsed, tilted, or sank because of unstable or settling soil and sediment.

Superficial ground accelerations in Kobe and adjacent Nishinomiya were measured at up to 50 to 80 percent of the acceleration of gravity—too high for most unreinforced structures to withstand. When materials are unconsolidated (soft soil, alluvial deposits, landfill) and especially when water-saturated, as after rains and in coastal regions, they lose strength and absorb energy when vibrated by seismic waves. Ground motions are amplified, and damage is intensified. This behavior, termed liquefaction, causes much worse damage than structures on firm bedrock receive. Some of the worst structural damage was thus along the Kobe waterfront, with its water-saturated landfill in place for port development and creation of habitable land for the expanding population, which faced high land prices and lack of available space along the narrow coastal plain.

Portions of the elevated Hanshin four-lane expressway, Japan's primary east-west traffic artery through coastal Kobe, collapsed. A section 656 yards (600 meters) long toppled over sideways to rest at a 45-degree angle. There was much ground failure, cracking, and sinking along the waterfront. The elevated rail line of the high-speed Shinkansen ("bullet") train, constructed to be almost indestructible, was snapped in eight places. Fortunately, the first train of the day had not yet left for Kobe.

Particularly vulnerable to the horizontal shaking of earthquake waves were the older two-story houses built of wood frames with heavy tile roofs. They collapsed, trapping their occupants, and were then burned in fires ignited by ruptured gas lines. There were over 300 fires in the area, and a dozen of them raged for twenty-four to forty-eight hours. Fire

fighting was impossible, because major utilities—water mains, as well as electricity, gas, and telephone lines—were severed and disabled. Further, the roadways were congested with fallen buildings, rubble, and people fleeing, checking on relatives, or engaged in rescue efforts. Roads, bridges, and rail lines (for the public transportation electric trains) were cut. With the loss of utilities, there was no heat for the cold January weather and no water for drinking, plumbing, or bathing.

Factories and shops that did survive the earthquake had to shut down operations because of lack of power and other utilities, toppled equipment, and lack of employees. Despite the destruction and abandonment of homes, stores, and shops, there was virtu-

The Kobe earthquake toppled part of the Hanshin expressway. (AP/Wide World Photos)

ally no looting or civil disturbance. The Japanese virtues of order and discipline, stoicism, and civility were evident and focused the citizenry on applying their perseverance and hard work to the task of survival and reconstructing their lives.

Damage and casualties occurred along the coast through Nishinomiya and as far as Osaka, Japan's second-largest city, which is 18 miles (30 kilometers) from Kobe. The latter had cracked walls, broken windows, and 11 earthquake-related deaths.

Japan is a nation with high cost of living and an elaborate urban infrastructure. Rebuilding costs, public and private, have been variously estimated from U.S. $40 to 100 billion—exceeding those of any other natural disaster. This figure does not include indirect losses such as lost economic productivity and business activity. Little of the residential losses was covered by insurance—only 9 percent of Japan's population has home earthquake insurance, and only 3 percent in Kobe, which was thought to be in a region of low seismic risk.

Rescue and Relief. The rescue efforts and distribution of emergency relief materials—food, water, fuel, and blankets—were hampered by an initially slow response by local government authorities and uncharacteristic disorganization. Assistance was also slowed by the congested urban destruction and impassable roadways. Roads that could have been cleared for emergency vehicles—fire, police, and search and rescue—were not cordoned off and were thus clogged with residents with their vehicles and possessions. The officials also delayed in calling in the national armed forces for assistance.

The lack of civic preparedness for such an earthquake disaster was surprising, considering the generally high awareness in Japan of the prospect of such an event. Many people have an earthquake-emergency kit of supplies in their homes. Every September 1, Disaster Prevention Day, on the anniversary of the Great Kwanto Earthquake that hit Tokyo and Yokohama in 1923, there are nationwide community drills on disaster response, evacuation, mock rescues, and protective measures. Ironically, Kobe rose to become a busy port and international trading city in 1923, when foreign merchants left the devastated port city of Yokohama after the earthquake there. In fact, some Japanese survivors of the 1923 earthquake had come to Kobe to settle and were still alive for the 1995 event—thus experiencing the two most devastating earthquakes in Japan in the twentieth century.

Reasons for the Scope of the Destruction. Kobe was not well prepared, psychologically and organizationally, for a major earthquake. First, it was some distance back from the seismically active zone of earthquakes associated with the oceanic trenches off Japan's southern and eastern margins. It was thus believed to have less potential of suffering a major shock. Second, there was a belief that modern engineering and building design had made structures less susceptible to being damaged and disabled by an earthquake. This event, having a fairly large magnitude and being shallow and nearby, demonstrated the continuing vulnerability of an urban infrastructure.

By coincidence and with regard to earthquake-resistant design, three years after the earthquake, in April, 1998, the world's longest suspension bridge opened there. The Akashi Kaikyo bridge connects the mainland west of Kobe across the Akashi Strait to Awaji Island. Its total length is 15 miles (24 kilometers), and the center suspension span is 1.2 miles (2 kilometers) long. The bridge was supposedly designed to withstand a magnitude 8.0 earthquake. Each of the tall towers supporting the center span is equipped with 20 vibration-control pendulums to reduce bridge movement if buffeted by earthquake waves or high winds.

Third, there was an expectation, or hope, that Japan's application of technology to the problems of understanding earthquake mechanisms, monitoring for precursory indications of an impending event, and public warnings issued to the citizenry would give advance warning of a likely event. Unfortunately, the earthquake struck on a then-unsuspected fault and without any obvious premonitory indicators such as minor foreshocks. However, there were reports of odd animal behavior near Kobe in the hours and days before the earthquake. These included fish near shore, birds, and sea lions at the zoo. The composition of well water used for local sake (rice wine) production varied unusually—especially for radon, a gas whose presence in deep groundwater has been linked to pre-earthquake straining.

Ironically, on the day the earthquake struck Kobe, the fourth Japan-United States Workshop on Urban Earthquake Hazard Reduction was beginning down the road in Osaka. After the earthquake, the meeting was canceled because the participants had gone to Kobe to assess and investigate the disaster and its consequences.

This was the biggest earthquake to hit a densely populated area of Japan since June, 1948, when one of magnitude 7.1 struck Fukui, on the north coast of Honshū island, killing about 5,000. With Kobe's death toll of 5,502, it was the most deadly seismic disaster since the September, 1923, Great Kwanto Earthquake of magnitude 8.3 that struck Tokyo and Yokohama and killed 143,000, mostly in the fires that raged after the shock.

The geological fact of life for Japan is that the island nation, with its scenic majesty and as the world's second-largest economic power, is constructed on vulnerable and unstable terrain. The inexorable movement and collision of tectonic plates—the Pacific and Philippine from the east, the Eurasian from the west, and the North American from the north— means that faults will continue to rupture and cause earthquakes into the foreseeable future.

Robert S. Carmichael

FOR FURTHER INFORMATION:

Abe, K. "Seismicity of Japan's Earthquakes and Tsunamis." *Impact of Science on Society* 37, no. 145 (1986): 63-74.

Reid, T. R. "Kobe Wakes to a Nightmare." *National Geographic*, July, 1995, 112-136.

Somerville, P. "Kobe Earthquake: An Urban Disaster." *EOS/Transactions of American Geophysical Union* 76, no. 6 (February 7, 1995): 49-51.

"Twenty Seconds of Terror." *Newsweek*, January 30, 1995, 19-30.

U.S. Geological Survey/National Earthquake Information Center, www.neic.cr.usgs.gov.

quently, the homes constructed on the island were not built with the idea of withstanding any significant tremors.

The town of Neftegorsk (meaning "oil town"), located near the northern tip of the island and comprising a population of 3,000 people, suffered the brunt of the damage. The town was completely destroyed, with over 1,800 people, 60 percent of the population, killed. Thirteen five-story houses collapsed during the quake, burying most of the residents beneath tons of rubble. Rescue workers were able to remove hundreds of injured, but the bodies of most of the 1,800 dead in the town were found beneath the ruins. An oil pipeline that ran north of the town—and was the basis for the town's name—was ruptured, spilling oil onto the landscape. Russian officials decided the town would not be rebuilt. In the town of Okha, located 55 miles north of Neftegorsk and containing a population of 35,000 people, balconies collapsed on a number of five-story buildings.

Sakhalin Island has been the source for much of the oil and gas shipped into eastern Russia. However, the island has been most noted as the site of Russian military bases. It was near Sakhalin Island in 1983 that a Korean Air Lines flight was shot down by Russian pilots, killing the 269 passengers.

Richard Adler

FOR FURTHER INFORMATION:

"Death Toll of 2,000 Is Feared in Quake on Russian Island." *The New York Times*, May 30, 1995, p. A1.

"Quake on Russian Island in Pacific Kills at Least 300." *The New York Times*, May 29, 1995, pp. A1, A3.

1995: Russia

DATE: May 28, 1995
PLACE: Sakhalin Island, Russia
MAGNITUDE: 7.5
RESULT: 2,400 dead, town of Neftegorsk destroyed

At 1:04 A.M. on the morning of May 28, 1995, what has been called the most devastating earthquake in Russian history occurred under the Russian island of Sakhalin. The region, on the Pacific coast of Russia, had not previously been considered part of the earthquake zone despite its proximity to Japan. Conse-

1997: Pakistan

DATE: February 28, 1997
PLACE: Southwestern Pakistan
MAGNITUDE: 7.3
RESULT: More than 100 dead

Southwestern Pakistan was devastated by an earthquake that struck before dawn on February 28, 1997. The tremor's epicenter was in Baluchistan Province, located along the Iran and Afghanistan borders. The earthquake woke up residents of Quetta, the provincial capital, who heard a loud roaring noise. Sixteen hours later, a second earthquake rocked northwestern Iran near the Azerbaijan border, but seismologists concluded that the two tremors were unrelated, noting that seismic activity was common in the area. Newspaper accounts discussed the Pakistani and Iranian earthquakes together, totaling casualties from both sites.

Pakistan officials determined that at least 48 people had died in that country during the earthquake and that hundreds were injured. Because the earthquake occurred in a mountainous region, authorities feared that more casualties would be discovered when rescuers reached isolated villages. The isolated Sibi District suffered the most damage because its mud-brick buildings collapsed on top of sleeping inhabitants. The earthquake also ruined roads and railway, hindering relief attempts. As more bodies were found, the death toll was raised to more than 100 people. Injured victims were transported to Quetta for medical attention. Due to the intensity of the earthquake and the resultant destruction, many Pakistanis believed that doomsday had arrived.

Elizabeth D. Schafer

FOR FURTHER INFORMATION:

"Death Toll Rises in Iran and Pakistan Quakes." *The New York Times*, March 2, 1997, p. 12.

"Pakistan-Iran Quakes Kill 150." *The New York Times*, March 1, 1997, p. 3.

1997: Iran

DATE: February 28 and March 2, 1997
PLACE: Northwestern Iran
MAGNITUDE: Both 6.1
RESULT: 965 dead, 2,600 injured

Two earthquakes struck Iran within a three-day period. The first tremor occurred the same day that an earthquake shook southwestern Pakistan. Seismologists decided that the two earthquakes were not linked, commenting that the region experienced much earthquake activity, such as a 1990 tremor that killed 50,000 Iranians. Initial news reports combined casualty figures from both the Pakistani and Iranian tremors, noting that the Iranian earthquake had caused more deaths. After the second earthquake hit Iran, separate statistics were kept for that country.

The first Iranian earthquake occurred in the northwest part of the country, close to the border with Azerbaijan. Located in an impoverished agricultural region, those communities and 80 surrounding villages were inhabited by Azerbaijanis, an ethnic minority in Iran. The Iranian settlements at Ardabīl, the provincial capital, and Meshkinshahr endured shaking for thirty seconds. The second earthquake, in March, caused more damage.

The earthquakes killed almost 1,000 people, injured thousands, and left 40,000 homeless. Rescuers feared thousands more might have died in remote regions in the Talish Mountains. Tehran officials claimed the first earthquake had an intensity of 5.5, but the U.S. National Earthquake Information Center said both tremors were 6.1-magnitude earthquakes. Two aftershocks increased panic among the residents, and Red Crescent Society workers tried to help earthquake sufferers despite snow and ice accumulations and scavenging wolves. The hot spring at Saraein was utilized to wash corpses according to Islamic rituals.

Elizabeth D. Schafer

FOR FURTHER INFORMATION:

"At Deadly Quake Site in Iran, More Destruction." *The New York Times*, March 3, 1997, p. A5.

"Quake Leaves Iranian Villagers Grief-Stricken and Homeless." *The New York Times*, March 4, 1997, p. A4.

1997: Iran

DATE: May 10, 1997
PLACE: Northeastern Iran
MAGNITUDE: 7.1
RESULT: 2,500 dead, 6,000 injured

At 12:28 P.M. on May 10, 1997, a severe earthquake struck the mountainous region of northeastern Iran. The epicenter of the quake was located near Qāyen, about 70 miles west of the border with Afghanistan. The most severe damage occurred in Khorāsān Province along a 60-mile region between the towns of Qāyen and Bīrjand, a rural area of small villages, subsistence farmers, and wheat and saffron fields approximately 300 miles east of the capital of Tehran. Damage extended across the border into Afghanistan, where 5 deaths were reported. The earthquake was the second major tremor to hit northern Iran in ten weeks, and the third within a year. More than 155 aftershocks were felt over the following twenty-four hours.

At least 2,000 people died in the region immediately surrounding Qāyen. About 110 children were killed in Ardakul alone when their schoolhouse collapsed over their heads. Another 400 people were killed in Bīrjand. The final toll from the earthquake, in addition to the dead and injured, included severe damage to over 200 villages, totaling some 10,000 homes.

Most of the rescue efforts were coordinated by the Iranian Red Crescent. France sent a cargo plane loaded with food and rescue supplies, while Switzerland sent a rescue team and trained dogs to search for survivors. A relief team from Great Britain was refused entry.

In early February, 1997, an earthquake measuring 6.1 struck northwestern Iran around the city of Ardabīl, killing nearly 1,000 people and leaving another 40,000 homeless. A series of earthquakes in June, 1990, left nearly 50,000 Iranians dead and 500,000 homeless.

Richard Adler

FOR FURTHER INFORMATION:

"Earthquake Toll in Iran Estimated to Climb to 2,400." *The New York Times*, May 12, 1997, p. A1.

"Second Quake in 10 Weeks Hits Iran." *The New York Times*, May 11, 1997, p. A1.

The bell tower in Foligno, Italy, was damaged after the 1997 temblor. (AP/Wide World Photos)

1997: Italy

DATE: September 26, 1997
PLACE: Central Italy
MAGNITUDE: 5.5 and 5.7
RESULT: 11 dead, Basilica of St. Francis of Assisi damaged

Two earthquakes inflicted cultural and religious damage in addition to human casualties. The first tremor hit central Italy at 2:33 A.M. and measured 5.5 on the Richter scale. The Basilica of St. Francis of Assisi in Umbria, a thirteenth century Roman Catholic shrine with fresco-covered walls, was near the earthquake's epicenter at Colfiorito. After the tremor subsided, a group entered the basilica to assess the damage to the building and its artwork, when a second earthquake struck at 11:42 in the morning. This tremor was 5.7 in magnitude. The building's vaulted roof fell, killing 4 people. Valuable frescoes were shattered. In nearby villages, medieval churches and monuments were also damaged. Thousands became homeless, and most casualties resulted from people being killed while sleeping during the first earthquake. The earthquake was felt in Venice and in Rome, where an iron lamp fell in the Senate.

By November of 1999, the basilica had been repaired, reinforced, and reopened, exhibiting some of its legendary art, which was reconstructed from fragments. Approximately 10,000 earthquake victims were still housed in temporary shelters. Fraud, inspection permit requirements, and insufficient supply plagued rebuilding efforts.

Elizabeth D. Schafer

FOR FURTHER INFORMATION:
Bohlen, Celestine. "A Fatal Quake Shatters Fresco in Assisi Shrine." *The New York Times*, September 27, 1997, p. A1.
"Quake Harm in Assisi Is Considered Irreparable." *The New York Times*, September 28, 1997, p. 8.

1998: Afghanistan

DATE: February 4, 1998
PLACE: Northeastern Afghanistan
MAGNITUDE: 6.1
RESULT: 5,000 dead, 20 villages destroyed

At approximately 7:35 on the night of Wednesday, February 4, 1998, an earthquake shook regions of Takhar Province in Afghanistan, approximately 200 miles north of the capital of Kabul. The area, one of mud houses and small villages situated in a remote mountainous region already struggling through a harsh winter, had been subjected to significant earthquakes in the past. An aftershock measuring a magnitude of 5.4 followed five days later. While neither quake was of a size comparable to earlier recorded events, they still produced significant damage and loss of life in a region of poorly constructed houses and public buildings.

The first shocks destroyed approximately 20 villages in the region around Rustaq, one of the largest towns in the area, though Rustaq itself suffered little significant damage. The quake resulted in massive landslides that covered homes and small villages in their path. The death toll was ultimately estimated at approximately 5,000 people, with thousands more left injured or homeless.

Recovery efforts were hampered by the harsh winter conditions in the remote mountainous areas. Relief teams were unable to travel by road and had to fly

in on helicopters. The Islamic State of Afghanistan, as the government was known, appealed for international aid. The first international agency to reach the region was Doctors Without Borders, members of which set up hospital tents to handle the injured. Additional aid was supplied from Pakistan and the former Soviet state of Tajikistan, and disaster relief arrived through the auspices of the United Nations.

Richard Adler

FOR FURTHER INFORMATION:
McFadden, Robert. "Thousands Said to Have Been Killed in Afghan Quake." *The New York Times*, February 7, 1998, p. A3.

1999: Colombia

DATE: January 25, 1999
PLACE: Armenia, Colombia
MAGNITUDE: 6.0
RESULT: 1,124 dead, 250,000 homeless, $1.8 billion in damage

At 1:19 P.M. local time on January 25, 1999, an earthquake with a magnitude of 6.0 struck western Colombia (4.26 degrees north, 75.43 degrees west). The quake was detected in real time by Colombia's National Seismic Network via satellite from the Instituto de Investigaciones en Geociencias, Miner'a y Qu'mica, Observatorio del Sur Occidente, and the Red Sismológica del Eje Cafetero. Causing skyscrapers to sway in downtown Bogotá, the quake was Colombia's worst since 1875, when a tremor killed 1,000 people near the border with Venezuela. The quake's focus was near the Cauca-Almaguer fault, part of the Romeral system of faults that cross Colombia in a north-south direction following the Patía and Cauca Rivers. Ordinarily, quakes within this region strike deep within the earth's mantle. However, the January 25 event was centered less than 9 miles (15 kilometers) below the surface. Although its magnitude was not considered large enough to be classified in the "great" or "major" category, the relative shallowness of the quake's focus and the presence of soft soils of volcanic origin may have amplified its destructive force.

Destruction in the region surrounding the quake

was widespread and affected over 30 municipalities within six Colombian departments (states). Hardest hit was Armenia, a city of about 290,000, located 12.4 miles (20 kilometers) from the epicenter in the Andes Mountains midway between Bogotá, Cali, and Medellín. Armenia has been affected by other earthquakes during the twentieth century: Temblors in 1938, 1961, 1962, and 1979 remain in the memory of many residents. Armenia is located within an area known as the Zona Cafeteria, which is a principal agricultural region and one of the most important economic areas in Colombia, where nearly half of the country's 2.2 million acres of coffee are grown. About 50,000 structures in the region sustained damage from the quake, representing an economic loss of approximately $1.8 billion (U.S. dollars) or 1.5 percent of Colombia's gross national product. Of the structures that were damaged, it is estimated that only 36 percent were covered by insurance. Many buildings had insurance coverage for only 72 percent of their value.

Within six days of the earthquake, the death toll in Armenia had reached 543 persons, with 1,700 injured and nearly 60 percent of buildings damaged or destroyed. Buildings destroyed within the city included a major hotel, the police and fire stations, a theater, and the city jail. The city's airport was also damaged, along with a majority of its churches. Much of the destruction was concentrated in the southern and central parts of the city, where older construction can be found. The largest number of collapses occurred among poorly constructed buildings or those built on poor-quality soil. Damage was most concentrated in buildings constructed prior to the enforcement of a national earthquake-resistant construction code that was introduced following a 1983 quake that damaged the city of Popaýan. The principal type of structural failure involved in-fill masonry walls and unreinforced hollow clay tile. Fill located inside walls contributed to the inertia of a swaying motion during the quake, leading to the collapse of many structures. Remarkably, some local buildings

Victims await food in Armenia, Colombia, after the 1999 earthquake. (AP/Wide World Photos)

constructed using "bahareque de guadua" (bamboo frames with an earth and mud-tile covering) held up extremely well.

Rescue and relief efforts were hampered by the loss of telecommunications and the inaccessibility of some areas as a result of rubble and debris piled in the streets, along with heavy rains. Four separate landslides in the Department of Quindío blocked roads with numerous other landslides reported between the cities of Armenia and Pijao. Although the landslides themselves caused minimal damage, they delayed the arrival of assistance to the disaster zone. Also slowing relief efforts were powerful aftershocks that continued to rock the region following the quake and measured as high as 4.3 on the Richter scale. Although some heavy machinery was available, rescue workers used picks and shovels or dug by hand for fear of injuring survivors trapped beneath tons of debris. Some of the injured were evacuated by air to Medellín, Bogotá, and Cali. A shortage of coffins for the dead resulted in price gouging by merchants. In some cases rescue workers resorted to wrapping the bodies of victims in plastic sheets. In the days immediately following the quake many of the residents who lost homes constructed makeshift shelters on curbs or in parks or empty lots. Damage was also extensive in Pereira, a city of approximately 695,000 inhabitants located 31 miles (50 kilometers) from the epicenter, where 44 people were killed, 650 were injured, and 390 buildings were destroyed or damaged.

One day after the earthquake, Colombian president Andrés Pastrana Arango declared a state of natural disaster and implemented a plan to mobilize government agencies and relief agencies. Public facilities throughout the region were equipped as temporary shelters. A variety of relief agencies, including the Colombian Red Cross, sent out urgent calls for supplies such as blankets, tents, and plastic tarps to assist residents displaced by the quake who chose to remain outside for fear of aftershocks. More than 500 tons of relief supplies were sent by the Colombian government, the United Nations World Food Program, and the U.S.-based relief agency AmeriCares. The European Union pledged $1 million, and the Inter-American Development bank promised $10 million in aid. Despite shipments of supplies, government troops clashed with hungry mobs in search of food. Market areas in Armenia were sacked with looters taking stoves, fans, furniture, computers, and

other goods. Armed citizens guarded their belongings on street corners while heavily armed police and military personnel patrolled streets, enforcing a curfew. The lack of running water and toilets contributed to a growing health problem. The final death toll for the disaster was 1,124, with 250,000 left homeless.

Thomas A. Wikle

FOR FURTHER INFORMATION:

Barrionuevo, Alexei. "Hunger, Looting Plague Colombia." *USA Today,* January 29, 1999.

Ojito, Mirta. "After Quake, a Sorrowful Journey to Colombia." *The New York Times,* February 1, 1999.

Semple, Kirk. "All of Colombia Quakes." *U.S. News & World Report,* February 8, 1999.

1999: Turkey

DATE: August 17, 1999
PLACE: Northwestern Turkey
MAGNITUDE: 7.4
RESULT: More than 17,000 dead, 25,000 injured, more than 250,000 homeless, 17,000 buildings destroyed, 25,000 buildings badly damaged, total economic cost estimated at $15 billion

The Northern Anatolian fault, which is some 600 miles long, runs east to west through northern Turkey, paralleling the coastline of the Black Sea. It marks the division of the Eurasian Plate to the north and the Anatolian Plate to the south. The Anatolian Plate itself is a small plate, wedged between the north-thrusting Arabian and African Plates. It is highly unstable—both the Northern and Southern Anatolian faults have given rise to frequent earthquakes over the centuries. Like the San Andreas fault in California, the Anatolian fault is a right lateral strike-slip fault, about 10 miles deep. Also like the San Andreas fault, it moves about an eighth of an inch a year and has branches at either end.

Seismologists noted a steady east-to-west shift of earthquake epicenters along the North Anatolian fault in the twentieth century, thrusting the Anatolian Plate in a westward direction. An earthquake occurred in eastern Turkey, for example, with a magnitude of 7.9 on the Richter scale, followed by another,

some 100 miles to the west, in 1942, with a magnitude of 7.1. Then, just two years later, in an area north of the capital Ankara, in central Turkey, another earthquake occurred, with a magnitude of 7.3.

Since then, earthquakes occurred along the fault in 1957 and 1967, each one moving further west, of approximately the same magnitude. Seismologists warned the Turkish government that the next earthquake along the fault could be in northwestern Turkey, and that suitable preparations needed to be made. More specifically, in 1997, Ross Stein, a geophysicist at the U.S. Geological Survey at Menlo Park, California, suggested, together with two colleagues, that there was "an increased probability" that the next earthquake would be around İzmit, some 50 miles east of Istanbul, Turkey's largest city.

Northwestern Turkey is the most densely populated area in the country. With 20 million inhabitants, it contains nearly a third of Turkey's population.

In it lies Istanbul, with 8 million inhabitants, growing at a rate of almost half a million a year; the new industrial areas round İzmit, with over half a million inhabitants; and Bursa, with nearly 1 million residents. Some new resort areas along the south coast of the Sea of Marmara, especially on the Gulf of İzmit around the town of Yalova, are also located in northwest Turkey. Half the nation's production takes place in the eleven provinces (or counties) surrounding Istanbul. Many migrants from the relatively poor areas of eastern Turkey come to these cities and towns to find work. A major oil refinery was constructed by the government-owned gas company just outside İzmit, as well as Honda and Toyota vehicle factories, a Pirelli tire factory, and several other multimillion-dollar construction projects largely financed by Western companies. Many small-scale businesses also sprang up. New hotels and apartment blocks were quickly constructed to deal with the sudden boom in workers and tourists. Swampland was drained around the Gulf of İzmit to create more building space.

To guard against earthquake hazards, the Turkish government laid down strict building codes, equal, it claimed, to those in force in other earthquake-prone areas, such as California and Japan. These included regulations of the height of buildings (a two-story maximum in many cases), quality of concrete, strength of steel rods, and depth of foundations. Unfortunately, the inspection and control of these regulations was left in the hands of local city and town officials, who were subject to political pressures, bribery, and lack of expertise. Enforcement procedures were generally weak.

Turkey itself is a centralized secular country, even though 99 percent of its population is Muslim. It has had a number of military regimes, and the army has always been large for the size of the country—some 800,000 personnel. Turkey's democratic structures have been considered weak and open to corruption. Nevertheless, respect for the country has been continuously inculcated into the population, particularly in an effort to keep the state secular—its ideal when the country became a republic after World War I. The economy grew during the 1990's at a rate of 7 to 8 percent yearly. At the time of the 1999 earthquake it was economically sound, despite some loss of tourist revenue over recent terrorist attacks by Kurdish rebels. Its annual gross national product stood at $200 billion.

The Earthquake. At 3:02 A.M. on Tuesday, August 17, a temblor shook northwestern Turkey with its epicenter near İzmit. It lasted forty-five seconds. First estimates of its magnitude were put at 7.1 by the National Earthquake Information Center at Golden, Colorado, and at 6.8 by the Turkish authorities. Both figures were later revised to 7.4, making it one of the worst quakes to hit Turkey in the twentieth century. It was felt as far away as Ankara, 270 miles to the east.

At the time the quake hit, the population was asleep, so first reports were confused. A few deaths at Adama, Eskisehir, and Istanbul, 162 in total, were reported on Turkish television at daylight. One of the worst-hit areas was Bursa, the foreign press reported, where an oil refinery was blazing out of control. (In fact, the refinery was at İzmit.) As the day wore on, it became clear that the worst-hit areas were İzmit; Gölcük, where there was a naval base; and Yalova, where 90 percent of the houses had collapsed. At Gölcük 248 sailors and officers were reported trapped under collapsed buildings.

It soon became apparent that initial numbers were hopelessly underestimated. Large parts of many towns and cities had been totally devastated, many buildings had simply collapsed on their sleeping occupants, and many others that remained standing were in too perilous a condition for people to remain. A seawall had given way in the Bay of Haldere, and further along the coast, a mile of shoreline had sunk into the sea. Many places within an area of 100 miles east of Istanbul were without electricity and water. Road and rail communications were severely disrupted by fallen bridges and sunken pavements, although telephone communications between the main cities were quickly restored. So many aftershocks occurred (250 within the first twenty-four hours, 1,000 in the ensuing month) that people were afraid to stay indoors even when their houses stood secure.

Rescue and Relief Efforts. By the end of the first day, the Turkish government had reported 13,000 injured. Hospital beds were set up in the streets of İzmit. In one of the suburbs of Istanbul, reporters saw piles of debris 20 feet higher than the bulldozers that were working to rescue people from the collapsed buildings. In fact, bulldozers and other heavy moving equipment were in very short supply over the first few days, and most early rescue attempts were characterized by families and neighbors working by hand or with small-scale machinery—often begged or stolen—to rescue their kin. Many inhabitants seemed too shocked and dazed to do anything.

Soon, great tent cities sprang up for the homeless, whose numbers were constantly being revised upward, finally reaching half a million people. Some of the shortage of suitable vehicles could be explained by their being trapped or destroyed in collapsed buildings, as could the shortage of medical supplies. However, the biggest feature of the first few weeks after the quake was the complete lack of any large-scale local rescue plans. There were no militias or civil-defense personnel, no official rescue workers seen by the vast majority of inhabitants, nor any sign of the army becoming immediately involved.

In fact, it was the foreign rescue teams who were the first to reach many of the stricken areas. An Israeli team was the first to arrive, the morning after the quake. The Israeli rescue team was also the largest. The Israelis sent 2 fire-fighting planes, teams of dogs, and 350 rescue workers. They also sent a field hospital and 200 medical workers. Eventually 80 countries and international organizations sent rescue teams or aid, with about 2,000 personnel directly involved. Besides the response from Israel, immediate responses were also made by Germany, the United States, France, Switzerland, and Great Britain, among others. The U.S. 70-person rescue team from Fairfax, Virginia, was typical of many. It naturally took several days to assemble and fly out, not reaching Turkey until two days after the quake. The unit was rushed to İzmit. A much larger U.S. relief effort was then promised, consisting of 3 naval vessels equipped with 80 beds, operating tables, doctors, dentists, and paramedics, as well as 22 rescue helicopters. This could not arrive until the weekend, however.

Those teams that were near at hand found movement difficult, with blocked roads and little direction or coordination from the Turkish government. Many foreign teams, as has been stated, found no local network at all and had to devise their own plans and organization. In the end, many rescue teams felt they had accomplished far less than they might have in better circumstances.

The government did slowly begin to make specific requests for help: body bags, tents, flashlights, blankets, garbage trucks, disinfectant, and tetanus vaccine. At the same time it imposed a blockage on aid by insisting that it be channeled through the Red Crescent (the Muslim equivalent of the Red Cross). National pride and religious feelings seemed to be the main cause for this demand. Indeed, the minister of health, Osman Durmus, declared Turks should not accept blood donated by Greece nor medical aid from the United States, and that foreigners should not actually deliver any relief aid. Aid from Islamic countries and groups was also blocked, the government fearing that any sympathy gained for political Muslims would undermine the secularity of the state.

The Turkish Red Crescent appealed to the International Red Cross for $6.92 million in aid. At the same time, the European Union sent $2.1 million, Britain $800,000, Germany $560,000, and other countries and charities smaller amounts for immediate help. The United States gave some $3 million. Most of these amounts were quickly increased as the scale of the disaster became apparent. A private German television appeal raised $7 million, a Dutch one $13 million. Even traditional foes of Turkey—Armenians, Kurds, and Greeks—sent gifts.

Turkish television broadcast graphic scenes of the devastation and early rescue attempts to drag people out of the wreckage. This caused an unorganized stream of Turkish volunteers from other parts of the country to make their way toward the devastated area. Some did sterling work in helping with the rescue efforts, especially groups of students from Istanbul, but many efforts were counterproductive, causing 20-mile traffic jams along already damaged highways, thus preventing heavy equipment and much-needed supplies from reaching their destination. Such volunteers often brought aid that was not actually needed, such as bottled water or bread. On the positive side, very little looting was reported.

As stated, the epicenter was near the industrial city of İzmit. One of the main dangers there was the oil refinery on the edge of the city, which had caught fire immediately and blazed uncontrollably for three days, despite aerial attempts to douse the flames. A nearby fertilizer plant with 8,000 tons of inflammable ammonia could have exploded easily, so all the nearby inhabitants had to be evacuated. At the hospital, medical supplies ran out, and nearby pharmacies were raided. An astonishing number of buildings less than five years old had collapsed, and the mayor declared he would need 250 teams to rescue everyone.

At Gölcük, the naval base and most of the town were flattened. One of the prominent features here, as elsewhere, was the haphazard nature of the building collapse. Some buildings were left standing; others appeared to be until it was clear that the first floor had sunk completely into the ground. Other buildings stood tilting sideways at 45-degree angles; many had cracks and fissures running through them. Each building had to be assessed separately for rescuing those still trapped inside, and it was often difficult to obtain the ground plans for the structures. It was feared that up to 10,000 people were trapped in the town.

Criticism was leveled against the government that its main rescue efforts, using Israeli as well as naval personnel, had been directed toward the army barracks, leaving individuals on their own. In fact, the navy did set up a crisis center, but it was in the town center and few trucks could reach it.

By Friday the death toll in Gölcük had reached 7,000, and bodies were being lined up in an ice rink for identification. Voices could still be heard in the rubble two and a half days after the quake, but lack of equipment or the wrong equipment continued to hinder the rescue teams. In other towns, the death toll also continued to rise: İzmit reported 3,242 dead and 8,759 injured; Adapazari 2,995 dead and 5,081 injured; Yalova 1,442 dead and 4,300 injured; and Istanbul, 984 dead and 9,541 injured. In Adapazari 963 bodies were interred in a mass grave. Not until Saturday, August 21, did soldiers appear, reaching a total of 50,000 eventually. Their first jobs were to pick up the rotting garbage, to spray disinfectant, and to set out lime. The stench of rotting bodies and garbage was giving rise to fears of an epidemic of cholera or typhoid, but in fact there was little medical evidence to support such fears. Nevertheless, dysentery and scabies were real threats to the tent-dwellers.

By the weekend, hope of pulling more survivors from the wreckage was fading. On Saturday the 21st, Austrian rescue workers pulled a ninety-five-year-old woman from a seaside complex at Yalova; on Sunday just two survivors were found. The last survivor to be pulled out was a small boy who had somehow survived for six days. At this stage, some foreign rescue teams began to pull out.

In some areas, it was reported that the army had intervened in these final rescue attempts, taking over from the foreign teams, but had only made a bad situation worse through their inexperience. However, the army's presence helped to stem the tide of volunteers and ease the massive traffic jams. Rain began falling the second week, keeping up for three straight days. To add to the misery of the homeless, many of the army-supplied tents were found not to be waterproof.

Public Criticism. After the initial shock of the quake, the severity of which affected the whole nation deeply, public criticism and anger quickly took over, on the part of both the survivors and the mass media. It was pointed in two directions: at the government for its inaction and lack of preparedness, and at the contractors and local officials who had allowed substandard buildings to be erected. Both criticisms point to the fact that the extent of the destruction was human-made—that a 7.4 earthquake should not have had such a deleterious effect.

The government tried to allay this criticism in a number of ways. On the evening of the quake Prime Minister Bülent Ecevit made a national broadcast. Parliament met in special session on Thursday, August 19, when Koray Aydin, minister of public works and housing, gave a report, stating that this was the greatest natural disaster in the history of Turkey. On the same day, the prime minister broadcast again, trying again to allay public anger, but the only positive step he took was to announce plans for more tents. The next day he ordered immediate burial of the dead and asked for more body bags. The much more robust response of the government and military to a November earthquake did lessen immediate criticism, even though confusion and delay were still very much in evidence.

The minister of the interior, Sadettin Tantan, promised harsh punishment for contractors, engineers, and building owners. In Duzce alone, magistrates arrested 33 very quickly. Three provincial governors were also dismissed for their failure to coordinate efforts, being replaced by cabinet ministers. However, some politicians were willing to avoid a cover-up. The minister of tourism, Erkan Mumcu, declared the lack of response was symptomatic of the Turkish political and economic system. By contrast, on August 25, Ecevit criticized the press for its "demoralizing" earthquake reporting and shut down one of the more outspoken private television stations under an anti-incitement law.

The case against contractors and local officials was overwhelming. For example, in Avcilar, the worst-hit suburb of Istanbul, a five-story building had collapsed in twenty-seven seconds, while a mosque standing nearby stood firm. The reasons the building collapsed were clear: cheap iron for support rods, too much sand mixed with the concrete, some buildings built without permits, and some with stories added without permission. In one case, local officials had ordered a halt three times to a building, but it had been completed just the same, demonstrating the weak enforcement laws, even when local inspectors were doing the job properly. A report by the Turkish Architects and Engineers Association suggested that 65 percent of new buildings put up in Istanbul were not in compliance with the building regulations. The strength of the quake by the time it had reached Istanbul was only 5.5, and all the buildings should theoretically have been able to withstand that magnitude quake. Other claims were made that of Turkey's forty thousand contractors, most were unqualified.

In Yalova, for example, survivors burned the car and stoned the house of one local contractor by the name of Veli Gocer. Seven of the 16 buildings he had constructed had collapsed. He quickly fled to Germany but is reported in an interview with the newspaper *Bild am Sonntaq* to have said that while he sympathized with the victims, he should not be made a scapegoat. His training was in literature, he said, not in civil engineering, and he had believed the builders when they had told him he could mix large quantities of beach sand with his concrete as a way of cutting costs.

The Geological Aftermath. Besides the many small aftershocks, two major aftershocks caused panic and some further deaths and damage. The first of these was on August 31, lasting ten seconds, with a 5.2 magnitude and its epicenter east of İzmit. The second was on September 13, registering 5.8 on the Richter scale. The Anatolian fault had ruptured for at least 60 miles east of İzmit, and in some places the ground was offset by 12 feet. One possible reason for this was that the original quake may in fact have been caused by two fault segments splitting thirty seconds apart, thus causing such a large shock.

Mehmet Au Iskari, director of Turkey's leading observatory, observed continuing unusual seismic movements that could suggest another temblor soon. On Monday, November 15, a temblor of some 7.2 magnitude struck with its epicenter at Düzce, 90 miles east of Istanbul. At least 370 people were killed and 3,000 injured.

The U.S. government, aware of the similarities between the San Andreas fault and the Anatolian, quickly dispatched a team of experts from Menlo Park, California, and Golden, Colorado, as well as from the University of Southern California and San Diego State University. They were to investigate what lessons could be learned from a country where building regulations were, in theory, as strict as those in California, and especially the lessons from those buildings that were left standing and the type of soil they were built on.

Geologists and seismologists made a prediction that the next big quake on the fault will be in Istanbul itself, or a little to the south, in the Sea of Marmara, in perhaps thirty to fifty years. Istanbul is somewhat more secure than the İzmit area in that it is built on harder rock and is 6 to 10 miles from the fault line. However, if the standard of building construction is not improved, that will clearly be of little advantage in the next big quake.

The Economic Aftermath. The northwest region of Turkey was the base for the country's economic growth during the late twentieth century, with many new industries creating new jobs. The destruction of much of this area was bound to have enormous economic consequences. Reconstruction of houses, apartments, shops, hotels, and factories, as well as the infrastructure of roads, railways, bridges, sewerage, and water supply, would cost billions of dollars. Added to this was the unemployment that followed the loss of workplaces and small businesses, the loss of stock and capital, and the loss of production. Worst hit were the small to medium-sized businesses that had fueled the economic progress of the 1990's. Fewer than 10 percent of houses were covered by insurance, adding to the financial loss.

Turkey's hopes of being in an economically sound position to apply for membership in the European Union (EU), whatever its democratic weaknesses, were thoroughly dashed. However, the EU did express sympathy for Turkey's plight. President Jacques Chirac of France wrote to each of the EU states asking for a "new strategy" for dealing with Turkey, after a two-year freeze in dialogue.

Turkey had also been in negotiation with the International Monetary Fund (IMF), especially since it had been in financial difficulties in 1999. It had been seeking to put the IMF's recommendations into practice. The loan originally requested had been $5 billion, but with the estimated $25 billion total loss, such a sum had clearly become too small. The government announced that it would endeavor to stick to the previously agreed fiscal measures. The government also immediately put aside $4 billion to repair businesses and $2 to $3 billion to repair the oil refinery. However, foreign aid would clearly be needed to supplement the long-term IMF loan. The World Bank pledged $200 million for emergency housing, and the EU gave $41.8 million. The future of Turkey's economy looked considerably bleaker than it had for many years, however.

The Political Aftermath. Potentially the most damaging results of the quake were in the political arena. The country's disillusionment with the government went deeper than particular individual politicians. It reflected a questioning of the paternalistic state that hitherto had been trusted by its citizens to care for them. Such an attitude had been fostered to bring unity to a country whose secular basis lay counter to the traditionalism of many of its conservative Muslims, who would prefer an Islamic republic.

The exposure of corruption at a local level, although well known by the population before, added to public anger and frustration, as did the inept bureaucracy. Most of the country's residents had experienced this frustration daily in a minor way, but the earthquake brought years of simmering annoyances to the boil. In a country where the state was treated with great respect, the depth of such anger and criticism may well have permanently undermined such trust, making the job of future governments that much harder. Indeed, some politicians and academics took the opportunity to call for reform, even to the extent of rewriting the constitution.

Not all the political aftermath was negative, however. International relationships were improved in a wave of sympathy, however frustrated individual foreign relief and rescue teams were (the U.S. naval ships were barely used in the end, for example). Prime Minister Ecevit arranged a meeting with U.S. president Bill Clinton to ask for more U.S. aid; with Turkey having been a loyal North Atlantic Treaty Organization (NATO) ally for many years, the request would certainly be granted. Turkish-Israeli relationships were also strengthened by the early and efficient arrival of Israeli rescue teams. Even the Kurdish rebels in the southeast of the country offered a temporary cease-fire.

Perhaps the most remarkable benefit politically was the blossoming of Turkish-Greek relationships. Enemies for centuries, these neighboring countries became antagonistic over the island of Cyprus, which was divided into Greek and Turkish sectors after a Turkish military invasion in the 1970's. The sending of a small Greek rescue team to the quake site was therefore an important symbolic gesture. This gesture was returned by the Turks when Athens was hit by an earthquake on September 9, 1999. A spontaneous response of reconciliation was released between the two populations and taken up by the media and politicians. The following month, President Clinton sought to seize on this goodwill by offering to broker talks over Cyprus. Rarely does an earthquake have such a profound effect politically and economically, as well as in terms of human tragedy.

David Barratt

FOR FURTHER INFORMATION:
The New York Times, August 17-September 14, 1999.

1999: Taiwan

DATE: September 21, 1999
PLACE: Nantou and Taichung, Taiwan
MAGNITUDE: 7.6

RESULT: More than 2,100 dead, 8,700 injured, more than 12,000 homes destroyed, more than 100,000 homeless, nearly 8,000 aftershocks, more than $3 billion in damage

Taiwan's strongest earthquake in over a decade struck at approximately 1:47 A.M. on September 21, 1999, destroying a twelve-story hotel in Taipei, shaking millions of people out of their beds, and killing more than 2,100. Thousands of people spent the rest of the night in tents, in fields, or in parks, either homeless or terrified that aftershocks would send their damaged homes tumbling down on them. The earthquake came just two days before Taiwan's Autumn Festival. Rescuers, many with trained dogs, scrambled desperately throughout the night to unearth thousands of people trapped under the debris. Most of the victims were found in the central cities of Taichung and nearby Nantou.

The quake's magnitude was estimated to be 7.6 on the Richter scale and was centered 90 miles south-southwest of the capital city of Taipei, near Nantou. Five aftershocks, all measuring about 6.0 on the Richter scale, occurred within thirty minutes after the initial quake. One week after the main quake, nearly eight thousand aftershocks had been recorded in Taiwan, with twenty to fifty tremors occurring every hour. The last time that Taiwan experienced an earthquake of this magnitude on land was in 1935, resulting in 3,276 deaths. The island's last tremor of similar magnitude occurred on November 14, 1986, but it was centered under the Pacific Ocean, resulting in 15 deaths.

The quake of September 21 toppled houses and high-rise apartment complexes throughout central Taiwan. Roads buckled, landslides blocked streams to create new lakes, bridges were broken, and pieces of land rose up to create new hills. Many cities in and around Nantou County desperately needed food, water, clothing, quilts, sleeping bags, tents, and medical supplies to care for the injured and homeless. In the summer heat, there was also a pressing need for body bags and freezers, as morgues filled up with bodies.

The main buildings to collapse in central Taiwan were the new high-rise apartments. Although Taiwan had strict building codes, due to a boom in construction in central Taiwan in the 1990's many buildings were built with shoddy materials. A fourteen-story building toppled over in Dongshi, primarily due to foundation problems. In Tungshih, a city of 60,000,

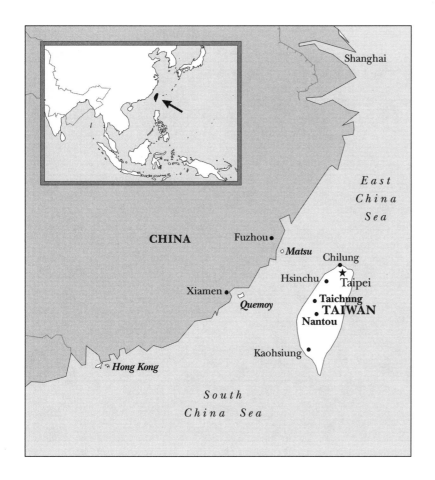

degree angle, only the top four floors of the twelve-story hotel remained visible, with smoke billowing out from fires that had erupted in the eight crushed floors below. Electrical power was out in large areas of Taipei, and transportation was badly disrupted. Numerous buildings had collapsed roofs, large cracks in the walls, or big piles of shattered tiles. Fires were reported throughout the city, as well as in the countryside, but Taipei and the surrounding region escaped with relatively minor damage.

Rescue crews from the United States, Singapore, Japan, Switzerland, South Korea, and Russia provided assistance, as did a United Nations disaster-assessment team. The Taiwanese vented anger at their own government for reacting too slowly. There was lack of central coordination and inefficient use of workers and supplies. Autumn Festival travelers and private efforts to deliver aid snarled traffic and complicated distribution of needed supplies.

nearly every house received damage, and all power, water, and communication links were cut off. There were not enough bulldozers or other machinery to dig through all the rubble.

Spectacular vertical offsets were visible in the river northeast of the central city of Fengyuen. At one site near a collapsed bridge, a new waterfall formed from an estimated 26-foot (8-meter) vertical fault offset. Approximately half a mile (1 kilometer) from this site, the dam of one of Taiwan's largest reservoirs, Sun Moon Lake, was cut by the fault, and the road running along the top of the dam was vertically offset by 26 feet (8 meters). People living below the dam were warned to evacuate. In the hills above Fengyuen, a concrete Buddhist temple folded in on itself during the quake, killing at least 3 people.

In Taipei, the bottom stories of the Sungshan Hotel collapsed, causing the badly damaged structure to lean on a neighboring commercial building. This collapse was most likely due to the removal of many internal walls during remodeling. Tilted at a 45-

Taiwan accepted China's offer of $100,000 in cash, but due to political posturing by China, Taiwan rebuffed its offer of seismological and medical experts and $60,000 worth of supplies. Taiwan felt that China was exploiting Taiwan's misfortune in China's unceasing bid to bring Taiwan under its sovereignty.

The island of Taiwan is located in a very seismically active region at a compressive tectonic boundary between the Eurasian Plate and the Philippine Plate. To the north of the island, the relatively small Philippine Plate is being forced under the very large Eurasian Plate, while to the south, the opposite is happening, with the Eurasian Plate subducting beneath the Philippine Plate. As a result, several large faults extend across the length of Taiwan. Dozens of quakes occur each year around Taiwan, but most are centered in the Pacific Ocean east of the island and cause no damage.

The earthquake that occurred on September 21 was primarily generated along the active, north-south

This running track in Taichung, Taiwan, shows the uplift caused by the powerful 1999 quake. (AP/Wide World Photos)

trending Chelongpu fault. After the quake, surface ruptures were located along this fault for over 37 miles (60 kilometers), beginning near Chushan in Nantou County in the south and extending to Fengyuen in Taichung County in the north. Vertical displacements of 3 to 13 feet (1 to 4 meters) were found along the fault. Northeast of Fengyuen, the faulting is complicated, and vertical displacements of 13 to 26 feet (4 to 8 meters) were found, as well as lateral displacements of 3 to 30 feet (1 to 9 meters) at scattered sites. There was little observed movement along the Shundong fault, which runs parallel to the Chelongpu fault.

Alvin K. Benson

FOR FURTHER INFORMATION:

Beveridge, Dirk. "Searchers Comb Wreckage in Taiwan; Toll Rises." *The Washington Post*, September 21, 1999.

Bonilla, M. G. "A Note on Historic and Quaternary Faults in Western Taiwan." In U.S.G.S. open-file report 99-447. Menlo Park, Calif.: U.S. Geological Survey, 1999.

Chichi, Taiwan Earthquake of September 21, 1999 (M7.6): An EQE Briefing. Oakland, Calif.: EQE International, 1999.

Liou, J. G., and L. Y. Hsiao. *Report #4 on the Chi-Chi (Taiwan) Earthquake.* Menlo Park, Calif.: U.S. Geological Survey, 1999.

El Niño

El Niño is a recurring weather phenomenon involving large-scale alterations in sea surface temperatures, air pressure, and precipitation patterns in the Pacific Ocean. It can cause severe storms and droughts in the bordering continents and has effects worldwide.

(AP/Wide World Photos)

FACTORS INVOLVED: Geography, rain, temperature, weather conditions
REGIONS AFFECTED: All

SCIENCE

The Spanish words *El Niño* (the boy) allude to the infant Christ. It is the traditional term used by Peruvian fishermen to refer to a slight warming of the ocean during the Christmas season. Scientists borrowed the name and reapplied it to abnormal, irregularly recurring fluctuations in sea surface temperature, air pressure, wind strength, and precipitation in the equatorial Pacific Ocean. These conditions are part of a weather phenomenon that scientists call the El Niño-Southern Oscillation (ENSO). El Niño conditions can last up to two years.

Under normal conditions westward-blowing trade winds push water in a broad band along the equator toward Indonesia and northern Australia. A bulge of water builds up that is about 1.5 feet higher than the surface of the eastern Pacific. The western Pacific is also warmer, as much as 46 degrees Fahrenheit (8 degrees Celsius), and the thermocline, the border between warm water and cold water, is much deeper. The air above this vast pool of warm water is moist, and evaporation is rapid. As a result, clouds form and rain falls abundantly. The average air pressure is low. Meanwhile, in the eastern Pacific, off the South American northern coast, the sea surface is cold as water wells up from the depths. Evaporation is slow, and there is little cloud formation or rain. The air pressure is high.

Sometimes the trade winds weaken. Scientists do not fully understand why this happens, although weather patterns to the north and south are known to influence the change. The trade winds can no longer hold back the bulge of warm water in the western Pacific. It flows eastward, generally within 5 degrees of latitude north and south of the equator. As the water bulge flows into the central Pacific, two sets of huge subsurface waves, Kelvin waves moving east and Rossby waves moving west, are created. They move slowly. The Kelvin waves take as much as two and a half months to cross the ocean to South America, and the Rossby waves reach the western Pacific boundary after six to ten months. As they spread, the Kelvin waves deepen the shallow central and eastern thermoclines as much as 98 feet (30 meters) and help propel the band of warm water, while the Rossby waves raise the deep western thermocline slightly.

An El Niño begins when the long finger of warm water extends to South America, raising the average surface temperature there. Scientists gauge the severity of an El Niño by the amount of temperature rise. A moderate El Niño involves an increase of 36 to 37 degrees Fahrenheit (2 to 3 degrees Celsius) above the normal summer and autumn temperatures for the Southern Hemisphere, a strong El Niño has a 37 to 41 degrees Fahrenheit (3 to 5 degrees Celsius) increase, and a severe El Niño can warm the sea surface nearly 46 degrees Fahrenheit (8 degrees Celsius).

The effects of the warm water are relatively rapid and dramatic. The warm layer blocks the normal upwelling of cold water near Peru and Ecuador, diverting it southward. The increased surface temperature accelerates evaporation. The coastal air turns more humid, and as it rises, the water vapor injects tremendous thermal energy into the atmosphere. As clouds form from the vapor, winds are generated that push the clouds inland in large storms. The storms bring downpours to regions that are normally desert. There is a rise in the sea level because of the warm water, which is less dense; that rise, together with high waves from the storms battering the coast, causes beaches to disappear in some areas and pile up in others. A huge low-pressure system settles in the central Pacific, approximately centered on Tahiti.

In the Australia-Indonesia region, conditions are nearly the reverse. The air pressure becomes abnormally high—in fact, this large-scale variation from low to high air pressure makes up the Southern Oscillation part of ENSO. Drought strikes areas that normally receive substantial rainfall. Sea levels fall, sometimes exposing coral reefs. There are further abnormal weather conditions in more distant regions, which scientists call teleconnections to El Niño.

When the Kelvin waves hit the South American coast and the Rossby waves reach the westernmost Pacific, they rebound. The western thermocline is deepened, and the eastern thermocline rises. This action begins the reversal of El Niño effects. The warm water retreats westward, pushed back by strengthening trade winds. Eventually, normal weather patterns resume.

If these oscillations came regularly, El Niños would simply be the extreme of a pattern. However, the period is not regular. For at least the last five thousand years, scientists believe, an El Niño occurred every two to ten years. Sometimes a decade, or even several decades, passes without one. Some, but not all events, are separated by abnormally cold weather in the eastern Pacific, a phenomenon known as La Niña, anti-El Niño, or El Viejo.

GEOGRAPHY

El Niños profoundly influence weather patterns in the Pacific Ocean. In addition to increasing rainfall along the northwestern South American seaboard, the warm water can increase the number of Pacific Ocean hurricanes, which can strike Central and North America and the Pacific islands. Above-normal water temperatures also have been recorded along the California coast of North America. Accordingly, there is more precipitation, causing coastal flooding and piling up large snowpacks in the Sierra Nevada. The Pacific Northwest, southern Alaska, the north coast of China, Korea, and Japan have above-average winter air temperatures. Australia and the maritime area of Indonesia and Southeast Asia suffer coastal and inland drought as rainfall is sparse throughout the western equatorial Pacific.

Teleconnections disrupt normal weather patterns throughout much of the Southern Hemisphere. Sections of the eastern Amazon River basin experience drought, and the monsoons in northern India may be short or fail entirely. Low rainfall occurs in southeastern Africa and drought in Sahelian Africa, particularly Ethiopia. There are also indications that El Niños affect Atlantic Ocean weather patterns. Northern Europe can be unusually cold, while across the Atlantic mild conditions prevail along the eastern seaboard of the United States, and the American Southeast has a wet winter. During the Atlantic hurricane season, fewer and weaker hurricanes arise.

PREVENTION AND PREPARATIONS

No El Niños are identical because external weather forces cause variations in the development, duration, and severity of each. Moreover, El Niños do not recur regularly. Predicting them is therefore difficult. Since the late 1950's, however, intensive basic scientific research has identified the dynamics of the phenomena, and technological developments have made prediction and tracking of El Niños ever more reliable, allowing potentially affected areas to prepare for harsh weather.

Weather stations in the western and eastern Pacific look for changes in air pressure and signs of declining precipitation. The Tropical Atmosphere-Ocean (TAO) array comprises hundreds of buoys; most monitor water temperature and atmospheric conditions, but some also measure the depth of the thermocline. Weather satellites can use infrared imaging and laser range-finding to follow the path of expanding warm waters and to gauge sea surface level. Data from all such sources is fed into computers with special software that compares it with past El Niños and fits it into empirically derived formulas in order to model the potential development of a new event.

While computer modeling is not foolproof, it is accurate enough that Pacific-bordering nations make preparations based upon the forecasts. Disaster relief agencies, such as the United States Federal Emergency Management Administration (FEMA), stockpile food, medicines, and sanitation and construction supplies in anticipation of floods and hurricanes. Some governments, as well as the World Meteorolog-

ical Organization, maintain Web sites with the latest information on El Niños so citizens can make preparations of their own. Governments of countries in potential drought areas have staved off disaster by encouraging farmers to plant drought-resistant crops or those that mature before the El Niño season. Moving people away from canyons and low-lying lands that are subject to flooding can sometimes save lives.

RESCUE AND RELIEF EFFORTS

El Niños do not directly threaten life and property. Instead, the storms that they spawn do the damage. The chief danger comes from flash floods in deserts, such as those in coastal Peru and Ecuador, flooding from rain-swollen rivers, and high winds from tropical storms. Since it is difficult to predict exactly where one of these conditions will occur, emergency workers usually respond only after a crisis develops. Their efforts follow the pattern for all flooding and windstorms: Move residents out of the area of danger and institute searches for those swept away by flash floods or caught in collapsed buildings.

Because flooding can be sudden, serious, and widespread, sometimes appearing simultaneously in widely separate locales, a substantial danger exists to public health from polluted drinking water. This is particularly true in areas that lack sewer systems, but even sophisticated city sewers can overflow. In such cases, water-borne diseases, such as cholera and typhoid, may wreak far greater harm to the populace than flooding or winds. Rescue workers must therefore provide clean water and treat outbreaks as they appear.

IMPACT

Because an El Niño prevents nutrient-rich cold water from rising near the coast of South America, fish must change their feeding grounds. Important commercial species, such as the anchoveta, seek cooler water to the south. This is a boon to Chilean fishers, but the fisheries of Peru and Ecuador are drastically reduced. Fishing boats make few, small catches, and the crews suffer economically, as do industries dependent upon them, such as fishmeal production. Seabirds that feed on the fish also suffer; large-scale die-offs have been recorded. Similar alterations in fishing patterns off the coasts of Central and North America occur, forcing fishers to travel farther for their catches and causing starvation among birds and seals.

Severe storms can decimate crops and kill livestock in the eastern Pacific nations, while drought does the same in Australia and the western Pacific. In Indonesia, dry forests often ignite and burn out of control, lifting smoke into the atmosphere and destroying property. The economic damage of a severe El Niño can easily exceed $1 billion on the West Coast of the United States alone, and many times that amount worldwide. The death toll from windstorms, flooding and attendant disease outbreaks, and drought-caused famine may reach into the thousands, principally in South America. Scientists suspect that global warming may make future El Niños more powerful, raising the potential for yet greater destructiveness.

Roger Smith

BIBLIOGRAPHY

Allan, Rob, Janette Lindesay, and David Parker. *El Niño Southern Oscillation and Climatic Variability.* Collingwood, Australia: CSIRO, 1997. Offers a scholarly introduction to the history of El Niño studies, the oceanic-atmospheric forces behind the phenomenon, and forecasting methods, followed by hundreds of color graphs displaying data on conditions during El Niños from 1871 to 1994.

Arnold, Caroline. *El Niño: Stormy Weather for People and Wildlife.* New York: Clarion, 1998. Intended for young readers, a richly illustrated explanation of the mechanics of El Niño, its effects, and forecasting methods. A clear introduction for general readers who are science-shy.

Diaz, Henry F., and Vera Markgraf, eds. *El Niño: Historical and Paleoclimatic Aspects of the Southern Oscillation.* New York: Cambridge University Press, 1992. Twenty-two essays discuss the historical, geological, and biological evidence concerning historic and prehistoric El Niños to shed light on modern questions, such as whether global warming will bring more powerful El Niños.

Fagan, Brian. *Floods, Famines, and Emperors: El Niño and the Fate of Civilization.* New York: Basic Books, 1999. Following a popular explanation of El Niño, Fagan examines evidence of its influence on ancient civilizations, concluding with an overview of the 1982-1983 and 1997-1998 episodes.

Glantz, Michael H. *Currents of Change: El Niño's Impact on Climate and Society.* New York: Cambridge University Press, 1996. Glantz, an environmental scientist, outlines the natural causes of El Niños for nonscientists and discusses the phenomenon's effects on society at length.

Lyons, Walter A. *The Handy Weather Answer Book.* Detroit: Visible Ink Press, 1997. Explains the fundamental science of weather systems and describes forecasting and the instruments used to gather meteorological data. A chapter address El Niños and climate change. The question-and-answer text is simple and clear, accompanied by illustrations.

Philander, S. George. *Is the Temperature Rising? The Uncertain Science of Global Warming.* Princeton, N.J.: Princeton University Press, 1998. Intended for college students, an enjoyable survey of the science behind climatic phenomena, with a lucid chapter on ENSO.

Notable Events

1982: Pacific Ocean

DATE: June, 1982-August, 1983
PLACE: Equatorial Pacific Ocean and bordering continents
RESULT: More than 2,000 dead, $13 billion in damage

Before 1982, "El Niño" was a term known almost strictly to scientists studying the ocean, atmosphere, and weather. After 1983, so widespread and serious were El Niño's destructive consequences, the phenomenon became known worldwide as the largest force disrupting world weather patterns.

The El Niño of 1982 developed anomalously. Previous El Niños had begun in April with waters warming off the Peruvian coast and spreading westward. In this case the temperature rise started in the central Pacific and flowed eastward in June and August, and the barometric pressure increased in the western Pacific. Moreover, while the warm water moved slowly eastward toward South America, the westerly trade winds continued blowing unabated; normally they weaken. Volcanic dust lofted into the atmosphere from the eruption of El Chichón in Mexico masked some of these developments from satellites, and partly because of this, the beginning of a full-blown El Niño in November took observers by surprise. Before it ended in August, 1983, five continents had suffered its devastating effects.

Its intensity was unheralded. The Southern Oscillation—indicated by the difference in air pressure between Darwin, Australia, and Tahiti—was never before so great. Sea surface temperatures off the South American coast soared to almost 46 degrees Fahrenheit (8 degrees Celsius) above normal, another record. The mass of warm water increased evaporation, which fueled storms that lashed the coasts and Pacific islands near the equator.

Six hurricanes swept over Tahiti and nearby Tuamotu archipelago in the central Pacific; the area had not seen a hurricane for seventy-five years. More than 7,500 houses were flattened or lost their roofs, and 15 people died. The destruction ended tourism for the season, a main source of income. A hurricane also hit the Hawaiian Islands, which otherwise had a drought. Elsewhere in the Pacific scientists noticed that millions of seabirds deserted their nests and the warm water damaged reefs.

Ecuador and Peru were first hurt economically, then physically. The planktonic nutrients that normally rise from the seafloor with upwelling cold currents dwindled when El Niño's warm water arrived. Schools of commercial fish vanished. Fishermen were idled, as were industries dependent upon fishing, such as fishmeal production. Because the coast of both countries is very arid, when El Niño-spawned storms arrived, their torrential rains turned into floods that swelled rivers and raged through canyons. As a result, thousands of houses, mostly in rural towns or urban slums, were washed away, along with sections of roads and more than a dozen major bridges. At least 600 people were killed in the process. Important export crops—particularly rice, cacao, and bananas—also were heavily damaged, further crippling the national economies.

The west coasts of Central and North America soon experienced similar conditions. California was especially hard hit. Salmon and other cold-water fish departed north, hurting the local fishing industry, while seabirds died and tropical fish, such as barracuda, invaded the coastal waters. High sea levels, as much as 8 inches above normal, combined with storm-propelled waves, battered the coast. Wind gusts damaged houses, and a tornado even tore the roof off the Los Angeles Convention Center before ravaging the Watts district. Rain fell until rivers overflowed and hillsides were so soaked that mudslides

Homes in Pacifica, California, had to be demolished after being battered by El Niño storms. (AP/Wide World Photos)

occurred at record rates. In the Sierra and Rock Mountains, snowpacks reached record depths. Altogether, more than 10,000 buildings were damaged or destroyed, and the economic toll on the West Coast, which included extensive damage to roads and agriculture, was estimated at $1.8 billion. Meanwhile, in the American South, heavy rains fell, nearly pushing the Mississippi River over its levees. The Atlantic hurricane season, however, was short and mild.

Across the Pacific, under the abnormally high pressure over the Indonesia-Australia region, conditions were dry. The drought in Australia starved thousands of livestock and wild animals and turned brushland parched and dusty. Immense dust storms dumped tons of dirt on cities, Melbourne most spectacularly, and brush fires raced out of control. At least 8,000 people were made homeless in the fires, and there were 75 fatalities. Late in the El Niño, downpours in eastern Australia led to flooding that drowned yet more livestock. Indonesia saw crops fail

in the drought. In one area 340 people starved because of it. On the island of Borneo, forest fires, spread from land burned off by farmers, expanded unchecked. The smoke fouled cities, endangered air traffic, and caused one port to close temporarily. The fires were called one of the worst environmental disasters of the century,

Record drought also came to Africa, hurting the southern and Sahelian regions most. In some areas of South Africa 90 percent of cattle died as the grassland turned to barren hardpan. Tens of thousands of wild animals, from rodents to elephants, perished. To escape famine, the poor countries of the region had to rely on food shipments from North America. Many other effects, such as delayed monsoons in southern India and droughts in Brazil and Mexico, were teleconnections to El Niño. Scientists suspect that a cold snap in Europe and droughts in the Midwest, northern China, and central Russia might also have occurred because of El Niño, at least in part.

In addition to bringing the El Niño phenomenon forcefully to public awareness, the 1982-1983 event had three consequences. It spurred much scientific research aimed at making predictions of future El Niños reliable. It encouraged farmers in affected areas to reconsider how they manage their crops and livestock. Finally, it demonstrated dramatically that coastal cities, which are growing increasingly crowded, are vulnerable to El Niño-related natural disasters.

Roger Smith

FOR FURTHER INFORMATION:

Canby, Thomas Y. "El Niño's Ill Wind." *National Geographic*, February, 1984, 144.

Fagan, Brian. "El Niños That Shook the World." In *Floods, Famines, and Emperors: El Niño and the Fate of Civilization*. New York: Basic Books, 1999.

1997: Pacific Ocean

DATE: Early 1997-August, 1998
PLACE: Equatorial Pacific Ocean and bordering continents
RESULT: More than 900 dead, approximately $20 billion in damage

Early in 1997, scientists detected a large pool of abnormally warm water in the southwestern Pacific. As it spread eastward along the equator, they knew what it meant—a developing El Niño. They could also predict its likely career, thanks to more than two decades of intense research and improvements in computer weather modeling. Accordingly, many of the countries that had suffered from previous El Niños made preparations. Still, the 1997-1998 El Niño's strength surprised forecasters and overpowered most precautionary measures.

By August, sea surface temperatures were as high as they were during the 1982-1983 El Niño, and forecasters began to expect the worst. In October, the pool of warm water swelled to an area larger than that of the United States. In early November, with ocean temperature nearly 46 degrees Fahrenheit (8 degrees Celsius) above normal, heavy storms began to gather and blow ashore along the North American, Central American, and South American Pacific coastline.

Stung by losses during previous El Niños, Peru had borrowed $250 million and Ecuador $180 million to pay for disaster relief supplies and construction. They cleared out waterways, built dikes, and shored up bridges. Despite these preparations, the two countries were again devastated. More rain fell in Ecuador than during the record deluges of 1982-1983. Nineteen bridges were washed out, and more than 1,554 miles (2,500 kilometers) of roadway were damaged. In some areas transportation was cut off completely, disrupting commerce. Flooding left 50,000 people homeless, many of them in poor towns and slums on the outskirts of cities. Fouled water sources spread diarrheal diseases.

In Peru, conditions were even worse. About 373 miles (600 kilometers) of roadway and 30 bridges were rendered impassable because of floods inland, while the south coast, which forecasters expected to remain dry, was also flooded. In the north the Sechura Desert turned into a vast shallow lake. Rain soaked the Andean foothills, and the consequent landslides were deadly. In one slide, 20 people died. More than 350,000 people eventually lost their homes. The destruction to agriculture and the collapse of the anchoveta fishery offshore left many more without a livelihood.

Just south of Peru, Chile's Atacama Desert, the driest place on earth, erupted in flowers after the rainfall, and the increased snowpack in the Andes gave the country its longest skiing season on record. Chile also suffered, however: Crops were destroyed, and 80,000 people became homeless because of flooding. Flooding in Argentina, especially along the Paraná River, cost the nation $3 billion in lost crops—40 percent of its cotton, 30 percent of its rice, and 50 percent of its tobacco—and left 150,000 homeless. Brazil lost even more in cattle and withered crops as drought came to its northeast. Drought also plagued Venezuela, Guyana, and Suriname. Receiving half its normal rainfall, Columbia lost 7 percent of its agricultural output.

Central America suffered similarly. Drought ruined 30 percent of El Salvador's coffee and 10 percent of Guatemala's grain. Water levels were so low in Panama that shipping was restricted through the Panama Canal, which cut into the nation's principal revenue source, and electrical output from hydroelectric plants declined. Mexico, as well as having drought in some areas, was lashed by three powerful hurricanes. One that came ashore at Acapulco leveled sections of the city, ending tourism for the season and idling 150,000 workers. The Caribbean was short of rain, causing forest fires in Cuba to burn out of control; some eastern Caribbean islands had to ration water.

North America (as well as Europe and eastern Asia) saw unusually warm weather, including the hottest February on record. As during the 1982-1983 El Niño, the West Coast, California especially, received storms with exceptionally heavy rain. During a nine-hour period in December, for example, Orange County received 8 inches of rain, and the resulting flood did an estimated $10 million in property damage. Elsewhere roads washed out, and bridges crumbled. The Sierra Nevada accumulated a deep snowpack, raising the possibility of spring flooding. On the coast, seabirds and seals starved because their prey, fish, had fled the warming seawater. Meanwhile, near Alaska, fishers were hauling in tuna and sunfish and spotting great white sharks, all of which normally swim the Southern Californian waters.

Across the Pacific Ocean, drought parched the western Pacific islands. The Philippines endured the worst dry spell in four decades. It ruined rice crops, killed off livestock, and sent thousands of farmers to cities looking for jobs. Indonesia, however, was the site of the most influential calamity. Farmers there burn off new fields every year and expect the seasonal rains to put out the fires. In 1998, the rains failed to come. The field burns escaped into forests and burned out of control for weeks. The smoke drifted throughout the region, so intensifying the smog in some cities that businesses and schools

Debris from flooding attributed to El Niño in Peru is cleared by Peruvian president Alberto Fujimori. (AP/Wide World Photos)

closed. The smog caused an airline crash that killed 234 passengers. The fires and the drought damage to crops brought $1.3 billion in losses and serious food shortages, contributing significantly to the Asian economic crisis.

By the time the pool of warm water receded in August, 1998, the 1997-1998 El Niño was the most studied weather phenomenon in history—"the climate event of the century," in the words of U.S. vice president Al Gore. Scientists wondered if the 1997-1998 event was evidence that global warming would eventually fuel even more powerful El Niños.

Roger Smith

FOR FURTHER INFORMATION:

Fagan, Brian. "El Niños That Shook the World." In *Floods, Famines, and Emperors: El Niño and the Fate of Civilization.* New York: Basic Books, 1999.

"The Season of El Niño." *The Economist* 347 (May 9, 1998): 35-38.

Epidemics

(AP/Wide World Photos)

An epidemic is the spreading of an infectious disease over a wide range of a human population that historically leads to a dramatic loss of life. Preventive measures, which include aggressive sanitation procedures, reduced the impact of epidemics on human life during the late twentieth century.

FACTORS INVOLVED: Animals, human activity, microorganisms, plants, temperature, weather conditions
REGIONS AFFECTED: Cities, forests, islands, towns

SCIENCE

Contagious or communicable diseases are those transmitted from one organism to another. Living microorganisms, also known as parasites, such as bacteria, fungi, or viruses, may invade or attach themselves to a host organism and replicate, thus creating infectious diseases. A disease that affects a large human population is called an epidemic.

In a disease situation the host organism serves as the environment where the parasite thrives. With many diseases, such as syphilis, the parasite remains present throughout the lifetime of the host unless it is destroyed by treatment. Generally, the parasite appears to have a degree of specificity with regard to the host. Thus, microorganisms adapted to plant hosts are rarely capable of attacking an animal host and vice versa. However, a given parasite may attack different types of animal hosts, including both vertebrates and invertebrates.

Many times the parasite emigrates from one host to another by means of an insect carrier or other vector. In other cases the parasites may spend one part of their life in an intermediate host. This may enhance or decrease the harmful effect the parasite will have on the host, as the intermediate host may or may not interact constructively with the parasite. As a result geographic or seasonal differences in the disease outbreak are very likely to occur.

Occasionally, diseases are spread among rodents by an intermediate host, such as fleas. The rodent-flea-rodent sequence is called enzootic, meaning the infection is present in an animal community at all times but manifests itself only in a small fraction of instances. However, once the environmental conditions are favorable the condition becomes epizootic, and a large number of animals become infected at the same time. As the rodent population is reduced by death, fleas from the dead animals fail to find other host rodents and begin infecting other animals that are present in the immediate area, including humans. The overall infestation is slow at the beginning but quickly explodes, with a devastating number of victims. The human involvement in this progression is therefore more coincidental than programmed.

Most pathogenic parasites adapt comfortably to their hosts and do not survive the conditions outside the host's tissues. Exceptions to this case are those microorganisms whose lives involve a resistant-spore stage. Such examples include the *Coccidioides* fungus, which is responsible for desert fever and the anthrax bacillus that affects cows, sheep, goats, and even humans. An animal disease that can also be transferred to humans is called zoonosis.

Epidemiology is the medical field that studies the distribution of disease among human populations, as well as the factors responsible for this distribution. Contrary to most other medical branches, however, epidemiology is concerned more with groups of people rather than with the patients themselves. As a result, the field relies heavily on statistical patterns and historical trends. Its development arose as a result of the great epidemics of the last few centuries that led to an immeasurable loss of human lives. Scientists at the time began looking into the identification of the high risk associated with certain diseases in an attempt to establish preventive measures. Epidemiological studies are classified as descriptive or analytic. In descriptive epidemiology, scientists survey the nature of the population affected by the disorder in question. Data on factors such as ethnicity, age, sex, geographic description, occupation, and time trends are closely monitored and recorded. The most common measures of disease are mortality, which is the number of yearly deaths per 1,000 of population at risk; the incidence, which is defined as the number of new cases yearly per 100,000 of population at risk; and prevalence, which is the number of existing cases at a given time per 100 of population at risk.

In analytic epidemiology, a careful analysis of the collected data is made in an attempt to draw conclusions. For instance, in the prospective-cohort study members of a population are observed over a long period of time, and their health status is evaluated. The analytic studies can be either observational or experimental. In observational studies, the researcher does not alter the behavior or exposure of the study subjects but instead monitors them in order to learn whether those exposed to different factors differ in disease rates. On the other hand, in experimental studies the scientist alters the behavior, exposure, or treatment of people to determine the result of intervention on the disease. The weighted data are often statistically analyzed using t-tests, analysis of variance, and multiple logistic regression.

An epidemic that takes place over a large geographical area is known as a pandemic. Its rise and decline is mainly affected by the ability of the infectious invading agent to transfer the disease to the susceptible individual host. Interestingly enough, the population of infected individuals that survives the parasite usually acquires a type of immunity. This immunity diminishes the epidemic and prevents it from reoccurring within a certain time period in the same geographic area. As a result the invading parasite is unable to reproduce itself in this immunity-equipped host population. This may be the reason why areas that have exhibited the Ebola epidemic for several

Types of Viral Infection

Family		Conditions
Adenoviruses		Respiratory and eye infections
Arenaviruses		Lassa fever
Coronaviruses		Common cold
Herpesviruses		Cold sores, genital herpes, chickenpox, herpes zoster (shingles), glandular fever, congenital abnormalities (cytomegalovirus)
Orthomyxoviruses		Influenza
Papovaviruses		Warts
Paramyxoviruses		Mumps, measles, rubella
Picornaviruses		Poliomyelitis, viral hepatitis types A and B, respiratory infections, myocarditis
Poxviruses		Cowpox, smallpox (eradicated), molluscum contagiosum
Retroviruses		AIDS, degenerative brain diseases, possibly various kinds of cancer
Rhabdoviruses		Rabies
Togaviruses		Yellow fever, dengue, encephalitis

months with a death rate of almost 95 percent suddenly displayed a suppressed outbreak.

Within a certain time frame, however, the host's susceptibility to the invader may be reproduced due to several factors. These include the removal of the immune generation by death, the deterioration of the individual immunity by external conditions, and the birth of offspring who do not have the ability to naturally resist the disease.

In some cases, such as syphilis, the disease severity appears to be less now than a few centuries ago. One theory suggests that the ability of the parasite to infect as many hosts as possible has produced a negative effect on the parasite itself. Eliminating all hosts steadfastly will lead to the extinction of the parasite itself. Therefore, once the adaptation of the parasite to the host has become close, the tendency for the disease outbreak appears less severe. Ecological studies suggest, however, that it is incorrect to assume that the host-parasite antagonism will reduce in intensity and that the continuous fight for dominance remains in full force.

GEOGRAPHY

Epidemics can take place anywhere on earth as long as the conditions allow it. Historically these conditions favor an isolated environment with animal or insect carriers, unsanitary conditions, and large human populations. The infectious disease can be spread easily to other areas and have an equally strong impact there. Rodents have long served as one of the primary factors in spreading diseases to people, especially if the human population is contained. The tsutsugamushi disease (also known as scrub typhus) is transmitted by the bite of a rat mite.

One of the first epidemics in history that involved infected rats occurred at the beginning of the Peloponnesian War in Greece (431-404 B.C.E.), in which the rats were transferred by ships. The Athenians, who were the dominant naval force in the conflict, were besieged by the Spartan army inside Athens. The infected rats were brought in the city unintentionally via ships that were transporting food from Egypt. The ensuing Plague of Athens led to the decline of the Pericles regime and tilted the scales of the war toward the Spartan army.

The historically devastating bubonic plague in Europe occurred in the fourteenth century, almost two centuries after the so-called Black Death originated in Mesopotamia. The mass spreading of rats is greatly attributed by many historians to the onset of the Crusades and led to an estimated 25 million lives lost in Europe alone. France was particularly affected (1348-1350), with many cities losing about one-third of their populations. Nothing appeared to check the disease in populations without immunity: neither bonfires to disinfect air, nor demonstrations of pertinence, nor persecutions of Jews and Gypsies. Ocean-going ships also appear to have been responsible for the epidemic in China during the end of the nineteenth century.

It is believed by many scholars that the origins of venereal syphilis were in America, since historical accounts of the outbreak first appeared in Europe after Christopher Columbus's return trip from the New World at the end of the fifteenth century. Moreover, skeletal remains of pre-Columbian American Indians indicate the presence of the *Treponema pallidum* spirochete, which is responsible for the disease. Among the victims of that disease were England's king Henry VIII and several members of the Italian Borgia family in the middle of the sixteenth century.

PREVENTION AND PREPARATIONS

There seems to be a variable degree of natural susceptibility to a specific disease among different people. This occurs because the outcome of the interaction of parasite and host is variable in each individual case. As a result individuals who have low resistance quickly show symptoms of the disease and easily display the infection. On the other hand, people with strong resistance do not show the symptoms, and the infection is not recognizable.

Most diseases seem to be preventable unless they are idiopathic (particular to the individual), such as inherited metabolic defects. Diseases that are caused by environmental factors may be avoided by eliminating or greatly reducing the effectiveness of the factors responsible. The various epidemics in Europe, such as the Black Death and the London plague, had much less impact on the upper classes. More affluent groups that had sufficient land or wages that would allow for the replacement of tools and isolation from the infected areas suffered much less. On the other hand, the poor, who had very few possessions and a great lack of sanitation and pure water, were forced to live under miserable conditions that allowed diseases to thrive.

Transmission of infection may be avoided by preventing contact between the susceptible host and the parasite. Historically, the easiest application of this principle has been quarantine, which in several cases had very limited success. It is nearly impossible to prevent diseases from spreading across borders because of airborne factors, such as mosquitoes infected with malaria and flies with the plague. Rocky Mountain spotted fever, which is believed to have originated in the northwestern part of the United States but spread to Mexico, South America, and Africa, is transmitted to humans via tick bites and is native to many rodents.

Syphilis would not have been so devastating in Europe if prostitutes did not spread the disease to their patrons. The consequences would not have been as severe if mercury treatment, the most popular method of combating syphilis at the time, was given to prostitutes. However, the expense, together with the social belief that such women were not worth the treatment, prohibited the remedy.

The last two cases of the plague in European urban areas were in Marseilles, France (1720), and Messina, Italy (1740), which were not as destructive as previous plagues because of more elaborate and organized methods of quarantine. The same was true during the last months of the Great Plague of London (1665). Some historians give credit for the containment of epidemics to the isolation of lepers, many of whom modern scientists believe were carrying communicable diseases other than leprosy. Another way to prevent the spread of disease is to exterminate animals that may carry the infectious factors, which has taken place as late as the 1990's, in the case of bovine spongiform encephalopathy, commonly called mad cow disease.

The spreading of plagues is greatly confined by controlling rat populations, particularly those on ships, and by preventing rodents from landing on uninfected ports. One plague bacillus can infect as many as 80 rodents, giving rise to the sylvatic plague. Using sprays to eliminate mosquitoes reduces outbreaks of malaria, which occur especially in swampy areas. Louse-borne typhus may be regulated in humans by strong disinfecting methods. Typhus has become virtually nonexistent in industrialized societies through the extermination of lice and fleas, while typhoid fever has been eliminated by the use of sanitized water. Examples of this involve the chlorination of water in swimming pools and municipal water sources, as well as pasteurization of milk. Despite the fact that plague epidemics have come under control in recent centuries, there still exist many foci of infection.

The explosive development of medical technology after World War II led to the synthesis and administration of significant medications, such as antibiotics, and vaccines, which led to the decisive control of epidemics. Developing an artificial immunity, such as through vaccination, appears to be extremely effective because it becomes impossible for the infecting agent to inhabit the organism after the virus has been administered to it. This has been the case with the diphtheria, smallpox, and poliomyelitis (polio) vaccines that were designed for children after World War II. The polio vaccine against infantile paralysis is a combination of the killed virus, which is injected, and the attenuated or weakened virus, which is given orally.

In the early 1980's the epidemic acquired immunodeficiency syndrome (AIDS) appeared. During this decade many thousands, possibly millions, of people died all over the world. Although quarantine is generally not possible in the society of industrialized countries, other measures of prevention are lessening the disease's spread. The use of prophylactics during sexual contact, extensive screening of blood transfusions, and education about the impact of the virus all seem to have had a positive effect on the number of people affected. To a much lesser degree the various forms of hepatitis have claimed a large number of victims. Although not as in the public eye as AIDS, the disease is communicable, and municipal health departments have tried to control its spreading by monitoring the conditions of restaurants for sanitation.

RESCUE AND RELIEF EFFORTS

Radical combat of the responsible bacteria has definitely relieved people from epidemics. The fact that the Great Plague of London never reappeared is attributed, according to some scholars, to the great fire of the city that occurred in September, 1666. People were often buried with caustic bases in the eighteenth century. The pioneering work of English scientist Joseph Lister in the nineteenth century introduced doctors to antiseptics, and detergents were used more frequently. The various laboratory procedures that were developed in the twentieth century provided first the detection of the disease and then the prescribed routes for cure. Thus, the eradication of syphilis started with the development of the serological test for syphilis (STS), which detects syphilis reagin and the treponemal antibody, two antibodies formed by the organism once the virus has invaded it. Penicillin and other antibiotics helped curb the number of syphilis victims.

American doctor Jonas Salk's polio vaccine in the 1950's gave all children the chance to walk without crutches. The wide availability of quinine has saved millions of people from malaria. A vaccine against the plague is currently available and is being used in areas where the epidemic is flourishing.

The World Health Organization (WHO) was set up in 1948 to increase the international effort toward improved health conditions, particularly to poor areas of Africa, Asia, and South America. The WHO was the successor of the Health Organization of the League of Nations, established in 1923, and the Office International d'Hygiene Publique, created in 1907. Unlike the other two organizations, whose duties included quarantine measures, drug standardization, and epidemic control, WHO undertakes the task of promoting the highest possible conditions for universal health to all populations. Its responsibilities include the revising and updating of health regulations, support of research services, and the dissemination of information that concerns any potential pestilent-disease outbreak. The organization also collaborates and shares information with all member countries on the latest developments of nutrition research, updated vaccinations, drug addiction, cancer research, hazards of nuclear radiation, and efforts to curb the spread of AIDS.

Much credit has been given to the WHO for its mass campaign against infectious diseases, which led to the control of a large number of epidemics. As a result, smallpox has been eradicated, cholera and the plague have been practically eliminated, and most other diseases have been substantially reduced. Intensive programs that have provided pure water, antibiotics, pesticides, primary health care facilities, and clean sanitation systems to underdeveloped countries helped to reduce infant mortality and increase the average life span in these places.

During the late 1980's and throughout the 1990's a huge concentrated effort was coordinated by the WHO and the governments of its member countries toward the war against AIDS. Data collection, education campaigns, promotion for safe sex, continuous research, health providers, and infection control served as the tools the organization used to overcome dangerous and unsanitary trends of susceptible people in the underdeveloped world.

It should also be noted that many of the countries that are vulnerable to natural disasters, such as floods, mudslides, earthquakes, tornadoes, and ty-phoons, face the menacing problem of refugees and homeless people after the event. The lack of sanitary conditions and an efficient way to remove the dead, a reduced number of medical supplies and personnel, and poverty and political indifference add more casualties to many disasters. The WHO has been helped in these situations by other international relief organizations, such as the Red Cross and the Peace Corps, together with the voluntary contributions of other countries.

IMPACT

Epidemics have had a strong effect in checking the human population. The Great Plague of London claimed more than 75,000 of a total population of 460,000 and forced the king and his court to flee to the suburbs for more than eight months, while the parliament kept a short session at Oxford. The outbreak in Canton and Hong Kong left almost 100,000 dead. Severe epidemics of poliomyelitis have been reported in many parts of the world, especially during the twentieth century. About 300,000 cases were recorded in the United States alone during the 1942-1953 period. Western Europe, and especially Germany, Belgium, and Denmark, as well as Japan, Korea, Singapore, and the Philippines, also suffered many casualties in the early 1950's.

When the carriers of the epidemic are rodents, the economic damage of the afflicted area is also immense. Norway rats, black rats, and the house mouse had devastating effects on crops of wheat, sugar beets, and potatoes in Germany at the end of the World War I, Russia in 1932-1935, and especially France in 1790-1935, where at least 20 mouse plagues have been reported.

Epidemiological studies and comparisons have shown that the twentieth century was pivotal in transforming the patterns of frequent death from disease to the lowest in human history. Infant and children mortality were reduced dramatically, cases of famine and epidemic were lessened, and modern science shifted many of its efforts to degenerative diseases that affect the elderly. Many countries still faced epidemics of relatively minor proportions in areas where civil strife occurred, especially Somalia, Rwanda, the Sudan, even in the 1990's. The hurricanes in Bangladesh and the Caribbean in that decade proved that epidemics were not fully eliminated from society.

During the twentieth century the epidemiologic transition of the human race shifted. Until the early part of that century the pattern of mortality and disease afflicted infants and children as well as younger adults and was related to bacteriological epidemics. In contrast, in the late twentieth century, with the exception of AIDS and occasional outbreaks of epidemics in underdeveloped countries, most diseases were human-made and degenerative, such as the ones attributed to drug use, smoking, and drinking. As a result the average life span increased sharply, by almost twenty-five years after the early 1960's. This holds true for industrialized countries; however, the pattern is only slowly changing in developing countries, which have not had the same socioeconomic development of industrial countries. Nevertheless, the twentieth century decline in mortality in developing countries was significantly more rapid that that of the nineteenth century in countries now classified as industrialized.

Soraya Ghayourmanesh

BIBLIOGRAPHY

Ernester, Virginia L. "Epidemiology." In *McGraw-Hill Encyclopedia of Science and Technology.* 8th ed. New York: McGraw-Hill, 1997. This article discusses epidemiology and its branches, including descriptive and analytic approaches, with emphasis on observational and experimental studies.

Ghayourmanesh, Soraya. "Ebola Virus." In *Magill's Medical Guide.* Rev. ed. Pasadena, Calif.: Salem Press, 1998. This short article describes the outbreak of the Ebola virus in Africa.

_____. "Typhoid Fever and Typhus." In *Magill's Medical Guide: Health and Illness.* Pasadena, Calif.: Salem Press, 1995-1996. This article discusses the history of typhoid fever and its effect on humans. More articles related to epidemics are included in this reference book.

Karlen, Arno. *Man and Microbes: Disease and Plagues in History and Modern Times.* New York: Putnam, 1995. Describes the history of communicable diseases, such as cholera, leprosy, AIDS, viral encephalitis, lethal Ebola viruses, and streptococcal infections.

Lampton, Christopher F. *Epidemic.* Brookfield, Wis.: Millbrook Press, 1992. This text, designed for young adults, discusses how epidemics begin and spread and what can be done to prevent them. Emphasis is on the Black Death and AIDS.

McNeill, William Hardy. *Plagues and Peoples.* Garden City, N.Y.: Doubleday, 1998. Topics include the impact of the Mongol Empire on transoceanic exchanges and the ecological impact of Mediterranean science after 1700.

Ranger, Terence, and Paul Slack, eds. *Epidemics and Ideas: Essays in the Historical Perception of Pestilence.* New York: Cambridge University Press, 1997. This book views medicine and disease as conceived by different civilizations, including those of classical Athens, the Dark Ages, Hawaii, and India.

Thomas, Gordon. *Anatomy of an Epidemic.* Garden City, N.Y.: Doubleday, 1982. Analysis and causes of epidemics are thoroughly investigated by the author.

Turkington, Carol. *Hepatitis C: The Silent Killer.* Lincolnwood, Ill.: Contemporary Books, 1998. The author discusses all aspects of hepatitis C, from the history of its first detection to modern treatments available.

Watts, Sheldon J. *Epidemics and History: Disease, Power, and Imperialism.* New Haven, Conn.: Yale University Press, 1998. This book discusses the human response to plagues in Europe and the Middle East from 1347-1844, with special chapters on leprosy, smallpox, syphilis, cholera, and yellow fever.

Notable Events

Historical Overview

Epidemic diseases are the greatest destructive force in human history. Epidemics have killed millions across continents and even more so influenced cultural, economic, and political institutions. Great empires, powerful armies, and a host of human endeavors have crumbled under the wake of disease and, likewise, factored in subsequent societal changes. Epidemics are contagious diseases that spread rapidly and extensively through a community, region, or country. When they sweep across the globe they are referred to as pandemics. Prior to the introduction of vaccination and antibiotics, viral and bacterial infections posed a constant and often widespread threat to human existence. The history of epidemics dates from the earliest of written records, an influence upon human life throughout time. In Western cul-

Milestones

11th century B.C.E.:	Biblical passage Samuel I tells of the Philistine plague, a pestilence outbreak that occurred after the capture of the Ark of the Covenant.
7th century B.C.E.:	Assyrian pestilence slays 185,000 Asssyrians, forcing King Sennacherib to retreat from Judah without capturing Jerusalem.
451 B.C.E.:	The Roman pestilence, an unidentified disease but probably anthrax, kills a large portion of the slave population and some in the citizenry and prevents the Aequians of Latium from attacking Rome.
387 B.C.E.:	According the records of Livy, a series of 11 epidemics strikes Rome through the end of the republic.
250-243 B.C.E.:	"Hunpox," or perhaps smallpox, strikes China.
48 B.C.E.:	Epidemic, flood, and famine occur in China.
542-543 C.E.:	Plague of Justinian is the first pandemic of bubonic plague that devastates Africa, Asia Minor, and Europe. The first year the plague kills 300,000 in Constantinople; the infection resurfaces repeatedly over the next half century.
585-587:	The Japanese smallpox epidemic, probably the country's first documented episode of the disease, infects peasants and nobility alike. Because it occurs after the acceptance of Buddhism, it is believed to be a punishment from the Shinto gods and results in burning of temples and attacks on Buddhist nuns and priests.
1347-1380:	The Black Death (bubonic plague) rages across Asia and Europe. It kills an estimated 25 million in Asia before reaching Europe. A reported two-thirds of the population in China succumbs. In the aftermath of devastation, the Mongolian dynasty collapses and is replaced by the Ming in 1368.
1494-1495:	French army syphilis epidemic strikes in Naples and is considered the first appearance of this venereal infection in Europe.
1507:	Hispaniola smallpox is the first recorded epidemic in the New World, representing the first wave of diseases that eventually depopulate America of most of its native inhabitants. In the next two centuries, the population plunges by an estimated 80 percent.
1918-1920:	Spanish influenza pandemic sweeps the globe, killing 20 to 25 million, perhaps the largest single biological event in human history.
1976:	Zairean Ebola epidemic kills 218 people and proves one of the deadliest diseases of the late twentieth century.
1981:	U.S. epidemic reported by U.S. Center for Disease Control in June and given the name acquired immunodeficiency syndrome (AIDS). In some regions of Africa the infection touches 90 percent of the population and poses a constant pandemic threat.
1995:	An outbreak of Ebola virus in Kitwit, Zaire, leaves 245 dead.
1999:	7 die in an epidemic of encephalitis in New England and New York.

ture an epidemic is often referred to as a pestilence, which is symbolized in the Bible's Book of Revelation as one of the three great enemies of humanity, along with famine and war. Characterized as the Horsemen of the Apocalypse, these three serve as a convoy for a fourth rider, death.

Peoples throughout ages, regions, and religions explained illness and death as divine judgment for the sins of humanity, psychologically interlacing poor health with their own moral depravity. Illness was punishment; cast from the hands of God, disease tortured individuals and often entire populations with more than the hardships of sickness. Modern medical science, together with the social sciences, has since revealed secular connections between social disorder and the spread of contagious infections. Still, many cultures maintain the belief that sickness and death are a form of divine retribution. However, medical theory also has ancient roots.

Healers and medical practitioners speculated on the origins of disease and epidemics throughout recorded history. The Greeks developed a more formalized framework for understanding the causes of illness and periodic epidemics, rejecting the idea of divine retribution. Hippocrates (c. 460-370 B.C.E.) is considered the "father of medicine" and the most prominent physician of the ancient world. His name is associated with the high ideals of medical practice. The *Corpus Hippocraticum*, a collection of nearly sixty treatises written by his students following his death, established the foundation of medical knowledge, especially relating to endemic and epidemic diseases. The most notable treatise, *Airs, Waters, and Places*, discusses the links between the environment and disease. It states that some diseases maintain a constant presence in a population and are referred to as "endemic." Other diseases flare infrequently but with deadly force; these are termed "epidemics." We still employ these terms today. Less enduring were early notions of the body, which, according to Hippocratic doctrine, consisted of four humors: blood, phlegm, yellow bile, and black bile. Good health meant keeping the humors in balance through proper diet, temperament, and correction of bodily deficiencies. Disease occurred when the humoral balance was upset, and epidemics resulted from excesses in the natural environment. In the latter, changing seasons and atmospheric conditions corresponded to the prevalence of vast instances of contagious diseases. Thus, drastic changes that upset the natural environment produced widespread sickness in humans. The ideal for human health was to live a balanced and unstressed life within a harmonic environment. Hippocratic doctrine related epidemics as a natural force in nature without understanding the role of microorganisms.

It was only within the last one hundred years that science expanded upon the Hippocratic doctrine to understand the mechanics of disease, how it spreads, and how it may be prevented or cured. The outbreak of an epidemic is dependent upon a variety of factors, some of which are seemingly unrelated to the actual spread of contagious infections. Among the important factors to consider in the formation of an epidemic are the general health of a population; living conditions, including hygiene and sanitation practices; immunity to a particular disease; access to medical treatment; community public health responses; and, of course, environmental conditions. Less obvious factors favoring the spread of disease may include economic disarray; the introduction of new people or products, especially after a period of isolation; a massive disruption resulting from war or natural disasters, such as earthquakes, famines, and floods; or an explosion in insect or rodent populations. Thus, epidemics are often dependent on a variety of factors that may work independently or in tandem to cause widespread destruction.

Historical references to epidemics are found in a variety of ancient texts. *The Gilgamesh Epic* (2000 B.C.E.) mentions the impact of natural disasters, floods in particular, and affirms the destructive force of the god of pestilence. The ancient writings illustrate how disease can have far more extensive effects than simply reducing populations. Histories of the great civilizations in Babylon, China, and Egypt document a host of diseases and widespread sickness. Many of these, such as bubonic plague, diphtheria, smallpox, and typhus, have paralleled human existence into the modern world. Other population-decimating diseases are difficult to define clearly given the lack of precise descriptions. For example, the last plague of Egypt, recounted in Exodus, offers little scientific evidence for identification of a specific disease other than it killed the firstborn children.

Similarly, the Plague of Athens in 430 B.C.E., which struck during the Peloponnesian War between Athens and Sparta, not only influenced the outcome of an important historic event but also produced a turning point in world history. Athenians were infected by an epidemic that killed 25 percent of the population. Thucydides, the Greek historian and witness to the plague and war, described the ailment as causing "violent sensations of heat in the head," sneezing and hoarseness, unquenchable thirst, and death in seven to ten days. He also described the collapse of morality within the city where without the "fear of gods or law of men there was none to restrain them." The plague, a disease without clear identification, in this case lengthened the war and thereby facilitated the eventual downfall of the Athenian Empire.

The Roman Empire also experienced several epidemics with significant consequences. Malaria may have been endemic in the Mediterranean region during much of antiquity and produced major problems in the Roman Empire from 100 B.C.E. The vastness of the empire, which extended from the African Sahara to Scotland and from the Caspian Sea to Spain, meant that infections from the hinterland found easy transportation to vulnerable populations. For example, the Plague of Antonius attacked the Empire between 164-189 C.E. and produced a ghastly mortality rate. Galen, the famous Roman physician, described victims with high fevers, throat inflammation, diarrhea, skin eruptions after a week of illness, and then death. Medical scholars maintain that this may have been one of the first smallpox epidemics in Western history. The disease may have started in Mongolia and moved eastward into the Germanic tribes, with whom the Romans were at war.

Of historical importance, the Antonius plague helped stimulate the acceptance and spread of Christianity within the Empire. Christianity provided hope for believers in miraculous cures, resurrection, and eternal salvation. In addition, the teachings of Christ, which stressed care for the sick, fit perfectly into an era marked by widespread illnesses. The establishment of charitable hospitals for the sick and indigent became a foundation of the faith. During the fourth century, a woman named Fabiola founded the first such hospital in Rome and institutionalized with medical care the religion's tenets, which have lasted into the twenty-first century. The epidemic in this instance promoted a religion that beforehand was of little significance.

Powerful epidemics not only devastated populations but also shattered the authority of governments, religions, and economic systems. The Black Death of the fourteenth century offers the best example of the destructive force of epidemics or, in this case, pandemics, because the affliction spread from Central Asia to East Asia and west to Europe. Fleas served as the vector, or agent that carries a pathogen, from rats to humans. In this manner, the causative bacillus *Pasteurella pestis* or *Yersinia pestis* spread through the movement of rats along caravan routes and accompanied the Mongol invasions in Central Asia. The regions suffered massive devastation. In Europe the bubonic plague swept urban and rural communities in huge waves, claiming perhaps 50 percent of the population. The loss of life fractured the feudal economic and social order, splintered control of the Roman Catholic Church's dominance, and helped usher in a new political order. The plague continued as a serious threat to Europeans into the eighteenth century. In other parts of the world, especially Asia, the plague flared, frequently with enormous loss of life and institutional destruction.

In 1911 an epidemic of bubonic plague swept the Manchurian region of northern China. The death toll, perhaps 60 percent of the population, could have been much worse had modern public health initiatives not held the disease in check. Chinese people traditionally believed that heaven sends a natural disaster as a sign of the end of an empire. The decaying Qing Dynasty, the last imperial dynasty in China's history, collapsed under the combined weight of social disruption and the force of the epidemic.

In the twentieth century, epidemics were checked by the development of antibiotics, widespread inoculations, and international public health measures. Still, the so-called Spanish influenza pandemic of 1918, arguably the greatest single biological event in human history, killed 25 million people worldwide, 600,000 in the United States alone. In the modern age, where an infected person can travel the globe in a few hours, a ghastly potential exists for natural disasters of giant proportions. Thus, government health organizations, such as the United States Public Health Service and the World Health Organization (WHO) of the United Nations continually monitor disease and varying social and environmental conditions to prevent the outbreak of epidemics.

Nicholas Casner

430 B.C.E.: The Plague of Athens

CAUSE UNKNOWN
DATE: 430-427 B.C.E.
PLACE: Athens, Greece
RESULT: About 30,000 dead

As the early battles of the Peloponnesian War (431-404 B.C.E.) were being waged between the ancient Greek city-states of Athens and Sparta, urban crowding in several major cities reached an unprecedented level. Perhaps the worst of these overpopulated centers was Athens itself. It had been the strategy of the Athenian general and statesman Pericles to protect the entire populace of Attica, the region in which Athens is located, by permitting any resident of this area who wished to do so to take refuge within the Athenian city walls. While this policy won much support because it protected most of the citizenry from Spartan raids, it also caused such intense crowding within central Athens that the city became vulnerable to the swift spread of disease.

The plague that befell Athens in 430 B.C.E. was first observed in Ethiopia, Egypt, Libya, and the island of Lemnos. Scholars assume that it was carried to Athens aboard ship, a theory given credence by the illness's first arrival in mainland Europe at Piraeus, the port of Athens. Because of the state of war that then existed between Athens and Sparta, initial suspicions fell upon the Spartans. They were accused of poisoning the Athenian water supply in an attempt to win victories through deceit that they could not win on the battlefield. Nevertheless, as the disease spread, ultimately killing as many as a quarter to a third of the entire Athenian population, it became apparent that the cause of the disaster was not an enemy conspiracy but a new form of contagion that had a natural (or, as some thought, a divine) origin.

Symptoms of the Athenian Plague. The symptoms of the Athenian plague have been detailed with far greater precision than those of any other ancient epidemic because the Greek historian Thucydides (c. 459-c. 402 B.C.E.) provided a full account of it in his history of the Peloponnesian War. Thucydides himself had suffered from the plague, but, like a number of other fortunate individuals, he survived. The description that Thucydides provided of the plague includes little speculation as to its cause but extensive analysis of its symptoms. Thucydides relates that he provided this information in the hope that future generations would recognize later outbreaks of the disease and understand its prognosis. By taking this approach, Thucydides revealed that he was under the influence of the "father of Greek medicine," Hippocrates of Cos (c. 460-c. 370 B.C.E.), then at the height of his prestige among the Athenian intelligentsia. Hippocrates, too, had stressed diagnosis and prognosis over vain attempts to find cures.

Thucydides notes that the onset of the plague was sudden. During a year that had otherwise been remarkably free of other illnesses, apparently healthy people would unexpectedly develop a high fever. Inflammation of the eyes, throat, and tongue soon followed, turning the victim's breath extremely foul. Several of the plague's initial symptoms resembled those of a severe cold. Patients suffered from sneezing, hoarseness, and coughs. The standard treatments of these symptoms had, however, little effect upon the rapid progress of the plague.

In its second stage, the plague moved from victims' heads to their stomachs. Vomiting and great pain were followed by dry heaves (or, some scholars believe, violent hiccups) and prolonged spasms. Then, as the fever began to subside, the patient's skin turned sensitive. Many victims found that they could not tolerate being touched in any way or even being covered by either clothing or blankets. The patient's skin turned deep red or black-and-blue in spots, with sores breaking out over large areas of the body. Sleep proved to be impossible, both from the pain of the illness and from a general restlessness. Unquenchable thirst caused many victims to throw themselves into public rain basins in their desire to drink as much water as possible.

By this stage in the illness, seven or eight days had elapsed; many of the plague's victims died at this point. Those who survived the plague's initial ravages, however, quickly developed severe diarrhea. The general weakness that resulted from sustained dysentery then caused additional deaths among the very young and very old. Those in the prime of life, however, might begin to regain their health at this point. The severe fevers caused some victims to develop amnesia. Others became blind or lost the use of their extremities.

As the plague lingered in Athens, it increasingly took its toll upon those with weakened immune systems. Thucydides notes that, as the winter continued, nearly any disease that an individual developed eventually turned into the plague. Victims also remained contagious after they died. Thucydides reports that animals did not feed on the corpses of plague victims or, if they did, they died soon after. Human patients who survived appeared to be immune to further attacks of plague. Several of those who repeatedly developed plague symptoms found that subsequent infections were increasingly less severe. In their elation at their restored health, many former victims imagined that they were now immune to illness of any kind. As evidence emerged that this was not true, however, a number of these survivors were plunged into a deep depression.

Subsequent History of the Plague. One unanticipated outcome of the Athenian plague was the emergence of an almost citywide sense of fatalism. The sudden, indiscriminate death caused by the plague suggested to many individuals that no human action or remedy was useful. Victims died regardless of whether they were ignored or well treated by physicians. Death occurred without respect for a victim's character or individual piety. Diet, exercise, and a person's general state of health had little bearing on the rapid progress of the disease. What was worse in the eyes of many was that the merciful appeared to be dying in even greater numbers than the callous. Compassionate individuals were more likely to treat others suffering from the disease and thus were more likely to be exposed to it themselves. As a result, many Athenians felt that all the virtues they had once cherished—piety, fitness, civic-mindedness, integrity—were of little practical value. In a matter of days, the plague did more to harden the hearts of many Athenians than did all the months of the war against Sparta.

The public disorder caused by the plague, combined with the psychic trauma resulting from daily exposure to victims dying or in intense agony, produced a state of chaos throughout Athens. The law provided no deterrent to citizens who imagined that they would die soon anyway. Crimes of all sorts began to increase. People ceased planning for the future, preferring to direct their efforts toward the satisfaction of immediate pleasures. The worship of the gods declined because many people felt that religion provided no guarantee of health. Even the literature and art of the city was affected by the plague. The god Apollo, until then regarded as a source of inspiration and light in Athenian literature, took on an increasingly negative image in many works, including the tragedies of the playwright Euripides (c. 485-406 B.C.E.). Apollo's oracle at Delphi had

promised aid to the Spartans, and, as the Athenians remembered well, Apollo was the god of plagues in Homer's *Iliad* (c. 800 B.C.E.).

When, in the spring of 429 B.C.E., the Spartans again invaded Attica and once more laid waste to the fields, public opinion began to turn against Pericles. The Athenians claimed it was his fault that no crops could be planted for two years and that the city was sufficiently crowded to spread the plague. In part, at least, these criticisms were justified. It had been Pericles' policy to protect behind the city's walls thousands of Athenian citizens who ordinarily would have remained unaffected by the plague in the countryside. As an urban phenomenon, the plague was largely confined to Athens itself and a few other large cities. It did not enter the Peloponnisos, sparing Sparta, a less-populated city than Athens.

Pericles was removed from office as general of Athens. Two of his own sons died in the plague. History, perhaps unreliably, reports that his mistress Aspasia and two of his friends, the philosopher Protagoras and the sculptor Phidias, were placed on trial by the Athenians in an effort to discredit Pericles. Pericles himself was fined for misuse of public funds. Soon, however, public opinion shifted yet again, and Pericles was restored to public office. Nevertheless, by this time, his health was in decline. Calling the plague "the one thing that I did not foresee," Pericles became its most prominent victim. He died in 429 B.C.E., and even afterward the plague continued to ravage the dense population centers of Attica. After its initial outbreak in 430 and 429, the plague returned to claim more victims in 427 B.C.E.

In 1994, a mass grave dating to the fifth and fourth centuries B.C.E. was discovered as preparations were being made for a subway station near the ancient Kerameikos cemetery in Athens. Numerous bodies were uncovered, hastily thrown into multiple shafts. One shaft alone contained more than 90 skeletons, 10 of which belonged to children. Because of the date of the burial and the cursory manner in which the interment appeared to be carried out, many scholars speculated that the site might have been associated with the great Plague of Athens. In his account of the plague, Thucydides had mentioned that the sheer number of casualties had necessitated swift burial in mass graves. Although the date and general location of the burial are appropriate for the Plague of Athens, final identification will never be possible because the site was destroyed as construction continued.

Precise Causes of the Athenian Plague. Historians and epidemiologists cannot agree as to the precise nature of the organism responsible for the Athenian plague. Some scholars believe that the illness was either identical or closely related to various illnesses known in the modern world. Others believe that, because of the rapid evolution of microbes, it was a unique contagion having no parallel in contemporary society. Candidates put forward as possible causes of the Athenian plague have included the Ebola virus, influenza, measles, typhus, ergotism (a disease caused by the ingestion of contaminated grain products), and toxic shock syndrome. The latter two of these possibilities seem unlikely because they would not have been spread in the highly contagious manner attributed to the Athenian plague. The other candidates for the disease all lack at least one of the major symptoms described by Thucydides. Although the precise nature of the Athenian plague will probably never be determined, one thing remains clear: The cause of this disease cannot be identified with that of another famous plague, the Black Death that ravaged Europe during the fourteenth century. Nowhere in Thucydides' account is there any mention of the buboes, those enlarged lymph nodes in the groin or armpits that gave the bubonic plague its name. In the history of epidemics, the Plague of Athens appears to remain unique.

Jeffrey L. Buller

FOR FURTHER INFORMATION:

Holladay, A. J., and J. C. F. Poole. "Thucydides and the Plague of Athens." *Classical Quarterly* 29 (1979): 282-300.

Langmuir, A. D. "The Thucydides Syndrome: A New Hypothesis for the Cause of the Plague of Athens." *The New England Journal of Medicine* 313 (October, 1985): 1027-1030.

Morens, D. M., and R. J. Littman. "Epidemiology of the Plague of Athens." *Transactions of the American Philological Association* 122 (1992): 271-304.

———. "The Thucydides Syndrome Reconsidered: New Thoughts on the Plague of Athens." *American Journal of Epidemiology* 140, no. 62 (1994): 1-7.

Morgan, Thomas E. "Plague or Poetry? Thucydides on the Epidemic at Athens." *Transactions of the American Philological Association* 124 (1994): 197-209.

Page, Denys L. "Thucydides' Description of the Great Plague." *Classical Quarterly*, n.s. 47, no. 3 (1953): 97-119.

Scarrow, G. D. "The Athenian Plague: A Possible Diagnosis." *Ancient History Bulletin* 11 (1988): 4-8.

---

541 C.E.: The Plague of Justinian

BUBONIC PLAGUE
DATE: 541-542 C.E.
PLACE: Constantinople and the Mediterranean
RESULT: About 300,000 dead in Constantinople

The first known pandemic (widespread epidemic) of bubonic plague struck while Justinian I was was emperor of the Roman Empire. Justinian himself contracted the plague and was incapacitated for months. Accordingly, this pandemic is known as the Plague of Justinian. It began in southern Egypt in 541 and, by May of 542, shipping had spread it to Constantinople. During the next fifty years plague visited the Mediterranean world and even India, creating so much personal and economic devastation that some historians consider it a contributing factor to the start of the Dark Ages.

The primary source of information on the plague is Procopius of Caesarea, a military historian and Byzantine court familiar who also provided the first detailed description of the disease, based on his observations in Constantinople. He relates that a mild, seemingly innocuous fever was the first symptom. It would strike the victim suddenly, at no particular time of day. Within a few hours or sometimes a few days, swellings appeared in the groin and armpits and sometimes behind the ears and on the thighs—the buboes for which this form of the plague is named. Some victims then fell into a coma. Others became delirious, while some died without falling into either a coma or delirium. Some but not all cases exhibited an outbreak of egg-sized black pustules all over the body. According to Procopius, in Constantinople the appearance of the pustules was a sign of imminent death, as was the vomiting of blood. However, if the buboes began to discharge pus, the victim was likely to survive. Puzzled physicians autopsied some of the victims. Since the bubonic swellings seemed the focus of the disease, they opened some of these and were surprised but not enlightened at finding swollen lymph nodes, which they judged to be some kind of carbuncle.

Victims had to be constantly restrained from falling out of bed, throwing themselves out of windows, or rushing from the house. Some tried to drown or starve themselves out of dementia or despair. Those who attended the patients were soon exhausted by the effort.

The seemingly random way the disease selected victims and the speed of onset terrified the population. It was not reassuring that the doctors could not predict the course of the disease. No precautions seemed effective, and, once the disease took hold, no cure availed. People assumed demons were responsible and made frantic efforts to evade them. Doors and windows were barred against the demons, but family and friends were also effectively excluded, so that social structures rapidly broke down. Work in the city ceased as people sought to avoid exposure. Eventually, the growing fear constricted food delivery to the city, creating hunger and further debilitating victims.

The plague persisted for four months in Constantinople, during which time an estimated 300,000 people died. Procopius claims daily death tolls ran from 5,000 to 10,000 throughout most of that time, with a peak of 16,000 people on the worst day. Reportedly, officials stopped keeping records once the count exceeded 230,000. While this estimated death toll may seem excessive, it amounts to about 40 percent of the population, a not unreasonable figure in comparison with better established results from later plague epidemics.

Justinian appointed a court official to supervise the disposal of those bodies not tended to by relatives. The official, in turn, enlisted as many helpers as he could find, but their efforts were quickly swamped. Once available tombs were filled, bodies were set adrift in boats or thrown into towers intended as fortifications. Laborers were hired to dig two trenches, each to hold 70,000 bodies. Corpses were thrown into the trenches and then trampled to compact them.

As with later pandemics, the impact on the economy of the empire and on personal opportunities was enormous. When food was available, its cost rose, even during the epidemic. The labor pool was devastated but quickly discovered the advantages of survivorship and began to demand higher wages. Prices of both goods and labor doubled and even tripled. The effect was to decrease the differences between the poor and the wealthy.

Procopius made a number of what are, in retrospect, highly significant observations. He noted that the disease always moved from the coast into the interior of a region. He was, of course, unaware that the plague was carried by the fleas of shipborne rats. His interest in the transmission of the disease prompted him to note the lack of contagion. That is, he observed that caregivers and those charged with disposing of bodies did not contract the disease from contact with the victims. This implies that this outbreak was entirely the bubonic form of the disease, with no admixture of the highly contagious pneumonic form. Furthermore, Procopius points out that those who had had the disease were not susceptible to it later, indicating that exposure led to immunity.

The plague was a disaster for Justinian. He was finally at peace with Persia, and his military campaigns had returned North Africa and much of Italy to the empire. His dream of reconstituting the full extent of the old Roman Empire seemed finally within his grasp. Then the plague struck empire and emperor alike. As he languished, tended by his notoriously corrupt wife, Theodora, and watched by anxious courtiers, the opportunity withered away. His recovery lasted for months. During that time the government was mostly run by Theodora, who took the opportunity to take revenge on those whom she disliked. Although the recovered Justinian restored a number of these victims, the episode damaged many relationships and undermined key governmental institutions, particularly the military. The plague-depleted population could not supply enough soldiers, and the army was forced to recruit increasingly from barbarian mercenaries, further weakening morale and military effectiveness.

John A. Cramer

For Further Information:

Kohn, George C., ed. *Encyclopedia of Plague and Pestilence.* New York: Facts on File, 1995.

Procopius of Caesarea. *History of the Wars.* New York: Twayne, 1967.

1320: The Black Death

Also known as: The Plague, the Black Plague, the Pestilence, the Great Mortality
Bubonic plague
Date: 1320-1352
Place: Europe, Asia, Middle East, and Africa

RESULT: 25 million estimated dead in Europe, perhaps more than double that amount worldwide

The Black Death was the worst pandemic in human history, one that annihilated at least one-third of all humanity during its thirty-year killing spree in the fourteenth century. No other disease has killed so many people so quickly as the Black Death. Some scholars call it the "greatest biological-environmental event" in history.

Despite many attempts to explain the reasons for the Plague, no one at the time understood what caused the disease or how it was spread. Today, however, medical experts know that the deadly disease was caused by the *Yersinia pestis* bacterium. Many researchers also believe the disease manifested itself in four distinct forms as it raged across most of the known world during the fourteenth century. The most common form was the bubonic plague. Victims of this malady suffered headaches, weakness, and feverish chills. A white coating on the tongue appeared along with slurred speech and a rapid pulse. Within days painful swellings the size of eggs, called buboes, erupted in the lymph nodes of the groin and armpits. Black purplish spots formed by subcutaneous hemorrhaging also appeared on the skin of most victims. This discoloration may have earned the disease the name the Black Death, though many historians believe this designation did not become commonplace until two centuries later, when Scandinavian writers used the term *swarta doden* (black death) to emphasize the dreadful aspects of the disease.

Most sufferers of the bubonic plague died within a week of contracting the disease. Though highly contagious, this form of the plague was not transmitted from one human to another as many fourteenth century observers believed. The real carrier of the disease was the *Xenopsylla cheopsis*, a flea that lived as a parasite on the European black rat and other rodents. In a complicated cycle of contagion, fleas were the first to become infected by the bacterium, eventually transmitting the disease to their rodent hosts. When rats died and became scarce, the infectious fleas searched for new warm-blooded hosts, such as human beings. Because so many people in the fourteenth century lived in cramped, squalid conditions, rats and fleas were ever-present in their daily lives. As result, plague-carrying fleas easily carried the disease from rats to people.

A pneumonic form of the plague that infected the lungs also developed during the colder periods of the pandemic. Death resulted from vomiting blood, coughing, and choking. Unlike the bubonic plague, the pneumonic form was transmitted by one human to another by sneezing and coughing contaminated mucous particles. Though less common than the bubonic form, the pneumonic plague was more lethal and killed up to 95 percent of its victims.

The deadliest of all the Plague's manifestations were two very rare forms of the Black Death. Septicemic plague attacked the bloodstream; death often came within hours. Almost no one survived. Equally lethal was enteric plague, which devastated digestive systems.

Spread of the Disease. Although historical records of the disease are imprecise, many historians believe the first major outbreak of the Black Death in human populations took place among the nomadic tribes of Mongolia in 1320. Alternating periods of drought, intense rain, and locust attacks throughout Asia may have produced severe ecological disturbances that upset the normal balance between plague fleas and rats in the wild. This disruption may have also caused rodents to come into closer proximity to humans. The result was an epidemic among humans unlike any ever seen before or since.

From the steppes of Mongolia, the Plague spread throughout China, India, and other Asian lands, killing tens of millions. Next, infected rats, fleas, and humans headed west by accompanying the numerous ships, barges, and caravans that traveled the trade routes connecting the East and West. By 1346 the Plague had spread into the lands along the Black Sea, but it had not yet reached medieval Western Europe. Europe's apparent immunity to the disease soon changed as a result of human conflict. According to Italian chronicler Gabriele de Mussis, a dispute broke out one day between local Turkish Muslims, or Tatars, and merchants from Genoa, Italy, who had established a trading post near the city of Kaffa (today called Feodosiya) on the Crimea. When fighting erupted, the Genoans retreated to their walled compound nearby and managed to keep their enemy at bay for months. The stalemate broke when the Black Death arrived and killed Tatars in great numbers. Distraught by their misfortune, the Muslims reportedly catapulted the corpses of their dead comrades into the Genoa compound to share the disease with their Christian enemies. Though modern scientists

Transmission of Plague

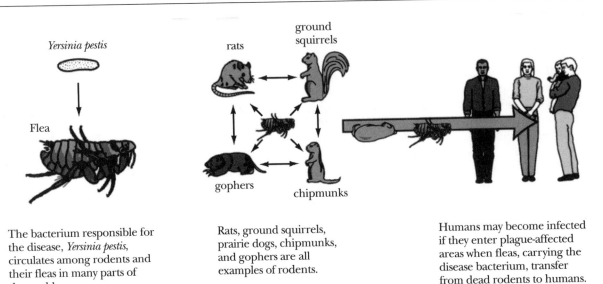

The bacterium responsible for the disease, *Yersinia pestis*, circulates among rodents and their fleas in many parts of the world.

Rats, ground squirrels, prairie dogs, chipmunks, and gophers are all examples of rodents.

Humans may become infected if they enter plague-affected areas when fleas, carrying the disease bacterium, transfer from dead rodents to humans.

The bacterium Yersinia pestis, *which causes plague, follows a path from fleas to rodents to humans.*

think it is unlikely that the Plague could be spread in this way, the volley of corpses prompted the Genoans to escape in their galley ships and head for friendlier ports in the West. They took with them the Black Death, presumably brought aboard by infected rats.

The returning Genoa ships, along with other seagoing vessels plying the trade routes, most likely introduced the disease to the various populated ports of the Aegean and the Mediterranean. Within a year, the disease swept through the Middle East, Arabia, Corsica, Sardinia, Sicily, and Africa. Muslim pilgrims making their way to Mecca may have helped spread the disease through the Islamic world. Genoese ships also arrived in the Sicilian port of Messina in October, 1347. On the ships were infected sailors. Though the terrified people of Messina drove the vessels away, the disease managed to infect the local human and rodent populations before departure. Soon, the residents of Catania, a nearby town, also began to die, and within weeks the disease raged across Sicily.

The Black Death next entered Italy through its many seaports and fishing villages. Millions of Italians, already weakened by famine, earthquakes, civil strife, and severe economic problems, quickly succumbed to the pestilence as it rushed across the pen-

insula. Venice lost 600 people a day during the worst of the disease; ultimately an estimated total of 100,000 Venetians died. As many as 80,000 may have perished in Siena. Matteo Villani, a plague survivor, estimated that 3 out of every 5 died in Florence.

The disease soon went beyond Italy. In 1357, it entered the port of Marseilles and swept through France, Europe's most populated country. In Narbonne, 30,000 died. The Plague destroyed half the population of Avignon, and in Paris 50,000 were killed. Within months the north and west of France also lay in the grip of the Plague. Mortality in many villages and towns often exceeded 40 percent. Next, the Low Countries (today Belgium, Luxembourg, and the Netherlands) became infected. By this time, Spain, Switzerland, Austria, Germany, and Hungary also suffered.

During the summer of 1348, while the Plague ravaged continental Europe and many other areas of the world, the English Channel seemed to offer a protective barrier to those living in the British Isles. Their security was breached in August, however, when plague-bearing ships finally arrived in England at the ports of Weymouth and Melcombe. Soon, Dorset, Devon, Somerset, and other settlements in the south of England were hit. Within months the disease had moved northward to London, where as many as 100,000 eventually died. By the summer of 1349 East Anglia and Yorkshire were also infected.

For a short while, many Scots welcomed the Plague as a divinely inspired punishment sent to strike down their enemy, the English. However, such wishful thinking soon vanished when the disease swept into Scotland. It also spread into Wales and made its way to Ireland. Before the year ended, infected ships reached Sweden and Norway, where the pneumonic form of the Plague may have destroyed 50 percent of the population. According to some accounts, the Black Death even reached Scandinavian settlements in Iceland and Greenland. The Plague also raced eastward and infected vast areas in Russia that had not yet been infected.

No place seemed safe from the Black Death. Outbreaks of the disease occurred in cities, towns, and villages throughout most of the known world. Though the rich were less likely than the destitute to contract the disease, all social classes suffered catastrophic losses. Everywhere, people died horrible deaths in their homes, on the streets, and in the fields. Animals died as well: Dead rats, dogs, cats, and livestock lay rotting alongside odiferous human cadavers. The living were horrified to see rats, vultures, crows, and wolves devouring the diseased bodies of beasts and humans alike.

By 1352, the worst of the Black Death was over, but the disease had not gone away forever. Instead it had become endemic to most countries it had struck. This new ecological situation meant that the plague recurred many times well into the eighteenth century. When it struck again in 1361 and killed a disproportionate number of the young, it became known as the "Pestilence of the Children." Wherever and whenever the plague took root, stunned survivors struggled to understand the calamity that had overwhelmed them.

The Search for Answers. From every land came a host of explanations of why and how the Plague had come into being. Many religious leaders claimed God sent the disease as a punishment for the sins of humanity, such as avarice, usury, adultery, and blasphemy. Others blamed the devil or an antichrist. Even the most learned minds of Christendom and Islam believed in astrology during the fourteenth century, and many scholars cited astrological influences as causes of the disease. When asked by Pope Clem-

ent VI to explain the presence of the Black Death, an esteemed panel of doctors in Paris concluded that a conjunction of the planets Saturn, Mars, and Jupiter at 1 P.M. on March 20, 1345, caused the disease.

Phantoms were also accused of spreading the Black Death. Among them was an apparition called the Plague Maiden. Many panic-stricken Europeans claimed to have witnessed her ghostly form sailing into one home after another to spread her deadly contagion. Some believed the Black Death materialized when frogs, toads, and reptiles rained down on earth. Priests in England insisted that immoral living and indecent clothing fashions were responsible. Comets were also blamed. The fourteenth century French surgeon Guy de Chauliac believed sick people spread the Plague merely by looking at another person.

Inordinate fear generated by the Black Death also produced theories based on hatred and hysteria, which resulted in massive scapegoatism and persecution. Witches, Gypsies, Muslims, lepers, and other minorities were often accused of starting the Plague and were killed by crazed mobs. The worst abuses, however, were reserved for Europe's Jewish population, a religious minority that had long faced persecution in Europe. Despite condemnation from the papacy, mobs in Switzerland, Germany, France, Spain, Italy, and parts of Central Europe tortured, hanged, and burned alive tens of thousands of Jews in revenge for allegedly spreading the disease with secret poisonous potions. Though political leaders in a few countries such as Poland and Lithuania offered sanctuary to Jews, most civil authorities either did nothing to protect them or officially authorized the mass executions.

Others, meanwhile, sought more rational explanations for the presence of the pestilence. Basing their opinions on the ideas of ancient Greeks, many Christian and Muslim physicians of the fourteenth century suggested that bad air brought on contagion. This contamination was believed to have been caused by foul odors released by earthquakes, decaying corpses on battlefields, or stagnant swamps. Fogs and winds from the south were also suspected of producing plagues. Many medieval physicians also subscribed to another ancient Greek teaching, which claimed that illness resulted from an imbalance of the four humors—phlegm, blood, black bile, and yellow bile—believed to have made up the human body. At special risk, according to many physicians, were poor people whose "bodies were replete with humours."

Medieval Preventatives and Cures. Balancing the humors in the body through corrective dieting was one preventive measure undertaken by Europeans. Many people also burned pleasant-smelling woods, such as juniper and ash, to produce counterbodies in the air to ward off the Plague. Rosewater and vinegar solutions also were used to purify household air. Women often held bouquets of flowers to their noses to counteract bad air. Birds were allowed to fly free in some homes to keep the air stirred up and free of the Plague; bowls of milk and pieces of bread were also left out in various rooms with the hope of soaking up bad air.

Medieval physicians told their patients to shun more than bad air. They also recommended avoiding hot baths, sexual intercourse, physical exertion, daytime slumber, and excessive consumption of deserts. On the other hand, diets of bread, nuts, eggs, pepper, onions, and leeks were recommended to ward off disease. Antiplague pills were also available and consisted of dozens of substances, ranging from saffron to snake meat and various toxins. Europeans were also urged to keep their minds healthy and sound as the Plague approached. Physicians advised others to purge their minds of all ideas of death and to think only pleasant thoughts.

Another fourteenth century theory held the opposite view and contended that bad air should be counteracted with something foul. Accordingly, some Europeans bathed in urine or menstrual blood or deliberately inhaled the fumes of fecal matter to fumigate themselves of any plague-causing agents.

In addition to these preventive measures, medieval physicians relied on common medical procedures of their day to cure those stricken by the Black Death. Because medical knowledge was limited to mostly inaccurate theories from the ancient world rather than research and experimentation, their efforts invariably failed. Nonetheless, doctors practiced their craft the best they could. Many bled their patients to alter the balance of humors in a sick or dying person. Some punctured buboes to release evil vapors or applied dead toads or poultices directly to these swellings to absorb toxins. Muslim physicians treated the buboes with cold water. Above all, doctors urged their patients to pray for good health.

Spiritual Weapons. The appeal to prayer found a receptive audience among most fourteenth century Christians and Muslims, who put more faith in their religious beliefs and institutions than anything their physicians had to offer. Both private and group prayer were rendered constantly to gain heavenly favor during the Black Death. In addition, religious pilgrimages, the construction of new shrines, and public processions of piety became commonplace attempts to gain spiritual strength in the fight against the Plague. Christians and Muslims also donned special religious

A victim of the plague shows physicians the bubo under his arm. (Library of Congress)

charms to protect themselves. Not all clerics tried to stave off the Plague, however. Many stressed an acceptance of God's will. Muslim religious leaders, for example, often taught that fleeing the Plague was futile, if not contrary, to divine plan. Allah, they said, was responsible for all things, including pestilence.

Sometimes, the panic-stricken took spiritual matters into their own hands. Many Christians dug up graves of various Catholic saints to obtain relics of skull fragments or bones believed to have antiplague powers. Others launched spiritual crusades against the disease. The biggest such campaign was the Flagellant Movement, which emerged in Germany and spread into France and the Low Countries. Detached from the Catholic Church, the movement urged atonement for personal sins and an end to the Plague through public acts of penitence and self-debasement. Members of the movement were called Flagellants because of the flagella or barbed whips they used to lash their naked backs in mass public demonstrations carried out in churchyards or town centers.

Sometimes numbering in the tens of thousands, the Flagellants marched on bare feet from one community to the next debasing themselves with whips, praying, singing, and seeking forgiveness before the eyes of thousands of onlookers. At times, their exhibitions also became fiercely anti-Semitic and resulted in mob violence against local Jews. Convinced the Flagellants were heretical and usurping Church authority, Pope Clement VI eventually ordered an end to their activities. Secular officials, including the kings of England and France, equally worried about civil disorder, provided enforcement of the papal order, and by 1350 the movement ceased to exist.

Human Response. Wherever the Black Death raged, terrified humans responded in various ways. Displays of fear, rancor, suspicion, apathy, violence, and resignation, along with nobler responses of altruism, self-sacrifice, and heroism, all appeared wherever the Plague struck. Some people faithfully nursed those who lay sick and dying, while others shunned all Black Death victims and fled. Many, terrified of contagion, refused to tend to even their loved ones; many physicians and priests abandoned their duties and ran away. Fear even prompted many to avoid the possessions of the dead and dying. According to Italian author Giovanni Boccaccio in his collection of stories *Decameron: O, Prencipe Galetto* (1349-1351; *The Decameron*, 1620), many people of Florence isolated themselves from the sick and spent their time carousing and living lives of wild abandon until death came or the disease went away. Similar behavior was reported in other plague-stricken cities.

The Black Death caused panic and social breakdown wherever it struck. Merchants closed shops. Trade ceased. Construction projects halted. Crops and livestock were abandoned. Even some churches closed their gates to keep away terrified mobs. The English Parliament shut down twice during the worst days of the Plague. Though many civil authorities died or fled the disease, most governments did not entirely cease to function. Hard-pressed to maintain a semblance of law and order, those left in charge of civil matters often passed antiplague ordinances. Some of these decrees were designed to fight the Plague by improving public moral behavior to please God. Authorities in Tournai, France, for example, ordered men and women, who lived together outside of matrimony, to marry at once. They also banned swearing, playing dice, and working on Sundays. Medieval officials also imposed travel bans and quarantines on travelers to reduce contact with the infected. In many places, the sick were forced into buildings hastily designated as Plague hospitals, where they invariably died. Authorities in Milan took even more drastic measures by ordering laborers to seal up homes of Plague victims, entombing both the alive and the dead.

Disposal of the dead became a logistical nightmare for both church and civil authorities. Because most European Catholics believed Christian burials in consecrated graves were necessary for salvation, church graveyards quickly filled. As a result, grave diggers, if they could be hired, hastily dug new mass graves, into which corpses were unceremoniously dumped. In many communities, only the abject poor and released criminals were willing to nurse the dying or bury the dead. In Italy, for example, slaves from galley ships were freed and ordered to undertake these tasks. All too soon, however, the new class of grave diggers—called the Becchini—took advantage of their newfound freedom and robbed, raped, murdered, and extorted the living. Civil authorities, exhausted by death and desertion within their own ranks, were often too weak to control the Becchini and their counterparts in other cities and towns.

Aftermath. Humanity had never before witnessed such a massive death toll as that of the Black Death. According to a study commissioned by papal authorities, the Plague killed more than 24 million Europeans. Throughout Africa, the Middle East, and Asia, the Plague killed anywhere from 25 to 40 percent of local populations. Some scholars estimate that as many as 1 out of every 3 died throughout the Muslim Empire. Although exact figures will never be known, and many may have been exaggerated by shocked survivors of the disease, most modern historians agree the impact of untold millions of human deaths caused great trauma among the living. Some scholars, in fact, suggest that the widespread mental suffering caused by the Plague paralleled that of the world wars of the twentieth century.

Many people responded to the pestilence by becoming more pious, in an attempt to appease God and keep such a calamity from recurring. Religious faith for others, however, was shaken or destroyed by the horrors of the Black Death. Many disillusioned Christians failed to understand how a loving god they had worshiped had failed to protect them from the terrors of the Plague, nor could they readily forgive the priests who had fled and failed to administer last rites to dying Christians.

Some disenchanted Christians, including religious reformers such as England's John Wyclif and Bohemia's Jan Hus, openly questioned many Church doctrines and practices and may have paved the way for the Protestant Reformation two centuries later. Others rejected Christianity altogether and joined various new cults based on mysticism or even satanic beliefs. Though the Catholic Church remained a powerful institution in Europe, its authority was forever weakened.

The Black Death also brought about other major changes. According to many firsthand reports, outbreaks of immorality, crime, violence, and civil breakdown followed in the wake of the Black Death. In addition, a preoccupation with death and the macabre expressed itself in many areas. Young people, for example, in many plague-stricken areas began to socialize in graveyards, where they danced and played games, as if to flaunt their indifference to death. Various folk dances that emphasized death also appeared in parts of Europe. The death dance also became a popular subject for artists and writers who concentrated on the ghoulish and inescapable aspects of dying.

Although cities and towns were growing, a majority of Europeans lived as feudal peasants or poor urban laborers when the Black Death first struck. This situation began to change in the wake of the Plague, however. The massive loss of life caused by the disease produced a severe widespread labor shortage that ultimately benefited the working poor. For one thing, the dearth of workers caused a rise in wages and gave laborers more negotiating power with employers and greater mobility than they had ever had before. Farm workers, artisans, and workers of all types no longer felt obliged to adhere to fixed working conditions imposed by a ruling nobility. In response to the newfound economic strength of workers, the ruling classes imposed various sumptuary laws both to prevent chaos and to control inflation generated by rising wages. Some of these new laws set wages and fined any employer who violated the restrictions, but many others were established primarily to maintain distinctions among the social classes. Some of these rules, for example, attempted to control what kinds of clothes and foods the poor could buy to prevent them from trying to imitate their social superiors. Though often effective, the sumptuary laws proved unpopular and hard to enforce.

Despite such attempts to maintain the old order, the shake-up caused by the Black Death helped to dismantle many of the centuries-old assumptions, traditions, and institutions of medieval Europe. The changes wrought by the Plague also lead to widespread questioning of the social and economic order that had existed in Europe for centuries. This assault on the old manner that had benefited a privileged class of nobles and the Church for centuries now opened the door for the coming of the Renaissance, the Enlightenment, and the modern age.

John M. Dunn

FOR FURTHER INFORMATION:

Bowsky, William M., ed. *The Black Death: A Turning Point in History?* New York: Holt, Rinehart and Winston, 1971.

Gasquet, Francis Aidan. *The Black Death of 1348 and 1349.* London: George Bell and Sons, 1908.

Gottfried, Robert S. G. *The Black Death: Natural and Human Disaster in Medieval Europe.* New York: Free Press, 1983.

Herlitly, David. *The Black Death and the Transformation of the West.* Cambridge, Mass.: Harvard University Press, 1997.

Horrox, Rosemary, trans. and ed. *The Black Death.* Manchester, England: Manchester University Press, 1994.

Karlen, Arno. *Man and Microbes: Disease and Plagues in*

History and Modern Times. New York: Putnam, 1995.

Nohl, Johannes. *The Black Death: A Chronicle of the Plague Compiled from Contemporary Sources.* Translated by C. H. Clarke. London: Unwin Books, 1961.

FOR FURTHER INFORMATION:

Kohn, George C., ed. *Encyclopedia of Plague and Pestilence.* New York: Facts on File, 1995.

McNeill, William H. *Plagues and Peoples.* Garden City, N.Y.: Anchor Press/Doubleday, 1976.

Marks, Geoffrey, and William K. Beatty. *Epidemics: The Story of Mankind's Most Lethal and Elusive Enemies from Ancient Times to the Present.* 8 vols. New York: Charles Scribner's Sons, 1976.

1490: Europe

SYPHILIS

DATE: 1490's onward
PLACE: France, Italy, Germany, Holland, Greece, England, Scotland, Hungary, Russia, and Poland
RESULT: Thousands dead

The first appearance of syphilis in Europe occasioned a military disaster. King Charles VIII of France claimed sovereignty over Naples, Italy. In pursuit of the claim, in 1494 he took a polyglot army into Italy and laid siege to and eventually occupied the city. Like the French army, the Neapolitan defenders were a mixed lot. Both armies claimed the attentions of a sizable contingent of camp followers, and soon many were demoralized by the horrible symptoms of virulent syphilis. In no condition to continue operations, both armies disbanded and went home, carrying the disease with them. They thus created the first and only real epidemic of syphilis.

The disease first appeared in France, Italy, and Germany in 1495, Holland and Greece in 1496, England and Scotland in 1497, and Hungary, Russia, and Poland in 1498. By 1498 it had also spread to Africa and India, and it reached China and Japan in 1505. In each place it was seen as an entirely new disease. Since then, syphilis has been endemic worldwide (maintaining a constant presence in a population) but not usually epidemic (flaring infrequently but with deadly force).

Physicians had no idea of effective treatment. Early on, the disease was confused with smallpox because of the scabs and pustules that appear within several weeks of infection. Indeed, the eventual recognition of syphilis as a distinct disease forced the "poxes" to be distinguished between "the great pox" and "the small pox." Mercury was the only reasonably effective treatment until antibiotics became available in the twentieth century.

John A. Cramer

1520: Aztec Empire

SMALLPOX

DATE: 1520-1521
PLACE: Tenochtitlán, Aztec Empire
RESULT: 2 to 5 million dead

Spanish conquest and colonization of Mexico began in 1519 when Hernán Cortés was ordered by Diego Velázquez, governor of Cuba, to command an expedition to the mainland of Mesoamerica. The smallpox epidemic of 1520-1521 figured importantly in the unlikely conquest of an empire of millions by a much smaller force of Spaniards accompanied by their Native American allies. Landing on the Yucatán peninsula, Cortés marched inland, collecting allies en route to the capital of the Aztec Empire, Tenochtitlán, where he took the emperor, Moctezuma II, prisoner. In 1520, Cortés left Tenochtitlán, leaving some of his men behind to hold the city, in order to meet an expedition on the coast sent by Velázquez, who suspected Cortés of exceeding his orders to further his own ambition. Cortés convinced these forces to join him rather than arrest him, and he returned to Tenochtitlán. He found a capital where the Indians were in the throes of rebellion against the Spanish. In June of 1520 the Aztecs succeeded in repelling the Spanish. Few Spaniards survived *la noche triste* (the sad night). Cortés and the remainder of his troops retreated to Tlaxcala to rebuild his fighting forces.

Meanwhile, a smallpox epidemic was proceeding from Yucatán to Tenochtitlán. A soldier who had an active case of smallpox came with the expedition to arrest Cortés. According to some chroniclers his name was Francisco Eguia. He infected Indians with the viral disease, and it was quickly spread from person to person and from village to village, progressing rapidly from the coast to the interior. The disease was reported to have arrived in April or May of 1520; it spread inland from May to September, and it reached Tenochtitlán in September or October.

The effects of the outbreak in America were far greater than were experienced during an outbreak in Europe during the same period. The susceptibility of the American Indians compared to the Spanish can be accounted for by the fact that this disease was unknown to them. The Aztecs had no specific word in their language for smallpox and usually described it in their writings by its characteristic pustules. In Europe the disease had been extant for centuries, and when it reappeared there were usually many persons who were immune because of previous exposure. In contrast, the Indian population was extremely vulnerable to the disease. There were no immune persons in the population, and the people were highly homogeneous genetically, which meant that the virus did not have to adapt to various genetic makeups to be successful in infecting the host. In addition, the first outbreak of a disease within a group is generally the most severe.

This disease wreaked disaster on the indigenous population. It is estimated that one-third to one-half of the population died during the epidemic. In contrast, only about 10 percent of a European population died in an outbreak in the sixteenth century. Because all segments of the population in America were vulnerable, there were few healthy caregivers to sustain the sick. In addition, many rulers were struck down. In Cortés's letters to the king, he reported that he was asked by many Indian groups who were allied with him against the Aztecs to choose a leader to replace the person who had died of smallpox.

Most important, the epidemic reached Tenochtitlán at a crucial moment in history. The Aztecs had forced Cortés to retreat, but during his time of rest and rebuilding he sent spies into Tenochtitlán to determine the strength of his opponents. He learned that the Aztecs had been struck down with smallpox and were greatly weakened. At times, the disease struck so many persons that no one in a family was able to give care to the others, and whole families died, not only of smallpox but also of thirst and starvation. Homes were destroyed with the corpses inside, to diminish the fetid odor wafting through the once-great city. Other bodies were thrown into the water, offering a wretched sight of bloated, bobbing flesh. Warriors who survived were weakened by the disease, and their chain of command was compromised. The emperor named to replace Moctezuma died of smallpox. The loss of continuity and experience in leadership greatly weakened the ability of the Aztecs to mount a defense against the Spaniards.

Having replenished his forces, Cortés struck Tenochtitlán again in May of 1521, and within months he had conquered the seat of the Aztec Empire. Debate continues over the role of the smallpox epidemic in this conquest. Cortés did not give it much weight in his chronicles, but Indian chronicles of the time emphasize its importance. The year 1520 is called the year of the pustules, according to Aztec chronicles. Though there is great disagreement among historians over the number of deaths and the importance of the smallpox epidemic in the conquest, there is no doubt that this epidemic was one of the most serious disasters in Mexico in the sixteenth century.

Bonnie L. Ford

FOR FURTHER INFORMATION:

Crosby, Alfred, Jr. *The Columbian Exchange: Biological and Cultural Consequences of 1492.* Westport, Conn.: Greenwood Press, 1972.

Diamond, Jared. *Guns, Germs, and Steel: The Fates of Human Societies.* New York: W. W. Norton, 1997.

McCaa, Robert. "Spanish and Nahuatl Views on Smallpox and Demographic Catastrophe in Mexico." *The Journal of Interdisciplinary History* 25 (Winter, 1995): 397-432.

Noble, David Cook. *Born to Die: Disease and New World Conquest, 1492-1650.* Cambridge, England: Cambridge University Press, 1998.

1665: The Great Plague of London

BUBONIC PLAGUE
DATE: May-December, 1665
PLACE: London, England
RESULT: Approximately 100,000 dead

Plague in England was a constant visitor for many centuries. The Black Death of the mid-fourteenth century had killed off between one-fourth and one-third of the country s population. In London, before the devastating Great Plague of 1665, there were serious epidemics in 1593 that killed 15,000; in 1603, 33,000; in 1625, 41,000; in 1636, 10,000; and in 1647, 3,600. In the interval between 1603 and 1665, there were only a few years in which London did not record any plague deaths.

Reasons for the Plague. In 1665, London was a city of a little less than 500,000 people. The core of this vast metropolis was the city itself, the historic area of about 1 square mile still enclosed by an impressive wall. Surrounding the city were growing suburbs, where most of the poor lived under wretched conditions. It is not known what brought the plague to London, but it is likely that it either came from abroad—perhaps from Holland, which experienced a terrible plague the previous year—or was already endemic to England and waiting for favorable conditions to break out. The Bills of Mortality, the official statistics that recorded deaths in London, reveal only 3 deaths from plague in the first four months of the year, but plague deaths jumped to double digits in May, and for the first time there was widespread concern about the plague. By the end of June, the weekly total had risen to 267; the plague was definitely spreading.

Unfortunately, neither the civic authorities nor the medical professionals had any knowledge of what the plague was or how it was transmitted. In fact, it was not until 1894 that the bacillus that caused the disease was isolated, discovered almost simultaneously by two scientists working independently of each other, Swiss bacteriologist Alexandre Yersin and Japanese physician Shibasaburo Kitasato. It was given the name *Pasteurella pestis*, and eventually the method of transmission was also discovered. It was carried by the black rat, which in turn infected fleas. Unfortunately, the black rat was a sociable creature that lived comfortably with human beings, and this close proximity made it easier for fleas to transfer themselves from the rats, which became plague victims, to nearby human hosts.

The reason the plague was most ferocious in the summer months was likely due to the fact that rat fleas tended to flourish in hot weather. The type of plague that afflicted London was the bubonic variety, characterized chiefly by the telltale buboes that appeared on the body of victims, large swellings about the size of eggs that appeared in the joints, groin, armpits, and neck. The disease had an incubation period of usually two to five days, and the victim suffered from fever, chills, weakness, and headaches, eventu-

ally becoming lethargic or delirious. Bubonic plague had a death rate of 50 to 90 percent.

At the time of the plague, London was a filthy, unsanitary city, made up mostly of dilapidated, unventilated wooden dwellings, fronted by open sewers masquerading as streets and having no proper methods for disposal of garbage and human waste—in short, an ideal environment for rats. Conditions were most appalling in the suburbs, and the plague broke out in one of the worst slum areas, St. Giles-in-the-Fields, eventually spreading eastward, as well as to the south and west.

By the end of July the weekly plague figure had risen to over 1,800 victims, but the deadliest moments of the epidemic were in August and September, when the total plague deaths exceeded 46,000. In late October, the figures began to decline noticeably, and by the first week of December only 210 deaths were recorded. For the entire year, the official total was 68,596, of which the ravished suburbs accounted for 85 percent of the deaths. In general, this was a "poor man's plague" and a suburban phenomena. As alarming as these figures were, scholars believe the death toll was seriously undercounted, and a more likely total is about 100,000. Still, the plague lingered, and in the following year over 1,700 died. It was not until 1670 that London recorded no plague deaths for the entire year.

Methods of Containment. A series of events conspired to make the death tolls even higher than they should have been, since the authorities often took measures that were counterproductive. For example, civic authorities mistakenly believed that dogs and cats may well have carried the disease, and officials ordered their extermination, resulting in the killing of tens of thousands of the creatures. Yet these were the very animals that could have possibly checked the rat population.

The most disastrous decision was to invoke a quarantine as the principal method of containing the plague. Authorities decreed that any house containing a case of plague was to be closed and locked, with all the residents sealed inside. Armed watchmen guarded the house to ensure that no one escaped from the infected dwelling. The door of the house was painted with a large red cross with the words "Lord Have Mercy upon Us" inscribed on it. This action simply guaranteed that the plague would likely spread to everyone trapped inside, and it was common for entire families to perish, one member after the other. In retrospect, a more successful policy would have been to separate the infected from the uninfected, perhaps by transferring all the infected to the local pesthouse or other such building, thus isolating the sick from the healthy.

Authorities believed that the contagion was carried in the air. Therefore, the city officials decreed in early September that fires should be burned throughout London, and for three days the city's air was fouled by a heavy pall of suffocating smoke and a terrible stench until rains mercifully doused these fires. Individuals had their own remedies for fighting the plague but all too frequently relied upon quack potions, amulets, charms, and mystical signs and numbers.

Aftereffects. London still managed to function during the plague, however imperfectly, despite the fact that the king, his court, and parliament fled the city for safety reasons. Among the few heroes to emerge from this period otherwise filled with much cowardice and stupidity were the Lord Mayor Sir John Lawrence and several of the city's aldermen. During the plague, they ensured a steady supply of food from the surrounding farmlands, kept prices from rising, prevented any riots, and raised money, mostly from private charities, to offer assistance to an increasingly destitute population.

A bureaucracy of sorts was established to cope with the demands of the plague. Watchmen were appointed to guard the infected houses. Nurses lived in the infected dwellings and administered to the needs of the sick. However, this dangerous and depressing work was done only by the truly desperate, who quickly established a reputation for venality and callousness, frequently misusing their position to steal from their patients and even expedite their deaths.

Perhaps the most notorious workers were the "searchers," people who were to visit the houses of the deceased and establish the cause of death. This dangerous job was usually taken only by elderly impoverished women, who were often ignorant, illiterate, and corrupt. Frequently, they either misdiagnosed the cause of death or were bribed to attribute the cause of death to something other than the plague, so that family members could leave the house immediately and not be placed under further quarantine. Other unfortunates pushed their carts through the city during the night in order to collect those who died, shouting "Bring out your dead" to announce their arrival. Gravediggers, who were al-

most overwhelmed at times by the tide of thousands of people dying weekly, frequently had to dig mass pits into which bodies, nude or wrapped in sacks or cloths, were tossed, without the dignity of a coffin or proper burial service.

Economic Results. London was economically devastated during the plague. Commercial activity almost vanished from the city. Shops were closed, the houses of the wealthy were shuttered, and many dwellings were kept under quarantine. Even the port of London, one of the most active in the world, saw deserted docks and little cargo, with foreign ships fearing to sail to this plague-infested destination and foreign customers reluctant to accept London goods that might be contaminated.

When the nobility and the professional classes fled the city by the tens of thousands, they often dismissed their workers or servants from employment. Newly impoverished, these unemployed sought cheap housing, which meant they were forced to live in the very suburbs that had the highest death tolls, thereby providing the human fodder that fed the deadly toll. There was a dramatic decline in human interaction. The authorities either forbade or discouraged large gatherings of people, whether in churches, alehouses, funerals, or inns. London, once one of the most noisy, bustling, and industrious of cities, became strangely silent and largely devoid of human activity.

The Last Plague. This was the last major plague epidemic to afflict London. The question of why a plague never struck London again is one of the great historical mysteries. Although a precise answer has confounded both the historical and the medical professions, there are a number of possible explanations. First, it has been argued that the Great Fire of 1666, which burned almost the entire city within its ancient walls, destroyed the plague by burning the old unsanitary wooden city and killing off the rats in the process. However, this does not explain why the plague did not return to the unsanitary suburbs, which were untouched by the Great Fire.

Another popular explanation is that the brown or Norwegian rat supplanted the black rat as the chief urban rodent. Unlike its predecessor, the brown rat tended to avoid human contact, preferring sewers, garbage dumps, and other areas free of human beings. This may have eventually been an important component in containing the plague, but the brown rat did not supplant the black rat immediately after 1665. Rather, the displacement occurred over a period of several decades, thereby not accounting for the era before it became dominant. There are also medical theories concerning how human beings may have developed immunities to bubonic plague or that the plague's bacillus had mutated into a more benign form, but these ideas are considered suspect by medical authorities.

Perhaps the most persuasive explanation emphasizes measures undertaken by public authorities. Central governments around the globe developed sophisticated methods of isolating their nations from plagues by strict quarantines imposed upon ships and cargoes from infected regions of the world. Also, societies witnessed important developments in the areas of public health and standards of public sanitation. Over a period of decades and centuries, people have become healthier, water supplies purer, housing more sanitary, refuse collection more efficient, and disposal of human waste more effective. All these measures have made cities more healthy and safe places to live. Undoubtedly, it was a combination of several of the above explanations that have helped modern society escape the horrors that London experienced in 1665.

David C. Lukowitz

FOR FURTHER INFORMATION:

Bell, Walter George. *The Great Plague in London in 1965*. New York: Dodd, Mead, 1924.

Butler, Thomas. *Plague and Other Yersinia Infections*. London: Plenum Medical Books, 1983.

Cowie, Leonard W. *Plague and Fire: London 1665-66*. New York: G. P. Putnam's Sons, 1970.

Leasor, James. *The Plague and the Fire*. New York: McGraw-Hill, 1961.

Mullett, Charles F. "London's Last Dreadful Visitation" and "The Plague of 1965 in Literature." In *The Bubonic Plague and England*. Lexington: University of Kentucky Press, 1956.

Ross, Sutherland. *The Plague and the Fire of London*. London: Faber & Faber, 1965.

1722: Russia

ERGOTISM
DATE: 1722
PLACE: Russia
RESULT: 20,000 dead

Ergotism is a disease of the central nervous system caused by ingesting the alkaloids (one of which is LSD) of the ergot fungus, *Claviceps purpurea*, which infects rye grain. It was endemic to areas of Europe where rye was the preferred cereal crop and only disappeared when potatoes replaced rye bread as the main source of dietary starch. Symptoms include numbness of the extremities, vomiting and diarrhea, dizziness, and delusions and convulsions usually ending in a painful death. The Romans called it "holy fire," and in Europe of the Middle Ages it was known as Saint Anthony's fire.

Perhaps the most disastrous outbreak of ergotism destroyed the dreams of Russian czar Peter the Great. Seeking an ice-free deep-water port for his navy and for Russian commerce, in 1722 he assembled his Cossack armies at Astrakhan, near where the Volga entered the Caspian Sea. He was preparing simultaneous attacks on the Turkish empire, hoping the advance of his Cossacks would lure its armies out of the Ukraine and, at the same time, the efforts of his navy would sweep all Turkish ships out of the Black Sea. Then, seizing control of the Dardanelles, he would turn the backward Russia into the greatest nation of the world.

Peter's army lived off the land, as did all armies of the time. The seemingly good rye brought in by the serfs from the surrounding area made fine bread, but it was infected with ergot. The first to go down was a horse. Within hours, hundreds of horses were paralyzed. Within a day, many soldiers in camp were screaming and writhing in their beds. Within a week, horses and riders were dying by the hundreds. The nightmare did not end until some 20,000 soldiers and serfs were dead. With them went Peter's dreams of empire.

John A. Cramer

FOR FURTHER INFORMATION:

Carefoot, G. L., and E. R. Sprott. *Famine on the Wind*. Skokie, Ill.: Rand McNally, 1967.

Kohn, George C., ed. *Encyclopedia of Plague and Pestilence*. New York: Facts on File, 1995.

1735: New England

DIPHTHERIA
DATE: 1735-1740

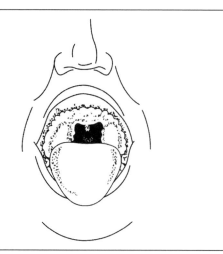

Diphtheria causes a thick, grayish-green membrane to form over the larynx, tonsils, pharynx, and sinus cavities.

PLACE: New England, primarily New Hampshire, Massachusetts, and Connecticut
RESULT: Thousands of children dead

The first clear case of diphtheria in the American colonies was described by American author Cotton Mather as an outbreak of a new "throat distemper" with "bladders in the windpipe." It began in late 1659 and killed a number of children. There are reports of other outbreaks of "throat distemper," but some of these were probably scarlet fever, which produces sore throat with a red rash but without the ulcers and the thick, grayish-green membrane over the larynx, tonsils, pharynx, and sinus cavities that characterize diphtheria. In diphtheria, the bacterium (*Corynebacterium diphtheriae*) may produce a toxin that causes inflammation of the heart and nervous system.

The first large-scale outbreak of diphtheria began in 1735 in Kingston, New Hampshire, with a few cases in western Connecticut. In New Hampshire, all of the first 40 victims died, a shockingly high mortality rate. In the first fourteen months, 1,106 people died in 16 New Hampshire towns. Of these, 95 percent were twenty or younger, and more than 80 percent were children under ten. Many families lost all of their children.

The disease spread slowly down the coast into Massachusetts and eastward along the Connecticut coast. Over the next five years, these two areas expanded until they joined in 1740. Each area claimed on the order of 1,000 deaths annually, so the total death count for this epidemic must have been well over 10,000. After 1740, diphtheria became episodic and endemic in the northern and central colonies.

John A. Cramer

FOR FURTHER INFORMATION:

Duffy, John. *Epidemics in Colonial America.* Baton Rouge: Louisiana State University Press, 1953.

Kohn, George C., ed. *Encyclopedia of Plague and Pestilence.* New York: Facts on File, 1995.

Marks, Geoffrey, and William K. Beatty. *Epidemics: The Story of Mankind's Most Lethal and Elusive Enemies from Ancient Times to the Present.* 8 vols. New York: Charles Scribner's Sons, 1976.

1793: Philadelphia

YELLOW FEVER
DATE: 1793
PLACE: Philadelphia, Pennsylvania
RESULT: 5,000 dead

Yellow fever, like malaria, is a mosquito-borne disease of African origin. Both seem to have arrived in the New World around 1650. The earliest adequately reported outbreak of yellow fever in the American colonies was brought to Boston from Barbados by a British fleet in 1693. The disease is carried by yellow-fever mosquitoes (*Aedes aegypti*), and the liver, kidneys, and heart are affected. American author Cotton Mather described its symptoms as "turning yellow, vomiting and bleeding every way." Other symptoms are headache, fever, and muscle pain. In severe cases, delirium occurs and the skin becomes jaundiced, or yellow. Mortality was very high.

Often called "the black vomit" because of victims' tendencies to vomit blood, yellow fever appeared episodically in the colonies throughout the eighteenth century. The worst of these was the terrible Philadelphia epidemic of 1793. In the summer of that year, refugees from a "plague" in the Caribbean poured into Philadelphia. A drought caused a stench in the city from dead fish and rotting vegetation. These set the scene for the disease and for the medical confusion that followed.

Dr. Benjamin Rush was one of the first to recognize the presence of the yellow fever. Believing the disease was due to bad sanitation, he urged that rotting coffee be cleared from the waterfront, while others urged even more energetic sanitary improvements. The populace as a whole and the federal government, including President George Washington, were more inclined to evacuate the town. Eventually, the entire federal government plus about a third of the population fled to outlying areas.

Under pressures from the panic as well as the lack of personnel, the local government collapsed. Mayor Matthew Clarkson heroically organized volunteers to nurse the sick and bury the dead. A hospital was set up, staffed by doctor Jean Duvèze, who had had yellow fever twice. By the end of September the daily death toll was 70, rising to 111 on October 12. By October 26, the count was down to about 20, after which the coming of cold weather ended the epidemic.

John A. Cramer

FOR FURTHER INFORMATION:

Kohn, George C., ed. *Encyclopedia of Plague and Pestilence.* New York: Facts on File, 1995.

Powell, J. H. *Bring out Your Dead: The Great Plague of Yellow Fever in Philadelphia in 1793.* Reprint. Philadelphia: University of Pennsylvania Press, 1993.

1799: Spain, North Africa

YELLOW FEVER
DATE: 1799-1802
PLACE: North Africa, beginning in Sierra Leone, and Spain, especially Andalusia
RESULT: 80,000 dead

Yellow-fever epidemics have been responsible for killing hundreds of thousands of people and have changed the course of history. Spain and northern Africa were especially hard hit by yellow fever in 1799 and 1800.

Yellow fever is caused by a virus and transmitted to humans through the bite of an *Aedes aegypti* mosquito that had been infected two weeks previously. Three to six days after being bitten by an infected mosquito, symptoms occur. Early symptoms include sudden onset of fever (102 to 104 degrees Fahrenheit or 39 to 40 degrees Celsius), initially rapid pulse which slows on the second day, nausea, vomiting, constipation, head-

ache, muscle pains, and restlessness. A mild case could end at this stage after one to three days. In severe cases, the fever falls between the second and fifth days, only to shoot up again, accompanied by jaundice (a yellow coloring of the skin), and by bloody, black vomit. Delirium and death follow.

Yellow fever, called "Yellow Jack" by sailors, was the disease most dreaded by seafarers at the end of the eighteenth century. If yellow fever infected a ship, 70 to 100 percent of the crew could die. Unfortunately, the fresh water stored in barrels aboard ships provided the perfect breeding ground for the mosquitoes that carried the yellow fever. As the mosquitoes bred and multiplied, they could continue to infect crew members throughout the entire voyage, even if it lasted months. Thus, yellow fever easily passed back and forth between Africa, Spain, and the New World on the other side of the ocean.

Spain was involved in a variety of shipping ventures to the New World at the end of the eighteenth century. The active slave trade from Africa to the Americas furthered the spread of yellow fever. Unlike Europeans and those who were indigenous to the Americas, Africans did not become very ill when infected with yellow fever. Africans were therefore favored over indigenous people or European indentured workers as laborers in the Caribbean because of their immunity to yellow fever.

Historical research indicates that there are two possible routes by which yellow fever may have arrived in Spain in 1799. It may have been brought to Spain from the Americas on one of the Spanish sailing vessels, or it may have spread to Spain from North Africa. Possibly, both of these routes operating simultaneously contributed to the devastating epidemic that followed.

Lack of early, complete records makes it difficult to determine whether yellow fever originated in Africa or came to Africa from elsewhere. Accounts of a yellow-fever epidemic in Senegal in 1778 definitely establish the presence of the disease in Africa at that time. This epidemic was traced to Sierra Leone, a small country in West Africa, where records show yellow fever was present as early as 1764. Yellow fever spread from Sierra Leone to territories in northern Africa, to the south and into the West African islands. The southern coast of Spain was only a short distance away from the northern coast of Africa.

The effects of the yellow-fever epidemic of 1799 to 1802 changed the course of history for Spain, France, and the United States. When yellow fever struck Spain and North Africa in 1799 and 1800, it had a tremendous impact on the area. The population of Spain in 1797 was 10,541,000 people. It is estimated that 80,000 of those citizens died during the years 1799 and 1800, mostly in Andalusia, a region in the southern part of Spain. This was close to 1 percent of the population. Thus, on the average, 110 people died each day during those two years in an area slightly larger than the state of California.

Apart from the human suffering, Spain could not afford this loss of population. The economic and political situation in Spain was grievous. Tensions existed between Napoleon I of France and the government of Spain. The Spanish treasury was drained, yet France was demanding financial payments from Spain. The yellow-fever epidemic was one more loss that Spain had to absorb. Napoleon would face his own difficulties with yellow fever. Of 60,000 troops and seamen he sent in 1802 to quell a rebellion in Haiti, 27,000 died of yellow fever. This was about 45 percent of the contingent. Napoleon's disgust with the Americas and his view that the area was nothing more than a pesthole led him to sell to the United States the land that comprised Louisiana in the Louisiana Purchase in 1803. Spain was extremely unhappy about the Louisiana Purchase and, as a consequence, refused to align itself with France in its war against England. France demanded that Spain pay a fee for the privilege to remain neutral. Spain used the devastation of its land by disease as a continuing reason to delay paying that fee. Although yellow fever hurt Spain within its borders, it weakened France, which made it possible for Spain to deal with France on a more equal basis.

Louise Magoon

FOR FURTHER INFORMATION:

Berkow, Robert, and Andrew J. Fletcher, eds. *The Merck Manual of Diagnosis and Therapy.* 16th ed. Rahway, N.J.: Merck, 1992. Provides a thorough description of the clinical course that yellow fever follows.

Desowitz, Robert S. *Who Gave Pinta to the Santa Maria?* New York: Harcourt Brace, 1977. Shows how diseases have impacted human history.

McNeill, William H. *Plagues and Peoples.* New York: Doubleday, 1976. Describes the life span of mosquitoes, yellow fever on ships, and sailors' dread of Yellow Jack.

Marks, Geoffrey, and William K. Beatty. *Epidemics: The Story of Mankind's Most Lethal and Elusive Enemies from Ancient Times to the Present.* 8 vols. New York: Charles Scribner's Sons, 1976. Describes the path of yellow fever in Africa in the eighteenth century.

Mitchell, B. R. *European Statistics, 1750-1975.* New York: Facts on File, 1980. Provides population statistics for European countries.

Oldstone, Michael B. A. *Viruses, Plagues, and History.* New York: Oxford University Press, 1998. Explores the relationship between political events and the courses of disease.

1829: Europe

CHOLERA OR ASIATIC CHOLERA
DATE: 1829-1838
PLACE: Beginning in Russia and spreading to Poland, Hungary, and much of Europe
RESULT: Hundreds of thousands dead

The cholera epidemic of 1826-1837 was but one of six cholera epidemics that struck parts of Asia, Europe, North Africa, and the Americas during the course of the nineteenth century. Originating in India in 1817, the first pandemic spread into the Caucasus of central Asia before petering out in 1823. However, in 1829 the "Asiatic cholera" reappeared in Russia, taking upward of 20,000 lives in Astrakhan Province during the summer of 1830. After overrunning Russia, it quickly spread to Poland, Hungary, and much of Europe. Cholera took thousands upon thousands of lives, particularly in larger cities such as Paris and London. As the epidemic peaked in 1831-1832, social problems connected with industrialization and urbanization exacerbated the deadliness of the disease. Pervasive overcrowding, poor sanitation, and the generally filthy conditions of Europe's burgeoning cities contributed to high death rates.

Although mortality estimates vary, most records indicate that about 50 percent of those contracting cholera died from it. In 1831-1832, cholera took approximately 23,000 lives in England and Wales, 20,000 in Ireland, and nearly 10,000 in Scotland. The epidemic reached its zenith in the spring and summer months. In 1832, cholera killed more than 5,500 Parisians during one week in April, while in Glasgow, Scotland, it wiped out over 1,200 in August alone. After reaching its peak in 1832, the epidemic spread into Spain and Portugal (1833), the south of France (1834), and Italy (1835-1836). In 1837, it hit Austria, the German states, the Baltic ports, and Poland. Though taking fewer lives after 1833, cholera recurred in most parts of Europe before subsiding in early 1838. A decade passed before an even deadlier cholera epidemic reached Western Europe in 1848.

Cholera's degrading symptoms were particularly disturbing to contemporaries. Describing several early English cases, one observer noted in 1831:

> Allison . . . was attacked at 4 A.M. on the 5th of August with vomiting and purging of a watery whitish fluid, like oatmeal and water. His hands and feet were cold, his skin covered with clammy sweat, his face livid and the expression anxious, his eyes sunken, his lips blue, thirst excessive, his breath cold, his voice weak and husky, and his pulse almost imperceptible. . . . Arnott, a farm-labourer . . . was seized at 2 A.M. on the 8th of August with precisely the same symptoms, and died in twelve hours.

Severe watery diarrhea (losing up to 4 gallons of fluid per day), intermittent vomiting, extreme thirst, and violent muscle cramps characterized the disease. Once contracted, cholera killed quickly and gruesomely. This new disease reminded many Europeans of the bubonic plague.

Throughout the epidemic, cholera remained a mysterious disease. Little agreement existed regarding its causes or reasons for its spread. Some said it was a general punishment from God, while others claimed that God was rebuking individuals for their sins, such as drunkenness, laziness, and blasphemy. Still others contended that corrupted air or "miasma" caused the disease. It was established later in the century that cholera spread via polluted water, but no one understood this connection in the 1830's. Modern medicine has determined that cholera bacilli thrive in warm water, explaining the seasonal nature of the disease.

Because no one knew its true cause, cholera often intensified unrest and suspicions among different segments of society. As it spread across Europe, the lower classes frequently blamed government or medical authorities, precipitating a series of riots and disturbances. Peasants and the urban poor contended that the authorities were either poisoning them or purposely allowing the disease to spread in order to reduce their numbers. Throughout Russia and parts of central and Eastern Europe, conspiracy theories flourished among the peasantry. Such sentiments blamed the feudal nobility and their agents. In some cases, these fears led to massacres of nobles, military personnel, and other state officials. Although there were no similar antigovernment reactions in England, several crowds attacked physicians, believing that they were purposely allowing deaths to provide human corpses for dissection.

Given the state of medical knowledge, little could be done to fight cholera effectively in the 1830's. Some of the many treatments attempted included bloodletting, laudanum (and other forms of opium), and saline solutions (oral and intravenous). Some observers also pointed out the correlation between poverty and disease. Being associated with dirt and filth, cholera expectedly struck the poor in working-class urban slums the hardest. Others noticed that foul bedding and clothing carried the poison that spread the disease. Limited attempts at cleaning were short-lived, having little impact in European cities. Sanitary reform movements, pushing for improved water supply and sewage systems, occured later in the century.

Robinson M. Yost

FOR FURTHER INFORMATION:

Bynum, W. F. "Medicine in the Community." In *Science and the Practice of Medicine in the Nineteenth Century*. Cambridge, England: Cambridge University Press, 1994.

Creighton, Charles. "Asiatic Cholera." In *A History of Epidemics in Britain*. Vol. 2. Cambridge, England: Cambridge University Press, 1894.

Delaporte, François. *Disease and Civilization: The Cholera in Paris, 1832*. Cambridge, Mass.: MIT Press, 1986.

Durey, Michael. *The Return of the Plague: British Society and the Cholera, 1831-32*. Dublin: Gill and Macmillan, 1979.

Evans, Richard J. "Epidemics and Revolutions: Cholera in Nineteenth-Century Europe." *Past and Present*, no. 120 (August, 1988): 123-146.

Hays, J. N. "Cholera and Sanitation." In *The Burdens of Disease: Epidemics and Human Response in Western History*. New Brunswick, N.J.: Rutgers University Press, 1998.

McGrew, Roderick. *Russia and the Cholera, 1823-32*. Madison: University of Wisconsin Press, 1965.

1832: New York City

CHOLERA
DATE: June-October, 1832
PLACE: New York City
RESULT: More than 3,000 dead

Though believed to have existed as far back as Neolithic times, cholera was contained to the Ganges River region of India for most of world history. It struck epidemically at intervals until the seventeenth and eighteenth centuries, when religious pilgrimages, tourist travel, and economic trade greatly increased the number of people who visited the region. The first cholera epidemic to spread beyond the containment of the Ganges Delta struck in 1817. Spread by soldiers, travelers, and traders throughout the surrounding areas and Russia, it killed thousands. Before the 1832 New York epidemic, America had been spared from attack.

The Industrial Revolution increased the frequency and scope of trade and transportation around the world. At the same time thousands of rural families moved to urban areas in search of employment. Cities were ill equipped to handle such large influxes of people. Cramped living quarters and little or no public sanitation caused overcrowded neighborhoods to became breeding grounds for disease. Cholera was spread through tainted food or water or contact with an infected person, their linens, or their clothing.

In 1826, cholera moved beyond India's borders again. Pilgrims and traders brought the disease to Russia, and Russian troops spread cholera to Poland and German invaders there. A German vessel is believed to have transported cholera to Northern England, where it spread to Scotland, Wales, and Ireland, which was already in the midst of a savage potato famine.

One of the most frightening aspects of cholera was its swiftness of course. The bacterium, *Vibrio cholerae*, entered the body and settled in the intestinal tract, where it released powerful toxins into the digestive system. Patients suffered severe cramping, vomiting, and diarrhea, then quickly became dehydrated. Bodily organs shut down, and victims frequently died within four to forty-eight hours of onset. Cholera had a 20 to 50 percent death rate.

Americans followed the terrible course of the disease in newspapers as it struck Europe and Russia during the winter of 1831-1832. Many hoped the great distance created by the Atlantic Ocean would protect America from attack. However, thousands of Irish immigrants fled to America and Canada in the 1830's. The cramped, poorly ventilated underbellies of immigrant ships created a perfect breeding ground for cholera. Vessels brought the disease to Canada, where it spread throughout major cities. By June 14, 1832, 1,220 people were dead in Montreal.

The disease moved southward, striking town after town along the Saint Lawrence and Hudson Rivers. New York City had experienced shifts in population and urban sanitation problems similar to Europe's, though on a smaller scale. Large numbers of traders, immigrants, and visitors arrived daily. New York City could not keep up with rising populations and over-crowded and unsanitary conditions. People and animals lived in close quarters; livestock roamed unrestrained in city streets. Garbage and human and animal waste were routinely strewn into alleyways and avenues.

To stave off cholera, New York City appropriated $50,000 to clean up the city. Garbage was collected, and streets were swept and disinfected with lime. New York instituted strict quarantine regulations for ships arriving at city ports. Mayor Walter Browne forbade vessels with sick passengers from coming within 300 yards of the city. No one departed without permission, and any vehicle conveying ill persons was forbidden within 1.5 miles of city hall.

Unfortunately, cholera had already struck New York City. On June 26, 1832, a physician visited an immigrant by the name of Fitzgerald stricken with cholera. It is probable his case was not the first but that previous cases had remained undiagnosed or unreported. Though Fitzgerald recovered, his wife and two children died within the next three days. The deaths were not made known to the public until June 30, probably to avoid a panic. By the end of the week, cholera had claimed more victims.

Cholera struck poorer, overcrowded parts of the city first. Poorhouses, jails, and saloons were hardest hit. Daily bulletins were issued listing the stricken and the dead. Homes and buildings were quarantined, and numerous victims were sent to offshore cholera islands or the 5 cholera hospitals that were established. The city contracted 8 doctors to care for those who could not afford physician's care, but doctors did not know how to treat the disease. The purgative calomel, laudanum, opium, and prayer were the most commonly used treatments. Ten physicians were among the dead.

Rumors spread quickly. Many citizens panicked at the rising death tolls and left: An estimated 70,000 of 220,000 residents fled the city. Cholera soon broke free of poorer neighborhoods, moving throughout the city and indiscriminately killing rich and poor, frail and healthy. By the middle of July, when the disease reached its peak, cholera was killing 100 people a day. The disease then began a slow but steady decline. By the end of August only 1 cholera hospital was still open, and citizens began filtering back into the city. The death toll was down to 50 people a week in September and 14 a week by October. Over 3,000 New Yorkers were dead by the time cholera disappeared in the fall of 1832. Many more cases were probably unreported by overworked physicians or patients who wished to conceal their illness.

New York citizens who fled the city effectively spread the disease to nearby communities. Cholera had spread to Philadelphia by July of 1832. It attacked along the Ohio River in Kentucky, Indiana, and Ohio and was spread westward by soldiers in the Black Hawk War. The disease eventually reached New Orleans in December, 1832, where it killed at least 6,000 residents before receding.

Cholera epidemics would strike again. Yet even before London anesthesiologist John Snow traced the cause of the disease in 1849, the 1831-1832 cholera epidemic emphasized the need for citywide sanitation measures. Many cities established public health commissions and provided for garbage cleanups. These and other sanitary measures created somewhat healthier urban living conditions.

Leslie Stricker

FOR FURTHER INFORMATION:

Chambers, J.S. *The Conquest of Cholera: America's Greatest Scourge.* New York: Macmillan, 1938.

Karlen, Arno. *Man and Microbes: Disease and Plagues in History and Modern Times.* New York: Putnam, 1995.

Rosenberg, Charles E. *The Cholera Years: The United States in 1823, 1849, and 1866.* Chicago: University of Chicago Press, 1987.

1832: New Orleans

CHOLERA

DATE: October, 1832

PLACE: New Orleans, Louisiana

RESULT: At least 4,340 dead, with estimates as high as 6,000

During the night of October 24, 1832, two steamboats arrived in the port of New Orleans carrying several passengers suffering from the symptoms of cholera. Some had died during the passage. The following day two men died on the levee after only a few hours of noticeable symptoms. The swift and cruel nature of the unfamiliar disease troubled many in the city. Large crowds soon began to assemble near the levee as fear of the unfamiliar overcame otherwise rational individuals.

The arrival of the pestilence was not an unexpected occurrence. Throughout the previous winter an epidemic of cholera has spread through Europe, moving in a westerly direction from Poland. New Orleans newspapers had reported the advance of the deadly disease, but few expressed concern that it could cross the salt-laden air of the Atlantic Ocean. It was generally believed by the medical professionals of that time that cholera was spread by poisonous air produced in swamps and noxious fumes rising from the squalor of cities. Known as the atmospheric theory, this hypothesis was embraced by most in the medical community despite vocal protests by a small minority who demanded a quarantine law to halt city trade, which they believed was somehow responsible for the spread of the disease.

Rumors circulated throughout New Orleans as early as January that cholera was present in the city, but all reports proved to be false. Similar reports circulated of outbreaks in Memphis, Tennessee; Mobile, Alabama; and St. Louis, Missouri. Concern turned to hysteria as news arrived in July of confirmed cases of cholera in Montreal and New York City. Forced by public pressure to take some type of action but still doubtful that the disease would ever threaten the city, the New Orleans City Council established a board of health in the spring of 1832. Composed of 7 physicians and 3 pharmacists, the body of respected men was successful in temporarily quelling public concern. Unfortunately, however, the men concluded that the malady was not contagious and therefore no quarantine was necessary. No effort was made to clean the open ditches and canals that would soon harbor the bacteria causing the plague.

Even after the arrival of cholera in October, physicians encouraged citizens to remain calm. Convinced that the pestilence was airborne, the board of health directed the burning of tar and pitch in an effort to cleanse and purify the poisonous air believed to be the source of the devastation. Frequent bathing was encouraged, and citizens were directed to abstain from consuming unripe fruit and alcoholic beverages. Small but numerous meals were also suggested as a way of keeping the internal organs active and in good health.

By the second day of the outbreak, reports began to circulate that large numbers were becoming ill, and most were dying. The virility of the disease seemed to be increasing. Terror and despair gripped the city. Hundreds fled New Orleans and surrounding communities in fear of their lives, many later found dead along the roads leaving the city. Individuals who tried to flee had little success, as no means of transport was available. Horses and mules were sold at exorbitant prices, and vessels leaving via the river were unable to accommodate the overwhelming demands for passage. The dead and dying could be found on every corner. Desperate parents waited in lines at apothecaries hoping to purchase drugs that would ease the suffering of dying children. Physicians who were not sick themselves were soon overwhelmed by the patients seeking treatment. Many collapsed from exhaustion while treating dying patients.

Hundreds lay stacked in piles at cemeteries, awaiting burial. Unable to secure coffins, city leaders directed that the bodies be disposed of in mass graves. Prisoners and inmates released from jails to assist with the effort fled or returned to their cells rather than risk exposure to the dreadful pestilence. Laborers needed to assist with the sick and dying could not be found at any price. Hospitals reported frustration with the situation as employees became disabled by the disease and care for the hordes of patients arriving daily became impossible to administer. Some hospitals were forced to close their doors when no one remained to provide assistance to the sick. In less than two weeks the disease had spread throughout the city, leaving no family untouched. Some estimate that as many as 6,000 died during a two-week period.

Faced with the reality of the devastation caused by cholera, the New Orleans City Council finally took actions necessary to protect the citizenry. Quarantines were placed in infected areas, and stagnant water present in canals and ditches was treated with lime or removed. Individuals violating sanitary laws were vigorously prosecuted, and hospitals and cemeteries were constantly monitored. Unfortunately, however, the action was taken too late and was not enforced uniformly enough to save the city from the horrors of cholera in the future.

Dr. John Evans, who traveled to New Orleans and the interior of the American West during that period, is credited by many as the first to realize how cholera spread. Evans studied the commerce along the Mississippi River and observed that river steamers had spread the disease up the river from New Orleans. Although at first dismissed by his contemporaries, the physician who established both Northwestern University and the University of Denver was instrumental in saving many New Orleanians from future outbreaks.

Donald C. Simmons, Jr.

FOR FURTHER INFORMATION:

Cornell, James. *The Great International Disaster Book.* New York: Charles Scribner's Sons, 1976.

Dunlop, Richard. *Doctors of the American Frontier.* Garden City, N.Y.: Doubleday, 1965.

Fossier, Albert. *New Orleans: The Glamour Period, 1800-1840.* New Orleans: Pelican, 1957.

1840: Worldwide

CHOLERA

DATE: 1840-1862

PLACE: Worldwide, including China, Russia, Europe, and North America

RESULT: Millions dead

Because cholera outbreaks were frequent during the nineteenth century, it is difficult to define pandemics with precision. However, the largest cholera pandemic, as measured by number of deaths, geographical coverage, and duration, occurred between roughly 1840 and 1862. Appearing first in India in 1817, cholera soon spread to China. There it became endemic for the following quarter of a century. The disease followed land trade routes west from China through central Asia, arriving in Russia in 1829. Simultaneously, commercial shipping carried cholera west. It struck the major European seaports of Naples, Genoa, Marseilles, Hamburg, London, and Liverpool, also in 1829. Immigrant ships brought cholera to North America in 1832: New York recorded its first fatalities in that year. The disease ravaged the cities of Europe and North America from 1847 to 1852. Localized outbreaks followed, with more serious epidemics in 1859 and 1866.

The mortality rate is difficult to estimate, especially for Eastern Europe and eastern Asia, where governments had less supervisory ability than European states. Between 1847 and 1851, cholera killed at least 2 million people in China, 1 million in Russia, and about 200,000 in the rest of Europe and North America. In 1849 alone, 20,000 died in Paris and 7,000 in London. Chicago lost 4,520 to the epidemic.

Cholera was horrifying because it challenged basic assumptions about what death should be like. Nineteenth century people, especially in Europe and North America, were accustomed to death's nearness, for infant mortality was high, famines frequent, and infectious disease ever-present. However, they expected death to be edifying and even ennobling. The literature of the age was full of deathbed scenes—the most famous being the death of Little Nell in Charles Dickens's *The Old Curiosity Shop* (1840-1841)—in which death came upon people slowly, transformed them into figures of otherworldly beauty, and gave them time to attain moral purity. Society also treated sudden and violent death, especially on the battlefield, as heroic and self-sacrificial.

Cholera was different and terrifying. Its onset was sudden, and its symptoms were offensive to middle-class sensibilities. Victims looked like the living dead as their skin turned blue, their eyes grew dull and sunken, and painful convulsions twisted their bodies. One might be struck with massive vomiting and diarrhea on the street, in a restaurant, or in a shop. Such symptoms were especially threatening in an era that felt bodily functions to be shameful.

The era's dominant medical ideas also labeled the disease as shameful. Some physicians believed in the contagionist theory, which taught that cholera was an infectious material transmitted through persons' breath, clothing, excretions, and items they touched. Because quarantining had failed to prevent the spread of disease during the earlier cholera epidemic of 1826-1837, most physicians advocated the miasmatic theory, which taught that bad-smelling vapors gave people the disease. Physicians argued that orderly personal behavior, correct morality, and especially moderation in the consumption of alcohol were the best preventatives. Therefore, cholera was to some extent a "lifestyle disease," or the victim's fault.

Governments, especially in Great Britain, France, and Germany, attempted to quell the epidemic by enforcing sanitary regulations, whitewashing tenement houses, cleaning streets, and unblocking sewers. The local governments were inadequate, however. Britain was forced to enact sanitary legislation and create a national board of health in the 1850's.

The epidemic stimulated much scientific research. By the 1860's, German scientist Max Josef von Pettenkofer's prolific publications had convinced most physicians that cholera was not spread by contaminated drinking water, but rather by contaminated groundwater, which produced a miasma that transmitted the disease. He therefore believed that quarantining victims and improving the drinking-water supply were pointless. Rather, hygiene primarily depended on individual people living temperate lives, keeping clean, eating well, and breathing fresh air. His theory appealed to middle-class values because it stressed individual responsibility and minimized state intervention. Even after the bacteriologist Robert Koch identified the cholera bacillus in the 1880's, many physicians continued to accept Pettenkofer's theory.

The epidemic provoked fear, rumors, and civil unrest. Town dwellers in Italy, France, and Germany rioted as rumors spread that body snatchers were stealing corpses to sell to medical schools for dissection. In Eastern Europe and Russia, serfs, most of them illiterate, killed physicians and government officials and burned the estates of landowners who tried to impose quarantines in affected areas.

The worst case of civil unrest occurred in China, where the population grew from 150 million to 400 million between 1700 and 1850. Food production failed to keep pace, and natural calamities of unprecedented proportions, including droughts, famines, and floods, worsened living standards. The Qing Dynasty neglected public works and failed to relieve the people's misery. The cholera epidemic of the 1840's and 1850's, which led directly to the death of 2 million Chinese, tipped the scales toward social chaos. Influenced by Protestant missionaries, a village schoolmaster named Hong Xiuquan developed a movement that combined Christianity and traditional Chinese beliefs. In 1850, he launched the Taiping Rebellion. After fourteen years of warfare, some 30 million Chinese had died from all causes, including disease. Although the Qing government defeated the rebellion, the uprising so weakened the dynasty that China's economic decline and social chaos accelerated and ended in the overthrow of the last emperor in 1911, the most profound political consequence of the mid-nineteenth century cholera epidemic.

D. G. Paz

FOR FURTHER INFORMATION:
Beatty, William K. "When Cholera Scourged Chicago." *Chicago History* 11 (1982): 2-13.
Coleman, William. *Death Is a Social Disease: Public Health and Political Economy in Early Industrial France.* Madison: University of Wisconsin Press, 1982.
Evans, Richard J. *Death in Hamburg: Society and Politics in the Cholera Years, 1830-1910.* New York: Oxford University Press, 1987.
Fairbank, John King. *The Great Chinese Revolution, 1800-1985.* New York: Harper & Row, 1986.
Kudlick, Catherine Jean. *Cholera in Post-Revolutionary Paris: A Cultural History.* Berkeley: University of California Press, 1966.
Pelling, Margaret. *The Public Health: Cholera Epidemics and English Medicine, 1825-1865.* Oxford, England: Oxford University Press, 1978.
Rosenberg, Charles E. *The Cholera Years: The United States in 1832, 1849, and 1866.* Chicago: University of Chicago Press, 1962.

1848: New York City

CHOLERA
DATE: 1848-1849
PLACE: New York City
RESULT: 5,071 dead

The cholera epidemic of 1848 eased its way into New York City on December 1, 1848, with the arrival of the ship *New York* from Le Havre, France. Upon arrival the New York City deputy health inspector met the ship in the harbor, only to find 7 of the 331 steerage passengers dead from cholera. Many more were sick, and all had been exposed. Common sense and public policy dictated the quarantining of all the passengers. With no facilities available or hospitals willing to take them, the Staten Island customs warehouses were converted into containment facilities.

Before January 1, 1849, 60 of those quarantined were displaying cholera symptoms, and more than 30 were dead. Panic spread throughout the facility, and more than half of those quarantined escaped into the city of New York, some also heading for New Jersey. Within seven days outbreaks were documented within the lower-rent districts of New York City. These areas were notoriously overcrowded and filthy, providing the perfect breeding ground for the disease. This outbreak was short-lived though. The cold winter weather provided a short respite from immediate epidemic conditions. No new cases were reported until the spring of 1849.

With the arrival of spring came the first reports of death due to cholera. Again, the victims lived in squalor in the filthiest area of New York City. James Gilligan and four female companions resided in the cellar of 20 Orange Street. On May 11, 1849, Gilligan and his companions sat at their makeshift table, two barrels with the door to the cellar laid across the top, and ate their usual dinner of spoiled ham. By Monday, May 14, 1849, Gilligan and two of his companions were found lying on the dirt floor suffering from severe cramps, vomiting, diarrhea, and dehydration. The three were dead before nightfall, and one of the other women residing with them began displaying the unmistakable symptoms. She was dead before sunrise of the following day.

Most New York City residents were not too worried about the incident. Gilligan's residence and neighborhood were considered to be the dirtiest areas in the city. Pigs and dogs, wandering the streets freely, provided much of the sanitation for these neighborhoods. The pigs, fed from garbage discarded into the streets by the residents, were a cheap source of meat for the poor. A residence just two units away from Gilligan's housed over one hundred pigs. Most city residents believed if those who lived there chose to exist under such conditions they deserved to die in their own filth. The belief that cholera was a disease that afflicted the poor, immigrants, drunks, prostitutes, and atheists was still widely held among the upper classes. The fact that all reported cholera cases thus far were contained to Orange Street helped to foster this false belief.

The New York City Board of Health looked upon the emerging epidemic a bit more seriously and scientifically. The members began seeking buildings in December to house cholera hospitals. Acquiring space became nearly impossible due to the stigma that would be forever attached to the residence. When a tentative site was chosen either the landlord raised the rent so high the board could not afford it or the neighborhood residents would threaten to burn the building down to keep the hospital from opening. All city residents agreed the hospitals were necessary, but no one wanted the hospital on their block. The board of health was not able to establish a hospital until May 16, 1849. They were able to obtain the second floor of a building whose main floor housed a tavern. As the disease spread throughout the city and the classes, the board of health, under great protest from the school board and the teachers, was able to open four of the city's public school buildings as cholera hospitals.

Meanwhile, the New York Academy of Medicine met with the board of health and reiterated its stance on cleanliness. They believed the streets must be cleaned, the garbage hauled away, and the animals relocated in order to stop the proliferation of the disease. The academy and the board of health alerted the mayor to take whatever steps necessary to clean up the streets. The board formed a Sanatory Committee, appointing three physicians who would meet daily to provide medical advice. A committee was appointed to find more hospital sites, and the board of health met with the aldermen of each ward in order to get a street-cleaning plan in motion. The aldermen were told to hire four inspectors for each ward to supervise the cleanup efforts. Streets were to be washed, landlords were ordered to thoroughly clean filthy rental units, and the sale of produce and meat from open street vendor carts was prohibited.

The cholera death toll had risen from 35 in May, 1849, to 775 by the end of June, 1849. The city inhabitants began to panic, and those who could afford to fled to the countryside, where they believed the cleaner air would protect them. Those who remained procured the usual cholera remedies such as calomel, laudanum, and lime. Some tried the newer cures of sulphur pills and camphor. Others put their fate in the hands of God. Puritans believed the epidemic was God's way of scoffing at the theories of natural science. Others thought cholera was God's punishment of sinners and atheists. This theory was based upon the fact that the outbreak began with the poorest and filthiest of the city's inhabitants. About 40 percent of the New York City cholera victims were Irish immigrants whose religious profile did not fit that of the American Puritan. The upper classes based the spread of the disease upon the lower-class and immigrant victims' way of life and lack of worship. When an upper-class citizen died of cholera the family would insist the death certificate be falsified by changing the cause of death. Some attributed a family member's contraction of and subsequent death from cholera to some secret misgiving the victim harbored.

As a result of this belief system, a formal fasting day, June 28, was enacted by the Dutch Reform Church and the Old School Presbyterians. Church doors were opened to all in honor of the fasting, and many workers were released from their duties in order to attend. The board of health and its committees, in an attempt to end the cholera scourge, pleaded with the ministers to address their congregation about the importance of cleanliness. Attending church had become as much a social as a religious event for the middle and upper classes. The poor neither could nor wanted to attend such affairs. In effect, the people who were hardest hit by the epidemic were out of reach as far as education concerning transmission of the disease. Many of the residents of Orange Street and the surrounding neighborhoods were seen instead frequenting taverns, hiring prostitutes, and sleeping off drunkenness in streets among the filth that was promoting the spread of the disease.

By the end of July the death toll was at a new high, 2,625 for that month. Only one theater remained open, and twenty-four churches had closed their doors. The pigs and dogs still roamed freely, and the garbage was piling higher. The street-cleaning efforts were at a standstill. Conflicts arose between the city and state governments over property and procedural issues, and local authorities and contractors argued over unfulfilled contracts. Compounding the matter, the Croton Water Board of New York City was refusing use of their water for street cleaning, claiming their reservoirs were too low for those purposes. Private landowners refused to be forced to clean their property, citing ownership rights with regard to property conditions. The vast governmental and legal procedures basically rendered the New York City Board of Health, the mayor, and the Sanatory Committee powerless.

When the ward aldermen were able to force their cleaning contractors to perform services, the dirt and garbage was left in heaps on the streets, where the cholera bacteria proliferated. The heaps of debris were then dumped off the ends of piers, where they stagnated and contaminated the water. More often than not, contractors refused to oblige their contracts. Some who were forced to fulfill the agreement filed petitions asking the city to release them from their contracts, stating "grave financial loss" as a direct result of performing their duties.

With the death toll rising rapidly, human body disposal was quickly becoming a problem. Bodies were left in the street for hours and sometimes days. The Catholic Church began to open plots to non-Catholics. Most churchyards allowed burial of caskets three deep. Men owning horses were hired to drive buckboards around the city and pick up the bodies lying in the streets. They were piled atop one another and driven out to a scow (a flat-bottomed boat) for final disposal on Randall's Island, the city cemetery site. Many preferred to die at home or even in the street; only those who were without family or friends died in the cholera hospitals. At Randall's Island trenches were dug for mass graves. Some of them were piled with bodies to within 1 foot of the surface, then quickly covered with dirt. No caskets were used due to lack of space. Literally thousands of rats swam to the island every day and feasted upon the contents of the shallow graves.

The Sanatory Committee began attacking the poor's only source of meat, the pigs. The pigs were eating from the debris piles, infecting themselves, and then being butchered and eaten by the residents. The establishments that disposed of the butchered carcasses were ordered closed as "menaces to the public health." The butchers, having no place else to dispose of the waste, dumped the carcasses into the river. When the tides came back in, the bacteria came with them. The Sanatory Committee and the police, although confronted with riots, were finally successful in removing the pigs to the city's less crowded northern wards. As a result the cholera began to dissipate at the city's point of origin but spread to formerly untouched neighborhoods.

The cholera death toll for the month of August, 1849, was recorded at 1,452. By the end of September the toll had declined to 161. Businessmen began to return from the country, and New York City saw its first boatload of immigrants since May of the same year. Only one cholera hospital was in operation. October's cholera death toll was 16, and November's 7 victims brought an end to the yearlong epidemic. The total cholera death toll for New York City, as reported by the New York City Inspector, was 5,071 people.

Christine L. Martin

FOR FURTHER INFORMATION:

Duffy, John. *A History of Public Health in New York City, 1625-1866.* New York: Russell Sage Foundation, 1968.

Pollitzer, R. *Cholera.* Geneva, Switzerland: World Health Organization, 1959.

Rosenberg, Charles F. *The Cholera Years in 1832, 1849, and 1866.* Chicago: University of Chicago Press, 1962.

1853: New Orleans

YELLOW FEVER
DATE: 1853
PLACE: New Orleans, Louisiana
RESULT: 7,790 dead

The first victim of the yellow-fever epidemic of 1853 was a crew member on the ship *Augusta,* newly arrived at New Orleans directly from Bremen, Germany. Apparently, the fever came with another ship, *Camboden Castle,* arriving from Kingston, Jamaica, where there was a "great deal of yellow fever," according to contemporary accounts, and the captain and several crewmen had died of the fever.

The sick of the *Augusta* were taken into the city to the charity hospital, from which site the fever spread around the city, appearing next near the U.S. Mint. Panic soon gripped the city, and many fled to outlying areas, where the fever also began to appear. Urged by the board of health, Mayor Abdil Daily Crossman ordered that cannons be fired at dawn and dusk to purify the air. Tar pots burned continually, a surprisingly effective measure that did control mosquitoes.

From June 1 until November 1 there were some 16,000 cases of yellow fever in New Orleans alone. Of these, about 5,600 died. The epidemic eased only with the arrival of cold weather.

John A. Cramer

FOR FURTHER INFORMATION:

Carter, Hoding, ed. *The Past as Prelude: New Orleans, 1718-1968.* New Orleans: Pelican, 1968.

Duffy, John. *Sword of Pestilence.* Baton Rouge: Louisiana State University Press, 1966.

Garvey, Joan B., and Mary Lou Widmer. *Beautiful Crescent: A History of New Orleans.* New Orleans: Garmer Press, 1982.

Kohn, George C., ed. *Encyclopedia of Plague and Pestilence.* New York: Facts on File, 1995.

1867: New Orleans

YELLOW FEVER
DATE: 1867
PLACE: New Orleans, Louisiana
RESULT: 3,093 dead

Throughout the nineteenth century, yellow fever was an almost annual summer visitor in New Orleans. Beginning in 1862, a hiatus occurred during the Civil War federal occupation under General Benjamin Franklin Butler. Using federal funds, Butler hired 2,000 unemployed residents to clean the streets, and yellow fever virtually disappeared. With the end of the war and military rule, sanitation declined while the numbers of susceptible residents increased. Accordingly, in 1867, yellow fever returned to the city in epidemic form. Contemporary accounts list 3,093 dead, although John Duffy, the twentieth century medical historian, believed the number closer to 1,600. As in the past, only cold weather finally ended the outbreak.

John A. Cramer

FOR FURTHER INFORMATION:

Carter, Hoding, ed. *The Past as Prelude: New Orleans, 1718-1968.* New Orleans: Pelican, 1968.

Garvey, Joan B., and Mary Lou Widmer. *Beautiful Crescent: A History of New Orleans.* New Orleans: Garmer Press, 1982.

1878: Mississippi Valley

YELLOW FEVER
DATE: August 13-October 29, 1878
PLACE: Memphis, Tennessee
RESULT: Over 100,000 cases of yellow fever, over 20,000 dead in lower Mississippi Valley

The summer of 1878 was wet and hot in the lower Mississippi Valley. The climate provided the ideal breeding grounds for the *Aedes aegypti* mosquito, which dwelt up and down the Mississippi River. The female *Aedes aegypti* mosquito is the carrier, or vector, of the yellow-fever disease. When the female mosquito bites a person whose blood contains the yellow-fever virus, subsequent bites infect susceptible individuals. However, in 1878, yellow fever, also known as Yellow Jack or the yellow plague, was still a mysterious disease of unknown cause. Yellow fever is endemic to West Africa and traveled to the Americas aboard trading ships importing slaves from Africa. With the open water casks on the ships, the mosquitoes easily survived the ocean crossings. Yellow fever then flourished wherever its vector could—where the temperature remained above 72 degrees Fahrenheit and where there was still water for the female mosquito to lay eggs.

The symptoms of yellow fever appear three to six days after the bite of an infected mosquito and range from mild, flulike symptoms to a severe, three-stage course of infection. Most Africans and their descendants exhibit mild to moderate symptoms of headache, fever, nausea, and vomiting. However, most victims recover within a few days. For Caucasians, Native Americans, and Asians, the first stage of the infection begins with a fever of 102 to 105 degrees Fahrenheit. The fever lasts three to four days and is accompanied by severe headache, backache, nausea, and vomiting. It is during this first stage that the patient is infectious and can pass the virus to a mosquito. In the second stage, which may last only a few hours, a remission of the fever occurs, the headache disappears, and the patient feels better. Thereafter, in the third stage, the temperature rises rapidly again and the pulse rate drops. The first-stage symptoms recur but in a more severe form. Liver injury from the infection disrupts normal blood clotting, and some patients vomit blood, or a black vomit, and may also bleed from the nose, gums, and spots on the skin. Jaundice from liver and renal failure may yellow the skin, but the color is seldom as pronounced as the name "yellow fever" may suggest. Liver, heart, and renal failure often result in delirium. Most deaths occur on the sixth or seventh day after the reappearance of symptoms. Survivors remain ill for another seventeen to thirty days.

Reports of outbreaks of yellow fever in North American port cities began to appear in the late seventeenth century. The plagues in northern port cities, such as New York and Philadelphia, occurred only in the summer because the *Aedes aegypti* mosquito does not survive after a frost. It was in the tropical climates of the southern United States that the mosquito flourished and caused repeated epidemics. New Orleans' first reported epidemic occurred in 1796, and over the next century epidemics occurred regularly. Once people knew of the devastation of yellow fever, they lived in dread of its return. For people of the nineteenth century, the greatest fear of yellow fever came from a fear of the unknown—how it came about and how it was spread. What was known about yellow fever was that once it entered a city, it spread rapidly and easily among the people.

Yellow Fever Strikes Memphis. Before the Civil War, Memphis had a population of 22,000. By 1878, the population had risen to 48,000. At that time, Memphis was a major hub of cotton production in the United States. The city was located on the Mississippi River—a major trade route—and had three railroad lines. Yellow fever was no stranger to the citizens of Memphis. It had visited Memphis three times before, killing 75 people in 1855, 250 people in 1867, and 2,000 in 1873. As the city grew, the people realized that the attacks of yellow fever were growing worse. Although the disease was not spread from person to person by direct contact, it was understood that people fleeing from a city where yellow fever had struck could spread the disease to another community. Realizing that yellow-fever patients must be isolated from other patients, staff members of a British hospital dressed the segregated patients in gowns with yellow patches to warn of their disease. The patients were nicknamed "Yellow Jackets" and the yellow flag flown over the quarantine area was known as the "Yellow Jack." Cities would also attempt to prevent escapees from other diseased communities from entry and prohibit their own inhabitants from entering affected areas.

When outbreaks of yellow fever in the West Indies, islands involved in trade with cities along the Mississippi River, were reported in the late spring of 1878, Memphis began to fear the possibility of another epidemic. Physicians and board of health members argued for quarantine measures. The city council rejected the quarantine so as to not interfere with Memphis's lucrative trade. In protest, the president of the Memphis board of health resigned his position. Outbreaks of yellow fever were reported in New Orleans by late July; however, a Memphis newspaper reassured the public that the sanitary conditions of the streets and private premises would prevent the arrival of the disease as long as the sanitary laws were enforced. When yellow fever was reported in Vicksburg, only 240 miles away from Memphis, on July 27, Memphis established quarantine stations for goods and people from cities south of Memphis on the Mississippi River.

On August 1, 1878, William Warren, a hand on a quarantined steamboat, slipped into Memphis and stopped at a restaurant located in Front Row along the Mississippi River. This small establishment was run by Kate Bionda and her husband, whose main trade was to cater food and drink to riverboat men. On August 2, William Warren became sick and was admitted to the city hospital. His illness was diagnosed as yellow fever, and he was moved to a quarantine hospital on President's Island, where he died on August 5.

Fear began to spread through Memphis as rumors of the riverboat hand's death multiplied, and on August 9, yellow fever was reported in the city of Grenada, Mississippi—only 90 miles south of Memphis. Again, newspapers tried to calm the public, cautioning them to avoid patent medicines and bad whiskey and to be cheerful and laugh as much as possible. By

this time, Kate Bionda, age thirty-four, had become ill. On August 13, in her rooms above the snack shop, she died. A physician saw her, noted her symptoms and her jaundice and, after consulting with other physicians, diagnosed her as the first official case of yellow fever in Memphis in 1878.

On August 14, an additional 55 cases of yellow fever were announced. By August 15 and 16, the city of Memphis was in full panic. Thousands of people began to leave the city. There were processions of wagons piled high with possessions. Railroad companies attached extra cars, yet these were not enough for all of the people trying to flee the city. The city council members fled, and one-third of the police force deserted the city.

By August 17, four days after Kate Bionda's death, more than 25,000 people, over half the population of Memphis, had fled the city. However, news of the Memphis epidemic had spread just as swiftly. Other communities established quarantines against those coming from Memphis. Barricades were enforced with shotguns. Railroad trains from Memphis were refused by many cities, and refugees on riverboats were forced to stay on board for months as port after port denied them permission to land.

The refugees camped in forests and fled to small towns along the Mississippi River as well as to St. Louis, Louisville, Cincinnati, East Tennessee, and Virginia. Many did carry the yellow-fever virus, and over 100 Memphis citizens died outside the city. When the infected refugees entered areas where the *Aedes aegypti* mosquito lived, they continued the spread of the disease.

Of the 20,000 citizens who remained in Memphis, approximately 14,000 were African Americans and

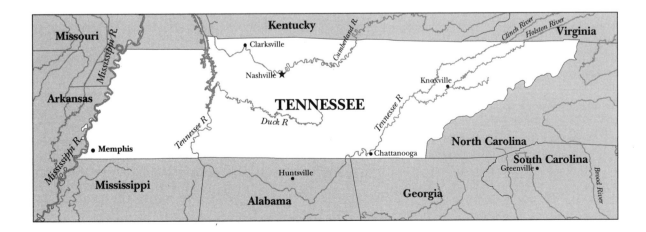

6,000 were Caucasians. Through the first half of September of 1878, at least 200 people died per day. Survivors of the epidemic described some of the terrible conditions in the city. Carts would be loaded with 8 or 9 corpses in rough-hewn boxes, and the coffins were piled in tiers on the sidewalk in front of the undertaker's shop. Entire families were wiped out, and many victims died alone, covered with the black vomit characteristic of the disease. Survivors recalled sights of piles of burned clothing and bedding outside houses—each a reminder that someone had died there. At first funeral bells tolled continuously, but the custom was suspended so as not to upset the sick and the dying. The stillness in the streets was occasionally broken by loud blasts of gunpowder, and at night burning tar barrels lit the streets—both futile attempts to clear the air of yellow fever. The weather remained unseasonably hot and humid for September and October, and ironically, one newspaper editor remarked that the mosquitoes were as vigorous and desperate as ever.

The African American population, which is usually resistant to the disease, also succumbed to the infection as never before. More than 11,000 African Americans in Memphis were infected, approximately 77 percent of their population. Of those infected, 946 died—a 10 percent mortality rate, considerably higher than in other epidemics. For Caucasians, the mortality rate was around 70 percent, with more than 4,000 deaths among the 6,000 that remained in the city. Other states quickly sent supplies and funds.

Aid to the Victims. Volunteer agencies arose to take care of the government and of the sick. The Citizen's Relief Committee was formed, composed mostly of prominent and wealthy citizens. Their first act was to establish a camp outside the city in an effort to remove any uninfected persons. About 1,000 persons occupied Camp Joe Williams, named for a Memphis physician who died of yellow fever in 1873, and only a few people died in the camp. The committee also assumed command of what remained of the police force. Under command of the African American janitor and cook, thirteen other African Americans were added to the police force. Fear of looting prompted them to call up the local militia, with both white and black companies guarding the city. Because business and commercial activity had ceased, people began to fear starvation. With donations of money and supplies from Memphis and elsewhere, the committee set up a welfare and rations program.

The difficult task of medical care was assumed by the Howard Association. Formed in Memphis in 1867, it was patterned after a similar group founded in New Orleans during the yellow-fever epidemic of 1837. Its membership was composed mostly of businessmen, and its sole task was to serve in yellow-fever epidemics. The members met on the day of Mrs. Bionda's death and assembled a corps of nearly 3,000 nurses and 111 physicians. Seventy-two of those physicians came from other states, because physicians in Memphis had enormous loads of patients. To treat yellow fever, many physicians relied on heavy medication, such as purges of calomel, rhubarb, or jalap (a plant root). Others used cold bath treatments, dousing the patients with cold water and then covering them with blankets to induce perspiration.

Most physicians, however, came to realize they could not cure yellow fever but could only alleviate its symptoms. Deeply frustrated, most Memphis physicians could only reduce fevers with sponge baths, alleviate warm chills with blankets, and give medicine to calm delirium. Few patients were admitted to hospitals as there were not enough beds for the thousands that were sick. Most of the sick were cared for in their homes by nurses. Both Caucasian and African American, male and female, most of the nurses were Memphians. Nursing was not yet a recognized profession, and their function was mainly to sit with the patient. Much criticism was directed at the nurses. Although their motives ranged from a selfless devotion to the sick to a desire to make money, reports of theft, drinking, and misconduct by the nurses were common.

Despite physical and mental exhaustion, the physicians made attempts to understand the disease and performed about 300 autopsies. Yet afterward, they knew no more than they had before except that they had probably been confronted by a new and deadlier strain of the virus. More than 60 percent of these physicians gave their lives caring for the victims of the epidemic.

When the frosts of October 18 and 19 came, so did a decrease in the rate of yellow-fever infection. On October 29, 1878, eleven weeks after the first reported case, the epidemic was declared over. Those who had fled the city returned home, and on November 28, Thanksgiving Day, the city held a mass meeting to praise the heroes of the epidemic, to thank the nation for its assistance, and to mourn their dead.

The Results of the Epidemic. The yellow-fever epidemic of 1878 had begun in New Orleans. It traveled up the Mississippi River to Vicksburg, then to Memphis, and to Cairo, Illinois, eventually reaching St. Louis. It was carried up the Tennessee River to Chattanooga, and up the Ohio River to Louisville and Cincinnati. Throughout the Mississippi Valley, over 100,000 had yellow fever, and more than 20,000 died. It was Memphis with its large population that felt the worst impact, however. Of the fewer than 20,000 who remained in the city, over 17,000 had yellow fever. Of the 14,000 African Americans, roughly 11,000 contracted the disease and 946 died. Of the 6,000 Caucasians, nearly all, 4,204, died of yellow fever.

The future of Memphis was now in doubt, as it was considered an incurable pesthole. The value of lives lost was incalculable. Loss of trade was estimated as high as $100 million. Some outsiders suggested that the city be abandoned. However, under the direction of a new and more powerful board of health, Memphis began to clean itself up and accomplished remarkable improvements in public sanitation, with the creation of a waste-disposal system, approved water supply, street-paving program, and rigid health ordinances. Although still unaware of the cause of the disease, these cleanup measures did reduce the risk of yellow fever by eliminating the open sewers and outside privies where the mosquitoes bred.

The epidemic of 1878 also generated widespread interest in public health. The U.S. Congress instituted the National Board of Health, and a full-scale research program was also prompted by the epidemic. However, it would be another twenty-two years before members of the U.S. Army Yellow Fever Commission would discover that yellow fever was transmitted by the *Aedes aegypti* mosquito and that the agent of the disease was a virus.

The impact of the epidemic would be felt by Memphis for many years. The population had declined drastically, many businesses left the city, and others were dissuaded from moving to Memphis. Meanwhile, other cities such as Atlanta and Birmingham attracted new wealth and population in the South. Yet the city of Memphis would not forget the devastation of the 1878 epidemic nor the heroes who stayed to help its victims. Dr. John Erskine was the Memphis Health Officer in 1878. His fearlessness and tireless work to treat the plague victims were inspirational to his fellow physicians, yet he himself died of yellow fever. In 1974, the city of Memphis named one of its libraries in his memory and filled its shelves with accounts of the city's health disasters and triumphs. In 1990, St. Jude Children's Hospital in Memphis established an annual lectureship to honor his memory.

Mary Bosch Farone

FOR FURTHER INFORMATION:

Baker, Thomas H. "Yellow Jack: The Yellow Fever Epidemic of 1878 in Memphis, Tennessee." *Bulletin of the History of Medicine* 42 (1968): 241-264.

Marks, Geoffrey, and William K. Beatty. *Epidemics: The Story of Mankind's Most Lethal and Elusive Enemies from Ancient Times to the Present.* 8 vols. New York: Charles Scribner's Sons, 1976.

Oldstone, Michael B. A. *Viruses, Plagues, and History.* New York: Oxford University Press, 1998.

1892: Worldwide

CHOLERA

DATE: 1892-1894

PLACE: India, Russia, Asia, the United States, Great Britain, Europe, and Africa

RESULT: Millions dead, development of health departments and infectious disease surveillance

Cholera epidemics plagued humankind for most of the nineteenth century. The final worldwide cholera epidemic of that century occurred between 1892 and 1894. This epidemic was similar to the cholera epidemics that had preceded it in that it caused great devastation; millions of people died. The 1892 to 1894 epidemic was unique, however, in that it occurred just at the time when science was determining beyond a doubt that the cause of cholera was bacterial infection passed through contaminated water.

Cholera is caused by the organism *Vibrio cholerae*. It lives in various marine animals, which are consumed by humans, and it is present in contaminated water. Most humans become infected by eating raw fish or shellfish, or by drinking contaminated water. Not all people infected with cholera show symptoms, and they can spread the disease unknowingly. Cholera causes severe diarrhea and vomiting, which leads to a drastic loss of fluids within the body. Dehydration, collapse of the circulatory system, and death occur if the fluids are not replaced. Without treatment, cholera kills 20 to 50 percent of its victims and death occurs within hours. Today, prompt treatment can bring the death toll down to 1 percent.

Ancient Sanskrit writings from 2,500 years ago described a disease with symptoms that were similar to cholera. Although cholera existed before the 1800's, it remained primarily in the area of Bengal, with some brief occurrences in China. Originating in the Bengal basin at the delta of the Ganges and Brahmaputra Rivers, *V. cholerae* lived in the shellfish present in the waters. Hindu pilgrimages drew crowds of faithful to the Ganges River for ceremonies, where many were infected with cholera. Some died promptly; others carried the disease back to their villages, causing local infestations. These outbreaks of cholera remained local; thus, when cholera made its appearance throughout the world in the early 1800's, it was described as a new disease. In 1817, cholera spread from Bengal to other parts of the world. Over the next one hundred years the world would suffer six major outbreaks of cholera.

The spread of cholera was closely linked to the increase in international commerce, military actions, the increase in travel, and the increase in immigration of people. When cholera broke out in India in 1817, English ships and troops were stationed there. They carried cholera overland to Nepal and Afghanistan. Far more critically, their ships passed cholera along to Ceylon (now Sri Lanka), Indonesia, China, Japan, Arabia, and Africa. The Industrial Revolution and an increase in urban population and crowded living conditions also contributed to the spread of cholera.

The devastation caused by cholera was so great that port towns made attempts to control it by mandating quarantines. Ship were not allowed to disembark for weeks until they were determined to be free of disease. Scientists struggled to find the cause of the dreaded disease. Although Robert Koch, one of the great microbiologists of the nineteenth century, had found the bacillus that caused cholera back in 1883, his explanation was not accepted by other experts of the time. In 1887, the federal government of the United States ordered a study of cholera to begin. Dr. Joseph Kinyoun directed the program, which later evolved into the National Institutes of Health. Dr. Kinyoun's research became more urgent in 1892, when an Asiatic cholera epidemic reached the United States.

When the cholera epidemic of 1892 struck the city of Hamburg, Germany, a unique situation within the area gave credence to Koch's theory that germ-contaminated water was responsible for spreading cholera. Hamburg obtained its water directly from the Elbe River, which was untreated. An adjacent town, Altona, had installed a water-filtration plant, so its citizens drank treated water. When the epidemic hit, the people in Hamburg succumbed, but the people of Altona were spared. The street that divided the towns experienced cholera on one side and none on the other side. Since the air was the same on both sides of the street and the ground was the same, it was apparently the water that made the difference.

The cholera epidemic of 1892-1894 appeared in India, Russia, Asia, the United States, Great Britain, Europe, and Africa. In Russia alone, over 1 million people died, including the great composer Peter Tchaikovsky. The exact circumstances surrounding his death were unclear. Some speculate that Tchaikovsky committed suicide by drinking water known to be contaminated; others believe that he took a poison that mimicked the symptoms of cholera. Tchaikovsky's doctor, however, pronounced him dead of cholera on November 6, 1893.

One result of the cholera epidemic of 1892 was the improvement in sanitation measures taken by the large cities. Water-treatment systems were instituted, and sanitation was greatly improved. Even in Asia, Africa, and Latin America, where resources were not available to provide sanitary water and sewage systems for all citizens, simple precautions like boiling drinking water made it possible to avoid exposure to waterborne infections. Cholera epidemics prompted the formation of public health departments, which conducted surveillance and reporting of the disease. In the international classification of diseases, the code for cholera is 001 because it was the first disease for which public health surveillance was developed. Although cholera is still present in various parts of the world, improved sanitation, increased surveillance, and modern medical treatment have helped prevent the occurrence of new, widespread epidemics.

Louise Magoon

FOR FURTHER INFORMATION:

Brown, David. *The Final Years (1885-1893)*. Vol. 4 in *Tchaikovsky*. New York: W. W. Norton, 1991. Provides a description of the composer's death from cholera.

Evans, Alfred S., and Philip S. Brachman. *Bacterial Infections of Humans: Epidemiology and Control.* 3d ed. New York: Plenum Medical Book Company, 1998. A thorough chapter on cholera describes the nature of the disease, its history, and its current prevalence in the world.

Karlen, Arno. *Man and Microbes: Disease and Plagues in History and Modern Times.* New York: Putnam, 1995. Describes the global terror that cholera evoked and the social and economic conditions of the times that promoted the spread of cholera worldwide.

McNeill, William H. *Plagues and Peoples.* New York: Anchor Press/Doubleday, 1998. Examines the impact that disease had on economies and public policies.

FOR FURTHER INFORMATION:

Kohn, George C., ed. *Encyclopedia of Plague and Pestilence.* New York: Facts on File, 1995.

Marks, Geoffrey, and William K. Beatty. *Epidemics: The Story of Mankind's Most Lethal and Elusive Enemies from Ancient Times to the Present.* 8 vols. New York: Charles Scribner's Sons, 1976.

1900: Uganda

AFRICAN SLEEPING SICKNESS
DATE: 1900-1907
PLACE: Lake Victoria, Uganda
RESULT: At least 200,000 dead, with 100,000 permanently displaced

The largest well-documented epidemic of African sleeping sickness occurred between 1900 and 1907 on the northern shores of Lake Victoria in Uganda, where two-thirds of the 300,000 inhabitants of the area died and the rest were relocated to remove them from danger. Between 1896 and 1906, an estimated 500,000 had succumbed to the disease in the Congo River basin, although documentation is weak. For the rest of the twentieth century, eruptions of sleeping sickness occurred across tropical Africa, although none were on the scale of either of these early events, which were particularly devastating because the illness was not well understood and treatments had not been developed. While modern treatments are fully effective, especially if diagnosed early, the development of drug resistance, as well as inadequate surveillance and treatment, carry the potential for major future epidemics among the 55 million people at risk for the disease.

Sleeping sickness is caused by one of several trypanosome species transmitted by tsetse flies between humans, with wild and domesticated animals serving as reservoirs of the disease. Trypanosomes are protozoa, or single-celled organisms, whose life cycle can require a vertebrate and an invertebrate host. Those that cause sleeping sickness need the bloodstream of a person or animal and tsetse flies, which inhabit the vast region of tropical Africa between the Sahara Desert on the north and the Kalahari Desert on the south. These insects do not survive in arid regions and are inactive at tempera-

1892: Worldwide

BUBONIC PLAGUE
DATE: Beginning in 1892
PLACE: India, as well as China, Egypt, Africa, and South America
RESULT: Millions dead

The third great pandemic of the bubonic plague began in China around 1892 and reached Canton and Hong Kong in 1894. From Hong Kong it spread rapidly, appearing in India in 1896. It appeared in Egypt, Madagascar, Hawaii, and South America in 1899; by 1904 it had reached Thailand.

Alexandre-Émile-John Yersin isolated the causative bacillus, *Yersinia pestis,* in 1894, and vaccines began to be used in India in 1897. Nevertheless, in the next fifty years some 12.5 million people died of the disease in India alone. Almost half of these died in the first decade. Indeed, plague was the cause of death in almost 50 percent of all deaths in India in that period.

Bombay was hit in the summer of 1896, where some 30,000 died of plague by the end of 1898. It then moved to Calcutta, where the hospitals experienced mortality of about 80 percent. In Bombay, 31,000 people were hired to clean and disinfect the streets. This did help to control the local rat population, but it did so by pushing the rats into outlying regions, thereby spreading the plague.

John A. Cramer

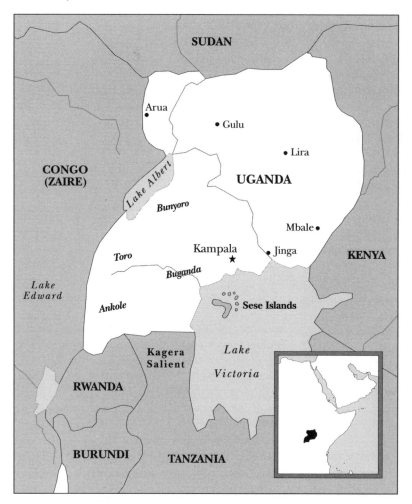

Two disease types are recognized that differ in their time courses. In the chronic form, the invasion of the central nervous system is delayed, and death of the untreated person may not occur for several years; months are spent in an emaciated and lethargic state, which gives the disease its name. In the acute form, the development is rapid, and untreated patients usually die within a few weeks or months. The distribution of both forms is discontinuous in space and time. For reasons that are not clear, some areas infested with tsetse flies have never experienced cases of sleeping sickness, while others have periodic explosions of the disease.

Well before 1880, sleeping sickness, primarily the chronic type, was known in isolated areas from western to central Africa, from Gambia to the northern reaches of the Congo River. The epidemics of sleeping sickness in central and eastern Africa at the beginning of the twentieth century accompanied early European colonization. In the Congo, steamers on the river system likely facilitated the rapid movement of pathological trypanosomes (in people and animals) to areas that had not been previously exposed. In Uganda, exploration or military campaigns probably moved people from or through affected regions to a place that had no previous experience of the disease. The resultant epidemics could not be arrested because of the lack of knowledge and the absence of treatments. In Uganda, the survivors were moved away from the tsetse breeding grounds to protect them from the disease. The initial hope was that, after several years without a human host, the disease-causing trypanosome would disappear from tsetse flies in these areas and people could return. However, subsequent experiments have shown that trypanosomes can retain their virulence against humans despite more than twenty years of passage through animal hosts.

tures below 60 degrees Fahrenheit. While several species of tsetse fly are recognized, with some preferring the rain forest and others the savanna, all depend on vertebrate blood for nourishment. For millions of years, tsetse flies have been in Africa, feeding on the blood of wild animals and facilitating the life cycle of trypanosomes that depend on both. Wild animals have developed a tolerance for the parasites and do not appear to be deleteriously affected by their presence in the circulation. Humans, as relatively recent arrivals on earth, have little natural resistance and can die from trypanosomiasis infection transmitted by the tsetse fly.

In sleeping sickness, trypanosomes reproduce in the blood, leading to anemia, and invade the central nervous system, causing coma and death. The first clinical signs, which include swollen lymph glands, are fairly general, making early diagnosis difficult.

Starting in 1905, drugs were developed to treat patients infected with pathogenic trypanosomes. Four drugs were available at the end of the twentieth century, with treatment more effective early in the disease process, before the central nervous system is affected. However, trypanosomes are developing resistance to these drugs, and new drugs are not being developed because of the relatively small number of affected persons and their poverty. This may be setting the stage for an epidemic of drug-resistant African sleeping sickness. In 1996, 30,000 new cases of the disease were reported. Actual cases were probably over 300,000, and the population at risk numbers 55 million. Limited financial resources in the region, and their mismanagement, are exacerbating the potential for future major epidemics. Developing vaccines against the disease has not been successful because trypanosomes assume a variety of forms during their life cycle within vertebrate hosts. Eradicating the tsetse fly would end the scourge of African sleeping sickness, as well as a more widespread trypanosomiasis that affects domesticated livestock and severely limits animal agriculture in much of tropical Africa. While tsetse flies have been eliminated from some isolated or peripheral areas, their complete elimination would be a monumental biological and logistical challenge in an impoverished region of the world.

James L. Robinson

FOR FURTHER INFORMATION:

Carpenter, G. D. Hale. *A Naturalist on Lake Victoria, with an Account of Sleeping Sickness and the Tse-tse Fly.* New York: E. P. Dutton, 1920.

Duggan, A. J. "An Historical Perspective." In *The African Trypanosomiases*, edited by H. W. Mulligan. London: George Allen and Unwin, 1970.

Jordan, Anthony M. *Trypanosomiasis Control and African Rural Development.* New York: Longman, 1986.

Langlands, B. W. *Sleeping Sickness Epidemic of Uganda 1900-1920: A Study in Historical Geography.* Kampala, Uganda: Makerere University Press, 1967.

Musere, Jonathan. *African Sleeping Sickness: Political Ecology, Colonialism, and Control in Uganda.* Lewiston, N.Y.: Edwin Mellen Press, 1990.

Oswald, Felix. *Alone in the Sleeping Sickness Country.* London: Kegan Paul, Trench, Trubner, 1915.

Soff, Harvey G. *Sleeping Sickness in the Lake Victoria Region of British East Africa, 1900-1915.* Syracuse, N.Y.: Maxwell Graduate School of Citizenship and Public Affairs, 1968.

1900: New York State

TYPHOID FEVER
DATE: 1900-1915
PLACE: New York State
RESULT: 3 dead, more than 50 ill from contact with "Typhoid Mary" Mallon

Mary Mallon, an Irish immigrant who served as a cook for various families and institutions, unwittingly spread typhoid fever to more than 50 people between the years of 1900 and 1915, and three deaths are linked directly to her.

Typhoid fever is a highly infectious disease caused by *Salmonella typhosa* bacteria and spread through contaminated food and water. Typhoid fever was a common epidemic until the early twentieth century, due to poor sewage and sanitation methods. The most common way of contraction was through contaminated drinking water. Symptoms include a high fever lasting a few weeks, pains, headache, cough, drowsiness, and chills. The bacteria lodge in the small intestine, where they proliferate and in severe cases may perforate the intestine or cause hemorrhaging. Typhoid ranges from mild, flulike symptoms to severe cases resulting in death within one or two weeks.

About 3 percent of individuals who have suffered from typhoid become carriers, which means that although they appear healthy and show no symptoms of the disease, their bodies contain the bacteria and they may spread it to others. Such is the case with Mallon, who either had typhoid before she could remember or had such a slight case in her early life that she thought it to be a minor influenza.

Mary Mallon was born in Ireland in 1869 and immigrated to the United States in 1883, where she began working as a domestic servant, cooking and cleaning in the homes of wealthy New Yorkers. In the summer of 1906, Mallon was working as a cook for a New York banker. When 6 of the 11 members of the household contracted typhoid fever, the house's owner hired George Soper, a sanitary engineer and specialist in typhoid fever outbreaks, to investigate the possible cause. Soper determined that Mallon had begun working for the family shortly before the outbreak began. He traced Mallon's work history back through eight families she had worked for and discovered that seven of the families had been affected by the fever. All totaled, Soper found 22 cases

Development of Typhoid Fever

Salmonella typhi bacteria enter digestive system after ingestion of contaminated water or food.

Phase 1 (2 weeks):
Bacteria invade intestines' lymphoid tissue. Usually no symptoms.

Phase 2 (10 days):
Bacteria invade bloodstream often causing toxemia. Fever, immune system response.

Phase 3:
Bacteria are localized in intestines' lymphoid tissue, mesenteric nodes, gallbladder, liver, spleen, occasionally bones. Lesions are caused by local tissue death (necrosis).

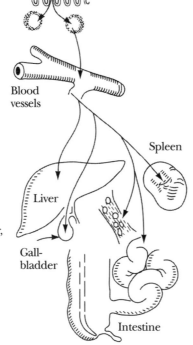

Blood vessels

Spleen

Liver

Gall-bladder

Intestine

and Mallon was moved to an isolated cottage on North Brother Island, close to the Bronx in New York City and the site of Riverside Hospital.

Mallon was kept in isolation in the cottage for two years. In 1909 she sued the health department for release; the judge was sympathetic but sent Mallon back to the island. In 1910 a new city health commissioner allowed her to leave, on the promise that she would no longer work as a cook. Around 1914 the health department lost track of Mallon. She most likely had trouble making a living outside her expertise and returned to cooking. In 1915, after a typhoid fever breakout in Manhattan's Sloane Maternity Hospital, Mallon was found working in the kitchen, under the pseudonym "Mrs. Brown." She had infected 25 more people, 2 of whom died. She was apprehended and returned to the island, where she lived for the rest of her life.

Mallon came to be known as "Typhoid Mary," a term that began among the medical community as a descriptive term, perhaps to protect her identity, but came to signify anyone who is a public health threat. News reporters sensationalized "Typhoid Mary," turning her into a further outcast. Although the popular view in society declared that Mallon purposely infected others, there is no evidence to show this is true. Rather, her refusal to believe that she was a carrier was probably an extreme disbelief in new scientific thought. She denied the accusations until the end of her life, convinced that health officials were picking on her. Mallon resented her imprisonment and was extremely distrustful of the health personnel involved in her case. Her feces and urine were tested frequently, at times on several occasions per week, which added to her reportedly sullen and irritable nature with doctors.

of typhoid that he believed were linked to contact with food that Mallon had prepared.

The idea of a disease carrier was new to doctors and scientists, and the general public knew nothing about it. Soper believed Mallon to be a carrier but needed laboratory proof of his hypothesis. He approached Mallon, telling her she was spreading typhoid fever through the food she prepared, and that samples of her urine, blood, and feces were needed for testing. Mallon refused, and after further unsuccessful attempts the New York City Health Department called in the police to remove her. Laboratory tests showed high levels of typhoid bacilli in her feces,

Mallon was one of hundreds of healthy typhoid carriers tracked over a period of time in New York City, but she was the first to be monitored and the only to be isolated for life. At the time of her first capture, the number of typhoid cases was greatly expanding. In New York City alone, it was estimated that about 100 new carriers were added each year between 1907 and 1911, and this became the main cause of infection. New York State began following those who had recovered from typhoid but was able to find fewer than 20 of the estimated number of carriers.

The state had more success through epidemiological investigations into typhoid outbreaks, such as Soper's. Once a potential carrier was identified, their feces were tested for the presence of typhoid bacilli. If a person tested positively, the health department opened an individual record for the carrier, keeping close contact and checking to make sure carriers were not involved in food industries, teaching, or nursing. This was time and labor intensive and relied on much cooperation by the carriers themselves, most of whom were living under free conditions but had to submit to frequent testing. Some carriers became lost or refused to be tested, and some were traced to outbreaks and deaths as severe as those linked to Mallon. The problem of typhoid carriers continued on well into the 1920's.

Michelle C. K. McKowen

FOR FURTHER INFORMATION:

Leavitt, Judith Walzer. *Typhoid Mary: Captive to the Public's Health.* Boston: Beacon Press, 1996.

1916: United States

POLIO

DATE: 1916
PLACE: 26 states, pariculary New York
RESULT: At least 7,000 deaths, 27,000 reported cases

Nearly all Americans coming of age during the first half of the twentieth century have childhood memories that include the apprehension each summer brought, when polio epidemics could begin without warning, leaving many paralyzed or dead in their wake. Although poliomyelitis, or infantile paralysis, as it was also called, had existed for hundreds of years, the first large-scale epidemic of the disease hit the United States in 1916. An earlier outbreak had occurred in Stockholm in 1887, with 44 cases reported. There were also outbreaks in New York City in 1907,

New York City and Cincinnati in 1911, and Buffalo, New York, in 1912, but none approached the horror and severity of the 1916 epidemic. Indeed, the 1916 polio epidemic set the pattern for polio epidemics through the middle of the twentieth century, both in the virulence of the disease and in the public's response.

Rate of Infection. Typically, in the early years of the twentieth century, the rate of polio infection in the United States was less than 7.9 cases per 100,000 people. In 1916, that figure rose dramatically, topping out at 28.5 cases per 100,000. People in 26 states were affected by the disease. All told, between roughly July of 1916 and October of 1916 some 27,000 cases were reported. Of these, about 7,000 people died. In New York City, the hardest hit area of the country, there were about 9,000 cases, and nearly all of these cases occurred in children younger than sixteen years of age. During the week of August 5, 1916, at the height of the epidemic, there were 1,151 cases reported in the city and 301 deaths. Many cases went unreported because the families of victims feared that they would be quarantined and unable to leave their homes.

Many victims of the disease suffered mild or no symptoms, often only complaining of a low-grade fever. However, others complained of stiff necks and backs and increasingly painful limbs. Sometimes, this muscular distress grew more severe, with the limbs becoming paralyzed. In the worst cases, the virus destroyed the nerves controlling the muscles responsible for breathing, leading inevitably to death. The swift onset of the disease, the often dire consequences, the mysterious nature of transmission, and its predilection for attacking adolescents and young adults in the prime of life made polio a terrifying word. During epidemics, horrified populations submitted to intrusive public health regulations that they never would have endured otherwise, all in the hope of quelling the infection's spread.

Polio Becomes Epidemic. Ironically, some researchers believe that the improved sanitation in American cities in the twentieth century changed the way the population experienced the virus. The improved sanitation, while a boon in preventing many forms of illnesses, may have contributed to polio becoming a typically epidemic disease. In the years before the twentieth century, human feces containing large amounts of polio virus were the most common form of transmission. Water contaminated with feces led to many cases. Thus, before the twentieth century, polio infected almost all babies. These babies only suffered a mild reaction, generally no more than a low-grade fever or cold symptoms.

Sometimes babies who were infected did not exhibit symptoms at all. They were, nonetheless, immune to future infection by the virus. Further, polio had always been a far more serious disease in adults than in infants. Improved sanitation meant that fewer babies were exposed to the virus. As a result, more adults were susceptible to the disease. When the virus struck the largely unprotected population, it reached epidemic proportions as adolescents and adults passed the disease to other adolescents and adults, often with disastrous consequences. The illness this population suffered was of a far more serious nature, often leading to paralysis or death.

Although the cause of polio had been identified as a virus as early as 1909, no vaccine existed in 1916. Further, the medical community was uncertain how the disease was passed from person to person, and they did not know why the disease always peaked in the summer, only to ease in the winter. At the time of the 1916 outbreak, popular wisdom attributed polio to wildly different sources. Many believed that the disease was caused by poisonous caterpillars or moldy flour. Others thought that gooseberries or contaminated milk could cause polio. Still others thought that contact with human spit or sewage odors might be the culprit.

In spite of popular opinion, in 1916 medical researchers generally subscribed to the germ theory. That is, they believed that disease was passed from person to person via invisible germs. Much of the general public and some epidemiologists, however, still believed that most disease was caused by dirt. If there were such a thing as germs, they reasoned, then they must be spread by dirty people. Such reasoning led to the extreme measures to enforce quarantine and isolation that characterized the 1916 epidemic, particularly in New York City.

Public Health Response. Public health officials undertook many measures to try to slow the spread of the disease in the summer of 1916. They placed quarantine signs on the doors of victims, instructed that all bed clothing be disinfected, and required nurses to change their clothing immediately after visiting with patients. In the mistaken notion that dogs and cats could spread the disease, pets were not permitted to go into rooms with people suffering from polio. As the epidemic wore on, public health officials gathered up and destroyed many dogs and cats. On July 14, 1916, New York officials announced a new regulation forbidding travel in or out of parts of the city stricken with the epidemic. Further, New York City children had to carry identification cards certifying that neither they nor anyone in their families had polio before they were allowed to leave the city.

Jonas Salk, who developed the polio vaccine in 1953, thirty-seven years after the first large-scale American polio epidemic. (AP/Wide World Photos)

The public reaction in New York to the 1916 epidemic is particularly interesting because it reveals the deep resentment the upper and middle classes bore toward the poor and immigrant populations. When most public health and elected officials attributed the epidemic to dirty people, they did not have far to look in New York City, with its large, poverty-stricken immigrant population. As a group, the poor were generally ill educated and did not wield political clout. Consequently, public officials took restrictive measures that were directly aimed at this population. For example, a New York City law required that any sick child living in a home without a private toilet and whose family could not provide a private nurse must be hospitalized. Thus, virtually any sick child who also had the misfortune to be poor was hospitalized. Since hospitals were often the sites of secondary infections, such hospitalization was not always in the best interest of the child. Even more extreme, poor children without symptoms were also quarantined, due to the public's belief that such children spread the illness to their middle-class and upper-class neighbors.

Residents attributed the large outbreak of polio in New Rochelle, New York, to its immigrant population. Indeed, the immigrant population was looked upon with growing suspicion as the epidemic dragged on through the summer. Immigrant children were banned from city functions and camps. In contrast, middle-class and wealthy children were sent out of the city for the summer, to places their parents deemed were "safe," often meaning to places that had low immigrant populations. More than 50,000 children were sent out of New York City over the course of the summer.

Several wealthy New York suburbs isolated themselves from the rest of New York, forbidding nonresidents from entering their towns. Hastings-on-Hudson, for example, refused to admit 150 families who wanted to summer there, and police intervention was needed to send them away. Some communities closed their beaches to nonresidents.

The polio epidemic of 1916, then, shows clearly how a public health issue can quickly become an issue of politics, race, economics, and class. In some places, such as Oyster Bay, a summer resort town, the interests of the less wealthy permanent residents were at odds with the wealthier summer guests. J. N. Hayes, in *The Burdens of Disease: Epidemics and Human Response in Western History* (1998), cites a study by

Guenter Risse of the public reaction in Oyster Bay during the time of the epidemic. The permanent residents, many of whom made their living by supplying the summer residents with services, did not want a quarantine imposed that would destroy their livelihoods. At the same time, they did not want to pay through their taxes for health services for the rich guests. That many of the permanent residents were of Irish or Polish descent further convinced the summer guests that they were at risk in the resort.

As the epidemic continued, it became clear that the transmission model that most middle-class and upper-class members held was not accurate. Contact with poor and immigrant populations did not lead to the transmission of the disease; victims seemed randomly chosen. Some public health officials began to advocate for the eradication of the fly, on the grounds that flies spread filth and disease. Once again, the public backed these measures because it gave them a sense that there was something they could do. Nonetheless, killing flies did not stop the spread of polio.

Conclusions. While such reactions seem extreme, it is difficult to overestimate the panic the population felt with a serious epidemic underway, an epidemic that seemed impervious to modern medicine, and to all contemporary public health measures. During the 1916 epidemic, parents began keeping their children indoors and away from crowds, a pattern that repeated itself each summer until a vaccine was discovered.

During the polio epidemic of 1916, federal health officials kept many records and statistics in their efforts to better understand the cause and transmission of the disease. It took over two years to assemble and analyze the data and to release their report. The results of the report did nothing to allay public fear over future epidemics. The report said that the quarantine efforts had been a failure, and the federal health officials were unable to establish the way polio moved through communities. There was no indication that the disease was linked to family socioeconomic status or ethnic background. The report did raise hope that a cure or vaccine could be found if research efforts were focused on those people who had contracted the disease but had not become ill.

The polio epidemic of 1916 was only the first of a series of major polio epidemics that raced through the nation in the subsequent summers. This epidemic, along with the influenza epidemic of 1918, undermined public trust in modern medicine, which had held out such hope for the eradication of disease just a few years earlier. It would not be until nearly 1960 before children would once again populate beaches and pools in the heat of summer.

Diane Andrews Henningfeld

FOR FURTHER INFORMATION:

Daniel, Thomas M., and Frederick C. Robbins, eds. *Polio.* Rochester, N.Y.: University of Rochester Press, 1997.

Gould, Tony. *A Summer Plague: Polio and Its Survivors.* New Haven, Conn.: Yale University Press, 1995.

Hayes, J. N. *The Burdens of Disease: Epidemics and Human Response in Western History.* New Brunswick, N.J.: Rutgers University Press, 1998.

Paul, John R. *A History of Poliomyelitis.* New Haven, Conn.: Yale University Press, 1971.

Rogers, Naomi. *Dirt and Disease: Polio Before FDR.* New Brunswick, N.J.: Rutgers University Press, 1992.

Smith, Jane S. *Patenting the Sun: Polio and the Salk Vaccine.* New York: William Morrow, 1990.

1918: Worldwide

INFLUENZA

DATE: 1918-1920

PLACE: The United States, Europe, Africa, India, Japan, Russia, South America, and the South Seas

RESULT: 550,000 dead in the United States, more than 30 million dead worldwide

Influenza, an illness caused by a highly contagious, highly mutable virus, has been a part of human history for many years. It has been described as the kind of illness a doctor loves: everyone ill, but no one dying. Also known by a variety of names, including the grippe, catarrh, and knock-me-down fever, influenza generally kills only the very young and very old. However, in the spring of 1918, a new influenza virus began spreading throughout the world. Before the pandemic burned itself out sometime in late 1919 or early 1920, it had circled the globe and killed more people in less time than any other illness in recorded history. Even more frightening, it had targeted young, robust people in the prime of their lives.

Symptoms for most influenza viruses mimic a bad cold. The 1918 strain, however, devastated the human body, causing hemorrhages in the nose and in the lungs. People who were exposed to the disease came down with it in under three days and were often dead within three days of their first symptoms. It is little wonder that contemporary doctors at first doubted that they were dealing with influenza at all, thinking perhaps that the world was being visited with a new plague of hemorrhagic fever.

Background. Influenza is caused not by one virus, but rather by several related viruses, which attack the respiratory system and are highly contagious. In general, influenza symptoms include sore throat, fever, sniffles, cough, and aches and pains. Sometimes it is difficult to differentiate influenza from the common cold; however, when large numbers of people in a given population begin to suffer the symptoms in a very short period of time, it is nearly always an influenza virus causing the problems.

One of the most troubling aspects of the flu virus is its ability to mutate quickly. Indeed, as it replicates itself, it makes small changes in its surface genetic material. Eventually, enough changes take place to render the virus impervious to the human immune system. That is, although the immune system produces enough antibodies to protect the person from further attacks by the same virus, once the virus mutates sufficiently, it is no longer the same strain that the person has become immune to. The immune system simply does not recognize the virus.

In 1889, the world saw the first influenza pandemic in history. Across the globe, many people suffered from the same strain of the virus. The pandemic reflected both the increased amount of travel and the increased speed of travel that the late nineteenth century technological revolution provided. As people moved around the globe, they carried their viruses with them.

Overview. It is likely that the 1918 influenza pandemic began in the midwestern United States. Many researchers believe that a widespread illness among the pig population of Iowa (a population that vastly outnumbered the human population of that state) presaged the human epidemic. Pig farmers fell ill, as did many sheep, bison, moose, and elk. Although the 1918 influenza is generally known as the Spanish influenza, all evidence points to an American origin.

Beginning in the United States in the spring of 1918, the pandemic spread to Europe and on to Africa, India, Japan, Russia, South America, and the South Seas, returning to the United States for a second, more deadly, round of illnesses. By very conservative estimates, some 30 million people died worldwide, with as many as 20 million dying in India alone.

Many have argued that World War I was the cause of the pandemic's devastating sweep of the world. While it is not possible to attribute the influenza epidemic to the war itself, certainly the war created conditions conducive to the spread and the virulence of the disease. Young, healthy men, a favorite target for this strain of influenza, were housed in close quarters as part of the armies of the combatants. In addition, they moved across the globe, pursuing their countries' political and military objectives. Consequently, they spread their viruses with them to each country they visited. Social upheaval and poor economic conditions also contributed to the high death rates in some nations.

Spring and Summer, 1918. In the spring of 1918, Europe was in the heat of combat. The United States had recently entered the war, and American troops were being rushed to the western front to fight a German offensive. Between March and April, over 200,000 troops left for Europe. These were the topics that grabbed the headlines in the spring of 1918; few noticed a flu epidemic that made its way across the United States. At that time, flu was not a reportable illness. As a result, although cases of influenza occurred in virtually every corner of the United States, the lack of a coordinated information-gathering system meant that health care workers could not assess the wave of flu for what it was: the first shot across the bow of what would become the worst pandemic in history. While there are few records from civilian sources, military and prison records suggest a pattern to the illness that was striking the country at large.

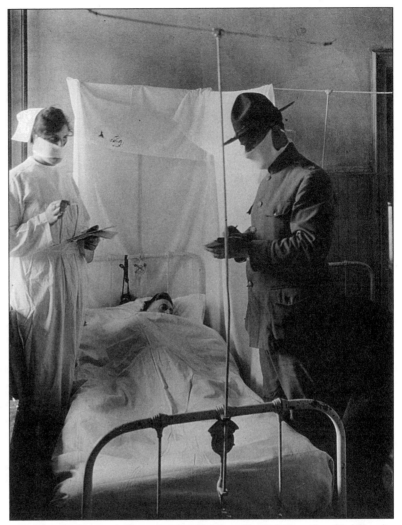

A soldier suffering from influenza in a New York Army Hospital. (American Red Cross)

First, many of the cases of influenza were followed by pneumonia. Second, the virus seemed to strike and kill not only children and the elderly but also young, healthy adults. While there was not a high death rate during March and April, the death rate for the latter group was considerably higher than one would expect.

Perhaps even more significant was the high rate of infection among men being prepared to fight the war in Europe. For example, an epidemic of influenza struck the Fifteenth U.S. Cavalry while en route to Europe. Consequently, the flu began to appear in and around the ports of disembarkation of American troops. By May, the virus was firmly entrenched in Europe. It had appeared in British and German troops in April. Not surprisingly, the German troops with the closest proximity to American and British troops were the earliest victims. It was widespread among French troops by May. From there, the virus spread to Italy and Spain. At this point, the influenza was named "Spanish influenza," not because it had originated in that country but because Spain did not censor the news from its borders, as did the countries actively involved in the war. Consequently, news of the European epidemic was largely limited to the cases reported by the Spanish, and people began to identify the influenza as a Spanish disease. Indeed, along with its many other nicknames, this flu was known as "the Spanish Lady."

Soon, the disease appeared in the civilian populations of Europe. Like the epidemic in the United States, the virus did not kill many of its victims at this time; however, a surprising number of the mortalities were among the young and healthy, a group that would be expected to survive an influenza epidemic. By June, the virus seemed to be dying out in the United States. However, it had appeared in Russia, North Africa, India, Japan, China, New Zealand, and the Philippines. In the following month, it appeared in Hawaii, the Panama Canal Zone, Cuba, and Puerto Rico.

The first cases were nearly always reported in port towns, where ships from nations already infected with the virus made landfall. Frequently, the sailors on the vessels were infected when their ships landed. From the port towns, the disease fanned rapidly outward among the indigenous populations. Roughly four months after its first appearance in the United States, the flu had circled the world. The disease, although widespread, was fairly mild. Nonetheless, estimates suggest that it had killed more than 10,000 people by the end of the summer.

August, 1918. By August, the death rates for respiratory illnesses began to inch upward in the United States, something that could not have been predicted by actuarial tables. Further, the virus had mutated as it traveled around the globe, sometimes manifesting itself in a milder form, sometimes in a horrifying, virulent form. During the third week of August, the flu exploded on 3 different continents, at 3 different ports. Alfred Crosby, one of the foremost historians of the pandemic, suggests that at this time, the milder form of the illness was homegrown. For example, English people who contracted the disease in England generally developed mild cases. On the other hand,

when a British ship landed at Freetown, Sierra Leone, with 200 sailors ill with mild flu, the local workers who entered the ship became violently ill. On August 27, 500 out of 600 dock laborers in Freetown were unable to come to work due to illness.

The Sierra Leone workers then passed the virus back to the British on a different ship. This time, the British sailors were violently ill, and 59 died. Meanwhile, the civilian population of Sierra Leone became sicker and sicker. By the time this wave of influenza retreated, 70 percent of the population had flu and about 3 percent of the entire population had died.

A second port affected by the mixing of the flu virus through hosts of different nationalities was Brest, France, where most members of the American expeditionary force disembarked. Here, ill French soldiers and ill American soldiers passed the virus back and forth. Between August 22 and September 15, 370 had died and 1,350 had been hospitalized.

Boston, Massachusetts, was the first American city to experience the second wave of the flu virus. In the course of two weeks, the flu swept through 2,000 sailors before moving out into other military installations and to the civilian population.

September, 1918. In 1918, the American army was as healthy as it had ever been. New sanitation methods and improved nutrition meant the army suffered far fewer illnesses. However, the ranks of the Army were swelling in 1918, as the United States sent an ever-growing number of young men to fight in World War I. Consequently, many Army bases were grossly overcrowded, in spite of relatively good conditions for the men.

In September of 1918, an illness began striking men in Camp Devens, Massachusetts, and then quickly spread to other camps. At first, the disease was not even recognized as influenza; it bore little resemblance to the flu that had become epidemic during the previous spring. The illness the Fort Devens soldiers contracted came on abruptly and devastated its victims. In addition, many of the men contracted pneumonia. Between September 7 and September 23, 12,604 soldiers out of a total population of 45,000 contracted influenza.

Even as the number of new cases of flu went down, the number of cases of pneumonia went up, and many were dying. The hospital at the base and the medical staff were completely overwhelmed, as was the morgue. When doctors performed autopsies on the dead, they discovered that the lungs of men who had been healthy and robust just days before were filled with bloody liquid. Some doctors speculated that this was some new form of hemorrhagic fever before they realized that it was a new, more deadly strain of influenza causing the illness. In any event, the doctors were horrified by the scope and the devastation of the disease.

The Epidemic in the United States. The influenza spread rapidly throughout the United States. In general, while the U.S. Navy tended to spread the infection at the ports and at training centers, such as Great Lakes Naval Training Station, the Army moved across the interior of the United States by rail, infecting civilian populations along the way. The overcrowded conditions on troop trains meant that a highly contagious, airborne infection would spread rapidly to all those on the train. In addition, the camps the new soldiers were moving to were overcrowded.

To make the situation even worse, the country was gripped by patriotic fervor. The United States, in need of more money to support the war effort, kicked off a Liberty Loan war-bond drive on October 4, 1918. Across the country, cities planned and carried out large-scale parades and systematic door-to-door solicitations in order to draw attention to the sale of bonds. While the sale of the bonds certainly raised money for the war effort, it also had the effect of spreading the influenza virus at a rapid rate.

The waves of influenza sweeping the country moved at different rates in different populations. The week ending September 28 marked the high point of the pandemic in the Navy, with 880 deaths due to influenza and pneumonia reported. In the Army, the peak occurred about two weeks later. In the week ending October 11, 1918, 6,170 soldiers died of influenza and pneumonia. In general, civilian populations became part of the pandemic a bit later than did the military.

Perhaps the hardest hit American city was Philadelphia. Alfred Crosby offers a horrifying look at the spread of the disease through that city in his book *America's Forgotten Pandemic: The Influenza of 1918* (1989). He attributes part of the problem to Philadelphia's proximity to Fort Dix and Fort Meade as well as the fact that the city had its own naval yard. In addition, Philadelphia had a huge Liberty Loan parade on September 28. Shortly after the parade, the virus ravaged the city. Schools, churches, and pool halls—any places that people gathered—were closed. By the

time this happened, however, it was already too late, and there is little indication that the closing of public buildings did anything to prevent or ameliorate the spread of the flu.

Large cities such as Philadelphia and New York often had shortages of essential medical personnel. In 1918, the situation was worse than usual, however. During the pandemic, many doctors and nurses had gone to Europe to help care for the sick and the wounded on the western front. Thus, the medical and hospital facilities of large cities during the pandemic were totally inadequate to handle the numbers of sick and dying.

The infrastructure of large cities had trouble keeping up with the virus in other ways. Although by 1918 most cities had telephone services, there were too few operators healthy and on the job for the systems to work adequately. Garbage collectors stayed home sick, and garbage piled up in the streets.

The most grisly problem that large cities faced, and Philadelphia in particular, was what to do with the ever-increasing dead bodies. Crosby reports that the Philadelphia morgue was prepared to handle only 36 bodies. At the height of the epidemic, there were several hundred bodies stacked up in the corridors. Furthermore, there were not enough hearses to collect the dead bodies, and often corpses would stay in their homes or on the streets for days at a time. There were not enough coffins to bury the dead; cities that were not yet affected by the epidemic were warned by their not-so-fortunate sister cities to begin making coffins immediately in preparation for the inevitable arrival of the infection. Finally, there were not enough grave diggers to make enough graves for all the dead.

Between September 29 and November 2, 12,162 Philadelphians died of influenza and pneumonia. Although the very young and the very old died in the epidemic, the largest group affected consisted of people between the ages of twenty-five and thirty-four, just as they had been in the earlier, milder version of the influenza epidemic.

The Epidemic Spreads. In September of 1918, a group of American soldiers were put on British troopships and sent, along with a troopship of Italians, to Archangel, Russia, an area under British control in the midst of the Russian Revolution. The soldiers brought influenza with them. Although there are no records of how many people in Russia ultimately died during the pandemic, it is estimated that about 10,000 in Archangel alone contracted the flu during October. As many as 30 people per day died during that month.

The effects of the pandemic were felt worldwide. As terrible as influenza was in the United States and Europe, it was many times worse in other parts of the world. In the United States, about 5 people per 1,000 died of the flu. Outside the United States, these figures were much higher. K. David Patterson and Gerald F. Pyle, in an important study, "The Geography and Mortality of the 1918 Influenza Epidemic" (1991), provide careful estimates of deaths worldwide. In Latin America, about 10 people per 1,000 died, while in Africa 15 per 1,000 died. In Asia, researchers estimate that as few as 20 and as many as 35 people per 1,000 died.

It appears that India was the most severely hit country in the world. In that country alone, researchers estimate that between 17 and 20 million people died. This works out to about 60 deaths per 1,000 people. In addition, although young men were the group most hard hit by the disease in the United States and in Europe, in India a disproportionate number of deaths occurred among women. Some scholars attribute the death toll among women to the stresses put on women by pregnancy. Others argue that the death toll was due to caregiving arrangements in India. Women almost exclusively provided care for the ill and dying. This rendered them most susceptible to becoming infected with the illness. In addition, when they fell ill in large numbers, there were few remaining women to provide care for them.

Colonial Africa was also hit extremely hard. The war in Europe certainly contributed to high death tolls among the indigenous people, for two reasons. In the first place, the African nations under European control had large numbers of European troops coming and going through their ports. European troops were stationed in Africa to protect these properties from other European troops. Thus, the Europeans brought their virus to Africa and exposed the civilian populations. Second, the demands of the war meant that there were few doctors or nurses available to help care for the colonial population. In addition, medical supplies, always in short supply in these areas, were diverted to the European front for use on soldiers there. As a result, the death figures were extraordinarily high. In modern-day Ghana, for example, there were about 100,000 deaths from influenza in just six months.

Research on the pandemic outside of Europe and the United States reveals that the poor tended to die in greater frequency than did the wealthy. The poor tend to have inferior nutrition, less accessibility to safe water supplies, and less adequate housing than do wealthier people, and these conditions render them susceptible to the bacterial infections that followed swiftly behind the viral influenza. Furthermore, there is some indication that deaths from other sources, such as kidney disease, heart disease, and diabetes, were much higher during the influenza epidemic. This may be partially due to the lack of health care in general or to the stress on the immune system that even a mild case of the flu caused.

Not only the heavily populated areas of the world and the large cities were affected, however. Often, small isolated areas fared worse than did larger countries. While the total death counts from these areas are not as high in total numbers as those from Philadelphia, for example, the death count per capita is often extraordinarily high. The South Pacific islands, often considered tropical paradises, became islands of death. In Tahiti, 10 percent of the entire population died in just three weeks. The influenza was brought to Tahiti by ship and immediately ravaged the civilian population. On Western Samoa, another island nation, 7,500 people died. This figure represents nearly 20 percent of Western Samoa's total population of 38,000.

In addition to these extraordinary figures, there were long-term, serious consequences for the nations involved. In most places, birth rates dropped dramatically. In India, the high death rate among women of childbearing age led to a much smaller number of women becoming pregnant.

Conclusions. The second and most deadly wave of influenza burned itself out by the spring of 1919. Although influenza made one more global sweep in 1920, it was less catastrophic, in all probability because so much of the surviving population was already immune. Scientists estimate that from 1918 through 1919, about 25 percent of the population of the United States suffered from influenza. The figures could be a good deal higher, however, for several reasons. First, flu was not a reportable illness in many places until the epidemic was well underway. Second, the shortage of doctors and nurses during the peak of the epidemic made it difficult for the remaining medical personnel to spend time compiling and reporting statistics. Finally, there were, in all probability, many people who had mild cases of the flu who never saw a doctor or reported their illness.

Another startling statistic to come out of the research is the number of deaths in the military due to influenza. More soldiers and sailors died of influenza than died of wounds during World War I. Crosby reminds readers that the total number of Americans killed by influenza in ten months, about 550,000, is higher than the total numbers of Americans killed in World War I, World War II, the Korean War, and the Vietnam War combined.

If it is difficult to ascertain how many Americans died in sum, it is nearly impossible to arrive at a worldwide figure. Some estimate that 30 million died; others suggest that the figures are far higher, at least 40 million or more. Even more elusive is the answer to the question of why this influenza virus turned so deadly. Researchers continue to investigate the causes and effects of the influenza pandemic. In the 1990's, frozen tissue from the lungs of influenza victims was scrutinized with technology unavailable in the early years of the century. Although preliminary reports suggested that the virus is a swine influenza, opinion would remain divided on the connection between the flu virus and the linked bacterial infections.

Another important question is why the virus attacked young people. Some researchers hypothesize that the immune system in young adults responded too strongly to the virus and caused the buildup of fluid in the lungs. Although there are no firm answers to all the questions surrounding the pandemic of 1918, there is little question that some strain of influenza virus will return every several years. Whether or not a pandemic of the scale of 1918 will ever happen again remains to be seen.

Diane Andrews Henningfeld

FOR FURTHER INFORMATION:

Collier, Richard. *The Plague of the Spanish Lady: The Influenza Pandemic of 1918-1919.* New York: Atheneum, 1974.

Crosby, Alfred W. *America's Forgotten Pandemic: The Influenza of 1918.* Cambridge, England: Cambridge University Press, 1989.

Fincher, Jack. "America's Deadly Rendezvous with the 'Spanish Lady.'" *Smithsonian* (January, 1989): 130-132.

Gladwell, Malcolm. "The Dead Zone." *The New Yorker,* September 29, 1997, 52-58.

Hayes, J. N. *The Burdens of Disease: Epidemics and Human Response in Western History.* New Brunswick, N.J.: Rutgers University Press, 1998.

Iezzoni, Lynette. *Influenza 1918: The Worst Epidemic in American History.* New York: TV Books, 1999.

Nikiforuk, Andrews. "Influenza: Viral Waves." *The Fourth Horseman: A Short History of Epidemics, Plagues, Famine, and Other Scourges.* New York: M. Evans, 1991.

Patterson, K. David, and Gerald F. Pyle. "The Geography and Mortality of the 1918 Influenza Epidemic." *Bulletin of the History of Medicine* 65 (Spring, 1991): 4-21.

1976: Zaire, Sudan

EBOLA VIRUS

DATE: Late June-November 20, 1976, in Sudan and September 1-October 24, 1976, in Zaire

PLACE: Southern Sudan and northern Zaire (now Democratic Republic of Congo)

RESULT: 151 dead out of 284 cases (53 percent mortality), 280 dead out of 318 cases (88 percent mortality)

In 1967, 23 commercial laboratory workers were hospitalized in Marburg, Germany, for a hemorrhagic fever that was traced to the handling of vervets (African green monkeys) imported from Uganda. Six more medical workers in Frankfurt, Germany, who were involved in the treatment of these patients, also became sick. At the same time, a veterinarian who handled monkeys and his wife were infected in Belgrade, Yugoslavia. Electron microscopy work determined that the disease agent was an unusual-looking ribonucleic acid virus. It had a unique, slender filamentous comma shape or branched shape and caused 23 percent mortality. As of 1999 there were only three detected recurrences of this disease after its discovery. However, a serologically distinct but related virus with similar effects, now known as Ebola hemorrhagic fever (EHF), was identified during two almost simultaneous epidemics during 1976.

The diseases begin four to sixteen days after infection as an increasingly severe influenza-like illness, with high fever, headaches, chest pains, and weakness for about two days. This is followed in the majority of

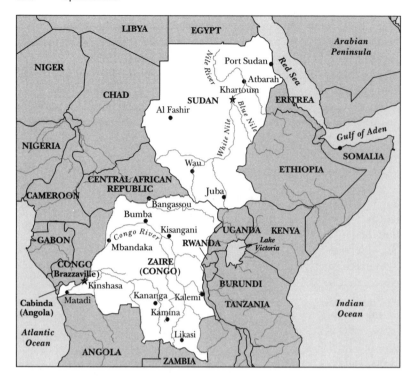

Another storekeeper who worked with the deceased storekeeper entered the hospital on July 12 and died July 14. His wife took ill and died on July 19. Another factory worker employed in the cloth room next to the store where the two deceased employees worked became sick on July 18, entered the hospital on July 24, and died on July 27. None of the men lived near each other nor socialized together, and their lives were very different. Eventually associates of the third employee became ill, and one individual who managed the jazz club, a social center in Nzara, journeyed to the Maridi hospital, where he died. Forty-eight cases and 27 deaths in Nzara could be traced to the third employee. By July, September, and October, additional factory employees were getting sick but could not be tied directly to previously infected individuals. Most were cared for by family members in isolated homesteads. This helped limit the spread of the disease.

The individual who died in Maridi was cared for by close friends and several hospital employees, all of whom came down with the fever. They were cared for by others, who managed to spread the disease to various regions around the Maridi township. An additional source of infection arrived when a nurse from Nzara came in for treatment. Many of the hospital staff were also infected.

By the time the World Health Organization (WHO) team arrived in Maridi on October 29, the situation was dire there but improving in Nzara. The Maridi hospital was virtually emptied of patients; 33 of the 61 on the nursing staff had died, and 1 doctor had developed the disease. Eight additional people associated with hospital maintenance also died. Thus, the local community viewed the hospital as the source of their woes. Isolation measures were quickly adopted, and protective clothing was distributed within the hospital.

Five teams of 7 individuals each, including schoolteachers and older school boys led by a public health official, were to visit every homestead and identify in-

cases by severe diarrhea, vomiting, dry throat, cough, and rash. Bleeding from body openings is very common, and patients can become aggressive and difficult to manage. The virus reaches high levels in the blood and other body fluids, and the resulting tissue infections are so extensive that organ damage can be widespread. Within seven to ten days the patient is severely exhausted and dehydrated and often dies of shock. The natural animal reservoir for this virus is not known, and human-to-human transmission mostly results from close, intimate contact. There is presently no known treatment.

Sudan. The epidemic started in Nzara township, where most residents live in mud-walled, thatched-roof houses in the thick woodlands adjacent to the African rain-forest zone. The first persons infected with Ebola hemorrhagic fever are believed to be three employees of a cotton factory, part of an agricultural cooperative, in Nzara; local raw cotton is converted to cloth by the 455 employees of this factory. A factory storekeeper became ill on June 27, 1976, with a high fever, headache, and chest pains. He bled from the nose and mouth and had bloody diarrhea by the fifth day, was hospitalized in Nzara on June 30, and died on July 6. His brother nursed him and also became sick but recovered after two weeks.

fected individuals in the community, who were then requested to come to the hospital. If they preferred to stay at home, relatives were warned to restrict contact with the patient. Funeral rituals also hastened the spread of the disease because ritual called for the body being prepared for burial by removing all food and excreta by hand. Local leaders were apprised of the situation, and they encouraged people to bring their dead to Maridi, where medical personnel would cleanse the bodies. Their support accelerated the work of the surveillance teams, which expanded their efforts to include a 30-mile radius around Maridi by November 17.

The final count of 284 cases was distributed as 67 in Nzara, 213 in Maridi, 3 in Tembura, and 1 in Juba. Epidemiological analysis indicated that Nzara was the source of the epidemic, and the cotton factory was studied most intensively. Infections developed in the cloth room and nearby store, the weaving areas, and the drawing-in areas only. There were no infections in the spinning area, where most of the employees worked.

Zaire. The focus of the epidemic in Zaire was in a region where more than three-quarters of the 275,000 people of the Bumba zone live in villages with fewer than 5,000 people. This region is part of the middle Congo River basin and is largely a tropical rain forest. The Yambuku Catholic Mission was founded by Belgian missionaries in 1935 and provided medicines to a region of about 60,000 people in the Yandongi collectivity (county). In 1976 there were 120 beds supervised by a medical staff of seventeen, including a Zairean medical assistant and three Belgian nuns who worked as nurses and midwives. Around 6,000 to 12,000 people were treated monthly. Five syringes and needles were distributed to the nursing staff every morning for use at the outpatient, prenatal, and inpatient clinics. Unfortunately, they were only rinsed in warm water between uses, unlike in the surgical ward, which had its own equipment that was sterilized after every use.

The first person to exhibit definitive signs of the Ebola virus was a forty-four-year-old male teacher at the Mission School who had recently toured the most northern areas of Zaire, the Mobayi-Mbongo zone, by automobile with other Mission employees from August 10 to August 22. His fever was suggestive of malaria, so he was injected with chloroquine on August 26 at the outpatient clinic. His fever disappeared and then reappeared on September 1, along with

other symptoms. He was admitted with gastrointestinal bleeding to the Yambuku Mission Hospital (YMH) on September 5. The medical staff gave him antibiotics, chloroquine, vitamins, and intravenous fluids but nothing worked. He died on September 8.

Records for the outpatient clinic were too incomplete to trace easily possible earlier cases, but there may have been one individual with EHF treated on August 28, who was described as having an odd combination of symptoms: nosebleeds and diarrhea. He may have been the source of the infection, but he left the clinic and was never found. Nine additional conclusive cases occurred in people who had received treatment for other diseases at the outpatient clinic at YMH. A sixteen-year-old female was given transfusions for her anemia. An adult woman was given vitamin injections so that she could care for her husband recovering from hernia surgery. Another adult woman was recovering from malaria, tended by her husband. All later succumbed and died of EHF, and soon those who had nursed these individuals or prepared their bodies for burial also came down with the disease. The disease struck 21 family members and friends of the first patient, and 18 died.

This new, mysterious disease that caused people to bleed to death and to go crazy was soon causing a panic in the local villages. On September 12 a nun became sick, and other nuns radioed for help. The provincial physician arrived on September 15 and, equally baffled, gathered as much information as he could and then returned to Bumba, where he requested help from administrators in Kinshasa. On September 19, the nun died; by then, the bleeding illness was responsible for deaths in more than 40 villages.

Two professors of epidemiology and microbiology from the National University of Zaire were sent to Yambuki. They arrived on September 23, expecting to study the situation for six days, but left after a day of collecting blood and tissue samples from cadavers and patients. The professors also took two nuns and a father back with them to Kinshasa for treatment. Thirteen of the 17 staff members at YMH had become infected and 11 had died, so the hospital was closed on October 3. At least 85 out of 288 cases, where transmission could be traced, had received injections at YMH. Another 149 patients had had close contact with infected patients, and 49 had been subject to injections and patient contact.

The former physician of Zairean president Mobutu Sese Seko, Dr. William Close, was contacted by the Minister of Health in order to gain assistance from the United States. He contacted the Centers for Disease Control (CDC) in Atlanta, Georgia, which provided laboratory support. By mid-October medical authorities had imposed a quarantine on the Bumba zone. Village elders requested their community members to stay in their homes, and all activities stopped. By now officials were aware that there was a similar epidemic in southern Sudan, and blood samples from both locales were shipped to the virus unit of the WHO in Geneva, which then forwarded them to the CDC. On October 15, the WHO reported the presence of a new virus, later named Ebola for a local river.

What followed was an internationally coordinated investigation of both Zaire and Sudan by at least eight nations, several international organizations, and Zaire's entire medical community. The most up-to-date isolation strategies were used, and patients were attended by personnel in protective suits. A complete epidemiological investigation was conducted, studying 550 villages and interviewing 34,000 families. Scientists took blood samples from 442 people in the communities where the infection was most prevalent. They also collected local insects and animals, with no success at finding the animal reservoir.

Although geographically and chronologically close, the two epidemics appear to have been independent events. There were relatively few travelers and no Ebola cases between the two locales. Molecular analyses also indicated the two strains of Ebola were different. The Nzara virus is relatively more infectious, and the Yambuku virus is more lethal. Both Ebola virus strains were placed in the new filovirus family.

It was not until 1995 that another major Ebola epidemic occurred, this time in Kikwit, Zaire. EHF outbreaks before 1995 were sporadic and small, including 1 death in Tandala, Zaire, in 1977; 34 cases and 22 dead in Nzara and Yambio, Zaire, in 1979; and 1 case in Tai, Ivory Coast. There may have been a near miss when macaque monkeys from the Philippines residing in a facility in Reston, Virginia, died from an Ebola-like filovirus in 1989. The virus did not affect humans. Scientists continued to search for a cure, knowing that the prevention of future epidemics hinges on identification of the animal reservoir and the presence of adequate health care facilities in some of the poorest regions of the world.

Joan C. Stevenson

FOR FURTHER INFORMATION:

Garrett, Laurie. *The Coming Plague: Newly Emerging Diseases in a World out of Balance.* New York: Penguin Books, 1994. Garrett describes the personalities involved in fighting both epidemics in chapter 5, entitled "Yambuku." The political and social contextual variables are discussed in chapter 7, "N'zara." The Marburg virus is detailed in chapter 3.

Murphy, Frederick A., and Clarence J. Peters. "Ebola Virus: Where Does It Come from and Where Is It Going?" In *Emerging Infections*, edited by Richard M. Krause. San Diego: Academic Press, 1998. This is up-to-date biological knowledge for advanced readers.

Preston, Richard. *The Hot Zone.* New York: Anchor Books/Doubleday, 1995. An excellent account of the Marburg and Ebola epidemics from the scientist's perspective.

WHO/International Study Team. "Ebola Haemorrhagic Fever in Sudan, 1976. Ebola Haemorrhagic Fever in Zaire, 1976." *Bulletin of the World Health Organization* 56, no. 2 (1978): 247-293. Clear, concise descriptions of the communities, the course of the disease, and scientific data collection and analysis.

1976: Philadelphia

LEGIONNAIRES' DISEASE (LEGIONELLOSIS)
DATE: July 21-August 4, 1976
PLACE: Philadelphia, Pennsylvania
RESULT: 29 dead, 221 infected

Yearlong U.S. bicentennial celebrations reached a peak on July 4, 1976, in the city of Philadelphia. Philadelphians proudly displayed American flags on the porches of their row houses, welcoming the thousands of visitors who came to witness the United States celebration of the two hundredth anniversary of the signing of the Declaration of Independence. President Gerald Ford gave a speech at Independence Hall in Philadelphia to record the occasion for posterity. Later that afternoon, the historic Liberty Bell monument, which had been silent for many decades, was struck. Bells in towns across the country simultaneously echoed the toll of the Liberty Bell. By nightfall the excitement escalated. The light from red, white, and blue fireworks lit up skies from coast to coast.

Less than three weeks later, after so many jubilant festivities, Pennsylvanians were stunned and helpless when the city witnessed a major event in medical history and found it was again the focus of media attention. The stifling July heat and drizzling rain that fell during the legionnaires' parade added to the sticky humidity but did not offer much relief to spectators and legionnaire families lining the center city streets in Philadelphia. The veterans with the American Legion held parades to kick off their annual gatherings. The Bellvue-Stratford Hotel, a national and historic Philadelphia landmark built in the early 1900's, hosted the fifty-eighth Pennsylvania State American Legion Convention, where an outbreak of a pneumonia-like illness mysteriously occurred among a group of attendees. More than 4,000 delegates attended the four-day convention at the hotel, which lasted from July 21 to 24, 1976. One week after the convention, American Legion officials in Pennsylvania began receiving calls from members statewide: They reported several legionnaires had died and dozens of others were hospitalized with severe pneumonia. Leaders from the American Legion quickly alerted city and state health department personnel and media to the rapidly increasing number of legionnaires stricken by the mysterious illness.

The Legionnaires' disease epidemic of 1976 began at the Bellevue Hotel in Philadelphia. (AP/Wide World Photos)

The epidemic pneumonia that emerged following the American Legion convention was subsequently described as "one of the most publicized epidemics" in which the elite Centers for Disease Control (CDC) medical investigators had participated. State and national newspapers covering the story reported the link of the illness to legionnaire members, calling the mysterious pneumonia "Le-

gionnaires' disease," and they constantly pressed researchers for information on the official death tolls and progress reports on the investigation of the outbreak. Ten days after the convention concluded, publishing a brief account in the *Morbidity and Mortality Weekly Report* of August 6, 1976, researchers from the CDC in Atlanta stated 22 people had died from pneumonia caused by Philadelphia Respiratory Disease. State and city physicians and epidemiologists investigating the cause of the illness that was later officially named Legionnaires' disease were not initially able to identify the agent responsible because it mimicked other illnesses and could not be cultured using standard laboratory techniques.

Four months passed before investigators were able to find the answers and to unlock the mystery that accompanied the sometimes-fatal infection. Then, on January 14, 1976, Joseph McDade, a CDC research microbiologist, isolated a bacterium that caused the epidemic. The bacteria responsible for the disease was named *Legionella pneumophila* (lung-loving). It was difficult to isolate and culture, and the patterns seen in chest X rays of the victims resembled patterns that had previously been associated with viral infections. Eventually, in this outbreak legionellosis caused 29 deaths (various sources list 29-34 deaths) and sickened 221 people, some of whom were not directly associated with the convention.

Classification and Definition. In 1999 scientists characterized *Legionella pneumophila* as a naturally occurring aquatic microorganism. *Legionella* species are now recognized as a leading cause of community-acquired pneumonia. The CDC has estimated that 17,000 to 23,000 cases of Legionnaires' disease occur annually in America, with less than 1,000 of these cases being confirmed and reported. The resulting mortality rate, which ranges up to 25 percent in untreated immunity-compromised patients, can be lowered if the disease is diagnosed rapidly and appropriate antimicrobial therapy instituted early. *Legionella pneumophila* is estimated to be responsible for 80 to 85 percent of reported cases of *Legionella* infections, with the majority of cases being caused specifically by *Legionella pneumophilia*.

Risk Factors, Symptoms, and Treatment. Those at risk for Legionnaires' disease include people fifty years of age and older, smokers, and those with pulmonary disease. People with weakened immune systems, such as organ transplant patients, kidney dialysis patients, and those suffering from cancer and AIDS, are also at risk, as are those who are exposed to water vapor containing *Legionella pneumophila*. Males are 2.5 times more likely to contract the disease than females.

People with legionellosis usually first display a mild cough and low fever and, if untreated, can quickly advance through progressive pneumonia and coma. The incubation period for *Legionella pneumo-*

phila is two to ten days. Other early symptoms of this disease include malaise, muscle aches, and a slight headache. In later stages, victims have displayed high fevers (105 degrees Fahrenheit); dry, unproductive coughs; and shortness of breath. Gastrointestinal symptoms observed include vomiting, diarrhea, nausea, and abdominal pain. Since identification of *Legionella pneumophila*, clinicians have reported it is effectively treated with either erythromycin or a combination of erythromycin and rifampin.

Reservoirs and Amplifiers. Scientists sampling lakes, ponds, streams, marine and fresh waters, and soils have isolated the *Legionella pneumophila* bacterium in nature. Amplifiers are defined by scientists as any natural or human-made system that provides suitable conditions for the growth of the bacterium. In 1999, controversy still surrounded the exact location of the bacterial agent responsible for the Philadelphia outbreak; however, most articles listed the hotel air conditioner water cooling tower as the source.

Scientific publications after 1978 reported the isolation of *Legionella pneumophila* from human-made plumbing systems, including showers, faucets, hot-water tanks, cooling towers, evaporative condensers, humidifiers, whirlpools, spas, decorative fountains, dental water units, grocery produce misters, and respiratory-therapy equipment. The plumbing systems of hotels, dental offices, hospitals, grocery stores, gymnasiums, and homes have also been documented as sources for the bacterium. Environmental factors associated with survival of this bacterium are water temperatures between 68 and 122 degrees Fahrenheit (20 and 50 degrees Celsius), stagnant water, pH ranges of 2.0-8.5, microbiotically nutrient sediments, and host microorganisms (algae, protozoa, flavobacteria, and *Pseudomonas* bacteria).

Transmission. In 1980, CDC investigators published six key events required for the transmission of *Legionella*. The first three events—survival in nature, amplification, and aerosolization—are influenced by environmental parameters (reservoir temperature and pH, microorganism populations, climate, humidity, and biocides). In contrast, the last three events—susceptible exposure, intracellular multiplication in human phagocytes, and diagnosis of Legionnaires' disease—are clinical parameters (patient risk factors, virulence, symptoms, laboratory testing, and diagnosis).

Anthony Newsome and Mary Etta Boulden

FOR FURTHER INFORMATION:

Altas, Ronald, Jeffrey F. Williams, and Mark K. Huntington. "Legionella Contamination of Dental-Unit Waters." *Applied and Environmental Microbiology* 61, no. 4 (1995): 1208-1213. This academic article by microbiologists at the University of Louisville, Kentucky, reports that high concentrations of *Legionella pneumophila* developed frequently in the dental-unit water lines sampled.

Altman, Lawrence K. "Twenty Flu-like Deaths in Pennsylvania, 115 Ill: A Mystery." *The New York Times*, August 4, 1976. A 1976 newspaper account from Harrisburg, Pennsylvania, describing the death toll and health officials' search for the cause of the epidemic.

Chandler, Francis, Martin Hicklin, and John A. Blackmon. "Demonstration of the Agent of Legionnaires' Disease in Tissue." *New England Journal of Medicine* 297 (1977): 1218-1220. The authors describe successful culture and staining of the bacterial agent causing Legionnaires' disease in specimen tissues from Pennsylvania pneumonia victims.

Fraser, David W., et al. "Legionnaires' Disease: Description of an Epidemic of Pneumonia." *New England Journal of Medicine* 297 (1977): 1189-1197. A scientific report issued by the Chief of Special Pathogens and leader of the Centers for Disease Control investigation team following the Philadelphia legionellosis epidemic.

Stout, Jane E., and Victor L. Yu. "Legionellosis." *New England Journal of Medicine* 337 (1997): 682-687. A review article describing the origin, risk factors, transmission, and treatment of the epidemic by *Legionella* experts from the Veterans Affairs Medical Center at the University of Pittsburgh.

Thomas, Gordon, and Max Morgan-Witts. *Anatomy of an Epidemic.* New York: Doubleday, 1982. The authors describe the personal accounts of the victims, survivors, and key medical researchers whose lives were touched by the epidemic.

Wooten, James T. "Mystery Disease Search Is Pressed as 2 More Die." *The New York Times*, August 5, 1976. A journalist's account of the state and federal researchers' struggle to identify legionellosis.

Yu, Victor L. "Resolving the Controversy on Environmental Cultures for *Legionella*: A Modest Proposal." *Infection Control and Hospital Epidemiology* 19, no. 12 (1998): 893-897. An editorial by an infectious-disease expert discussing the scientific

findings of *Legionella* investigators searching for the source of *Legionella pneumophila* bacteria in hospital outbreaks of the disease.

1979: Soviet Union

ANTHRAX
DATE: 1979
PLACE: Ekaterinburg, Soviet Union
RESULT: 64 dead, 32 ill

On April 2, 1979, the first of 94 cases of anthrax appeared in Ekaterinburg, Soviet Union (now Sverdlovsk, Russia). The outbreak lasted six weeks, and 64 people died; the first death occurred on April 6.

The Soviet government reported the outbreak and attributed it to tainted meat. Western observers were suspicious because a biological weapons plant was located in Ekaterinburg. In 1992, Russian president Boris Yeltsin admitted the outbreak was due to an accidental release of anthrax spores from the weapons facility; maintenance workers apparently neglected to replace a critical filter. Victims, including livestock, all lived directly downwind of the plant. The incident would have claimed many more lives, but, fortunately, the wind was blowing away from the city at the time of the accident.

John A. Cramer

FOR FURTHER INFORMATION:

Cornell, James, Jr. *The Great International Disaster Book.* New York: Charles Scribner's Sons, 1976.

1980: Worldwide

ACQUIRED IMMUNODEFICIENCY SYNDROME (AIDS)
DATE: Originating perhaps in the 1940's or 1950's, at pandemic levels by the 1980's
PLACE: Worldwide, especially Africa
RESULT: Millions dead and infected

At the beginning of the twenty-first century, human immunodeficiency virus (HIV) was infecting 6 million new individuals and killing about 2 million each year. Most of the 40 million infected during the 1990's were expected to die in the first decade of the new century. Prospects for a vaccine were poor, and chemotherapeutic drugs were too expensive for most.

Science. HIV causes the almost total destruction of CD4 helper T lymphocytes (CD4 lymphocytes). These cells are necessary for the development and maintenance of the immune response against myriad viruses and microorganisms. A person infected with HIV who has a very low CD4 lymphocyte count and one or more severe infectious diseases has acquired immunodeficiency syndrome (AIDS).

HIV, like all viruses, is unable to proliferate on its own. The only way it can reproduce is to get its hereditary information into an appropriate host cell. The hereditary information subsequently directs the synthesis of viral proteins and new hereditary information. New viruses "self-assemble" as they bud from the cell.

One of the proteins in the viral envelope, a glycoprotein called GP120, attaches the virus to an appropriate host cell. The viral attachment protein is designated GP120 because it has sugars attached to it and a molecular weight of 120 daltons. GP120 attaches the virus to the primary cellular receptor, CD4, embedded in the membranes of macrophages and CD4 lymphocytes. Cells are distinguished by cluster differentiation (CD) molecules in their membranes. After attaching the virus to CD4, the viral attachment protein binds a coreceptor, usually CCR5 on macrophages but CXCR4 on CD4 lymphocytes. Viral attachment to a coreceptor results in the subsequent fusion of the viral membrane with the host's membrane. Upon membrane fusion, the viral core diffuses into the host's cytoplasm, and a viral enzyme trapped inside the core converts the viral ribonucleic acid (RNA) into double-stranded deoxyribonucleic acid (DNA). The conversion of RNA into DNA is called reverse transcription and is carried out by the viral enzyme reverse transcriptase. The newly synthesized viral DNA is transported into the nucleus, where another viral enzyme called integrase modifies the DNA and promotes its integration into one of the host's chromosomes.

The integrated viral DNA, called the provirus, functions as a template for the synthesis of new viral RNA. Some of this viral RNA serves as messenger RNA (mRNA), which directs the synthesis of viral proteins. Full-length RNAs also serve as new hereditary information.

HIV is transmitted from one person to another in body fluids: blood, mothers' milk, semen, and vaginal secretions. Although the virus can be found in saliva and tears, it is present in such low concentrations that it is almost never transmitted through these fluids. Generally, in adults, HIV is transmitted during sexual intercourse. Viruses containing vaginal fluid deposit viruses on the mucous membranes of the mouth and genitals. Similarly, virus-laden semen may introduce viruses on the mucous membranes of the mouth, vagina, uterus, and colon. All these tissues are protected by macrophages that engulf the viruses and degrade them. If there are too many viruses, however, some of the macrophages become infected and the virus reproduces in them. Usually, CD4 lymphocytes are not infected until GP120 mutates to a form that binds the coreceptor on CD4 lymphocytes.

A fetus occasionally becomes infected when the virus passes through the placenta from infected mother to fetus; however, most infections in babies occur at birth because of exposure to contaminated blood or soon after birth because of drinking mother's milk. Viruses in the blood and milk are deposited on the mucous membranes of the mouth and throat, where they infect macrophages.

About one-quarter of the blood used for medical purposes (mostly transfusions) in nonindustrialized countries is contaminated with HIV. In Africa and Southeast Asia, medical quacks and unprofessional doctors may infect their patients with HIV by reusing contaminated needles. Transfused or contaminated blood releases viruses in the circulatory and lymphatic systems. Circulatory and lymphatic macrophages destroy most of the introduced viruses, but a few of the macrophages become infected. In some countries, as many as 50 percent of those who become infected with HIV have shared contaminated hypodermic needles when abusing cocaine, heroine, or opium.

Once HIV infects skin or circulatory and lymphatic system macrophages, it spreads rapidly to other macrophages in the lymph and blood. Four to six weeks after the initial infection, there may be as many as 1 million viruses per milliliter of blood produced each day. A person infected with this many viruses usually develops a headache, fever, enlarged lymph nodes, muscle aches, pharyngitis (sore throat), and a rash that may last a week or so. Some individuals experience an outbreak of oral candidiasis, caused by the yeast *Candida albicans*. CD4 lymphocytes sustain heavy casualties because of the high viral concentration. Typically, CD4 lymphocytes drop from about 1,000 cubic millimeters of blood to 500 cubic millimeters of blood, but in some cases the numbers may go as low as 250 cubic millimeters of blood.

The destruction of 50 to 75 percent of blood CD4 lymphocytes is caused by the massive binding of viruses or viral attachment proteins (GP120) to the lymphocyte receptors (CD4). This extensive binding of proteins to CD4 induces CD4 lymphocytes to commit suicide. Programmed suicide is used to eliminate cells that might be dangerous or that are no longer needed. This early in the infection, almost no CD4 lymphocytes are infected. Thus, their destruction is not caused by viruses infecting the cells or an immune system attack by CD8-cytotoxic T lymphocytes (CD8 lymphocytes). Macrophages are not significantly killed by viral or GP120 binding because they have very few CD4 molecules on their surface in comparison to CD4 lymphocytes.

About six weeks after the initial infection, the immune system begins to reduce the number of circulating viruses and the number of infected macrophages. Antibodies secreted by plasma cells into the lymph and blood link viruses together. Antibody-linked viruses are readily engulfed by macrophages and destroyed. CD8 lymphocytes, on the other hand, destroy infected macrophages. The number of circulating viruses goes from a high of about 1 million to as few as 1,000 per millileter of blood. This decline in viruses results in a partial recovery of CD4 lymphocytes. The number of CD4 lymphocytes may go from about 500 to 700 cubic millimeters of blood. The immune system is unable to eliminate all the viruses and infected macrophages. Proviruses are able to hide in Langerhans cells in the skin, glial cells and astrocytes in the brain, and dendrites in the testes and lymph nodes. Often, infected macrophages in these tissues fail to attract the attention of CD8 lymphocytes.

A balance between the immune system and the proliferating virus may exist anywhere from three years to fifteen years. During this period, the infected person may show little or no signs of disease and is said to be asymptomatic. Although a person may appear to be well, they are infective because viruses are produced by some infected Langerhans cells. During the asymptomatic phase of the disease, genetically diverse populations of the virus evolve. Some populations gain the ability to infect CD4 lymphocytes. As vi-

ral clones become increasingly more efficient at infecting CD4 lymphocytes, the viral populations gradually increase in number. The more viruses there are, the more binding of viruses (and/or GP120) to CD4 lymphocytes occurs. CD4 lymphocytes once again commit suicide at an increasing rate. Generally, the new clones of HIV able to infect CD4 lymphocytes cause these cells to fuse together and form giant multinucleated cells called syncytia. The efficiency of the immune system decreases drastically as syncytia-inducing HIV appear.

Although CD8 lymphocytes attack and destroy infected CD4 lymphocytes, this only accounts for about 1 percent of the CD4 cell loss each day. Most of the CD4 lymphocytes lost to viral (and/or GP120) binding and subsequent formation of syncytia are not infected. The destruction of uninfected CD4 lymphocytes increasingly weakens the immune system. The weakened immune system is no longer able to check HIV or fight off opportunistic pathogens. Thus, individuals infected with the new HIV clones begin to develop severe forms of common and less common diseases. HIV infected individuals that suffer from these various diseases are said to have acquired immunodeficiency syndrome (AIDS). Without vigorous chemotherapy, death usually occurs within a year of an AIDS diagnosis.

The diseases most frequently seen in adults with AIDS are tuberculosis induced by *Mycobacterium avium* or *M. intracellulare* (10-68 percent); *Pneumocytis carinii* pneumonia (14-62 percent); *Candida albicans* (yeast) infections of the mouth, pharynx, lungs, and vagina (10-50 percent); bacterial and viral diarrheas (45 percent); Kaposi's sarcoma, induced by human herpesvirus-8 (5-36 percent); cold sores, induced by human herpesvirus-1 and -2 (30 percent); HIV-associated central nervous system disease (15-30 percent), which includes HIV-associated dementia (15-20 percent) and cognitive/motor disorder (30 percent); *Toxoplasma gondii* infections of the central nervous system (3-27 percent); cytomegalovirus (CMV) infections of the intestines and eyes induced by human herpesvirus-5 (10-25 percent) and CMV pneumonia (6 percent); bacterial pneumonias (20 percent); shingles or varicella-zoster virus, induced by human herpesvirus-3 (15 percent); *Cryptosporidium*-caused diarrhea (10 percent); and *Cryptococcus neoformans*-induced meningitis (5 percent) and pneumonia (1 percent). The percent infected varies significantly when different populations are considered. For example, about 5 percent of persons who acquire HIV through intravenous drug abuse also become infected by human herpesvirus-8, whereas more than 30 percent of those who acquire HIV through sexual intercourse become infected with human herpesvirus-8. This accounts for the higher incidence of Kaposi's sarcoma in male homosexuals with AIDS as compared to intravenous drug abusers with the disease.

Origins. A growing body of evidence suggests that the virus responsible for the AIDS pandemic appeared in the 1940's or 1950's in one of the African countries dominated by rain forests and chimpanzees: Cameroon, Gabon, Congo, or Zaire (now Democratic Republic of Congo). HIV-1 arose when a chimpanzee retrovirus, simian immunodeficiency virus (SIVcpz), infected a human. As HIV-1 spread, it evolved into ten distinct subtypes, designated MA through MJ. The viruses responsible for the AIDS pandemic belong to the "major" group of HIV-1, designated HIV-1:M. One of twelve hundred frozen blood samples taken in 1959 from a native of Zaire was positive for antibodies against HIV-1 and contained a portion of the viral hereditary information. Analysis of this information suggests that the virus existed just after HIV-1 began to diverge into distinct subtypes. The 1959 virus is most closely related to HIV-1:MD subtype but is also very closely related to HIV-1:MB and HIV-1:MF.

During the early 1970's, some of the evolving subtypes became established in prostitutes along the highways that link Zaire to East African countries. Truckers and military spread HIV-1:MA, HIV-1:MB, HIV-1:MC, and other subtypes from Zaire into Uganda, Rwanda, Burundi, Tanzania, and Kenya. The HIV-1:MC subtype spread north from Kenya into Ethiopia and south from Tanzania into Zambia. In the 1990's, HIV-1:MC was most frequently detected in heterosexuals of South Africa. At about the same time, subtype HIV-1:MD spread from Zaire as far west as Senegal.

In the early 1970's, subtype HIV-1:MB spread from central Africa to Europe and to the United States, where it became the predominant subtype in homosexual and bisexual men. Thousands of men from America and Europe visited Kinshasa, Zaire, in late 1974 to view the heavyweight boxing championship bout between Muhammad Ali and George Foreman. Because of this event, HIV-1:MA and HIV-1:MB had many chances to spread to America and Europe. The

first two deaths from AIDS in homosexual men were reported in the United States in 1978; a four-year incubation period is not unusual. In North America and in Europe, HIV-1:MB became associated with homosexual and bisexual males and their sex partners. On the other hand, in South America and in the Caribbean, HIV-1:MB became dominant in heterosexuals.

In the 1980's, various subtypes of HIV-1:M spread throughout the world. HIV-1:MA from East Africa, HIV-1:MB from North America and Europe, HIV-1:MC from South Africa, and HIV-2 from West Africa entered India to begin at least four separate AIDS epidemics. From India, HIV-1:MC spread north into China and south into Malaysia. From America and Europe, HIV-1:MB and HIV-1:MBs spread to Japan, Taiwan, the Philippines, Indonesia, and Australia. HIV-1:MB became the subtype associated with homosexual and bisexual men, whereas the HIV-1:Bs became the subtype associated with intravenous drug abuse. A number of epidemics raged in Southeast Asia during the 1990's. In this region of the world, HIV-1:MC and HIV-1:ME were dominant in heterosexuals, whereas HIV-1:MB and HIV-1:MBs were dominant in homosexual men and intravenous drug abusers.

Two strains of HIV-1 were discovered in central Africa during the 1990's which were so different from pandemic HIV-1:M that they could not be detected by the standard antibody tests. HIV-1:O circulated in Zaire, Congo, Gabon, and Cameroon but infected only a few thousand individuals. This virus originated from another chimpanzee virus very similar to the one that gave rise to pandemic HIV-1:M. The small number of individuals infected with HIV-1:O suggested that it might have appeared in the 1980's, but its great evolutionary distance from SIVcpz indicated that it has been around much longer than pandemic HIV-1:M (the "major" group). Possibly, HIV-1:O (the "old" group) first infected humans at the beginning of the twentieth century. HIV-1:N (the "new" group), designated YBF30, was found in Congo and Gabon. The small number of infections by HIV-1:N and the short evolutionary distance from SIVcpz suggested that this virus may first have infected humans just a little bit later than pandemic HIV-1:M.

HIV-2 is closely related to monkey retroviruses that infect macaque monkeys (SIVmac) and sooty mangabey monkeys (SIVsm). It is distantly related to the retroviruses that infect African green monkeys

(SIVagm) and those that infect mandrill baboons of West Africa (SIVmnd). In the 1990's, HIV-2 was found predominantly in West Africa, from Ghana to Senegal. The variability of HIV-2 subtypes is nearly as great as that seen for HIV-1:M subtypes. This indicates that HIV-2 jumped from monkeys to humans in the late 1940's or 1950's. By the 1980's HIV-2 had spread to Western Europe; it was responsible for about 10 percent of the AIDS cases in Portugal. HIV-2 also managed to reach India a few years later.

Although AIDS induced by HIV-2 usually does not develop for ten to twenty years after the initial infection, it eventually kills. HIV-2 does not spread as efficiently as HIV-1:M through heterosexual intercourse or through mother's milk. Clearly, the infectivity of HIV-2 is much less than pandemic HIV-1:M. Nevertheless, approximately 200,000 West Africans were infected with HIV-2 during the 1990's. In fact, HIV-2 infections out numbered HIV-1 infections in Guinea Bissau, Senegal, and Gambia. In 1992, more people were infected with HIV-2 in Guinea Bissau than in any other country. Up to 13 percent of young men between fifteen and thirty-five years of age were infected. Many people in West Africa were infected with both HIV-1 and HIV-2.

AIDS came into prominence quietly in the United States. In 1978, AIDS was reported in two homosexual men who were suffering from multiple infections, extreme loss of weight, swollen lymph nodes, and malaise. It is estimated that these individuals were infected sometime in the early 1970's. This was the beginning of the AIDS epidemic in the United States. By 1985, 72 percent of the AIDS cases were in homosexual or bisexual men, and 17 percent were heterosexual intravenous drug abusers. These two risk groups accounted for 89 percent of the AIDS cases. In addition, about 4 percent were transfusion recipients and hemophilia patients. Approximately 4 percent of the cases were in heterosexual men and women, and 2 percent were in heterosexuals of African descent, mostly from Haiti.

The AIDS epidemic continued to expand in the United States. By 1995, AIDS cases totaled more than 400,000, whereas deaths added to more than 200,000. The numbers were getting so high that new AIDS cases and deaths per year were being reported instead of totals. In 1995, there were approximately 60,000 new cases and 50,000 deaths. The risk groups for contracting AIDS were changing. Many more heterosexuals were developing AIDS. In 1995, homosex-

ual and bisexual men accounted for 50 percent of the AIDS cases, whereas heterosexual intravenous drug abusers accounted for 30 percent. Heterosexuals having sexual intercourse with HIV-infected persons became a major risk group, accounting for nearly 20 percent of the AIDS cases. The distribution of new infections in the mid-1990's suggested that by 2005 homosexuals would account for less than 25 percent of AIDS cases, intravenous drug abusers would represent about 50 percent of AIDS cases, and heterosexuals would make up the remaining 25 percent of AIDS cases.

Although education, medical treatments, and new chemotherapies reduced the number of new cases of AIDS and the number of deaths by the late 1990's, most of this reduction occurred in Caucasians. The percent of white AIDS patients in 1986, 1996, and 2005 (projected) decreased—61 percent to 38 percent to 19 percent, respectively. However, the percent of black or Hispanic AIDS patients went up in 1986, 1996, and 2005 (projected)—for blacks, 24 percent to 42 percent to 56 percent, respectively, and for Hispanics, 14 percent, to 19 percent to 23 percent, respectively. The uninformed and poor were disproportionally developing AIDS and dying.

Treatment. By 1985, researchers in France and the United States developed a test for antibodies against HIV-1. All persons diagnosed with AIDS had antibodies against HIV-1 and were presumably infected with the virus. Persons not in high-risk categories were free of the antibodies and the virus. The antibody test for HIV-1 is important because it can be used to determine if asymptomatic people are infected many years before they develop AIDS. Early treatment prevents significant damage to the immune system, inhibits the spread of HIV-1, and delays the onset of AIDS. Nearly 100 percent of those infected with HIV-1 without aggressive chemotherapy die of AIDS.

A drug called azidothymidine (AZT), also called zidovudine, a nucleoside analog that blocks viral DNA synthesis, was introduced in the mid-1980's. In most cases, AZT was found to be useful for less than six months because of its toxicity and because of the rapid rate at which the viral reverse transcriptase becomes resistant to the drug. Beginning in 1996, AZT was used in conjunction with certain other nucleoside analogs (such as 3'sulfhydryl-2'deoxycytidine, abbreviated 3TC) that blocked viral reverse transcriptase. Resistance to the two-drug-combination therapy did not occur for a year or two. By 1997, there was a significant drop in the number of new AIDS cases and deaths in the United States. In 1998, the use of three-drug combinations (usually AZT, 3TC, and a protease inhibitor) effectively reduced HIV to undetectable levels in most people. The protease inhibitors blocked the viral protease needed for viral protein synthesis. The number of AIDS cases and deaths in the United States dropped more because of the three-drug therapy.

The first three-drug combinations had serious side effects. Some patients developed disfiguring fat deposits on their bodies (stomachs, chests, and neck) and lost excessive fat from their faces and limbs. The first protease inhibitors were also linked to an increase in diabetes. In some cases, patients with diabetes became sick, and their lives were threatened by continued use of the protease inhibitors.

Impact. Approximately 30 percent of babies born to HIV-infected mothers become infected. During the early 1990's, the number of babies infected per year in the United States amounted to more than 2,000. Treating infected mothers with AZT for a month before birth reduced the number of infected babies by 67 percent. In 1999, a study demonstrated that AZT treatment of the mother combined with cesarean delivery of the baby would reduce the number of babies born to HIV-infected mothers to less than 2 percent.

Worldwide at the beginning of the twenty-first century, more than 500,000 babies were infected each year. About 300,000 of these infections could have been prevented by treating the infected mothers with AZT for a month before birth and supplying the babies with a virus-free milk substitute. Almost all nonindustrialized countries failed to provide their poor with therapeutic drugs or milk substitutes.

A massive educational effort during the late 1980's and early 1990's alleviated the AIDS epidemics in the industrialized countries of North America and Western Europe, yet 100,000 new persons were infected during each of the last few years of the twentieth century. Male homosexual practices accounted for more than 25,000 of the new cases, whereas intravenous drug abuse was the cause of nearly 50,000. Although most older male homosexuals became monogamous and used condoms conscientiously, up to 50 percent of younger homosexuals had numerous sex partners and failed to use condoms regularly. More education might have convinced some of these young men to protect themselves by entering monogamous relationships with HIV-free partners and by using condoms conscientiously.

A number of studies demonstrated that education, drug rehabilitation programs, and the distribution of clean needles and bleach for sterilizing used needles reduced the number of persons infected by intravenous drug abuse. Education and services brought the death rates down in affluent communities in the United States; however, education, medical services, and chemotherapeutic drugs did not reach the poor blacks, Hispanics, whites, and Asians. Because these poor could not afford the $15,000-per-year treatment, their rates of infection, progression to AIDS, and death continued to increase as the twenty-first century began.

In the year 2000, four regions of the world accounted for more than 35 million (93 percent) HIV-infected persons: 25 million in sub-Saharan Africa, 8 million in Southeast Asia, 2 million in Latin America and the Caribbean, and 1 million in Asia). Each year, these four regions accounted for more than 5.5 million new infections and more than 2 million deaths.

The large number of persons infected and dying of AIDS at the beginning of the twenty-first century required massive worldwide intervention by the United Nations and the World Health Organization (WHO). However, these organizations were not up to the task of saving millions because they had myriad other agendas and lacked the tremendous amounts of money needed for education, medical services, and drugs to inhibit HIV.

The Future of the AIDS Pandemic. Greed and the struggle for power played an important role in the developing AIDS pandemic. Western governments, international corporations, politicians, drug lords, and rich profiteers backed dictators, civil wars, and attacks on indigenous peoples to gain control of cheap labor, markets, and natural resources (land, wood, water, and precious metals). Western governments and corporations are particularly interested in markets. For example, in the late 1990's, forty-one international pharmaceutical companies blocked attempts by African countries to make or obtain inexpensive chemotherapeutic drugs to treat the growing number of HIV-infected persons. These companies were protecting their drug patents and royalties worth billions of dollars. The U.S. government, in support of these companies, gave South Africa a sample of what would happen if they violated

U.S. intellectual property rights; the U.S. government denied preferential tariff treatment for a number of South African imports and restricted foreign aid to the country.

Nearly all the 40 million persons infected by HIV during the 1990's were expected to experience severe illnesses and painful deaths during the first ten years of the twenty-first century because they lacked the money for treatment. Secondary diseases from those dying of AIDS may spread and cause numerous localized epidemics that will further stress medical services. If anything substantial is to be done to save the uneducated and poor of the world from AIDS, everyone must realize how those in positions of power in the world are involved in the AIDS pandemic.

Jaime S. Colome

FOR FURTHER INFORMATION:

"Defeating AIDS: What Will It Take?" *Scientific American* 279, no. 1 (July, 1998): 81-107. This special report on AIDS contains nine papers written by various experts, including "HIV 1998: The Global Picture," "Improving HIV Therapy," "Preventing HIV Infection," and "Coping with HIV's Ethical Dilemmas." These papers contain excellent figures illustrating the extent of the AIDS pandemic and a discussion of the ethical dilemma that most people infected with HIV will receive no treatment because the drugs are too expensive.

Gao, Feng, et al. "Origin of HIV-1 in the Chimpanzee *Pan troglodytes troglodytes.*" *Nature* 397 (February 4, 1999): 436-440. Considers the evidence that a particular chimpanzee species has been the primary reservoir for HIV-1 groups M, N, and O and the source of at least three independent introductions of SIVcpz into the human population.

Goudsmit, Jaap. *Viral Sex: The Nature of AIDS.* New York: Oxford University Press, 1997. A leading AIDS researcher in Europe discusses the origin and nature of the AIDS pandemic. He postulates that new subtypes of HIV arise not only by acquiring mutations but also by recombining with each other. This recombination that produces new populations of HIV is viewed as viral sex.

Mann, Jonathan, and Daniel Tarantola, eds. *AIDS in the World II.* 3d ed. New York: Oxford University Press, 1996. Forty-one chapters and six appendices written by numerous authors summarize the epidemiology of the AIDS pandemic in 1996. Many useful maps, figures, and tables illustrate the extent of the pandemic and numerous articles suggest what needs to be done to quell the pandemic.

Piel, Jonathan, ed. *The Science of AIDS: Readings from Scientific American.* New York: W. H. Freeman, 1989. This summary of AIDS in the 1980's contains eleven articles written by experts in the area. The articles contain basic information and simple diagrams that are needed to understand the AIDS pandemic.

Tarantola, Daniel, and Jonathan Mann. "Global Expansion of HIV Infection and AIDS." *Hospital Practice* 31, no. 10 (October 15, 1996): 63-80. This review contains statistics and an analysis of the factors that affect the AIDS pandemic in different parts of the world.

1995: Zaire

EBOLA VIRUS
DATE: April-May, 1995
PLACE: Kitwit, near Kinshasa, Zaire (now Democratic Republic of Congo)
RESULT: 245 dead, 50 infected

Gaspard Menga died on January 13, 1995, in Kitwit General Hospital. For a week he struggled against some unknown enemy, suffering a soaring fever, headaches, horrible stomach pains, uncontrollable hiccups, and massive bleeding—blood in his vomit, diarrhea, nose, and ears. Bebe, Philemond, and Bibolo Menga all died in a similar manner within weeks of preparing Gaspard's body for burial, the preparation being a traditional procedure that involved washing the corpse. Philemond's nineteen-year-old daughter Veronique also died in the same manner, having helped care for her ailing father.

Of 23 members of the extended Menga-Nseke family, 13 perished because of the Ebola virus between January 6 and March 9, 1995. Four of them died in Kitwit General Hospital, which means the deadly virus probably lurked in the hospital for more than two months—perhaps mistaken for shigellosis, a common bacterial disease—before erupting in mid-April when surgery on an infected laboratory technician named Kimfumu spread Ebola to a dozen doctors and nurses. Kimfumu was a thirty-six-year-old laboratory technician who was responsible for collecting blood samples from suspected shigellosis cases. Kimfumu became ill, and his stomach was distended; the physicians thought he had an intestinal perforation caused by typhus. They operated twice. During the first operation, the physicians could not find any perforation, but they did remove Kimfumu's inflamed appendix on April 10, 1995. When Kimfumu's stomach remained severely distended, they operated again. This time when they opened the abdomen, they were horrified to see huge pools of blood—uncontrollable hemorrhaging from every organ. Kimfumu died, and soon, one after another, members of the two surgical teams that had operated on the man also died. The dead included 4 anesthesiologists, 4 doctors, 2 Zairean nurses, and 2 Italian nuns.

Symptoms and Spread of Ebola Virus. Symptoms of Ebola hemorrhagic fever (EHF) begin four to sixteen days after infection. Victims develop fever, chills, headaches, muscle aches, and loss of appetite. As the disease progresses, vomiting, diarrhea, abdominal pain, sore throat, and chest pain can occur. The blood fails to clot, and patients may bleed from infection sites, as well as into the gastrointestinal tract, skin, and internal organs.

Ebola virus is spread through close personal contact with a person who is very ill with the disease. In previous outbreaks, person-to-person spreading frequently occurred among hospital care workers or family members who were caring for an ill person infected with Ebola virus. Transmission of the virus also has occurred as a result of hypodermic needles being reused in the treatment of patients. Reusing needles is a common practice in developing countries, such as Zaire and Sudan, where the health care system is underfinanced. "The major means of transmission appears to be close and unprotected patient contact or preparation of the dead for burial," said a World Health Organization (WHO) statement.

Ebola virus can also be spread from person to person through sexual contact. Close personal contact with persons who are infected but show no signs of active disease is very unlikely to result in infection. Patients who have recovered from an illness caused by Ebola virus do not pose a serious risk for spreading the infection. However, the virus may be present in the genital secretions of such persons for a brief period after their recovery, and therefore it is possible they can spread the virus through sexual contact.

Epidemic Site and Sanitary Conditions. Kitwit, a community of between 250,000 and 400,000 people, is located about 260 miles (400 kilometers) northeast of Kinshasa, the capitol of Zaire, now the Democratic Republic of Congo. Kitwit, really no more than a huge village without running water, a sewage system, or electricity, became filled with fear. As of May 20, 1995, Ebola had infected 155 people and killed 97. Most of the fear in Kitwit was directed at the hospital, where the gruesome illness with mysterious origins spread slowly, doctors believed, unnoticed for months until magnified by nonsterile practices. These practices and conditions, including a lack of adequate medical supplies and the frequent reusing of needles and syringes, played a major role in the spread of disease. The outbreak was quickly controlled when appropriate medical supplies and equipment were made available and quarantine procedures were used. The same was true for earlier outbreaks of Ebola.

Birth of the Epidemic. The Mengas' experience, like the other chains of transmission, seem to show that Ebola initially simmered in Kitwit, spreading within families for two to three months. It exploded into an epidemic in mid-April of 1995 in the hospital. In all chains of transmission the virus seems to have hit hardest in the first rounds of spreading, waning in transmissibility and virulence over time, eventually burning itself out. For example, early in the epidemic a nurse at the Mosango Mission Hospital became infected tending a patient who had fled Kikwit, a ninety-minute drive from Mosango. The nurse died after particularly acute hemorrhaging. The terrified staff disinfected and scrubbed the room, burned the bed linens, and sealed the chamber for two weeks. Fifteen days after the nurse died, a young woman with an unrelated problem was placed in the room, Mosango physicians said. She contracted Ebola and died. Her only contact with the virus, scientists said, was the mattress upon which she had lain.

Physicians in Kitwit General Hospital were in a state of panic. Their patients were dying despite antibiotic therapy, and the medical staff and nuns were falling victim to the mysterious ailment as well. A tentative diagnosis of shigellosis—a bacterial disease that normally had a 30 percent fatality but should have been curable with antibiotics—was assigned to the crisis. The fatality rate from Ebola proved to be in the vicinity of 90 percent.

Aid from Belgium and Elsewhere. A Zairean doctor who arrived in Kitwit in mid-April radioed an urgent message to a contact in Brussels requesting ciproflaxin, one of the most powerful and expensive antibiotics on the market. The Zairean doctor also mentioned in his message to Brussels that the cases in Kitwit reminded him of an epidemic he had seen in 1976 in Yambuktu, Zaire, the country's first Ebola outbreak. Money was not available for the antibiotic, but the contact passed the message on to Antwerp's Institute of Tropical Medicine. The word Ebola stood out for an official of the Institute of Tropical Medicine who had been involved in the 1976 Ebola outbreak in Zaire. He told the Brussels contact to tell the Zairean doctor to send blood and tissue samples immediately. The samples arrived in Antwerp on May 6, 1995, but were quickly sent to the American Centers of Disease Control (CDC) in Atlanta. If it was Ebola, the official at the Institute of Tropical Medicine and officials from the World Health Organization (WHO) agreed, then it should be handled in the most secure facility available. Physicians from both the CDC and the WHO were dispatched to Kitwit, and a physician and a team of two volunteers arrived

from Médecins sans Frontières (MSF, or Doctors Without Borders).

Physicians and Volunteers Arrive. On May 10, 1995, the CDC physician, an American epidemiologist, arrived at the Kikwit General Hospital and surveyed the situation. He recalled that "[t]here was blood everywhere. Blood on the mattresses, the floors, the walls. Vomit, diarrhea . . . wards were full of Ebola cases. [Non-Ebola] patients and their families were milling around, wandering in and out. There was lots of exposure." The women mourners sat on a slab of concrete walkway that led from the wards, which were full of Ebola patients, to the morgue. Family after family sat on the walkway, rocking and wailing near the morgue.

The physician from MSF later said that the hospital was in a sorry state and the patients were in a sorrier state. The Kitwit General Hospital staff had no protection, and they had not been paid for risking their lives. So the MSF physician, Dr. Barbara Kierstein, and her team decided to focus on hospital sanitation and establishment of an isolation ward. On

Children try to protect themselves from the Ebola virus near a Kitwit, Zaire, hospital. (AP/Wide World Photos)

Thursday, May 11, 1995, Kierstein and her team began hooking up the hospital's ancient water system but gave up after realizing that all the pipes were blocked and rusted. Instead, they set up a plastic rainwater collection and filtration system. A thin, plastic wall was set up, isolating a ward for Ebola patients. The doctors dispensed gloves and masks to the hospital staff.

Supplies and the End of Quarantine. On Saturday, May 13, 1995, Kierstein decided that additional help was needed, and she and her team spent Saturday morning listing essential supplies, using a satellite telephone to pass the list to Brussels. The request was to send respirator masks, latex gloves, protective gowns, disinfectant, hospital linens and plastic mattress covers, plastic aprons, basic cleaning supplies, water pumps and filters, galoshes, and tents. Kierstein commented that she had seen many African countries, and even compared to others, the conditions at Kitwit General Hospital were shocking. She further stated that the only thing the hospital staff had to work with was their brains. For twenty-six days, however, the brains and dedication of the on-site rescue teams—as well as the numerous Zairean volunteers and medical workers—continued to be their main weapon. The supplies did not begin arriving in suitable amounts until May 27, 1995.

Meanwhile, Zairean officials had quarantined the Kitwit area. The quarantine was lifted on Sunday, May 21, 1995, so as to allow long-awaited food deliveries to reach Kinshasa. The road between Kitwit and Kinshasa carries much of the capital's food, grown in the fertile Bandundu region where Kitwit is located. Compulsory health checks continued on road travelers from Kitwit to Kinshasa until the number of recorded deaths remained static at 245. The road health checks ceased on Tuesday, June 6, 1995. The final count was 245 deaths recorded out of 315 people known to have been infected.

Even as a long-term investigation strategy was being prepared that would hopefully reveal the entire history of Kitwit's epidemic, officials in Zaire said that bloody diarrhea had broken out elsewhere in Kitwit's province of Bandundu. In an area 470 miles north of Kitwit, a town called Tendjuna, 25 people had died from the ailment. Experts initially assigned a diagnosis of shigellosis to the illness.

Researchers have begun to get a handle on the Ebola virus's high pathogenicity. Research work at the University of Michigan Medical Center in Ann Arbor reports results suggesting that the virus uses different versions of the same glycoprotein—a protein with sugar groups attached—to wage a two-pronged attack on the body. One glycoprotein, secreted by the virus, seems to paralyze the immune system response that should fight it off, while the other, which stays bound to Ebola, homes in on the endothelial cells lining the interior of blood vessels, helping the virus infect and damage them.

It seems that as Ebola invades and subverts the cells' genetic machinery to make more of itself, it also damages the endothelial cells, making blood vessels leaky and weak. The patient first bleeds and then goes into shock as failing blood pressure leaves the circulatory systems unable to pump blood to vital organs. Long before their immune systems can mount an antibody response—a process that can take weeks—most Ebola victims bleed to death. If confirmed in infected animals and humans, the findings suggest that these glycoproteins could be targets for anti-Ebola vaccines as well as for drugs that treat Ebola infections. A prototype vaccine, which has shown promising results in guinea pigs, was developed at the end of the twentieth century.

Dana P. McDermott

FOR FURTHER INFORMATION:

Centers for Disease Control and Prevention. "Outbreak of Ebola Viral Hemorrhagic Fever—Zaire, 1995." *Morbidity and Mortality Weekly Report* 44 (1995): 381-382.

———. "Update: Outbreak of Ebola Viral Hemorrhagic Fever—Zaire, 1995." *Morbidity and Mortality Weekly Report* 44 (1995): 399.

Cowley, Geoffrey. "Outbreak of Fear." *Newsweek* 125 (May 22, 1995): 48.

"Ebola's Lethal Secrets." *Discovery Magazine* 19, no. 1 (July 1, 1998): 24.

"The Hot Zone." *Scientific American* 271 (November, 1994): 114.

Preston, Richard. *The Hot Zone.* New York: Doubleday, 1995.

1997: Hong Kong

AVIAN INFLUENZA
DATE: May 19-December 28, 1997
PLACE: Hong Kong

RESULT: 8 dead, 18 humans infected, 70-100 percent mortality in affected chicken flocks, 1.6 million domestic fowl slaughtered

Influenza viruses mutate constantly, and there are at least three types, A with subtypes, B, and C. When changes result in a new influenza virus, in a process called antigenic shift, the population is not resistant, and some of these new viruses cause epidemics. In 1983 a particular influenza virus strain, A(H5N2), became more lethal as it spread among chickens and turkeys in Pennsylvania, leading to the isolation and butchering of more than 17 million birds at a direct cost of $60 million and an indirect cost of $250 million. There was no evidence this particular influenza strain could immediately spread to humans. Another epidemic of the same influenza virus strain occurred in domestic chickens in Mexico in 1994, leading to a decline in egg production. Only a mild infection at first, within months it had become lethal to poultry.

Molecular analysis of the Mexican strain indicated it was related to an A(H5N2) virus discovered in shorebirds (ruddy turnstones) in Delaware Bay in 1991. Aquatic birds are the likely natural reservoirs of all fifteen subtypes of influenza A viruses. The virus prefers to replicate in the lining cells of the intestinal tract, does not cause disease, and is eliminated in large concentrations in the feces. Thus, these viruses are likely passed through water supplies to other birds, and probably all mammalian influenza viruses are derived from this reservoir. The human and pig (swine) viruses are closely related and more readily passed between the two species. Pigs are sometimes fed untreated garbage or carcasses of dead birds, and they have also been observed under chicken houses (as noted during the Pennsylvania epidemic), where they have access to dead birds. Contact between wild birds and domestic chickens, or between pigs and chickens, facilitates transmission of viruses from one species to another. Once that transfer has been made, the main mechanism for more infections is respiratory transmission. Early symptoms include fever, cough, and chills.

The A(H5N1) virus was first identified between March and May, 1997, in chickens on three farms in the New Territories region of Hong Kong. The infection killed 6,800 birds but was not expected to transfer to humans. A previously healthy three-year-old boy developed a cough, profusely running nose, and fever that worsened during the week. He was hospi-talized but died six days later on May 19, 1997, from acute respiratory failure due to viral pneumonia complicated by Reye's syndrome associated with aspirin use. His type A influenza was not easily subtyped and had to be sent to laboratories in the United States, Netherlands, and United Kingdom, where it was identified as A(H5N1). The boy had previously been around sick chickens, and thus blood samples were taken from 502 persons who had connections with the child or the poultry, which included his family, neighbors, children and staff of the boy's childcare center, health care workers, poultry workers, and people at pig farms. Exposure to the virus was indicated only for 5 of the 29 poultry workers, 1 of the 54 health care workers, 1 of the 73 laboratory technicians, 1 of the 63 neighbors, and 1 of the 261 childcare center contacts.

Eighteen confirmed cases were identified all over Hong Kong and included 8 males and 10 females, with 3 cases in Hong Kong, 6 from Kowloon, 3 in the East New Territories, and 6 from the West New Territories. Both Hong Kong and Kowloon are densely populated, but the New Territories are where 90 percent of the domestic poultry farms are located. Except for 4 cases in 1 family, none of the infected individuals could be connected. Ten got sick in November and the rest in December. All importation of chickens from nearby areas was stopped on December 24, 1997, for four weeks. No one got sick after December 28, the same day that veterinary administrators began slaughtering and burying all chickens in wholesale and retail settings within Hong Kong. It was the beginning of the influenza season in Hong Kong, and medical personnel were worried that mixing of human strains with avian influenza viruses might lead to a strain that would easily be passed between people. H5 also kills chicken eggs and complicates the vaccine preparation process.

The mean age of the patients was seventeen years, ranging from one to sixty years. Nine of the cases (47 percent) were in people aged five years or less. Only 2 died in those aged under eighteen years (18 percent), whereas, 4 out of 7 (57 percent) individuals died who were eighteen years and older. (Ordinarily it is the very young and the elderly who are affected the most.) Molecular analyses indicate that the infected persons were probably independently infected by poultry; 7 out of the 18 had either purchased chickens or lived near chicken stalls. Thus, human-to-human transmission rates are likely very low, although there may have been a number of mild influenza infections that did not come to the attention of authorities.

The threat of another outbreak remains because wild birds harbor the virus, and Hong Kong has many migrating birds. Surveillance is key. The World Health Organization had just established a Pandemic Task Force in 1997, and this was its first challenge. Hong Kong has also expanded its monitoring efforts. In particular, live-bird markets need close monitoring, and chickens need to be raised separately from pigs and other avian species and protected from exposure to wild birds in order to prevent interspecies mixing of the influenza viruses. Mixing increases the odds that a new human pathogen will emerge.

Joan C. Stevenson

FOR FURTHER INFORMATION:

Belshe, Robert B. "Influenza as a Zoonosis: How Likely Is a Pandemic?" *The Lancet* 351, no. 9101 (February 14, 1998): 460-461. The difficulties of managing this disease are outlined.

Marwick, Charles. "Investigators Present Latest Findings on Hong Kong 'Bird Flu' to the FDA." *Journal of the American Medical Association* 279, no. 9 (March 4, 1998): 643-644. A succinct but detailed description and discussion of this epidemic.

Webster, Robert G. "Influenza: An Emerging Disease." *Emerging Infectious Diseases* 4, no. 3 (1998): 436-441. He provides a brief overview of the interrelationships of humans and their domestic animals relative to the spread and maintenance of influenza.

_____. "Influenza: An Emerging Microbial Pathogen." In *Emerging Infections*, edited by Richard M. Krause. New York: Academic Press, 1998. An excellent overview of the biology and ecology of influenza for more advanced readers.

1999: New York

ENCEPHALITIS

DATE: August-September, 1999

PLACE: Primarily New York; also New Jersey and Connecticut

RESULT: 7 dead, 56 confirmed or probable cases

The first cases of a suspected encephalitis outbreak were reported to the New York City Department of Health on August 23, 1999. Upon investigation, offi-

The Department of Public Works sprays insecticide in Shirley, New York, to kill mosquitoes carrying encephalitis. (AP/Wide World Photos)

cials found an initial cluster of eight cases in a 4-square-mile area of northern Queens. Based upon antibody studies using serum samples from patients, the original diagnosis was an outbreak of St. Louis encephalitis (SLE), with mosquitoes being the likely vector of the virus. On September 3, aerial and ground applications of insecticides were carried out to limit the size of the mosquito population.

Simultaneously with the outbreak among city residents, health officials observed a large incidence of mortality among local birds, primarily crows. Several exotic birds at the Bronx Zoo also died suddenly. Tissues obtained from the dead animals were sent to the Centers for Disease Control and Prevention (CDC) in Atlanta for analysis. On September 23, the CDC reported that the birds had died from an infection by West Nile virus, a virus similar to that which causes SLE. At the same time, specimens from human brain tissue were used to confirm that the encephalitis outbreak among the New York residents was due to the same virus. The presence of the virus was subsequently confirmed in a wide array of birds, including robins, ducks, and a bald eagle.

West Nile virus had originally been isolated in the West Nile region of Uganda. Though outbreaks have been common in Africa and the Middle East, the disease had never before been observed in the Western Hemisphere. The insect-borne nature of the virus was confirmed when the virus was found in mosquitoes in the New York area. It is unclear exactly how the virus appeared in the United States, but suspicion falls on the movement of migrating birds that may have carried the virus.

During September, intensive application of insecticides was carried out in the tristate area. It was recommended that people limit outdoor activity and avoid exposing skin when outdoors. The last reported onset of human infection was September 22; no human cases were reported outside of the New York City area, although one Canadian citizen developed the disease following a visit to the city. The danger associated with this epidemic was expected to subside following the first frost, but in July of 2000, birds were discovered carrying the West Nile virus in the New York City area. Trucks began spraying insecticide immediately, hoping that early action would prevent the spread of the virus from mosquitoes to humans.

Richard Adler

FOR FURTHER INFORMATION:

Allen, Mike. "Scientists Detect Encephalitis at 2 Connecticut Sites." *The New York Times*, September 22, 1999, p. B1.

Steinhauer, Jennifer. "African Virus May Be Culprit in Mosquito-Borne Illnesses." *The New York Times*, September 25, 1999, p. Al.

———. "Outbreak of Virus in New York Much Broader than Suspected." *The New York Times*, September 28, 1999, p. Al.

"Update: West Nile Virus Encephalitis—New York, 1999." *Morbidity and Mortality Weekly Report* 48 (1999): 944-955.

Explosions

(AP/Wide World Photos)

The detonation of pipes or storage tanks containing fuel and grain dust in silos occurs with little warning and often in densely populated areas, so that the explosions have devastating, although localized, effects on life and property.

FACTORS INVOLVED: Chemical reactions, human activity
REGIONS AFFECTED: Cities, towns

SCIENCE

For an explosion to occur, three conditions must exist. First, a fuel must be present in sufficiently concentrated form. Industrial society is awash with volatile materials—the hydrocarbons of petroleum and natural gas used for power, volatile chemicals for processing and fabrication, and the residue of manufacturing and agriculture. Second, there must be an ignition source. Third, oxygen must be present, and it is, except under special conditions, everywhere humans live.

When a fuel and an oxygen-bearing agent, or oxidant, react to produce heat, light, and fire, they are combusting. Explosions are fast combustion. More precisely, an explosion is combustion that expands so quickly that the fuel volume (and its container, if there is one) cannot shed energy rapidly enough to remain stable. The energy from the chemical reactions spreads into surrounding space. This runaway reaction, or self-acceleration, produces two types of explosions. If the rate is slower than the speed of sound, the reaction spreads outward as burning materials ignite the materials next to them. The process is called deflagration, and explosives that deflagrate are known as low explosives. If the rate is faster than the speed of sound, a shock wave progressively combusts materials by compressing them. This process is called detonation and occurs in high explosives.

Ignition starts an explosion. All materials have some minimum temperature, called a flash point, at which a combustible mixture of air and vapor exists, and increasing the pressure on the materials may lower this point. Beyond the flash point, the fuel awaits only an ignition source—electric spark, sharp blow, static electricity, or friction—to start the explosion. Some materials, in fact, combust spontaneously if they are sufficiently hot, as is the case, for instance, with oil-soaked rags. Most often the fuels are liquid, but many gases will also explode when the vapor forms a sufficiently dense cloud. Fuels that explode when ignited by a nonexplosive source are known as primary explosives. Additionally, some explosions occur when pressurized equipment, such as steam boilers, rupture, although these explosions are seldom catastrophic on their own.

The most common and easily obtainable commercial explosives in the United States are mixtures of ammonium nitrate (also used as fertilizer) and fuel oil mixtures (ANFOs), accounting for 95 percent of commercial applications. Unfortunately, late in the twentieth century ANFOs also became weapons in the form of car bombs used by terrorists.

Dust constitutes a special, important category of explosive materials. About 80 percent of industrial dusts are explosive, as is all the dust produced by milling and storing grain. All that is necessary for an explosion, in addition to an ignition source, is that the dust be dry, concentrated, mixed with air, and in a confined space. Under these conditions, dust that is only the thickness of a coin is exposable.

The power of commercial explosives is usually measured on a scale comparing them to trinitrotoluene (TNT), where TNT equals 100. Most primary explosives have a rating of about 50. The aluminum nitrate in ANFOs on its own, for instance, has a rating of 57, which rises considerably in the presence of fuel oil. Almost universally, however, the power of an accidental explosion is expressed as equivalent to tons of TNT.

After ignition, a shock wave continues beyond the initial flash point into the surrounding environment and gives the explosion its power to shatter and crush, or brisance. Following the shock wave is a region of vacuum, followed in turn by high pressure—a pair of effects called backlash. The shock wave and backlash together may produce subtle but serious damage. The shock wave can knock walls and supports out of place, and then the backlash can move them back into place, but in dangerously weakened condition. The damage is difficult to detect. Heat (often in the form of fire) also spreads out from the explosion, extending its impact with secondary detonations and deflagrations, while flying debris and ground vibrations worsen the damage.

GEOGRAPHY

Explosions are phenomena of industrial civilization—especially its energy production. About 80 percent of explosions in the United States take place in industrial plants. Because most industry is located near metropolitan areas, explosions are most likely to occur in cities. Naturally, facilities making or transporting commercial or military explosives run a high risk of accidental explosions, but petroleum refineries; storage tanks for natural gas; and liquefied petroleum gas, propane, and gasoline are also at risk and are more likely to occupy the outskirts of a city. Moreover, terrorists usually target heavily populated areas, especially those associated with a symbol of power or wealth, such as military headquarters or corporate offices.

Towns likewise suffer explosions from fuel processing and storage. In addition, agricultural communities in grain-producing regions store the grain in large silos. If the grain dust is ignited, the silos explode with spectacular, deadly violence.

The arteries of communication between inhabited areas also see explosions. Tanker trucks on highways and tanker cars on railways may explode if they rupture during a wreck, and leaks in pipelines conveying natural gas and petroleum products can also lead to explosions. Human-caused explosions in wilderness areas are rare, usually the by-product of an airplane crash or military accident.

PREVENTION AND PREPARATIONS

Preventing accidental industrial or residential explosions first requires that the three minimum conditions for an explosion do not exist. Fuels must be used, stored, and moved at conditions well below their flash points, and ignition sources, especially sparks from machinery, must be eliminated. In some cases, oxygen levels can be lowered.

Additionally, the design of fuel-handling buildings and equipment can ward off accidents or reduce their effects. Reinforcing buildings, locating hazardous equipment in the center of rooms, installing water systems to douse flames, venting rooms to the outside environment, and installing grating rather than solid decks all can serve to contain, suppress, or dispel an explosion's destructive force. Locating critical structures, such as storage tanks and processing plants, far from one another prevents secondary explosions. Automatic shutdown sensors on pipelines and temperature sensors in ovens, boilers, and processing machinery can eliminate the conditions for an explosion.

Government agencies, insurance companies, public utilities, and private contractors offer risk analysis of existing structures and equipment and may recommend safety improvements. Experts point out, however, that technology alone cannot prevent

Fires started by an initial explosion may ignite any leftover fuel, causing further damage. (AP/Wide World Photos)

accidents. Human error accounts for about 60 percent of accidental explosions. Proper training in handling and storing materials is therefore essential, both for workers on the job and people at home. Especially important is knowing how to avoid an accidental ignition.

Because explosive materials are usually highly toxic, preventive measures must also safeguard pollution of the environment. Fuels—in gas, liquid, or solid form—ejected from an explosion can poison wildlife and even lead to further explosions. For this reason, thorough cleanup of a disaster site is important.

RESCUE AND RELIEF EFFORTS

Immediately following a disastrous explosion, rescue workers have three paramount tasks: stopping fires, ensuring the injured are located and receive adequate medical care, and evacuating anyone who is threatened by the explosion's aftermath. All three tasks involve substantial risks.

An explosion of petroleum products or a natural gas leak often leaves some of the fuel unignited. This can form pools or, if it is a gas, collect in sewers or low-lying areas. Fires started by the initial detonation may then ignite the leftover fuel after rescuers have entered the disaster zone, placing them in peril. Likewise, buildings damaged in the explosion may look safe but then suddenly collapse as rescue workers search for survivors. Digging survivors from building rubble poses similar hazards and must be conducted with utmost care. Debris, disturbed by digging, may suddenly settle or shift, killing those trapped below and injuring rescuers.

Most industrial plants and surrounding cities maintain evacuation plans for disasters. The plans prescribe the areas to be cleared of residents in an emergency; who is to perform the evacuation; and places to set up emergency medical facilities, temporary lodging, and kitchens. Rescue officials allow residents back into the area only after thorough inspection shows that all fires have been put out and buildings are safe.

For small explosions, local police and firefighters conduct the rescue work, while medical personnel in area facilities take care of the injured. In large disasters, police, firefighters, and medical personnel from surrounding areas may be called. In the United States, state police, the National Guard, and federal armed forces, all coordinated by state or federal agencies, may become involved.

IMPACT

While uncommon, explosions cause great damage, and do so spectacularly. Between January of 1995 and July of 1997, for instance, 39 industrial explosions occurred, causing an average of almost $1.5 million in damage each. In 1998, the 18 grain-dust explosions alone cost about $30 million and killed 7 people. ANFOs have caused some of the worst disasters in American history. In 1947, a fire broke out in the *Grandcamp*, a cargo ship docked near the Monsanto Chemical Company factory in Texas City. The crew could not extinguish it, and 2,500 tons of ammonium nitrate exploded in its hold, also igniting the same cargo in a nearby ship. The factory was destroyed, as well as two-thirds of the buildings in Texas City. More than 500 people died. ANFOs also appeal to terrorists because they are cheap and relatively easy to obtain. In 1995, a truck full of ANFOs tore apart the Alfred P. Murrah Federal Building in Oklahoma City, killing 169 people.

Because of industrial accidents, state and federal legislators enacted regulations designed to minimize the danger of explosions and, should one occur, to safeguard life and property. The building codes, procedures, and technological measures that implement the regulations increase immediate production costs to industry but, by reducing the number of accidents, save money in the long run.

Likewise, to guard against terrorist bombs, increased control of explosive materials, security in public buildings and airports, and surveillance costs taxpayers billions of dollars. Measures to protect against accidental or terrorist explosions, critics maintain, make society ever more dependent upon technology and security forces, and to some degree affect individual liberty.

Roger Smith

BIBLIOGRAPHY

Bodurtha, Frank. *Industrial Explosion Prevention and Protection*. New York: McGraw-Hill, 1980. For readers sophisticated in science, this book offers a technical discussion of how industrial products—mainly gases—can ignite and how to prevent accidents.

Brown, G. I. *The Big Bang: A History of Explosives*. Gloucestershire, England: Sutton, 1998. Brown summarizes the history of explosives and their use, from gunpowder to nuclear bombs.

Cleary, Margot Keam. *Great Disasters of the Twentieth*

Century. New York: Gallery Books, 1990. A somewhat grisly picture book (mostly black-and-white photographs) of natural and human-caused disasters, accompanied by descriptive text.

Davis, Lee. *Man-Made Catastrophes: From the Burning of Rome to the Lockerbie Crash.* New York: Facts on File, 1993. Brief descriptions of various types of disasters illustrating, according to the author, how human folly and carelessness wreak havoc.

Fires and Explosives. Vol. 7 in *The Associated Press Library of Disasters.* Danbury, Conn.: Grolier Educational, 1998. Drawn from the story and photograph files of the Associated Press, this volume, written for young readers, tells about famous explosions worldwide.

Rossotti, Hazel. *Fire.* Oxford: Oxford University Press, 1993. A compellingly written history of fire and explosives that explains the basic science and discusses types of disasters, as well as practical uses.

Notable Events

Historical Overview

Explosions occur when there is a pressure differential on either side of a barrier or when inherently unstable chemicals ignite. A few explosions are entirely a result of natural situations. This is the case with volcanoes, a portion of whose cone may explode upon eruption, as was the case when Mount St. Helens

---

Milestones

June 3, 1816:	The steamboat *Washington* explodes on the Ohio River.
May, 1817:	The steamboat *Constitution* explodes on the Mississippi River.
April 27, 1865:	1,500 die in the explosion of the steamboat *Sultana* on the Mississippi River.
December 6, 1917:	Munitions ships in Halifax, Nova Scotia, harbor explode and burn; 2,000 die.
July 17, 1944:	Two ammunition ships in Port Chicago, California, explode, killing 300.
March 25, 1947:	A mine explosion in Centralia, Illinois, kills 111.
April 16, 1947:	A French vessel explodes in Texas City, Texas, killing 581.
April 25-26, 1986:	32 are killed when a nuclear reactor at Chernobyl, Russia, explodes.
June 8, 1988:	A Kansas grain elevator explodes, killing 6.
July 6, 1988:	The explosion of Piper Alpha oil rig in the North Sea kills 167.

---

erupted on May 18, 1980, but most are the consequence of human-made structures. The startling increase in human ability to create artificial structures since the onset of the Industrial Revolution is responsible for most of the memorable explosions in history.

Among the earliest explosions that caused a significant loss of life were those occurring in mines, especially coal mines, where significant accumulations of coal gas could arise. When most coal mining was at or near the surface, this was not a problem, but as mines were sunk deeper into the earth, as happened in the nineteenth century, the risk of explosion increased. Explosions in British coal mines killed 1.2 miners for every 1,000 employed between 1850 and 1870. However, the introduction of new machinery and government regulation dramatically reduced the number of accidents and fatalities in British mines in the twentieth century.

Coal mining in the United States expanded less quickly than in Great Britain because the United States had ample wood fuel for a longer period of time. However, from the middle of the nineteenth century, coal production grew rapidly, especially for industrial uses. Between 1900 and the U.S. entrance into World War I in 1917, there were 14 mine disasters in the United States in which more than 100 people died. One of the worst mining disasters in U.S.

history occurred in March, 1947, in Centralia, Illinois, when 111 miners were killed. In the United States, the shift to other fuels in the years after World War II, as well as the shift away from shaft mining to open-face mining, dramatically reduced the risk in coal mining. Coal mining in underdeveloped countries is highly labor intensive, and when explosions occur the loss of life is substantial. An explosion at the Chasnala coal mine in India on December 27, 1975, killed 431 miners.

Among the most spectacular explosions occurring in the United States in the early years of the nineteenth century were those on steamboats, especially those plying the midwestern rivers. The first major steamboat disaster on the midwestern river system occurred in 1816, when the *Washington* blew up on a trip between Wheeling, West Virginia, and Marietta, Ohio. The second occurred in May, 1817, when the *Constitution* blew up on the lower Mississippi River. Most steamboat explosions were attributed at the time to the preference for high-pressure steam engines on these rivers, but the fascination of the public with the speed of travel they provided (compared to horse-drawn land transportation) led to much overcrowding on the steamboats, partly accounting for the high number of casualties when explosions occurred. In 1848, the U.S. Commissioner of Patents estimated that 110 lives had been lost annually to steamboat explosions since 1830.

After the introduction of regulation of steamboats by the federal government in 1852, the number of explosions dropped somewhat. Still, a catastrophic explosion occurred in April of 1865, when the *Sultana* blew up near Memphis, Tennessee, taking the lives of 1,500 people. This was the worst steamboat explosion in U.S. history. After that, as railroads replaced steamboats, casualties dropped dramatically.

The increase in the use of military explosives from the middle of the nineteenth century onward led to many explosions of munitions. The most spectacular munitions explosion occurred during World War I, when two munitions ships collided in the harbor of Halifax, Nova Scotia, Canada; the resulting explosion and fire killed more than 1,500 people. A similar event in July, 1944, in Port Chicago, California, killed more than 300. In 1947, an explosion of a Norwegian vessel carrying nitrate outside Brest, France, killed 20 people and injured 500. An explosion at a naval torpedo and mine factory in Cadiz, Spain, also in 1947, killed 300 to 500 people. The same year, on July 29, a French vessel exploded in Texas City, Texas, killing 468.

The oil and gas industry has also experienced some major explosions. One of the most deadly was an explosion on the Piper Alpha oil rig in the North Sea, July 6, 1988; 167 people died. In September of 1998 an explosion at a gas plant in Australia killed only 2 persons but shut down the entire plant and cut off gas supplies to the entire state of Victoria for more than a week.

Although casualties have generally been few because few workers are involved, periodic explosions occur in grain elevators. On June 8, 1998, a Kansas grain elevator exploded, killing 6 workers trapped in a small tunnel.

The most fearsome explosion of the twentieth century was the explosion at the Russian atomic-energy plant at Chernobyl on April 25-26, 1986. Several explosions blew off the steel cover on the reactor, permitting the release of large amounts of radioactive material into the atmosphere. Prevailing winds carried this radioactive material over much of Eastern Europe. The entire reactor was shut down after the accident; 32 people were killed in the explosion.

Nancy M. Gordon

1880: England

MINE EXPLOSION
DATE: September 8, 1880
PLACE: Sunderland, England
RESULT: 164 dead

Under the rolling countryside of Durham County, located in the northeast corner of England, rested great coal fields. Evidence suggested that the early Romans who occupied England mined and burned coal in this region. The first recorded report of coal mining, however, came in the twelfth century. In 1183, Bolden Buke wrote of a coal miner providing coal for use at the ironworks of Coundon, a town located in Durham County. In the western part of the Durham coalfield, the coal seams were close to the surface of the earth and were relatively easy to mine. Most of the early mines were located along the bank of the Tyne River.

The Explosion. Coal mining in northeast England included a long history of disasters. One of the worst disasters occurred at Seaham Colliery on September 8, 1880. "Colliery" is the British term for "mine." Seaham Colliery, located near Durham and Sunderland, consisted of five seams of coal, one on top of another. These seams were between 38 and 600 yards below the surface. Three separate shafts connected the seams to the surface. The explosion occurred at 2:20 A.M., and it was loud enough to be heard by people on ships in the harbor and at a neighboring mine. Clouds of dust blowing skyward spewed from the shafts. The first people to arrive at the scene discovered that all three shafts of the mine were blocked. Cages used to raise and lower men from the mine were fastened in each shaft, blocking them.

A rope was tied around Mr. Stratton, a mine supervisor, and he was lowered a small distance down into the main seam. Although he was unable to proceed very far, he could hear men talking in the highest seam; they were believed to be safe and were later recovered alive. At the time of the explosion, roughly 230 men and boys were working in the mine. In 1880, it was against the law for boys younger than twelve years of age to work in mines.

Initial rescue attempts were hampered by the debris in the shafts. Twelve hours went by before volunteers could be lowered into the shafts. A kibble, an iron bucket, was used because the cages were out of action. The main rescue work was conducted from

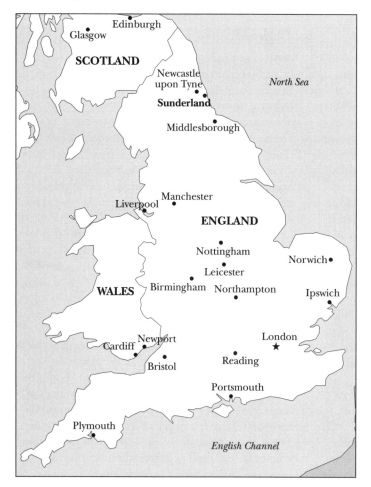

face by the kibble. Since the lamps were numbered, they aided in the process of identifying the bodies. Recovering the bodies was a slow and difficult procedure. By October 1, 1880, 136 bodies had been recovered. The final body was not retrieved until a full year after the explosion occurred.

Inquiry and Outcomes. In the seven months following the explosion, the Londonary Institute conducted an official inquiry. An official report was presented to Parliament in 1881. Two different theories were proposed regarding the cause of the explosion. The first theory stated that stones fell and released gases, which came into contact with a miner's safety lamp and triggered the explosion. The second theory focused on shots fired in the mine where holes were being enlarged. In the final report, the jury that studied the findings of the inquiry did not designate which theory was the actual cause. The report also stated that the issues of firing shots and clearing the dry coal dust, also considered a possible contributing factor to mine explosions, were best left to the mine managers.

The miners were unhappy that the report did not push for further study into the dangers of firing shots in mines and the presence of dry coal dust. Through their lawyer, Atherley Jones, the Miners Association—a union—requested that experimental chemists test the Seaham Colliery's coal dust. The miners' request was granted, and a series of experiments were initiated by Sir Frederick Abel at the Institute of Chemistry. Professor Abel amassed a document that included results of experiments conducted by him, as well as experiments from other countries. His work stressed the potential danger caused by large amounts of dry coal dust lying around. Despite this evidence, no new laws regarding mine safety were enacted until 1887.

Louise Magoon

what was called the High Pit shaft. From this shaft, 48 men were rescued alive and brought up in the kibble, while 19 survivors were brought up from the Low Pit shaft. Therefore, by midnight, twenty-one hours after the explosion, 67 men had been rescued alive. Tragically, 164 men and boys, some as young as fourteen, died in the explosion; 181 pit ponies, which were used to haul coal underground, were also killed.

Vast scenes of destruction met the rescue teams when they were finally able to reach the lower seams. Piles of stones were mixed with the mutilated bodies of miners and pit ponies. Several fires burning near the shafts needed to be put out before rescue attempts could continue. The potential for new explosions remained an ever-constant danger. As bodies were recovered, they were wrapped in flannel and canvas and numbered. The miner's lamp was placed with his body, which was then transported to the sur-

FOR FURTHER INFORMATION:
McCutcheon, John. *Troubled Seams: The Story of a Pit and Its People.* Seaham, England: J. Greenwood, 1955. Reprint. 1984.

Mitchell, William Cranmer. *A History of Sunderland.* 1919. Reprint. Manchester, England: E. J. Morten, 1972.

The New York Times, September 9-11, 1880.

Steinberg, S. H., and I. H. Evans, eds. *Steinberg's Dictionary of British History.* 2d ed. New York: St. Martin's Press, 1971.

Sunderland Daily Echo (England), September 8-10, 1880.

1884: Colorado

MINE EXPLOSION
DATE: February 24, 1884
PLACE: Crested Butte, Colorado
RESULT: 59 dead

On the morning of February 24, 1884, the Crested Butte coal mine, operated by the Colorado Coal and Iron Company, was hit by a massive explosion of coal gas. The mine, long considered by miners one of the most dangerous in the United States, had recently been modernized with the addition of a gigantic fan. The fan was supposed to prevent coal dust and gas from accumulating in the mine tunnels. Coal dust is extremely dangerous and is the major cause of coal-mine explosions. A single spark or flame could ignite the dust and cause major catastrophes.

On this day, 71 miners were in the main tunnel when someone carelessly lit a lamp; with a great roar, the resulting explosion ripped through the entire mine shaft. Coal cars and railroad tracks in the mine were broken into pieces, and flying debris knocked many miners to the floor. The giant fan became a tangled mass of steel, and more than 25 feet of the tunnel totally collapsed on the injured miners, crushing and killing most of them. Twelve of the men managed to struggle out of the devastation, but 59 others were dead. A new fan was brought in to prevent the buildup of more gas, but the rescue party failed to find any more survivors after the rubble was cleared.

Leslie V. Tischauser

FOR FURTHER INFORMATION:
The New York Times, February 25, 1884.

1884: Virginia

MINE EXPLOSION
DATE: March 13, 1884
PLACE: Pocahontas, Virginia
RESULT: 114 dead

Coal mining played a significant role in the history of Virginia. One of the major coal fields, called Pocahontas, was located in the western part of the state. The first man to mention the coal deposits in Pocahontas was Dr. Thomas Walker, a surveyor and explorer who wrote of coal in his journal in 1750. It was 1876 before an engineer and mineralogist, Major Jed Hotchkiss, publicized Dr. Walker's findings and financed an investigation of the coal resources. Knowing that both capital and labor would be needed to mine the coal, Major Hotchkiss convinced entrepreneurs to invest in the project. On March 9, 1880, the Virginia legislature granted a charter for the Southwest Virginia Improvement Company. Throughout 1880, approximately 31,000 acres of coal land was purchased for the company. In 1881, the town of Pocahontas, named for the American Indian, was established. The first superintendent of mines, William A. Lathrop, arrived in Pocahontas in 1881 and immediately began planning and constructing boarding houses, offices, and support buildings for the mine.

The mine consisted of a series of tunnels located just below the surface of the earth. The coal was removed from the earth by the miners and loaded into train cars. Although the men worked underground, air quality was controlled through the use of fans. Fans situated at one end of the tunnel operated as an exhaust system. They pulled stale and dust-filled air out of the mine, allowing fresh air to enter.

Located 1 mile from town, the mine had three entrances: the east mine, the west mine, and Pocahontas Number 1 Mine, which was nicknamed the "Baby Mine." Coal produced by the Baby Mine was mined so quickly that 40,000 tons accumulated in a few months. Work needed to be halted until a railroad could be built to transport the coal. The existence of the Pocahontas Coal Mine caused the western expansion of the Norfolk and Western Railway. The first train arrived in Pocahontas on March 10, 1883.

The promise of employment brought many men to Pocahontas. Immigrants newly arrived from Europe flocked to work in the mine, especially men from Hungary, Germany, and Wales. Men worked in the mine twenty-four hours a day; men working the night shift were the ones who lost their lives when the terrible explosion occurred.

On the evening of March 12, 1884, at 6 P.M., the night-shift workers replaced the day-shift workers in the mine. The day shift's mine boss, W. H. Cochran, reported that when he left the mine everything was in order and that there was good air circulation in all areas of the mine. He turned over charge to the night mine boss, L. M. Hampton. Work proceeded as usual until 1 in the morning of March 13, 1884. At that time, Hampton sent a messenger to the engineer who operated the fan at the mine's entrance and asked that the speed of the fan be lessened. Twenty minutes later a loud explosion was heard by all in the town, followed soon after by three more.

Although the cause of the explosion was not known because no one in the mine survived to report, the evidence of the explosion was everywhere. The force of the explosion damaged Cochran's house, which was located near the fan house at the entrance to the mine. His windows were blown in, his bed and other furniture were broken up, and coal dust filled his room. Mine cars that had been on the railroad tracks in the mine were forced out at terrific velocity and dashed to pieces against trees. Debris could be seen for 100 yards from the mine's en-

trance, and some of the miners' houses were completely destroyed.

The mine's records reported that 114 people were killed in the explosion. The casualties included a variety of ethnic groups: 65 were white, including 26 Hungarians; 49 were African Americans. Some reports listed the casualties as numbering between 155 and 166. Unauthorized men who had accompanied friends into the mines may account for the difference.

On the morning of March 14, two mine bosses entered the mine. Burning masses of coal forced them to retreat. Their report to Lathrop persuaded him that the mine was on fire. Hoping to keep the fire from spreading, he ordered the entrances of the mine closed. The mine was flooded to put out the fires. Shafts had to be sunk into the mine from the surface of the ground to provide an escape route for gases produced when the mine was flooded. The water remained in the mine for a month and then was drained into a creek that ran through the center of town. Two railcars full of disinfectant were spread along the banks of the creek to counteract the decay. Once the mine was drained, the difficult task of removing the bodies began.

Although the cause of this explosion cannot be known, mine explosions in general tended to occur when gases released by the coal accumulated, when

blasting powder was used, or when coal dust collected in dry mines. It was believed that the Pocahontas Mine was well managed and that the explosion was in no way caused by the management. Mining temporarily ceased at Pocahontas, but no wages were lost; all of the surviving miners were put to work controlling the mine fire, clearing debris, rebuilding, and preparing to reopen the mine. Collections were taken up for the widows of the miners, and the Southwest Virginia Improvement Company paid to send the wives of the immigrant miners back to the countries from which they had come.

The aftermath of the explosion at Pocahontas did not lead to the creation of new safety laws or mining practices. It did make men leery of working in mines, however. The danger was ever present. The explosion was costly in terms of both human life and financial loss. However, the mining company survived and continued to produce coal into the next century.

Louise Magoon

For Further Information:

Dixon, Thomas W. *Appalachian Coal Mines and Railroads.* Lynchburg, Va.: TLC, 1994.

Hotchkiss, Jed, ed. "The Pocahontas Coal Mine Explosion." *The Virginias* 5, no. 3 (March, 1884): 33-51.

Jones, Jack M. *Early Coal Mining in Pocahontas, Virginia.* Lynchburg, Va.: Author, 1983.

"Thirty-nine Years Ago First Coal Mine Explosion in This Field Took Toll of Many Lives." *Bluefield Daily Telegraph* (Bluefield, West Virginia), April 8, 1923.

1892: Oklahoma

Mine explosion
Date: January 7, 1892
Place: Krebs, Oklahoma
Result: 100 dead

At about 5:04 P.M. a massive explosion ripped through Mine Number 11 of the Osage Coal and Mining Company at Krebs, Oklahoma. The blast resulted from a mine worker carelessly setting off a small dynamite explosion deep in the mine that was supposed to open up a new vein of coal. The small explosion ignited a pocket of coal gas, and, although

400 hundred miners made it to safety, 100 suffered the horrible death associated with coal-mine disasters.

Rescuers found piles of mutilated bodies deep in the main shaft, buried under collapsed walls. Heads, arms, legs, and trunks were missing, and most were horribly burned and blackened beyond recognition. One father and son were found dead within each other's arms. The intensity of the heat from the blast had literally roasted away all the flesh on their bodies. Rescuers, who came from all areas of the mine field, were stunned by the mass destruction they uncovered. They tried to remove the bodies with great care, but this effort did not prevent arms, legs, and heads from being completely torn off as the victims were removed from the mine's interior. The final death count was never verified because of the bad conditions of the bodies, but it was almost certainly 100.

Leslie V. Tischauser

For Further Information:

Humphrey, Hiram B. *Historical Summary of Coal Mine Explosions in the United States, 1810-1958.* Washington, D.C.: U.S. Government Printing Office, Bureau of Mines, 1959.

The New York Times, January 8-9, 1892.

1902: Pennsylvania

Mine explosion
Date: July 10, 1902
Place: Cambria City, near Johnstown, Pennsylvania
Result: About 114 dead

On the morning of July 10, 1902, a miner carelessly set off a blast in one of the Cambria Steel Company's largest operations, the Rolling Mill Mine near Cambria City, Pennsylvania. The mine was one of the most productive in the state. It had deep deposits of high-quality coal but required a heavy use of dynamite to blast through to the highest-grade coal. Miners were required to drill holes 10 feet deep into the slate walls to reach these deposits.

Blasting was the most dangerous job in the mine and required skill and patience. On this morning, however, a new miner set off the blast. The miners had been complaining for two months about the excessive levels of gas they encountered in the shafts, but the company had done little to remedy the dangerous problem. At this point in history, there were few state or federal regulations aimed at enforcing mine safety rules. Thus, this small explosion set off a gigantic one, trapping more than 100 miners at their jobs. Many were immediately crushed to death by falling rock and debris, but some apparently survived the initial blast.

A twelve-man rescue party entered the mine to search for survivors. Three miners were found alive and brought to the surface by a seventeen-year-old miner, Mike Sabot. When he returned to the shaft he and all the other rescuers died when they encountered heavy levels of coal gas. All together, 114 mangled bodies were brought out of the mine, though the total number of dead was never known, and many miners insisted that some bodies still remained deep in the mine.

Leslie V. Tischauser

FOR FURTHER INFORMATION:
The New York Times, July 11-14, 1902.

1903: Wyoming

MINE EXPLOSION
DATE: June 30, 1903
PLACE: Hanna, Wyoming
RESULT: About 230 dead

At 10:30 A.M. on the morning of June 30, 1903, a huge explosion ripped through the Union Pacific Coal Company's newest mine, near Hanna, Wyoming. There had been complaints of dangerous levels of gas in some areas of the mine. At least 230 miners were killed, and hundreds were injured as the force of the explosion sent huge timbers shooting through the shafts. Many of the victims were buried alive or crushed by flying debris, while others suffocated from accumulations of coal gas. A rescue party found 46 miners still alive at one end of the devastated shaft and brought them to the surface. The exact cause of this disaster was never discovered.

Most of the survivors were unconscious when taken out and later reported mass terror and hysteria in the mine after the explosion. Many miners apparently could have escaped had it not been for the general panic. As some crazed miners desperately ran back and forth looking for a way out, others buried their faces in their hands and gave up all hope instead of trying to dig their way to safety. When the rescuers found them it was too late: The coal gas had taken its toll. The rescuers did, however, find 4 mules still breathing in the vicinity of the dead miners and brought them to safety. The total number of dead was subject to dispute, as mine officials had no idea how many people were in the mine at the time of the explosion. Newspapers reported at least 230 funerals in Hanna in the aftermath of the disaster.

Leslie V. Tischauser

FOR FURTHER INFORMATION:
Humphrey, Hiram B. *Historical Summary of Coal Mine Explosions in the United States, 1810-1958.* Washington, D.C.: U.S. Government Printing Office, 1959.
The New York Times, July 1-2, 1903.

1907: West Virginia

MINE EXPLOSION
DATE: December 6, 1907
PLACE: Monongah, West Virginia
RESULT: 362 dead, mine workings destroyed, some structural damage in nearby town

The Monongah Number 6 and Number 8 Mines were situated on the west fork of the Monongahela River, roughly 6 miles south of the town of Fairmount in Marion County, West Virginia. Operated by the Fairmount Coal Company, these mines were considered state-of-the-art for the early 1900's. They were equipped with mechanical ventilation fans, electrical coal-cutting machinery, and locomotives for hauling the extracted coal. In 1907 the Monongah mines, until then regarded as models of safety, became the site of the worst mining disaster the United States had experienced. The tragedy at Monongah also proved to be the worst U.S. mining disaster of the twentieth century.

Like many other major coal-mining accidents, the Monongah disaster occurred in winter, when the risk of fire and explosion in the mines is greatest. Low atmospheric pressures allow increased migration of

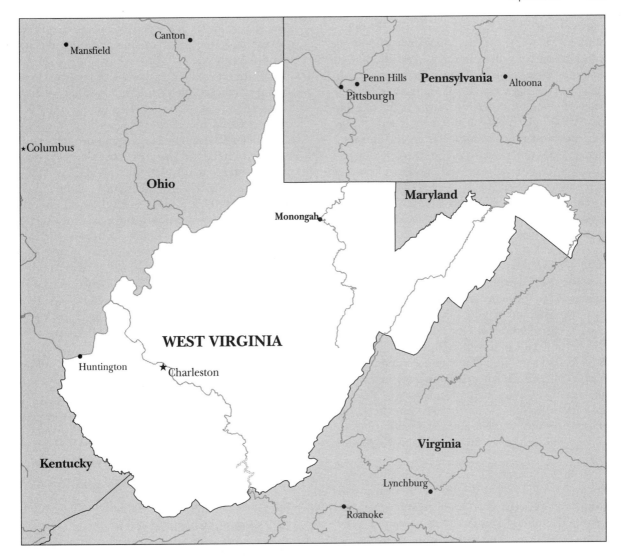

the highly flammable gas methane from coal seams into the ambient air of mines. Also, the colder weather leads to drier air within mines, which in turn means less moisture to trap dust particles suspended in the air. Like methane, airborne coal dust is capable of igniting and exploding. In this environment, an ignition source could easily touch off a fire or explosion.

In the case of the Monongah disaster, the ignition source is believed to have been the explosive used to blast coal free from the surrounding rock. The coroner's inquest conducted after the incident concluded that improper explosion of blasting powder was the probable cause, possibly in the form of a blown-out shot—that is, a charge of blasting powder whose energy was not absorbed by the surrounding coal. Instead of blasting the coal free from the mine walls, a blown-out shot would have sent a burst of flame out the back of the charged hole. There, it is thought, the flame ignited coal dust in the mine atmosphere. (The Monongah mines were purportedly free from explosive gas.) Because mines Number 6 and Number 8 were connected underground, the resulting blast rolled quickly through both mines.

The explosion that ripped through the Monongah mines at 10:20 A.M. on Friday, December 6, 1907, rattled the ground up to 8 miles away. In nearby Fairmount, buildings shuddered, pavement buckled, people and horses fell to the ground, and streetcars ran off their rails. Hastily forming rescue teams,

Fairmount residents hurried to the scene of the explosion. Volunteer rescuers crowded around the mines, along with the miners' wives and children anxiously awaiting news. Unable to locate any officials from the Fairmount Coal Company, or to determine whether the mines were on fire or full of explosive gas, volunteers began by clearing away timber, rail cars, and other wreckage from the mine entrance. Once they tried to enter the mines, they were quickly overcome by toxic and oxygen-deficient air and had to be rescued.

Shortly after the explosion, 4 dazed miners stumbled from the rubble. All had sustained only minor injuries. They had no idea whether any of their fellow miners lived through the blast. The volunteers, goaded on by the need to find and rescue any other survivors as soon as possible, braved the adverse conditions within the mines' remains. Rubble, wreckage, extreme heat, and stifling air impeded the volunteers' progress. The explosion destroyed mine Number 8's powerful ventilation fan and the partitions used to direct air through the mines, so a smaller fan had to make do. Choking coal dust hung in the mine air, and rescue and cleanup teams were sickened by toxic gases produced in the explosion. With more sophisticated means of clearing the air unavailable, volunteers flapped canvas curtains to disperse dust and gas.

At 4:00 on the afternoon of the explosion, rescuers pulled what was to be the last surviving miner from the wreckage. Search and rescue operations continued until December 12, but no additional survivors were found. The search teams recovered the bodies of 337 men and boys. During subsequent cleanup operations, an additional 25 victims were discovered. The 362 fatalities strained the community's resources. The bank was transformed into a makeshift morgue, embalmers worked around the clock in shifts, and churches conducted several funeral services a day. Many of the victims were difficult to identify, leading to disputes between grieving families laying claim to the same body. A special graveyard was dug in the nearby hillside, adjacent to company housing. The miners who lost their lives in the disaster left behind them over 1,000 widows and fatherless children.

A committee of the West Virginia legislature that investigated the accident concluded from testimony that the Monongah mines had been well equipped and safely run. These findings cast doubts on the safety of coal mines in general and pointed out the need for more research in coal-mining safety and accident prevention.

The Monongah disaster was one of a series of devastating mining accidents that brought the issue of mining safety to the attention of the American public and increased demands for the federal government to take action. Within two weeks, another coal-mine explosion claimed 239 lives in the Darr Mine at Jacob's Creek, Pennsylvania. In 1908, an accident at Marianna, Pennsylvania, killed 152 miners, and another 259 died in 1909 in a mine fire at Cherry, Illinois. Pressure on the federal government from unions and other miners' organizations, the press, and the public led to passage in 1910 of the Organic Act, which established the U.S. Bureau of Mines under the Department of the Interior. In its early years, the Bureau of Mines focused on reducing the mortality rate of miners through accident investigations, safety training for miners, and improved working conditions in the mines.

Karen N. Kähler

FOR FURTHER INFORMATION:

Graebner, William. *Coal-Mining Safety in the Progressive Period.* Lexington: University Press of Kentucky, 1976.

1907: Pennsylvania

MINE EXPLOSION
DATE: December 19, 1907
PLACE: Jacob's Creek, Pennsylvania
RESULT: 239 dead

At about 11:30 A.M. on December 19, 1907, an explosion ripped through the Darr Mine of the Pittsburgh Coal Company. The mine produced more than 2,000 tons of high-grade bituminous coal, making it one of the best-producing mines in the United States. The mine was located next to the Youghiogheny River and was extremely difficult to enter, making rescue efforts even more hazardous than normal. The only way of entering the mine was by a "sky ferry," a basketlike car suspended by a cable in which men pulled themselves back and forth across the river. Only six people at a time could fit into the ferry. Rescue efforts continued into the next day but proved mostly fruitless.

The cause of the explosion was never verified, but it seems likely it was another coal-gas catastrophe. Rescue parties found 239 bodies in the mine and only 2 survivors. Most of the bodies were so mangled, blackened, and scarred by the explosion they were left exactly where they were found. An immense cloud of smoke hung over the mine for days after the disaster, but rescuers found no sign of fire. Most of the dead were Greeks and Italians, and the total would have been much higher had it not been Saint Joseph's Day, a religious holiday celebrated by many Russians in the area. Russian miners did not go to work on that day, so perhaps as many as 400 lives were therefore saved.

Leslie V. Tischauser

FOR FURTHER INFORMATION:
The New York Times, December 20-23, 1907.

1908: Pennsylvania

MINE EXPLOSION
DATE: November 28, 1908
PLACE: Marianna, Pennsylvania
RESULT: 152 dead

At about 8:30 P.M. on the evening of November 28, 1908, a huge explosion roared through a mine owned by the Pittsburgh-Buffalo Coal Company a few miles outside of the city of Pittsburgh. The force of the explosion was so great it threw three miners totally out of the shaft onto the roof of a house several hundred feet away. They were killed instantly. The mine entrance was choked with debris and made rescue efforts very difficult and tedious. The explosion resulted from a miner carelessly exposing his flaming helmet lamp to coal dust. At this time, as dangerous as it seems and despite thousands of deaths in previous years, miners still received most of their light from flaming lamps in their helmets.

When rescuers finally entered the mine they miraculously found one badly injured survivor. Most of the bodies of the victims were never found, however—their bodies destroyed by the blast—so casualties could only be estimated. There was some discrep-

ancy in the final count, but most observers believed that between 152 and 155 miners were in the mine at the time of the explosion.

A fierce fire at the bottom of the shaft created a dense cloud of smoke that darkened the community for days after the disaster. Only two days before the explosion a state mine inspector had declared the mine safe and free of gas. The mine was considered a model of safety, but coal gas built up nevertheless and exploded with the full power of what one victim's wife thought was a massive earthquake.

Leslie V. Tischauser

FOR FURTHER INFORMATION:
The New York Times, November 29-30; December 1, 1908.

1913: New Mexico

MINE EXPLOSION
DATE: October 22, 1913
PLACE: Dawson, New Mexico
RESULT: 263 dead

At about 3:00 P.M. on October 22, 1913, the Stag Canyon Fuel Company's Number 2 Mine, owned by Phelps, Dodge & Company, was hit by an explosion so violent that everyone in the small town knew that hardly anyone in the shaft could have survived. The debris at the mouth of the mine was so thick it took almost eight hours for a rescue team to penetrate 100 feet. Rescuers were also slowed down when the huge fans bringing fresh air into the mine stopped and took four hours to fix. When the first bodies were found they were buried beneath tons of fallen earth, timber, and coal.

Miraculously, after two days of intense digging, 23 survivors were found deep in the mine and brought to safety, though most of them had broken and mangled arms and legs and suffered from exposure to coal gas. These miners were the only survivors of the 284 men in the mine when the explosion hit. Two rescuers died from coal-gas inhalation before the disaster was over.

The cause of the mine explosion was methane gas, which entered the mine from above after part of the roof collapsed. A vein of coal lay in a shaft directly above the roof of the lower shaft. It was from there that the deadly gas entered the mine and came in contact with an unprotected miner's lamp. Miners still used open flames in their lamps long after the deadly consequences of the practice were well known. Thousands of miners would continue to die yearly from these open flames until the invention of a simple substitute, battery-powered lights.

Leslie V. Tischauser

FOR FURTHER INFORMATION:

Humphrey, Hiram B. *Historical Summary of Coal Mine Explosions in the United States, 1810-1958.* Washington, D.C.: U.S. Government Printing Office, 1959.

The New York Times, October 23, 1924.

1914: West Virginia

MINE EXPLOSION
DATE: April 28, 1914
PLACE: Eccles (near Beckley), Raleigh County, West Virginia
RESULT: 181 dead

The Eccles Number 5 Mine was opened in 1905. It was owned by the Guggenheim family of New York City and managed by the New River Collieries Company until the Stoneage Coke and Coal Company took over operations in 1923. Stoneage operated the mine from 1923 until 1928. Eccles was a gaseous mine, as noted in the 1911 annual report of the Department of Mines of West Virginia. However, the ventilation required for gaseous mines was adequate and appeared to be up to standards. The Department of Mines was not expecting a major tragedy at Eccles.

At 2:10 P.M., an explosion in the Number 5 Mine killed every man among the 172 who were working there. While working the seam in the Number 6 mine, above the Number 5 Mine, 8 men were killed by the afterdamp from the Number 5 Mine explosion. Afterdamp, which killed the 8 men in the Number 6 Mine, is an asphyxiating gas left in a mine after an explosion of firedamp. Firedamp is a gas, largely methane, formed in coal mines and is explosive when mixed with air. Sixty-six men managed to escape from the Number 6 Mine. One of these men died later from injuries sustained while getting on the cage (the mine elevator) so as to escape from the Number 6 Mine.

The explosion originated in the Number 5 Mine. There the heat and violence were so great that few of the 172 men in those mine workings could have lived any real amount of time after the explosion. About ten minutes after the first explosion in the Number 5 Mine, a second and less violent explosion occurred, which carried debris out of the Number 5 Mine's shaft. The first and more violent explosion, accompanied by flame, carried timber and quantities of mud up both mines' shafts and blew off the explosion doors of the fanhouse at the Number 5 Mine's shaft. The explosion did not, however, damage the fan. The explosion wave in the Number 5 Mine traveling toward the Number 6 Mine's shaft blew a large quantity of water from a depression up the Number 5 Mine's shaft. This quenched the flame and prevented it from entering the Number 6 Mine. Rescue workers entered through the Number 6 Mine's shaft.

Reasons for the Explosion. The official report filed by the mine inspectors gives the cause of the explosion as a barrier of coal being shot out a short time before the explosion occurred. A contractor working on the south side of the coal barrier was notified not to take the barrier out, as that would disrupt the ventilation in that portion of the mine. This barrier was intact on the morning of the explosion, as testified to by the night boss who examined it.

> After the explosion the body of [Seth] Combs [the contractor] was found on the north side of the barrier . . . while his work was on the south side, and it is assumed that some time during the day he had blasted out a hole in the barrier that he might have a shorter travel way to the north section of the entry. In doing so, practically one-third of the mine was left without ventilation and it seems that the explosion originated in the main south sections of the mine.

The mine was known to liberate explosive gas, and the coal in this section, varying in thickness from 8 to 10 feet, would allow the gas to accumulate next to the roof. Conditions showed this explosion was caused by the ignition of gas and its propagation throughout the various parts of the mine. This was aided, to some extent, by the presence of coal dust, as the force of the explosion traveled in all directions. It dropped the Eccles Number 5 Mine 500 feet down into the Beckley coal seam.

The Aftermath. Of the 181 dead, 62 were positively identified. Of those, 15 percent were African American, 39 percent were married, and 23 percent were of Italian descent. Some had Slavic surnames. Many of the dead miners were immigrants. Those who could be identified were buried in family cemeteries if they were locals. Some of the Catholic immigrant miners were taken to Saint Sebastian cemetery in nearby Beckley. Those who were not identified were buried in the "Polish cemetery" above the tipple, where coal was emptied from the mine cars at the Eccles mines. In 1976, the bodies were moved to a new cemetery at the request of the Westmoreland Coal Company, which was then working the Eccles mines.

Dana P. McDermott

FOR FURTHER INFORMATION:

Humphrey, Hiram B. *Historical Summary of Coal Mine Explosions in the United States, 1810-1958.* Washington, D.C.: U.S. Government Printing Office, Bureau of Mines, 1959.

Wood, James L. *Raleigh County, West Virginia.* Beckley, W.V.: Raleigh County Historical Society, 1994.

1917: Colorado

MINE EXPLOSION
DATE: April 27, 1917
PLACE: Hastings, Colorado
RESULT: 120 dead

About 120 miners and company officials were killed on April 27, 1917, after a mine explosion and fire trapped them deep within a coal mine near Trinidad, Colorado. The blast took place as the men were riding to their work site on a train within the mine. Rescue efforts were quickly abandoned after poisonous coal gas built up in the area near the disaster. The victims were trapped and entombed behind thousands of tons of rubble, and their bodies were never recovered. Most of the men were caught and burned alive beneath a huge wall of fire that fell from the ceiling in the early morning hours of April 27.

The explosion was apparently caused by a match lit by one of the men to relight his lamp. No one sur-

vived; 100 of the dead were miners. The other casualties were mine company officials taking a safety tour of what some miners considered a highly dangerous "gas mine." An explosion four years earlier had killed several miners, but the company had made few improvements. A report issued by the Mine Workers Union labeled the mine a damp, treacherous place to work with poor safety and warning systems in place.

Criticisms were ignored, though, because of the great need for coal after America's entrance into World War I a few weeks before the explosion. Some local residents charged that a German spy had set off the blast, but accusations of a German plot were vigorously denied by government officials. The horrible tragedy was simply the result of coal gas and carelessness.

Leslie V. Tischauser

FOR FURTHER INFORMATION:

Humphrey, Hiram B. *Historical Summary of Coal Mine Explosions in the United States, 1810-1958.* Washington, D.C.: U.S. Government Printing Office, Bureau of Mines, 1959.

The New York Times, April 27-30; May 1, 1917.

1917: Nova Scotia

SHIP EXPLOSION
DATE: December 6, 1917
PLACE: Halifax, Nova Scotia, Canada
RESULT: Roughly 2,000 dead, 2,000 missing and presumed dead, 9,000 injured, city of Halifax virtually destroyed in explosion of the steamer *Mont Blanc*

Although the United States did not enter World War I until 1917, America's factories played a vital role in the success or failure of the Allied war effort. War material produced by the United States helped to stop the initial German advance, kept the Allied armies in the field, and reaped huge profits for American companies. American ammunition proved to be the product most in demand. The industrialized armies fighting the war required massive amounts of munitions far beyond what British and French factories could produce. Contracts for American munitions soon led Allied ships filled with American munitions

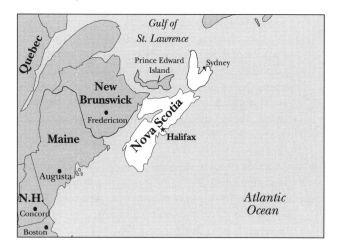

to cross the Atlantic in growing numbers, creating the growing possibility of a disaster.

First, the demand for American munitions required ships to be hastily loaded and unloaded. Inexperienced, overworked, or tired dockworkers could easily trigger a conflagration. Poorly loaded munitions also presented a safety hazard if the cargo shifted, a factor in the *Mont Blanc* explosion. Second, Germany, realizing the vital nature of American trade with the Allies, tried to sever the lifeline across the Atlantic Ocean with its submarine force, sinking scores of Allied merchant ships. A decrease in the most experienced Allied merchant crews forced the British and French to hire less skilled mariners to fill the ranks, leading to fatal miscues aboard the *Mont Blanc*. Last, the pressing demands to equip Allied armies in the face of the German submarine menace forced the British and French to use ships unsuitable for hauling munitions. The *Mont Blanc*, an old steamer, certainly fit into this category, again with fatal results.

The morning of December 6, 1917, found the French steamer *Mont Blanc* entering Halifax harbor. Loaded in New York with 2,600 tons of American explosives (TNT, benzine, picric acid, and guncotton), the *Mont Blanc* sailed to the Canadian harbor to join a convoy scheduled to make a run for Europe two days later. For unknown reasons *Mont Blanc* was not flying the red flags signifying its dangerous cargo. The weather was sunny and clear. Although known for potentially treacherous tides and weather, Halifax that December day enjoyed moderate tides and sunny weather. Despite the open, uncrowded harbor, easy tide, and sunny conditions, disaster loomed.

At this time a Norwegian steamship, the *Imo*, was heading out to sea. Despite plenty of clearance, the *Imo* gradually veered into the *Mont Blanc*'s steering channel and struck the *Mont Blanc* on the starboard bow at roughly 8:45 A.M. No reason has ever surfaced for the *Imo*'s erratic change of course. The collision, although not immediately disastrous, set in motion a chain of events that led to a catastrophe. The collision ruptured several benzine containers that burst into flames. The *Mont Blanc*'s crew, instead of immediately sinking the ship by flooding the explosive-filled holds, tried to fight the fire. The conflagration soon spread out of control, and, rather than destroy the burning ship, the crew fled in the lifeboats. The impact with the *Imo*, however, caused the boat to drift toward the shore and the crowded city beyond. Officers and crew of the Royal Canadian Navy warship HMCS *Niobe* and the harbor tug *Stella Maris* desperately attempted to tow the *Mont Blanc* away from the city. All were killed when, thirty minutes after the collision, the *Mont Blanc* exploded.

The eruption transformed the *Mont Blanc* into a storm of white-hot steel shrapnel. An enormous shock wave flattened more than 2 square miles of the harbor front as wooden buildings vaporized and concrete structures crumbled. *Mont Blanc*'s half-ton anchor landed more than 2 miles from the blast site. A mushroom cloud rose over Halifax to a height of 3 miles. The explosion shattered windows 20 miles away, and the detonation was felt on Prince Edward Island, more than 100 miles away. Many small boats simply disappeared, and several larger vessels capsized.

The harbor temporarily turned into a mudflat as a 15-foot-high seismic wave crashed into the shattered shore, carrying debris as far as a quarter mile inland. Fires, ignited by toppled coal stoves, spread out of control; the city's water mains had been severed. The detonation virtually erased Halifax's harbor. More than 1,600 buildings were destroyed, and another 12,000 were damaged. Nearly half of Halifax's population of roughly 50,000 were left homeless or lacked adequate shelter. Even more citizens became homeless when fears of unexploded ordnance forced massive evacuations. To add to the city's misery, a blizzard the next day seriously hampered relief efforts.

Financial and humanitarian assistance immediately flowed into Halifax, much from the United

States. In the months immediately after the blast, the Halifax Relief Commission received and disbursed nearly $30 million worth of food, clothing, and supplies. Because of its importance as a wartime port, the reconstruction of Halifax and its harbor facilities became a priority for the Canadian and British governments. Temporary housing sheltered most of the city's returning inhabitants until the city was completely rebuilt after the war.

As a human-made disaster, the Halifax explosion is without parallel. The accident triggered the most powerful explosion in history up to that time and remains the largest conventional explosion in history, surpassed only by nuclear explosions.

Steven J. Ramold

FOR FURTHER INFORMATION:

Beed, Blair. *1917 Halifax Explosion and American Response.* Halifax, N.S.: Dtours Visitor and Convention Service, 1998.

Bell, Francis M. *A Romance of the Halifax Disaster.* Halifax, N.S.: Royal Print, 1918.

Bird, Michael J. *The Town That Died: The True Story of the Greatest Manmade Explosion Before Hiroshima.* New York: G. P. Putnam's Sons, 1962.

Boning, Richard A. *Seventeen Minutes to Live.* Baldwin, N.Y.: Dexter & Westbrook, 1973.

Ground Zero: A Reassessment of the 1917 Explosion in Halifax Harbor. Halifax, N.S.: Nimbus, 1994.

Kitz, Janet F. *Shattered City: The Halifax Explosion and the Road to Recovery.* Halifax, N.S.: Nimbus, 1989.

Mahar, James G. *Too Many to Mourn: One Family's Tragedy in the Halifax Explosion.* Halifax, N.S.: Nimbus, 1998.

1923: Wyoming

MINE EXPLOSION
DATE: August 14, 1923
PLACE: Kemmerer, Wyoming
RESULT: 99 dead

On the morning of August 14, 1923, at about 8:20 A.M., a miner lit a match in the darkness of a mine tunnel in Frontier Number 1 Mine, causing a huge explosion of coal gas. Whoever the unfortunate miner was died instantly, and several other miners were blown to pieces. The sound of the explosion caused other men in the mine to panic. At least 70 miners started to run for the entrance, but they ran into a huge pocket of gas and suffocated to death before rescuers could reach them. Twenty-nine miners ran in the opposite direction, and their bodies were later found under a mountain of debris. Through some miracle, 36 miners survived the chaos because they built a makeshift wall around the area in which they worked. Rescuers found them still breathing but barely alive at about 3:00 P.M.

Investigators later concluded that all the miners who panicked and ran could have survived had they remained calm and followed the actions of their wall-building colleagues. However, deep within a mine it is extremely difficult to remain calm after hearing the sound of a huge explosion.

Leslie V. Tischauser

FOR FURTHER INFORMATION:

Humphrey, Hiram B. *Historical Summary of Coal Mine Explosions in the United States, 1810-1958.* Washington, D.C.: U.S. Government Printing Office, Bureau of Mines, 1959.

The New York Times, August 15-17, 1923.

1924: West Virginia

MINE EXPLOSION
DATE: April 28, 1924
PLACE: Benwood, West Virginia
RESULT: 119 dead

On the morning of April 28, 1924, the entire day shift of miners at the Benwood Mine was trapped by an explosion of gas only five minutes after entering the mine. The mine was located about 5 miles south of Wheeling, West Virginia, on the Ohio River. One of the oldest mines in the United States, it had one of the worst safety records in the nation. The force of the explosion destroyed the train on which the miners were riding, and the debris from the train temporarily blocked the mine's entrance, making rescue efforts difficult. Water, rock, and coal gas made rescue almost impossible.

As rescuers entered the mine, the families of the trapped men gathered at the entrance despite the drenching rain. Huge clouds of dust from the explosion hovered over the valley, further adding to the darkness of the day. A huge mass of stone blocked the passageway into the interior of the mine. Two men were found alive not far from the rubble, but they died as they were being carried to the surface. Many of the victims were found burned beyond recognition, bearing witness to the intense heat set off by the exploding gas. Others died from concussions caused by the explosion. What caused the explosion was never discovered.

Leslie V. Tischauser

FOR FURTHER INFORMATION:
Humphrey, Hiram B. *Historical Summary of Coal Mine Explosions in the United States, 1810-1958*. Washington, D.C.: U.S. Government Printing Office, 1959.
The New York Times, April 29-30, 1924.

1927: Pittsburgh

GAS TANK EXPLOSION
DATE: November 14, 1927
PLACE: Equitable Gas Company in the North Side district of Pittsburgh, Pennsylvania
RESULT: 28 dead, 1 missing, more than 600 injured and 5,000 homeless

Early in the morning shift of November 14, 1927, workmen were using torches to weld shut a leak in the main tank of the Equitable Gas Company in North Side, Pittsburgh. Capable of holding 5 million cubic feet of natural gas, the tank, 208 feet in diameter and 233 feet tall, was billed as the world's largest natural-gas container. In preparation for the repair, the tank had been emptied—supposedly. Apparently fumes and liquid gas remained, because at 8:43 A.M. an explosion occurred in it that sent a fireball more than 1,000 feet into the sky and lifted its top section, onlookers reported, like a balloon. Two tanks nearby were ruptured and set afire, and the air filled with black smoke. The blast leveled or broke open nearby factories, stores, homes, tenements, stables, hotels, and a fire station. Buildings within a 5-mile radius rocked, and their windows shattered. Within seconds, lengths of steel, bricks, and glass rained down on the area.

The 13 repairmen perished instantly, as well as workers in adjacent factories and those crushed in collapsed buildings. The last victim died in the hospital ten days later. Falling debris and glass injured more than 600 people, including children on their way to school. The injured streamed in panic away from the blast site, to be met almost immediately by police, firemen, and voluntary rescuers who took them to hastily erected treatment centers. The North Side gas tank explosion was only the third in the nation's history and the first to cause fatalities.

Roger Smith

FOR FURTHER INFORMATION:
The New York Times, November 15, 1927, p. 1-2.
The New York Times, November 16, 1927, p. 27.

1928: Pennsylvania

MINE EXPLOSION
DATE: May 19, 1928
PLACE: Mather, Pennsylvania
RESULT: 195 dead

One of the most severe explosions of the twentieth century hit a giant coal mine in western Pennsylvania on May 19, 1928. It blew apart most of the mine at 4:07 P.M., just as 400 men were changing shifts in a mine that produced more than 1 million tons of coal a year. An accumulation of bituminous coal gas was ignited by an arc from a storage battery illegally being used to operate a locomotive in the mine. The locomotive pulled the train that brought miners to and from the entrance.

The blast killed 193 men instantly. Two men were rescued but died from their injuries before they could be brought to safety. After three days of unsuccessful searching, the rescue party came upon a wall that had been hastily constructed. Behind it they discovered 14 men who had survived by successfully barricading themselves behind the wall, which protected them from the deadly effects of breathing coal gas. Another group of casualties included 100 canaries brought into the mine to signal, by their deaths, the presence of gas.

Leslie V. Tischauser

FOR FURTHER INFORMATION:

Humphrey, Hiram B. *Historical Summary of Coal Mine Explosions in the United States, 1810-1958*. Washington, D.C.: U.S. Government Printing Office, Bureau of Mines, 1959.

The New York Times, May 20, 1928.

FOR FURTHER INFORMATION:

Humphrey, Hiram B. *Historical Summary of Coal Mine Explosions in the United States, 1810-1958*. Washington, D.C.: U.S. Government Printing Office, Bureau of Mines, 1959.

The New York Times, March 21-23, 1929.

1929: Pennsylvania

MINE EXPLOSION
DATE: March 21, 1929
PLACE: Parnassus, Pennsylvania
RESULT: 46 dead

At about 7:25 A.M. on March 21, 1929, a violent explosion ripped through the Kinlock Mine outside of Parnassus, Pennsylvania. More than 250 men were in the mine at the time of the explosion. The mine was considered one of the safest in the area, and the disaster did not result from carelessness. Rather, it was blamed on faulty equipment, in this case a conveyor belt used to haul coal from the base of the shaft to the surface. The belt snapped, sending hundreds of tons of coal down into the mine, creating huge clouds of coal dust. A spark from an electric wire did the rest of the damage by igniting the dust. The explosion destroyed the entire conveyor system and blew through the entire mine, knocking out doors, fans, and other equipment.

Dozens of miners were blown into the sides of the sheds, smashing their skulls and dying instantly. Many others died from coal gas, which suffocated them before they could reach safety or build a protective wall. Forty-five miners died horrible deaths deep in the shaft, while another was burned alive close to the mine entrance.

Rescuers entered the mine only a few minutes after the explosion, although progress was slowed by the intense fire. Because of the heroic efforts of the rescue crew 212 miners were found alive deep in the mine. They still had to dig through the collapsed walls in floodwater up to their waists before reaching the surface, but they managed to get out alive. Later still, a single miner who had barricaded himself behind a wall was found alive, but his experience was so horrifying that he had become insane.

Leslie V. Tischauser

1931: China

MINE EXPLOSION
DATE: February 8, 1931
PLACE: Manchuria, northern China
RESULT: More than 3,000 dead

On the evening of February 8, 1931, a massive explosion roared through a coal mine in Japanese-occupied Manchuria. Perhaps more than 3,000 Chinese miners were killed in this catastrophe. If true, this would certainly be the worst coal mine explosion in history to date. The day after the initial report of the explosion was published in Chinese and Western newspapers, however, the Japanese government issued a retraction. No one had died, according to officials of the Japanese army, which ran the mine. All 3,000 miners had been rescued, the report said. The incident remained surrounded in controversy, though, as local Chinese mine officials and families of miners insisted that the men were still missing and no rescue attempts had been made. The exact nature of this event and the costs and casualties have never been verified. The event remains clouded in mystery.

Leslie V. Tischauser

FOR FURTHER INFORMATION:

The New York Times, February 9-11, 1931.

1937: Texas

SCHOOL EXPLOSION
DATE: March 18, 1937
PLACE: New London, Texas
RESULT: 412 dead, $300,000 Consolidated School building completely destroyed

The worst school disaster in U.S. history to date occurred in New London, Texas, on March 18, 1937, when a gas explosion demolished the Consolidated School. The death toll of 398 students and 14 teachers far exceeded the toll of 174 killed when an explosion ruined the Lakeview School of Collinwood, Ohio, in 1908.

New London, Texas, is located about 120 miles southeast of Dallas and about 70 miles from the Louisiana border in the heart of the East Texas oil fields. Royalties from these oil fields allowed the residents to build a very modern and well-equipped school. Described as "the finest rural school in the country," the school included model home-economics kitchens, sewing rooms, laboratories, and playgrounds. The school's enrollment of 1,500 included elementary and high school students.

On this Thursday afternoon, some of the elemen-

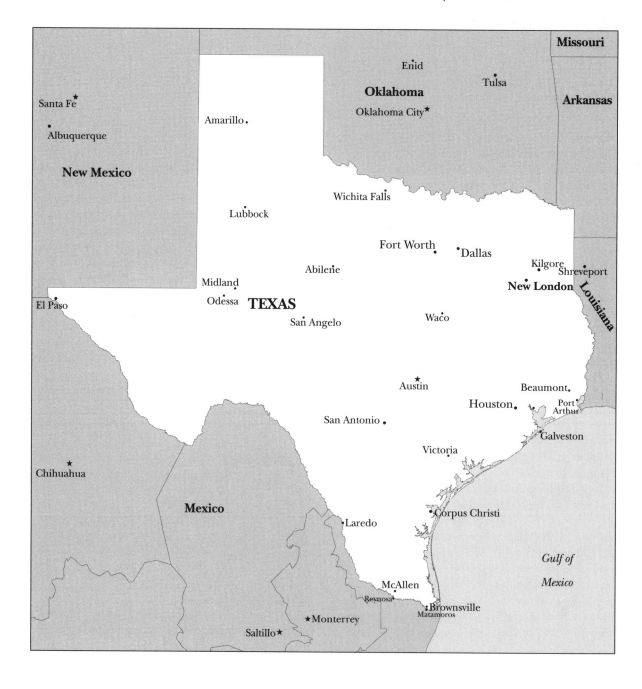

tary classes had been dismissed, and the students either had returned home or had stayed to play on the school grounds while waiting for buses. About one hundred parents were gathered in a nearby gymnasium waiting for a Parent-Teacher Association meeting to start. Nearly seven hundred students in grades seven through twelve remained in the building.

Meanwhile, in the school's basement a leaking natural-gas pipeline feeding into the heating system gradually filled every available air space. At approximately 3:15 P.M. a spark ignited the explosive gas and air mixture. A low rumble rolled beneath the building, followed by a tremendous explosion that buckled the walls and raised the roof before the entire structure collapsed into rubble.

Rescuers arriving at the scene of the explosion, including the parents from the gymnasium, found several of the victims who had been blown out of the building. Hundreds of rescue workers from the town and from the nearby oil fields dug through the debris trying to free trapped survivors. Rescue efforts continued throughout the night and into the morning. While there had been a sheet of flame produced momentarily during the explosion, there was no fire to extinguish. Some of the victims showed evidence of burns, but the vast majority of deaths resulted from either crushing or the impact of brick, steel, or other debris. Several of the victims apparently died from the concussive force of the explosion.

By 2 A.M. approximately 400 bodies had been recovered. Local mortuaries were unable to cope with the demand, and the dead were taken to morgues in neighboring towns within a 50-mile radius to be prepared for burial. Makeshift hospitals to treat the injured were established in schools, grocery stores, and churches. Governor James V. Allred declared martial law and sent National Guard units from Tyler, Longview, and Marshall to the scene. A military court of inquiry was established to begin an investigation into the blast.

Rain during the early morning hours following the blast hampered rescue and recovery efforts. In some cases, identification of the victims was difficult due to the extent of their injuries. Fingerprints of the children, taken a year before, were rushed to the scene from Dallas. On Sunday, March 21, the first funerals were held at the nearby Pleasant Hill cemetery. For the next several days there were almost constant processions to this cemetery.

The investigation into the blast revealed several factors contributing to the disaster. A connection to take natural gas from a waste line of the Parade Oil Company and pipe it into the school's heating system had been installed. The goal was to save from $250 to $350 per month on heating costs. Whether the oil company had sanctioned this action, or even had knowledge of it, was never clearly established. No expert had been called in to make or inspect the connection, and a gas leak had developed without anyone's knowledge. The United Gas Company indicated that until January of that year it had sold gas to the school with a telltale odorant. This odorant is added to natural gas so that leaks can be more easily detected. The waste gas from the Parade Oil Company was odorless, as is most natural gas. The school's heating system was relatively complex, with individual gas-fired heaters in each classroom instead of a central heating system. The basement was poorly ventilated, allowing the odorless gas to accumulate undetected.

Dr. E. P. Schoch, a chemistry professor at the University of Texas and an expert on gas explosions, inspected the wreckage and discovered that many of the gas heaters lacked proper flues. Of six heaters recovered intact, only one was found to be properly ventilated. Dr. Schoch came to the conclusion that the gas leak in the basement allowed an explosive gas and air mixture to fill the wall spaces. When the gas was ignited, the walls burst, causing the entire structure to collapse. The court of inquiry concurred with Dr. Schoch's findings.

School was resumed eleven days later, using whatever space could be found in New London. Attendance was very low, with less than 300 students reporting for classes. Parents and children were still in shock from the disaster that had claimed the lives of so many of their friends and classmates. A new school was eventually built on the site, and a memorial to the victims of the worst school disaster in U.S. history was erected.

Terrence A. Lee

FOR FURTHER INFORMATION:
Benson, Ragnar. "School Blast Kills 455 Students, Teachers in New London." In *Fire, Flash, and Fury: The Greatest Explosions in History.* Boulder, Colo.: Paladin Press, 1990.
Gelman, Woody, and Barbara Jackson. "School Explosion, 1937." In *Disaster Illustrated: Two Hundred Years of American Misfortune,* edited by Linda Sunshine. New York: Harmony Books, 1976.

Parnes, Seymour. "The Roof Fell In." In *Disaster*, edited by Ken Kartman and Leonard Brown. Freeport, N.Y.: Books for Libraries Press, 1948.

Perkes, Dan. "It Only Took a Spark." In *Eyewitness to Disaster*. New York: Gallery Books, 1985.

1937: The *Hindenburg* Disaster

AIRSHIP EXPLOSION
DATE: May 6, 1937
PLACE: Lakehurst, New Jersey
RESULT: 36 dead (22 crew members, 13 passengers, and 1 person on the ground), travel by airship comes to an end

On May 3, 1937, the huge airship *Hindenburg* took off from Frankfurt, Germany, headed for Lakehurst, New Jersey. On board were 97 people—61 passengers and 36 crew members. The *Hindenburg* had already completed more than thirty ocean crossings in its first year of operation, having safely delivered more than 2,000 passengers and 375,000 pounds of mail and freight. The *Hindenburg* was a Nazi propaganda showpiece, with large black swastikas displayed prominently on its tail fins.

Over the years, German-built airships (lighter-than-air aircrafts), often called zeppelins, had acquired an excellent record for safety and dependability. An earlier airship, called the *Graf Zeppelin*, had logged more than 1 million miles without mishap on regular trans-Atlantic flights from 1930 until it was retired in 1936.

The Creation of Airships. Ferdinand von Zeppelin (1838-1914) was born into a wealthy German family. As an army officer, he was sent to the United States in 1861 to observe military maneuvers during the Civil War. He had the opportunity to take a ride in a hot-air balloon, which can only drift with the air currents because it has no mechanism for steering or propulsion. That experience gave Zeppelin a lifelong motivation to design a lighter-than-air vehicle whose direction of flight could be controlled by a pilot on board. Other inventors had the same goal, but Zeppelin had the persistence and the financial resources to carry out his plan. By the time he died in 1914, Zeppelin had a fleet of thirty airships with a regular schedule of passenger flights between major cities in Europe.

The *Hindenburg* had the designation LZ-129, the one hundred twenty-ninth airship to be built by the Zeppelin factory since the first successful flight on the LZ-1 took place in the year 1900. The *Hindenburg* looked like an enormous sausage, 803 feet long and 135 feet in diameter. Most of its bulk consisted of a metal framework that held sixteen large gas bags filled with hydrogen. Hydrogen is much lighter than air, even lighter than the helium that is used in balloons. The total weight of the airship, including the framework, the gas bags, the passenger gondola, and the propulsion and steering apparatus must be less than the weight of air that it displaces in order for the airship to become buoyant. Like a submarine, which gets its buoyancy from the surrounding water, the airship literally floats in the air. Propulsion was provided by four 1150-horsepower diesel engines that turned two relatively small propellers. Cruising at an average speed of 80 miles per hour, the trans-Atlantic trip took only three days, less than half the time taken by the fastest ocean liners of the 1930's. The passenger gondola, about 60 feet long, was fastened to the bottom of the main balloon near its front end. It was designed for wealthy patrons who were accustomed to luxury. The sleeping cabins had comfortable beds and modern bathroom fixtures. The dining room had elegant furnishings, adjacent to a promenade deck with large observation windows. There was a dance floor with a stage for the band. The guest lounge was furnished with card tables and easy chairs. Because hydrogen gas is highly combustible, elaborate safety precautions were needed to prevent any open flame or sparks. Smoking was permitted only in a special smoking room, where the cigarette lighters were chained to the furniture. No cigarettes or matches were allowed anywhere else. The hallway walls had a rubberized coating to prevent buildup of static electricity. Riding in the gondola was very smooth compared to ocean liners because the great bulk of the balloon smoothed out any local air turbulence.

Because hydrogen gas is flammable, Germany had tried to buy helium gas from the United States. Helium is a lightweight, inert gas that provides almost the same amount of buoyancy as hydrogen. The U.S. government opposed exporting helium to Germany because Adolf Hitler's Nazi Party had come to power in 1933 and the threat of war was coming closer. During World War I, the German military had used zeppelins to drop bombs over London and other cities in

The Hindenburg *airship explodes near its landing base in Lakehurst, New Jersey.* (AP/Wide World Photos)

Great Britain. In some fifty air raids, large buildings had been destroyed and over 500 people were killed. The terror caused by these air attacks left a lasting memory that firmly opposed selling helium to Germany as it was rearming itself.

The *Hindenburg* Explodes. On May 6, 1937, after a routine three-day flight across the Atlantic, the *Hindenburg* passed over New York City. Just after 7 P.M., the airship arrived at its landing field at Lakehurst, New Jersey. As it hovered above the mooring tower, ropes were dropped from the front of the ship to tie it down for unloading. A radio announcer and a newsreel photographer were on hand to report on the arrival because the passenger list frequently included international celebrities.

Without warning, the tail section of the *Hindenburg* suddenly burst into flames. The fire spread very quickly, and the airship sank down toward the ground because of the loss of hydrogen. Some of the panicked passengers jumped from the gondola and survived, but others were killed upon impact with the ground. Some waited too long to jump and died when their clothing and hair caught fire. The radio announcer spoke into his microphone, where his eyewitness words of shock were recorded: "It's burst into flames! Get out of the way! . . . It's falling on the mooring mast and all the folks between us. . . . This is the worst thing I've ever witnessed!" Only thirty-four seconds after the initial explosion the *Hindenburg* lay on the ground with its metal skeleton twisted and wrecked. The fire did not last long because after the hydrogen had escaped, there was not much combustible material left to burn.

A circus performer named Joseph Spah was one of the miraculous survivors from the *Hindenburg* disaster. He was sitting in the dining room when the explosion happened. He smashed one of the window-panes and climbed out through the broken window, dangling from the ledge by his hands. He realized that he was too high to let go, so he waited for the burning airship to drop closer to the ground. The window ledge became very hot, searing his hands. When he thought he was about 40 feet from the ground, he let go, dropped to the ground, landed on his feet, and ran away from the fire. His only injury was a fractured heel.

There were some extraordinary acts of heroism during the disaster that helped to save lives. Some of the ground crew remained underneath the burning airship long enough to catch passengers who had jumped. Captain Max Pruss, who was in the control room, helped 7 crew members to escape through a window. He dragged an unconscious man to safety even after his own clothes had caught on fire. One of the casualties was Ernst Lehman, who had been in command of the *Hindenburg* on earlier flights. He was able to walk away from the blazing wreckage but died of burns later.

The *Hindenburg* disaster made headlines in all the major newspapers. Like the tragic sinking of the cruise ship *Titanic*, another technological marvel had come to a spectacular end, in spite of extensive safety precautions. In the 1930's, television was not available yet, but newsreel photography of major events was commonly shown at movie theaters before or after the feature film. Because a camera man was all set up to film the landing of the *Hindenburg*, he was able to capture the whole disaster from beginning to end. Together with the voice of the radio announcer, it was shown to horrified audiences. It was the first major disaster with eyewitness photography. Pictures of burning victims trying to run away from the flaming wreck left an indelible image that travel by airship was too dangerous. The age of the airships came to an end with the *Hindenburg* disaster.

Reasons for the Explosion. What caused the *Hindenburg* to explode? As is customary after a major disaster, there was a formal inquiry, at which some of the survivors were able to tell their stories. Three possible scenarios emerged from the investigation. One was that an electric discharge from the atmosphere had initiated the explosion. Although no one had seen any lightning, there is frequently a buildup of static electricity between low-lying clouds and the ground. It had been raining earlier that day in Lakehurst, and newsreels did show a cloudy sky above

the airship as it was landing. A second possibility was an electric discharge inside the balloon itself, perhaps produced by friction between gas bags rubbing against each other. It was almost impossible to prevent some leakage of hydrogen through the rubberized fabric of the bags, so a spark could have ignited the gas.

The third possibility, more of a speculation, was that it was an act of sabotage. Perhaps a member of the crew who was strongly opposed to Adolf Hitler's militarism and persecution of Jews had set a bomb that would bring a spectacular end to this airship that symbolized the dominance of German technology. However, no evidence of bomb material could be found in the wrecked remains of the *Hindenburg*.

Hans G. Graetzer

FOR FURTHER INFORMATION:
Archbold, Rick. *Hindenburg: An Illustrated History.* New York: Warner Books, 1994.
Danner, James F. *Graf Zeppelin and Hindenburg: A Handbook of Airship Memorabilia.* Whitesboro, N.Y.: Oceanair Specialties, 1975.
Dick, Harold G. *The Golden Age of the Great Passenger Airships: Graf Zeppelin and Hindenburg.* Washington, D.C.: Smithsonian Institution Press, 1985.
Mooney, Michael M. *The Hindenburg.* New York: Dodd Mead, 1972.
Robinson, Douglas H. *Famous Aircraft: The LZ-129 "Hindenburg."* Dallas: Morgan, 1964.
Tanaka, Shirley. *The Disaster of the Hindenburg: The Last Flight of the Greatest Airship Ever Built.* New York: Scholastic/Madison Press, 1993.
Wood, Peter. *When Zeppelins Flew.* New York: Time-Life Books, 1969.

1943: Montana

MINE EXPLOSION
DATE: February 27, 1943
PLACE: Washoe, Montana
RESULT: 104 dead

At about 9:30 A.M. on February 27, 1943, a massive explosion hit the Montana Coal and Iron Company's fifty-year-old mine near Washoe, Montana. About 30 miners working about 800 feet down in the shaft were killed instantly by the force of the explosion. Smoke poured from air vents in the shaft as an intense fire burned rapidly through the main tunnel. Sixty-nine miners were trapped behind a wall of debris, most of them still alive.

Rescue efforts were hampered by the fire, and the air was almost unbreathable. When rescuers finally reached the 69, they were all dead from suffocation. Some had left behind desperate, handwritten notes for their families. "It's 11 A.M.—time to go," was all one said. The mine had a reputation for low safety standards, but World War II was on and coal was needed by the military, so safety standards took second place to these demands.

An investigation of the disaster found the cause to be flames from an open lamp, which struck coal gas. It was also reported that, incredibly, smoking was still allowed in the shaft, which was an open invitation to suicide, as the investigator noted.

Leslie V. Tischauser

FOR FURTHER INFORMATION:
Humphrey, Hiram B. *Historical Summary of Coal Mine Explosions in the United States, 1810-1958*. Washington, D.C.: U.S. Government Printing Office, Bureau of Mines, 1959.
The New York Times, February 28, 1943.

1944: India

SHIP EXPLOSION
DATE: April 14, 1944
PLACE: Bombay, India
RESULT: 1,376 dead, 3,000 injured in explosion of the cargo ship *Fort Stikine*

The steamship *Fort Stikine* was an 8,000-ton ship built in Canada. It departed from Birkenhead, England, across the Mersey River from Liverpool, on February 24, 1944. After a stop in Karachi, Pakistan, its cargo included 708 bales of cotton, 300 tons of the powerful explosive TNT, more than $4 million worth of gold bullion, and a variety of other items. On April 14, 1944, this cargo was being unloaded at the Alexandra, Victoria, and Prince docks on the eastern shore of the port of Bombay, India.

Cotton bales are known for spontaneous combustion. This means that they can begin to burn without an external spark or heat. No one knows if the fire on the ship was caused by spontaneous combustion or a careless cigarette. The cotton bales were stowed in the lower part of the number 2 hold, while the TNT was stowed in the upper part of the hold. Wartime urgency had probably led to this dangerous combination.

Smoke was seen coming from the lower hold early in the afternoon. Lieutenant Colonel J. R. Sadler, the general manager of the Bombay Port Trust of Docks and Railways, dispatched firefighters and equipment to fight the fire. The ship was equipped with a steam system that could have been used to smother the fire. It is also possible that the fire could have been put out by rapidly and completely flooding the lower hold from the sea. Unfortunately, neither of these measures was tried. By midafternoon 7 fire engines, 66 firefighters, and 4 officers, including Colonel Sadler were at the scene. Some 30 fire hoses were pouring water on the fire at a rate of 4 tons per minute. All this water may have actually made the situation worse. The burning cotton bales floated on the water, which brought them closer to the deck between the upper and lower holds. Sitting on top of this deck was the TNT. Throughout the afternoon no attempt was made to unload the TNT from the upper hold, and no attempt was made to tow the ship out to sea.

At 4 P.M. the smoke changed from brown to milky white, and flames were observed. The chief of the fire brigade ordered the workers to abandon the ship, but they continued to fight the fire from the dock. A huge explosion erupted at 4:07 P.M. The ship and everything on the dock disappeared. A 4,000-ton ship tied up nearby was lifted onto a wharf. All the windows shattered in a house 1 mile from the ship, and a 28-pound gold bar worth $27,700 landed on the porch of the third floor. Twelve other ships totaling 50,000 tons were destroyed by the explosion, and a similar number were badly damaged.

Fires started by flying debris sprang up all over the port. A second large explosion occurred half an hour after the first. Police, firemen, and military troops from India, Great Britain, and the United States mobilized to fight the fire that threatened to burn the entire city of 1.5 million people to the ground. Warehouses in the port contained grain, paper, paint, and large quantities of baled cotton. As these burned they

set fire to residences nearby. Explosives experts demolished hundreds of buildings in an attempt to halt the progress of the fire. By the third day it was clear that the main business center, Ballard Estate, was saved. On the fourth day the fire was only smoldering.

Total damage to property and buildings ashore was estimated at 20 million British pounds. The insurance companies initially denied responsibility on the grounds that the root cause of the damage was an explosion, something that the insurance policies did not cover. Eventually a settlement was negotiated by which the insurance companies paid one-eighth of the cost and the Indian government paid seven-eighths.

A commission was appointed to investigate the disaster and make a formal report. This report was issued on September 12, 1944, nearly five months later.

Although sabotage by Japanese agents was suspected at first, there was no evidence to support this theory. In its findings the commission cited five causes of the disaster: Ships carrying explosives were brought directly to the dock because of the war effort, the stowage of cotton and TNT in the same hold was not proper, the cotton was ignited by accident, insufficient measures were taken to fight the fire early on, and no one had total authority over the situation.

Because the disaster occurred during World War II, news was suppressed by British-Indian censors. The first account of the explosion and fire was broadcast by Radio Saigon. The story first appeared in *The New York Times* on April 17, three days after the explosion; apparently this story was based on the Radio Saigon broadcast. More detailed accounts appeared in U.S. magazines (*Time* and *Life*) in late May. At that point the death toll was reported as 360. When the report of the investigation was issued in Bombay on September 12, it was written about in *The New York Times*. The death toll was given there as "at least 900 persons killed or missing." The death toll was eventually given as 1,376. Newspapers and magazines were filled with news of the war at that time. As a result, this explosion, which was not directly war-related, did not receive great attention outside India.

Edwin G. Wiggins

FOR FURTHER INFORMATION:

Barnaby, K. C. *Some Ship Disasters and Their Causes.* New York: A. S. Barnes, 1970.

"Bombay Blast Toll 128." *The New York Times*, April 17, 1944, p. 3.

"Fire in Bombay." *Time*, May 22, 1944, p. 36.

"Ship Smoker Blamed for Bombay Disaster." *The New York Times*, September 12, 1944, p. 10.

"War Explodes into Bombay." *Life*, May 22, 1944, 38.

1944: Cleveland

GAS TANK
DATE: October 20, 1944
PLACE: East Ohio Gas Company on the east side of Cleveland, Ohio

A burned man is led away from the explosion of two gas tanks in Cleveland. (AP/Wide World Photos)

RESULT: 130 dead, 215 injured, 1,500 homeless, estimated $10 million in damage

At 2:30 P.M. on October 20, 1944, scientists in a nearby laboratory saw white vapor leaking from the top of a natural-gas tank belonging to the East Ohio Gas Company in Cleveland. About ten minutes later, the spherical tank, 57 feet in diameter and containing 90 million cubic feet of natural gas, exploded. The blast spread sheets of flame through the surrounding half-mile area, and a fireball climbed 2,800 feet high. Twenty minutes later a smaller tank also ignited. Flames swept through a fifty-block area as the largest fire in the city's history burned out of control.

Residents of the area, just blocks from Lake Erie, fled in panic, as police, volunteer trucks, military personnel, and 95 percent of the municipal firefighters showed up to put out the blaze and search for the dead and injured. Fearing renewed fires and the collapse of damaged buildings, authorities evacuated 10,000 families; 1,500 remained homeless under the care of the Red Cross. The property damage included 79 houses, 2 factories, and 218 vehicles totally destroyed and dozens more damaged. Of the dead, 55 were never identified.

Experts concluded that uneven contraction of metal, caused by the minus 257 degree Fahrenheit temperature of the natural gas, made a steel plate rupture. When the gas mixed with air, it combusted. This analysis led to safer storage techniques for low-temperature gas.

Roger Smith

FOR FURTHER INFORMATION:

"Mystery Persists." *Business Week*, November 18, 1944, p. 52-53.

The New York Times, October 21, 1944, p. 19.

The New York Times, October 22, 1944, p. 41.

Van Tassel, David D., and John J. Grabowski, eds. "The East Ohio Gas Company Explosion and Fire." In *The Encyclopedia of Cleveland History*. 2d ed. Bloomington: Indiana University Press, 1996.

1947: Texas

SHIP EXPLOSION
DATE: April 16, 1947
PLACE: Texas City, Texas

RESULT: 581 dead, 3,500 injured, 539 homes damaged or destroyed, $100 million in property damage in explosion of the freighter *Grandcamp*

Various cargoes, including sisal twine, peanuts, cotton, tobacco, small arms ammunition, and ammonium nitrate fertilizer were being loaded into the French Liberty ship *Grandcamp* as it lay alongside a pier at Texas City, Texas. Under certain conditions, ammonium nitrate can explode violently, but this fact was not widely known at the time. As a result, the longshoremen loading the ship failed to take proper precautions as they handled this dangerous cargo. Smoking was forbidden, according to signs posted on the dock and on the ship, but this rule was often violated. The longshoremen not only often smoked while working in the ship's hold but also sometimes laid lighted cigarettes down on the paper bags containing fertilizer. On April 14, two days before the disaster, a cigarette started a small fire among the bags. Luck was with the workers that day, and the fire was put out quickly.

Events Leading to the Explosion. On the morning of April 16, 1947, longshoremen resumed loading ammonium nitrate into hold number 4 of the ill-fated ship. About 2,300 tons had already been loaded on previous days. Shortly after loading resumed at 8 A.M. someone saw smoke. It appeared to be coming from several layers deep in the hold. First the men poured a gallon jug of drinking water on the fire. Next, two of the ship's fire extinguishers were discharged. Unfortunately, neither of these measures did much good. A fire hose was lowered into the hold, but the captain refused to turn the water on, because he knew the water would ruin the cargo. As a precaution the captain instructed the longshoremen to remove the small arms ammunition from hold number 5.

As the fire worsened the workers left the hold, and the hatch covers were reinstalled. This meant laying long wooden boards across the deck opening and covering them with tarpaulins. The ventilating system that circulated fresh air through the hold was turned off, and the steam-smothering system was turned on. Steam was admitted to the hold in the hope that it would displace all air and deprive the fire of the oxygen it needed. This did not work, because ammonium nitrate contains oxygen in its molecules. This oxygen is released as the fertilizer decomposes during a fire.

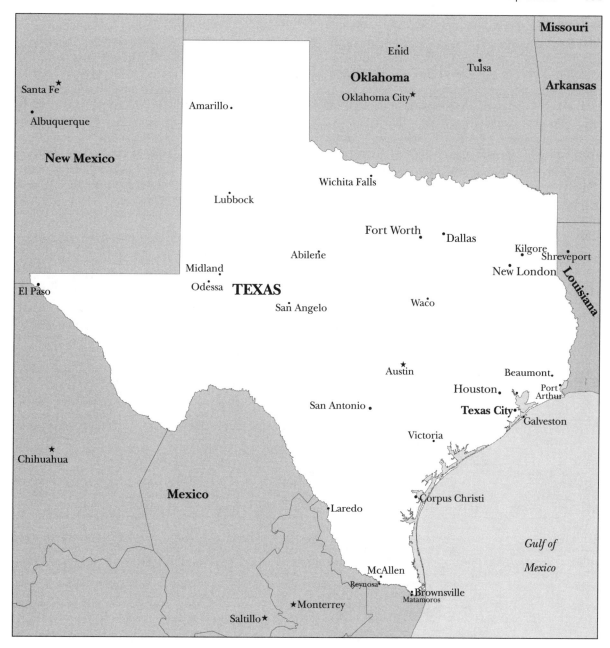

As steam pressure built up in the hold, it blew the hatch covers off at about 8:30 A.M. A photograph of the scene shows a fire hose spraying water onto the ship at about 8:45. Flames erupted from the open hatch around 9:00; at 9:12 there was a tremendous explosion that was heard as far as 150 miles away. Two small airplanes flying overhead were knocked out of the sky. A wall of water 15 feet high surged across the harbor and carried a large steel barge up onto dry land. Everyone still aboard the ship and in the immediate area on the dock was killed instantly. The ship's anchor, which weighed 1.5 tons, was later found about 2 miles from the site of the explosion.

Results of the Blast. Near the port area in Texas City were oil refineries, petroleum tank farms, and the Monsanto Chemical Company. Red-hot pieces of the exploding ship caused widespread damage at these facilities. Tanks of highly flammable chemicals exploded at various locations ashore. A residential area, inhabited mostly by poor African Americans and Hispanics, was just half a mile from the ship. Many homes in this area were damaged or destroyed, and many people were killed and injured.

The Monsanto plant was only about 350 feet from the explosion site; three-quarters of this facility was heavily damaged or destroyed. Monsanto's steam plant and powerhouse were destroyed. There were 574 people working at Monsanto that day. Of these, 234 were killed immediately or died of their injuries, and another 200 were injured.

Half of Texas City's firefighters, including its chief, and all of its fire-fighting equipment had been sent to fight the shipboard fire. These personnel and their equipment were wiped out by the explosion, seriously hampering efforts to extinguish the fires ashore.

Another Liberty ship, *High Flyer,* was tied up near *Grandcamp.* This ship was also loading ammonium nitrate fertilizer. When *Grandcamp* exploded, *High Flyer* was torn loose from its moorings and driven across the harbor, where it lodged against the *Wilson B. Keene.* The explosion killed one member of *High*

The explosion of the freighter Grandcamp *in Texas City, Texas.* (AP/Wide World Photos)

Flyer's crew. The others tied up their ship to the *Wilson B. Keene* and climbed over that ship to a dock. *High Flyer*'s hatch covers were blown off by the force of the explosion, which meant flying debris could fall into its holds and start fires.

Because the entire area was blanketed by heavy black smoke, officials were not aware that *High Flyer* was on fire. During the evening of April 16, a Coast Guard vessel discovered the burning ship, but the captain decided it was too dangerous to try to tow it out to sea. At about 1 A.M. on April 17, *High Flyer* exploded with a force at least as great as the earlier explosion of *Grandcamp*. It appears that 2 deaths and 24 injuries resulted from this second explosion. Casualties were relatively light because most people had left the port area.

Rescue Efforts. Texas City's police chief, William Ladish, was in his office when the explosion occurred. He was knocked to the floor by its force even though he was more than a mile from the ship. The police radio was knocked out by the blast, so Chief Ladish ran to the telephone exchange and called Captain Simpson of the Houston Police Department. Telephone-company officials called the National Guard and hospitals in Galveston and Goose Creek. Chief Ladish dispatched some of his men to set up roadblocks and some to assist the rescue efforts on the docks.

Mayor Curtis Trahan issued a disaster declaration and ordered the city's health officer, Dr. Clarence Quinn, to set up first-aid stations. Fred Dowdy, the assistant fire chief, was out of town when the explosion occurred. When he returned, he took charge of what was left of the fire department. George Gill and a group of volunteers from the Carbide and Carbon Chemical Company, located at the edge of town, rushed to the scene with fire-fighting equipment from their plant. About two hours after the blast, officers and enlisted men from the Galveston office of the Army Corps of Engineers arrived on the scene with trucks and heavy equipment.

Texas City's three medical clinics were immediately overwhelmed with injured people in urgent need of medical care. The nearby city of Galveston activated the part of its hurricane relief plan having to do with emergency medical care. Galveston's three large hospitals and its Red Cross chapter were put on alert. Ambulances and city buses assembled at the hospitals; doctors and nurses carrying medical supplies boarded these vehicles and were transported to Texas City. An unused army hospital at Fort Crockett in Galveston was reopened and used to treat the wounded. More than 500 seriously injured people were transported from Texas City to Galveston by ambulance, bus, truck, taxi, and private car. About 250 were taken to hospitals in Houston.

It was impossible to keep accurate records of the names of the injured and where they were sent. As a result it was hours or days before families knew whether loved ones who had been in the port area were dead or alive. Both the Red Cross and Galveston radio station KGBC tried to collect this information, but they met with little early success.

A variety of law enforcement personnel converged on Texas City to help maintain order. The Texas Highway Patrol set up roadblocks. Texas Rangers kept order within the city, and a Houston police captain was responsible for order in the port area. Local police departments, sheriff's departments, and the state police also sent personnel.

Efforts to control the situation after the explosion were poorly coordinated, because there was no emergency plan for the port. Port officials, city officials, U.S. Coast Guard, U.S. Army, Red Cross, and other organizations dispatched teams of people to help. Unfortunately, these groups were unable to communicate with each other. Telephones were knocked out by the explosions, and portable radio communications were not compatible between groups. Although the mayor of Texas City and the chief of police tried to establish a command center, they were unable to get a clear picture of the situation. Each individual group of rescuers did what seemed best at the time, and many heroic acts were performed, but no overall system of priorities was established.

Cause and Effects. Certainly the immediate cause of the disaster was careless handling of a very dangerous material, ammonium nitrate. During World War II this chemical was produced and transported under the supervision of the U.S. Army, and it was used as an explosive. The army insisted on very careful handling of the material. When the war ended factories continued to produce ammonium nitrate and sell it as fertilizer. Army supervision ended, and the people who handled the transportation of the fertilizer seem to have been unaware of its danger. The U.S. Coast Guard, which is responsible for the safety of ships, did not assume an active role. It appears that port officials and ship's officers did not know the potential for danger.

In the aftermath of the disaster some 273 lawsuits on behalf of 8,484 persons were filed against the United States government under the Federal Tort Claims Act. These suits were consolidated into a single case referred to as *Dalehite v. United States*. Early in 1950 Judge T. M. Kennerly of the U.S. District Court, Southern Division of Texas, found in favor of the people who sued. The judge's opinion stated,

> All of Said Fertilizer stored on the *Grandcamp* and *High Flyer* was manufactured or caused to be manufactured by Defendant [the U.S. government], shipped by Defendant to Texas City, and caused or permitted by Defendant to be loaded into such Steamships for shipment abroad. . . . All was done with full knowledge of Defendant that such fertilizer was an inherently dangerous explosive and fire hazard, and all without any warning to the public in Texas City or to persons handling same.

This decision was, however, overturned by the Fifth Circuit Court. In 1953 the Supreme Court voted four to three to uphold the action of the Fifth Circuit Court. Clark Thompson, U.S. Representative for Galveston, introduced a bill in Congress to compensate the victims. Enacted in 1955 this bill resulted in payments of almost $17 million to 1,394 individuals.

Perhaps some good came of this terrible event. It caused officials at many levels to reevaluate safety regulations and disaster plans. A hospital was finally built in Texas City in 1949. The National Red Cross, not satisfied with its ability to provide assistance to Texas City, revised its entire disaster relief program. Refineries and chemical plants upgraded their firefighting capabilities, and they entered into mutual assistance agreements. In 1950 the Coast Guard established a new port safety program, and in 1951 it reestablished the security provisions for handling dangerous cargoes, which had been in effect during World War II. These rules prohibited the handling of dangerous cargo near populated areas, required the stationing of trained guards, and restricted welding, smoking, and the movement of motor vehicles when such cargo was being handled.

Texas City recovered quickly from the disaster. Most of the people who fled were back in their homes within a few months. Retail businesses resumed normal operation, and many new homes were built. Refineries and chemical plants were rebuilt, and the city's population grew steadily. Port operations resumed, but cargo loading was limited to petroleum products. Ammonium nitrate was never shipped through Texas City again.

Edwin G. Wiggins

FOR FURTHER INFORMATION:

Barnaby, K. C. *Some Ship Disasters and Their Causes.* New York: A. S. Barnes, 1968.

Cross, Farrell, and Wilbur Cross. "When the World Blew up at Texas City." *Texas Parade,* September, 1972, 70-74.

Stephens, Hugh W. *The Texas City Disaster, 1947.* Austin: University of Texas Press, 1997.

1951: Illinois

MINE EXPLOSION
DATE: December 21, 1951
PLACE: West Frankfort, Illinois
RESULT: 119 dead

At about 6:30 P.M. on December 21, 1951, the worst mine disaster in Illinois history rocked the small southern Illinois community of West Frankfort. An explosion powerful enough to shake mines 12 miles away blew through the Orient Number 2 Mine. About 217 miners were in the shafts when the blast was ignited. The sound was so loud some miners were immediately deafened and never regained their hearing. The explosion created a strong wind that raced through the main tunnel, knocking out telephones and other equipment. The mine quickly filled with coal dust, coal gas, and intense flames. Rescue teams had to wait six hours for the gas to clear before they could enter the shaft. They eventually dragged 119 charred, mutilated, and blackened bodies out of the mine.

Investigators concluded that a spark from a piece of electrical equipment ignited the blast. They also blamed the state legislature for failing to pass a Coal Mine Safety Code that had been debated the previous term. It failed to pass mainly because of opposition from mine owners and coal mine union leaders. Both sides argued that the code would have increased the cost of digging coal, which would have

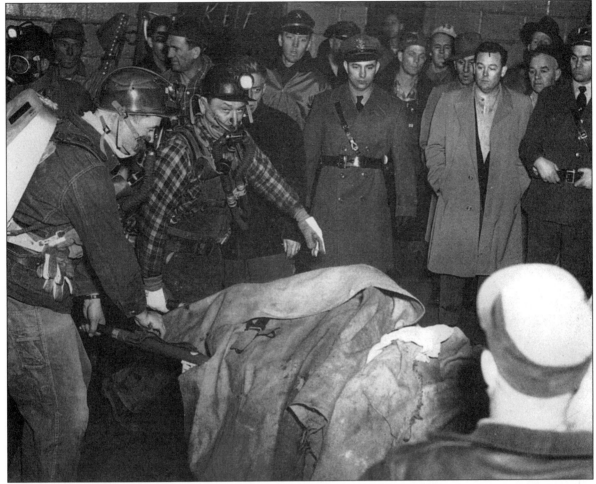

Rescue workers remove a victim from a coal mine in Franfort, Illinois, following a powerful explosion. (AP/Wide World Photos)

led to fewer jobs. Shortly after the West Frankfort disaster, a safety code was passed and signed into law.

Leslie V. Tischauser

FOR FURTHER INFORMATION:
Chicago Tribune, December 22-26, 1951.
Humphrey, Hiram B. *Historical Summary of Coal Mine Explosions in the United States, 1810-1958*. Washington, D.C.: U.S. Government Printing Office, Bureau of Mines, 1959.

1957: Virginia

MINE EXPLOSION
DATE: February 4, 1957

PLACE: Bishop, Virginia
RESULT: 37 dead

At 1:15 in the morning of February 4, 1957, a gigantic explosion roared through the Pocahontas Fuel Company Mine outside of Bishop, Virginia. The coal-gas explosion trapped 180 miners 337 feet below the surface. Dozens of miners struggled out of the various shafts, heading for the surface. The survivors told of smelling gas fumes shortly before they heard the blast.

A group of 37 miners remained far down in the mine, where they barricaded themselves behind a makeshift wall. Shortly after the explosion, rescuers contacted them by telephone and conversed with them for several hours. The frightened miners explained that they were still in good shape but warned that gas fumes were still very heavy. The last words heard from the 37 were, "O.K., if the fumes die down." By the time rescuers reached the area of the mine in which they were trapped, all the miners were found dead from suffocation, still holding onto their picks.

A postblast investigation traced the cause of the blast to an electric spark from a wire. Investigators found no reason to believe the explosion resulted from carelessness or human error. The Bishop disaster was the worst in Virginia coal fields in the twentieth century.

Leslie V. Tischauser

FOR FURTHER INFORMATION:
The New York Times, February 4, 1957.

1962: Germany

MINE EXPLOSION
DATE: February 7, 1962
PLACE: Volkingen, Germany
RESULT: 298 dead

The coal mine that exploded in Volkingen, West Germany, on February 7, 1962, was considered to be the safest and most modern in the industrial region of the Saarland, Germany's major mining region. However, at 8 A.M., methane (coal) gas exploded on the mine's second level, sending a roaring fire through the mine. The flames reached a region 1,800 feet below the surface where 480 miners were working, setting off a second blast.

The eruption of coal gas was caused by an electric spark. The force of the explosion crushed hundreds of miners, and many others' lungs were punctured by flying debris. After rescuers reached the level at which the miners were working, they recovered almost 300 headless bodies. None of the miners had survived. This was the second worst mine explosion in German history. The worst took place in 1946 at the Kamen Works, where 402 miners were blown apart by a massive gas explosion. The exact cause of the Volkingen blast was never discovered.

Leslie V. Tischauser

FOR FURTHER INFORMATION:
The New York Times, February 8, 1962.

1962: Pennsylvania

MINE EXPLOSION
DATE: December 6, 1962
PLACE: Carmichaels, Pennsylvania
RESULT: 37 dead

Two explosions ripped through the Robena Number 3 Mine at Carmichaels, Pennsylvania, on December 6, 1962. The first occurred at 1:05 P.M., and the second roared through the mine twenty minutes later. Thirty-seven miners were killed by the first blast, caused by a spark from a railroad car-puller motor. The spark set off an explosion of coal gas. Air flow to the main shaft was interrupted, allowing further buildup of coal gas, delaying for several vital hours rescue efforts.

The miners died from the force of the explosion, most being killed by flying debris. Forty-three miners came out of the mine shortly after the explosion. The victims' bodies were recovered and brought to the surface several days after the explosion. Investigators found inadequate measures had been taken to prevent coal-gas accumulation. The electric equipment used on the mine railroad was not well maintained, a fact that was directly linked to the explosion.

Leslie V. Tischauser

FOR FURTHER INFORMATION:
The New York Times, December 7-9, 1962.

1963: Japan

MINE EXPLOSION
DATE: November 9, 1963
PLACE: Omuta, Japan
RESULT: About 452 dead

A massive explosion swept through the Mitsui Miiki Coal Mine near Omuta, Japan, on November 9, 1963, killing an estimated 452 miners and severely wounding 450 more. Omuta is a port city on Japan's southernmost island of Kyūshū. Most of the killed or injured were trapped deep within the mine at an area 2,400 feet from the mine's opening. Lethal levels of coal gas contributed to the death toll, although most of the victims were killed by the force of the explosion and flying debris. A government investigation found inadequate safety measures in the mine, even though the government itself was accused by mine union officials of failing to provide sufficient safety measures for the mines.

The explosion took place on the same day 162 Japanese citizens were killed when two passenger trains crashed head on 10 miles north of Yokohama. Both accidents led to growing pressure to force industries to promote safety for workers. The Omuta mine disaster was the worst, in terms of loss of life, in Japan's history.

Leslie V. Tischauser

FOR FURTHER INFORMATION:
The New York Times, November 10, 1963.

1965: India

MINE EXPLOSION
DATE: May 28, 1965
PLACE: Dhanbad, India
RESULT: More than 475 dead

A huge blast destroyed the Dhori Coal Mine in Dharbad in the Indian state of Bihar on May 28, 1965. The mine was located about 225 miles northwest of Calcutta in east India. The explosion devastated the interior of the mine and obliterated several buildings in the vicinity. Rescue workers were hampered by intense fires and more explosions during the day. Accumulations of coal gas also made rescue efforts difficult. Investigators blamed an electric spark or a small flame from a match lighted by a miner that ignited coal dust.

One hundred miners at the surface were killed as huge timbers from the mine flew threw the air, smashing the men's heads and bodies. The force of the explosion rattled buildings more than 5 miles away. Eventually, 375 badly burned and mangled bodies were brought out of the mine. The disaster was the worst in the history of India's mining industry.

Leslie V. Tischauser

FOR FURTHER INFORMATION:
The New York Times, May 29-30, 1965.

1965: Japan

MINE EXPLOSION
DATE: June 1, 1965
PLACE: Fukuoka, Japan
RESULT: 237 dead

A coal gas explosion at the Yamano Coal Company Mine, 20 miles west of the city of Fukuoka on the island of Kyūshū, killed 237 miners. Thirty-seven others were badly injured, while 279 men survived the blast. Most of the dead were crushed by tons of rocks that crashed through the mine shafts following the gigantic explosion. A hot, intense fire added to the toll of death and destruction. Outside the mine 2,000 wives, relatives, and friends kept a two-day vigil as rescuers entered the mine looking for survivors. The bodies were found in groups of tens and twenties. All the victims were crushed to death or asphyxiated by coal gas. Only six years before, 10 miners had died and 24 were injured in the same mine. The Japanese Minister of Trade and Industries resigned after the 1965 disaster because he was held responsible for the tragedy. Investigators linked the explosion to an electric spark that set off an explosion of coal gas and dust. This explosion was the second worst in Japanese history. The worst disaster had taken place two years earlier at Omuta, where more than 400 miners were killed.

Leslie V. Tischauser

FOR FURTHER INFORMATION:
The New York Times, June 2-3, 1965.

1972: Rhodesia

MINE EXPLOSION
DATE: June 6, 1972
PLACE: Northwest Rhodesia (now Zimbabwe)
RESULT: 427 dead

An explosion in the Wankie Company Coal Mine in northwest Rhodesia (now Zimbabwe) trapped 468 men hundreds of feet underground in the sloping shafts of the country's largest mine. Rescue efforts could not begin until the day after the blast because of accumulations of coal gas resulting in two smaller explosions. The rescue operation was halted within

Rescue crews about to descend into the Wankie mine in Rhodesia after an explosion. (AP/Wide World Photos)

two days because, as the mine company president said, there was "no cause for hope." The final death toll was not announced for almost a month, and the bodies of the victims were never recovered. The explosion was probably caused by an accumulation of oil and grease on a machine that came in contact with an electrical wire. It was the worst disaster in the history of the south African nation. The toll of 427 dead made this blast one of the worst in the history of the worldwide coal mining industry.

Leslie V. Tischauser

FOR FURTHER INFORMATION:
The New York Times, June 7-9 and July 4, 1972.

1975: India

MINE EXPLOSION
DATE: December 27, 1975

PLACE: Dhanbad, India
RESULT: 430-700 dead

An explosion in the Chasnala Colliery took the lives of between 430 and 700 Indian miners on the evening of December 27, 1975. The huge discrepancy in numbers of the dead resulted from a conflict between the company's owners and officials of the union representing miners. Because most of the bodies were never recovered, an official toll was never agreed upon. The blast trapped hundreds of miners under thousands of tons of debris and caused water from a nearby reservoir to flood into the pits, causing more destruction. Many of the dead were working hundreds of feet below the surface and probably drowned under the estimated 140 million gallons of water that rushed into the mine. Survival would have been possible only as the result of a miracle, and no miracle was forthcoming.

The December disaster was the second in ten years that killed over 400 miners in the Indian state of

Bihar. A report issued by the Indian government suggested that the cause of the blast was a spark from an unknown source that ignited accumulated coal gas. No survivors or bodies were ever found, despite search efforts that continued until January 19, 1976.

Leslie V. Tischauser

FOR FURTHER INFORMATION:

The New York Times, December 28-29, 1975, and January 18, 1976.

1989: Soviet Union

PIPELINE EXPLOSION
DATE: June 3, 1989

PLACE: Near Asha, 750 miles east of Moscow in the Ural Mountains
RESULT: 460 dead, 720 hospitalized

During the morning of June 3, 1989, between the villages of Asha and Ufa in the Ural Mountains, a 28-inch pipeline cracked, and liquefied petroleum gas leaked out. Detecting a drop in pressure, a controller apparently turned up the pump, thereby increasing the leak, without checking further. The gas, a mixture of propane, benzene, and butane, evaporated, but because the vapor was heavier than air it collected in a gully. Overhead were two tracks of the Trans-Siberian Railway. In the evening, as two passenger trains passed each other on the tracks, a spark ignited the gas.

The resulting explosion had the force of 10,000 tons of TNT. It threw from the tracks both locomo-

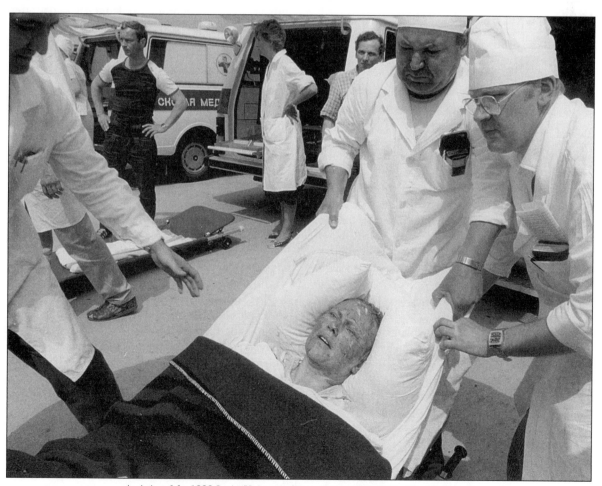

A victim of the 1989 Soviet Union pipeline explosion. (AP/Wide World Photos)

tives and 38 cars, 2 of which were completely vaporized. Of the 1,200 passengers, many of them families on their way to vacation sites, 460 died immediately, and most of the rest were injured. The blast flattened all trees for 3 miles around. The pipeline took six months to repair, and because of the explosion natural-gas delivery in the Soviet Union was down 20 percent for the year.

Roger Smith

FOR FURTHER INFORMATION:

Davis, Lee. *Man-Made Catastrophes: From the Burning of Rome to the Lockerbie Crash.* New York: Facts on File, 1993.

Wickens, Barbara. "A Deadly Explosion." *Maclean's*, June 19, 1989, 46-47.

1992: Mexico

SEWER EXPLOSION
DATE: April 22, 1992
PLACE: Guadalajara, Mexico
RESULT: More than 200 dead, more than 1,000 injured, several thousand left homeless, more than 1,000 buildings damaged

On the morning of April 22, 1992, at 10:20 A.M., the first of at least a dozen sewer explosions surprised the residents of the Reforma neighborhood of Guadalajara, a working-class area of Mexico's second-largest city. As sewer pipes exploded, they ripped up enormous trenches and craters in the streets, blasting cars and trucks off the streets and scattering debris everywhere. The explosions continued through the day, and the area took on an increasingly disastrous appearance. Buildings were leveled, people wandered the streets looking for relatives and friends, and crevices up to 20 feet deep gaped in the middle of what had been streets. The most catastrophic explosions occurred in a dense twelve-block area of about 150,000 residents, which contained mixed residential, industrial, and commercial buildings. In total, the area affected reached 20 to 30 square blocks, or several miles.

A state of emergency was declared. Hospitals quickly filled with victims. Many people died inside collapsed buildings in the direct line of the explosions, many of whom were children at home for the Easter school break. Corpses were extracted from the rubble by some of the 700 rescue workers and were carried to the Jalisco state sports complex. Electricity, telephone, water, and gas were cut off to the area, with power outages affecting other parts of the city as well. Certain areas of the city were blocked off, and about 20,000 families were evacuated.

As early as Sunday, three days prior to the explosions, Reforma residents complained of gaslike odors coming from the sewer drains in the neighborhoods. Some residents experienced nausea and stinging of the throat and eyes from gas fumes emanating from the sewer gratings. Complaints were made to the fire department, and both firefighters and officials from Pemex (the state-owned and -operated petroleum company) inspected the area and in some cases removed sewer covers but reportedly found nothing. Two newspapers reported on Tuesday that there were potential problems, but the fire chief and other officials claimed there was no danger. The day after the explosions, the governor of the state of Jalisco, Guillermo Cosio Vidaurri, announced that the inspectors had decided any possible danger was diminishing and had returned home because they were tired. About seven hours later the explosions began.

Immediate blame was placed by Pemex and the governor's spokesperson on a hexane leak from a local cooking-oil factory, which denied culpability. The governor admitted a day later that evidence blaming the factory was inconclusive. Later that day, President Carlos Salinas de Gortari ordered disaster relief aid and flew to the site to inspect the damage. He ordered Attorney General Ignacio Morales Lechuga to investigate the explosions and to prepare a report to name possible responsible parties and to determine if government officials had been negligent.

Morales Lechuga's report found Pemex and local leaders, not the cooking-oil factory, responsible for the explosions. The cause of the explosions was a leak of unleaded gas flowing from an underground Pemex pipeline carrying gas from a refinery over 100 miles away. The gasoline was estimated to have been leaking for several weeks prior to the explosions. The incident sparked further fury toward Pemex, which had a reputation as a bureaucratic and inefficient monopoly as well as a company practicing questionable health and safety measures. It was responsible for the deaths and injuries of Pemex workers across Mexico. The case also brought to light serious environmental safety problems; in addition to Pemex's

The wreckage from the 1992 sewer explosion in Guadalajara, Mexico. (AP/Wide World Photos)

fered $32.8 million toward the estimated $300 million in damages. In addition, Pemex was reorganized into four semiautonomous divisions in the hopes of improving efficiency. Pemex also hired a U.S. engineering firm to investigate its gasoline, oil, and gas pipelines and evaluate their maintenance guidelines.

Survivors of the explosions were paid about $16,000 each, while those severely injured were offered more. Weeks after the explosions, Pemex workers were still recovering gasoline from the sewer system and subsoil. Reconstruction of the Reforma neighborhood took over a year; months after the explosions, open trenches and rubble still filled the streets. The explosion was the worst in Mexico since the 1984 explosion in Mexico City, in which a propane depot exploded and killed at least 450 people. Pemex was also responsible for this explosion.

Michelle C. K. McKowen

FOR FURTHER INFORMATION:

Dabrowski, Andrea. "Guadalajara Survivors Still Puzzled by Blasts." *Washington Post*, April 24, 1992, p. A17.

Golden, Tim. "At Least 200 Dead as Blasts Rock a Mexican City." *The New York Times*, April 23, 1992, p. A1.

Katz, Gregory. "Mexico Blast Is Recuperating; Government Earns Praise, but Many Frustrations Linger." *Dallas Morning News*, October 4, 1992, p. 14.

"Mexico Blames Oil Trust and City for Blasts." *The New York Times*, April 27, 1992, p. A3.

negligence, the city sewer system was contaminated by industrial waste. Hazardous chemicals were routinely dumped into the city sewers, as there was no separate drainage system for industry.

Nine people were named in the charges; these included 4 Pemex employees, 4 government officials, and the Guadalajara mayor, Enrique Dau Flores, who resigned the day after the explosions. On April 27 the 9 individuals were jailed, facing charges of homicide, damage to public communications, damage and injury to others, and the breaking of environmental laws. Pemex accepted no immediate blame but of-

1998: Nigeria

PIPELINE EXPLOSION
DATE: October 18, 1998
PLACE: Jesse, in the Niger Delta of southern Nigeria
RESULT: More than 700 dead

Red Cross officials gather human remains after a pipeline explosion in Jesse, Nigeria. (AP/Wide World Photos)

Even though oil was Nigeria's primary export commodity, so little gasoline was reserved for domestic consumption during the late 1990's that it was constantly scarce. Thus when an aging 16-inch gasoline pipeline ruptured near Jesse on October 18, 1998, an impoverished farming village, area residents crowded around the leak to scavenge the fuel. The scene was like a marketplace, according to the local police chief.

The scavenging, called "bunkering," was illegal, and an oil company helicopter arrived to order the crowd away. Five minutes later, the spilled gasoline erupted in a fireball more than 60 feet high. Hundreds of people, mostly women and children, were incinerated immediately, and many more were severely burned. Exactly how many were killed and injured may never be known because victims' families, fearing that the government would prosecute survivors for theft, kept them away from hospitals, almost ensuring that they would not recover. The pipeline fire burned for six days until a crew of fire-fighting specialists from Houston, Texas, smothered it with foam.

Roger Smith

FOR FURTHER INFORMATION:

Walsh, James. "Holocaust in the Delta." *Time International,* November 2, 1998, 39.

Natural Disasters

Time Line

c. 65,000,000 B.C.E.:	Atlantic Ocean meteorite
c. 48,000-13,000 B.C.E.:	Arizona meteorite
c. 5000 B.C.E.:	Mazama eruption, Oregon
2400 B.C.E.:	The Great Flood, worldwide
c. 1470 B.C.E.:	Thera eruption, Aegean Sea
464 B.C.E.:	Sparta earthquake
430 B.C.E.:	The Plague of Athens
373 B.C.E.:	Greece earthquake
218 B.C.E.:	Alps avalanche, Italy
217 B.C.E.:	North Africa earthquake
64 C.E.:	The Great Fire of Rome
79:	Vesuvius eruption, Italy
c. 186:	Taupo eruption, New Zealand
365:	Egypt earthquake
365:	Egypt tsunami
526:	Syria earthquake
541:	The Plague of Justinian, Constantinople and the Mediterranean
1064:	Egypt famine
1169:	Etna eruption, Sicily
1200:	Egypt famine
1228:	Netherlands flood
1281:	Japan typhoon
1290:	China earthquake
1320:	The Black Death epidemic, Europe
1360:	France hailstorm
1362:	Öræfajökull eruption, Iceland
1421:	Netherlands flood
1490:	Europe syphilis epidemic
1502:	Dominican Republic hurricane
1520:	Aztec Empire smallpox epidemic
1556:	China earthquake
1559:	Florida hurricane
1570:	Netherlands flood
1574:	The Flood of Leiden, Netherlands
1586:	Kelut eruption, Indonesia
1591:	Taal eruption, Philippines
1596:	Japan tsunami
1601:	Russia famine
1622:	Cuba hurricane
1631:	Vesuvius eruption, Italy
1638:	England tornado
1640:	Japan tsunami
1642:	China flood
1657:	The Meireki Fire, Japan
1665:	The Great Plague of London
1666:	West Indies hurricane
1666:	The Great Fire of London
1669:	Etna eruption, Sicily
1683:	Timor eruption, Indonesia
1692:	Jamaica earthquakes
1703:	England hurricane
1703:	Japan earthquake
1713:	North Carolina hurricane
1715:	Florida hurricane
1718:	Switzerland avalanche
1722:	Russia ergotism epidemic
1722:	Jamaica hurricane
1735:	New England diphtheria epidemic
1737:	Bay of Bengal cyclone
1737:	India cyclone
1740:	Ireland famine
1741:	Cotopaxi eruption, Ecuador
1741:	Japan tsunami
1755:	Lisbon earthquake, Portugal
1759:	Jorullo eruption, Mexico
1766:	Mayon eruption, Philippines
1769:	India famine
1769:	Italy lightning strike
1772:	Papandayan eruption, Indonesia
1775:	The Hurricane of Independence, U.S. East Coast
1779:	Sakurajima eruption, Japan
1780:	The Great Hurricane of 1780, Caribbean
1783:	Asama eruption, Japan
1783:	Italy earthquake
1783:	Laki eruption, Iceland
1784:	South Carolina hailstorm
1788:	Jamaica famine
1790:	Kilauea eruption, Hawaii
1790:	Skull Famine, India
1792:	Unzen eruption, Japan
1793:	Philadelphia yellow fever epidemic
1794:	Tunquraohua eruption, Ecuador
1795:	Denmark fire
1797:	Ecuador earthquake
1798:	New England blizzard

1799:	Spain and North Africa yellow fever epidemic
1806:	Guadeloupe hurricane
1807:	Luxembourg lightning strike
1811:	New Madrid earthquakes, Missouri
1812:	Venezuela earthquake
1812:	La Soufrière eruption, St. Vincent
1814:	Mayon eruption, Philippines
1815:	Tambora eruption, Indonesia
1815:	Year Without a Summer famine, United States and Europe
1819:	Gulf Coast hurricane
1822:	Galung Gung eruption, Indonesia
1822:	Chile earthquake
1824:	Neva River flood, Russia
1825:	Puerto Rico hurricane
1825:	Canada fire
1829:	Europe cholera or Asiatic cholera epidemic
1831:	Caribbean and Gulf Coast hurricane
1832:	New York City cholera epidemic
1832:	New Orleans cholera epidemic
1833:	India famine
1835:	Cosigüina eruption, Nicaragua
1835:	Chile earthquake
1835:	Florida hurricane
1837:	West Indies hurricane
1840:	Worldwide cholera epidemic
1840:	Mississippi tornado
1841:	The October Gale, Massachusetts (hurricane)
1842:	Germany fire
1844:	Mexico hurricane
1845:	Nevado del Ruiz eruption, Colombia
1845:	The Great Irish Famine
1846:	Florida hurricane
1846:	The Donner Party famine, California
1848:	New York City cholera epidemic
1848:	Turkey fire
1851:	San Francisco fire
1853:	India hailstorm
1853:	Niuafo'ou eruption, Tonga
1853:	New Orleans yellow fever epidemic
1856:	Greece lightning strike
1856:	Louisiana hurricane
1857:	Fort Tejon earthquake, California
1859:	Ecuador earthquake
1860:	Iowa tornado
1862:	Massachusetts hurricane
1862:	China typhoon

1863:	Philippines earthquake
1866:	Georgia hurricane
1866:	Canada fire
1867:	New Orleans yellow fever epidemic
1867:	San Narciso Hurricane, Puerto Rico and Virgin Islands
1868:	South America earthquake
1868:	California earthquake
1869:	Sexby's Gale, Massachusetts (hurricane)
1870:	Turkey fire
1871:	Wisconsin fire
1871:	The Great Chicago Fire
1872:	Owens Valley earthquake, California
1872:	Zanzibar hurricane
1872:	Vesuvius eruption, Italy
1872:	The Great Boston Fire
1873:	The Great Nova Scotia Hurricane
1876:	India famine
1876:	China famine
1877:	Cotopaxi eruption, Ecuador
1878:	Mississippi Valley yellow fever epidemic
1879:	Scotland bridge collapse (wind gusts)
1880:	Missouri tornado
1880:	England mine explosion
1881:	Turkey earthquake
1882:	Iowa tornado
1883:	North Sea ship collision (fog)
1883:	Krakatau eruption, Indonesia
1883:	North Atlantic ship collision (fog)
1884:	U.S. South tornadoes
1884:	Colorado mine explosion
1884:	Virginia mine explosion
1885:	India earthquake
1886:	U.S. Midwest blizzard
1886:	Minnesota tornado
1886:	Texas hurricane
1886:	Charleston earthquake, South Carolina
1887:	Riviera earthquakes
1887:	Switzerland flood
1887:	Yellow River flood, China
1887:	English Channel ship collision (fog)
1888:	The Great Blizzard of 1888, U.S. Northeast
1888:	India hailstorm
1888:	Bandai eruption, Japan
1889:	The Johnstown Flood, Pennsylvania
1890:	Mississippi River flood
1890:	Kentucky tornado
1890:	English Channel shipwreck (fog)
1891:	U.S. Midwest blizzard

1891:	Japan earthquake	1907:	Jamaica earthquake
1892:	Worldwide cholera epidemic	1907:	West Virginia mine explosion
1892:	Worldwide bubonic plague epidemic	1907:	Pennsylvania mine explosion
1892:	Oklahoma mine explosion	1908:	Massachusetts fire
1892:	Switzerland avalanche	1908:	U.S. South tornadoes
1893:	The Sea Islands Hurricane, Georgia and the Carolinas	1908:	Siberia comet or meteorite
		1908:	Pennsylvania mine explosion
1893:	U.S. South hurricane	1908:	Italy earthquake
1894:	Minnesota fire	1909:	Caribbean and Mexico hurricane
1896:	Texas tornado	1909:	U.S. South hurricane
1896:	St. Louis tornado	1909:	Illinois fire
1896:	Japan tsunami	1910:	Washington State avalanche
1897:	India earthquake	1911:	Taal eruption, Philippines
1897:	Mayon eruption, Philippines	1911:	New York and Pennsylvania heat wave
1898:	U.S. Northeast blizzard	1911:	Yangtze River flood, China
1899:	Wisconsin tornado	1912:	Mississippi River flood
1899:	San Ciriaco Hurricane, Puerto Rico	1912:	The Sinking of *Titanic* (iceberg)
1899:	Alaska earthquake	1912:	Katmai eruption, Alaska
1900:	Galveston Hurricane, Texas	1912:	The Black River Hurricane, Jamaica
1900:	Uganda African sleeping sickness epidemic	1913:	Nebraska tornadoes
		1913:	Ohio, Indiana, and Illinois flood
1900:	New York State typhoid epidemic	1913:	New Mexico mine explosion
1900:	New Jersey fire	1914:	West Virginia mine explosion
1902:	Russia earthquake	1914:	Canada ship collision (fog)
1902:	Guatemala earthquake	1915:	Italy earthquake
1902:	La Soufrière eruption, St. Vincent	1915:	British Columbia avalanche
1902:	Pelée eruption, Martinique	1915:	Zhu River flood, China
1902:	Texas tornado	1915:	Texas and Louisiana hurricane
1902:	Pennsylvania mine explosion	1915:	Louisiana hurricane
1902:	Santa María eruption, Guatemala	1916:	Netherlands flood
1902:	Turkestan earthquake	1916:	Southern California flood
1903:	South Pacific tsunami	1916:	Chicago heat wave
1903:	Canada rockslide	1916:	United States polio epidemic
1903:	Armenia earthquake	1916:	Alps avalanche, Italy
1903:	Kansas and Missouri Rivers flood	1917:	English Channel ship collision (fog)
1903:	Georgia tornado	1917:	Colorado mine explosion
1903:	Willow Creek flood, Oregon	1917:	Illinois tornadoes
1903:	Wyoming mine explosion	1917:	Boquerón eruption, El Salvador
1904:	Maryland fire	1917:	New York City heat wave
1904:	Arkansas River flood, Colorado	1917:	Nova Scotia ship explosion
1905:	India earthquake	1918:	Worldwide influenza epidemic
1905:	Oklahoma tornado	1918:	Minnesota fire
1905:	Vesuvius eruption, Italy	1919:	Kelut eruption, Indonesia
1905:	Italy earthquake	1919:	Minnesota tornado
1906:	Masaya eruption, Nicaragua	1919:	Florida and Texas hurricane
1906:	Colombia and Ecuador earthquakes	1920:	Chicago tornado
1906:	Taiwan earthquake	1920:	U.S. South tornado
1906:	San Francisco earthquake	1920:	The Great Russian Famine
1906:	Chile earthquake	1920:	China earthquake
1906:	Florida hurricane	1921:	Arkansas River flood, Colorado

1921:	San Antonio River flood, Texas		1933:	France train collision (fog)
1922:	U.S. East Coast blizzard		1934:	India earthquake
1923:	Wyoming mine explosion		1934:	Japan fire
1923:	The Great Kwanto Earthquake, Japan		1935:	Florida hurricane
1923:	Northern California fire		1935:	The Hairpin Hurricane, Caribbean and Central America
1924:	West Virginia mine explosion		1936:	U.S. South tornadoes
1924:	U.S. South tornado		1937:	Ohio River flood, U.S. Midwest
1924:	Ohio tornado		1937:	Texas school explosion
1925:	The Great Tri-State Tornado, Missouri, Illinois, and Indiana		1937:	The *Hindenburg* Disaster, New Jersey (explosion)
1925:	Ohio airship crash (wind gusts)		1938:	Custer Creek flood, Montana
1926:	Mauna Loa eruption, Hawaii		1938:	The Great New England Hurricane of 1938
1926:	New Jersey lightning strike		1939:	Chile earthquake
1926:	The Great Miami Hurricane		1939:	Yellow River flood, China
1926:	Cuba hurricane		1939:	Japan blizzard
1926:	Colombia landslide		1939:	Turkey earthquake
1927:	Texas tornado		1940:	Washington State bridge collapse (wind gusts)
1927:	Mississippi River flood		1940:	U.S. Midwest blizzard
1927:	U.S. Midwest tornado		1941:	China freeze
1927:	China earthquake		1941:	U.S. Midwest blizzard
1927:	Kentucky River flood		1941:	Peru mudslide
1927:	St. Louis tornado		1942:	Mississippi tornadoes
1927:	New England flood		1943:	Paricutín eruption, Mexico
1927:	Pittsburgh factory explosion		1943:	Montana mine explosion
1928:	St. Francis Dam Collapse, Southern California (flood)		1943:	Black Wednesday smog, Los Angeles
1928:	Pennsylvania mine explosion		1944:	India ship explosion
1928:	Rokatenda eruption, Indonesia		1944:	West Virginia, Pennsylvania, and Maryland tornado
1928:	San Felipe Hurricane, Florida and Caribbean		1944:	Cleveland gas tanks explosion
1929:	Pennsylvania mine explosion		1944:	Typhoon Cobra, Philippines
1930:	Dominican Republic hurricane		1945:	U.S. Midwest tornadoes
1931:	Ecuador landslide		1945:	New York City plane crash (fog)
1931:	Italy avalanche		1946:	Hawaii tsunami
1931:	New Zealand earthquake		1946:	Japan tsunami
1931:	China mine explosion		1947:	Western Europe freeze
1931:	United States heat wave		1947:	Texas, Oklahoma, and Kansas tornadoes
1931:	Yangtze River flood, China		1947:	Texas ship explosion
1931:	The Great Belize Hurricane		1947:	Florida and Gulf Coast hurricane
1931:	Merapi eruption, Indonesia		1948:	U.S. South freeze
1932:	U.S. South tornadoes		1948:	U.S. Midwest and East freeze
1932:	Dust Bowl, Great Plains (dust storms)		1948:	Columbia River flood, U.S. Northwest
1932:	France mudslides		1948:	Japan earthquake
1932:	California airship unmooring (wind gusts)		1948:	New York City heat wave
1932:	San Ciprian Hurricane, Puerto Rico		1948:	Pennsylvania smog
1932:	Cuba hurricane		1949:	Missouri tornado
1933:	Japan tsunami		1949:	Ecuador earthquake
1933:	Long Beach earthquake			
1933:	Mexico hurricane			

1949:	China fire
1950:	India earthquake
1950:	Nebraska flood
1950:	Huai and Yangtze Rivers flood, China
1951:	Lamington eruption, New Guinea
1951:	Alps avalanche
1951:	Kansas and Missouri Rivers flood
1951:	Texas heat wave
1951:	Hurricane Charlie, Jamaica and Mexico
1951:	Po River flood, Italy
1951:	Hibok-Hibok eruption, Philippines
1951:	Illinois mine explosion
1952:	Sierra Nevada blizzard
1952:	Austria avalanches
1952:	U.S. South tornadoes
1952:	Kern County earthquake, California
1952:	The Great London Fog (smog)
1952:	Austria avalanche
1953:	North Sea flood, Netherlands, Great Britain, and Belgium
1953:	Texas tornado
1953:	The Flint-Beecher Tornado, Michigan and Ohio
1953:	Massachusetts tornado
1954:	Alps avalanche, Austria, Italy, Germany, Switzerland
1954:	Rio Grande flood, Texas and Mexico
1954:	Tibet flood
1954:	Iran flood
1954:	Hurricane Carol, U.S. East Coast
1954:	Algeria earthquake
1954:	Hurricane Hazel, Caribbean, U.S. East Coast, Canada
1954:	Haiti landslide
1955:	Kansas and Oklahoma tornadoes
1955:	Hurricanes Connie and Diane, U.S. East Coast
1955:	Typhoon Iris, China
1955:	California heat wave
1955:	Hurricane Hilda, Mexico
1955:	Hurricane Janet, Windward Islands, Belize, and Mexico
1955:	Mexico landslide
1955:	Northern California flood
1956:	Europe blizzard
1956:	New England ice storm
1956:	North Atlantic ship collision (fog)
1956:	Hurricane Flossy, southeastern United States
1956:	Cleveland National Forest fire
1957:	Virginia mine explosion
1957:	Missouri tornado
1957:	Hurricane Audrey, Louisiana and Texas
1957:	Western Europe heat wave
1957:	Iran earthquake
1957:	Finland lightning strike
1957:	Iraq hailstorm
1957:	England train collision (fog)
1958:	U.S. East Coast and Midwest blizzard
1958:	Saudi Arabia heat wave
1958:	Nova Scotia rockslide
1959:	The Great Leap Forward Famine, China
1959:	North Sea ship collision (iceberg)
1959:	St. Louis tornado
1959:	Malpasset Dam Collapse, France (flood)
1960:	South Africa rockslide
1960:	Philippines rockslide
1960:	Morocco earthquakes
1960:	Chile earthquake
1960:	Hawaii tsunami
1960:	India heat wave
1960:	Hurricane Donna, Caribbean, U.S. East Coast
1960:	New York City plane collision (fog)
1961:	Ukraine mudslide
1961:	Japan landslides and mudslides
1961:	Hurricane Carla, Texas
1961:	Hurricane Hattie, Belize
1962:	Peru avalanche
1962:	Germany mine explosion
1962:	Germany flood
1962:	Peru mudslide
1962:	Iran earthquake
1962:	Spain flood
1962:	London smog
1962:	Pennsylvania mine explosion
1963:	Agung eruption, Indonesia
1963:	Yugoslavia earthquake
1963:	Hurricane Flora, Haiti and Cuba
1963:	The Vaiont Dam Disaster, Italy (rockslide)
1963:	Surtsey Island eruption, Iceland
1963:	Japan mine explosion
1963:	Maryland lightning strike
1964:	The Great Alaska Earthquake
1964:	Hurricane Cleo, Caribbean and Florida
1965:	British Columbia avalanche
1965:	Chile earthquake
1965:	U.S. Midwest tornadoes
1965:	India mine explosion

1980: United States heat wave
1980: Hurricane Allen, Caribbean, Mexico, and Texas
1980: Algeria earthquake
1980: Italy earthquake
1981: Africa drought
1981: Yellow River flood, China
1982: San Francisco landslides and mudslides
1982: Austria avalanche
1982: Alps avalanches, France
1982: El Chichón eruption, Mexico
1982: Nicaragua and Honduras flood
1982: Pacific Ocean El Niño
1982: Ganges River flood, India
1982: North Yemen earthquake
1983: Australia fire
1983: Ganges and Brahmaputra Rivers flood, Bangladesh
1984: Africa famine
1984: The Carolinas tornadoes
1985: Canada, Ohio, and Pennsylvania tornadoes
1985: Italy flood
1985: Texas plane crash (wind gusts)
1985: Mexico City earthquake
1985: Nevado del Ruiz eruption, Colombia
1986: Lake Nyos eruption, Cameroon
1986: California drought
1987: Ecuador earthquake
1987: China fire
1987: Texas tornado
1987: Whittier earthquake, Southern California
1988: Bangladesh flood
1988: Yellowstone National Park fire
1988: Hurricane Gilbert, Jamaica and Mexico
1988: Armenia earthquakes
1989: Soviet Union pipeline explosion
1989: Hurricane Hugo, Caribbean and the Carolinas
1989: Loma Prieta earthquake, Northern California
1989: Alabama tornado
1990: Iran earthquake
1990: Philippines earthquake
1991: Italy ship collision (fog)
1991: Kansas tornado
1991: Bangladesh cyclone
1991: Pinatubo eruption, Philippines
1991: Yangtze River flood, China

1991: The Oakland Hills Fire, Northern California
1991: Tropical Storm Thelma, Philippines
1991: California dust storm
1992: Turkey earthquakes
1992: Mexico sewer explosion
1992: Landers and Big Bear earthquakes, Southern California
1992: Hurricane Andrew, Florida, Louisiana, and the Bahamas
1992: Indonesia earthquake
1993: U.S. East Coast blizzard
1993: The Great Mississippi River Flood of 1993
1993: India earthquakes
1993: Southern California fire
1994: Northridge earthquake, Southern California
1994: U.S. South tornado
1994: Bolivia earthquake
1994: Tropical Storm Gordon, Caribbean and Florida
1994: Merapi eruption, Indonesia
1995: California flood
1995: Northern Europe flood
1995: Kobe earthquake, Japan
1995: India avalanche
1995: Zaire Ebola virus epidemic
1995: Arizona dust storm
1995: Texas hailstorm
1995: Russia earthquake
1995: Honduras lightning strike
1995: India heat wave
1995: U.S. Midwest and Northwest heat wave
1995: Hurricane Luis, Caribbean
1995: Hurricane Marilyn, U.S. Virgin Islands
1995: Hurricane Opal, U.S. South
1995: Iceland avalanche
1996: The Blizzard of '96, U.S. East Coast
1996: India avalanches
1996: Sudan sandstorm
1996: Nepal blizzard
1996: Pakistan heat wave
1996: Oklahoma and Texas heat wave
1996: Hurricane Bertha, Puerto Rico, Virgin Islands, U.S. East Coast
1996: Yosemite National Park rockslide
1996: Spain flood
1996: India blizzard
1996: Hurricane Fran, U.S. East Coast

1996:	Hurricane Hortense, Dominican Republic and Puerto Rico
1996:	Iceland flooding (glacier)
1996:	Hurricane Lili, Central America, Cuba, and Great Britain
1996:	Oregon mudslides
1996:	Europe freeze
1996:	U.S. West Coast flood
1997:	Pacific Ocean El Niño
1997:	Iran earthquakes (northwest)
1997:	Pakistan earthquake
1997:	Red River flood, North Dakota and Minnesota
1997:	Egypt sandstorm
1997:	Iran earthquake (northeast)
1997:	Hong Kong avian influenza epidemic
1997:	Texas tornado
1997:	Soufrière Hills eruption, Montserrat
1997:	Rhine and Oder Rivers flood, Central Europe
1997:	Michigan tornado
1997:	Australia landslide
1997:	Colorado River flood, Arizona
1997:	Hurricane Nora, Mexico, California, and Arizona
1997:	Indonesia fire
1997:	Italy earthquakes
1997:	Hurricane Pauline, Mexico
1998:	Canada ice storm
1998:	U.S. Northeast ice storm
1998:	Afghanistan earthquake
1998:	Mississippi, Alabama, and Georgia tornado

1998:	U.S. South heat wave
1998:	U.S. East Coast and Midwest drought
1998:	Papua New Guinea tsunami
1998:	Yangtze River flood, China
1998:	Hurricane Georges, Caribbean and U.S. South
1998:	Texas flood
1998:	Nigeria pipeline explosion
1998:	Democratic Republic of Congo lightning strike
1998:	Hurricane Mitch, Central America
1999:	The Blizzard of '99, U.S. Midwest and East Coast
1999:	Colombia earthquake
1999:	France avalanche
1999:	Washington State avalanche
1999:	Switzerland avalanche
1999:	Austria avalanches
1999:	Alaska avalanche
1999:	Oklahoma and Kansas tornado
1999:	U.S. Midwest and East Coast heat wave
1999:	New York encephalitis epidemic
1999:	Utah tornado
1999:	Turkey earthquake
1999:	Mexico flood
1999:	Hurricane Floyd, Bahamas, U.S. East Coast
1999:	Taiwan earthquake
1999:	Venezuela flood
2000:	Georgia tornadoes
2000:	Mozambique flood
2000:	New Mexico fire

Geographical List

AFGHANISTAN
1971: Afghanistan landslide
1998: Afghanistan earthquake

AFRICA. *See also individual countries*
217 B.C.E.: North Africa earthquake
1799: Spain and North Africa yellow fever
  epidemic
1968: North Africa drought
1972: Africa, Asia famine
1981: Africa drought
1984: Africa famine

ALABAMA
1979: Hurricane Frederic, Alabama and Mississippi
1989: Alabama tornado
1995: Hurricane Opal, U.S. South

ALASKA
1899: Alaska earthquake
1912: Katmai eruption, Alaska
1964: The Great Alaska Earthquake
1999: Alaska avalanche

ALGERIA
1954: Algeria earthquake
1980: Algeria earthquake

ALPS
218 B.C.E.: Alps avalanche, Italy
1916: Alps avalanche, Italy
1951: Alps avalanche
1954: Alps avalanche, Austria, Italy, Germany,
  Switzerland
1982: Alps avalanches, France

ARGENTINA
1972: Argentina heat wave

ARIZONA
c. 48,000-13,000 B.C.E.: Arizona meteorite
1995: Arizona dust storm
1997: Colorado River flood, Arizona
1997: Hurricane Nora, Mexico, California, and
  Arizona

ARMENIA
1903: Armenia earthquake
1988: Armenia earthquakes

ASIA. *See also individual countries*
1972: Africa, Asia famine

ATLANTIC OCEAN
c. 65,000,000 B.C.E.: Atlantic Ocean meteorite
1883: North Sea ship collision (fog)
1883: North Atlantic ship collision (fog)
1887: English Channel ship collision (fog)
1890: English Channel shipwreck (fog)
1912: The Sinking of *Titanic* (iceberg)
1917: English Channel ship collision (fog)
1953: North Sea flood, Netherlands, Great Britain,
  and Belgium
1956: North Atlantic ship collision (fog)
1959: North Sea ship collision (iceberg)
1977: Tenerife plane collision, Canary Islands (fog)

AUSTRALIA
1974: Australia flood
1974: Cyclone Tracy, Australia
1983: Australia fire
1997: Australia landslide

AUSTRIA
1952: Austria avalanches
1952: Austria avalanche
1954: Alps avalanche, Austria, Italy, Germany,
  Switzerland
1982: Austria avalanche
1999: Austria avalanches

BAHAMAS
1992: Hurricane Andrew, Florida, Louisiana, and
  the Bahamas
1999: Hurricane Floyd, Bahamas, U.S. East Coast

BANGLADESH. *See also* EAST PAKISTAN
1972: Bangladesh tornado
1974: Bangladesh flood
1983: Ganges and Brahmaputra Rivers flood,
  Bangladesh

1988: Bangladesh flood
1991: Bangladesh cyclone

BELGIUM
1953: North Sea flood, Netherlands, Great Britain, and Belgium

BELIZE
1931: The Great Belize Hurricane
1955: Hurricane Janet, Windward Islands, Belize, and Mexico
1961: Hurricane Hattie, Belize
1974: Hurricane Fifi, Mexico, Central America

BOLIVIA
1994: Bolivia earthquake

BRAZIL
1965: Brazil heat wave
1966: Rio de Janeiro landslides, mudslides, and rockslides
1966: Brazil flood
1967: Brazil flood
1967: Rio de Janeiro landslides, mudslides, and rockslides
1969: Rio de Janeiro heat wave
1974: Tubarão River flood, Brazil

BRITISH COLUMBIA
1915: British Columbia avalanche
1965: British Columbia avalanche

CALIFORNIA
1846: The Donner Party famine, California
1851: San Francisco fire
1857: Fort Tejon earthquake, California
1868: California earthquake
1872: Owens Valley earthquake, California
1906: San Francisco earthquake
1916: Southern California flood
1923: Northern California fire
1928: St. Francis Dam Collapse, Southern California (flood)
1932: California airship unmooring (wind gusts)
1933: Long Beach earthquake
1943: Black Wednesday smog, Los Angeles
1952: Sierra Nevada blizzard
1952: Kern County earthquake, California
1955: California heat wave

1955: Northern California flood
1956: Cleveland National Forest fire
1969: Southern California mudslides
1971: Sylmar earthquake, Southern California
1982: San Francisco landslides and mudslides
1986: California drought
1987: Whittier earthquake, Southern California
1989: Loma Prieta earthquake, Northern California
1991: The Oakland Hills Fire, Northern California
1991: California dust storm
1992: Landers and Big Bear earthquakes, Southern California
1993: Southern California fire
1994: Northridge earthquake, Southern California
1995: California flood
1996: Yosemite National Park rockslide
1997: Hurricane Nora, Mexico, California, and Arizona

CAMEROON
1986: Lake Nyos eruption, Cameroon

CANADA
1825: Canada fire
1866: Canada fire
1873: The Great Nova Scotia Hurricane
1903: Canada rockslide
1914: Canada ship collision (fog)
1915: British Columbia avalanche
1917: Nova Scotia ship explosion
1954: Hurricane Hazel, Caribbean, U.S. East Coast, Canada
1958: Nova Scotia rockslide
1965: British Columbia avalanche
1985: Canada, Ohio, and Pennsylvania tornadoes
1998: Canada ice storm

CANARY ISLANDS
1977: Tenerife plane collision, Canary Islands (fog)

CARIBBEAN
1502: Dominican Republic hurricane
1622: Cuba hurricane
1666: West Indies hurricane
1692: Jamaica earthquakes
1722: Jamaica hurricane
1780: The Great Hurricane of 1780, Caribbean
1788: Jamaica famine
1806: Guadeloupe hurricane

1812: La Soufrière eruption, St. Vincent
1825: Puerto Rico hurricane
1831: Caribbean and Gulf Coast hurricane
1837: West Indies hurricane
1867: San Narciso Hurricane, Puerto Rico and
Virgin Islands
1899: San Ciriaco Hurricane, Puerto Rico
1902: La Soufrière eruption, St. Vincent
1902: Pelée eruption, Martinique
1907: Jamaica earthquake
1909: Caribbean and Mexico hurricane
1912: The Black River Hurricane, Jamaica
1926: Cuba hurricane
1928: San Felipe Hurricane, Florida and Caribbean
1930: Dominican Republic hurricane
1932: San Ciprian Hurricane, Puerto Rico
1932: Cuba hurricane
1935: The Hairpin Hurricane, Caribbean and
Central America
1951: Hurricane Charlie, Jamaica and Mexico
1954: Hurricane Hazel, Caribbean, U.S. East Coast,
Canada
1954: Haiti landslide
1955: Hurricane Janet, Windward Islands, Belize,
and Mexico
1960: Hurricane Donna, Caribbean, U.S. East
Coast
1963: Hurricane Flora, Haiti and Cuba
1964: Hurricane Cleo, Caribbean and Florida
1966: Hurricane Inez, Caribbean, Florida, and
Mexico
1979: Hurricane David, Dominican Republic,
Puerto Rico, and the U.S. South
1980: Hurricane Allen, Caribbean, Mexico, and
Texas
1988: Hurricane Gilbert, Jamaica and Mexico
1989: Hurricane Hugo, Caribbean and the
Carolinas
1992: Hurricane Andrew, Florida, Louisiana, and
the Bahamas
1994: Tropical Storm Gordon, Caribbean and
Florida
1995: Hurricane Luis, Caribbean
1995: Hurricane Marilyn, U.S. Virgin Islands and
Puerto Rico
1996: Hurricane Bertha, Puerto Rico, Virgin
Islands, U.S. East Coast
1996: Hurricane Hortense, Dominican Republic
and Puerto Rico

1996: Hurricane Lili, Central America, Cuba, and
Great Britain
1997: Soufrière Hills eruption, Montserrat
1998: Hurricane Georges, Caribbean and U.S.
South
1999: Hurricane Floyd, Bahamas, U.S. East Coast

CENTRAL AMERICA. *See also individual countries*
1935: The Hairpin Hurricane, Caribbean and
Central America
1998: Hurricane Mitch, Central America

CHILE
1822: Chile earthquake
1835: Chile earthquake
1906: Chile earthquake
1939: Chile earthquake
1960: Chile earthquake
1965: Chile earthquake

CHINA
1290: China earthquake
1556: China earthquake
1642: China flood
1862: China typhoon
1876: China famine
1887: Yellow River flood, China
1911: Yangtze River flood, China
1915: Zhu River flood, China
1920: China earthquake
1927: China earthquake
1931: China mine explosion
1931: Yangtze River flood, China
1939: Yellow River flood, China
1941: China freeze
1949: China fire
1950: Huai and Yangtze Rivers flood, China
1955: Typhoon Iris, China
1959: The Great Leap Forward Famine, China
1975: China earthquake
1976: China earthquake
1981: Yellow River flood, China
1987: China fire
1991: Yangtze River flood, China
1998: Yangtze River flood, China

COLOMBIA
1845: Nevado del Ruiz eruption, Colombia
1906: Colombia and Ecuador earthquakes

HAWAII
1790: Kilauea eruption, Hawaii
1926: Mauna Loa eruption, Hawaii
1946: Hawaii tsunami
1960: Hawaii tsunami

HONDURAS
1974: Hurricane Fifi, Mexico, Central America
1995: Honduras lightning strike
1996: Hurricane Lili, Central America, Cuba, and
  Great Britain

HONG KONG
1972: Hong Kong landslides
1997: Hong Kong avian influenza epidemic

ICELAND
1362: Öræfajökull eruption, Iceland
1783: Laki eruption, Iceland
1963: Surtsey Island eruption, Iceland
1973: Heimaey Island eruption, Iceland
1995: Iceland avalanche
1996: Iceland flooding (glacier)

IDAHO
1976: Teton Dam Collapse, Idaho (flood)
1988: Yellowstone National Park fire

ILLINOIS
1871: The Great Chicago Fire
1909: Illinois fire
1916: Chicago heat wave
1917: Illinois tornadoes
1920: Chicago tornado
1925: The Great Tri-State Tornado, Missouri,
  Illinois, and Indiana
1951: Illinois mine explosion

INDIA
1737: Bay of Bengal cyclone
1769: India famine
1790: Skull Famine, India
1833: India famine
1853: India hailstorm
1876: India famine
1885: India earthquake
1888: India hailstorm
1897: India earthquake
1905: India earthquake

1934: India earthquake
1944: India ship explosion
1950: India earthquake
1960: India heat wave
1965: India mine explosion
1965: India heat wave
1966: India heat wave
1968: India flood
1972: India heat wave
1975: India mine explosion
1978: Yamuna and Ganges Rivers flood, India
1982: Ganges River flood, India
1993: India earthquakes
1995: India avalanche
1995: India heat wave
1996: India avalanches
1996: India blizzard

INDIANA
1925: The Great Tri-State Tornado, Missouri,
  Illinois, and Indiana

INDONESIA
1586: Kelut eruption, Indonesia
1683: Timor eruption, Indonesia
1772: Papandayan eruption, Indonesia
1815: Tambora eruption, Indonesia
1822: Galung Gung eruption, Indonesia
1883: Krakatau eruption, Indonesia
1919: Kelut eruption, Indonesia
1928: Rokatenda eruption, Indonesia
1931: Merapi eruption, Indonesia
1963: Agung eruption, Indonesia
1992: Indonesia earthquake
1994: Merapi eruption, Indonesia
1997: Indonesia fire

IOWA
1860: Iowa tornado
1882: Iowa tornado

IRAN
1954: Iran flood
1957: Iran earthquake
1962: Iran earthquake
1968: Iran earthquake
1972: Iran blizzard
1972: Iran earthquake
1978: Iran earthquake

1990: Iran earthquake
1997: Iran earthquakes (northwest)
1997: Iran earthquake (northeast)

IRAQ
1957: Iraq hailstorm

IRELAND
1740: Ireland famine
1845: The Great Irish Famine

ITALY
218 B.C.E.: Alps avalanche, Italy
64 C.E.: The Great Fire of Rome
79: Vesuvius eruption, Italy
1169: Etna eruption, Sicily
1631: Vesuvius eruption, Italy
1669: Etna eruption, Sicily
1769: Italy lightning strike
1783: Italy earthquake
1872: Vesuvius eruption, Italy
1887: Riviera earthquakes
1905: Vesuvius eruption, Italy
1905: Italy earthquake
1908: Italy earthquake
1915: Italy earthquake
1916: Alps avalanche, Italy
1931: Italy avalanche
1951: Po River flood, Italy
1954: Alps avalanche, Austria, Italy, Germany,
      Switzerland
1963: The Vaiont Dam Disaster, Italy
      (rockslide)
1966: Italy flood
1976: Italy earthquake
1980: Italy earthquake
1985: Italy flood
1991: Italy ship collision (fog)
1997: Italy earthquakes

JAMAICA
1692: Jamaica earthquakes
1722: Jamaica hurricane
1788: Jamaica famine
1907: Jamaica earthquake
1912: The Black River Hurricane, Jamaica
1951: Hurricane Charlie, Jamaica and Mexico
1988: Hurricane Gilbert, Jamaica and Mexico

JAPAN
1281: Japan typhoon
1596: Japan tsunami
1640: Japan tsunami
1657: The Meireki Fire, Japan
1703: Japan earthquake
1741: Japan tsunami
1779: Sakurajima eruption, Japan
1783: Asama eruption, Japan
1792: Unzen eruption, Japan
1888: Bandai eruption, Japan
1891: Japan earthquake
1896: Japan tsunami
1923: The Great Kwanto Earthquake, Japan
1933: Japan tsunami
1934: Japan fire
1939: Japan blizzard
1946: Japan tsunami
1948: Japan earthquake
1961: Japan landslides and mudslides
1963: Japan mine explosion
1965: Japan mine explosion
1968: Japan heat wave
1995: Kobe earthquake, Japan

KANSAS
1903: Kansas and Missouri Rivers flood
1947: Texas, Oklahoma, and Kansas tornadoes
1951: Kansas and Missouri Rivers flood
1955: Kansas and Oklahoma tornadoes
1991: Kansas tornado

KENTUCKY
1890: Kentucky tornado
1927: Kentucky River flood

LOUISIANA
1832: New Orleans cholera epidemic
1853: New Orleans yellow fever epidemic
1856: Louisiana hurricane
1867: New Orleans yellow fever epidemic
1915: Texas and Louisiana hurricane
1915: Louisiana hurricane
1957: Hurricane Audrey, Louisiana and Texas
1965: Hurricane Betsy, Florida and Louisiana
1971: Mississippi Delta tornadoes
1992: Hurricane Andrew, Florida, Louisiana, and
      the Bahamas

MISSISSIPPI RIVER
1890: Mississippi River flood
1912: Mississippi River flood
1927: Mississippi River flood
1973: Mississippi River flood
1993: The Great Mississippi River Flood of 1993

MISSOURI
1811: New Madrid earthquakes, Missouri
1880: Missouri tornado
1896: St. Louis tornado
1903: Kansas and Missouri Rivers flood
1925: The Great Tri-State Tornado, Missouri,
    Illinois, and Indiana
1927: St. Louis tornado
1949: Missouri tornado
1951: Kansas and Missouri Rivers flood
1957: Missouri tornado
1959: St. Louis tornado

MONTANA
1938: Custer Creek flood, Montana
1943: Montana mine explosion
1988: Yellowstone National Park fire

MONTSERRAT
1997: Soufrière Hills eruption, Montserrat

MOROCCO
1960: Morocco earthquakes

MOZAMBIQUE
2000: Mozambique flood

NEBRASKA
1913: Nebraska tornadoes
1950: Nebraska flood

NEPAL
1996: Nepal blizzard

NETHERLANDS
1228: Netherlands flood
1421: Netherlands flood
1570: Netherlands flood
1574: The Flood of Leiden, Netherlands
1916: Netherlands flood
1953: North Sea flood, Netherlands, Great Britain,
    and Belgium

NEW ENGLAND
1735: New England diphtheria epidemic
1798: New England blizzard
1927: New England flood
1938: The Great New England Hurricane of 1938
1954: Hurricane Carol, U.S. East Coast
1956: New England ice storm
1960: Hurricane Donna, Caribbean, U.S. East
    Coast

NEW GUINEA
1951: Lamington eruption, New Guinea

NEW JERSEY
1900: New Jersey fire
1926: New Jersey lightning strike
1937: The *Hindenburg* Disaster, New Jersey
    (explosion)

NEW MEXICO
1913: New Mexico mine explosion
2000: New Mexico fire

NEW YORK
1832: New York City cholera epidemic
1848: New York City cholera epidemic
1900: New York State typhoid epidemic
1911: New York and Pennsylvania heat wave
1917: New York City heat wave
1945: New York City plane crash (fog)
1948: New York City heat wave
1960: New York City plane collision (fog)
1966: New York City heat wave
1999: New York encephalitis epidemic

NEW ZEALAND
c. 186: Taupo eruption, New Zealand
1931: New Zealand earthquake

NICARAGUA
1835: Cosigüina eruption, Nicaragua
1906: Masaya eruption, Nicaragua
1972: Nicaragua earthquakes
1982: Nicaragua and Honduras flood
1996: Hurricane Lili, Central America, Cuba, and
    Great Britain

NIGERIA
1998: Nigeria pipeline explosion

NORTH CAROLINA
1713: North Carolina hurricane
1893: The Sea Islands Hurricane, Georgia and the Carolinas
1954: Hurricane Carol, U.S. East Coast
1984: The Carolinas tornadoes
1989: Hurricane Hugo, Caribbean and the Carolinas
1995: Hurricane Opal, U.S. South
1996: Hurricane Fran, U.S. East Coast
1999: Hurricane Floyd, Bahamas, U.S. East Coast

NORTH DAKOTA
1997: Red River flood, North Dakota and Minnesota

NORTH SEA
1883: North Sea ship collision (fog)
1953: North Sea flood, Netherlands, Great Britain, and Belgium
1959: North Sea ship collision (iceberg)

NORTH YEMEN
1982: North Yemen earthquake

NOVA SCOTIA
1873: The Great Nova Scotia Hurricane
1917: Nova Scotia ship explosion
1958: Nova Scotia rockslide

OHIO
1913: Ohio, Indiana, and Illinois flood
1924: Ohio tornado
1925: Ohio airship crash (wind gusts)
1944: Cleveland gas tanks explosion
1953: The Flint-Beecher Tornado, Michigan and Ohio

OKLAHOMA
1892: Oklahoma mine explosion
1905: Oklahoma tornado
1947: Texas, Oklahoma, and Kansas tornadoes
1979: Texas and Oklahoma tornadoes
1996: Oklahoma and Texas heat wave
1999: Oklahoma and Kansas tornado

OREGON
c. 5000 B.C.E.: Mazama eruption, Oregon
1903: Willow Creek flood, Oregon
1996: Oregon mudslides

PACIFIC OCEAN
1853: Niuafo'ou eruption, Tonga
1903: South Pacific tsunami
1951: Lamington eruption, New Guinea
1982: Pacific Ocean El Niño
1997: Pacific Ocean El Niño

PAKISTAN
1974: Pakistan earthquake
1996: Pakistan heat wave
1997: Pakistan earthquake

PAPUA NEW GUINEA
1951: Lamington eruption, New Guinea
1998: Papua New Guinea tsunami

PENNSYLVANIA
1793: Philadelphia yellow fever epidemic
1889: The Johnstown Flood, Pennsylvania
1902: Pennsylvania mine explosion
1907: Pennsylvania mine explosion
1908: Pennsylvania mine explosion
1927: Pittsburgh factory explosion
1928: Pennsylvania mine explosion
1929: Pennsylvania mine explosion
1944: West Virginia, Pennsylvania, and Maryland tornado
1948: Pennsylvania smog
1962: Pennsylvania mine explosion
1976: Philadelphia Legionnaires' disease epidemic

PERU
1941: Peru mudslide
1962: Peru avalanche
1962: Peru mudslide
1970: Peru earthquake
1971: Peru avalanche

PHILIPPINES
1591: Taal eruption, Philippines
1766: Mayon eruption, Philippines
1814: Mayon eruption, Philippines
1863: Philippines earthquake
1897: Mayon eruption, Philippines
1911: Taal eruption, Philippines
1944: Typhoon Cobra, Philippines
1951: Hibok-Hibok eruption, Philippines
1960: Philippines rockslide

1965: Taal eruption, Philippines
1972: Philippines flood
1976: Philippines earthquake
1990: Philippines earthquake
1991: Pinatubo eruption, Philippines
1991: Tropical Storm Thelma,
　　　Philippines

PORTUGAL
1755: Lisbon earthquake, Portugal
1967: Portugal flood

PUERTO RICO
1825: Puerto Rico hurricane
1867: San Narciso Hurricane, Puerto Rico and
　　　Virgin Islands
1899: San Ciriaco Hurricane, Puerto Rico
1932: San Ciprian Hurricane, Puerto Rico
1979: Hurricane David, Dominican Republic,
　　　Puerto Rico, and the U.S. South
1995: Hurricane Marilyn, U.S. Virgin Islands and
　　　Puerto Rico
1996: Hurricane Bertha, Puerto Rico, Virgin
　　　Islands, U.S. East Coast
1996: Hurricane Hortense, Dominican Republic
　　　and Puerto Rico

RHODESIA
1972: Rhodesia mine explosion
1975: Rhodesia lightning strike

ROMANIA
1977: Romania earthquake

RUSSIA. *See also* SOVIET UNION
1601: Russia famine
1722: Russia ergotism epidemic
1824: Neva River flood, Russia
1902: Russia earthquake
1908: Siberia comet or meteorite
1920: The Great Russian Famine
1995: Russia earthquake

ST. VINCENT
1812: La Soufrière eruption, St. Vincent
1902: La Soufrière eruption, St. Vincent

SAUDI ARABIA
1958: Saudi Arabia heat wave

SCOTLAND
1879: Scotland bridge collapse (wind gusts)
1978: Scotland blizzard

SIBERIA
1908: Siberia comet or meteorite

SOUTH, U.S.
1884: South tornadoes
1893: South hurricane
1908: South tornadoes
1909: South hurricane
1920: South tornado
1924: South tornado
1932: South tornadoes
1936: South tornadoes
1948: South freeze
1952: South tornadoes
1969: Hurricane Camille, U.S. South
1979: Hurricane David, Dominican Republic,
　　　Puerto Rico, and the South
1994: South tornado
1998: South heat wave
1998: Hurricane Georges, Caribbean and South

SOUTH AFRICA
1960: South Africa rockslide

SOUTH CAROLINA
1784: South Carolina hailstorm
1886: Charleston earthquake, South Carolina
1893: The Sea Islands Hurricane, Georgia and the
　　　Carolinas
1984: The Carolinas tornadoes
1989: Hurricane Hugo, Caribbean and the
　　　Carolinas
1996: Hurricane Fran, U.S. East Coast

SOUTH DAKOTA
1972: Rapid Creek flood, South Dakota

SOVIET UNION. *See also* RUSSIA
1961: Ukraine mudslide
1979: Soviet Union anthrax epidemic
1989: Soviet Union pipeline explosion

SPAIN
1799: Spain and North Africa yellow fever epidemic
1962: Spain flood

1977: Tenerife plane collision, Canary Islands (fog)
1996: Spain flood

SUDAN
1976: Zaire, Sudan Ebola virus epidemic
1996: Sudan sandstorm

SWITZERLAND
1718: Switzerland avalanche
1887: Switzerland flood
1892: Switzerland avalanche
1954: Alps avalanche, Austria, Italy, Germany, Switzerland
1999: Switzerland avalanche

SYRIA
526: Syria earthquake

TAIWAN
1906: Taiwan earthquake
1999: Taiwan earthquake

TENERIFE
1977: Tenerife plane collision, Canary Islands (fog)

TENNESSEE
1971: Mississippi Delta tornadoes

TEXAS
1886: Texas hurricane
1896: Texas tornado
1900: Galveston Hurricane, Texas
1902: Texas tornado
1915: Texas and Louisiana hurricane
1919: Florida and Texas hurricane
1921: San Antonio River flood, Texas
1927: Texas tornado
1937: Texas school explosion
1947: Texas, Oklahoma, and Kansas tornadoes
1947: Texas ship explosion
1951: Texas heat wave
1953: Texas tornado
1954: Rio Grande flood, Texas and Mexico
1957: Hurricane Audrey, Louisiana and Texas
1961: Hurricane Carla, Texas
1970: Texas tornado
1979: Texas and Oklahoma tornadoes
1980: Hurricane Allen, Caribbean, Mexico, and Texas

1985: Texas plane crash (wind gusts)
1987: Texas tornado
1995: Texas hailstorm
1997: Texas tornado
1998: Texas flood

TIBET
1954: Tibet flood

TONGA
1853: Niuafo'ou eruption, Tonga

TUNISIA
1969: Tunisia flood

TURKESTAN
1902: Turkestan earthquake

TURKEY
541: The Plague of Justinian, Constantinople and the Mediterranean
1848: Turkey fire
1870: Turkey fire
1881: Turkey earthquake
1939: Turkey earthquake
1966: Turkey earthquake
1975: Turkey earthquake
1976: Turkey earthquake
1992: Turkey earthquakes
1999: Turkey earthquake

UGANDA
1900: Uganda African sleeping sickness epidemic

UKRAINE
1961: Ukraine mudslide

UNITED STATES. *See also individual states and regions*
1735: New England diphtheria epidemic
1775: The Hurricane of Independence, East Coast
1798: New England blizzard
1815: Year Without a Summer, United States and Europe
1884: South tornadoes
1886: Midwest blizzard
1888: The Great Blizzard of 1888, Northeast
1891: Midwest blizzard
1893: South hurricane

1898: Northeast blizzard
1908: South tornadoes
1909: South hurricane
1916: United States polio epidemic
1920: South tornado
1922: East Coast blizzard
1924: South tornado
1927: New England flood
1927: Midwest tornado
1931: United States heat wave
1932: South tornadoes
1932: Dust Bowl, Great Plains
1936: South tornadoes
1937: Ohio River flood, Midwest
1938: The Great New England Hurricane of 1938
1940: Midwest blizzard
1941: Midwest blizzard
1945: Midwest tornadoes
1948: South freeze
1948: Midwest and East freeze
1948: Columbia River flood, Northwest
1952: South tornadoes
1954: Hurricane Carol, U.S. East Coast
1954: Hurricane Hazel, Caribbean, U.S. East Coast, Canada
1955: Hurricanes Connie and Diane, U.S. East Coast
1956: New England ice storm
1956: Hurricane Flossy, U.S. Southeast
1958: East Coast and Midwest blizzard
1960: Hurricane Donna, Caribbean, U.S. East Coast
1965: Midwest tornadoes
1965: Arkansas and South Platte Rivers flood, Great Plains
1967: Southwest blizzard
1969: Hurricane Camille, U.S. South
1972: Hurricane Agnes, U.S. East Coast
1974: The Jumbo Tornado Outbreak, South, Midwest, and Canada
1976: Hurricane Belle, East Coast
1979: Hurricane David, Dominican Republic, Puerto Rico, and the South
1980: United States heat wave
1993: East Coast blizzard
1994: South tornado
1995: Midwest and Northwest heat wave
1996: The Blizzard of '96, East Coast

1996: Hurricane Bertha, Puerto Rico, Virgin Islands, U.S. East Coast
1996: West Coast flood
1998: Northeast ice storm
1998: South heat wave
1998: East Coast and Midwest drought
1998: Hurricane Georges, Caribbean and South
1999: The Blizzard of '99, Midwest and East Coast
1999: Midwest and East Coast heat wave
1999: New England encephalitis epidemic
1999: Hurricane Floyd, Bahamas, U.S. East Coast

UTAH
1999: Utah tornado

VENEZUELA
1812: Venezuela earthquake
1999: Venezuela flood

VIRGIN ISLANDS
1867: San Narciso Hurricane, Puerto Rico and Virgin Islands
1995: Hurricane Marilyn, U.S. Virgin Islands and Puerto Rico
1996: Hurricane Bertha, Puerto Rico, Virgin Islands, U.S. East Coast

VIRGINIA
1884: Virginia mine explosion
1957: Virginia mine explosion
1996: Hurricane Fran, U.S. East Coast

WALES
1966: The Aberfan Disaster, Wales (landslide)

WASHINGTON STATE
1910: Washington State avalanche
1940: Washington State bridge collapse (wind gusts)
1980: Mount St. Helens eruption, Washington
1999: Washington State avalanche

WEST INDIES
1666: West Indies hurricane
1806: Guadeloupe hurricane
1837: West Indies hurricane
1867: San Narciso Hurricane, Puerto Rico and Virgin Islands